# TRUCKING

# Tractor-Trailer Driver Handbook/Workbook

W9-AGF-012

96%

*Anthony Hernandez*

Senior Editor: Marilyn M. Martin
Managing Editor: William C. Klein
Assistant Editor: Laura M. Mertens
DP Specialists/Illustrators: Hector Arvizu
                             Alan Borie
Cover Design: Harris Graphics
Cover Photo: Truckshots

This publication is designed to provide accurate and authoritative information in regard to the subject matter covered. It is sold with the understanding that the publisher is not engaged in rendering legal, accounting or other professional service. If legal advice or other expert assistance is required, the service of a competent professional person should be sought.

**Disclaimer:** Information has been obtained by the Professional Truck Driver Institute and Career Publishing Inc., from sources believed to be reliable. However, because of the possibility of human or mechanical error by our sources, Career Publishing Inc., others, and the Professional Truck Driver Institute, do not guarantee the accuracy, adequacy, or completeness of any information and is not responsible for any errors or omissions or the results obtained from the use of such information. The publisher and editors shall not be held liable in any degree for any loss or injury by any such omission, error, misprinting or ambiguity. If you have questions regarding the content of this publication, the editorial staff is available to provide information and assistance.

ISBN 0-89262-500-7
Library of Congress Number 92-074427

Printed in the United States of America
4 5 6 7 8 9 10 XXX 05 04 03 02 01

**DELMAR**
★ ™
**THOMSON LEARNING**

Africa • Australia • Canada • Denmark • Japan • Mexico • New Zealand • Philippines
Puerto Rico • Singapore • Spain • United Kingdom • United States

# TABLE OF CONTENTS

**Chapter 1**
**An Introduction to Trucking**

Objectives .................................................................................................. 1.2
Introduction ............................................................................................... 1.3
Trucking Industry ..................................................................................... 1.4
Regulating Agencies ................................................................................. 1.6
Commercial Motor Vehicles .................................................................... 1.8
Trailers ....................................................................................................... 1.10
Becoming a Professional .......................................................................... 1.13
Safety .......................................................................................................... 1.15
Training and Instruction .......................................................................... 1.16
Summary ..................................................................................................... 1.17
Key Words .................................................................................................. 1.17
Learning Activities .................................................................................... 1.18

**Chapter 2**
**Control Systems**

Objectives .................................................................................................. 2.2
Introduction ............................................................................................... 2.3
Vehicle Controls ....................................................................................... 2.3
Driver Restraints ....................................................................................... 2.9
Vehicle Instruments .................................................................................. 2.9
Basic Instruments ...................................................................................... 2.9
Summary ..................................................................................................... 2.13
Key Words .................................................................................................. 2.13
Learning Activities .................................................................................... 2.14

**Chapter 3**
**Hours of Service**

Objectives .................................................................................................. 3.2
Introduction ............................................................................................... 3.3
Regulations ................................................................................................ 3.4
Definitions .................................................................................................. 3.4
Maximum Driving and On-Duty Time .................................................. 3.5
Record of Duty Status .............................................................................. 3.5
Driver Declared Out of Service .............................................................. 3.10
Penalties ..................................................................................................... 3.10
Summary ..................................................................................................... 3.11
Key Words .................................................................................................. 3.11
Learning Activities .................................................................................... 3.11

**Chapter 4**
**Vehicle Inspection**

Objectives .................................................................................................. 4.2
Introduction ............................................................................................... 4.3
Purpose, Importance and Types of Vehicle Inspection ...................... 4.3
What Makes a Good Inspection .............................................................. 4.4
Pre-Trip Inspection ................................................................................... 4.9
Step 1: Approach the Vehicle .................................................................. 4.10

Step 2: Check Under the Hood ............................................................................ 4.11
Step 3: Start the Engine, and Check Inside the Cab .......................................... 4.12
Step 4: Check the Lights and Mirrors ................................................................ 4.14
Step 5: Conduct a Walkaround Inspection ......................................................... 4.14
Step 6: Check the Signal Lights ......................................................................... 4.21
Step 7: Check the Air Brake System .................................................................. 4.21
Enroute and Post-Trip Inspections ..................................................................... 4.23
FMCSR 392.9 ...................................................................................................... 4.23
FMCSR 397.17 .................................................................................................... 4.23
Vehicle Inspection Report .................................................................................. 4.24
Summary .............................................................................................................. 4.24
Key Words ........................................................................................................... 4.24
Learning Activities ............................................................................................. 4.26

## Chapter 5
## Vehicle Systems

Objectives ............................................................................................................ 5.2
Introduction ......................................................................................................... 5.3
Frame, Suspension System, and Axles ............................................................... 5.3
Engines ................................................................................................................ 5.7
Fuel System ......................................................................................................... 5.8
Air Intake and Exhaust System .......................................................................... 5.10
Lubrication System .............................................................................................. 5.11
Cooling System ................................................................................................... 5.13
Electrical System ................................................................................................ 5.14
Drive Train .......................................................................................................... 5.16
Transmission ....................................................................................................... 5.18
Drive Shafts and Universal Joints ...................................................................... 5.19
Differential .......................................................................................................... 5.19
Braking System ................................................................................................... 5.20
Mixing Old and New Equipment ........................................................................ 5.25
Wheels ................................................................................................................. 5.25
Mounting Systems ............................................................................................... 5.26
Tires ..................................................................................................................... 5.27
Tread Design and Wheel Position ....................................................................... 5.28
Normal Tire Inflation .......................................................................................... 5.29
Steering Systems ................................................................................................. 5.31
Coupling Systems ................................................................................................ 5.32
Other Coupling Devices ...................................................................................... 5.34
Summary .............................................................................................................. 5.35
Key Words ........................................................................................................... 5.35
Learning Activities ............................................................................................. 5.36

## Chapter 6
## Basic Control

Objectives ............................................................................................................ 6.2
Introduction ......................................................................................................... 6.3
Definitions ........................................................................................................... 6.3
Diesel Engine ...................................................................................................... 6.3
Putting the Vehicle in Motion and Stopping ...................................................... 6.6
Backing in a Straight Line .................................................................................. 6.7
Turning the Vehicle ............................................................................................. 6.8
Range Practice ..................................................................................................... 6.13

Summary ............................................................................................................. 6.14
Key Words ......................................................................................................... 6.14
Learning Activities ............................................................................................ 6.14

## Chapter 7
## Shifting

Objectives .......................................................................................................... 7.2
Introduction ....................................................................................................... 7.3
Key Elements of Shifting .................................................................................. 7.3
Shift Controls .................................................................................................... 7.3
Coordination of Controls .................................................................................. 7.4
When to Shift ..................................................................................................... 7.4
Aids to Shifting ................................................................................................. 7.5
Nonsynchronized Transmissions ...................................................................... 7.7
Shifting Synchronized Transmissions .............................................................. 7.9
Importance of Proper Shifting .......................................................................... 7.9
Shifting Patterns and Procedures ...................................................................... 7.11
Summary of Good Shifting Habits .................................................................... 7.21
Key Words ......................................................................................................... 7.22
Learning Activities ............................................................................................ 7.22

## Chapter 8
## Backing

Objectives .......................................................................................................... 8.2
Introduction ....................................................................................................... 8.3
Backing Principles and Rules ............................................................................ 8.3
Basic Backing Maneuvers ................................................................................. 8.8
Summary ............................................................................................................ 8.11
Key Words ......................................................................................................... 8.11
Learning Activities ............................................................................................ 8.11

## Chapter 9
## Coupling and Uncoupling

Objectives .......................................................................................................... 9.2
Introduction ....................................................................................................... 9.3
Step-by-Step Coupling Procedures ................................................................... 9.3
Step-by-Step Uncoupling Procedures ............................................................... 9.10
Summary ............................................................................................................ 9.11
Key Words ......................................................................................................... 9.11
Learning Activities ............................................................................................ 9.11
Procedural Steps and Checklists ....................................................................... 9.14

## Chapter 10
## Visual Search

Objectives .......................................................................................................... 10.2
Introduction ....................................................................................................... 10.3
The Importance of Seeing ................................................................................. 10.3
Looking Ahead .................................................................................................. 10.4
Mirrors ............................................................................................................... 10.6
Summary ............................................................................................................ 10.9
Key Words ......................................................................................................... 10.10
Learning Activities ............................................................................................ 10.10

**Chapter 11**
**Communication**

Objectives ........................................................................................................ 11.2
Introduction ..................................................................................................... 11.3
Tell Your Intent .............................................................................................. 11.3
Signaling .......................................................................................................... 11.4
Summary .......................................................................................................... 11.7
Key Words ....................................................................................................... 11.7
Learning Activities ......................................................................................... 11.8

**Chapter 12**
**Space Management**

Objectives ........................................................................................................ 12.2
Introduction ..................................................................................................... 12.3
The Importance of Space Management ....................................................... 12.3
Space Ahead ................................................................................................... 12.3
Space Behind .................................................................................................. 12.5
Space to the Sides ......................................................................................... 12.6
Space Overhead ............................................................................................. 12.7
Space Below ................................................................................................... 12.8
Space for Turns ............................................................................................. 12.8
Space to Cross or Enter Traffic ................................................................. 12.9
Summary .......................................................................................................... 12.10
Key Word ........................................................................................................ 12.10
Learning Activities ......................................................................................... 12.10

**Chapter 13**
**Speed Management**

Objectives ........................................................................................................ 13.2
Introduction ..................................................................................................... 13.3
Speed and Stopping Distance ...................................................................... 13.3
Road Surfaces ................................................................................................. 13.4
Taking Curves ................................................................................................. 13.6
Hills .................................................................................................................. 13.7
How Far Can You See ................................................................................... 13.7
Speed and Traffic ........................................................................................... 13.8
Summary .......................................................................................................... 13.8
Key Words ....................................................................................................... 13.8
Learning Activities ......................................................................................... 13.9

**Chapter 14**
**Night Driving**

Objectives ........................................................................................................ 14.2
Introduction ..................................................................................................... 14.3
Night Driving Factors .................................................................................... 14.3
Night Driving Procedures ............................................................................. 14.7
Night Driving Adjustments ........................................................................... 14.8
Summary .......................................................................................................... 14.8
Key Words ....................................................................................................... 14.8
Learning Activities ......................................................................................... 14.9

**Chapter 15**
**Extreme Driving Conditions**

Objectives .................................................................................................. 15.2
Introduction ............................................................................................... 15.3
Extreme Weather ...................................................................................... 15.3
Tire Chains ................................................................................................ 15.6
Starting Your Engine in Cold Weather .................................................. 15.8
Bad Weather Operating Hazards ........................................................... 15.10
Operating in Bad Weather ...................................................................... 15.13
Hot Weather .............................................................................................. 15.16
Driving in the Desert ............................................................................... 15.17
Mountain Driving ..................................................................................... 15.17
Auxiliary Brakes and Speed Retarders .................................................. 15.21
Escape Ramps ............................................................................................ 15.22
Summary .................................................................................................... 15.23
Key Words .................................................................................................. 15.23
Learning Activities ................................................................................... 15.24

**Chapter 16**
**Hazard Awareness**

Objectives .................................................................................................. 16.2
Introduction ............................................................................................... 16.3
Importance of Recognizing Hazards ...................................................... 16.3
Road Conditions ....................................................................................... 16.5
Appearance of Other Road Users .......................................................... 16.8
Activities by Other Road Users .............................................................. 16.12
Summary .................................................................................................... 16.15
Key Words .................................................................................................. 16.15
Learning Activities ................................................................................... 16.16

**Chapter 17**
**Emergency Maneuvers**

Objectives .................................................................................................. 17.2
Introduction ............................................................................................... 17.3
Avoiding Emergencies .............................................................................. 17.3
Types of Emergency Maneuvers ............................................................. 17.4
Evasive Steering ....................................................................................... 17.4
Off-Road Recovery ................................................................................... 17.7
Emergency Stopping ................................................................................. 17.9
Brake Failure ............................................................................................. 17.10
Blowouts ..................................................................................................... 17.12
Summary .................................................................................................... 17.13
Key Words .................................................................................................. 17.13
Learning Activities ................................................................................... 17.13

**Chapter 18**
**Skid Control**

Objectives .................................................................................................. 18.2
Introduction ............................................................................................... 18.3
Vehicle Control Factors ........................................................................... 18.3
Preventing Skids ....................................................................................... 18.5
Causes of Skids ......................................................................................... 18.5

Causes of Skids ............................................................................ 18.5
Tractor-Trailer Skids ..................................................................... 18.7
Anti-Jackknife Devices .................................................................. 18.10
Antilock Brakes ............................................................................ 18.10
Skid Recovery .............................................................................. 18.10
Summary ...................................................................................... 18.12
Key Words .................................................................................... 18.12
Learning Activities ........................................................................ 18.12

## Chapter 19
## Accident Procedures

Objectives .................................................................................... 19.2
Introduction ................................................................................. 19.3
Accidents ..................................................................................... 19.3
Accident Reporting ....................................................................... 19.6
Giving First Aid ............................................................................ 19.17
Fires and Fire Fighting .................................................................. 19.23
Summary ...................................................................................... 19.27
Key Words .................................................................................... 19.27
Learning Activities ........................................................................ 19.28

## Chapter 20
## Sliding Fifth Wheels and Tandem Axles

Objectives .................................................................................... 20.2
Introduction ................................................................................. 20.3
Shifting Weight ............................................................................ 20.3
The Bridge Formula ....................................................................... 20.5
Maneuverability and Off-Tracking ................................................. 20.5
The Fifth Wheel ............................................................................ 20.6
Sliding the Fifth Wheel ................................................................. 20.7
Trailer Tandem Axles .................................................................... 20.9
Sliding the Trailer Tandem Axles ................................................... 20.10
Summary ...................................................................................... 20.13
Key Words .................................................................................... 20.13
Learning Activities ........................................................................ 20.14

## Chapter 21
## Special Rigs

Objectives .................................................................................... 21.2
Introduction ................................................................................. 21.3
Long Combination Vehicles ........................................................... 21.4
Special Trailer Types ..................................................................... 21.10
Low Clearance Vehicles ................................................................. 21.12
High Center of Gravity Vehicles .................................................... 21.14
Unstable Loads ............................................................................. 21.15
Special Cargo Vehicles .................................................................. 21.17
Special Handling Vehicles ............................................................. 21.18
Summary ...................................................................................... 21.19
Key Words .................................................................................... 21.19
Learning Activities ........................................................................ 21.19

**Chapter 22**
**Preventive Maintenance and Servicing**

Objectives .................................................................................... 22.2
Introduction ................................................................................. 22.3
Preventive Maintenance ............................................................. 22.4
Types of Maintenance ................................................................ 22.4
Federal Motor Vehicle Inspection and Maintenance Requirements .................. 22.6
Daily Vehicle Condition Report ............................................... 22.6
Basic Servicing and Routine Maintenance .............................. 22.8
Checking and Changing Engine Fluids, Filters, Lights, and Fuses ............. 22.9
Checking the Air Pressure and Changing Tires ..................... 22.14
Draining the Air Reservoirs ..................................................... 22.17
Adjusting the Tractor-Trailer Brakes ...................................... 22.17
Summary ...................................................................................... 22.17
Key Words ................................................................................... 22.18
Learning Activities ..................................................................... 22.18

**Chapter 23**
**Recognizing and Reporting Malfunctions**

Objectives .................................................................................... 23.2
Introduction ................................................................................. 23.3
Diagnosing and Reporting Malfunctions ................................ 23.4
Problem Solving Exercises ........................................................ 23.9
Emergency Starting Procedures ............................................... 23.16
Summary ...................................................................................... 23.18
Key Words ................................................................................... 23.18
Learning Activities ..................................................................... 23.18

**Chapter 24**
**Handling Cargo**

Objectives .................................................................................... 24.2
Introduction ................................................................................. 24.3
Importance of Handling Cargo Properly ................................ 24.3
The Driver's Responsibilities ................................................... 24.4
Regulations .................................................................................. 24.5
Securing Cargo ........................................................................... 24.6
Covering Cargo ........................................................................... 24.11
Accepting and Loading Freight ............................................... 24.13
Hazardous Materials ................................................................. 24.15
Vehicle Weight ........................................................................... 24.19
Distribution of Weight .............................................................. 24.21
Summary ...................................................................................... 24.23
Key Words ................................................................................... 24.23
Learning Activities ..................................................................... 24.24

**Chapter 25**
**Cargo Documentation**

Objectives .................................................................................... 25.2
Introduction ................................................................................. 25.3
Definition of Terms ................................................................... 25.3
Transportation Charges and Services ...................................... 25.5
Basic Shipping Documents ....................................................... 25.6

Driver's Signature and Responsibility ................................................................ 25.9
Previously Loaded Trailer .................................................................................. 25.10
Delivery of Freight ............................................................................................ 25.11
Interline Freight ................................................................................................. 25.11
Hazardous Material and Hazardous Waste ........................................................ 25.11
Summary ............................................................................................................ 25.16
Key Words .......................................................................................................... 25.16
Learning Activities ............................................................................................. 25.17

## Chapter 26
## Personal Health and Safety

Objectives .......................................................................................................... 26.2
Introduction ....................................................................................................... 26.3
Physical Condition ............................................................................................. 26.3
Fatigue ................................................................................................................ 26.5
Illness ................................................................................................................. 26.7
Alcohol ............................................................................................................... 26.7
Drugs .................................................................................................................. 26.10
Hazards to Safety ............................................................................................... 26.13
Roadside Emergencies ....................................................................................... 26.18
Causes of Accidents ........................................................................................... 26.20
On-Duty and Off-Duty Job Stress .................................................................... 26.21
Physical Demands of the Job ............................................................................. 26.22
Summary ............................................................................................................ 26.23
Key Words .......................................................................................................... 26.23
Learning Activities ............................................................................................. 26.24

## Chapter 27
## Trip Planning

Objectives .......................................................................................................... 27.2
Introduction ....................................................................................................... 27.3
Types of Truck Runs .......................................................................................... 27.3
Route Selection .................................................................................................. 27.6
Map Reading ...................................................................................................... 27.9
Calculating Travel Time and Fuel Usage .......................................................... 27.11
Keeping Records ................................................................................................ 27.13
Vehicle Licensing and Permits ......................................................................... 27.16
Federal Length and Weight Limits .................................................................... 27.17
State Limits ........................................................................................................ 27.18
Hazardous Material ............................................................................................ 27.20
Roadside Enforcement ....................................................................................... 27.21
Summary ............................................................................................................ 27.22
Key Words .......................................................................................................... 27.22
Learning Activities ............................................................................................. 27.23

## Chapter 28
## Public Relations and Employer-Employee Relations

Objectives .......................................................................................................... 28.2
Introduction ....................................................................................................... 28.3
Public Relations ................................................................................................. 28.3
Customer Relations ............................................................................................ 28.6
Employer Relations ............................................................................................ 28.7
Basic Job Requirements ..................................................................................... 28.8

Applying for the Job ............................................................................................ 28.12
Summary .............................................................................................................. 28.14
Key Words ........................................................................................................... 28.14
Learning Activities .............................................................................................. 28.15

## Chapter 29
## CDL: Commercial Driver License

What Tests Do You Need to Pass? ........................................................................ 29.2
Introduction ......................................................................................................... 29.5
The Law ............................................................................................................... 29.5
Classes of Licenses and Endorsements ................................................................. 29.7
CDL Knowledge Tests ......................................................................................... 29.7
CDL Skills Tests .................................................................................................. 29.8
Exceptions ........................................................................................................... 29.13
Why So Many Different Tests? ............................................................................. 29.13
Passing Scores .................................................................................................... 29.14
Your Commercial License is a . . . ....................................................................... 29.14

## Appendix A
## Trouble Shooting Guide

If You See. . . ...................................................................................................... A.2
If You Hear. . . .................................................................................................... A.4
If You Feel. . . ..................................................................................................... A.6
If You Smell. . ..................................................................................................... A.8

**Index** ...................................................................................................................... I.1

# PREFACE

A severe shortage of trained tractor-trailer drivers faces the trucking industry and the nation. *Trucking: Tractor-Trailer Driver Handbook/Workbook* is a result of the cooperative efforts of the Professional Truck Driver Institute of America, Inc. and Career Publishing Inc. The book will provide easy to use materials for use in training truck drivers for entry level positions in the industry.

The book is patterned after and meets the standards established by the FHWA in their Model Curriculum (Proposed Minimum Standards for Training Tractor-Trailer Drivers). It also meets the standards established by the Professional Truck Driver Institute of America, Inc. for their certification program.

The book addresses not only the body of knowledge a driver needs to know and understand, it teaches the procedures that, with practice, will enable the student to become a skilled driver. Safety practices are emphasized. There are also sections of the book that can be removed for the driver's later use. These will serve as aids for correctly performing certain procedures.

A variety of learning activities are presented. The emphasis is on reinforcing what was covered in the chapter. Many real-life driving problems and situations are presented for the driver to solve.

Because tractor-trailer drivers are placed in a unique position of being entrusted with expensive equipment and cargo as well as representing the industry to the public at large, this book stresses the importance of developing the traits and demonstrating the behavior that characterize true professionals.

The handbook/workbook also addresses the driver as a person. Emphasis is placed on good health and safety routines. There are many helpful suggestions the driver may follow while he or she is on a trip.

This edition of the book has a reduced level of readability for ease of understanding, added graphics, and improved teaching aids. Truck driver training schools, motor carriers, and individual teachers will find this book readily meets their needs as they seek to provide the trucking industry with professional drivers who are knowledgeable, safe, and skillful.

# ACKNOWLEDGMENTS

Many groups and individuals have made the development and publication of this handbook/workbook possible. Contributions of the following organizations are particularly appreciated.

**Owner-Operators Independent Drivers Association (OOIDA)** for reviewing manuscripts and offering constructive comments.

**The American Trucking Associations** and, in particular, the **Interstate Carriers Conference** for continuing cooperation, encouragement, and support.

Special thanks are expressed to:

**George Beaulieu**, SAFE, Inc., Waco, Texas.

**Robert M. Driscoll, Jr.**, General Vice President (OOIDA), Laurel Springs, New Jersey for detailed manuscript review and comments.

**Truck Driving Academy**, Sacramento, California for detailed manuscript review and comments.

**Tom Waite**, McFatter Vo-Tech, Davie, Florida for detailed manuscript review and comments.

**Denny Shollenberger**, Allstate Career Schools, Lester, Pennsylvania, for detailed manuscript review and comments.

**John Hale**, Redwing/Winona Technical College, Winona, Minnesota, for detailed manuscript review and comments.

**Tony Pepitone**, Commercial Driver Training, West Babylon, New York, for detailed manuscript review and comments.

**Deborah Strum**, Dundalk Community College, Baltimore, Maryland, for detailed manuscript review and comments.

**Van O'Neal**, Houston Community College, Houston, Texas, for detailed manuscript review and comments.

**Mark McNeely**, American Freightways, Indianapolis, Indiana, for detailed manuscript review and comments.

**Fran Bernard**, International Trucking School, Inc., Ypsilanti, Michigan, for detailed manuscript review and comments.

**Don Hess**, John Wood Community College, Quincy, Illinois, for detailed manuscript review and comments.

**Joe Elrod**, MTA Schools, Corona, California, for detailed manuscript review and comments.

**Ron Rath**, Kirkwood Community College, Cedar Rapids, Illinois, for detailed manuscript review and comments.

**Rich Clemente**, N.A.T.A., Detroit, Michigan, for detailed manuscript review and comments.

**Mike Burholder**, Landstar Inway, Inc., Rockford, Illinois, for detailed manuscript review and comments.

**Cliff Miller**, Contract Freighters, Joplin, Missouri, for detailed manuscript review and comments.

**James McKay**, Davis Cartage, Co., Carunna, Michigan, for detailed manuscript review and comments.

**Paul Murphy**, Ruan Transportation Management Systems, Madison, Wisconsin, for detailed manuscript review and comments.

**Rowland A. Fisher**, Orange Ball Trucking Company, Hayward, California for technical Assistance.

**Richard Rohrer**, President, Global Safety Services, Inc., Mechanicsburg, Pennsylvania for technical assistance.

**Dr. Allen Robinson**, University of Pennsylvania, Indiana, Pennsylvania for detailed manuscript review and comments.

**Mark McAtee**, Director of Training, C-1 Professional Training Center, Indianapolis, Indiana for detailed manuscript review and comments.

Special appreciation also to the following individuals who have performed most of the production tasks related to the original and most recent edition:

**Michael R. Calvin**, State Liaison, National Commercial Driver License Program, American Association of Motor Vehicle Administrators, Washington, DC (former PTDIA staff member), for screening and selection of content for the handbook/workbook.

**Robert M. Calvin**, Manager, Highway Safety Programs, Washington, DC and curriculum technical consultant to the Institute.

**Andrew Ryder,** Editor, Heavy Duty Trucking, Newport Communications, Newport Beach, California for his careful editing and revision of the existing material.

**Harold A. Haase**, Publisher, Career Publishing Inc., Orange, California for encouraging the Institute to develop better educational tools and providing the facilities to make this possible.

**Marilyn M. Martin**, Senior Editor/Project Coordinator, Career Publishing Inc. for detailed analysis and alteration of the readability level as well as the book design and layout.

## ABOUT THE DEVELOPERS OF
## TRUCKING: TRACTOR-TRAILER DRIVER HANDBOOK/WORKBOOK

**Professional Truck Driver Institute of America**

The Professional Truck Driver Institute of America is an independent, non-profit organization established in 1985 by the Trucking Industry Alliance. It has as its sole purpose the development of a system to evaluate and certify truck driver training programs. To that end, the PTDIA assists carriers, schools, and governments in establishing or improving their truck driver training courses. Currently, they are also developing recommended industry standards for training drivers.

**Career Publishing Company Inc.**

Career Publishing Company was founded in 1974 and is a textbook publisher specializing in transportation, medical, and computer courseware. They also serve as the publisher and distributor of all PTDIA driver training materials. Recognized by the industry for its unique approach to learning, Career's materials teach the student a life skill using a step-by-step, learn-by-doing method. Readability levels are kept low and many graphics are used to illustrate concepts, so the books are easy to read and easy to understand. The student learns by systematically progressing through a series of skill levels.

Career's CDL Test Study Books, videos, and audiotapes have been successfully used by countless drivers across the United States to prepare for their commercial driver license tests both prior to the April 1, 1992 deadline and currently.

## INTRODUCTION

*Trucking: Tractor-Trailer Driver Handbook/Workbook* is a book of fundamentals. It has been developed especially for training those persons who wish to enter the trucking industry as tractor-trailer drivers. It provides a sound foundation of entry-level knowledge and skill. If you are an aspiring driver, you will find this book the best source of information and instruction available.

You will learn what characterizes a professional driver and how to demonstrate those traits. You will learn the procedures needed by a truck driver. You will be taught how to maintain good customer relations, good will with the public, and proper and accurate records. You will be walked through the most common types of emergency situations and shown how to correctly deal with them.

Because you, the driver, are an important person, you will learn the best ways to stay in good shape so you can handle the rigorous job of being a tractor-trailer driver in the best possible way.

This book has been reviewed by professional truck drivers, educators, truck driver training specialists, and representative of the trucking industry. The information is as complete and up to date as possible. The handbook/workbook may be divided into six general sections.

# Chapter One
# AN INTRODUCTION TO TRUCKING

© 1997 Truckshots

**The Trucking Industry • Types of Carriers • A Regulated Industry
Regulating Agencies • CMVSA '86 • Commercial Motor Vehicles
Becoming a Professional • Training and Instruction**

**FROM NOW ON,**

**ONLY THE BEST WILL DRIVE**

# OBJECTIVES

When you have mastered this chapter, you will be able to:

- Introduce the potential driver to tractor-trailer driving

- Have a working knowledge of trucking

- Explain why the trucking industry is vital to our nation's economy

- Explain the rules and regulations under which it operates

- Understand the main systems and parts of tractor/trailers

- Describe the professionalism drivers should develop

## CHAPTER ONE

# AN INTRODUCTION TO TRUCKING

## INTRODUCTION

Those who drive tractor-trailers are vital team members of a major service industry. We could not get along without them. It has been said, "If someone has it, a truck brought it." Our whole economy depends on trucks. No family can exist without them, and trucks need well-trained, dedicated drivers.

Trucks carry almost everything we eat, wear, or use. The needs of families, farms, medicine, business, industry, government, and education are served by trucks. They haul farm products from the field to processing plants or markets; crude oil from the oil fields to refineries; fuel from the refineries to gas stations or homes; raw material like coal, ore, and chemicals to industry; and cars and appliances to sales rooms.

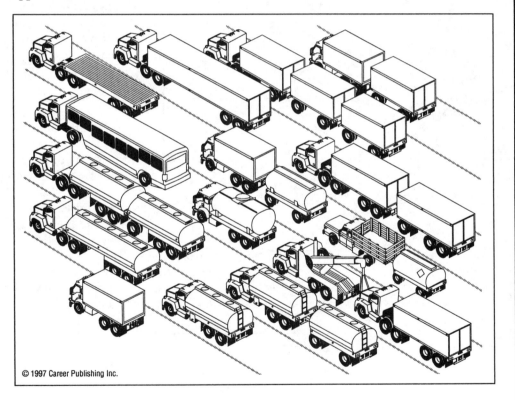

© 1997 Career Publishing Inc.

**Figure 1-1**

Trucks are the major way of transporting goods in our country. They haul more than rail, air, and water carriers. The 1.4 million tractor-trailer fleet hauls three out of every four tons of goods in our country. This means 735 billion ton-miles of freight each year is carried. (One ton-mile equals one ton of goods carried one mile.)

More than 7.8 million people have jobs in the trucking industry (not all are drivers). Almost 13% of the people in the U. S. depend on breadwinners employed in trucking. That's 33 million people. While not all jobs are driving, this job is the key one in the industry. The driver must:
- Meet schedules
- Keep maintenance costs down
- See that freight arrives safely

The statement *if you have it, a truck brought it* is true, and it is also true that without a good truck driver, you would not have it.

Figure 1-2

## TRUCKING INDUSTRY

The trucking industry is vital to America's economy. The lives of all of us are affected by trucks and their drivers. Tightly regulated by state and federal laws, the motor carrier industry maintains a constant effort to instill the desire to be professional and safe in its drivers.

Carriers that stay within state borders are known as **intrastate** carriers and are subject to state regulations. Carriers operating over state borders are known as **interstate** carriers and are subject to federal regulations, administered by the **Department of Transportation (DOT)**. These federal regulations were formerly administered by the Interstate Commerce Commision (ICC). State regulations are generally the same as federal regulations, but they can also impose their own size and weight rules as well as insurance requirements.

Interstate — Between states

Intrastate — Within a state

There are two general types of carriers.

**For-Hire Carrier**: An organization that has as its primary business hauling cargo by truck.

**Private Carrier**: An organization that uses trucks to transport its own goods in its own trucks.

The For-Hire Carriers can be divided into two groups.

**Common Carrier**: A motor carrier that offers its services to all individuals and businesses.

**Contract Carrier**: A motor carrier that is under contract to customers to transport their freight. The contract sets the rates and other terms of service.

Any common carrier transporting by truck in interstate or foreign commerce must first receive authority to

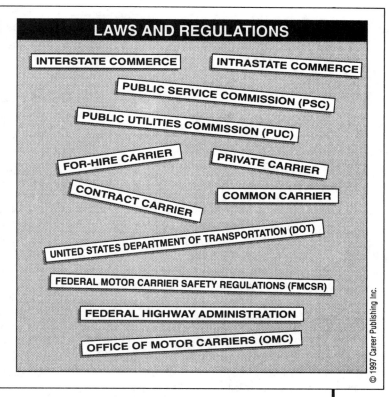

**Figure 1-3**

do this from the DOT and file its rates with them. Contract carriers and others do not have to file rates.

## A Regulated Industry

Many rules and regulations have been made to make sure the trucking industry and the public are safe. Over 80,000 different governments regulate trucking. These include federal, state, county, and city governments.

State governments include counties, cities and towns. They usually pass laws about routes, speed limits, truck loading, and parking; and are very concerned with weight and size limits on roads and bridges. The state governments also regulate commerce within their state.

The federal government is concerned about commerce that crosses state lines. The interstate truck operations are regulated principally by the **U. S. Department of Transportation (USDOT or DOT)**.

## State Regulations

Each state regulates motor carriers and sets vehicle laws. The **Department of Motor Vehicles (DMV)** usually assists in making these laws. States usually:
* Decide how much the trucks may carry
* Collect road and fuel taxes
* Limit length, width, and weight of **CMVs** (Commercial Motor Vehicles)
* Issue licenses
* Set minimum insurance requirements

Interstate truckers often are contacted by state officials at Ports of Entry where they display their permit number or get a one-trip permit. Professional truck drivers must know and obey all state laws and regulations.

## IN YOUR STATE

1. What is the speed limit for commercial vehicles on Interstate highways? County and local roads?
2. What is the maximum weight limit for a three-axle truck?
3. What is the maximum weight limit for a combination of vehicles such as a tractor-semitrailer? Straight truck pulling a trailer?
4. Who should you contact for an overweight or oversize vehicle?
5. What is the maximum legal length for a single vehicle?
6. What is the maximum legal length for a combination truck and single trailer? Double trailers, if allowed? Triples?
7. What is the maximum vehicle height allowed without a permit?
8. What is the maximum width allowed for a commercial vehicle?
9. How far can rearview mirrors extend from the side of the vehicle?
10. How far can a load extend from the vehicle?
11. How many hours can you legally drive?
12. How many hours can you legally be on duty?
13. If your vehicle is involved in an accident, what must you do?
14. What items do you need to bring to the licensing office to apply for your CDL?
15. Which commercial drivers need a CDL?
16. What class of CDL will you need?
17. Do experienced commercial drivers with a good driving record need to take the CDL knowledge (written) and skill (driving) tests to get their new CDL? Can you obtain a waiver?
18. What type of CDL endorsements do you need?
19. What group of drivers are exempted by state law from having to obtain a CDL?

**Figure 1-4**

## REGULATING AGENCIES

### U. S. Department of Transportation

All motor carriers operating in interstate or foreign commerce must follow the **Federal Motor Carrier Safety Regulations (FMCSR)** and the **Hazardous Materials Regulations** of the USDOT. Through the **Motor Carrier Safety Assistance Program (MCSAP)**, most states put these federal regulations in effect.

This means that these regulations probably also apply to intrastate commerce. In other words, they apply to all commercial motor vehicles (CMVs) with a gross vehicle weight rating (GVWR) more than 10,000 pounds. They also apply to any vehicle hauling cargo that needs placards.

The FMCSR applies to trucks and buses used by common carriers, contract carriers, and private motor carriers for interstate or foreign commerce. They list:
- Insurance requirements
- Driver qualifications
- Driving rules
- Hours of service
- How to report accidents
- How to inspect, repair and maintain CMVs
- Parts and accessories for safe operation

Within the **Federal Highway Administration (FHWA)**, the **Office of Motor Carriers (OMC)** issues and enforces the FMCSR. This Office was formerly named the Bureau of Motor Carrier Safety.

The **Research and Special Programs Administration (RSPA) Office of Hazardous Materials Transportation (OHMT)** classifies hazardous materials. It also sets standards for:
- Shipping containers
- Shipping documents
- Marking and labeling
- Placarding

Placards help fire and emergency personnel identify dangerous cargo in the event of an accident or spill. Hazardous material is also regulated by the **Environmental Protection Agency (EPA), Nuclear Regulatory Commission (NRC),** and the **Occupational Safety and Health Administration (OSHA).**

**The National Transportation Safety Board (NTSB)** investigates accidents and offers solutions to prevent future accidents.

Figure 1-5

At this time, the law has changed and many of the areas previously under ICC control have been deregulated. However, the details of determining the agencies that will oversee these areas in the future have not been resolved.

Carriers not regulated by the DOT include:
- Intrastate carriers
- Private carriers that do not infringe on the definition of "for-hire carriers"

## Commercial Motor Vehicle Safety Act of 1986

Before 1986 when the **Commercial Vehicle Safety Act of 1986 (CMVSA/86)** was passed, lack of cooperation among the states, loopholes in laws, and difficulty in knowing individual driver's records let some drivers continue to drive when they were clearly unfit to do so. The CMVSA/86 was passed to make sure all CMV drivers were qualified. It also prevented drivers from having more than one commercial driver license (CDL). For certain traffic law violations, it disqualified them from driving.

**YOUR COMMERCIAL DRIVER'S LICENSE**

| I.D.NUMBER | HT. | WGT. | CLASS |

ENDORSMENT :
Tanker N

SIGNATURE

NAME:
STREET:
CITY:                        ZIP

© 1997 Career Publishing Inc.

**Figure 1-6**

The CMVSA/86 applies to:
- Both interstate and intrastate drivers and carriers
- Drivers of CMVs with a GVWR of more than 26,000 pounds
- Drivers of vehicles carrying 16 or more passengers, including the driver
- Drivers of any vehicle transporting hazardous material that requires placards

The law says employers are not to let any employee drive a CMV:
- Who has more than one CDL
- Whose CDL has been suspended, revoked, or canceled
- Who has been disqualified from driving under the FMCSR

Drivers must:
- Have only one (1) CDL
- Notify their employer and the state that issued the CDL within 10 days of a conviction for any traffic violation except parking violations
- Provide the employer with information about all driving jobs held during the past 10 years

The FMCSR require drivers to notify their employers at once if their CDL is suspended, revoked, or canceled even though the CMVSA/86 does not.

## COMMERCIAL MOTOR VEHICLES

The purpose of this section is to show different types of tractor-trailer combinations.

### Truck Tractors

The following section is about **truck tractors**. They are used to pull other vehicles, such as semitrailers. The tractor is built so it carries only part of the load of the vehicle it pulls. There are two general cab styles:
- Conventional
- Cabover

**Conventional tractors** have a smoother ride because the driver sits between the front wheels and the rear wheels. Its main drawback is a longer wheelbase. Longer wheelbases make maneuvering in tight spaces harder.

In a COE tractor, the cab and driver are over the front wheels. This makes a firmer ride. The shorter wheelbase can pull a longer trailer and remain within the legal length and weight limits. A driver can see better in this type of tractor because of the higher cab. The hood also does not block part of the forward view. Many tractors have sleeper berths.

Both straight trucks and truck tractors have a front axle and one or more rear axles. The front axle is the steering axle. The rear axle that is powered is called the drive axle.

A truck or tractor with only one axle in the rear is called a two-axle truck with a single drive axle. A single drive axle tractor usually has a shorter wheelbase. A single drive axle tractor with dual rear wheels has six (6) wheels with tires. The shorter wheelbase allows it to turn in a smaller space. It also limits the amount of weight the truck can carry.

© 1997 Career Publishing Inc.

**Figure 1-7**

**Figure 1-8**

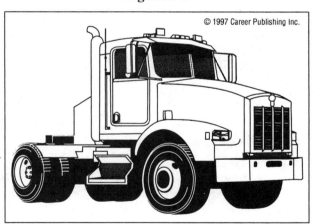

© 1997 Career Publishing Inc.

**Figure 1-9**

A conventional tractor with the engine under the hood.

The **cabover tractor** has a flat face with the engine beneath the cab. It is often called a cab-over-engine (COE) tractor.

A two-axle truck with a single drive axle.

To carry heavier loads, another axle must be added. This addition will lengthen the wheelbase. The two axles are called a tandem.

A tandem axle tractor generally has two drive axles. They are also called **twin-screws** and help give the truck more traction in slippery conditions.

A driveshaft runs between the differential of the front drive axle and the differential of the rear drive axle. Many twin-screws also have a differential lock to spread power evenly to each axle. The lock is engaged only in slippery conditions and at low speeds.

Some tandems have only one drive axle. The non-driven axle can be a **tag axle** (mounted behind the drive axle) or it can be a **pusher axle** (mounted ahead of the drive axle).

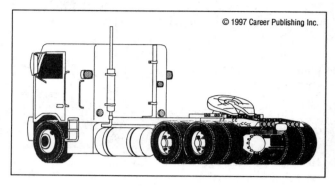

**Figure 1-10**

Wheels with tires, mounted in pairs, on each end of the axle are called **duals**. A tandem tractor with dual wheels on the rear axles has ten (10) wheels.

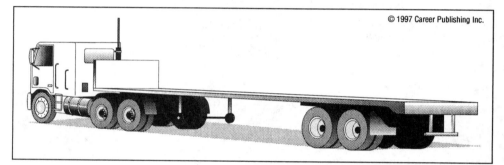

**Figure 1-11**

Each wheel on a tractor is identified in the drawing at right. If you have to report a tire problem to your dispatcher, use these IDs. Be sure to call each wheel by its proper name.

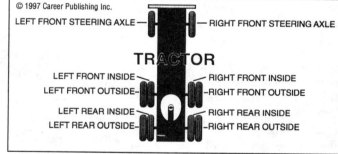

**Figure 1-12**

## TRAILERS

A **trailer** is a vehicle built for hauling cargo. It has one or more axles and two or more wheels. There are two types of trailers.

- Full trailers
- Semitrailers

Sometimes, both are just called trailers.

A **full trailer** is built so that no part of its weight rests upon the vehicle pulling it. A full trailer is fully supported by its own axles. It can be pulled by a straight truck or a truck tractor. Full trailers are often used as the second trailer in a double-trailer rig. They can also be used as the second and third trailers in a triple-trailer rig. Shown on the next page is a full trailer.

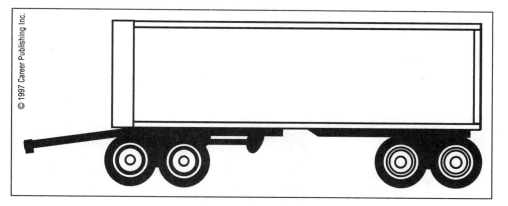

**Figure 1-13**

**Figure 1-14**

A **semitrailer** is the one most often used in a tractor-trailer combination. It has axles only at the rear of the trailer. The front of the trailer is supported by the tractor.

The front of the **semitrailer** rests on the fifth wheel of the tractor. The fifth wheel is a plate mounted over the rear axle of the tractor. It has a hole in the center into which the trailer's kingpin fits. This couples the units together. The fifth wheel is the pivot point between the tractor and the trailer. It bears the weight of the front of the semitrailer.

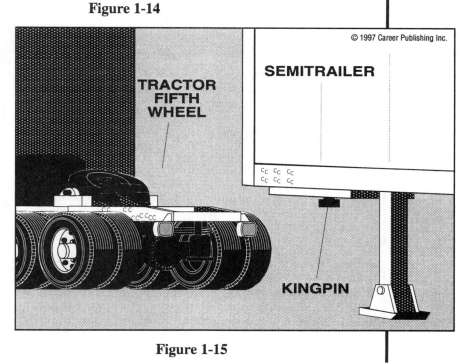

**Figure 1-15**

© 1997 Career Publishing Inc.

**Figure 1-16**

A semitrailer can be made into a full trailer by coupling it to the fifth wheel on a converter dolly. The dolly is hooked to the rear of another trailer. When you put a dolly on a semitrailer, it becomes a full trailer.

There are many different types of semitrailers. Some of them are shown in the drawing below.

When we add a trailer to a tractor or a straight truck, it is called a **combination vehicle**, or combination rig. Some of the many types of combination vehicles are shown in the drawing below. Combination rigs can have different types of wheel and axle arrangements.

Other types of combination vehicles include the following:

**Rocky Mountain Double:** This rig has double trailers. The truck has three axles. The 40'-45' semitrailer has tandem axles. Then there is a single axle dolly and a 27'-28' single axle semitrailer. There are a total of seven (7) axles on this rig. It is not legal in some states.

**Standard Double:** A single axle tractor pulling a 28' semitrailer and a 28' trailer. These are not legal in some states.

**Turnpike Double:** A tandem axle tractor pulling a 48' semitrailer and a 48' trailer. These are not legal in some states.

**18-wheeler:** The most familiar combination rig. The tractor has ten (10) wheels. The semitrailer has eight (8) wheels. There are five (5) axles on an 18-wheeler.

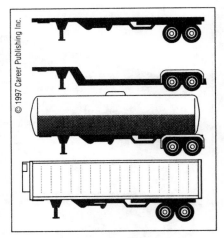

**Figure 1-17**

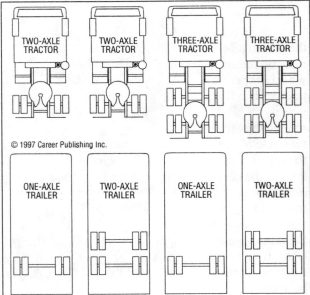

© 1997 Career Publishing Inc.

**Figure 1-18**

© 1997 Career Publishing Inc.

**Figure 1-19**

# BECOMING A PROFESSIONAL

The best truck drivers act in a professional manner. They:
- Are responsible
- Are skillful
- Have a good attitude
- Practice safety at all times
- Can make independent judgments
- Are accountable
- Understand trucks

What is a profession? A profession is a field that:
- Requires special knowledge, skill, and attitudes that are a result of long preparation and training
- Contains a specialized body of knowledge and established practices, procedures, and methods
- Often requires evidence of individual standing, such as a certificate or license

Professionals are expected to act and make independent judgments according to best of their ability. They are held accountable for their actions. They are expected to be ethical and committed to the public good.

Motor carriers want drivers who perform in a professional manner. They entrust expensive vehicles and valuable cargo to their care. They also know drivers present the corporate image of the company to the public. Competent, safe, courteous, and responsible drivers are invaluable to a company and a credit to their profession. Drivers who are a hazard or liability cannot be tolerated in this vital service industry.

A professional tractor-trailer driver must have strong personal qualities. They must be above the average driver in the following areas.

**Physical and mental abilities**: He or she meets government, industry, and company standards.

**Skill**: Is qualified by training and experience to operate specific vehicle types (tractor-trailer, etc.)

THERE ARE MANY MEN AND WOMEN IN
TRUCKING WHO DESERVE THE TITLE OF
# PROFESSIONAL DRIVER!

**Figure 1-20**

**Safety standards**: Understands and practices safe driving methods; obeys the law; knows more and is safer than an average driver; concentrates on avoiding accidents.

**Tolerance and courtesy**: Can accept bad traffic behavior from other drivers without getting mad or trying to get even; cooperates with other road users.

**Efficiency**: Delivers goods on time while obeying laws and regulations; recognizes the company cannot be successful unless schedules are met; does not waste fuel.

**Knowledge**: Knows government regulations; follows industry requirements for driving and handling cargo.

**Figure 1-21**

Professional drivers understand *they are the trucking industry* in the eyes of customers and the public. They know they must perform better than the average driver. They realize that driving well is not enough. They must also be polite and safe. Finally, they know they must keep on trying to improve. They take pride in doing these things.

Ensuring responsible driving among the nation's truck drivers is critical to improving highway safety. Carriers must try to qualify, hire, and train only the best and most professional people to drive. Drivers must use good judgment, common sense, and courtesy.

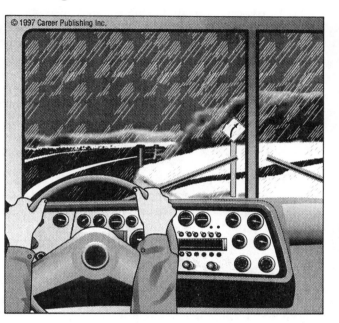

**Figure 1-22**

# SAFETY

A tractor-trailer driver's highest priority should be safety. The whole purpose of the industry is to move cargo from one point to another without

**Figure 1-23**

damage to the equipment, cargo, or people. Unsafe vehicles and unsafe driving threaten the economic well-being of the trucking industry as well as the nation as a whole.

It is not easy to be safe. Driving heavy trucks is one of the most dangerous and demanding jobs in the transportation industry. Tractor-trailer drivers must always be aware of what is going on around them. Accidents can easily happen.

Preventing accidents does not happen by chance. Truck drivers should not let themselves get into situations that could have been avoided if they had been thinking ahead. They must use common sense, always pay attention, and be trained how to avoid accidents.

# TRAINING AND INSTRUCTION

A driver must be prepared. The more driving skill he or she has gained while in training, the less there is to be learned on the job. Formal training is valuable when learning to drive any vehicle, but the value increases with the size of the vehicle.

Safe driving is more likely to occur when:
- Drivers understand their personal strengths and weaknesses.
- Drivers understand the capabilities and limitations of their vehicles.
- Instruction has been given for both good and bad driving conditions.
- Drivers have been taught to look for and identify potential hazards.

Looking for and identifying possible hazards is very important because most emergencies do not appear in a split second, they grow gradually. Drivers can be taught to *see them* before they have grown into full-scale problems. Drivers can then take steps to reduce the threat.

Of course, there are some emergencies that do happen quickly. These may be due to the road conditions, traffic, or unsafe actions of others. In these cases, drivers must know how to analyze the situation and decide what is the best course of action. Here again, training can be a major factor in how well the driver performs.

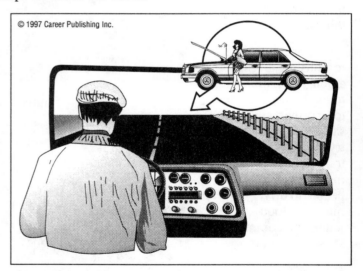

© 1997 Career Publishing Inc.

**Figure 1-24**

CMV drivers tend to have more accidents in the first few months they drive. This may be as a result of not enough training or experience. If training includes experience, and experience reduces accidents; then better training of tractor-trailer drivers can reduce the accident rate on our highways.

Truck drivers who perform in a professional manner can improve overall highway safety, promote courtesy on the road, and in general, provide better highway conditions for all drivers. They are an asset to their employers and are regarded with respect by all others.

## SUMMARY

In this chapter, you learned something about how the trucking industry operates. You now know there are different types of carriers and many regulations to follow. The differences between the types of trucks and trailers were shown. You also learned why you should be a professional and how to become one.

## KEY WORDS

**Carrier**: An organization that hauls cargo by truck

**CDL**: Commercial Driver License

**Combination vehicle**: A trailer combined with a tractor or a straight truck

**CMV:** Commercial Motor Vehicle

**DOT**: Department of Transportation

**EPA:** Environmental Protection Agency

**FHWA:** Federal Highway Administration

**FMCSR:** Federal Motor Carrier Safety Regulations

**Hazardous Materials Regulations**: Standards set by the **Research and Special Programs Administration (RSPA) Office of Hazardous Materials Transportation (OHMT)** that regulate how hazardous materials are shipped.

**Interstate**: Between states

**Intrastate**: Within the state

**MCSAP:** Motor Carrier Safety Assistance Program

**NRC:** Nuclear Regulatory Commission

**NTSB:** The National Transportation Safety Board

**OMC:** Office of Motor Carriers

**OSHA:** Occupational Safety and Health Administration

**PSC**: Public Service Commission

**PUC**: Public Utilities Commission

**Straight truck**: A single unit truck with the engine, cab, and cargo compartment all on the same frame.

**Trailer**: A vehicle built for hauling cargo.

**Truck Tractor**: A vehicle used to pull one or more other vehicles, such as a semitrailer.

# LEARNING ACTIVITIES

## Review Exercises

1. Name one advantage of the conventional tractor.

   _____

2. Name one disadvantage of the conventional tractor.

   _____

   _____

3. Name one advantage of the cabover tractor.

   _____

   _____

4. Name one disadvantage of the cabover tractor.

   _____

5. Name five types of tractor body styles.

   1. _____     4. _____

   2. _____     5. _____

   3. _____

6. Name six types of semitrailers.

   1. _____     4. _____

   2. _____     5. _____

   3. _____     6. _____

7. Name and describe each different type of truck-tractor.

   Name _____

   _____

   Name _____

   _____

   Name _____

   _____

8.  Name and describe several types of tractor-trailer vehicles.

    Name _____

    _____

    Name _____

    _____

    Name _____

    _____

9.  What do these terms mean?

    Converter dolly _____

    _____

    Fifth wheel _____

    _____

    Duals _____

    _____

    Drive axle _____

    _____

    Tandem axle tractor _____

    _____

    Twin-screws _____

    _____

    Turnpike double _____

    _____

    Semitrailer _____

    _____

    Full trailer _____

    _____

    Van body _____

    _____

    Combination vehicle _____

## True-False Questions ✓

If the statement is true, circle the T. If the statement is false, circle the F.

(T) F    1.    A tandem axle tractor has two rear axles.

(T) F    2.    A single axle tractor has one steering axle and one rear axle.

T (F)    3.    The rear axle, which is powered, is called a tag axle.

T (F)    4.    A conventional tractor has the cab over the front wheels.

(T) F    5.    Two wheels with tires together on each side of the same axle are called duals.

(T) F    6.    A cabover tractor has a shorter wheel base than a conventional tractor.

T (F)    7.    A semitrailer can be made into a full trailer by using a twin screw.

(T) F    8.    The front of a semitrailer has no axle.

(T) F    9.    A fifth wheel connects a trailer to a tractor.

(T) F    10.    A full trailer is completely supported by its own axles.

T (F)    11.    A tag axle is a drive axle.

(T) F    12.    A single drive axle tractor has a shorter wheelbase than a tandem axle tractor.

T (F)    13.    A turnpike double is a tractor with three trailers.

T (F)    14.    A tractor with dual rear axles is the only type of tractor that can be used to make a combination vehicle.

(T) F    15.    Professional truck drivers understand they **are** the trucking industry in the eyes of the public.

# Chapter Two
# CONTROL SYSTEMS

© 1997 Career Publishing Inc.

**Vehicle Controls • Engine Controls • Primary Vehicle Controls • Transmission Controls • Secondary Vehicle Controls • Driver Restraints • Instruments**

**FROM NOW ON,**

**ONLY THE BEST WILL DRIVE**

# OBJECTIVES

When you have mastered this chapter, you will be able to:

- Describe the engine controls, primary vehicle controls, and secondary vehicle controls

- State the name, location, and function of the controls for:
  Starting the engine              Accelerating
  Shutting down the engine         Braking
  Shifting                         Parking

- Know the location of the controls for lights, signals and comfort

- Understand the importance of using seatbelts

- Describe the acceptable operating range for the fuel, oil, air, cooling, exhaust, and electrical systems

- Discuss how checking these systems often can help you spot problems early

- Understand the use of warning devices

# CHAPTER TWO

# CONTROL SYSTEMS

## INTRODUCTION

Big rigs are as different on the inside as on the outside. One look at the controls and instruments in the cab lets you know it's a different ball game than driving a car. This chapter will help you learn the name, location, and function of these controls.

## VEHICLE CONTROLS

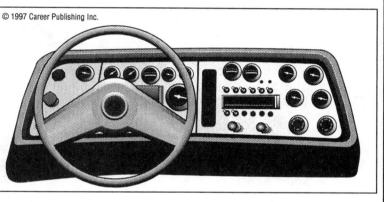
© 1997 Career Publishing Inc.

**Figure 2-1**

All drivers must learn how to operate the controls of any vehicle before driving. The three basic types of controls are the:

1. Engine controls
2. Primary vehicle controls
3. Secondary vehicle controls

### Engine Controls

The engine controls start the engine and shut it down. They do not control movement. Engine controls are similar in most vehicles. The differences depend on the type of engine, fuel used, and starters.

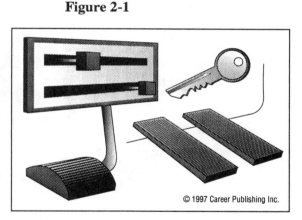
© 1997 Career Publishing Inc.

**Figure 2-2**

#### Engine Control Switch

The engine control switch allows the engine to start. Think of it as a gate through which an electrical current must pass to start the engine. If the switch is off, the engine will not start. You move the switch with your hand to turn the engine on or off.

#### Starter Button

Some trucks also have a starter button. To start the engine, turn the key to on and push the starter button.

Other controls that relate to starting or stopping the engine include the:

**Auxiliary Starter button**: Available on some cab-over-engine (COE) models. It lets you to start the engine with the cab tilted.

**Engine stop control knob**: Used in some diesel engines to shut off the engine. You pull the knob out and hold it until engine stops.

**Computerized idle timer**: A function of the engine's electronic controls, it will shut down the engine in a prescribed amount of time after the truck has come to a halt.

**Emergency engine stop control**: Shuts down the engine. Use this control in emergency situations only. Many companies insist that it be reset by a mechanic after each use.

## Primary Vehicle Controls

The primary vehicle controls allow the driver to control the truck. The clutch pedal, transmission control, accelerator pedal, steering wheel, and brake controls are primary vehicle controls. Truck drivers must know how to operate all of these.

### Clutch Pedal

To start the engine or shift gears, you must use the clutch pedal. There are three basic pedal positions:

**Figure 2-3**

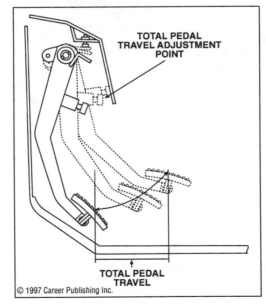

**Figure 2-4**

1. **Disengaged:** The pedal is pushed within 2" of the floor. When the pedal is in this position, the engine and drive train are separated. The clutch must be disengaged to start the engine and shift gears.
2. **Free Play**: This is the amount of pedal movement possible at the top of the stroke without engaging or disengaging the clutch. It should be between 1/2" and 2-1/2".
3. **Engaged**: The pedal is fully released. The driver is not applying any pressure. The word *engaged* means the engine and drive train are connected and moving together.

The clutch pedal also passes through a transition distance when the clutch is engaging or disengaging.

**Clutch brake**: Most transmissions use a clutch brake. It stops or controls the speed of the transmission input shaft and countershaft. The clutch brake is used to engage only the first gear or the reverse gear when the vehicle is stopped. It works when the pedal is within 1" or 2" of the floor, depending on its adjustment.

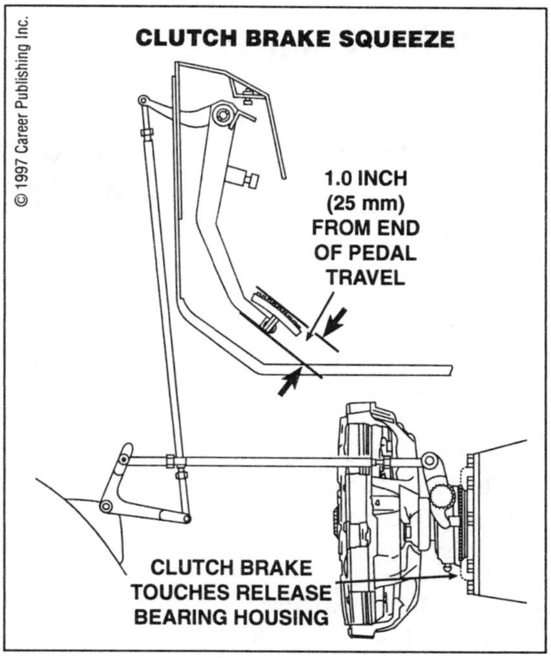

## Transmission Controls

Transmission controls vary with different types of transmissions. Most tractors

**CLUTCH BRAKE SQUEEZE**

© 1997 Career Publishing Inc.

1.0 INCH (25 mm) FROM END OF PEDAL TRAVEL

CLUTCH BRAKE TOUCHES RELEASE BEARING HOUSING

Figure 2-5

have a manual transmission with both a clutch and a gear lever. All gear changes are controlled by the driver. Some have semi-automatic transmissions which still include a clutch and gear lever, but some of the gear changes are controlled by an on-board computer. A few trucks have fully automatic transmissions with just a gear lever and no clutch. All gear changes are controlled by hydraulics or by an on-board computer.

**Controls on a typical manual transmission gear lever:** A range change lever on the front of the lever allows you to switch between ranges. The lever is in the down position for the low range (usually the bottom four or five gears) and in the up position for the high range (the top four or five gears).

**Splitter valve:** Some transmissions, such as the 13-speed and 18-speed Eaton Fuller, use a splitter valve to split gears into direct or overdrive. The valve is controlled with a button on the top of the gear shift knob.

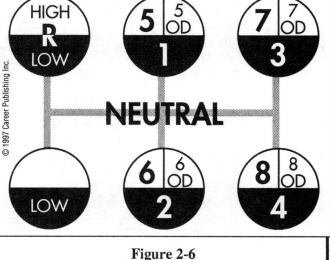

**CONTROLS AND OPERATION OF A 13-SPEED EATON FULLER**

HIGH R LOW

5 / 5 OD / 1

7 / 7 OD / 3

NEUTRAL

LOW

6 / 6 OD / 2

8 / 8 OD / 4

© 1997 Career Publishing Inc.

Figure 2-6

## Other Controls

**Accelerator Pedal**: Controls the vehicle's road speed (mph). Push the pedal down to increase speed and ease off to reduce speed.

**Steering Wheel**: Used to steer the rig. The steering wheel is 6-12" larger across (diameter) than on a car. The larger size gives the turning leverage needed to control big rigs.

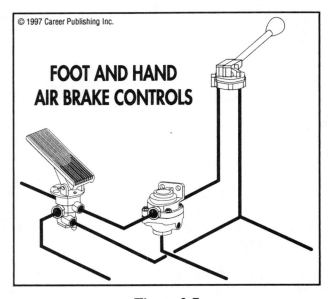

**FOOT AND HAND AIR BRAKE CONTROLS**

© 1997 Career Publishing Inc.

Figure 2-7

**Brake Controls**: Used to slow or stop the rig. Learning how to use the brake controls is very important. You will learn how to use the following controls.

- **Foot brake control valve** (also called foot valve or treadle valve): This valve operates the service brakes on both the tractor and trailer. When pushed in, it releases air pressure to all tractor and trailer brake chambers on the rig.

- **Trailer brake control valve** (also called hand valve, trolley valve, or independent trailer brake): Operates the service brakes on the trailer only. This hand brake is used only in special situations, not to hold the rig when parked.

- **Parking brake control valve**: A flip switch or push-pull knob that lets the driver put on the parking brake. The parking brake should be put on only after the rig is stopped.

- **Trailer air supply valve**: (also called tractor protection valve) In the open position, it provides air to the trailer brakes. In the closed position, it shuts off the air supply to the trailer. It is closed when there is no trailer. Never use this valve as a parking brake.

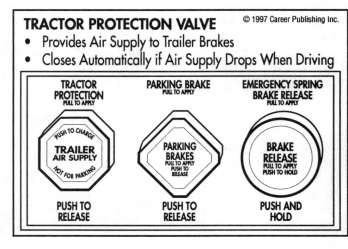

**TRACTOR PROTECTION VALVE** © 1997 Career Publishing Inc.
- Provides Air Supply to Trailer Brakes
- Closes Automatically if Air Supply Drops When Driving

| TRACTOR PROTECTION PULL TO APPLY | PARKING BRAKE PULL TO APPLY | EMERGENCY SPRING BRAKE RELEASE PULL TO APPLY |
|---|---|---|
| PUSH TO CHARGE **TRAILER AIR SUPPLY** NOT FOR PARKING | **PARKING BRAKES** PULL TO APPLY PUSH TO RELEASE | **BRAKE RELEASE** PULL TO APPLY PUSH TO HOLD |
| PUSH TO RELEASE | PUSH TO RELEASE | PUSH AND HOLD |

Figure 2-8

When the air supply drops to 20-45 psi, the valve closes automatically. This stops the flow of air and protects the tractor's air supply. The trailer air supply valve triggers the emergency relay valve that puts on the trailer brakes.

- **Trailer emergency relay valve**: Works only in an emergency when the air supply is lost. It will not keep the brakes applied on a parked trailer. If the air lines are crossed, the brakes will stay on.

Other primary controls found on some rigs include the:

**Antilock Brakes**: From March 1, 1997, all new tractors must be fitted with an anti-lock brake system (ABS). The system is largely invisible from the cab, except for a warning lamp to tell you if the system is malfunctioning and/or a warning label.

The ABS is designed to maintain vehicle stability while braking by preventing the wheels from locking and losing traction. Sensors at the wheels detect impending lock-up and electronically release and reapply the brakes so that traction is maintained. The whole process occurs in split seconds — much faster than you could physically pump the brakes. The most important thing to know about driving with ABS is to always hit the brakes and *hold* them. Do not pump them. Even though it may take longer to stop, ABS will prevent more accidents because it allows you to stay in control and steer around objects. Without ABS, it easy to lock the wheels and lose total control of the vehicle.

**Engine brakes and retarders**: Slow the rig without using the service brake system. They keep the rig operating at a reasonable speed. There are four basic types of auxiliary brakes or speed retarders.

1. **Exhaust brake**: Simplest form of retarder. It keeps the exhaust gases from escaping. The exhaust brake builds up back pressure in the engine. This keeps it from increasing speed. It is controlled by an on/off switch in the cab or automatically by a switch on the accelerator or clutch pedal.
2. **Engine brake**: Most widely used type of retarder; it alters valve timing and turns the engine into an air compressor. The engine brake can be operated by hand with a switch on the dash or automatically when the foot is removed from the accelerator pedal.

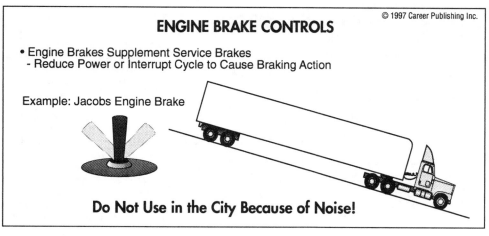

Figure 2-9

3. **Hydraulic retarder**: A type of drive line retarder, mounted on the drive line between the engine and the fly wheel or between the transmission and drive axles. It reduces speed by directing a flow of oil against the stator vanes. The retarder can be turned on by hand with a lever in the cab or automatically by an accelerator switch on the floor.

4. **Electric retarder**: Uses electromagnets to slow the rotors attached to the drive train. The driver turns it on or off with a switch in the cab.

**Interaxle Differential Lock Control**: Locks and unlocks rear tandem axles. Unlocked, the axles turn independently of one another on a dry surface. In the locked position, power to the axles is equalized to help keep the wheels without traction from spinning. This position is used on slippery roads. The control should be locked before the wheels begin to spin.

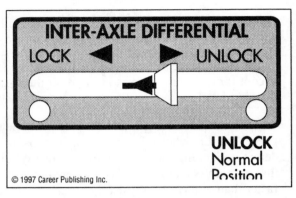

Figure 2-10

## Secondary Vehicle Controls

These controls do not affect the rig's power or movement. They have other jobs; they help the driver's:

- Vision:
    Lights
    Windshield wipers
    Defroster
- Communication:
    Horns
    Radios
    Lights (headlights, brake lights, 4-way flashers)
- Comfort:
    Seat position
    Air vents
    Air conditioner
    Heater
- Safety:
    Seatbelts
    Door locks

Many of these controls are similar to those found in cars. For example, the switches for the lights and windshield wipers. Others are found only on tractor-trailers. The number and function of the secondary controls vary with the design of the truck.

Other controls not related to driving include those for the:
- Hydraulic cab tilt operation
- Fifth wheel lock assembly

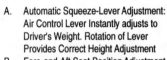

### Air Suspension Seat Controls

A. Automatic Squeeze-Lever Adjustment: Air Control Lever Instantly adjusts to Driver's Weight. Rotation of Lever Provides Correct Height Adjustment
B. Fore-and-Aft Seat Position Adjustment
C. Three-Position Seat Cushion Tilt
D. Shock Release Lever

Correct seat adjustment is vital. Over the years, not sitting in the right position can injure your back. Adjust the seat so that your knees are as high or higher than the bottom of your lower back. In this way, the weight of your legs will not pull on your lower back. Use the isolator to protect your back and kidneys from being slapped by the seat every time the drive wheels hit a bump. © 1997 Career Publishing Inc.

Figure 2-11

# DRIVER RESTRAINTS

The DOT is concerned with safety for big rig drivers and is urging enforcement of the law requiring drivers to wear seatbelts. In a study in 1990, the National Transportation Safety Board (NTSB) found that 92.3% of drivers who were killed in crashes had safety belts available but were not using them.

Most trucks are now fitted with full lap and shoulder belts. Although they will not prevent all fatalities and injuries, they can greatly improve your chance of survival. If the shoulder belt is uncomfortable because of the action of the suspended seat, get a special locking clip to keep the belt from constantly tightening. A safe company will encourage its drivers who wear seatbelts and discipline those who do not.

# VEHICLE INSTRUMENTS

Gauges and meters tell you about the condition of your rig and its parts. Keeping an eye on your gauges and meters can warn you of possible problems. To drive a tractor-trailer, you must learn to:
- Understand the purpose and function of each instrument.
- Know what the instruments are telling you. Temperature and pressure gauges can indicate improper or unsafe operating conditions that can damage your rig.
- Take the correct action when an improper reading appears.
- Know when your rig has reached the correct operating range. For example, what should the correct readings be for air pressure, oil pressure, and water temperature?

Instruments are divided into two types.
1. Basic instruments
2. Warning devices

# BASIC INSTRUMENTS

**Speedometer:** Indicates road speed in miles and kilometers per hour. A speedometer that works is required by law.

**Odometer:** Shows how many miles or kilometers the rig has been driven.

**Tachometer:** Displays the engine speed in revolutions per minute (rpm). It is a guide to knowing when to shift gears. The tachometer helps you use the engine and transmission effectively during acceleration and deceleration.

**Fuel Gauge:** Shows how much fuel is in the tanks. Since the gauge is not always accurate, a driver should check the tanks visually before each trip and at stopovers.

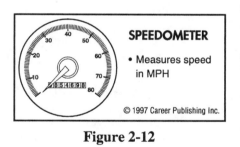

**Figure 2-12**

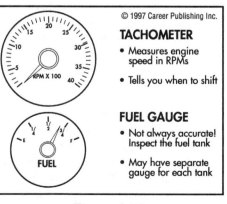

**Figure 2-13**

**Voltmeter**: Measures the voltage output of the battery. The meter needle should be between 13.0 and 14.5 volts during normal operation. The operator's manual will tell you if the reading should be different for your rig. Higher than normal voltage may boil away battery fluids and shorten the battery's life.

# MEASURING THE ELECTRICAL SYSTEM

**VOLTMETER**

**Starting**
• Green — Well Charged Battery
• Yellow — Low Battery Charge
• Red — Very Low Charge

**Operating**
• Green — Okay
• Red — Voltage Output Too High!

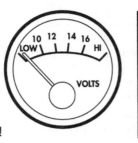

**AMMETER**
• Normal is ZERO
• Continuous High Charge +
  or Discharge –
  Means Problems With
  the Electrical System

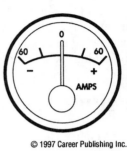

© 1997 Career Publishing Inc.

**Figure 2-14**

**Ammeter**: Measures how much the battery is being charged or discharged. Under normal operating conditions, the ammeter should read:

**Engine off** — zero
**Engine starts** — needle jumps to the charge side and flutters
**Engine warmed** — reading drops back to zero or slightly on the charged side

A constant high reading indicates the battery may be ready to fail. Continuous discharge means the battery is not receiving a charge from the alternator or generator. A number of things can cause these readings.
• The battery needs fluid.
• The voltage regulator is not working properly.
• A bare wire is causing a short circuit.
• The alternator is defective.
• There are loose or worn belts.

## Air Pressure Gauge

The air brake system is activated by air pressure. The air pressure gauge tells the amount of pressure in the tanks. Air pressure should start building as soon as the engine starts and continue until the maximum pressure is reached. This is usually 120 psi (pounds per square inch). In normal operation, when the air pressure drops to 90 psi, the air compressor will build it back to 120 psi. The air compressor governor controls this operation.

If the air pressure drops to 60 psi while driving, the low pressure warning alarm light will turn on. At 20-45 psi, the tractor protection valve will close and shut off the air supply to the trailer. Shutting off the air to the trailer triggers the emergency relay valve, which puts on the trailer brakes.

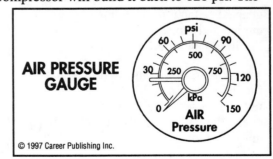

**AIR PRESSURE GAUGE**

© 1997 Career Publishing Inc.

**Figure 2-15**

Low air pressure can result from:
- Air leaks
- Failure of the compressor or compressor governor control
- Broken or kinked air lines
- An open air tank petcock

If you have a loss of air pressure, stop at once. Locate the source of the problem and get it fixed. Do not operate your rig without enough air pressure.

## Oil Pressure Gauge

Metal engine parts rub against each other and create friction (heat). A thin film of oil between the parts prevents overheating and too much wear. The lubrication

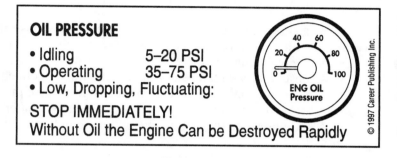

**OIL PRESSURE**
- Idling          5–20 PSI
- Operating       35–75 PSI
- Low, Dropping, Fluctuating:

**STOP IMMEDIATELY!**
Without Oil the Engine Can be Destroyed Rapidly

© 1997 Career Publishing Inc.

**Figure 2-16**

system provides the oil. The oil pressure gauge indicates the oil pressure within the system.

If pressure is lost, it means there is not enough lubrication in the system. Then the engine can be destroyed in a short period of time. Oil pressure should register within seconds after the engine is started. It should then rise slowly to the normal operating range. The normal range will depend on the type of vehicle and the engine rpm. You should stop and check if:
- Pressure does not register or if it fluctuates rapidly when starting.
- A loss in pressure occurs.

A number of things can cause low oil pressure.
- Not enough oil
- Oil leaks
- Oil pump failure

An adequate oil level with no leaks suggests a problem with the oil pump or a clogged oil line or filter.

## Other Gauges

The gauges found on vehicles will vary. The only gauges required by law are the speedometer and air pressure gauge. Most rigs do not have the following extra gauges.

**Air Brake Application Gauge:** It indicates in psi the amount of air pressure used when the brake pedal is pushed.

**Coolant Temperature Gauge:** This panel gauge shows the temperature of the coolant in the engine block. The cooling system protects engine parts against destruction from the heat created by the burning of fuel in the combustion chamber, rapid movement and friction. The normal operating range is 170-195° or the safe range indicated by the operator's manual.

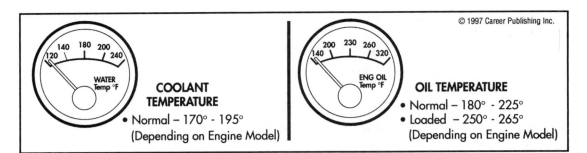

**Figure 2-17**

If the gauge registers above the normal range, the engine may be overheating. Shut down the engine at once. Overheating can be caused by:
- Not enough engine oil
- A loose or broken fan belt or malfunctioning fan clutch or control
- A blocked radiator – either from the inside or from the outside
- A broken thermostat, coolant pump, or radiator shutter
- A severe load on the engine (attempting to pull too much or pull too hard)
- The winter front may need to be removed

**Engine Oil Temperature Gauge**: This gauge indicates the temperature of the engine oil. The normal operating temperature for engine oil is 180-225°. This is 20-60° higher than the coolant temperature.

High oil temperature causes the oil to get thin (reduced viscosity). This decreases the oil pressure. Engine oil temperatures, however, can run as high as 250-265° for a short period without damaging the engine by overheating. Do not operate the engine above the safe operating range.

**Exhaust Pyrometer Gauge**: This gauge indicates the temperature of the gases in the exhaust manifold. If the gases are too hot, they can damage the turbocharger. Maximum safe operating temperatures may be shown on the pyrometer name plate or listed in the operator's manual.

**Gear Box Temperature Gauge**: This gauge shows the temperature of the lubricant in the transmission. The normal reading is 150-200°. A high reading may indicate a low oil level.

**Axle Temperature Gauge**: This gauge shows the temperature of the lubricant in the front and rear drive axles. The normal reading is 150-200°. This reading does not vary when the rig is loaded. Higher readings, up to 230-250° degrees, are all right for short periods. The readings for both drive axles should be within 10° of each other. Readings above the normal range can mean bad bearings or a flat tire. The forward rear axle in a twin screw will run hotter than the rear axle.

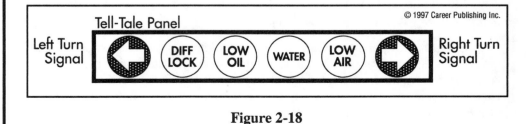

**Figure 2-18**

**Warning Devices**: Some rigs have warning lights and buzzers to tell when the fuel, air pressure, or temperature has reached a danger point. Some warning lights are on the dash. They will turn on or flash when there is a problem. Stop your rig when any warning devices sound or light up.

You should become familiar with the following warning lights or buzzers.

- **Low air pressure warning alarm**: Sounds or lights up when there is low pressure in the air brake system.

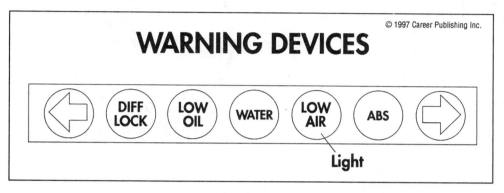

**Figure 2-19**

- **Coolant level alarm**: Lights up when the coolant level starts dropping, indicating a probable leak.
- **Oil level alarm**: Lights up when the oil level becomes too low for normal operation.
- **Coolant temperature warning**: Lights up when the temperature is too high.
- **Pyrometer warning**: Lights up when exhaust temperatures are too high.
- **Differential warning**: Flashes when the interaxle differential is in the *locked* position.

## SUMMARY

In this chapter, you have learned about the control systems for your rig. You now know where the readings should be for safe operation. As a driver concerned with safety on the highways, you understand the importance of wearing a seatbelt at all times. Warning devices were explained, as well as the need to pay attention to them if they should sound or light up.

## KEY WORDS

**Engine controls**: Start the engine and shut it down.

**Primary vehicle controls**: Allow the driver to control the truck.

**Seatbelts**: A safety restraint required by law for drivers and passengers of all vehicles.

**Secondary vehicle controls**: Do not affect the rig's power or movement but help the driver's vision, communication, comfort, and safety.

# LEARNING ACTIVITIES

Draw the needle at the correct setting for normal operation on each of the gauges, and write the normal range on the line below the drawing.

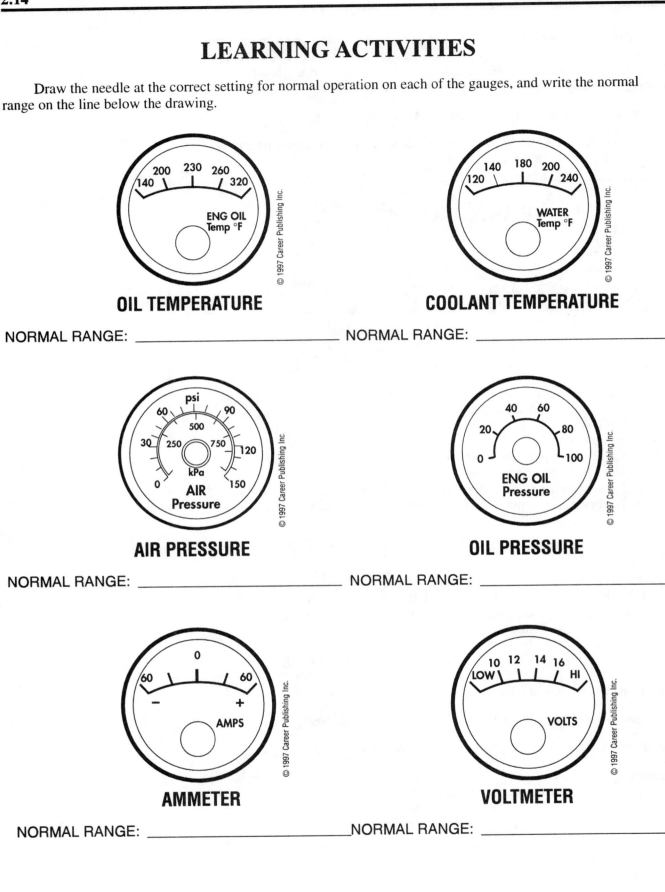

**OIL TEMPERATURE**

NORMAL RANGE: _____

**COOLANT TEMPERATURE**

NORMAL RANGE: _____

**AIR PRESSURE**

NORMAL RANGE: _____

**OIL PRESSURE**

NORMAL RANGE: _____

**AMMETER**

NORMAL RANGE: _____

**VOLTMETER**

NORMAL RANGE: _____

## True-False Questions   _- 3_

If the question is true, circle the T. If the question is false, circle the F.

T (F) 1. The engine is started and shut down by the primary vehicle controls.

(T) F 2. Engine control switches allow the engine to start.

(T) F 3. Pushing the clutch pedal to the floor engages the clutch. *(p. 2.4)*

T (F) 4. Clutch brake has nothing to do with controlling the speed of the transmission input shaft.

(T) F 5. Manual transmissions typically have two ranges.

(T) F 6. The tractor protection valve controls the compressed air supply that actuates the trailer brakes.

(T) F 7. Engine brakes and retarders slow the rig without using the service brake system.

(T) F 8. When the air supply to the trailer is lost, the trailer emergency relay valve is activated.

(T) F 9. The interaxle differential lock control is used to prevent the wheels from spinning on slippery surfaces.

(T) F 10. The independent trailer brake operates the emergency brake on the tractor. *(p. 2.6)*

T (F) 11. Once you have begun your trip, you do not need to be concerned about the readings on the gauges and meters.

(T) F 12. The speedometer, odometer, tachometer, and fuel gauge are classed as basic instruments.

T (F) 13. The air pressure gauge inside the cab of the tractor measures the amount of air in the tires.

(T) F 14. The air pressure warning alarm will activate if the air pressure drops to 60 psi while you are driving.

T (F) 15. The coolant temperature gauge may not be found on some trucks. *(p. 2.11)*

# Chapter Three
# HOURS OF SERVICE

© 1997 Career Publishing Inc.

**Definitions • Maximum Driving Time • Maximum On-Duty Time • Off-Duty Time
Records of Duty • Driver Declared Out-of-Service**

**FROM NOW ON,**

**ONLY THE BEST WILL DRIVE**

# OBJECTIVES

When you have mastered this chapter, you will be able to:

- Explain how to record the driver's time and activities while on the road

- Describe the format for making entries in a log book and what information must be included

- Compute on-duty hours and required rest stops while on the road

# CHAPTER THREE

# HOURS OF SERVICE

## INTRODUCTION

As a tractor-trailer driver, you will be responsible for maneuvering up to 40 tons of loaded equipment in all kinds of weather and traffic conditions. You will be expected to safely deliver valuable cargo to its destination in the shortest time possible. Many shipments are part of the **Just in Time,** or **JIT,** delivery system. This system gets rid of the costly overhead of warehousing stock by getting it there just in time for its use.

In order to wisely use your time behind the wheel and yet stay within the federal laws, you will need to know how to manage and record various activities when you transport freight. There is far more to hauling a shipment than just driving.

The human body must have rest in order to function. We often push ourselves beyond our natural limits to do the job we have set out to do. If we push too hard, often we do not do the job as well as we should.

**Figure 3-1**

Airline pilots have strict limitations on their flying hours and the required rest between flights. Federal laws have been passed to protect passengers by guaranteeing their pilot should not be unfit to fly because of fatigue.

Your responsibility as a tractor-trailer driver is similar to that of a pilot. You should not be unfit to drive because you are too tired. Your skills are at their best when you are well rested and alert. There are federal regulations that also apply to drivers of heavy vehicles to keep tired drivers from driving.

## REGULATIONS

The laws that govern maximum time on duty are found in Part 395 of the Federal Motor Carrier Safety Regulations (FMCSR). You must know and comply with them. The regs regarding **Hours of Service** (time on duty) apply to you if you drive a CMV that:

- Has a GVWR of 10,001 lbs. or more
- Transports more than 15 persons including the driver
- Transports cargo requiring hazmat placards

## DEFINITIONS

**On-Duty Time:** The time the driver begins work, or must be ready to go to work, until the time he or she is relieved from work of any kind. On-Duty Time includes all time spent:

- Working or waiting to be dispatched at your terminal or a shipper's facility
- Inspecting, servicing, or getting your tractor or trailer ready
- Driving or in the cab except for sleeper berth time
- Loading or unloading cargo, or supervising the loading or unloading
- Obtaining shipping documents
- Performing required duties at an accident involving your rig
- Repairing your rig or staying with it while repairs are being made
- Doing any work for pay for a carrier
- Performing any compensated work for any non-motor carrier

**No driver shall drive more than 10 hours after having 8 hours off duty.**

Figure 3-2

**Off-Duty Time:** Any time during which the driver is relieved of all on-duty time responsibilities.

**Driving Time:** All time spent at the controls of your tractor.

**Seven (7) Consecutive Days:** Seven days in a row, beginning on any day at a given time.

**Eight (8) Consecutive Days:** Eight days in a row, beginning on any day at a given time.

**Twenty-Four (24) Hour Period:** Twenty-four hours in a row beginning at a time set by the carrier.

**Regularly Employed Driver:** A driver who works for one motor carrier for any 7 consecutive days

**Sleeper Berth:** A berth in the tractor cab in which the driver can sleep. Its size and other specifications are determined by law.

**Driver-Salesman:** A driver who also sells products or provides services to the customer. An example is a beverage or baked goods delivery person. The driver works within 100 miles of his home terminal and spends at least half of his time selling or taking orders for restocking products.

**Multiple Stops:** Several stops in the same village, city, or town that can be entered as one stop.

**Principal Place of Business:** The main office of the carrier where all records are kept.

# MAXIMUM DRIVING AND ON-DUTY TIME

Federal laws provide that no carrier shall require or permit a driver to drive:
- More than 10 hours after having 8 hours off duty
- After being on duty for 15 hours following 8 hours off duty
- After being on duty for 60 hours in any 7 consecutive days if the carrier does not operate every day of the week
- After being on duty for 70 hours in any 8 consecutive days if the carrier operates every day of the week

These same regulations apply to an owner/operator. The laws say no commercial driver can drive more than the specified hours. Section 395.3 of the FMCSR provides for exceptions to the rules for maximum hours in certain cases.

## Travel Time

If an employer requires a driver to travel, even though he is not driving, the time must be counted as on-duty time unless the driver is given 8 consecutive hours off duty when he or she arrives at the destination. Then the travel time will be counted as off-duty time.

## Adverse Driving Conditions

**Figure 3-3**

Snow, sleet, fog, icy pavement, and unusual road or traffic conditions may prevent the driver from completing his scheduled run in the 10 hours allowed by law. In such cases, the driver may be able to drive for 2 hours more to reach the original destination or a safe place to park the rig. Adverse driving conditions must be noted on the driver's log to show the reason for the extra driving time.

# RECORD OF DUTY STATUS

There are only two ways permitted by federal laws to record a driver's duty status. The status must be noted in the:
1. Driver's Log
   or
2. Carrier's Time Record

The **Carrier's Time Record** may be used only when:
- The driver operates within a 100-mile radius of his home terminal.
- The driver reports back to his home terminal and was not on duty more than 12 hours.
- The driver has at least 8 hours off duty after each 12 hours on duty.
- The driver does not drive more than 10 hours following 8 hours off.
- For 6 months, the carrier prepares and maintains records showing the time drivers go on duty and go off duty, the total hours per day, and the preceding 7-day record for new or part-time drivers.

The form shown below is used for first time or intermittent drivers.

The **Driver's Daily Log** is the most commonly used record of duty status for drivers. Other than pick-up and delivery operations, most tractor-trailers are driven over 100 miles from their home terminal.

Federal laws require every carrier to make sure each driver records, in duplicate, his or her duty status for all 24-hour periods. It must be recorded on the specified form.

The form (Figure 3-5 on the next page) shows the entries the driver

**HOURS OF SERVICE RECORD FOR FIRST TIME OR INTERMITTENT DRIVERS**

Name (Print) _____
First        Middle        Last

| DAY | TOTAL TIME ON DUTY |
|---|---|
| 1 | _____ |
| 2 | _____ |
| 3 | _____ |
| 4 | _____ |
| 5 | _____ |
| 6 | _____ |
| 7 | _____ |

TOTAL _____

I hereby certify that the information contained heron is true to the best of my knowledge and belief, and that my last period of release from duty was from

_____ to _____
(Hour/Date)              (Hour/Date)

Signature_____ Date _____

© 1997 Career Publishing Inc.

**Figure 3-4**

must make on the daily log. The correct blanks in which to make the entries are identified by the number of the duty status or other information that is required.

Duty status must be recorded as:
1. Off-duty; or OFF
2. Sleeper Berth; or SB, (if a sleeper berth is used)
3. Driving; or D
4. On-duty, Not driving; or ON
5. Each change of duty status must show the name of the nearest city, town, or village and the state abbreviation in the Remarks Section.

The form must also show the:
6. Date by month, day, and year
7. Number of miles driven each day
8. Tractor and trailer number or license plate number
9. Name of the carrier, or carriers: when you drive for more than one carrier in a 24-hour period, you must show the names of all carriers and the time you started and finished work for each.
10. Address of the carrier's main office
11. Driver's signature on certification
12. Name of the co-driver (if there is one)
13. Starting time for the 24 hour period
14. Total hours in each on-duty status
15. Total hours of duty status: Line 14 + Line 15 must = 24.
16. Shipping document number or the name of the shipper and the product

17. When noting the city and state where the change of duty status took place, include such information as adverse weather or emergency conditions in the remarks section.
18. On some Driver's Daily Log forms, the starting point and final delivery, or turn around, point may be entered. If the run is a turn around back to the original terminal, enter the name of the most distant point, and then the words *and return.*
19. Although it is not required by law, it is a good idea, and often company policy, for a driver to complete the recap section of the Driver's Daily Log. List the number of hours remaining on duty and state whether you will be driving. Figure 3-6 on the next page shows how one type of recap may be completed.

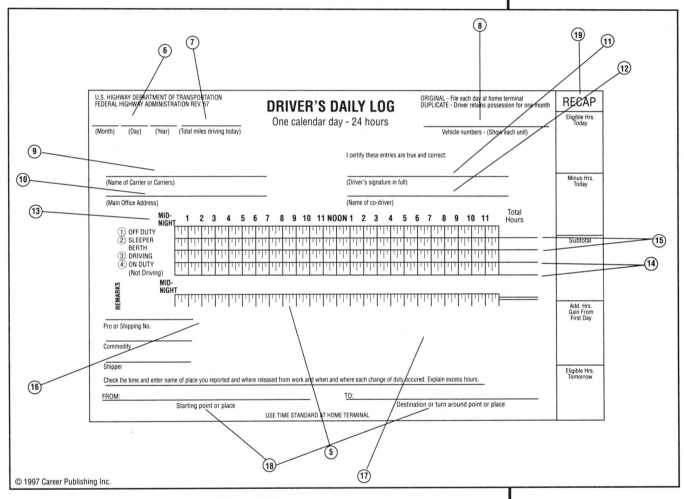

© 1997 Career Publishing Inc.

**Figure 3-5**

## Driver's Daily Log Entries

The **Driver's Log** is his or her personal record of duty status and the time worked for each employer. If the driver was paid for work for a non-carrier, he or she must also record this as On-duty time.

All entries must:
- Be made only by the driver
- Be legible

- Be current to the last change of duty status
- Be made using the time zone of the driver's home terminal: for example, a driver on a run to New York from his or her home terminal in California will make all entries using Pacific time. If the return run starts at 7:00 a.m. out of New York, he or she will enter the time as 4:00 a.m. Carriers with multiple terminals assign a home terminal to each driver.
- Be certified as correct by the drivers signature
- Be made on the correct section of the grid: a solid line will mark every 24-hour period
- Be readable on the duplicate copy: press hard to make sure

# Recap



| 1 | 2 | 3 | 4 | 5 |
|---|---|---|---|---|
| DAILY TOTAL DUTY & DR. HRS. | | | | |
| LAST SEVEN CONSECUTIVE DAYS IN PRECEDING MONTH | | 8 DAYS – 70 HOURS | | |
| | | TOTAL ON DUTY HOURS LAST 8 DAYS | TOTAL ON DUTY HOURS LAST 7 DAYS | HOURS AVAILABLE FOR ON DUTY TIME NEXT DAY (70 MINUS) (COL. 4) |
| | | | | |
| | | | | |
| | | | | |
| | | | | |
| | | | | |
| | | | | |
| | | | | |
| 1 | | | | |
| 2 | | | | |
| 3 | | | | |
| 4 | | | | |
| 5 | | | | |
| 6 | | | | |
| 7 | | | | |
| 8 | | | | |
| 9 | | | | |
| 10 | | | | |
| 11 | | | | |
| 12 | | | | |
| 13 | | | | |
| 14 | | | | |

**RECORD OF TIME WORKED**

DRIVER:

MONTH:

BOOK NUMBER:

INSTRUCTIONS

This form is designed for use in maintaining a running record of a driver's time on-duty each day. It may be used equally well for drivers working on a midnight-to-midnight or noon-to-noon basis and, by using the proper chart, for drivers eligible to work 60 hours in 7 consecutive days or 70 hours in 8 consecutive days. The person using the chart can also determine the time that a driver has available for work the next day in compliance with the Hours of Service Regulations of the Department of Transportation.

In keeping the record, be sure to use the proper chart. For a driver working 70 hours in 8 consecutive days, use the chart on the left. For a driver working 60 hours in 7 consecutive days, use the chart on the right.

Column 1 of each sections lists days of the month, 1-31 inclusive, plus the last days of the preceding month that must be counted.

In column 2 of the proper section enter the time on-duty for the day, (the total of Line 3, Driving, and Line 4, On-Duty Not Driving of the Drivers Daily Log). If the driver does not work on any day, enter a "0" for that day and compute other figures in accordance with the instructions below, as though he had worked.

| 1 | 2 | 3 | 4 | 5 |
|---|---|---|---|---|
| LAST SIX CONSECUTIVE DAYS IN PRECEDING MONTH | DAILY TOTAL DUTY & DR. HRS. | 7 DAYS – 60 HOURS | | |
| | 10 | TOTAL ON DUTY HOURS LAST 7 DAYS | TOTAL ON DUTY HOURS LAST 6 DAYS | HOURS AVAILABLE FOR ON DUTY TIME NEXT DAY (60 MINUS) (COL. 4) |
| | 10 | | | |
| | 15 | | | |
| | 4 | | | |
| | 15 | | | |
| | 0 | | | |
| 1 | 0 | 54 | 44 | 16 |
| 2 | 10 1/2 | 54 1/2 | 44 1/2 | 15 1/2 |
| 3 | 10 3/4 | 45 1/4 | 40 1/4 | 19 3/4 |
| 4 | 10 1/2 | 50 3/4 | 46 3/4 | 13 1/4 |
| 5 | 10 | 56 3/4 | 41 3/4 | 18 1/4 |
| 6 | 3 1/4 | 45 | 45 | 15 |
| 7 | | | | |
| 8 | | | | |
| 9 | | | | |
| 10 | | | | |
| 11 | | | | |
| 12 | | | | |
| 13 | | | | |
| 14 | | | | |

**Figure 3-6**

## Recording Your Duty Status

- Two or more consecutive 24-hour periods off duty may be recorded on one daily log.
- **Sleeper berth time** is only the time spent resting in an approved type of sleeper berth. Time spent sleeping on the seat or while sitting in the cab cannot be counted as sleeper berth time.
- All time spent at the controls of the rig must be counted as driving time.
- Changes in duty status must be recorded to the nearest 1/4 hour.
- The driver must have daily logs for the previous seven days.

All daily logs must be:
- Kept by the driver for seven days.
- Turned in to the carrier within 13 days, either in person or by mail.
- Kept temporarily at the home terminal by the carrier. Then they should be kept at the carrier's main office for at least six months from the date on the log.

The Driver's Daily Log shown in Figure 3-7 shows entries made by a driver on a midnight-to-midnight run from Richmond, VA to Newark, NJ. Notice how the 24-hour period contains a solid line made by the entries.

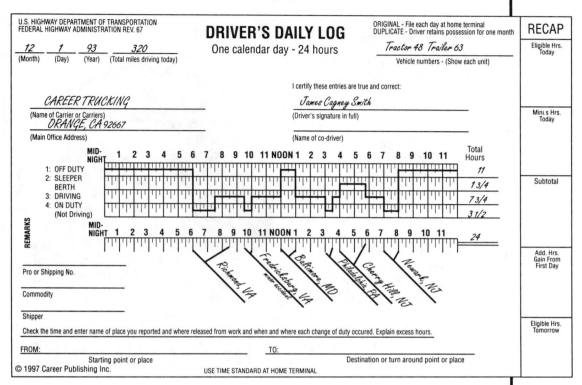

**Figure 3-7**

## Schedule

6:00 a.m. - 7:15 a.m.: Driver reported for work at his home terminal in Richmond and helped load his trailer.

7:15 a.m. - 7:30 a.m.: Picked up the shipping documents and did the pre-trip inspection.

7:30 a.m.: Driver got behind the wheel and began driving.

9:30 a.m. - 10:00 a.m.: Driver was in minor accident near Fredricksburg, VA. Filed police report.

12:00 noon: Driver arrived at the company's terminal in Baltimore, MD. Was relieved from duty to go to lunch while repairs were made to his tractor. The driver returned to the terminal at 1:00 p.m. and resumed his trip.

3:00 p.m. - 3:30 p.m.: Made deliveries to 2 locations in Philadelphia, PA.

4:00 p.m.: Stopped at rest area in Cherry Hill, NJ.

4:00 p.m. - 5:45 p.m.: Slept in sleeper berth.

5:45 p.m.: Started driving again.

7:00 p.m.: Arrived at Newark, NJ terminal. Parked rig and went to driver's room to complete paperwork.

7:00 p.m. - 8:00 p.m.: Driver completed daily log, vehicle condition report, and insurance report on the accident.

8:00 p.m.: Driver went off duty.

## DRIVER DECLARED OUT OF SERVICE

A driver may be declared out of service by any agent of the Federal Highway Administration (FHWA) for either of the following reasons:
- The driver has been on duty too many hours.
- The driver does not have Daily Logs for the previous 7 days.

> NOTE: A driver who has not completed the log for the current day and the day before, but has logs for the previous six days, will be given a chance to bring his logs up to date without being declared out of service.

© 1997 Career Publishing Inc.

## OUT OF SERVICE

**Figure 3-8**

If a driver is declared out of service because of too many hours on duty, he or she cannot drive until they have been off-duty long enough to be eligible to legally drive again.

If the driver is declared out of service for not having the daily logs, he or she may not drive until they have been off duty for 8 hours in a row and can legally drive again.

## PENALTIES

Drivers who make false entries on their Daily Logs, do not prepare a Daily Log, or drive more than the allowable hours, are subject to:
- Heavy fines
- Being declared out of service by an agent of the FHWA

They may also face delays in delivering their cargo. If a driver has driven too long, he or she can have an accident. As a result of this accident, both the driver and the carrier may face civil and criminal liability.

Carriers who do not keep proper records on all their drivers are also subject to heavy fines and civil liability if there is an accident because the driver violated the regulations.

A current log that is neat and readable means the driver has a professional attitude about knowing and obeying the trucking laws.

## SUMMARY

In this chapter, you have learned the importance of keeping a Daily Log accurately. The details of the on-duty and off-duty time requirements were explained. The penalties for both drivers and carriers if they break these laws were outlined. Finally, you have also learned a neat and readable log is the result of a driver's professional attitude.

## KEY WORDS

**Carrier's Time Record:** A record maintained by the carrier that records a driver's duty status.

**Driver's Daily Log, or Driver's Log:** The most commonly used record of duty status for drivers.

**Driving time:** All time spent at the controls of the rig.

**Hours of Service:** The amount of time you may spend on duty.

**Just in Time (JIT) delivery system:** A method of shipping that gets rid of the costly overhead of warehousing stock.

**Sleeper berth time:** Time spent resting in an approved type of sleeper berth.

# LEARNING ACTIVITIES

You are on a run from your home terminal in Los Angeles, California to Amarillo, Texas, and then on to Wichita, Kansas. You are following the Interstate Highways all the way. You do not exceed the speed limit at any time. You have engine trouble in Kingman, Arizona and must have repairs made to the truck. You also have a delay in Texas due to flooding and accidents. Fill in the Driver's Daily Log with all the necessary information.

U.S. HIGHWAY DEPARTMENT OF TRANSPORTATION
FEDERAL HIGHWAY ADMINISTRATION REV. 67

# DRIVER'S DAILY LOG
One calendar day - 24 hours

ORIGINAL - File each day at home terminal
DUPLICATE - Driver retains possession for one month

## RECAP

Eligible Hrs.
Today

_____ (Month) _____ (Day) _____ (Year) _____ (Total miles driving today)

Vehicle numbers - (Show each unit)

I certify these entries are true and correct:

_____ (Name of Carrier or Carriers)

_____ (Driver's signature in full)

Minus Hrs.
Today

_____ (Main Office Address)

_____ (Name of co-driver)

| | MID-NIGHT | 1 | 2 | 3 | 4 | 5 | 6 | 7 | 8 | 9 | 10 | 11 | NOON | 1 | 2 | 3 | 4 | 5 | 6 | 7 | 8 | 9 | 10 | 11 | Total Hours |

1: OFF DUTY
2: SLEEPER BERTH
3: DRIVING
4: ON DUTY (Not Driving)

Subtotal

REMARKS

| MID-NIGHT | 1 | 2 | 3 | 4 | 5 | 6 | 7 | 8 | 9 | 10 | 11 | NOON | 1 | 2 | 3 | 4 | 5 | 6 | 7 | 8 | 9 | 10 | 11 |

Add. Hrs.
Gain From
First Day

Pro or Shipping No.

Commodity

Shipper

Eligible Hrs.
Tomorrow

Check the time and enter name of place you reported and where released from work and when and where each change of duty occured. Explain excess hours.

FROM: _____
_____ Starting point or place

TO: _____
_____ Destination or turn around point or place

© 1997 Career Publishing Inc.                    USE TIME STANDARD AT HOME TERMINAL

---

U.S. HIGHWAY DEPARTMENT OF TRANSPORTATION
FEDERAL HIGHWAY ADMINISTRATION REV. 67

# DRIVER'S DAILY LOG
One calendar day - 24 hours

ORIGINAL - File each day at home terminal
DUPLICATE - Driver retains possession for one month

## RECAP

Eligible Hrs.
Today

_____ (Month) _____ (Day) _____ (Year) _____ (Total miles driving today)

Vehicle numbers - (Show each unit)

I certify these entries are true and correct:

_____ (Name of Carrier or Carriers)

_____ (Driver's signature in full)

Minus Hrs.
Today

_____ (Main Office Address)

_____ (Name of co-driver)

| | MID-NIGHT | 1 | 2 | 3 | 4 | 5 | 6 | 7 | 8 | 9 | 10 | 11 | NOON | 1 | 2 | 3 | 4 | 5 | 6 | 7 | 8 | 9 | 10 | 11 | Total Hours |

1: OFF DUTY
2: SLEEPER BERTH
3: DRIVING
4: ON DUTY (Not Driving)

Subtotal

REMARKS

| MID-NIGHT | 1 | 2 | 3 | 4 | 5 | 6 | 7 | 8 | 9 | 10 | 11 | NOON | 1 | 2 | 3 | 4 | 5 | 6 | 7 | 8 | 9 | 10 | 11 |

Add. Hrs.
Gain From
First Day

Pro or Shipping No.

Commodity

Shipper

Eligible Hrs.
Tomorrow

Check the time and enter name of place you reported and where released from work and when and where each change of duty occured. Explain excess hours.

FROM: _____
_____ Starting point or place

TO: _____
_____ Destination or turn around point or place

© 1997 Career Publishing Inc.                    USE TIME STANDARD AT HOME TERMINAL

## True-False Questions

If the question is true, circle the T. If the question is false, circle the F.

T  F  1.  On-duty time may include many activities in addition to driving.

T  F  2.  All time spent in the tractor is considered driving time.

T  F  3.  In the event of unexpected bad weather, a driver may be permitted to drive two extra hours to reach the original destination or a safe place to park the rig.

T  F  4.  The driver's log is the only method permitted by federal law to record a driver's duty status.

T  F  5.  The carrier's time record may be used to record a driver's duty status when the driver operates within a 100-mile radius of the home terminal.

T  F  6.  The driver's log is the most commonly used record of duty status for tractor-trailer drivers.

T  F  7.  Federal rules require every carrier to make sure each driver records his or her duty status in duplicate.

T  F  8.  Only the driver is permitted to make entries in the daily log.

T  F  9.  Time spent sleeping on the seat or while sitting in the cab may be counted as sleeper berth time.

T  F  10.  All time spent at the controls of the tractor-trailer must be considered driving time.

T  F  11.  All of his or her daily logs for the previous 7-day period must be kept by the driver.

T  F  12.  A driver may be declared out of service by any agent of the FHWA if he or she has been on duty more than the maximum hours permitted.

T  F  13.  Drivers who make false entries on daily logs may be disciplined by their companies but not by other authorities.

T  F  14.  A neat and readable log is the result of a driver's professional attitude.

T  F  15.  As long as a driver updates his or her log book on a monthly basis, he or she cannot be declared out of service.

# Chapter Four
# VEHICLE INSPECTION

**Pre-trip Inspection • Enroute Inspection • Post-trip Inspection • What to Look For • FMCSR 392.9 • FMCSR 397.17 • Vehicle Inspection Report**

**FROM NOW ON,**

**ONLY THE BEST WILL DRIVE**

# OBJECTIVES

When you have mastered this chapter, you will will be able to:

- Describe ways to make a quick and complete pre-trip inspection

- Discuss the effect of unknown malfunctions.

- Explain the importance of correcting malfunctions quickly.

- Provide a working knowledge of federal and state regulations for inspection.

- Explain the procedures for enroute and post-trip inspections

# CHAPTER FOUR
# VEHICLE INSPECTION

## INTRODUCTION

A tractor-trailer rig is a large and complex vehicle. For a rig's best operation, each part must be in a safe condition. The driver is mainly responsible for the state of all equipment. Timely, step-by-step inspections are a major way to ensure proper vehicle maintenance. This chapter will show the importance of inspections and how to correctly inspect your rig.

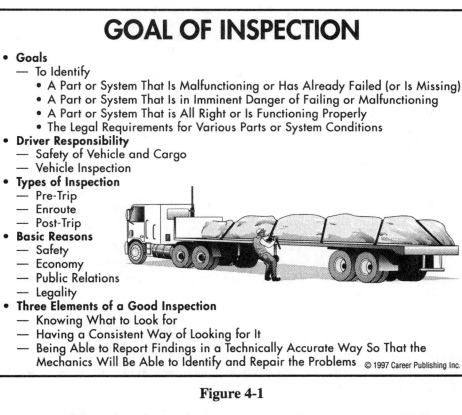

## GOAL OF INSPECTION

- **Goals**
  - To Identify
    - A Part or System That Is Malfunctioning or Has Already Failed (or Is Missing)
    - A Part or System That Is in Imminent Danger of Failing or Malfunctioning
    - A Part or System That is All Right or Is Functioning Properly
    - The Legal Requirements for Various Parts or System Conditions
- **Driver Responsibility**
  - Safety of Vehicle and Cargo
  - Vehicle Inspection
- **Types of Inspection**
  - Pre-Trip
  - Enroute
  - Post-Trip
- **Basic Reasons**
  - Safety
  - Economy
  - Public Relations
  - Legality
- **Three Elements of a Good Inspection**
  - Knowing What to Look for
  - Having a Consistent Way of Looking for It
  - Being Able to Report Findings in a Technically Accurate Way So That the Mechanics Will Be Able to Identify and Repair the Problems  © 1997 Career Publishing Inc.

**Figure 4-1**

## PURPOSE, IMPORTANCE AND TYPES OF VEHICLE INSPECTION

The goal of all tractor-trailer inspections is safety. Inspections identify systems or parts that are:
- Working properly
- Not working properly
- Failing
- Missing
- In danger of failing or malfunctioning

The law requires certain levels of performance for some parts and systems. A vital part of your job as a driver is to perform safety inspections on your rig. The driver is responsible for the:
- Safety of the rig
- Safe delivery of cargo

The driver is responsible for three types of vehicle inspections:
1. Pre-trip inspection
2. Enroute inspection
3. Post-trip inspection

The **pre-trip inspection** is a systematic parts and system check done before each trip. Its purpose is to find problems that can cause accidents, breakdowns, or poor performance. Such inspections are required by law for interstate trucking. Many states have adopted these federal laws. In most cases, pre-trip inspections are required by company policy. It makes sense to always do one. Use a company form if one is available.

During the **enroute inspection**, the driver checks the rig's controls and instruments while driving. At each stop, he also checks critical items.

The **post-trip inspection** is a thorough check at the end of a trip. The inspection is to be made on every vehicle driven. The driver must fill out a **vehicle condition report** (VCR) listing any defect noted during operation. Such reports are often required by law and by company policy.

Vehicle safety inspections are important for:
- Safety
- Economy
- Public relations
- Legal reasons

Safety is the most important and obvious benefit. Inspections help avoid mechanical defects and malfunctions that can lead to accidents.

Skipped or sloppy inspections cost money in the long run. Maintenance costs rise. Small problems become major repairs. Problems that are not attended to cut vehicle life. Also, careless or missed inspections can lead to rising fuel costs, high breakdown costs, and out-of-service time.

The trucking industry needs the good will of the public. Careful inspections are good public relations because they cut down on bad reports about the industry. For example, accidents and breakdowns cause traffic tie-ups. Inspections help cut down exhaust smoke and noise and may improve the rig's appearance.

Federal and state laws require certain types of commercial vehicle inspections by approved inspectors. If your rig does not meet their requirements, you can be put *out of service*.

## WHAT MAKES A GOOD INSPECTION?

Proper inspection of a tractor-trailer rig requires knowledge, a desire to do it right, and effort. You also have to know what you are doing and why you are doing it.

In performing inspections on your tractor-trailer, you should:
- Know what you are looking for
- Have a regular routine to follow
- Report findings in a way that mechanics can identify and repair the problem

## What To Look For

As a driver, you need to know:
- If a system or part is working correctly
- When a system or part is in danger of failing or malfunctioning
- The difference between major and minor defects
- Defects that are illegal and cause the rig to be put *out of service* by federal or state inspectors

Out-of-service regulations are found in **Federal Motor Carrier Safety Regulations (FMCSR), Part 396, Inspection, Repair, and Maintenance of Motor Vehicles**. You must, by law, know the requirements of **FMCSR 396.9(c), Motor Vehicle Declared Out-of-Service**. This regulation:
- Prohibits a driver from operating a vehicle that is *imminently hazardous to operate*
- Prohibits a motor carrier from requiring or permitting a driver to operate such a vehicle

A vehicle that is *imminently hazardous to operate* can be put out-of-service by federal or state inspectors during a roadside inspection. Safety defects considered *imminently hazardous* include:
- A defective steering system.
- Brake shoes that are missing or do not work
- Cracked brake drums
- Serious air loss in the brake system
- Missing lights or ones that do not work
- Bad tires
- Cracked wheels or ones that have missing lug nuts
- Fuel system leaks
- Cargo that is not properly secured
- A defective coupling system

## Fluid Leaks

Serious engine damage or breakdowns can occur because of loss of coolant or lubricant. Fuel leaks can result in fire. During any inspection, you should check all fluid levels including oil, coolant, battery, and fuel. You should also check for signs of fluid loss under the vehicle. You must check the gauges often while driving.

## Bad Tires

Tire defects increase the chance of a blowout and make the rig hard to handle. Federal regulations forbid driving with faulty tires. When inspecting, look for tires that are:
- Under-inflated, flat, or have a leak you can hear
- Badly worn, cut, or damaged in any way
- Not matching (radials and bias-ply used together)
- Touching other tires or parts of the rig
- Mismatched sizes

## Wheels and Rims

Defective wheels or rims can cause a tire to come off and cause a serious accident. Look for:

- Dented or damaged rims or cracks starting at the lug nut holes; these can cause tires to lose air pressure or come off the rim in a turn.
- Rust trails indicating a loose wheel; check lug snugness with a lug wrench.
- Missing clamps, spacers, studs, or lugs
- Unevenly tightened lugs: this can cause the wheel to wobble. Wobble causes vibration and early tire failure.
- Mismatched, bent, or cracked lock rings
- Welded wheels or rims: these may be weak and unsafe.
- Loose rims that can spin and cut valve stems when the driver puts on the brakes
- Look for rims that have already spun. Most open-well wheels have safety catches to protect the valve stem. If the lug wedges are against them, check them for damage, or have them checked.

© 1997 Career Publishing Inc.

**Figure 4-2**

© 1997 Career Publishing Inc.

**Figure 4-3**

## Braking System Defects

You must be able to control slowing and stopping to drive a rig safely. Your braking system must be in top shape.

### Air Pressure

You should not hear any air leaks. The sound of air coming from any part of the air brake system means the system is defective and can be dangerous.

To check for air brake system pressure loss (leaks):

1. Start the engine and build the air brake system until it is fully charged-usually about 125 psi.

2. Turn off the engine. Release the service brake, and time the air pressure drop. The air pressure loss should be less than:
   a. 2 psi in one minute for single tractors
   b. 3 psi in one minute for a tractor with a trailer
   c. 5 psi in one minute for a tractor with three trailers

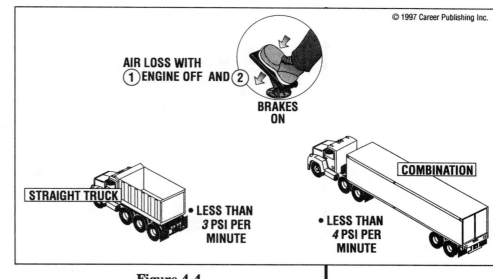

Figure 4-4

3. Then apply 90 psi or more of air with the brake pedal. The pressure should drop and hold steady. After the initial drop, it should not fall more than:
   a. 3 psi in one minute for tractor
   b. 4 psi in one minute for a tractor and trailer
   c. 6 psi in one minute for a tractor and three trailers

Air leaks that can be heard or are more than the amounts listed above should be repaired before the truck or combination is driven because they are unsafe and violate safety regulations.

## Brake Lines

You should not hear any air leaks. You should check for air lines that are:
• Not secured properly
• Hardened or swollen
• Chafed or worn to the fabric or steel braid
• Cut or cracked
• Crimped, pinched, or in any way restricted
• Taped or not spliced right

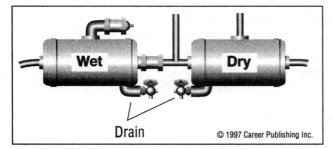

Figure 4-5

## Brake Adjustment

Adjustment procedures will be covered in a later chapter.

## Air Reservoir

The air reservoir(s) must be properly attached to the rig. They must be bled each day to remove moisture. A good time to bleed them is during the pre-trip or post-trip inspection.

NOTE: Many trucks have air dryers. These may or may not have automatic drain valves.

## Steering System Defects

Steering system defects are very unsafe. They may affect your control of the vehicle. The higher your speed and the heavier your front-end load, the more these defects will affect your rig. When you inspect, look for:

- Bent, loose, or broken parts such as the steering column, steering gear box, tie rods, Pitman arm, and drag link
- More than 10 degrees of steering wheel play. When any of the values are met or exceeded, the vehicle shall be considered out-of-service

| Steering Wheel Diameter | Manual System Movement 30° or | Power System Movement 45° or |
|---|---|---|
| 16" | 4-1/2" | 6-3/4" |
| 18" | 4-3/4" | 7-1/8" |
| 19" | 5" | 7-1/2" |
| 20" | 5-1/4" | 7-7/8" |
| 21" | 5-1/2" | 8-1/4" |
| 22" | 5-3/4" | 8-5/8" |

- For power steering, if the movement exceeds 45° before the steering axle tires move, rock the wheel left-to-right between the points of power steering valve resistance. If it is more than 30°, the rig is out-of-service.
- Missing nuts, bolts, cotter keys, or other securing devices

If the vehicle has power steering, check the condition of the hoses and pumps and the fluid level in the power steering fluid reservoir. Finally, check for air and fluid leaks.

## Suspension System Defects

The suspension system supports the rig's load and maintains axle attachment and alignment. Failure can have tragic results. Check for:

- Cracked or broken torque arms and U-bolts
- Hangers that let the axle move from its proper position
- Missing or broken leaves in a spring leaf cluster: the rig will be put out of service if one-fourth or more of them are missing. Any broken or missing leaves can be dangerous.
- Leaking or faulty shock absorbers
- Cracked or broken spring hangers
- Missing or damaged spring hangers or other axle positioning parts
- Damaged or leaking air suspension systems
- Broken leaves or leaves that have shifted and are touching the tires, wheels, frame, or body in multi-leaf springs
- Missing or broken torque rods
- Loose, cracked, broken, or missing frame members

## Exhaust System Defects

Faulty exhaust systems can lead to noxious fumes in the cab or sleeper berth. Look for:

- Loose, broken, or missing exhaust pipes, mufflers, tailpipes, or vertical stacks.
- Loose, broken, or failing clamps, bolts, nuts, or mounting brackets.
- Exhaust system parts in contact with fuel system parts, tires, wiring, or other parts of the rig.

- Exhaust system parts that leak in an area where the air stream will carry the fumes into the cab or sleeper.
- Black soot around the coupling means exhaust leaks.

## Coupling System Defects

Failure of the coupling system (upper or lower fifth wheel) can cause cargo damage or serious accidents. Check for:
- Too much slack in the fifth wheel locking mechanism.
- Cracks or breaks in any part of the fifth wheel assembly.
- Bent, broken, or missing parts of the locking mechanism.
- Missing pins or other defects in the slide mechanism of the sliding fifth wheel.
- Bent, cracked, or very worn kingpins.
- Missing U-bolts, cracked or broken welds, or other defects in the fifth wheel mounting devices(s).
- More than 3/8" horizontal movement between the pivot bracket pin and bracket.
- Pivot bracket pin missing or not secured.

## Cargo Problems

Cargo must be checked to make sure it cannot move. Unsecured cargo often causes accidents. Cargo handling will be covered in detail in a later chapter.

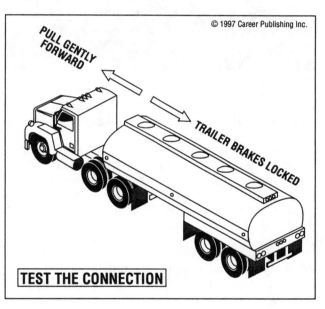

Figure 4-6

## PRE-TRIP INSPECTION

You have a moral and legal duty to your employer, other motorists, and yourself to conduct a thorough pre-trip inspection of any rig you drive. It takes much longer to learn how to do a quality pre-trip inspection than it takes to do one. After a lot of practice, you will be able to do the job well in less than 15 minutes. The secret to making a rapid and accurate inspection is to learn a regular, step-by-step routine. If you inspect your rig the same way each time, you will do it more quickly and you will not accidentally forget to check some key part.

NOTE: Many companies have specific policies on vehicle inspection. Some carriers require drivers to conduct a more extensive inspection. Some carriers prohibit certain checks. All drivers must establish a procedure that is consistent with company policy. Career Publishing Inc. has a complete pre-trip vehicle inspection training course available.

The routine explained here is called the **Seven Step Pre-Trip Inspection Procedure**. The steps are:

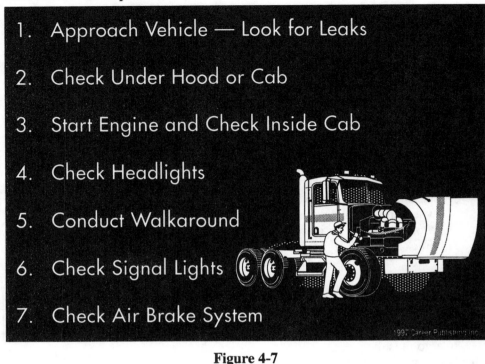

1. Approach Vehicle — Look for Leaks

2. Check Under Hood or Cab

3. Start Engine and Check Inside Cab

4. Check Headlights

5. Conduct Walkaround

6. Check Signal Lights

7. Check Air Brake System

1997 Career Publishing Inc

**Figure 4-7**

## STEP 1: APPROACH THE VEHICLE

While walking toward the rig, look for signs of damage. Also look for anything that may be in the way when you try to move the vehicle. As you approach the rig, look at the following items:

**Vehicle Posture**: A truck sagging to one side may mean flat tires, overloading, shifted cargo, or suspension problems.

**Cargo**: Make sure the trailer or cargo compartment doors are closed and properly fastened. On flat-bed trailers and other open cargo compartments, make sure the cargo is not hanging over the side and that restraints can stand 1-1/2 times any pressure from the load.

# INSPECTING CARGO

© 1997 Career Publishing Inc.

**Figure 4-8**

**Damaged, Loose, or Missing Parts:** Look for cracked glass, dents, or missing parts such as fenders, mud flaps, and lights. Check for loose parts like a fuel tank hanging with unsecured straps.

**Leaks**: Glance under the truck for puddles of fresh oil, engine coolant, grease, or fuel. Check for other signs of leakage.

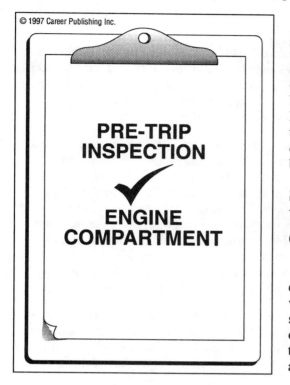

© 1997 Career Publishing Inc.

**PRE-TRIP INSPECTION**

✓

**ENGINE COMPARTMENT**

**Figure 4-9**

**Area Around Vehicle**: Look for anything that may be damaged by the rig or damage it as you drive away. Include objects on the ground such as glass or boards with nails. Look up for low hanging branches, electric or telephone wires, and any other overhead objects that may be hit by the tractor or trailer.

## STEP 2: CHECK UNDER THE HOOD OR CAB

Check the engine compartment to make sure the vehicle has been properly serviced. Look for signs of damage or possible problems with the engine, steering mechanism, and suspension system.

**Fluid Levels**: Check the crankcase oil, radiator coolant, battery fluid, windshield washer fluid, and any other fluids such as automatic transmission fluid and engine oil in the make-up reservoir. Make sure all fluids are at the right level before starting the engine.

**Leaks**: Look for leaks of oil, water, or hydraulic fluid in the engine compartment. Check around the entire compartment for any grease, soot, or other signs of fluid leaks. Inspect the exhaust manifold for signs of blow-by. If your vehicle's main air tanks are under the hood or cab, listen carefully for the sound of leaking air.

**Electrical System**: Make sure the battery is secured and the terminals are not corroded. Check for loose electrical wires. Check the insulation to make sure it is not cracked or worn through. If your rig has spark plugs, check for secure electrical connection.

**Belts and Pulleys**: Inspect the alternator, air compressor, and water pump belts for cracks or frays. Pull the belts to test for tension and slippage. If you can slide a belt over a pulley, it is too loose and should be tightened or replaced.

**Coolant System**: Check the radiator, its shroud and shutters to make sure it is structurally sound and free of dents or other damage. Make sure all parts of the coolant system are properly secured. Check the hoses for cracks or breaks. Inspect the fan for missing blades. Look for hanging wires or hoses that can catch on the blades.

**Steering System**: Check the steering linkage and gear box closely. Make sure they are secure. Look for signs of wear such as paint rubbed off. If the rig has power steering, make sure the power steering lines are securely connected and there are no leaks.

**Braking System**: Look for cracked brake drums, missing brake shoes, and missing or disconnected brake hoses and slack adjusters. If the rig has air brakes, make sure the air intake screen (if there is one) is not clogged with dirt, leaves, or other debris. Open the air tank petcocks and drain the tanks. Check for oil contamination. Make sure to close the petcocks when you are through.

**Suspension System**: Check the U-bolts, spring pins, spring brackets, and torque arms for cracks, bends, missing bolts, etc. Check the axles for signs of rubbing. If the truck has adjustable axles, make sure all locking pins are in the proper position and fully engaged. Make sure the safety clamps holding the locking pins are securely in place. Look for cracks in the truck's frame and cross members. Check the whole suspension system for rust or shiny spots that may indicate excessive wear. Look at all leaf springs for missing, out of place, or broken leaves. Leaves sticking out from a leaf spring may touch the tires, rims, or frame. Look for leaking or defective shock absorbers. If the rig has an air suspension system, make sure the air bags are not damaged or leaking.

**Exhaust System**: Look at the muffler. Be sure it is securely connected and has no holes, large dents or is crushed. Make sure all lines and hoses connected to the system are securely fastened. Report all damage found before your trip. Be sure the fuel and electric lines will not come too close to any part of the exhaust system that gets hot.

**Hood or Cab**: When you have finished the under-the-hood checks, lower and fasten the hood or cab. Make sure all fastenings are secure.

## STEP 3: START THE ENGINE, AND CHECK INSIDE THE CAB

After checking the engine compartment, get into the cab and get ready to start the engine. You are not yet ready to move the vehicle. This part of the inspection is to make sure the cab and all controls and instruments are in good working order.

**Vehicle Entry**: Check to see that the ladder, grab handle, and door handles are secure and free of oil, grease, or ice. Make sure the door opens and closes freely and latches securely.

**Emergency and Safety Equipment**: Be sure you have all the required emergency and safety equipment. Always have a fully charged and mounted fire extinguisher and at least three reflective triangles.

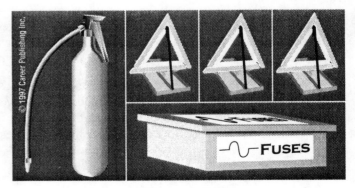

Figure 4-10

**Mirrors and Glass**: Clean all window glass before you drive. Check for cracks and breaks. Dirty windshields and windows are hard to see through, especially at night. Make sure the windshield wipers work. Run your hand along the wiper blades to feel for worn spots. The rubber should be soft and pliable. Make sure your mirrors are securely mounted. Check them for cracks. Adjust the seat to a driving position that is right for you. Then check the mirrors and adjust them if needed.

**Engine Start-Up**: Make sure the parking brake is on and the transmission is in a position for starting the engine. Start the engine at zero throttle. Don't crank over 15 seconds. Listen for unusual noises from the engine and exhaust system (knocking, pinging, skipping, etc.) Let the engine idle.

**Instruments and Gauges**: With the engine running, check to see that all instruments and gauges are working. Be sure the major systems are within proper limits. Look at the:

- **Oil pressure gauge:** It should begin to register a few seconds after engine start-up and gradually rise to the normal range.
- **Ammeter/voltmeter:** The needle should jump, flutter, and then register "charge" or "+."
- **Coolant temperature gauge:** It should gradually rise to the normal operating range.
- **Warning lights:** The oil, coolant, and generator warning lights should go out almost as soon as the engine is started.
- **Low air pressure warning buzzer:** The buzzer or alarm should sound until the air pressure builds to about 60 psi. At this point, the buzzer or alarm should stop.
- **Air pressure gauge:** Pressure should build steadily. Check the time needed for the pressure to build from 50 psi to 90 psi. If it is within three minutes, the buildup is OK. If it takes longer, adjustments are needed.
- **Air pressure governor cut-off:** Pressure buildup should stop between 100 and 125 psi. If the buildup stops below or above that range, adjustments are necessary.

NOTE: In trucks with electronically controlled engines, the needles on all gauges will make a full sweep right after the engine is turned on. This is a self-check function to ensure all gauges are working.

**Primary Controls**: With the engine still running, check the vehicle's main controls.

- **Steering mechanism:** Check steering for freeplay. Open the cab door and lean out so you can see the left front tire of the truck. While watching the tire, turn the wheel until the tire starts to move. The steering wheel should turn less than 10 degrees. More than 10 degrees of freeplay is unsafe.
- **Clutch:** Depress the clutch until you feel a little resistance. For most clutches, one to two inches of freeplay is normal. Too much or too little freeplay can cause hard shifting, gear clashing, and clutch or transmission damage.
- **Transmission:** With the clutch depressed, check to see that the transmission lets you shift freely from neutral into the other gears.
- **Accelerator and brake pedals:** Check both pedals for looseness or sticking. Be sure there is no dirt build-up underneath.

**Secondary Controls**: Check the controls for the:
- Defroster
- Fan
- Horn
- Interior lights
- Turn signal
- High-beam indicator
- Heater
- Lanyard to the airhorn
- Windshield washers and wipers
- Dash lights
- Four-way flashers

Be sure they are all in working order.

**Cab Housekeeping**: Make sure all cab parts are where they belong. Check the dashboard knobs, rubber pedal covers, and door handles. Everything in the cab should be in place and properly secured. Make sure nothing is in the way to limit your vision or movement. Remove papers, cans, and trash. Loose trash in the cab can get under the accelerator, brake, or clutch pedals and become a danger.

**Prepare to Leave the Cab**: When the air pressure has built to the governor cut-out pressure, turn off the engine. If the engine shut-off is the pull-out type, leave it in the pulled out position until you start the engine again. Put the rig into the lowest forward gear. Set the parking brake. Turn on the low beam headlights and four-way flashers. Remove the starter switch key and place it in your pocket to keep someone else from moving the rig while you are making the outside inspections.

## STEP 4: CHECK THE LIGHTS AND MIRRORS

After you get out of the cab, go to the front of the rig. Check the:
- Low beam headlights: Do they work? Are they aligned?
- Four-way flashers: Do both of them work?

Reach into the cab and switch the lights to high beam.
- Do they work?
- Are they aligned?

Inspect the mirrors.
- Are they clean?
- Adjust the mirrors if you need to.

## STEP 5: CONDUCT A WALKAROUND INSPECTION

Go back to the cab. Turn off the headlights and four-way flashers. Turn on the right turn signal. Leave the cab, and start a walkaround inspection.

The walkaround inspection is a 14-point routine. During this part of the pre-trip inspection, you will be looking at vehicle parts that are outside the cab.

### Left Side of the Cab

How does it look, in general? Check the:
- **Driver's door glass, latches and lock**
- **Left front wheel and rim:** Check for damage. A bent or damaged rim can make a tire lose pressure or separate from the wheel. If the rims have

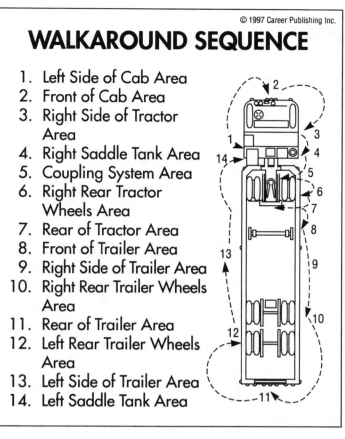

© 1997 Career Publishing Inc.

# WALKAROUND SEQUENCE

1. Left Side of Cab Area
2. Front of Cab Area
3. Right Side of Tractor Area
4. Right Saddle Tank Area
5. Coupling System Area
6. Right Rear Tractor Wheels Area
7. Rear of Tractor Area
8. Front of Trailer Area
9. Right Side of Trailer Area
10. Right Rear Trailer Wheels Area
11. Rear of Trailer Area
12. Left Rear Trailer Wheels Area
13. Left Side of Trailer Area
14. Left Saddle Tank Area

**Figure 4-11**

more than one piece, they are under extreme pressure and can explode from the wheel if damaged, mismatched, or not mounted properly. Always let the experts adjust them for you. Such adjustments are regulated by standards set by OSHA.

Check for improperly mounted tires. Loose or missing lugs put too much stress on the other lugs. They could break off and cause the wheel to come off. Look for a rust trail around the lugs. This tells you they may be loose.

Use a lug wrench to check the lugs. Look for signs of lubricant leaking from the wheel bearings or seals. Lost lubricant can cause a wheel to lock up. Check the hub oil level.

- **Left front tire:** Check the:
  - Air pressure
  - Tread
  - General condition

Low tire pressure makes the rig hard to handle. It can increase the chance of a blowout or tire fire. It also reduces tire life. Always check the tire air pressure with a gauge.

Bald or worn tires can cause a blowout or make it hard to stop. They also make the rig harder to handle. If the road surface is wet, driving on worn treads causes the rig to hydroplane. Cuts, separated treads, bulges, and missing or broken valve stems may cause tire failure. Remove any objects, such as stones, nails, and glass that have become wedged in the tread.

- **Left front Brake:** Check the condition of the:
  - Brake drum
  - Hoses
  - Shoes (if they can be seen)

- **Air tanks**
  - Drain

- **Left front suspension:** Check the condition of:
  - Springs and spring hangers
  - U-bolts

- **Shock absorbers:** Look for:
  - Leaks
  - Defects

## Front of Cab

Check the condition of the:
- Front axle
- Steering system: no loose, worn, bent, or damaged parts. The driver must grab the steering mechanism to test for looseness.

Make sure the license plates are on tightly. Check that all legally required inspection stickers, tax plates, decals, etc. are in place.

Check the condition of the windshield. Make sure it is clean and undamaged. Check the windshield wiper arms for proper spring tension. Check the wiper blades for damage and to be sure they are attached right.

Check the parking, clearance, and ID lights to be sure they are:
- Clean
- The right color
- Working

Make sure all reflectors are clean and not damaged. Check the right turn signal light to be sure it is:
- Clean
- The right color
- Working

## Right Side of Cab

Check all items on the right side of the cab that you checked on the left side. If your tractor has a cabover engine (COE), check the cab tilt mechanism to be sure it is working right. Check all primary and safety locks. Make sure they are engaged.

## Right Saddle Tank Area

Check the:
- **Right fuel tank(s):** The tank(s) should be in good condition and securely mounted. The fuel crossover line should be secure. The tanks should be full of fuel and the caps on firmly.
- **Rear of engine:** No leaks should be seen.
- **Transmission:** No leaks should be seen.
- **Drive shaft:** Check how it looks in general. Is it in position and secured both on the front and on the rear?
- **Exhaust system:** Are the brackets, pipes, and other parts secure and free of leaks? Be sure no fuel lines, air lines, or wires are in contact with exhaust parts.
- **Frame and cross members:** Look for bends and cracks in the parts you can see.

- **Air lines and electrical wiring:** Be sure they are secure and will not catch on or rub against anything.
- **Spare tire carrier and rack:** Make sure they are sturdy, strong enough to carry the load, and not damaged.
- **Spare tire and wheel:** They should be firmly mounted in the rack. Make sure they are in good condition. Check the tire to be sure it is the right size and properly inflated.

## Coupling System Area

Inspect the following:
- **Lower fifth wheel:** Is it properly lubricated? Is it firmly mounted to the frame? Are any parts missing or damaged? You should see no space between the upper and lower fifth wheels. Be sure the locking jaws are securely fastened around the shank of the kingpin. Never leave them around the head of the kingpin. The release arm must be properly seated and the safety latch/lock must be engaged.
- **Upper fifth wheel:** The guide plate should be firmly mounted on the trailer frame. The kingpin should not be worn, bent, or damaged.
- **Air and electrical lines to the trailer:** These lines should be in good condition. Be sure they will not get tangled, catch on, or rub against anything.

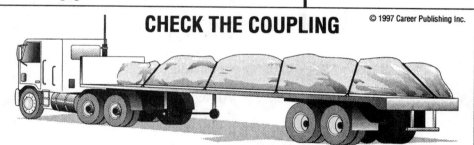

CHECK THE COUPLING
© 1997 Career Publishing Inc.

**No gap between fifth-wheel and trailer upper plate**

**Figure 4-12**

They should not be oily, greasy, or damaged. The air lines must be properly connected to glad hands. Be sure there are no leaks. Electrical lines should be firmly seated and locked in place.
- **Sliding fifth wheel (if your rig has one):** The sliding fifth wheel should not be worn, bent, or damaged. Make sure there are no missing parts. It should be properly lubricated. All lock pins should be there and locked in place. If it is air powered, make sure there are no air leaks. The fifth wheel should not be too far forward. If it is, the trailer could hit the cab, tractor frame, or landing gear during turns.

## Right Rear Tractor Wheels Area

Inspect the following parts:
- **Dual wheels and rims:** All wheels and rims should be on and in good condition. Spacers, studs, clamps, or lugs should not be missing, bent, or broken.
- **Dual tires:** All tires should be properly inflated with the valve stems and caps in good condition. There should be no cuts, bulges, or serious tread wear. Tires should not rub each other. Make sure nothing is stuck between them. All tires should be the same type and size. Check for any leaks from the wheel bearings.

- **Suspension:** Make sure the springs, spring hangers, shackles, and U-bolts are in good shape. Check the torque rod arms, bushings, and shock absorbers to be sure they are OK.
- **Brakes:** Inspect all brake chambers to make sure everything is connected and in good working order. Where you can see them, check the brake drums for cracks and signs of rust or wear. Be sure the brake shoes are evenly adjusted. If they are not, the vehicle will pull to the side during braking.

Check the manual slack adjusters on S-cam brakes. Park on level ground. Chock the wheels. Turn off the parking brakes so you can move the slack adjusters. Wear gloves. Pull hard on each adjuster you can reach. It should not move more than 1" where the push rod attaches to it. Adjust them or have them adjusted if they move more. Too much brake slack can make the rig hard to stop.

## Rear of Tractor

- The **frame and cross members** should not be:
  - Bent
  - Cracked
  - Damaged
  - Missing

- All **lights and reflectors** should be:
  - The proper color
  - Clean
  - In good condition
  - Working

- **License plates** should be:
  - Clean
  - Firmly mounted

- All **splash guards** should be:
  - Present
  - Properly fastened on
  - Not rubbing the wheels

- **Air and electrical lines** should be:
  - Secured
  - Not damaged
  - Not rubbing against anything

## Front Area of the Trailer

- The **license/registration holder** should be:
  - Present
  - Firmly mounted with the cover closed

- The **header board** should be:
  - Securely mounted
  - Not damaged

- **Canvas or tarp carrier** (if your rig has one):
  - Securely mounted
  - Damage-free
  - Tarps should be secured in the carrier

- **Clearance and ID lights** should be:
  - The proper color
  - Clean
  - In good condition
  - Working

Reflectors and reflective tape should also be clean and damage-free.

## Right Side of Trailer

The following items should be inspected:
- **Front trailer support (landing gear or dolly):** This device should be fully raised with no parts bent, damaged, or missing. The crank handle should be present, properly secured, and in low gear if possible. If the crank handle is power operated, there should be no air or hydraulic leaks.
- **Spare tire carrier or rack:** It should be strong enough to carry the load. Make sure it is in good condition.
- **Spare tires and wheels:** Make sure the rack is secure. The spare tires and wheels should be in good condition. They should be the right size and inflated.
- **Lights and reflectors:** Trailer side clearance lights and reflectors should be:
  - Clean
  - The proper color
  - In good condition
  - Operating
- **Frame and body:** The frame and cross members should not be:
  - Bent
  - Cracked
  - Damaged
  - Missing
- **Cargo:** The cargo should be properly blocked, braced, tied, chained, etc. Side boards and stakes should be strong, properly mounted, and not damaged. Canvas or tarps should be properly lashed down to prevent water damage, tearing, blowing about, or blocking the view from the rear-view mirrors. Side doors should be securely latched with the security seals in place.

## Right-Rear Trailer Wheel Area

The following areas should be inspected:

- **Dual tires and rims:** Spacers, studs, clamps, or lugs should not be bent, broken, or missing. The tires should be properly inflated with valve stems and caps in good condition. They should be free of cuts, bulges, and serious tread wear and should not rub together. Check to be sure nothing is stuck between them. Tires should be the same size and type.
- **Tandem axles:** If the rig has sliding axles, check their position and alignment. Also check for damaged, worn, or missing parts. All locks should be present, in place, and secured. Air lines should be checked for cracks, cuts, crimping, and other damage. Be sure they are not tangled, dragging, or rubbing against anything.
- **Suspension:** The springs, spring hangers, shackles, U-bolts, torque rod arms, bushings, and shock absorbers should be in good condition.

- **Brakes:** Inspect all brake chambers. Make sure everything is connected and in good working order. Where you can see them, check the brake drums for cracks and rust or wear. The brake shoes should be evenly adjusted. Uneven adjustment can cause the vehicle to pull to the side during braking.

Check the manual slack adjusters on S-cam brakes. Park on level ground. Chock the wheels. Turn off the parking brakes so you can move the slack adjusters. Wear gloves. Pull hard on each adjuster you can reach. It should not move more than 1" where the push rod attaches to it. Adjust them or have them adjusted if they move more. Too much brake slack can make the rig hard to stop.

- **Park on Level**
- **Brakes Off**
- **Chock Wheels**
- **Check Free Play**

Slack Adjuster

© 1997 Career Publishing Inc.

**Figure 4-13**

Also check the spring brakes (if your rig has them). Drain the moisture from the air reservoir and close the petcock.

## Rear of Trailer

Inspect the following items:

- **Lights and reflectors:** The rear clearance lights, ID lights, tail lights, license plate lights, and right rear turn signal lights should be clean and in good condition.
- **ICC underride prevention bumper:** Present and sound.
- **License plates:** They should be present, current, clean, and fastened on securely.
- **Splash guards:** Properly attached and undamaged.
- **Cargo:** See that cargo is properly blocked, braced, tied or chained. Tailboards should be up and properly secured. End gates should be free of damage and secured in the stake pockets. Canvas or tarps should be properly lashed down to prevent water damage, tearing, or blowing about. Make sure the rear-view mirrors and rear lights are not blocked. The rear door should be securely locked, with the required security seals in place.

## Left Rear Trailer Wheel Area

Inspect the same things that you did on the right side except for the air tank.

## Left Side of Trailer

Inspect it in the same way you inspected the right side.

## Left Saddle Tank Area

Check the same items that you did on the right side tank area except for the spare tire. Also check the:

- **Battery box:** See that it is firmly mounted to the vehicle and its cover is in place.
- **Battery** (if not mounted in engine compartment): Be sure it will not move, and the case is not broken or leaking. The fluid should be at the proper level. All caps should be tight. The vents in all cell caps should be free of anything that could block the escape of gases.

# STEP 6: CHECK THE SIGNAL LIGHTS

- Return to the cab.
- Turn off all the lights.
- Walk around the vehicle.
- Check the left front and rear of the tractor.
- Check the left rear trailer turn signal lights. Make sure they are:
  - Clean
  - The right color
  - Working
- Check both tractor and trailer stop lights.

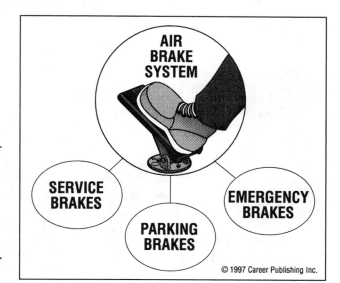

**Figure 4-14**

# STEP 7: CHECK THE AIR BRAKE SYSTEM

- Return to the cab.
- Turn off all the lights.
- Make sure you have all trip manifests, permits, and required documents.
- Secure all loose articles in the cab so they will not be in the way while you are driving the rig.
- Fasten your seat belt!

Now you are ready to test the air brake system. Be sure to check all of the following items.

## Low Pressure Alarm and/or Light

Start *fanning* off the air pressure by rapidly applying and releasing the treadle valve. At approximately 60 pounds of pressure, the low air pressure warning alarm should sound and/or the light should go on.

## Tractor Protection Valve

Continue to fan off the air pressure. At approximately 40 pounds of pressure, the tractor protection valve should go from the *normal* to the *emergency* position. This action must cause the trailer brakes to lock up. If they do not, there is a defect in the system.

## Air Pressure Buildup

With the engine at operating rpm, the pressure should build from 85 to 100 psi within 45 seconds in dual air systems. If the air tanks are larger than minimum, build-up time can be longer and still be safe. In single air systems, pressure should build from 50 to 90 psi within 3 minutes with the engine idling at 600-900 rpm.

**Figure 4-15**

## Parking Brake

Put on the brake. Put the transmission in gear and engage the clutch slowly to see if the parking brake holds.

## Trailer Hand Valve Brake

Put on the trailer brakes. Try to drive away. If the unit moves, there is a defect, or air is not reaching the trailer brakes.

CAUTION: If the trailer is empty, it is possible to pull it with the brakes locked. This causes undue wear. It can also be pulled out from under the trailer if the fifth wheel is not latched properly.

## Too Much Slack in the Fifth Wheel

Put on the trailer brakes. Now, carefully and very gently, rock the tractor in first and reverse gears. Feel and listen for too much slack in the kingpin locking jaws. If there seems to be too much slack, check it out! Also be sure the clutch is working right during this procedure.

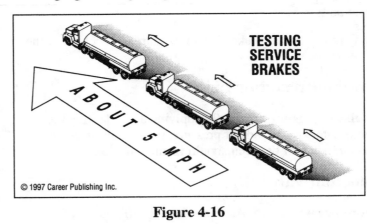

**Figure 4-16**

## Brake System Balance and Adjustment

While still in an off-street area, build the vehicle speed up to 5-7 mph. Put on the service brakes sharply. Note if the rig is *pulling* to one side or the other. If the stopping rate or adjustment of the brakes does not *feel* right, get it checked out right away. Do not drive the rig until you are certain the brakes are working right.

# ENROUTE AND POST-TRIP INSPECTIONS

## Enroute Inspection

These specific enroute driver inspections are required by the Federal Motor Carrier Safety Regulations (FMCSR).

### FMCSR 392.9 (b) (2)

You must examine the cargo and its securing devices within the first 25 miles of a trip. Make adjustments as needed to maintain a secure load. Keep on making periodic exams of the cargo. Fix as needed. This requirement does not apply to a sealed trailer.

### FMCSR 397.17

If you are carrying hazardous material and your vehicle has dual tires on any axle, you must stop at a safe location every two hours, or 100 miles, and check the tires.

- Identify and take off overheated tires at once to prevent a fire.
- Identify and repair or correct tires with not enough air pressure.

One of your major jobs as a driver is to know what your instruments are reading. This should be done every few minutes while driving.

© 1997 Career Publishing Inc.

**Figure 4-17**

Conduct walkaround safety inspections every 150 miles or every three hours (whichever comes first). Check the following:
- **Tires:** Check the air pressure and whether they are getting too hot.
- **Brakes:** Check the adjustment and temperature.
- **Cargo:** Check the doors and whether the cargo is still secure.
- **Coupling device:** Check to be sure it is still firmly attached.
- **Lights:** Check the vehicle lights before dark and at every stop while driving at night.

## Post-Trip Inspection

After the trip, you will be required to:
- Drain the moisture from the air tanks and fill the fuel tanks as instructed by your employer.
- Identify any problems found during the enroute inspection; e.g., unusual noises, vibrations, etc.

- Inspect the rig to further identify or locate these problems and to discover any developing problems.
- Identify or diagnose the source of problems. This will be covered in detail in Chapter 20.
- Complete an accurate vehicle inspection report.

### Reporting Findings

Inspections have no meaning unless you take action. Your job as a driver is to:

- Report findings to your supervisor and/or maintenance department as directed by your company policy.
- Report to the mechanics if you need to.
- Prepare an accurate, written report (required by law) for each rig driven during each day or work shift.

## VEHICLE INSPECTION REPORT

A written vehicle inspection report at the end of a trip is required by law for companies in interstate or foreign commerce (FMCSR 396.11). The report must cover the following parts.

- Service brakes including trailer brake connections
- Parking brake
- Steering mechanism
- Lights and reflectors
- Windshield wipers
- Rear-view mirrors
- Wheels and rims
- Tires
- Horn
- Coupling devices
- Emergency equipment

The U.S. Department of Transportation has prepared a recommended Vehicle Condition Report (VCR). There are several versions of this report. All serve as the record of what the driver finds.

One copy of the report must be kept in the company files for at least three (3) months. Another copy must be kept in the vehicle until the next Vehicle Condition Report is made. This will tell the next driver about defects or problems. The items should be fixed by this time. As a driver you must, by law, review the previous driver's report and sign it.

## SUMMARY

Now that you have completed this chapter, you are able to describe ways to make a quick and complete pre-trip inspection. You are also able to discuss the effect of unknown malfunctions and explain the importance of correcting malfunctions quickly. Because you have completed this chapter, you can provide a working knowledge of federal and state regulations for inspection and explain the procedures for enroute and post-trip inspections.

# Example of Driver's Inspection Report

---

## DRIVER'S INSPECTION REPORT

MAINTENANCE   (SEE INSTRUCTIONS ON REVERSE SIDE)
CHECK DEFECTS ONLY. Explain under REMARKS
COMPLETION OF THIS REPORT REQUIRED BY FEDERAL LAW, 49CFR 396.11 & 396.13.
Mileage (No Tenths)

Truck or
Tractor No. _____   |__|__|__|__|__|__|   Trailer No. _____

Dolly No. _____   Trailer No. _____   Location: _____

### POWER UNIT

**GENERAL CONDITION**
- ☐ 02 Cab/Doors/Windows
- ☐ 02 Body/Doors
- ☐ ____ Oil Leak _____
- ☐ ____ Grease Leak _____
- ☐ 42 Coolant Leak
- ☐ 44 Fuel Leak
- ☐ ____ Other _____
  _____
  (IDENTIFY)

**ENGINE COMPARTMENT**
- ☐ 45 Oil Level
- ☐ ____ Belts _____
- ☐ ____ Other _____
  _____
  (IDENTIFY)

**IN CAB**
- ☐ 03 Gauges/Warning Indicators
- ☐ 02 Windshield Wipers/Washers
- ☐ 54 Horn(s)
- ☐ 01 Heater/Defroster
- ☐ 02 Mirrors
- ☐ 15 Steering
- ☐ 23 Clutch
- ☐ 13 Service Brake
- ☐ 13 Parking Brake
- ☐ 13 Emergency Brake
- ☐ 53 Triangles
- ☐ 53 Fire Extinguisher
- ☐ 53 Other Safety Equipment
- ☐ 34 Spare Fuses
- ☐ 02 Seat Belts
- ☐ ____ Other _____
  _____
  (IDENTIFY)

**EXTERIOR**
- ☐ 34 Lights
- ☐ 34 Reflectors
- ☐ 16 Suspension
- ☐ 17 Tires
- ☐ 18 Wheels/Rims/Lugs
- ☐ 32 Battery
- ☐ 43 Exhaust
- ☐ 13 Brakes
- ☐ 13 Air Lines
- ☐ 34 Light Line
- ☐ 49 Fifth-Wheel
- ☐ 49 Other Coupling
- ☐ 71 Tie-Downs
- ☐ 14 Rear-End Protection
- ☐ ____ Other _____
  (IDENTIFY)
- ☐ NO DEFECTS

### TOWED UNIT(S)

- ☐ 71 Body/Doors
- ☐ 71 Tie-Downs
- ☐ 34 Lights
- ☐ 34 Reflectors
- ☐ 16 Suspension
- ☐ 17 Tires
- ☐ 18 Wheels/Rims/Lugs
- ☐ 13 Brakes
- ☐ 77 Landing Gear
- ☐ 59 Kingpin Upper Plate
- ☐ 59 Fifth-Wheel (Dolly)
- ☐ 59 Other Coupling Devices
- ☐ 79 Rear-End Protection
- ☐ ____ Other _____
  _____
  (IDENTIFY)
- ☐ NO DEFECTS

REMARKS: _____
_____
_____
_____

REPORTING DRIVER:   Date _____
Name _____ Emp. No. _____

REVIEWING DRIVER:   Date _____
Name _____ Emp. No. _____

MAINTENANCE ACTION:   Date _____
Repairs Made ☐   No Repairs Needed ☐
R.O.#s _____
Certified By: _____
Location: _____

SHOP REMARKS: _____
_____

**Figure 4-18**

## KEY WORDS

**Enroute Inspection**: A rig's control and instrument check while driving and a check of critical items at each stop.

**DOT**: Department of Transportation.

**Federal Motor Carrier Safety Regulations (FMCSR)**: Federal laws that regulate commercial vehicle operation.

**Pre-trip Inspection**: A systematic parts and system check made before each trip.

**Post-trip Inspection**: A thorough check of the rig at the end of a trip.

**Vehicle Condition Report (VCR)**: A written report that a driver must fill out listing any problem or defect noted while he or she was driving the rig.

# LEARNING ACTIVITIES

## Review Questions

1.  Why is a safety inspection performed? *Safety inspections identify systems or parts that are: working properly; not working properly; failing; missing; danger of failing or malfunctioning*

2.  What are the three basic types of vehicle inspections? What is the purpose of each?
    *① pre-trip insp, to find problems that can cause accidents or Breakdowns or poor performance ② Enroute clnsp, Driver checks the rigs controls + instruments while driving at each stop he also check critical items ③ Post trip insp, (VCR) report list any defects noted during operation*

3.  What are the four basic reasons for vehicle safety inspections? Explain each.
    *to identify (A part of system that is malfunctioning or has already failed) (a part or system that is in danger of failing or malfunctioning) :(a part or system that is OK or is functioning properly) :The legal requirements for various parts or system conditions*

4.  Explain Federal Motor Carrier Safety Regulations (FMCSR), Parts 396.9 (Motor Vehicle Declared Out of Service), 392.9 (Secure Cargo Check), and 397.17 (Hazardous Material Tire Check).
    *(396.9): Prohibits a driver from operating a vehicle that is imminently hazardous to operate. Prohibits a driver motor carrier from requiring or permitting a driver to operate such a vehicle.*
    *(392.9) you must examine cargo + securing devices within 25 miles of a trip. maintain a secure load. make periodic exams of cargo fix as needed*
    *(397.17)*

5.  Why is it important to have a step-by-step routine for a pre-trip inspection?

_____

_____

6.  Describe each of the seven steps that make up the "Seven Step Pre-trip Inspection Procedure."

_____

_____

_____

_____

_____

_____

_____

_____

_____

_____

_____

7.  What is a vehicle inspection report? Does the law require it?

_____

_____

_____

8.  What are the three basic points of a good inspection?

_____

_____

_____

9.  List five safety defects that are considered very dangerous.

_____

_____

_____

_____

_____

10.    Why is it important to file a written vehicle condition report (VCR)?

_____

_____

_____

# Review Quiz, Part A

## Problems

In column A are things that can occur because of a defect or malfunction. Column B shows a step in the pre-trip inspection. Draw a line from the problem to the step in the inspection that might have told you there was a problem.

**Column A**

**A problem you don't want to happen**

1.    Engine failed and serious damage occurred as a result

2.    Vehicle declared "out of service" because of defective steering

3.    Pieces of cargo fell off trailer

4.    A blowout in the right front tire that made the rig run off the road

5.    Brakes reacted too slowly and the rig had an accident

**Column B**

**An inspection step that might have told you there was a problem**

A.    Checked under front end of tractor for bent, worn or missing parts

B.    Checked tire pressure gauge and inspected tread wear

C.    Conducted air pressure check of braking system

D.    Looked under the vehicle hood and checked dash instruments

E.    Inspected cargo

# Review Quiz, Part B

## Inspection Sequences

Listed below are the seven steps in a pre-trip inspection. Put them in the best order. (Number them 1, 2, 3, 4, 5, 6, and 7).

_____ Shut off the engine. Secure the rig, and check the high and low headlight beams and four-way flashers.

_____ Raise the cab or hood. Check the engine compartment.

_____ Start the engine. Check the instruments, controls, and emergency equipment.

_____ Walk toward the rig. Look it over for damage and fluid leaks.

_____ Do a walkaround inspection with the right turn signal on.

_____ Do a standing and rolling air brake system test and a last check of the instruments.

_____ Check the operation of the left turn signal and the stop lights.

## Review Quiz, Part C

## Federal Requirements

Put a T in front of the statements that are required by the law.

As well as inspecting your rig to be sure it is safe to drive, federal laws say you must:

_____ Make out a Vehicle Condition Report (VCR) at the end of the day or tour of duty.

_____ Be able to repair any vehicle defect you identify.

_____ Inspect for hot tires and low pressure every 100 miles or two hours when pulling a cargo of hazardous material.

_____ Have a CB radio that works during a pre-trip inspection.

_____ Review the previous Vehicle Condition Report to determine if reported defects were corrected.

## True or False Questions  - |

Circle the T if the statement is True. Circle the F if the statement if False.

**T** F 1. The best way to check for loose lugs is to use a lug wrench.

T **F** 2. Low tire pressure makes the rig hard to handle, but it makes a fire less likely to occur.

T **F** 3. To check steering wheel free play on a rig with power steering, the engine may be either on or off.

T **F** 4. On most rigs, the brake low pressure alarm and/or light will go on when the air pressure drops to 80 psi.

**T** F 5. Rust around the lugs is most often a sign the lug nuts are loose.

**T** F 6. *Thumping* a tire with a tire iron to check for proper air pressure is a quick and accurate method. *(p. 4. 15)*

**T** F 7. There should be no more than 10 degrees of steering wheel free play.

T **F** 8. To check for air pressure loss in the brake system, watch the air pressure gauge while you put on the foot brake with the engine running.

**T** F 9. The proper way to inspect air tanks for oil is to open the petcocks and allow the tanks to drain.

T **F** 10. With the engine off and the foot brake applied for one minute, the air pressure should be no more than 10-12 psi.

**T** F 11. According to FMCSR 396, a vehicle will be declared out of service if the steering wheel free play is 30 degrees.

**T** F 12. According to FMCSR 392.9, you must stop to examine the cargo securing devices within 25 miles of the start of a trip.

**T** F 13. According to FMCSR 397.17, if you are hauling hazardous material and your vehicle has dual tires, you must stop and check the tires every two hours or 100 miles.

T (F) 14.  The tractor protection valve should automatically go from the *normal* to *emergency* position when the air pressure drops to 60 psi.

(T) F  15.  You must stop and do an enroute walkaround safety inspection every 150 miles or every three hours.

T (F) 16.  For most clutches, normal free play is two to three inches.

# THREE-AXLE TRACTOR WITH TWO-AXLE TRAILER
# PRE-TRIP INSPECTION ROUTINE
## *REVIEW CHECKLIST*

USE THIS CHECKLIST TO REVIEW THE ITEMS TO BE INSPECTED ON YOUR RIG. DO YOU KNOW THE CHECK POINTS FOR EACH OF THE ITEMS LISTED? IF NOT, MARK OR CHECK THE ITEM FOR FURTHER REVIEW.

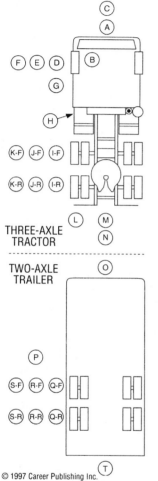

THREE-AXLE TRACTOR

TWO-AXLE TRAILER

© 1997 Career Publishing Inc.

**A.  ENGINE COMPARTMENT**
— Oil Level
— Coolant Level
— Power Steering Fluid
— Water Pump
— Alternator
— Air Compressor
— Any Leaks

**B.  ENGINE START**
— Clutch/Gearshift
— Air Buzzer Sounds
— Oil Pressure Builds
— Ammeter/Voltmeter
— Air Brake Check*
— Steering Play

— Parking Brake
— Mirrors — Windshield
— Wipers
— Lighting Indicators
— Horn(s)
— Heater/Defroster
— Safety/Emergency Equipment

**C.  FRONT OF TRACTOR**
— Lights
— Steering Box
— Steering Linkage

**D.  FRONT SUSPENSION**
— Springs
— Spring Mounts
— Shock Absorber

**E.  FRONT WHEEL**
— Rim
— Tire
— Lug Nuts
— Hub Oil Seal

**F.  FRONT BRAKE**
— Slack Adjuster
— Chamber
— Hoses
— Drum

**G.  DRIVER/FUEL AREA**
— Door, Mirror
— Fuel Tank
— Leaks
— Battery/Battery Box

**H.  UNDER TRACTOR**
— Drive Shaft
— Exhaust System
— Frame

**I-F.  REAR WHEELS (FRONT AXLE)**
— Rims
— Tires
— Axle Seals
— Lug Nuts
— Spacers

**I-R.  REAR WHEELS (REAR AXLE)**
— Rims
— Tires
— Axle Seals
— Lug Nuts
— Spacers

**J-F.  REAR SUSPENSION (FRONT AXLE)**
— Springs
— Spring Mounts
— Torsion, Shocks
— Air Bags
— Torque Arm

**J-R.  REAR SUSPENSION (REAR AXLE)**
— Springs
— Spring Mounts
— Torsion, Shocks
— Air Bags
— Torque Arm

**K-F.  REAR BRAKES (FRONT AXLE)**
— Slack Adjuster
— Chamber
— Hoses
— Drums

**K-R.  REAR BRAKES (REAR AXLE)**
— Slack Adjuster
— Chamber
— Hoses
— Drums

**L.  COUPLING SYSTEM**
— Mounting Bolts
— Safety Latch
— Platform/Catwalk
— Release Arm
— Kingpin/Apron
— Air/Electric Lines
— Locking Jaws
— Gap
— Guide Plate
— Fifth Wheel Plate

**M.  SLIDING 5th WHEEL**
— Locking Pins

**N.  REAR OF TRACTOR**
— Lights, Reflectors
— Signal/Brake Lights
— Splash Guards

**O.  TRAILER FRONT**
— Air/Electric Connect
— Header Board
— Lights, Reflectors

**P.  SIDE OF TRAILER**
— Landing Gear
— Lights, Reflectors
— Doors, Ties
— Frame
— Tandem Release

**Q-F.  WHEELS (FRONT AXLE)**
— Rims
— Tires
— Axle Seals
— Lug Nuts
— Spacers

**Q-R.  WHEELS (REAR AXLE)**
— Rims
— Tires
— Axle Seals
— Lug Nuts
— Spacers

**R-F.  SUSPENSION (FRONT AXLE)**
— Springs
— Spring Mounts

**R-R.  SUSPENSION (REAR AXLE)**
— Springs
— Spring Mounts

**S-F.  BRAKES (FRONT AXLE)**
— Slack Adjuster
— Chamber
— Hoses
— Drums

**S-R.  BRAKES (REAR AXLE)**
— Slack Adjuster
— Chamber
— Hoses
— Drums

**T.  REAR OF TRAILER**
— Lights, Reflectors
— Doors, Ties
— Splash Guards

**Figure 4-19**

# Chapter Five
# VEHICLE SYSTEMS

**Wheels • Tires • Axles • Brakes • Steering System • Exhaust System • Coupling System • Cooling System • Air Intake System • Suspension • Engine • Frame • Electrical System • Fuel System • Drive Train • Bearings**

**FROM NOW ON,**

**ONLY THE BEST WILL DRIVE**

# OBJECTIVES

When you have mastered this chapter, you will be able to:

- Describe the suspension, fuel, air intake and exhaust, lubrication, cooling, electrical, steering, and coupling systems

- Explain where the frame, axles, wheels and their parts, engine, drive train, and brakes are located and how they operate

- Show how all these parts relate to one another

# CHAPTER FIVE

# VEHICLE SYSTEMS

## INTRODUCTION

A tractor-trailer is made up of many parts and systems. Just as the human body has a system to circulate blood through its organs, the tractor of your rig has a system to send oil through its parts. Each system must do its part if the truck is to work properly.

This chapter will teach you:
- The reason for each of the rig's systems
- The function of the system's major parts
- The relationship of the system to safety and economy of operation

Remember, this chapter is only an overview. If you want to learn more about the various parts and systems of trucks and how they operate, ask your instructor for the best manual.

© 1997 Career Publishing Inc.

**Figure 5-1**

## FRAME, SUSPENSION SYSTEM, AND AXLES

### Frame

Many van trailers and cargo tanks are of frameless construction. **Frameless construction** means the exterior of the van or truck, instead of the frame, is the weight carrying part.

On many other tractors and trailers, however, the **frame** is the *backbone* of the truck tractor and many trailers. Engine mounts are attached to the frame to hold the engine in place. The body is connected to and strengthened by the frame. The frame is the unit through which the axles and wheels are connected to the suspension system.

The frame includes two steel rails that run the entire length of the vehicle. Lightweight tractors may have aluminum rails. Tractors that haul oversized or overweight loads usually have extra strength steel rails. Cross members connect the two rails and provide strength and support to the frame.

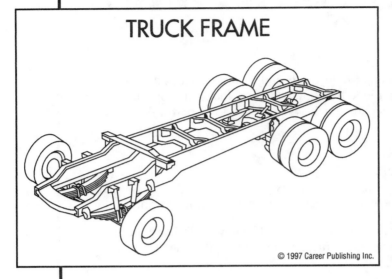

TRUCK FRAME

© 1997 Career Publishing Inc.

**Figure 5-2**

## Suspension System

The **suspension system** supports, distributes, and carries the weight of the truck. This system is made up of springs and spring hangers. The front and rear axles are attached to it, and the frame rests on it. As the ground changes, the system allows the axles to move up and down without seriously affecting the cargo. By securing the suspension system at several points along the frame, the stress of road shocks can be evenly distributed.

How strong and durable the system must be is determined by the weight and type of cargo the rig will transport. A good suspension system should be able to support the load and transmit full engine or braking power to the chassis frame.

The suspension system should hold the axles securely to insure correct drive-line alignment. It should also cushion the ride for the driver and cargo, whether the trailer is empty or loaded. Ready access to the system will make it easy to maintain.

Most tractor-trailers use one of two types of suspension systems:
• Leaf spring suspension system
• Air bag suspension system
Most suspension systems use leaf springs for deadening shocks, but the air bag suspension is becoming more popular.

**Leaf spring suspension**: Narrow metal strips of varying lengths bolted together and attached to frame hangers. There are many types of leaf springs. The most commonly used spring on heavy duty systems is the stack, or multi-leaf, spring. The tapered leaf spring is used mostly on lighter weight, tandem axle vehicles.

**Air suspension**: Uses bags of air placed between the axle and frame. Widely used on trailers, air suspension is now also being used on truck tractors. These systems give a smooth ride and decrease damage to both the rig and cargo. With air suspension, loaded and empty vehicles differ little in their ride.

Air pressure for the air suspension system comes from the tractor air compressor. Some systems have valves to let the driver adjust air pressure for specific loads. Frame height can also be changed for different loads.

There are more tandem suspensions now that most states have increased the legal gross weight limits. One popular system uses both the leaf spring suspension and air pressure suspension. The combination results in a sturdy, yet smooth ride. It can be installed on a single-axle, dual-axle, or three-axle setup.

While combining the two systems reduces many common air cushion problems, some trouble spots continue to need attention. Leaks and other problems can occur around the leveling valves and linkage. Loads with a high center of gravity are unstable and rock easily. The leaf springs help improve these situations.

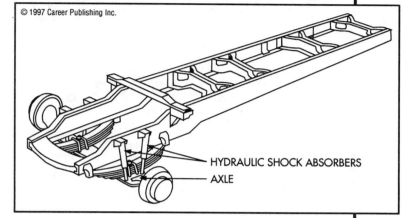
HYDRAULIC SHOCK ABSORBERS
AXLE

**Figure 5-3**

**Shock Absorbers**: Reduce the motion of the vehicle body as the wheels move over uneven surfaces. They are usually needed in the independent coil and air bag suspension systems.

A shock absorber operates like a piston in a cylinder with a hole in it. Since liquid is almost impossible to compress, liquid is forced through the tiny hole as the shock is compressed. The liquid resists the pressure and smooths out the ride.

## Axles

**Axles** connect the wheels to the rest of the trailer-tractor. They also support the weight of the vehicle and its cargo. Different axles perform different functions. While all axles support the weight of the vehicle, each type of axle performs a special function.

The front tractor axle connects the steering mechanism and brakes. The tractor drive axle transfers power from the engine and drive train to the wheels. Along with trailer axles, it also serves as a connecting point for the brakes.

All axles fall into two basic types.
• Dead
• Live

## Dead Axles

A **dead axle** is not powered. It:
• Receives, or houses, the wheel
• Supports vehicle weight
• Provides a place to connect steering mechanisms and brake components

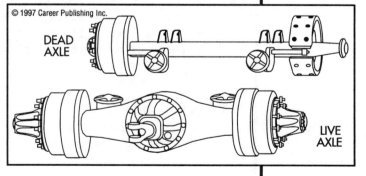
DEAD AXLE
LIVE AXLE

**Figure 5-4**

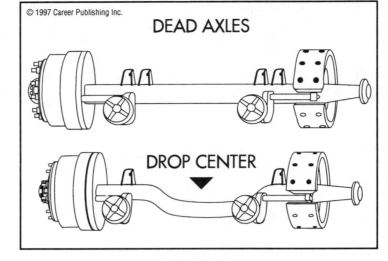

**Figure 5-5**

Most dead axles are straight, but some have a drop center design that allows space for the drive shaft. Some are I-beam construction while others consist of a hollow tube or box.

There are several types of dead axles including the:

- **Ordinary trailer axle**: Connects the trailer wheels to the trailer body.

- **Tractor steering axle**: Supports and steers the front end of the tractor. The front wheel assemblies at each end of the axle turn. The axle does not turn.

- **Converter dolly axle**: Attaches to the front end of the trailer. This axle steers the second trailer in a set of doubles. The entire axle turns for steering.

- **Multiple axle assembly**: Two or more dead axles together. They spread the rig's weight over more axles. This reduces the amount of weight on any one axle.

- **Lift axle**: Can be raised off the pavement when loaded to reduce tire and axle wear. It is usually kept in the raised position.

- **Variable load suspension axle (VLS)**: Allows adjustment of the weight carried by each axle. One type uses air or hydraulic suspension. The other type has springs.

- **Sliding tandem**: Used on semitrailers. Allows the trailer axles to be moved forward and backward on a track. Weight can be transferred back and forth between the tractor and trailer. When the axle is moved backward, more weight is placed on the tractor.

## Live Axles

A **live axle** is powered. It:
- Supports the vehicle's weight
- Sends power to the wheels
- Is hollow

Because the live axle is hollow, the gears and axles can transmit power through this space to the wheels. Some examples of live axles include:
- **Single Drive Axles**: Found on the rear of the tractor.
- **Tandem Axles**: Two axles that work together. There are three types of tandem axles.

1. **Twin Screw**: Both axles are powered.
2. **Pusher Tandem**: The rear axle is powered (live) and the forward axle is not powered (dead). The forward axle must have a drop center so the drive shaft can be attached to the live axle.
3. **Tag Tandem**: The forward axle is live and the rear axle is dead. The dead axle *tags* along behind the live axle.
- **Tri-drive Axles**: Three axles in the same assembly. They are used where a load carrying advantage is needed.

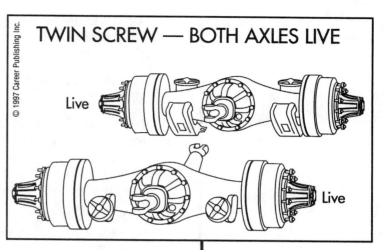

**Figure 5-6**

# ENGINES

This chapter will not go into great detail about the many types of engines and how they work. If you want that information, you should take a mechanic's training course. However, tractor-trailer drivers should be aware there are many types of engines. Drivers should also know something about how they operate.

The engines on truck tractors are internal combustion engines. The engines may be:
- Gasoline
- Diesel
   Two-stroke cycle or four-stroke cycle

An **internal combustion engine** burns fuel inside itself, within enclosed chambers. These chambers are called cylinders. The cylinders are the heart of the engine. They are where power is generated to turn the wheels that run the tractor and pull the trailer.

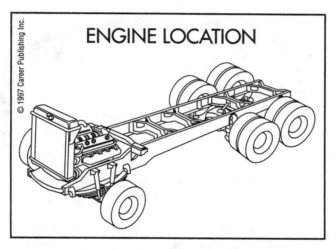

**Figure 5-7**

The basic parts of the engine are the:
- Block
- Cylinders
- Pistons
- Connecting rods
- Crank shaft

Think of an **engine block** as a large block of steel with holes, or cylinders, drilled into it. Think of a cylinder as a coffee can. One end of the can is sealed shut. The other end is open. A plunger (piston) fits snugly against the cylinder wall, but it can move up and down the wall. When fuel burns within the cylinder (combustion), it creates the expansion that forcefully moves the piston.

A rod attached to the piston moves with it. Since the rod is connected to a crank, it turns the crank. Therefore, the up and down movement of the piston is converted into the rotary, or circular, motion of the crankshaft.

The rotary motion is the force that is applied to the wheels to move the vehicle.

Fuel alone will not run an internal combustion engine. In the case of the **gasoline engine** (used on most cars and smaller vehicles), fuel (gasoline) must be mixed with air when it is sent to the cylinders for burning. This mixing takes place in the carburetor. A mass of pressurized air is forced over a thin jet of gasoline. This breaks the fuel into a mist, or vapor, of very small droplets and air.

Today, almost all tractors have **diesel engines**. Diesel engines do not have carburetors. They have fuel injectors to supply fuel to the cylinders. The air intake system supplies the air to the cylinders.

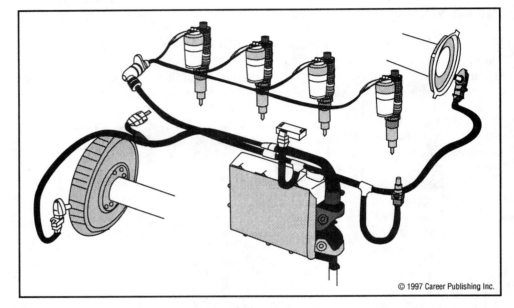

© 1997 Career Publishing Inc.

**Figure 5-8**

Another difference between gasoline and diesel engines is that:
• In a gasoline engine, the fuel/air mixture is ignited by an electrical spark from a spark plug.
• In a diesel engine, the extreme compression of the fuel/air mixture in the cylinder by the piston squeezes it so much the diesel fuel ignites.

No matter what type of engine the tractor has, the fuel/air mixture is burned in the cylinders. After burning has expanded it, the burned fuel is forced out of the cylinder through exhaust valves and manifolds.

## FUEL SYSTEM

The **fuel system** sends fuel to the engine. It regulates the amount of fuel that is sent and the how often it is injected into the cylinders. The basic components of the fuel system are:
• The injector
• A tank containing fuel
• An engine-driven pump

The pump moves the fuel from the tank, through the filtering system, and into the injector. Usually the pump delivers more fuel than is needed, so there is a pipe to return the extra fuel to the tank.

Just before the fuel reaches the injector, a filter cleans it. Even a small speck of dirt can ruin an injector, so the oil can never be too clean. Because dirt can also harm the engine and its operation so greatly, there is often another filter between the tank and the pump.

The injector must figure just the right amount of fuel and inject it into the cylinder at exactly the right time and at the right pressure. This is not easy. The amount of fuel needed varies because of power needs. Most new engines use electronic controls to do this. Electronics are more efficient than the old mechanical controls.

## Fuel Tank

The **fuel tank** is a container that holds fuel. Sometimes larger trucks have two tanks: one tank strapped to each side of the frame. On straight trucks, a single tank may be placed behind the cab. If a straight truck has more than one tank, the fuel lines are joined with a **Y** or an **I** type of connection.

Fuel tanks are vented to maintain equal pressure on the inside and outside. The vent hole is usually in the filter pipe cap or at the top of the tank.

The fuel cap area must be kept clean at all times. The fuel filter cap and the neck of the tank should be completely clean before removing the cap. If the tank is under the chassis, use *great care* when cleaning the cap to keep dirt from getting into the fuel system.

## Fuel Filters

**Filters** in the fuel system clean the fuel as it goes from the entry tube of the tank, through the tank and fuel lines, and into the injectors. A coarse filter is the first dirt block. A finer filter is next. Finally a filter/water separator protects the injector jets and engine from water, rust, and other contaminants. This filter is the most important one because water can seriously harm the fuel system. Rust and corrosion destroy engine parts.

## Fuel System Heaters

Trucks driven in cold weather should have fuel system heaters. Many kinds of heaters are available.
- Some units heat the fuel in the tank.
- In-line units heat the fuel when it is going from the tank to the injector system.
- Filter heaters heat the filters, which then heat the fuel as it passes through the injection system.

When a truck is driven in severely cold weather, all three types may be needed. Chemicals are also used to help the fuel flow in cold and sub-zero weather. The chemicals prevent the fuel from jelling and keep wax crystals from forming. Some even clean the injectors and improve the fuel.

## Diesel Fuel

**Diesel fuel** has an advantage over gasoline. It has a low vaporizing rate. It does not create an explosive air-fuel mixture when it is accidentally spilled or leaked. This can be very important when hauling highly volatile fluids or explosives.

Cetane number is an indicator of diesel fuel quality. It tells the amount of time needed for the fuel to ignite the hot air in the combustion chamber of the cylinder. Cetane numbers generally range from 30 to 60. The higher the number, the faster the fuel mixture will ignite.

If the cetane number is too low, the engine will be difficult to start, it will knock, and there may be puffs of white smoke from the exhaust. This is often seen during the warm-up period and during light road operation. If it continues, harmful deposits can collect in the cylinders.

A bad characteristic of diesel fuel is that it creates wax crystals in cold weather. The crystals make starting and operating difficult. If too many crystals collect, the engine will not start. Lower density fuel is less likely to crystallize or jell.

## AIR INTAKE AND EXHAUST SYSTEM

The air intake and exhaust system is another vital element of the diesel engine. A lot of fresh air is needed and must be easily available for use in the engine's air supply system.

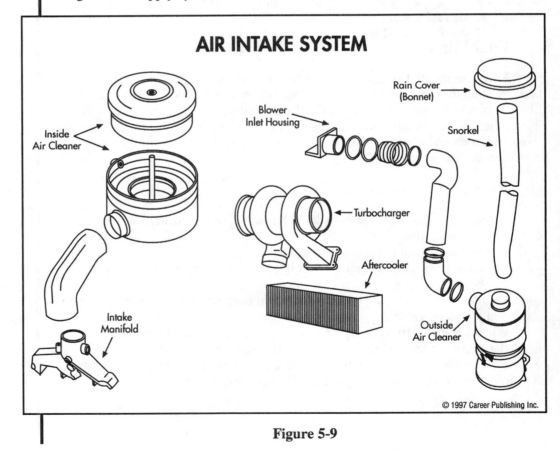

**Figure 5-9**

## Air Intake System

The **air intake system** delivers fresh air to the cylinders. An air cleaner removes dirt, dust, and water from the fresh air. There are two types of cleaners.
1. Oil bath (wet)
2. Disposable cartridge (dry)

The air cleaners must be kept clean for the engine to operate at its best. If the weather is dusty or rainy, you may have to check the cleaners each day.

The clean air flows into the air intake manifold. The manifold is simply a pipe with an equal number of outlets and cylinders. Each outlet from the manifold is an intake port for a cylinder. Valves regulate the flow of air into the cylinders. The cylinders act as combustion chambers.

## Exhaust System

After combustion (burning), the **exhaust system** expels used gases. Exhaust valves open in each cylinder. A stroke of the piston expels the used gases through ports in the exhaust manifold. The gases pass through the exhaust pipe and a muffler. The muffler quiets the noise. The gases are discharged from the vehicle through a vertical stack or tail pipe. A vertical exhaust stack has a movable rain cap that opens to let the gases escape and closes to keep the rain out.

## Pyrometer

Some instrument panels have a **pyrometer** that measures the temperature of exhaust gases. This gauge lets the driver know how hot the exhaust gas is. The temperature may be anywhere from 600°-1,000° F. The normal operating range varies from truck to truck, so you must learn the normal range for your truck.

You must be careful the temperature of the gas does not get too high. This is especially important on mountain roads or long sloping grades. If the exhaust temperature gets too high, you can damage the engine. An exhaust temperature that is too hot usually results from lugging the engine because the driver did not downshift when needed, or the engine is receiving too much fuel. Take your foot off the accelerator if the engine begins to lug or the pyrometer temperature does not drop. Shift the transmission.

## LUBRICATION SYSTEM

The **lubrication system** distributes oil to the parts of the engine. The film of oil between the moving parts keeps them from rubbing together. Instead, they ride or slide on the oil. This reduces the friction between the surface of the parts. When you keep friction to a minimum, you:
• Increase engine efficiency
• Increase engine part life

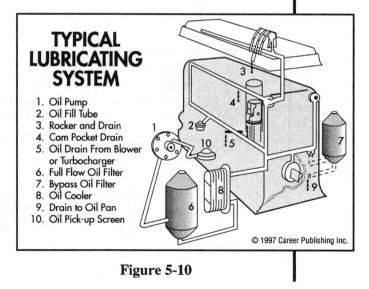

**TYPICAL LUBRICATING SYSTEM**

1. Oil Pump
2. Oil Fill Tube
3. Rocker and Drain
4. Cam Pocket Drain
5. Oil Drain From Blower or Turbocharger
6. Full Flow Oil Filter
7. Bypass Oil Filter
8. Oil Cooler
9. Drain to Oil Pan
10. Oil Pick-up Screen

© 1997 Career Publishing Inc.

**Figure 5-10**

A lot of heat is created by the rapid movement of parts. With the oil film present, some of the heat is absorbed into the oil instead of into the metal parts. The flowing oil carries the heat away. This helps keep the engine operating at a safe temperature.

Oil also cleans the engine. As it flows through the engine, it collects bits of dirt, carbon, and even worn metal. The biggest particles settle to the bottom of the oil pan. The smaller ones are filtered out.

Another vital function of the oil is to prevent the loss of pressure between the pistons and cylinder walls. When pressure is lost, power is also lost.

When there is an oil film between these parts, the force of combustion delivers a firm push against the piston. This sends the maximum amount of power to the drive shaft and the wheels. Without an oil seal, a great deal of power would be lost.

Oil also protects engine parts from corrosion, wear, and rust. It coats the surfaces that do not move and protects them from rust. When rust collects, it flakes off and damages other parts of the engine.

Finally, engine oil absorbs shocks. It forms a cushion between surfaces that are subjected to shocks. For example, each time ignition occurs in the combustion chamber, a sudden force hits the piston. This, in turn, sends the force through a wrist pin, connecting rod, and crankshaft. The oil helps absorb the shock to these parts as well as reduce noise and wear.

## Operation

Bolted to the bottom of the engine is a container, or reservoir, called the **oil pan**. When lubricating oil is poured into the engine, it flows down to the oil pan. When the engine is operating, oil is pumped under pressure from the pan to all the vital friction and pressure points of the engine.

Vital friction and pressure points are:
* The **crankshaft bearings** (sometimes called the main bearings). The bearings are inserts between the crankshaft and its holder, the crankcase.
* **Wristpins**: Used to fasten the connecting rods to the pistons
* The **inserts**, or bearings, where the connecting rods are joined to the crankshaft.

Oil is not pumped directly to many engine parts that need lubrication. Instead, they get oil by the *splash method*. The bearings and many other rapidly moving engine parts throw off oil. With the constant motion, a fine oily mist reaches those parts not included in the pressure line of the system. The area between the pistons and cylinder walls is lubricated in this way.

## Oil Changes

You must drain the old oil before you change to new oil. You cannot tell the quality of the oil by its color or feeling it with your fingers. Detergents have been added to prevent or slow the corrosion of the bearings and formation of sludge and deposits in the engine. These additives may cover up the *feel* of dirty oil. It is better to follow the manufacturer's recommendations for changing the oil.

## Oil Filters

Another way of prolonging the life of the oil and the life of the engine is by carefully filtering the oil. As the oil circulates and does its work of cooling the engine and reducing friction between moving parts, it collects foreign matter and holds it in suspension. Such grit, dirt, small bits of metal, etc. must be removed before they damage the engine. **Oil filters** strain out the impurities.

There are several different types of oil filtering systems. They are the:
- Full flow system
- Bypass system
- Combination full flow/bypass system

**Full Flow System:** In a full flow oil filtration system, all oil leaving the oil pump passes through an oil filter. The filter uses what is called a *one-pass method*. All contaminants, dirt, and floating particles must be filtered out during this one trip through the filter.

Because the filter must remove all of the floating material, it often becomes clogged. Then the flow of oil to the engine is restricted. A valve opens to let the oil flow. Even though impurities may be carried to the engine, keeping oil from the bearings would create more damage.

**Bypass System:** The bypass, or part-flow, oil filtration system filters a small amount (about 10%) of the oil flow. It is normally used along with the full flow system. It filters the excess oil that does not go through the bearings but is normally returned to the oil pan. The flow of oil through the bypass filter is controlled by an opening.

**Combination Bypass/Full Flow System:** This is the best type of filtration system. Oil from the full flow filter goes to the bearings. Oil from the bypass filter returns to the oil pan.

The thorough cleaning of the full flow system is combined with the added protection of the bypass system. As a result, the oil and filters last longer because there is less contamination. The longer life of the oil and filters cuts costs.

**Centrifugal Filter:** This is a type of bypass filter. The oil entering the permanent housing spins the filter at high speed forcing the dirt and particles out of the oil for more efficient cleaning of the oil. It is used in addition to the other oil filters.

## COOLING SYSTEM

Heat is the basis of the internal combustion engine. However, intense heat can quickly destroy an engine. The cooling system keeps the temperature down.

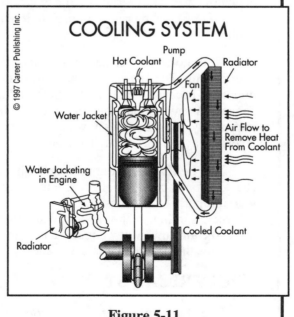

**Figure 5-11**

The engine is cooled by coolant that circulates through the engine block and cylinder head. Remember, we said to think about the block as a solid block of steel into which large holes (cylinders) were drilled. The block is actually a bit more complex than that. In addition to the cylinder holes, the block is honeycombed with a channel that comes very close to all the cylinders. This channel is called the water jacket.

Coolant flows through the jacket. It picks up heat as it goes. The channel then takes the coolant to the radiator. In the radiator, the coolant flows through small, thin walled tubes that are surrounded by air. The coolant is cooled in the tubes.

Then it is pulled into the pump and forced back into the engine. When the coolant enters the water jacket, the process is repeated and the coolant is again cooled.

In addition to the water jacket, radiator, fan, and water pump, the cooling system also includes a thermostat and the coolant.

> NOTE: Water should not be used in the cooling system because alone it can cause rust or other damage to the system and engine. It seldom has the correct pH (acid-alkaline balance). Commercial antifreeze cools better and should be changed every year.

**Coolant**: A fluid, usually water and anti-freeze, that circulates within the system. It absorbs heat from the engine and takes it to the radiator for cooling. The coolant then returns to the engine to repeat the process.

The coolant should always be carefully selected according to the manufacturer's specs for the type of engine and conditions through which the truck will travel.

**Thermostat**: A valve in the water jacket located at the point where the coolant leaves the engine. Until the engine runs long enough to heat the coolant, the thermostat is closed. When the engine reaches operating temperature (usually about 180° F), the thermostat opens to let the coolant go to the radiator for cooling.

**Radiator cap**: Located at the top of the radiator. It keeps the coolant from overflowing. The cap also maintains pressure on the coolant. The pressure is important because the higher the pressure, the higher the boiling point of the coolant. A leaking radiator cap can cause the entire cooling system to operate improperly. Most engines now have separate coolant reservoirs to check coolant levels. They are see-through and easy to open so that coolant can be added.

**Fan belt**: A belt from the engine that drives the fan. The belt must be checked for slack. It should be tightened or replaced as needed. The fan must work properly at all times. This is very important in stop-and-go driving or when the truck is idling. A shroud or cowling usually surrounds the fan to protect it and direct the air flow. Many engines have fan clutches or viscous drives that disengage the fan when it is not needed.

## ELECTRICAL SYSTEM

The **electrical system** is very complex on a tractor-trailer. For more detailed information than this book provides, read a manual on electrical systems.

There are four basic parts of the electrical system.
1. Charging circuit
2. Cranking circuit
3. Ignition circuit
4. Lighting and accessory circuit

## Charging Circuit

The **charging circuit** produces electricity to keep the battery charged and run the electrical circuits. The parts of the charging circuit are the:
- Battery
- Alternator or generator
- Voltage regulator
- Ammeter or voltmeter
- Electrical wires
- Battery cables

**Battery:** Creates (through chemical reactions) or receives and stores electrical energy. This is the energy that activates the starter. It is a backup source of electricity for a number of accessories when the alternator cannot keep up with electrical needs.

The battery has two posts — positive and negative — through which electricity flows. The negative post and electrical parts are attached to the vehicle frame. Electricity travels from the positive post through wires to the electrical equipment, on to the frame, and back through the negative post to the battery.

**Generators and Alternators:** Devices that recharge the battery when it loses electricity. They create electricity that can be used by the battery and electrical system. Most systems today use alternators. In either case, the device is run by a fan belt that receives its power from the engine crankshaft.

In other words, when the engine is running, the alternator (or generator) is creating electricity. Through an automatic control system, the electricity used for operating, except starting the engine, is provided by the alternator or generator.

In summary, the battery provides the energy to start the engine and is a backup for extra energy when needed. The alternator or generator furnishes all other electricity.

**Ammeter:** A gauge on the instrument panel that shows the current output of the alternator. It indicates whether the battery is being charged by the alternator or is discharging.

**Voltmeter:** Gives an overview of the charging system. It tells the state of charge of the battery and whether the charging system is keeping up with the demands for electricity. It can warn of battery, alternator or regulator failures; a loose and slipping fan belt; and broken, loose, or corroded wires and cables.

**Voltage Regulator:** Controls the voltage produced by the alternator or generator. The regulator keeps the battery voltage from getting too high. This is so the battery does not overcharge and boil off the battery fluid. It also keeps the other electrical parts from burning themselves out.

## Cranking Circuit

The **cranking circuit** sends electricity from the battery to a small starter motor. This starter motor is connected to a large disc (flywheel) by a gear. The disc turns the crankshaft and starts the engine. All a driver needs to know is that activating the starter switch puts this process in motion. A few trucks still have air starters that use compressed air instead of electricity to crank the engine.

## Ignition Circuit

In a gasoline engine, the **ignition circuit** provides the sparks for each cylinder to ignite the gasoline/air mixture. An ignition circuit is not needed for diesel trucks because the compression of the air ignites the fuel and is its own ignition circuit.

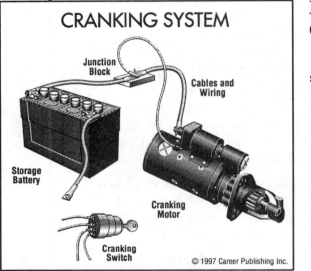

**Figure 5-12**

## Lighting and Accessory Circuits

The lighting and accessory circuits send electricity to all:
- **Lights:**
    Headlights
    Taillights
    Turn signals
    Running lights
- **Horns**
- **Instrument lights:**
    Speedometer
    Odometer
    Gauges, etc.
- **Windshield cleaners:**
    Wipers
    Washers

## DRIVE TRAIN

The **drive train** takes the power generated by the engine and applies it to the tractor's rear wheels. As the wheels turn, the rig moves. The drive train has five main parts.
- Clutch
- Transmission
- Drive shaft
- Universal joints
- Differential

They perform four basic functions.
1. Connect the engine (source of power) to and disconnect it from the drive train.
2. Modify the torque (twist) and engine speed (rpm) produced by the engine to let the vehicle operate at its best.
3. Carry the power of the engine to the rear axle and drive wheels.
4. Change the direction of the torque, or twist, to propel the rear wheels.

The simple explanations that follow show what happens when you put various parts of the power train into action with your pedals and levers. Remember again, this is not a complete explanation. It is simply an overview.

## Clutch

As the driver uses it, the **clutch** connects or disconnects the engine from the rest of the power train. On most trucks, this is done by three plates. The plates can be engaged (together) or disengaged (apart). The middle plate, or clutch disc, is the driven member. It is connected to a shaft leading to the transmission. The other two are driving members. They connect to the engine.

A strong spring forces the two driving members toward each other. This squeezes them against the middle plate until they all turn together as one unit. When they are together, the clutch is *engaged*. When they are apart, the clutch is *disengaged*.

The engine flywheel is the first driving member. Its surface is very smooth where it squeezes the driven plate. The other driving member is called the pressure plate. It is a fairly heavy cast iron disc that is smooth on one side. It is fastened to the cover, which is bolted to the flywheel so they all turn together. The disc can slide toward and away from the driven plate.

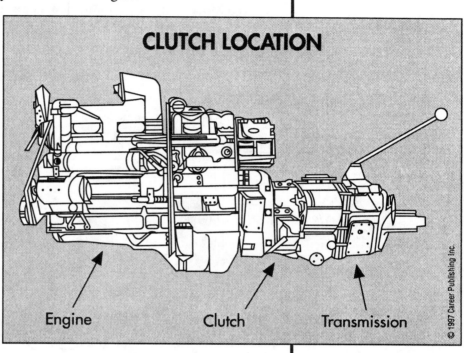

**CLUTCH LOCATION**

Engine        Clutch        Transmission

© 1997 Career Publishing Inc.

**Figure 5-13**

The driven plate, or clutch disc, is a flat disc of steel with a friction facing on each side. The plate is fastened by splines (grooves or slots) to a shaft connected to the transmission. The disc fits into the grooves on the shaft so that the plate and shaft turn together. The plate can slide backward and forward on the shaft.

The clutch disc is softer than the other plates. Thus, it will be destroyed before damage can occur to other parts of the drive train. When a clutch goes out, it is usually this part that is worn out and must be replaced.

To prevent damage or excess wear, clutches can be adjusted. They have an access hole to permit this adjustment.

A series of coil springs, or sometimes one large flat spring, act between the clutch cover and the pressure plate. They push (or pull) the pressure plate toward the flywheel. This action squeezes the clutch disc between the cover and the plate.

The springs exert a constant force trying to engage the clutch. Usually they are strong enough to keep the clutch from slipping.

To disengage the clutch, the driver pushes down on the pedal. The pedal causes levers to pull or push the pressure plate against the springs. This loosens and finally separates the driving plates from the driven plate. The clutch disengages and disconnects the engine from the rest of the power train.

## TRANSMISSION

The **transmission** is a case, or box, of gears located behind the clutch. The case is usually fastened to the clutch housing. The clutch and transmission look like an extension of the engine.

The transmission adjusts the power generated by the engine so it provides the right speed and torque for the job. For example, when the loaded rig moves from a stopped position, a great deal of power is needed.

The driver adjusts the gears in the transmission to provide the needed combination of power, torque, and speed. The transmission then sends, or *transmits* the power from its source, the engine, to the drive, or powered, axles. This is the power that propels the vehicle.

The gears in the transmission help control the speed and power of the vehicle. The engine can be kept at a relatively constant speed. The rig, however, can be moved either slowly or rapidly with much the same power output. Once underway, the vehicle needs less power to keep it going than it needed to start it rolling. Gears make all this possible.

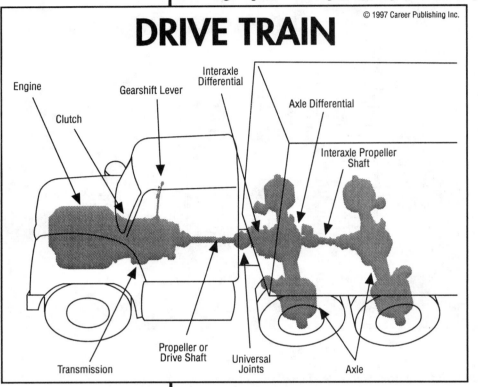

# DRIVE TRAIN

© 1997 Career Publishing Inc.

**Figure 5-14**

You need to understand two basic, related facts when selecting gears.
1. More torque, or power, means less speed.
2. More speed means less torque.

In other words, as the gears increase torque, they decrease speed at about the same rate. This means the driver can change the ratio between the engine and the drive wheels to get either more speed or more torque. The lower the gear, the more torque. The higher the gear, the more speed.

## Types of Transmissions

There are many types of transmissions. They may have:
- Different numbers of forward speeds
- One or more shift levers
- Single or multiple gear housings
- Single or dual drive axles
- Different types of gear selector switches
- Manual, power-assisted, or auxiliary units
- Different combinations of main transmissions and variable speed rear ends

We will not go into detail about the many possible combinations and why they are needed. However, new drivers should be aware that operating the transmission correctly is an important part of learning to drive a tractor-trailer.

# DRIVE SHAFTS AND UNIVERSAL JOINTS

Behind the transmission is a propeller called the drive shaft. The **drive shaft** is a steel shaft that runs from the transmission to the rear of the vehicle. Usually it is hollow. On trucks with a long wheel base, **carrier bearings** join two drive shafts. It is in a metal casting mounted on a cross member between the two drive shafts.

At each end (front and rear) of the shaft are the **universal joints**, or U-joints. They are called universal joints because they can move in almost any direction. They are usually made of two U-shaped pieces set at right angles to one another and fastened together by cross arms of equal length. As the drive shaft spins, it transfers, or carries, the twisting motion back to the rear axle. The U-joints let the drive shaft change its angle of operation.

The U-shaped pieces (yokes) pivot on the arms of the cross. Since there are two pivots, the shaft can be at an angle and still transmit power. The U-joints do not have to be in a straight line. This is very important because they become somewhat misaligned with each bump in the road. The rear axle moves up and down with the wheels at every bump while the transmission does not move as much. The U-joints let the propeller shaft turn even though its two ends are shifting in relation to one another.

# DIFFERENTIAL

The **differential** transfers driving power to the wheels through the drive axle shafts. At the rear end of the propeller shaft is a short shaft with a small gear at the end. This gear is called the **pinion gear**. The pinion gear meshes with the **ring gear** in the differential box on the rear axle. The pinion and ring gears have two jobs.
1. They turn the force, or torque, of the pinion shaft at right angles so the wheels can turn and drive the vehicle.
2. They can reduce speed and increase torque because the pinion gear is much smaller than the ring gear.

## Differential Gears

As you know, the pinion gear sends the power to the ring gear in the differential gear box. The rear wheels of the vehicle must be able to turn at different speeds when turning a corner. The wheels that are farther from the corner travel a greater distance, so they must be able to turn faster.

This turning of the wheels at different speeds is made possible by the differential. The differential is a group of gears that connect the right and left rear axles. It divides the driving force equally between the axles and permits one axle to turn faster than the other. This is a complex gear arrangement, and a driver does not need to understand how it works, but just that it does work.

## Twin Screw Interaxle Differential

As one wheel begins to spin, the differential takes power away from the wheel that has better traction. Almost at once, one wheel is turning while the other one is not. This is helpful when turning a corner.

However, it can create trouble on slippery pavement. Having one wheel stand still on firm ground while the other is turning is a good way to get stuck.

When you expect poor traction, place the inter-axle differential in the *lock* position. This insures equal power will be sent to each axle of a tandem. You should do this before the wheels lose traction and start to spin. When a drive wheel spins quickly at high speed, it throws the oil off the bearing and causes it to run without lubrication. This shortens the life of the bearing.

As soon as you get back traction, the interaxle differential should be returned to the *unlock* position. Be sure to let up on the accelerator to interrupt torque to the wheels when *shifting* between the locked and unlocked positions.

Driving on dry pavement with the interaxle differential in the locked position is not recommended. Switch immediately to *unlock* when you are back on a good surface.

# BRAKING SYSTEM

A good **braking system** is very important. A smoothly operating engine and drive train are needed for the rig to do its work. However, if the braking system is not in tip-top shape, the driver, the load, and other roadway users are in great danger.

A truck's braking system consists of three separate elements.
1. Service brakes
2. Secondary brakes
3. Parking brakes

The **service brake system** is normally used to slow down or stop the vehicle. The **secondary braking system** can slow or even stop the rig if the service brake system fails. The **parking brake system** is used to hold the rig in place when it is parked.

There are two basic types of foundation brakes used in the service brake system.
1. Drum brakes
2. Disc brakes

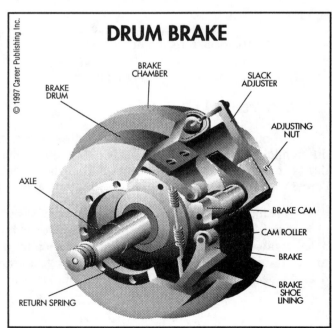

**DRUM BRAKE**

© 1997 Career Publishing Inc.

BRAKE CHAMBER
BRAKE DRUM
SLACK ADJUSTER
ADJUSTING NUT
AXLE
BRAKE CAM
CAM ROLLER
BRAKE
BRAKE SHOE LINING
RETURN SPRING

**Figure 5-15**

**Drum Brakes:** This brake is a metal cylinder that looks something like a drum. It is bolted to each end of the axle. The drum rotates with the turning wheels. To stop the vehicle, the brake shoe linings are forced against the inside surface of the brake drums. This creates the friction that slows or stops the rig when enough friction is created. Friction creates heat. When too much heat is created, the drums expand out away from the shoe lining. This causes brake fade, and the truck is hard or impossible to stop.

**Disc Brakes:** A modern disc brake system usually has a fixed disc attached to the inside of the wheel. It rotates with the wheel. This circular part is flat and made of steel that is machined on both sides. To slow down or stop, the linings are squeezed against each side of the disc. This looks something like a wide-jawed vice closing quickly on a spinning disk. It creates the friction that slows or stops the rig.

## Air Brake Systems

Air is compressible; that is, it can be squeezed into a smaller space than it normally occupies. The smaller the space into which it is forced, the more resistance, or pressure, it can exert.

In an **air brake system**, this pressure is used to increase the braking force. The compressed air can multiply the force of mechanical braking many times.

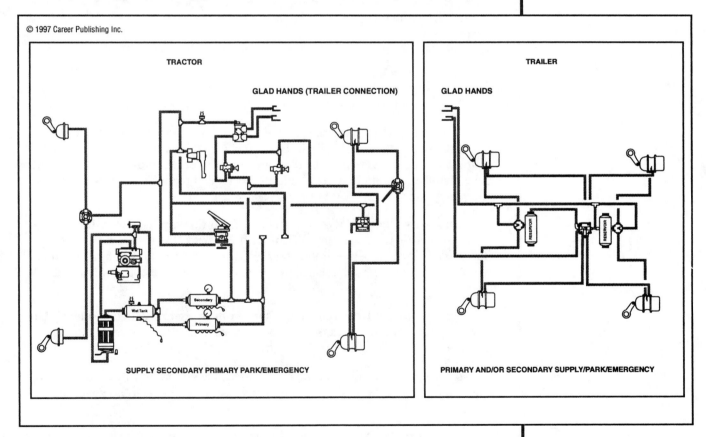

Figure 5-16

A number of parts make up the air brake system. They include:

- Compressor
- Governor
- Air reservoirs
- Brake chambers
- One-way check valve
- Safety valve
- Drain cocks
- Air pressure gauge
- Low pressure warning signal
- Treadle valve
- Highway valve
- Independent trailer brakes
- Glad hands
- Tractor protection system
- Tractor parking valve
- Quick release valve
- Relay valve
- Emergency relay valve

**Compressor:** Squeezes the air into a smaller space. This increases the force the air exerts. Compressors operate in different ways. They may use belts and pulleys or shafts and gears, but they are always run by the engine. When the engine runs, they run.

Even though the compressor runs with the engine on, it is not always pumping. The compressor pumps, or compresses, air until the pressure of the air in the cylinder reaches around 125 pounds per square inch (psi). Then it stops pumping until it is needed again.

**Governor:** Regulates the air flow to maintain the desired pressure. As the pressure approaches 125 psi, the inlet valves are held open. This releases air. When the pressure drops below 100 psi, the governor closes the inlet valve to let the pressure build up again.

**Air Reservoirs:** Hold the compressed air supply. There are three tanks.

1. Wet tank
2. Dry tank
3. Trailer Reservoir

The size of the tank varies, depending on how many tanks there are and the size of the brake chambers. The wet tank receives the hot moist air from the compressor and delivers it to the dry tank. The trailer reservoir is near the trailer brake chambers. Compressed air held in this tank is ready for both normal and emergency use.

**One-Way Check Valve:** Prevents air from flowing back into the compressor from the reservoirs. When air flows back, the brakes do not work. This valve is located between the compressor and the wet tanks on the tractor. If two of the valves are used, the second one is located between the wet and dry tanks.

**Safety Valves:** Keep the air pressure from rising to a dangerous level. One valve is placed in each air tank. It usually opens and releases air when the pressure reaches 150 psi. This lowers the pressure in the system.

After the safety valve has been activated, the governor will need servicing. This is a job for a qualified mechanic. Never attempt to adjust the governor yourself.

**Drain Cocks:** Drain moisture from the air brake system reservoirs. Air becomes hot when it is squeezed by the compressor. When it reaches a reservoir it expands, cools, and releases moisture. This moisture condenses in the tank. If the moisture is not removed, it damages the system.

Drain this moisture each day. Drive your rig onto a level surface. Chock the wheels to keep the rig from rolling. Be sure to allow all of the air to escape so the moisture can drain out. Some trucks also have air dryers to remove moisture. These should also be drained regularly.

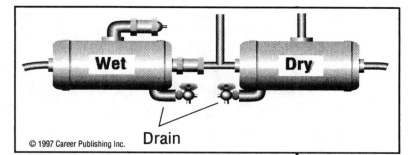

Figure 5-17

**Air Pressure Gauge:** Tells how much air pressure is in the system in pounds per square inch (psi). This gauge is found on the instrument panel. The normal operating range is 90-120 psi.

**Low Pressure Warning Signal**: Tells the driver the air pressure has dropped below 60 psi. A red warning light will turn on, a buzzer will sound, or both will happen.

If one of these signals activates, stop at once. 60 psi is still enough air pressure to put on the brakes. If you do not stop at once, you may lose more pressure and not be able to stop. The cause of the low air pressure must be fixed before you go on.

**Air Application Pressure Gauge:** Shows the amount of air pressure being applied to the brakes. When the brakes are not in use, the gauge will read zero psi (0 psi).

**Treadle Valve:** Controls the air that operates the brakes. It is also called the foot brake. The further down the pedal is pushed, the more air is sent into the system. Letting up on the pedal releases the brakes by letting the air exhaust from the brakes.

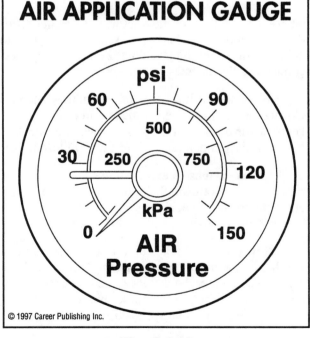

Figure 5-18

**Highway Valve:** Allows air from the hand valve to flow through the air line to put on only the trailer brakes. It also allows the foot valve to use the same air line and put on both the tractor and trailer brakes.

**Independent Trailer Brake:** A hand valve that regulates the air flow to only the trailer unit and puts on the brakes. It is usually called the trolley valve and is normally on the right side of the steering column.

**Tractor Parking Valve:** A round blue knob you can push in to release the tractor parking brake. You pull it out to put on the parking brake. It also operates the spring brakes.

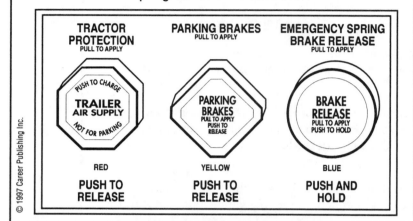

**TRACTOR PROTECTION VALVE & EMERGENCY TRAILER BRAKE OPERATION**

**Tractor protection valve**
• Provides Air Supply
• Closes Automatically if Air Supply Drops When Driving
The parking brakes, when applied, close the tractor protection valve and set the spring brakes at the same time.

Figure 5-19

**Tractor Protection System:** Secures the tractor's air pressure if the trailer should break away from the tractor and snap the air lines. The tractor protection system is made up of two valves.
1. Tractor protection valve
2. Emergency valve

The tractor protection valve is closed by the driver to keep air from going out of the tractor. When it is pulled, it sets the tractor's spring brake. When it is pushed, it supplies air to the maxi-chamber to compress the spring and release the brakes.

**Glad Hands:** Connect the service and emergency air lines of the tractor to the trailer. The connections are secure when the glad hands lock. An O-ring seals the coupling to prevent air loss. Because it is important for nothing to damage the O-ring, check for dirt and sand before connecting the air lines.

When the air lines are unhooked, they should be sealed to keep dirt out. Covers, protection plates, or dead-end (dummy) couplers may be used. They will keep the air lines from dropping down onto the drive shaft and being torn off. You will have much less risk of brake failure if you keep the air lines clean.

**Quick-Release Valve:** Allows the brakes to release swiftly. When you remove your foot from the brakes, air escapes from the chambers into the atmosphere. This quickly releases the brake shoes regardless of the distance between the foot valve and the brake chamber.

**Relay Valve:** Makes up for brake lag on a long wheelbase vehicle. When you brake, the distance between the brake pedal and the brake chambers is a factor. The greater the distance, the longer the period of time before the brakes apply. This means the rear trailer brakes will not apply as soon as the tractor brakes. The relay valve speeds up the action of the brakes.

**Emergency Relay Valve:** Relays air from the trailer air tank to the brake chambers. If there is a break in the lines between the tractor and trailer, the valve sends air from the trailer reservoir to the brake chambers.

This is part of the emergency brake system and activates automatically. You can also put on the trailer brakes in an emergency with the cab-mounted emergency valve. The emergency relay valve can also help release the trailer brakes quickly.

## Operation of the Air Brake System

The one-way check valve is between the compressor and wet tank. The compressor pumps pressurized air to the wet tank where most of the moisture is removed. The air then passes through the one-way check valve to the dry reservoir.

When the driver puts on the foot brake, the air flows through the service air lines to the front and rear tractor brake chambers. At the same time, air is sent through the tractor protection valve to the trailer brake chambers.

When the brake pedal is released, air escapes through the foot valve, or relay valve, in the tractor and through the quick release, or relay valve, in the trailer.

## Antilock Brake System

An antilock brake system is needed to keep the rig from moving outside its lane while coming to a stop. The antilock system prevents wheel lock-up by sensing the speed of each wheel electronically.

When the sensor detects an impending lock-up, it adjusts the application of air to prevent lock-up and a possible skid. Thus, the system uses a computer to replace the driver's manual efforts of pumping the brakes to prevent lock-up. The computer operated system can apply the brakes 3-5 times per second faster than a driver can.

## Spring Brake System

Many vehicles with air brakes also have spring brakes, which serve as dependable parking or emergency brake systems. The brakes are applied or released by using a control in the cab.

# MIXING OLD AND NEW EQUIPMENT

One problem you will face as a driver is the mix of equipment that does not work well together. Some trailers built before 1975 are still in operation. The brake application time for most of these older trailers is much slower than for current tractors. Some new tractors have air-operated disc brakes, so the problem is even worse. You must know what equipment you are operating, so that it can be handled properly.

# WHEELS

There are two basic types of wheels.
1. Spoke
2. Disc

### Spoke Wheel

Usually called a *Dayton*, the **spoke wheel** is of made of two pieces. It is more difficult to balance spoke wheels and align the tires and rims. Also, the lug nuts must be checked often for tightness.

### Disc Wheel

The **disc wheel**, commonly called a *Budd*, is made of aluminum or high-tensile steel. Alignment is simpler because these wheels can be fastened together with 6-10 wheel studs.

## MOUNTING SYSTEMS

Two types of wheel mounting systems are used.
1.   Stud piloted
2.   Hub piloted

A stud piloted system uses the studs on the wheel hub to guide and center the wheel. A hub piloted system uses the wheel hub itself to guide and center the wheel during mounting. The two types of mounting systems cannot be intermixed.

Wheels are fastened by two methods:
1.   Ball-seat nuts
2.   Flange nuts

Ball seat nuts clamp the wheel on by seating in a tapered part of the stud hole. Flange nuts clamp onto a flat surface and provide more even clamping torque. These two types cannot be interchanged.

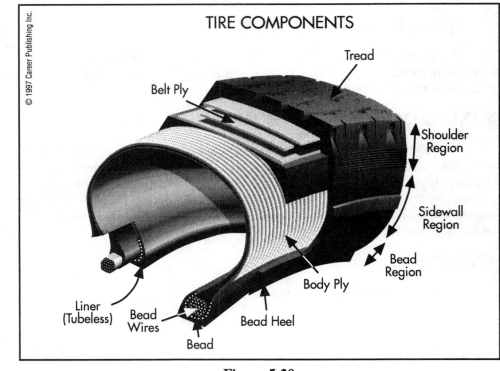

**Figure 5-20**

## TIRES

There are three basic types of tires.
1. Radial
2. Bias ply
3. Bias belted

### Radial Tires

On **radial tires**, the body ply cords run across the tire perpendicular to the tread. There are also belt plies around the tire, parallel to the tread along the part that makes contact with the road. These hold the body ply cords tight and provide sturdiness for the tread.

Radial tires cost more to buy than other tires, but they have a number of advantages. Radial treads last 40-100% longer. Because more of the surface of radials comes in contact with the road, they provide greater traction. They also give better fuel mileage.

### Bias Ply Tires

**Bias ply tires** have body cords running across the tire at an angle. There may also be breakers, or narrow plies, just under the tread that angle like the ply cords.

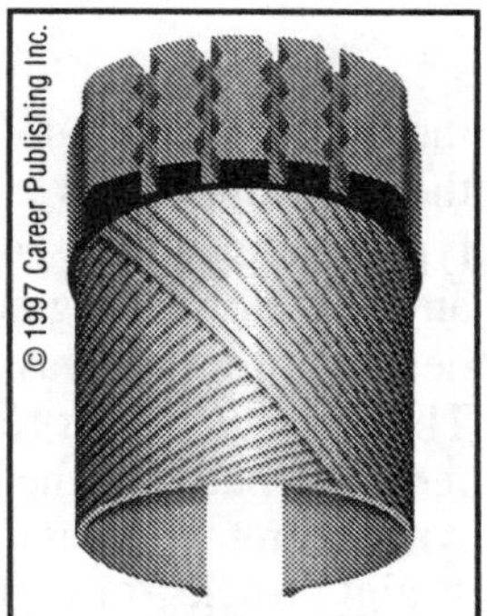

### Belted Bias Tires

**Belted bias tires** have body ply cords that run across the tread at an angle. The belt plies run around the tire under the tread.

### Mixing Radial and Bias Ply Tires

In general, it is best not to use radial and bias ply tires together. Tires should be the same size and of the same type. To save money, however, you may use radial and bias ply tires on the same vehicle if you carefully follow the manufacturer's guidelines.

The recommendation for combining radial and bias ply tires applies to tractor wheels with a 20" or larger rim and 15" trailer tires.

> NOTE: NEVER put tires of different size or construction on the same axle. NEVER mix radial and bias tires on a tandem-drive assembly.

### Tire Tubes

Truck tires may or may not have tubes. Both radial and bias-ply tires can operate with tubes. Tubes can be used only with multi-piece wheels, however.

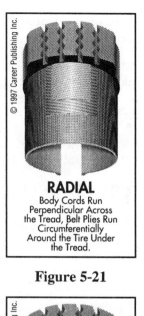

**RADIAL**
Body Cords Run Perpendicular Across the Tread, Belt Plies Run Circumferentially Around the Tire Under the Tread.

**Figure 5-21**

**BIAS PLY**
Body Cords Run Diagonally Across the Tread

**Figure 5-22**

**BELTED BIAS**
Body Cords Run Diagonally Across the Tread. Belt Plies Run Circumferentially Around the Tire Under the Tread.

**Figure 5-23**

In tires that have tubes, the tube fits between the tire and the rim. The air that keeps the tire inflated and supports the vehicle is held in the tube.

Tubeless tires are mounted on single-piece wheels. The tire itself holds the air that supports the rig. The advantages of using tubeless tires are:
- The wheels are much lighter
- The tires run cooler
- They are more efficient

The wheels are also lighter because the parts of the multiple piece wheel (flap, side ring, and lock ring) are not needed.

## TREAD DESIGN AND WHEEL POSITION

For highway use, there are two basic truck tire **tread** designs.
1. Rib
2. Lug

**Rib Tread:** Grooves in the tire tread run parallel to the sidewalls. Tires with a rib-type tread can be used anywhere on the rig and are designed for highway speed. These *all-position* tires are recommended for the front wheels on tractors and large straight trucks for high-speed, long-haul service. These tires help the driver maintain control of the vehicle and avoid skids. Be careful when choosing tires. There is a tire made for trailer use only that looks like the all position tire.

**Lug Tread:** Deep grooves in the tire shoulders run perpendicular to the sidewalls. These tires are best for the drive wheels. In high-torque road service, they wear better and have greater traction. They also have higher rolling resistance than the rib types. If you do not operate in cold areas, it may be wiser to use rib tires on the drive wheels for greater fuel efficiency.

© 1997 Career Publishing Inc.

**Figure 5-24**

© 1997 Career Publishing Inc.

**Figure 5-25**

# NORMAL TIRE INFLATION

Tires must be inflated correctly for the rig to perform at its best. For the right number of pounds per square inch (psi), refer to the truck's owner manual and Federal Tire Regulations FMC 393.75.

Pressure should be checked with an accurate gauge at least once a week. For a true reading of tire pressure, check when the tire is cool. Inspect the tires thoroughly and check the pressure with an accurate tire gauge. Driving causes the tires to heat and increase the pressure. The pressure in sizes 9R22.5 tubeless or 8.25R230 and smaller tube-type tires may increase by as much as 10 psi. Sizes 10R22.5 tubeless and 9.00R20 and larger tube-type tires may increase approximately 15 psi.

If you test your tires after they have been used and they show less than these increases, inflate them to the proper pressure. If the pressure of the heated tires is more than the recommended pressure, do not release any air. Wait until the tires cool. Check them again, and then correct the pressure if you need to.

When you inflate tires, keep in mind the maximum pressure for the load you will be carrying. Do not exceed the rim or wheel rating. Check the pressure in new tires after 24 hours of operation to get an accurate reading. Always replace the valve stem caps to maintain a tight air seal and keep dirt and moisture out.

If tire pressure increases more than 10-15 psi during normal operation:
- The tires may be underinflated
- The rig may be overloaded
- The tires may not be the right size
- The rig may have been speeding

The increase may also be any combination of these causes. Correct the cause of the increase.

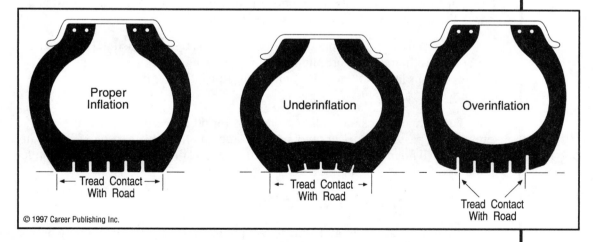

© 1997 Career Publishing Inc.

**Figure 5-26**

## Underinflation

Underinflation increases tread wear and reduces tire life.
- When the temperature increases in an underinflated tire, it can cause the tread to separate from the body or belt ply of the tire.
- The tire can flex excessively. As a soft tire travels over the road, this flexing builds up heat. Heat weakens the body cords. If it continues, the body cord deteriorates and may catch fire from the high internal temperature.

Tires that are underinflated can make the rig very hard to control. This can be dangerous in emergencies.

If you are driving on duals and one is under-inflated or flat, a fire can result. Because it is overloaded, the other tire may also fail. Both of these are very dangerous conditions.

NOTE: Radial tires at the correct pressure can show a bulge on the side that may make them appear to be underinflated. Check them to be sure the pressure does not get too low and cause too much wear.

## Overinflation

Overinflation can damage tires and create hazards. It can also greatly reduce the stopping distance of an empty or lightly loaded rig.
- Rigid tires are damaged more easily by roadway objects.
- Roadway shock is not absorbed as well. This can cause stress and rim failure.

## How Heat Affects Tire Rubber

A tire can become very, very hot during long-distance, high-speed driving. This can happen very easily during hot weather or when the tire is underinflated. Check the temperature often to prevent problems.

Internal friction heats the tire. When it reaches the combustion point, a tire can burst into flame. This usually happens in a dual assembly when one of the tires is underinflated. Often, just after the rig stops, the tire explodes. Such fires are very hard to put out.

Tire temperatures must also be checked for other reasons. As the tire's temperature passes 250° F, components weaken and the rubber softens. Tires can be more easily damaged if they rub against a curb, railroad track, or pit rail guide at the terminal dock.

## Matching and Spacing Duals

If two tires of different diameters are put together, the larger tire may bulge at the sides. This happens because it is carrying more than its share of the load. The smaller tire may wear unevenly because it does not contact the road properly. The tread can then separate.

With some tire types, there may be a difference in diameter even if they have equal inflation pressures. There can be 1/4" difference in diameter for an 8.25 cross section 9.22.5 or smaller tubeless tire. For a 9.00 cross section 10.22.5 or larger tubeless tire, there can be a 1/2" difference.

To get true dual diameter readings, you should measure the tires with a steel pi tape 24 hours after they are inflated. If you measure them while they are on the rig, use a string gauge, straight edge, tire caliper, or large square.

To be on the safe side, keep the differences in diameter to less than 1/4" no matter what the size of the tires. Keep the space between the tires at the recommended distance to keep the tires from *kissing* (rubbing together).

## Tread Life

Because conditions vary, no one can predict the life of the tire tread exactly. Quality of the tire, how the vehicle was handled, tire inflation, load distribution, and care of the tire will all affect the life of the tread.

Average tread life for a given tire is known. This is good information for the driver because it serves as a guide. If the driver shifts gears smoothly and is generally responsible, he or she may be able to get greater than average tread wear. On the other hand, the driver can cut tread wear in half by speeding or braking sharply.

NOTE: Tire wear depends on the type of operation, whether it is a light or heavy load, the type and grade of the tire, and the road surface.

## STEERING SYSTEMS

To control your rig, the **steering system** must be working properly. There are a number of parts that must be checked often to insure smooth operation.

- **Steering wheel**: Connected to the steering shaft and controls the direction of the vehicle
- **Steering shaft**: Connects the steering wheel to the steering gear box
- **Steering gear box**: Transfers the turning of the steering shaft to the Pitman arm
- **Pitman arm**: Connected to and moves the drag link

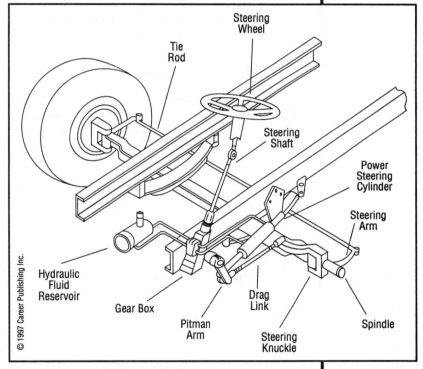

Figure 5-27

- **Drag link**: Transfers movement from the Pitman arm to the left steering arm
- **Steering arm**: The one on the right side attaches the tie rod to the wheels. The one on the left side is attached to the drag link
- **Tie rod**: Connects the front wheels together and adjusts their operating angle

Proper placement of the parts is known as *correct steering geometry*. All of these parts must be correctly aligned or the rig will be hard to steer. A rig that is hard to steer can be dangerous.

## Wheel Alignment

The following **alignment features** on the front end of the rig are built in by the manufacturer. They may be changed as needed.

**Caster:** The amount the axle kingpin is tilted backward at the top. It is measured in degrees. The axle should have a positive caster. That is, it should tilt forward. When set in this manner, the vehicle has a natural tendency to go straight. It will also recover from turns more quickly. Positive caster makes steering easier.

**Camber:** The amount the front wheels are tilted outward at the top. It is best for trucks to have positive camber. The distance between the tires is greater at the top than at the bottom. With this kind of setting, the loaded truck tends to straighten the tires in relation to the road surface.

Other tendencies of alignment can result from wear and damage. Most noticeable are toe-in and toe-out.
- **Toe-in**: The amount the front wheels are closer together at the front than they are at the rear.
- **Toe-out**: The amount the front wheels are farther apart at the front than they are at the rear.

## Power Steering

**Power steering** lets the driver control the tractor with less effort and stress. This is of great help when you have a blow-out. You can retain control of the rig and be able to slowly lift your foot off of the accelerator. There are two types of power steering systems.
1. Hydraulic
2. Air

A hydraulic system uses fluid to make steering easier. An air system uses the force of air.

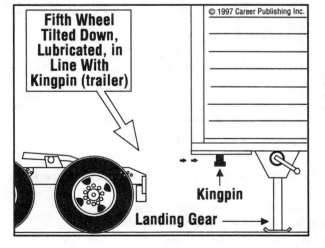

**Figure 5-28**

## COUPLING SYSTEMS

The **coupling system** connects the tractor to the trailer. Coupling systems have two main parts.
1. Fifth wheel
2. Trailer kingpin

To correctly couple the tractor to the trailer with a single 2" kingpin is one of the biggest responsibilities a driver of big rigs has.

## Fifth Wheel

The **fifth wheel** is not really a wheel. It is a flat disk on the tractor. The kingpin of the trailer fits into and is held by the fifth wheel. The linking of the fifth wheel and kingpin lets the tractor pull the trailer.

Because of the type of coupling, some sideways, or lateral, motion of the rig is possible. Moving the truck

**GREASE RETENTION GROOVE**

© 1997 Career Publishing Inc.

**Figure 5-29**

*pulls* the trailer along. When the truck turns, it moves somewhat independently of the trailer. The trailer follows the truck but along a different path of travel.

The trailer receives from the tractor:
- Stability
- Support
- Direction of movement

At the same time, the trailer enjoys some independent sideways movement. This lets the whole rig make turns better.

There are several fifth wheel options a tractor may have to make it easier to couple and uncouple. All of the following help cut down on wear to the fifth wheel and kingpin.
- Approach rails
- Tapered frames
- Complex locking mechanisms that remove excess movement between the kingpin and fifth wheel

There are different types of fifth wheel styles. Which type you use will depend on the kind of cargo you are carrying.

**Fixed-Mount Type:** The most common type. A fixed-mount fifth wheel is secured in a fixed position behind the cab. It has three parts.
1. Top, or base, plate
2. Bracket sub-assemblies
3. Frame mounting members

The top plate includes the locking mechanism and bears much of the stress of coupling. The bracket sub-assemblies hold the top plate in place. The frame mounting members are usually structural steel angles bolted to the fifth wheel.

**Sliding (adjustable) Type:** Slides backward and forward. It can be locked into place to adapt to different loads. It greatly increases the flexibility of the total rig. The sliding fifth wheel, or slider, helps the trucking industry conform to state laws regarding the length of vehicles and distribution of weight over the axles. This would not be possible with a permanent, or fixed-mount, fifth wheel assembly.

Sliding fifth wheels may be locked in place in one of two ways.
1. Pins fit into matching holes in the slider track and hold it in place.
2. A plunger fits into a row of slotted holes in the base to keep it from moving.

The slider can be adjusted by hand or automatically. To adjust it by hand, the driver moves the pins or plunger himself, and then adjusts the fifth wheel by moving it forward or backward.

When it is done automatically, an air activated control in the cab unlocks the locking device. The driver sets the trailer brakes and moves the tractor forward or backward until the fifth wheel is in the correct position.

## Fifth Wheel Slack Adjusters

The slack adjuster on a fifth wheel adjusts the kingpin locking mechanism so it will fit snugly around the kingpin. Slack adjusters are used on most mechanical locking mechanisms. Compression locking mechanisms reduce problems with slack.

## Kingpins

Kingpins are attached to the upper fifth wheel plate, which is underneath the front of the trailer. The kingpin is usually a 2" steel pin that is locked into the jaws of the fifth wheel to couple the tractor to the trailer. It is made of high strength steel and will usually last as long as the trailer.

# OTHER COUPLING DEVICES

There are other devices that are often used when coupling a truck to a tractor; and after a trailer has been uncoupled, to support the front of the trailer. The purpose of each part is explained in the section that follows.

## Converter Dolly

There are two types of **converter dollies**.
• Conventional dolly
• Jifflox, or Universal, converter dolly

**Conventional converter dollies**: Used to change semitrailers into full trailers. The dolly becomes the front axle of the trailer.

**Jifflox converter dolly**: Used in the eastern U.S., it is hooked behind the axle of a single axle tractor. This converts it to a tandem axle tractor. The tractor then can pull a loaded trailer.

Both dolly types are similar and include the same parts.
• Fifth wheel
• Draw-bar and eye
• Safety chains
• Air hose
• Electrical cable connections

## Trailer Landing Gears

When it is not coupled to a tractor, a trailer needs support for its front end. The landing gear supports the trailer when it is not attached to a tractor. It also moves the front of the trailer up and down as needed. The landing gear is usually hand cranked and may have either wheels or skid feet. Landing gears will not resist pressure from the side, front, or rear. They are only a means of stationary support.

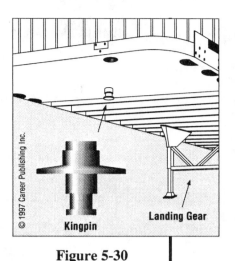

Figure 5-30

## SUMMARY

In this chapter, you have learned about most of the systems on a tractor-trailer. You have studied about the suspension, fuel, air intake and exhaust, lubrication, cooling, electrical steering, and coupling systems. You also now know where the frame, axles, wheels and their parts, engine, drive train, and brakes are located and how they operate.

## KEY WORDS

**Air intake system**: Delivers fresh air to the cylinders. An air cleaner removes dirt, dust, and water from the fresh air.

**Axles**: Connect the wheels to the rest of the rig and support the weight of the vehicle and its cargo.

**Braking system**: Used to slow or stop the rig. The braking system uses service brakes, secondary brakes, and parking brakes.

**Cooling system**: Keeps the temperature down in the engine.

**Coupling system**: Connects the tractor to the trailer.

**Dead axle:** An axle that is not powered.

**Differential**: Transfers driving power to the wheels through the drive axle shafts.

**Drive train**: Takes the power generated by the engine and applies it to the tractor's rear wheels.

**Electrical system**: Provides electricity to power the charging, cranking, ignition, lighting and accessory circuits.

**Exhaust system**: Expels used gases after combustion (burning).

**Fifth wheel**: A flat disk on the tractor that the kingpin of the trailer fits into to couple the tractor to the trailer.

**Frameless construction**: The exterior of the van or tank is the weight carrying part instead of the frame.

**Fuel system**: Regulates the amount of fuel that is sent to the engine and how often it is injected into the cylinders.

**Internal combustion engine**: Burns fuel within enclosed chambers called cylinders.

**Lubrication system**: Distributes oil between the moving parts to keep them from rubbing together.

**Pyrometer**: Gauge that measures the temperature of exhaust gases.

**Steering system**: The system that lets the driver control the movement of the rig.

**Suspension system**: Supports, distributes, and carries the weight of the truck.

**Tire tread**: The part of the tire that makes contact with the road.

# LEARNING ACTIVITIES

## Identify the Diagrams

**Instructions**: Write the name of the part on the line below the drawing. Tell its function on the lines beside the drawing.

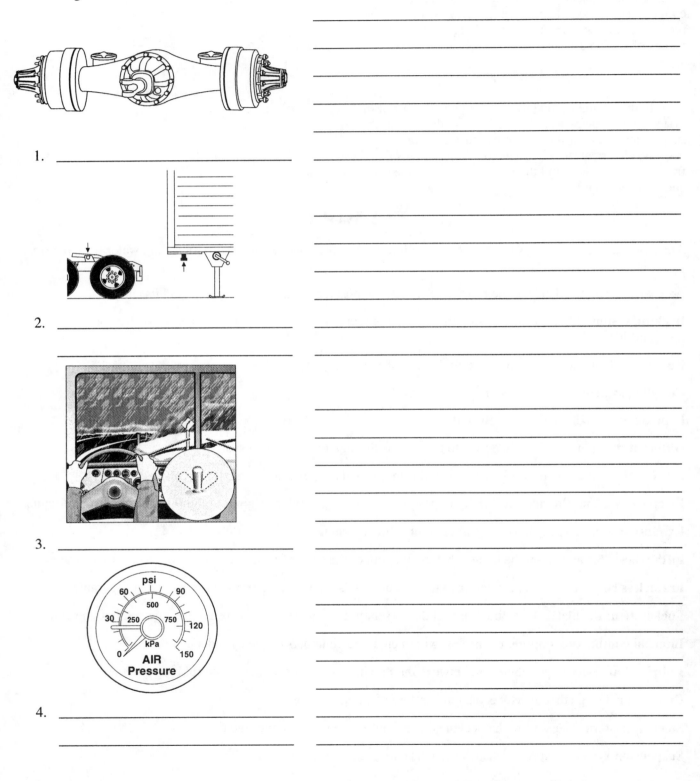

1. _____

2. _____

3. _____

4. _____

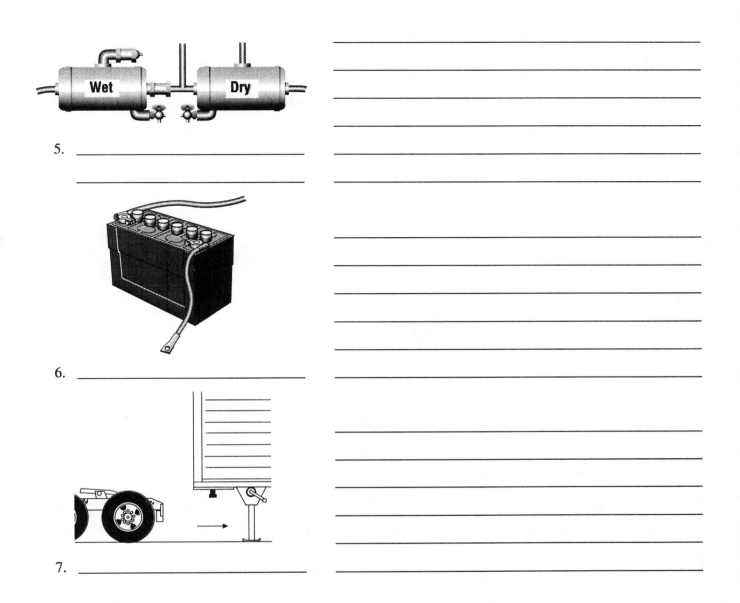

5. _____

   _____

6. _____

7. _____

## True-False Questions

Circle the T if the statement is true. Circle the F if the statement is false.

T F 1. A tractor frame serves much the same purpose as the skeleton of the human body. It provides support for all other parts of the system.

T F 2. The suspension system supports, distributes, and carries the weight of the truck.

T F 3. The only important difference between the front and rear tractor axles is the steering capability of the front axle.

T F 4. A lift axle is sometimes called a landing gear.

T F 5. *Live* axles are those that power the vehicle.

T F 6. *Live* axles are always on the road surface while *dead* axles are retractable and may be raised above the ground surface.

T F 7. Trucks are powered by internal combustion engines.

T F 8. Diesel engines do not have a carburetor or spark plugs.

T F 9. Power from the engine turns the *fifth* wheel, which pulls the trailer.

T F 10. Fuel injectors can be ruined by a small speck of dirt.

T F 11. One disadvantage of diesel fuel is its tendency to form waxy crystals in cold temperatures.

T F 12. Air temperature, like fuel temperature, must be monitored to prevent inefficient engine operation and damage.

T F 13. The most important function of the lubrication system is to distribute oil to reduce friction between the surfaces of engine parts.

T F 14. The lubrication system prevents loss of power and protects engine surfaces against corrosion.

T F 15. If it is necessary to add oil on a trip, any quality brand containing additives may be used.

T F 16. Damage from an overheated engine can generally be avoided by carefully monitoring lubrication and cooling system gauges.

T F 17. When the electrical system is working properly and not over-taxed, the battery provides electricity for starting the engine, and the alternator or generator provides for other electrical needs.

T F 18. The power train may be thought of as a series of parts that transfer the power generated by the engine to the drive wheels and road.

T F 19. By pushing in the clutch pedal, the driver can disconnect the engine from the rest of the vehicle. When the clutch pedal is released, the engine is connected to the rest of the vehicle again.

T F 20. The main purpose of transmission gears is to turn the torque of the drive shaft at right angles.

T F 21. The links at either end of the drive shaft are called universal joints because they can move up, down, or sideways as the tractor moves along the road.

T F 22. Rear wheels are able to turn at different speeds because of the rear universal joint.

T F 23. Tandem axles are able to carry greater loads than single axle rigs.

T    F    24.    One advantage of all tandem axles is that they increase traction.

T    F    25.    The primary braking system is used to reduce speed and stop the vehicle.

T    F    26.    The primary braking system may include both disc and drum brakes, both of which are mechanical.

T    F    27.    With an air brake system, compressed air can multiply the force of mechanical brakes.

T    F    28.    An air brake system will work with disc brakes, but not with drum brakes.

T    F    29.    Moisture should be drained from the air pressure system daily to protect against damage to the system.

T    F    30.    You must be careful and prevent the rig from rolling during the moisture draining process.

T    F    31.    If the low pressure warning system (red light or buzzer) comes on, you should pull into the next convenient rest area and search for the cause.

T    F    32.    An antilock brake system helps keep the truck moving in a straight line during hard braking.

T    F    33.    Advice not to mix radial and bias ply tires is a phony attempt to sell more tires.

T    F    34.    The most accurate reading of tire pressure will be achieved when the tires are cool.

T    F    35.    Overheated tires can result from a number of conditions including underinflation, mixing tires of unequal size, and long distance high speed operation.

T    F    36.    The fifth wheel is one of the two main components of a tractor-trailer coupling system.

# Chapter Six
# BASIC CONTROL

© 1997 Career Publishing Inc.

**Starting an Engine • Types of Diesel Engines • Gasoline Engine • Warm-up Period Engine Shutdown • Cooldown Period • Testing Trailer Hook-up • Idling • Putting the Rig into Motion • Stopping the Rig • Backing • Turning • Off-Tracking**

# OBJECTIVES

When you have mastered this chapter, you will be able to:

- Explain the routines for starting, warming up, cooling down, and shutting off two-cycle and four-cycle diesel engines

- Show how to test the trailer hook-up

- Explain the proper way to put a rig into motion

- Describe the correct way to stop a rig

- Describe backing in a straight line

- Explain the correct procedures for turning right and turning left

- Define off-tracking

## CHAPTER SIX

# BASIC CONTROL

## INTRODUCTION

Driving a tractor-trailer is a complicated job. You must master a number of basic skills. Big rigs are built to be started, steered, turned, stopped, and maneuvered in a certain way. In this chapter, you will learn some of these basic skills. Of course, you will have to do more than just read this material to be able to control your rig; you may have a chance to get in the cab and perform the skills.

Keep in mind, as you review the facts given here, this is just the beginning. Driving by yourself successfully means a lot of practice to polish the skills and knowledge you gain here. Getting the *feel* of basic control from this chapter and the range activities will help you greatly when you are out on the road.

## DEFINITIONS

Knowing the meanings of certain terms will help as you study this chapter. You will learn what is actually meant by starting the engine and shutting it down.
- **Starting routine** — Steps used to start the engine.
- **Warm-up** — The period of time after starting the engine and before moving the vehicle. During this time, the engine will warm up. Gauges in the vehicle will show you when the engine is operating within the manufacturer's specified range.
- **Engine shutdown** — The period of time from stopping the rig until the engine is turned off. Shutting down an engine requires a cooling off period. This prevents damage if the engine has a turbo-charger.

Routines vary according to the engine type.
- Two-cycle diesel engine
- Four-cycle diesel engine

When you drive a rig, you need to know the kind of engine it has and the basic operating procedures for the engine. If you do not, serious engine damage can result.

## DIESEL ENGINE

Before starting the engine you should always check the trailer coupling. How to check the coupling is described in detail in a later section.

### Two-cycle Diesel Engine

Always start a two-cycle diesel engine in this way.
1. Put on the parking brake.
2. Place the **STOP** and **EMERGENCY STOP** controls in the **RUN** position (if your rig has them).
3. Make sure transmission is in neutral. Depress the clutch pedal (prevents the starting motor from turning the transmission gears).

4. Turn on the switch-key.
5. Operate the starter. If the engine does not start in 15 to 20 seconds, turn off the starter. Allow it to cool for at least one (1) minute. Then try again. The reason for allowing it to cool is that trucks start on 24 volts and then drop to 12 volts. The extra volts can overheat or burn out the starter.
6. Control the engine speed with the foot throttle until it is running smoothly.
7. During warm-up, the engine should never be run at a higher rpm than is needed to keep it running. Turbocharged engines should not be run at a higher rpm until the engine oil pressure has built up and stabilized. Until the engine has reached this point, there is not enough oil at the turbocharger bearings to meet the lubrication needs of higher speeds.
8. Check the instruments for system malfunctions.

## Four-cycle Diesel engine

The start-up routine for a four-cycle diesel engine follows.
1. Put on the parking brake.
2. Close the throttle. Depress the clutch pedal. Make sure the transmission is in neutral.
3. Turn on the switch-key.
4. Operate the starter.
5. Crank for three or four seconds.
6. Check the instruments.
7. Warm up the engine.
8. During warm-up, the engine should never be run at a higher rpm than is needed to keep it running. Turbocharged engines should not be run at a higher rpm until engine oil pressure has built up and stabilized. Until the engine has reached this point, there is not enough oil at the turbocharger bearings to meet the lubrication needs of higher speeds.

## Fuel Efficient Starting

Keep these points in mind when starting an engine. They will help you save fuel.
• Pumping the throttle is a waste of fuel. It will only flood the engine.
• Rapidly revving the engine wastes fuel.

## Engine Warm up for Operating at Low rpm

The purpose of warming up an engine is to:
• Allow the engine to reach a beginning operating temperature.
• Circulate oil.
• Reach a favorable clearance between moving parts. This occurs at operating temperature.
• Build the oil pressure to the proper level.
• Coat the cylinder walls with a film of oil.
• Lubricate the bearings.
• Increase the coolant temperature. This may not show on the gauge.
• Heat the oil to the proper temperature.
• Build up air pressure.

## Fuel-Efficient Warm up

While warming up, do not idle the engine any more than needed. Keep the rpms low and the speed under 30 mph. The owner's manual will tell you the idling time. Idling time should be kept to a few minutes. Many rigs warm up best while moving at slow speeds. Keep the speed to 30 mph or less until the engine is warm. Use creeping speed when first moving to lubricate the dry wheel, transmission, and rear end bearings. Use extra care in cold weather.

## Results of Not Warming Up

Rapid acceleration or over revving before the engine is warm causes:
• Crankshaft and bearing damage
• Turbocharger bearing damage from lack of lubrication
• Damage to most parts that have not been properly lubricated

## Normal Instrument Readings

When the instrument readings reach normal, it is safe to drive your rig at cruising speed. Be sure to check the operator's manual for the proper oil pressure, air pressure, coolant temperature, oil temperature, and voltmeter or ammeter readings. These vary with the rig.

## Engine Shutdown

The steps in engine shutdown vary from one type of truck to another. The basic steps in turning off a diesel engine are:

1. Depress the clutch.
2. Shift to neutral and release the clutch.
3. Cool the engine.
4. Turn off the switch-key.
5. If the engine has a stop control, move it to the off position. The fuel flow is now cut off from the fuel injectors.

## Cool-down Period

In diesel engines, the cool-down period is the key step. It is as important as the warm-up. During the cool-down, the:
• Engine idles for up to five minutes.
• Coolant and oil flow at reduced temperatures.
• The heat from highway driving is distributed.

The cool-down period varies according to the:
• Manufacturer's specifications
• Type of trip completed: a longer period is needed for high-speed, long-haul trips
• Type of load that was pulled: heavy vs. empty (hot, overworked engines require longer periods)

### Excessive Idling

Too much idling wastes fuel. When idling, the vehicle is getting zero miles per gallon. Idling can waste as much as 1 gallon of fuel in an hour. It can also clog the fuel injectors. The engine may not be hot enough for complete combustion. The unburned fuel can cause harmful deposits.

Today's engines do not need to idle more than five minutes. Fleet surveys show that many truckers idle for long periods at truck stops during the warm-up and cool-down periods. One hour of idling causes the same amount of wear as two hours of driving. The typical over-the-road truck idles about 800 hours. That is equal to driving 64,000 miles.

## PUTTING THE VEHICLE IN MOTION AND STOPPING

Moving a tractor-trailer differs from moving an automobile. It takes more skill and practice. The driver must test the tractor-trailer hook-up, put the vehicle in motion, and bring it to a stop.

### Testing the Trailer Hook-up

Each time the trailer is hooked up, a hook-up test must be made. The test is different for a vehicle that has an independent trailer brake control than for one that does not have the control.

### Testing the Trailer Hook-up With Independent Brake Control

- Depress the clutch.
- Shift into the lowest forward gear.
- Put on the independent trailer brakes.
- Release the clutch to the friction point.
- Pull gently forward against the locked trailer brakes.
- Disengage the clutch.
- Repeat the whole procedure.

This routine also shows whether the trailer brakes are working.

### Testing the Trailer Hook-up Without Independent Brake Control

- Push in the clutch.
- Shift into the lowest forward gear.
- Switch the tractor protection valve from **normal** to **emergency**.
- Partly engage the clutch.
- Gently pull forward against the locked trailer brakes.
- Repeat the whole procedure.

### Putting the Tractor-Trailer in Motion

Moving the rig smoothly with ease is a skill you learn from practice. There is no subsititute. To move a rig, follow these steps:
- Push in the clutch all the way.
- Shift to the lowest forward gear.

- When the vehicle starts to move, slowly increase the engine rpm to increase the rig's speed.
- When the vehicle is in motion with the clutch fully engaged, take your foot off the clutch. Get ready to shift to another gear or stop.

## Hints:

- Engage the clutch quickly to avoid slippage.
- As the clutch engages, release the brakes.
- When starting on an upgrade, set the independent trailer brakes. Shift into the lowest forward gear. Slowly release the clutch. As the clutch engages, release the parking and trailer brakes.
- Allow for brake lag.

© 1997 Career Publishing Inc.

**Figure 6-1**

## Stopping the Tractor-Trailer

Stopping a big rig smoothly is a skill also learned from practice. To stop a rig, follow these steps:

- Push the brake pedal down.
- Control the pressure so the rig comes to a smooth, safe stop.
- If you have a manual transmission, do not push in the clutch until the engine rpm is almost to idle.
- When you have stopped, select a starting gear.

If you have stopped properly, there should be no nose rebound or bouncing of the cab.

## BACKING IN A STRAIGHT LINE

Backing is difficult and is covered in detail in a later chapter. Only basic information is presented here. It should help prepare you for straight line backing.

### Step 1.  Position the Vehicle Properly

Move forward until the tractor and trailer are aligned and the front (steering) wheels are straight.

## Step 2.  Speed Control

Shift to reverse gear. Back as slowly as you can using idle speed. Do not ride the clutch or brake pedals.

## Step 3.  Check Behind Your Rig

Use both mirrors to constantly check behind the rig while backing. Be aware and careful of pedestrians. In later exercises, you will need to guard against backing into an object. Keep the doors closed.

## Step 4.  Steering

The best way to keep your vehicle on course is not to oversteer. To correct drifting, turn the steering wheel toward the drift as soon as it occurs. If you catch the drift right away, a very slight movement will correct it. Little drifts need small corrections. Big drifts need big corrections.

Use the push-pull method to keep the trailer in a straight line. When the trailer gets bigger in the mirror, push the steering wheel toward that mirror. Immediately pull the steering wheel back to straighten the rig out. The biggest error in using the push-pull method is not returning the wheel to a straight position. This must be done as soon as you correct the drift.

## Step 5.  Pull Up and Start Again if Too Far Out of Position

If your rig is getting too far out of alignment, remember it is easier to correct a drift moving forward than moving backward. Stop and pull forward to realign the tractor and trailer. Then continue backing.

## TURNING THE VEHICLE

This section will describe basic turning maneuvers. Detailed instruction will be given in a later chapter.

A few basics to keep in mind when turning your vehicle:
- Know your vehicle.
- Allow for off-tracking.
- Plan your turn in advance.

## Off-Tracking

What, exactly, is off-tracking? It happens when you turn. The rear wheels do not follow the same path as the front wheels. They follow a

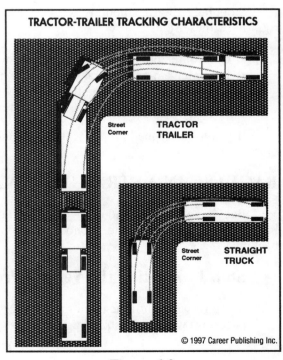

Figure 6-2

shorter path than the front wheels. The more distance between the front wheels and the rear wheels and the sharper the turn, the more the rear wheels off-track. Keep off-tracking in mind when making turns or taking curves.

## Off-Tracking in Tractor-Trailer Rigs

Two key factors determine the off-tracking of a trailer.
1. The distance between the kingpin and the rear trailer wheels
2. The amount of sideway drag of the rear tires.

The greater the distance between the kingpin and the rear trailer wheels, the more the off-tracking. For single axle trailers, measure the distance from the center of the kingpin to the center of the rear axle. For tandem axle trailers, measure the distance from the center of the kingpin to the center point between the axles.

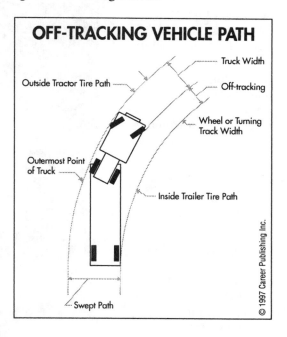

**Figure 6-3**

Sideway drag of the rear tires increases with the number of tires. The more sideway drag, the more off-tracking. Tandem axles have more sideway drag and greater off-tracking than does a single rear axle.

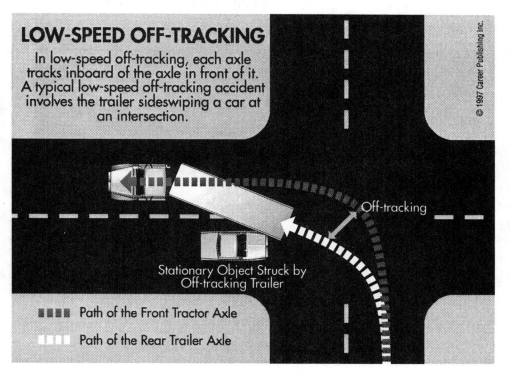

**Figure 6-4**

### Right Turns

Most right turns are tighter than the turning radius of your truck. To make it safely around the corner without hitting a curb or other object, you will need to use more traffic lanes than you would in a car. At the same time, you do not want to obstruct traffic.

Do not make the turn if you cannot clear the corner using the available space. Choose a different route. Sometimes you can continue straight ahead for another block and then make three left turns to get to the street you want.

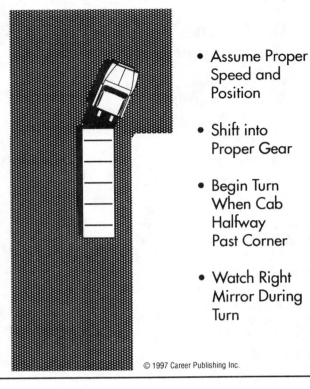

## MAKING A RIGHT TURN

- Assume Proper Speed and Position

- Shift into Proper Gear

- Begin Turn When Cab Halfway Past Corner

- Watch Right Mirror During Turn

© 1997 Career Publishing Inc.

**Figure 6-5**

The diagram below shows two possible ways to make a right turn. One of them is a good method. The other is not.

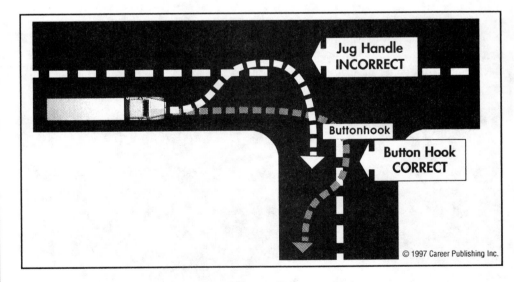

**Figure 6-6**

**Incorrect: Jug Handle Turn**

A jug handle turn is a common, but sloppy and dangerous, way to make a right turn. It is bad for the following reasons:

- Little, if any, real advantage is gained because the trailer tires do not have time to move away from the curb.
- As well as using extra cross-traffic lanes, one more lane in your direction is blocked.
- If you signal right but move left, you confuse traffic. Someone behind you may even try to squeeze between the trailer and the curb.

### Correct: Buttonhook Turn

A buttonhook turn will let you clear the corner without these problems. You use the extra space in front of you in this manner:

- Approach the intersection in the right lane.
- If the lane width allows, position your truck about four or five feet from the curb. You want as much space on the right as you can have without letting a car slip in.
- Turn on your right turn signal.
- Scan the intersection. Watch for a break in cross-traffic.
- Proceed straight ahead until the trailer tires will clear the corner in a hard right turn.
- Turn hard to the right.
- Finish the turn in the right lane.
- Cancel your turn signal.

**BUTTONHOOK**

© 1997 Career Publishing Inc.

**Figure 6-7**

Plan ahead as you enter a turn, so you will have done as much as you can to make the turn properly. Your plan should include:

- Signaling in advance
- Adjusting your speed
- Shifting into the proper gear
- Postioning your rig properly

## Signal in Advance

You must warn traffic that you plan to turn. Signal early enough that they will not be in your way when you need to turn.

## Adjust Your Speed

Adjust your speed as you approach the

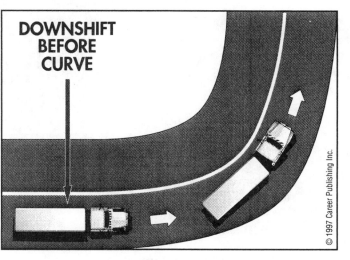

**DOWNSHIFT BEFORE CURVE**

© 1997 Career Publishing Inc.

**Figure 6-8**

intersection or turning point. Then you will be able to speed up slightly as you make the turn.

## Shift Gears

Shift into the proper gear before entering the turn. Then you will be able to complete the turn in the same gear. In this way, you can keep both hands on the steering wheel during the turn.

## Get into the Proper Position

You must pull your rig farther into the intersection than you would a smaller vehicle. By doing this, you will not run over the curb during the turn due to off-tracking. A good rule-of-thumb for a right angle turn is to pull about one-half the length of the rig past the corner point of the intersection before beginning the turn. Keep the vehicle wheels straight before turning.

## Making the Turn

Turn the steering wheel to the right and speed up slightly for a smooth turn. Watch the right hand mirror carefully for:
- The position of the trailer wheels
- Other traffic

As you finish the turn, turn the steering wheel back to the left to straighten the wheels.

## Errors in Making Right Turns

Major errors in making right turns include:
- Approaching the intersection too fast.
- Not down-shifting before the turn.
- Shifting gears while turning.
- Not allowing for off-tracking of the trailer.
- Not getting far enough into the intersection before making the turn.

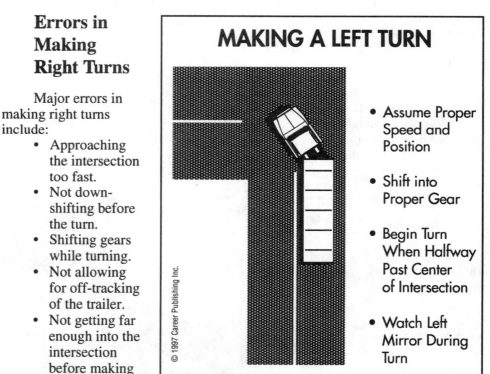

**MAKING A LEFT TURN**

- Assume Proper Speed and Position

- Shift into Proper Gear

- Begin Turn When Halfway Past Center of Intersection

- Watch Left Mirror During Turn

© 1997 Career Publishing Inc.

Figure 6-9

## Left Turns

Plan ahead for a left turn just as you would for a right turn. Follow these steps.
- Slow down as you approach the intersection.
- Put the rig into the right gear for the turn.

- Keep your wheels straight.
- Be as far to the right in the left turn lane as you can.
- Watch the left mirror during the turn.
- After turning, turn the steering wheel back to the right to straighten the wheels.

### Errors in Making Left Turns

Common errors in making left turns are:
- Approaching the intersection too fast.
- Shifting gears while turning.

### Highway Curves

Position yourself carefully for highway curves. For right curves, keep the front of your vehicle toward the center of the road. If you do not, the rear of the trailer may run off the road during the turn. For left curves, keep the tractor as close to the outer (right) edge of the road as you can. This will keep the trailer from running over the center line.

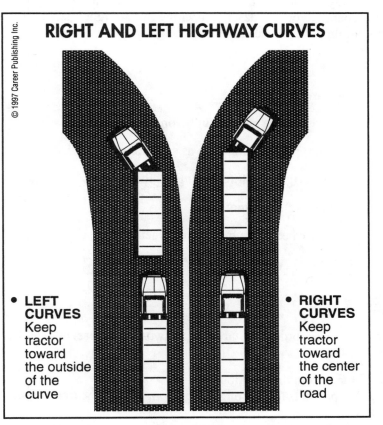

**RIGHT AND LEFT HIGHWAY CURVES**

© 1997 Career Publishing Inc.

- **LEFT CURVES** Keep tractor toward the outside of the curve

- **RIGHT CURVES** Keep tractor toward the center of the road

**Figure 6-10**

## RANGE PRACTICE

After you have learned the correct methods of operating your rig, your instructor may take you out for range practice. You will be expected to:
- Start, warm up, and shut down the engine as directed by the manufacturer.
- Put the rig into motion and accelerate smoothly.
- Come to a smooth stop.
- Back in a straight line.
- Make turns correctly from the proper position.

To meet these goals, you will need other skills. They include:
- Coordinated use of the accelerator and clutch
- Learning the proper way to put on air brakes
- Coordinated use of all controls needed to drive forward or back in a straight line

• Knowing the path the trailer will take as the entire rig takes curves or makes turns

All of these driving skills can be mastered as you practice on the range. Using care in operating your rig will bring you success as a driver and profit to your company.

## SUMMARY

Now that you have completed this chapter, you are able to explain the routines for starting, warming up, cooling down, and shutting off two-cycle and four-cycle diesel engines. You are also able to show how to test the trailer hook-up, explain the proper way to put a rig into motion, and describe the correct way to stop a rig. Because you have completed this chapter, you can describe backing in a straight line, explain the correct procedures for turning right and turning left, and define off-tracking.

## KEY WORDS

**Start-up** — The routine followed for starting an engine.

**Warm-up** — The period of time after starting the engine but before moving the rig.

**Articulation** — Movement between two separate parts, such as a tractor and a trailer.

**Cool-down** — The period after stopping a rig but before turning off the engine.

**Idling** — Letting the engine run while the rig is not moving.

**Off-tracking** — The shorter path the rear wheels of a trailer take when making a turn.

# LEARNING ACTIVITIES

## Review Quiz — Part A

List the following steps in the correct order for starting up a two-cycle diesel engine. Each step is used only once, so you can cross it off as you list it.

    A.   Check the instruments for system malfunctions.
    B.   Depress the clutch pedal (prevents the starting motor from turning the transmission gears).
    C.   Turn on the switch-key.
    D.   Operate the starter. If the engine does not start in 15 to 20 seconds, turn off the starter. Allow it to cool for at least one (1) minute then try again.
    E.   Place the **STOP** and **EMERGENCY STOP** controls in the **RUN** position (if your rig has them).
    F.   Control the engine speed with the foot throttle until it is running smoothly.
    G.   Put on the parking brakes.

1. _____   2. _____   3. _____   4. _____

5. _____   6. _____   7. _____

## Review Quiz — Part B

List the following steps in the correct order for starting up a four-cycle diesel engine. Each step is used only once, so you can cross it off as you list it.

    A.   Turn on the switch-key.
    B.   Crank for three or four seconds.
    C.   Close the throttle. Depress the clutch pedal.
    D.   Check the instruments.

E. Operate the starter.
F. Warm up the engine.
G. Put on the parking brake.

1. _____     2. _____     3. _____     4. _____

5. _____     6. _____     7. _____

## True/False Questions

If the question is true, circle the T. If the question is false, circle the F.

T **F** 1. Pumping the throttle when starting is fuel efficient. It assures enough fuel will enter the engine for a smooth start.

T **F** 2. Some engines warm up better while being driven at slower speeds than while idling. *(p. 6.5)*

**T** F 3. Rapidly revving the engine wastes fuel.

**T** F 4. Engine warm-up is important because it aids lubrication, raises the coolant temperature, and builds up air pressure.

**T** F 5. Not warming up the engine can cause serious and costly damage.

**T** F 6. The steps in engine shut-down vary from one vehicle to another.

**T** F 7. In diesel engines, the cool-down is as important as the warm up.

**T** F 8. Idling the engine can waste a lot of fuel.

T **F** 9. Idling is one method of cleaning fuel injectors.

T **F** 10. Once a driver has mastered the trailer hook-up process, it becomes habit and testing the hook-up on later occasions becomes unnecessary.

T **F** 11. Putting the tractor-trailer in motion is a skill that can be mastered quickly by reading and memorizing the proper steps.

**T** F 12. Stopping a big rig smoothly is a skill that must be learned from practice.

**T** F 13. When attempting to back in a straight line, if the trailer gets bigger in the mirror, push the steering wheel toward the mirror.

**T** F 14. In turning a tractor-trailer, the rear wheels follow a shorter path than the front wheels.

**T** F 15. The longer the vehicle, the greater the off-tracking.

# Diagrams

1. Draw the correct path a rig should take when taking a right curve.

2. Draw the correct path a rig should take when taking a left curve.

3. Draw the path the front wheels will take when the truck makes a left turn. Then draw the path the rear wheels will take in the turn. Label each path.

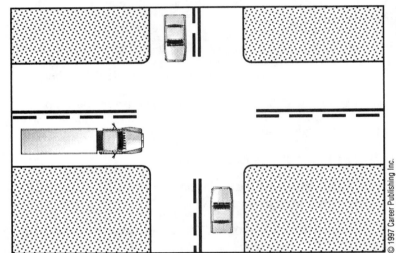

4. Draw the proper path for making a right turn.

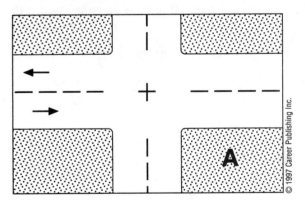

5. Draw the proper path for making a left turn.

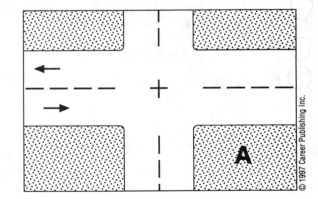

# Chapter Seven
# SHIFTING

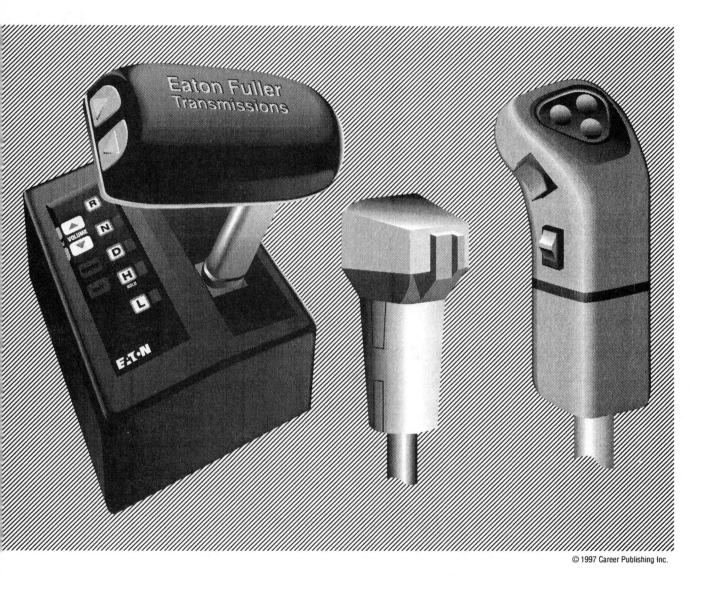

© 1997 Career Publishing Inc.

**Key Elements of Shifting • Shift Controls • Coordination of Controls • When to Shift
Upshifting • Downshifting • Aids to Shifting • Double Clutching • Types of
Transmissions • Shifting Patterns • Progressive Shifting • Good Shifting Habits**

**FROM NOW ON,**

**ONLY THE BEST WILL DRIVE**

# OBJECTIVES

When you have mastered this chapter, you will be able to:

- Describe the basic gear shifting patterns

- Explain the shift patterns for major types of transmissions

- Present methods of shifting up and down through the gears of all major types of conventional transmissions

- Describe double clutching and the timing of the shift for a smooth and fuel-efficient performance

- Explain how to select the proper gears for speed and road conditions

- Describe shifting with both fully automatic and semi-automatic transmissions

- Describe the different procedures needed to operate synchronized and nonsynchronized transmissions

- Explain the instruments and controls needed to shift gears properly

- Understand the common shifting errors and their results

- Demonstrate the proper use of hands, feet, sight, and hearing in shifting to obtain the best performance

- Explain how the improper use of the clutch and transmission can damage the rig

# CHAPTER SEVEN

# SHIFTING

## INTRODUCTION

Shifting gears in a heavy vehicle is more difficult than it is in an automobile. Experience with a manual transmission in an automobile helps, but it is only slightly similar and is far less demanding.

This section introduces you to the differences among shifting patterns and explain clutch and accelerator control. It also explains how to coordinate the eyes, hands, feet, sound, and feel to handle the transmissions found in tractor-trailers.

You will not learn all you need to master shifting from reading this chapter. You also need behind-the-wheel practice. What you learn will serve as a reference when you practice in your rig. Proper gear shifting involves both knowledge and skill.

## KEY ELEMENTS OF SHIFTING

To drive a tractor-trailer, you need to know the controls that are used in shifting. You also need to understand how to coordinate them when shifting, and when to shift.

## SHIFT CONTROLS

With a manual transmission, the controls used in shifting are the:

- Accelerator
- Gearshift lever
- Clutch

They are shown in Figure 7-1.

### Accelerator

The accelerator controls the flow of fuel to the engine and sets the speed of the engine. This is not new information, but it is important to remember because engine speed and shifting are closely related.

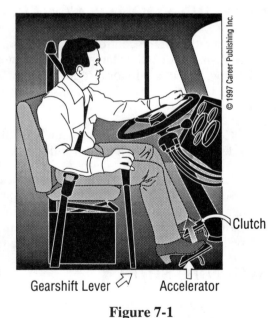

© 1997 Career Publishing Inc.

Gearshift Lever 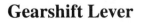    Accelerator    Clutch

**Figure 7-1**

### Gearshift Lever

The gearshift lever selects the gear. The gear determines how the engine speed is transferred into road speed. For example, at a given engine speed, placing the transmission in a low gear may produce a lot of power but little road speed. A low gear multiplies the power of the engine and supplies the power needed to build up road speed. In low gear, the power of the engine can be multiplied 10-15 times. In a high gear, high road speed is attainable but available power is reduced.

## Clutch

The clutch connects or disconnects the transmission and engine. It makes shifting gears possible. When the driver pushes down the clutch pedal, the engine is discon-nected (disengaged) from the transmis-sion, and the gears may be safely shifted.

If the idea of engaged and disengaged is hard to understand, think of it as with people. Engaged people are together. If the engagement is broken, they are disengaged, or separated.

**AUTOMATIC, SEMI-AUTOMATIC, MANUAL TRANSMISSION GEARSHIFT LEVERS**

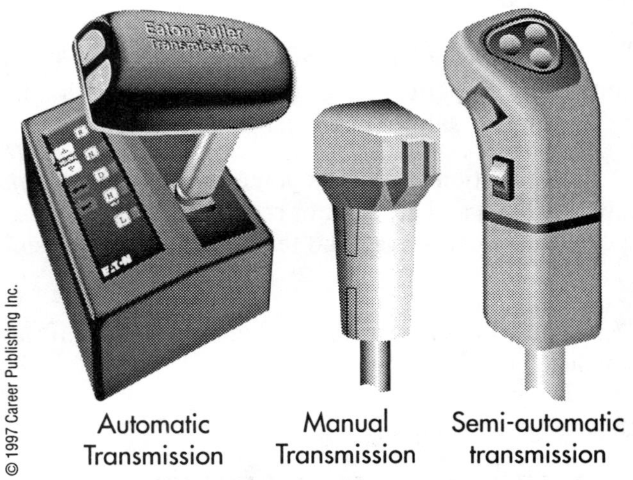

Automatic Transmission    Manual Transmission    Semi-automatic transmission

© 1997 Career Publishing Inc.

**Figure 7-2**

## COORDINATION OF CONTROLS

Operation of the controls requires coordination and careful timing. We know pushing down the clutch pedal separates the engine from the transmission. We know, too, it is safe to shift gears only when the engine and transmission are separated. Plainly, it would be foolish to try to shift gears when the clutch pedal is not pushed down.

Coordinating the use of the clutch pedal and the gearshift lever is logical. First depress the clutch, and then shift gears.

Lack of coordination of the accelerator and clutch pedal can cause revving of the engine. When this happens, engine speed increases before the transmission is engaged. If there is not enough acceleration when engaging the clutch again, the momentum can push the tractor and damage the drive line components. If you are on a slippery surface, this can cause you to skid or lose control of the rig.

## WHEN TO SHIFT

Gears can be shifted either up or down depending on what is needed. The following section explains when to upshift and when to downshift.

## Upshifting

A vehicle requires more power to start moving than to keep moving. Low gears provide a great deal of power but little speed. Thus, we select low gear to get the rig in motion. Always select the lowest gear needed to move the vehicle without slipping the clutch or jerking the vehicle.

As the speed increases, shift to a higher gear to gain more speed. The purpose of upshifting is to allow the rig to gain speed. Power to the wheels decreases as the speed increases but less power is needed to maintain speed.

## Downshifting

A vehicle that is reducing speed will, at certain points, require more power to prevent lugging (overstraining) the engine. For example, when you must slow down or go down a hill, you may need to shift down one or more gears as you slow. Shifting down increases engine power to the drive wheels while giving up some speed.

**Figure 7-3**

Downshifting too early can result in the vehicle having too much momentum or speed for the next lower gear. This can cause the engine to rev beyond its operating range and strain its parts. Also, you may not be able to complete the shift. Downshifting too early may also prevent rapid acceleration if it is needed.

## AIDS TO SHIFTING

The speedometer, tachometer, governor, and clutch brake are all useful or, in some cases, necessary tools for shifting.

### Speedometer

While speed ranges vary with the type of transmission, there is a range of road speeds to correspond to every gear. A driver must learn the speed ranges for the rig. Then the driver can upshift or downshift as needed.

When the top of a speed range is reached for a given gear, the driver has to upshift. When the bottom of a speed range is reached for a gear, he or she has to downshift.

## Tachometer

The tachometer displays the engine speed in revolutions per minute (rpm). Just as there is a road speed range for each gear, there is an rpm range for each gear. Upshifting and downshifting should be coordinated with rpm ranges the same as it is with road speed ranges.

## Governor

The governor is a device that keeps the engine from revving up too much while downshifting. It also reduces the fuel supply to the engine when the maximum rpm is reached. In today's new electronic engines, this is controlled by a computer chip or module.

## Clutch Brake

A clutch has three phases.
1. Free Play
2. Working
3. Clutch Brake

The clutch brake stops the gears from turning. To engage it, push the clutch pedal all the way to the floor. It keeps the gears from clashing when shifting into low or reverse. **Use the clutch brake only when the vehicle is completely stopped.**

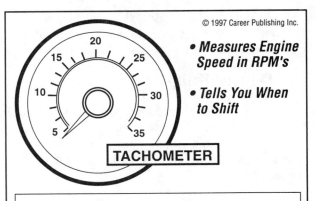

© 1997 Career Publishing Inc.

- Measures Engine Speed in RPM's
- Tells You When to Shift

**TACHOMETER**

### Groundspeed and Gear

Examples of Specific Gear to Groundspeed Relationships for a Nine-Speed Transmission

| Gear | MPH at 1300 RPMs | MPH at 1800 RPMs |
|---|---|---|
| Low | 0 | 4 |
| 1 | 4 | 7 |
| 2 | 7 | 10 |
| 3 | 10 | 14 |
| 4 | 14 | 19 |
| 5 | 19 | 26 |
| 6 | 26 | 38 |
| 7 | 38 | 53 |
| 8 | 53 | 65 * |

* Governor set at 1640 RPMs

**Figure 7-4**

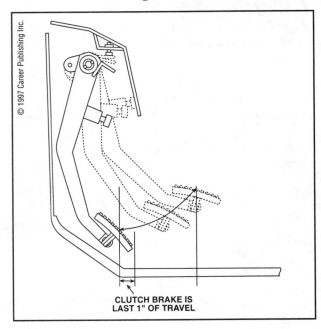

CLUTCH BRAKE IS LAST 1" OF TRAVEL

**Figure 7-5**

# NONSYNCHRONIZED TRANSMISSIONS

Later in this chapter, we will deal with synchronized transmissions. The following information is for nonsynchronized transmissions, which require double clutching.

## Double Clutching

Double clutching is used to let the driver control the engine rpms and the gears, so the gears can be shifted smoothly. While the method involves more than the simple routine shown here, it is important to understand and master this basic sequence.

### Upshifting

1. Release the accelerator.
2. Push the clutch pedal down, disengaging the clutch. Be careful not to engage the clutch brake.
3. Move the gearshift lever to neutral.
4. Release the clutch pedal, engaging the clutch.
5. Push the clutch down when the proper rpm for the next gear is reached.
6. Move the gearshift lever to the next higher gear.
7. Release the clutch pedal, engaging the clutch and transmission.
8. Accelerate.

### Downshifting

1. Release the accelerator.
2. Push the clutch down.
3. Move the gearshift lever to neutral.
4. Release the clutch.
5. Accelerate the engine enough to match the rpms with the road speed. This avoids clashing gears.
6. Push the clutch down.
7. Shift into the next lower gear.
8. Release the clutch.

Be sure to maintain the correct engine speed throughout the procedure.

## Synchronizing Skills

Although depressing and engaging the clutch two times on each shift is a very big part of handling a nonsynchronized transmission, it is not the main shifting event. The key action — the one that requires special shifting skills — is synchronizing (bringing to the same speed) the teeth of the mating gears (the driving gear and the driven gear). When this is done properly, there is no grinding, or clashing, of the gears.

Engine speed can be read on the tachometer and can be heard. It can also be felt in the tractor. Some drivers think they are using engine rpms to tell them when to shift when they are really using their sense of rpm.

A skilled driver of a nonsynchronized transmission rig uses his or her sense of rpm to know when to shift. Three basic skills are necessary to shift this kind of a rig. They are:

1. Being able to identify engine rpm
2. Knowing the rpm at which the engine should be turning
3. Being able to bring the engine to the correct rpm

What, exactly, does the driver do to control the tooth speed of the driving gear? After depressing the clutch and shifting into neutral, the driver releases the clutch. This allows the engine rpms to drop (upshift) or speed up (downshift). This adjusts the tooth speed of the next driving gear to the speed/rpms of the engine.

How does the driver know how much to increase or decrease the engine speed? Based on manufacturers' recommendations, a general rule of thumb is, "when you change gears you must change the rpm by about 25 percent (25%) or 500 rpms." Some transmissions differ from this rule of thumb.

As long as shifts are started at the same rpm, the synchronizing rpm will be about the same for each shift. For this reason, shifts are a matter of timing and coordination.

In more complex shifts, the synchronizing rpm is not always in the same place. Shifts may be started at various rpms, so the rpm at which the next gear will synchronize will also vary. On upgrades, the rig loses speed during shifts. On downgrades, speed increases. On upgrades, start your shift a little earlier than you would on flat ground.

Any change in vehicle speed that occurs during shifting will affect the synchronizing rpm. A skilled driver is able to deal with these variations.

Besides shifting up and shifting down, handling a nonsynchronized transmission demands a third shifting skill. When a vehicle is rolling in neutral, the driver must get the transmission into the proper gear. This process is known by many names, such as:

- Picking a gear
- Hunting a gear
- Finding a gear
- Hitting a gear

The possible mph/gear/rpm combinations can be worked out either by math or by *sense* or *feel*. In general, for each possible mph there will be only one possible gear.

Most drivers handle this situation by sense or feel. The skill is to sense the truck's mph and recall where the stick should be when the truck feels as it does. Then simply put the stick in front of that gear position.

Think how the engine should feel at that speed in that gear. Then, with the clutch engaged, throttle up or down until the engine feels right and push the stick.

It may drop into gear. If it does not, work the throttle and feel how changing the engine rpm changes the stick vibrations. If the rpms are too high, the grinding noise will be high. If they are too low, the sound will be deep and hollow. Close to the proper rpm, the stick vibrations will feel larger and farther apart. When the correct rpm is reached, the stick will begin to fall into gear. At that point, disengage the clutch and push the stick into place. Release the clutch and speed up.

Being able to find the synchronizing rpm under all possible shifting conditions is the major skill needed to handle a nonsynchronized transmission.

## Summary of Shifting Skills

Good shifting technique is a sign of a professional driver. Skills include:
• Good timing and coordination
• Shifting without forcing, raking, or grinding the gears
• Never riding the clutch pedal
• Always using the clutch to shift
• Selecting the proper gear for the best fuel economy
• Anticipating changes in terrain or traffic

A driver needs to know:
• What gear he or she is in at any given time
• The top mph and rpm for each gear

When using the engine to cut the speed of the rig, the range selector should be shifted to the next lower range. If the vehicle exceeds the maximum speed for the lower gear, use the service brakes to reduce speed. Downshifting at too high a speed causes damage to internal gears and synchronizers. Automatic transmissions have a longer *coast down* time than manual transmissions. You will need to learn to slow down earlier or use the service brakes until the downshift occurs.

## IMPORTANCE OF PROPER SHIFTING

Proper shifting is the sign of a skilled driver. These drivers do not grind, clash, or force the gears. Shifting is not a matter of strength. It can be done with the thumb and index finger. When done correctly, the gears practically fall into place.

Keys to Shifting:
• Use good timing and coordination (the driver matches the road speed, rpm, and gear).

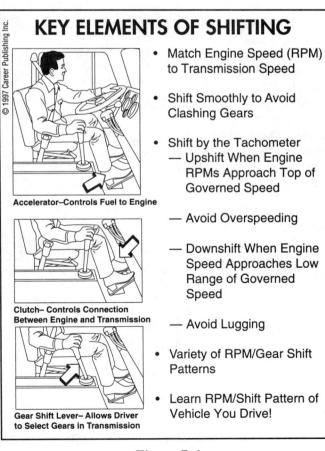

### KEY ELEMENTS OF SHIFTING

Accelerator–Controls Fuel to Engine

Clutch– Controls Connection Between Engine and Transmission

Gear Shift Lever– Allows Driver to Select Gears in Transmission

• Match Engine Speed (RPM) to Transmission Speed
• Shift Smoothly to Avoid Clashing Gears
• Shift by the Tachometer
  — Upshift When Engine RPMs Approach Top of Governed Speed
  — Avoid Overspeeding
  — Downshift When Engine Speed Approaches Low Range of Governed Speed
  — Avoid Lugging
• Variety of RPM/Gear Shift Patterns
• Learn RPM/Shift Pattern of Vehicle You Drive!

© 1997 Career Publishing Inc.

**Figure 7-6**

- Always know what gear the transmission is in.
- Know the top mph and the maximum and minimum rpm for each gear.
- Anticipate changes in terrain or traffic.

Important Knowledge:
- Know the vehicle.
- Know the top tachometer readings for each gear and road speed.
- Know the load and road. For example, do not attempt to shift to a higher gear until the trailer (not just the tractor) is over the crest of a hill.

## Results of Shifting into Too Low a Gear by Mistake

The engine runs too fast. This can damage the clutch, engine, transmission, or drive shaft. It can also cause loss of vehicle control.

## Lugging

Lugging occurs when the driver fails to downshift when the engine speed starts to fall below the normal operating range. In this condition, the tractor produces too little power and lugs, or struggles. Such straining can cause engine overheating, damage to the drive train, and stress on most of the rig's systems. It can also affect the life of all drive train components.

### Progressive Shifting

Progressive shifting is shifting before you reach the maximum governed rpm. It allows you to take the most advantage of the engine's power and save fuel at the same time.

All drivers should learn the technique. This is shown in Figure 7-7.

### Shifting Procedure

Upshifting
- Shift when the engine reaches cruise rpm instead of the maximum set by the governor.
- In lower gears, shift at the lowest rpm possible without lugging the engine.

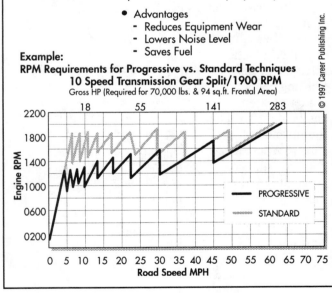

Figure 7-7

Downshifting
- Shift as soon as the rpm reaches peak torque (1,300 rpm on most engines. Check the operator's manual).

## Benefits

Progressive shifting is advised by many companies because it:
- Reduces equipment wear
- Lowers the noise level
- Saves fuel
- Allows smoother shifts

## SHIFTING PATTERNS AND PROCEDURES

In this section, we will look at the shift patterns of five common transmissions: the *Spicer Pro-Shift Seven Speed, Eaton Fuller Nine Speed, Eaton Fuller Super Ten, Rockwell Ten Speed, Eaton Fuller Thirteen Speed, Eaton Fuller Top 2, Spicer Automate-2,* and *Rockwell Engine Synchro Shift (ESS)*.

### Spicer Pro-Shift Seven Speed

The Spicer Pro-Shift Seven Speed is a constant mesh (non-synchronized) twin-countershaft transmission with a single range operation.

**Figure 7-8**

### Shift Pattern

The transmission uses a simple no-repeat shift pattern, starting with first at the bottom left and working up through the gears to seventh at the bottom right (see Figure 7-8). No levers or buttons are needed for any of the shifts.

### Shifting Procedures

Upshifting:
- Depress the clutch.
- Move the gear down and as far left as possible for first gear.
- To shift to second, double-clutch, move the lever up and slightly to the right.
- Shift up through the next five gears using the normal double clutching and following the standard "H" pattern.

Downshifting:
- Shift from seventh to sixth by double clutching, moving the lever straight forward, and matching the engine speed to the road speed before shifting.
- Use the same procedure for all further downshifts, following the "H" pattern back down to first.

## Eaton Fuller Nine Speed

The Eaton Fuller Nine Speed is a constant mesh (non-synchronized) twin-countershaft transmission with high and low range operation.

### Shift Pattern

Low range has five forward gears: Low through 4th gear. To use high range, you lift the range control lever. High range has four more gears (5th through 8th). The shifting sequence is commonly known as the Double H pattern (see Figure 7-9). You start in first at the top left, then straight down to second, up and right to third, and straight down to fourth. To engage fifth, you flip up the range lever and move the lever back to where you started in first. Then you go through the "H" pattern again for the top three gears.

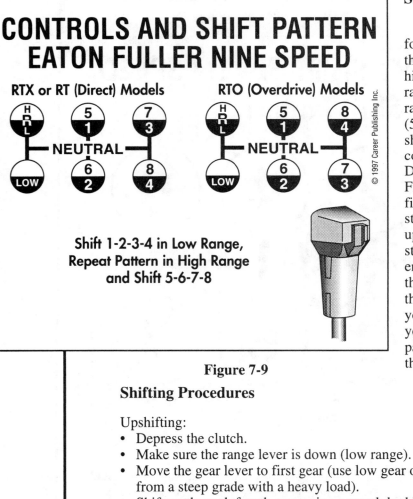

Figure 7-9

### Shifting Procedures

Upshifting:
- Depress the clutch.
- Make sure the range lever is down (low range).
- Move the gear lever to first gear (use low gear only if you are starting from a steep grade with a heavy load).
- Shift up through fourth gear using normal double clutching.

- To shift from fourth to fifth, lift the range control lever up before moving the gear lever.
- As the gear lever passes through neutral, the transmission automatically shifts to high range.
- Shift from fifth to eighth using normal double clutching.

Downshifting:
- Shift down from eighth to fifth using normal double clutching and engine and road speed matching.
- To shift down from fifth to fourth, push the range lever down before moving the gear lever.
- As the gear lever passes through neutral, the transmission automatically shifts to low range.
- Shift down from fourth to first using normal double clutching and engine and road speed matching.

### Eaton Fuller Super Ten

The Eaton Fuller Super Ten is a constant mesh (non-synchronized) twin-countershaft transmission with a low-inertia design and auto-range actuation to make shifting easier. With low-inertia technology, the main shaft is disconnected from the back box during compound shifts. Drivers can preselect all button shifts up and down, helping to speed shifts and reducing misshifts.

# CONTROLS AND OPERATION OF AN EATON FULLER SUPER TEN

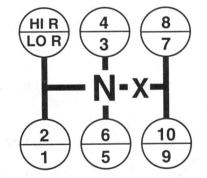

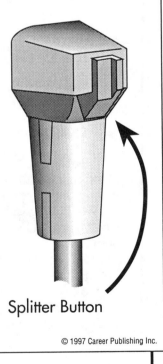

With the auto-range feature, the actual number of conventional lever shifts is half that of conventional ten speeds. The range shift is triggered automatically at "X" location as the operator moves the lever toward the third rail.

**When starting in first gear, preselect the next gear with the splitter button, release the throttle, and accelerate when you are in gear.**

Splitter Button

**Figure 7-10**

### Shift Pattern

Unlike other dual range transmissions, the Super 10 does not have a range change lever. Instead, you just have five gear positions that you split, reducing gear lever movements by half. For example, you start in first gear at the bottom left (see diagram shown on the previous page). Then you preselect the next gear with a splitter button. To engage the gear, all you need to do is release the throttle to break torque, and then accelerate again when you are in gear. You only need to move the gear lever from second to third, fourth to fifth, sixth to seventh, and eighth to ninth.

### Shifting Procedures

Upshifting:
* Depress the clutch.
* Move the gear lever to first gear (use low gear only if you are starting from a steep grade with a heavy load).
* To make a splitter shift (first to second, third to fourth, fifth to sixth, seventh to eighth, or ninth to tenth), move the splitter button forward, take your foot off the throttle, wait a few seconds for the gear to engage, and then accelerate.
* To make a lever shift (second to third, fourth to fifth, sixth to seventh, or eighth to ninth), move the splitter button back, double clutch, and make a normal shift

Downshifting:
* To make a splitter shift down (tenth to ninth, eighth to seventh, sixth to fifth, fourth to third, or second to first), simply move the splitter button back and whenever you are ready, release the throttle, wait a few seconds for the gear to engage, and accelerate again.
* To make a lever shift down one gear, move the splitter button forward, double clutch, match the engine rpm to road speed, and make the shift.

## Rockwell Ten Speed

The Rockwell Ten Speed is a constant mesh (non-synchronized) twin-countershaft transmission with high and low range operation.

### Shift Pattern

Low range has five forward gears: first through fifth gear. To use high range, you lift the range control lever. High range has five more gears — 6th through 10th (see Figure 7-11). You start in first at the bottom left, then up and slightly to the right for second, and through the normal "H" pattern to fifth. To engage sixth, you flip up the range lever and move the lever back to the bottom left where you started in first. Then you repeat the "H" pattern again for the top four gears.

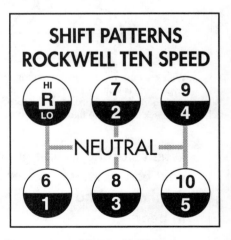

Figure 7-11

## Shifting Procedures

Upshifting:
- Depress the clutch.
- Make sure the range lever is down (low range).
- Move the gear lever to first gear at the bottom left.
- Shift up through fifth gear using normal double clutching.
- To shift from fifth to sixth, lift the range control lever up before moving the gear lever.
- As the gear lever passes through neutral, the transmission automatically shifts to high range.
- Shift from sixth to tenth using normal double clutching.

Downshifting:
- Shift down from tenth to sixth using normal double clutching and engine and road speed matching.
- To shift down from sixth to fifth, push the range lever down before moving the gear lever.
- As the gear lever passes through neutral, the transmission automatically shifts to low range.
- Shift down from fifth to first using normal double clutching and engine and road speed matching.

## Eaton Fuller Thirteen Speed

The Eaton Fuller Thirteen Speed is a constant mesh (non-synchronized) twin-countershaft transmission with high and low range operation, as well as a splitter on high range gears.

### Shift Pattern

The transmission has five gears in low range, including a low over low gear. High range has four direct ratios, as well as another four overdrive ratios. Overdrive can be engaged in high range with a splitter switch. The shift pattern is the basic *double H*. You start in first at the top left (see Figure 7-12), then move through the "H" to fourth, flip the range lever up, move to fifth, and repeat the pattern.

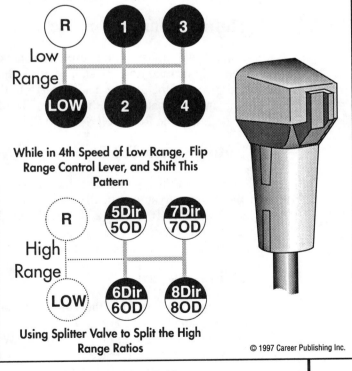

Figure 7-12

### Shifting Procedures

Upshifting:
- Depress the clutch.
- Make sure the range lever is down (low range).
- Move the gear lever to first gear (use low-low only if you are starting from a steep grade with a heavy load).
- Shift up through fourth gear using normal double clutching.
- To shift from fourth to fifth, lift the range control lever up before moving the gear lever.
- As the gear lever passes through neutral, the transmission automatically shifts to high range.
- Shift from fifth to eighth using normal double clutching.
- To split a gear in high range (go from direct to overdrive), flip the splitter switch, release the accelerator, depress and release the clutch, and accelerate again.
- To shift from overdrive to direct drive in the next higher gear, move the gear lever into the next gear and flip the splitter switch just before your foot has come off the clutch

Downshifting:
- To split down from overdrive to direct in the same gear, flip the splitter switch, release the accelerator, depress and release the clutch, and accelerate again.
- To shift down from direct in one gear to overdrive in the next lower gear, flip the splitter switch to overdrive and make a normal downshift.
- To shift from fifth direct to fourth, push the range lever down, double clutch, and make a normal downshift.

## Shifting Semi-Automatic Transmissions

Some newer transmissions use electronic controls to help you shift. They are essentially manual transmissions, with a clutch and a similar-looking gear lever, but some of the gears are automated. In this chapter, we will look at the operation and shift patterns of three types: The Eaton Fuller Top 2, the Spicer AutoMate-2, and the Rockwell Synchro Shift (ESS).

## Eaton Fuller Top 2

The Eaton Fuller Top 2 uses the control module of an electronically-controlled engine to automatically change the top two gears. It comes in two versions: the Super 10 Top 2 (a 10-speed) and the Super 13 Top 2 (a 13-speed). Both are twin-countershaft nonsynchronized transmissions with low-inertia technology which disconnects the back box during compound shifts.

### Shifting Pattern

The Super 10 Top 2 has the same shift pattern as the standard Super 10 (see instructions under Super 10 on p. 7.13) and the Super 13 Top 2 has the same change pattern as the Eaton Fuller 13-speed. With both transmissions, the top gear position is marked A. Once the gear lever is in this position, all upshifts and downshifts between the top two gears are automatic.

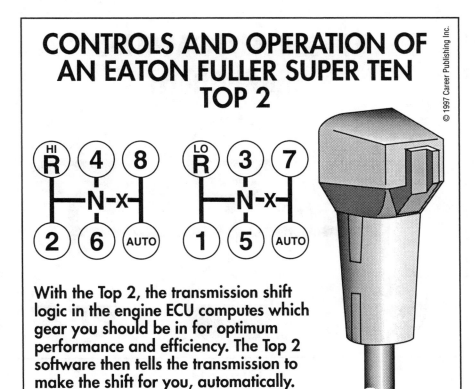

# CONTROLS AND OPERATION OF AN EATON FULLER SUPER TEN TOP 2

© 1997 Career Publishing Inc.

With the Top 2, the transmission shift logic in the engine ECU computes which gear you should be in for optimum performance and efficiency. The Top 2 software then tells the transmission to make the shift for you, automatically.

When starting in first gear, preselect the next gear with the splitter button, release the throttle, and accelerate when you are in gear.

**Figure 7-13**

### Shifting Procedure

- Both transmissions are operated as normal nonsynchro transmissions in all gears but the top two.
- Automatic mode can only be engaged when the vehicle is travelling over 40 mph.
- With the Super 10 Top 2, you change normally to 8th, then double clutch and move into the "A" position.
- With the Super 13 Top 2, you shift normally to 11th, then double clutch and move into "A".
- While in the "A" position, the engine and transmission work together to change, up or down, when needed. When a shift point is reached, the engine speed automatically changes to match road speed and the change is made — all without driver input.
- You can delay an upshift by applying more throttle or delay a downshift by easing off the throttle.
- With the engine brake on, the electronic controls automatically extend governed engine speed by 200 rpm to help maintain the lower gear on a downgrade.

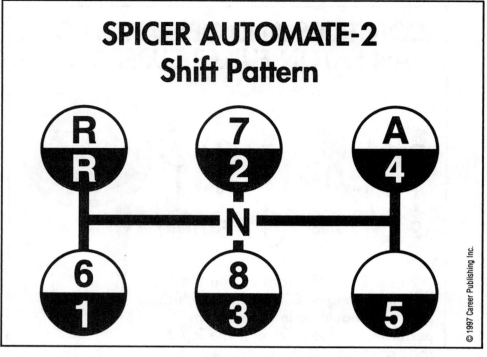

**Figure 7-14**

## Spicer AutoMate-2

The Spicer AutoMate-2 is a 10-speed transmission that uses electronic controls on the transmission to automatically change the top two gears. It is available in direct-drive and overdrive versions.

### Shifting Pattern

The AutoMate-2 has a familiar 10-speed shifting pattern. First gear is at the bottom left, second is up and to the middle, third straight down, etc. When you reach fifth, you flip the range lever up and come back to the bottom left, then up and the middle for 7th and straight down for 8th. The letter A is where 9th would normally be. Once the lever is moved to that position, the transmission automatically senses road and engine speed and changes up to 10th and back down to 9th when necessary.

### Shifting Procedure

- The AutoMate-2 is operated as a normal non-synchro transmission in the bottom eight gears. You first use the clutch and then change up or down by manually matching the road and engine speeds.
- The truck must be travelling over 38 mph to engage the automatic mode.
- When you reach 8th gear, double clutch and move to the A mode.
- No driver input is needed to change gears in 9th and 10th. The transmission automatically senses when a change is needed, adjusts the engine speed (no matter where the driver has the throttle), and makes the change.
- Upshifts in the A mode can be delayed by applying more throttle, and downshifts can be delayed by easing off the throttle.

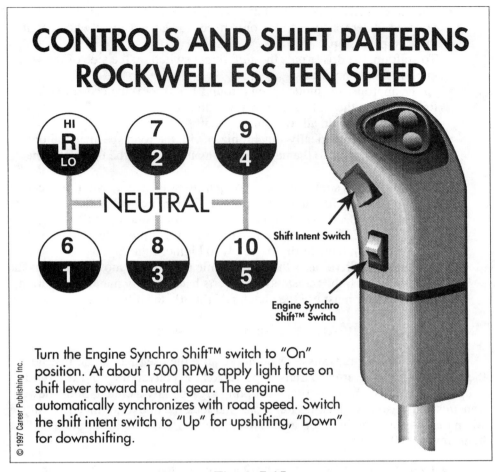

## CONTROLS AND SHIFT PATTERNS ROCKWELL ESS TEN SPEED

Turn the Engine Synchro Shift™ switch to "On" position. At about 1500 RPMs apply light force on shift lever toward neutral gear. The engine automatically synchronizes with road speed. Switch the shift intent switch to "Up" for upshifting, "Down" for downshifting.

© 1997 Career Publishing Inc.

**Figure 7-15**

### Rockwell Engine Synchro Shift (ESS)

The Rockwell Engine Synchro Shift (ESS) uses engine electronic controls to automatically synchronize the engine speed to road speed during shifts in all gears. The system reads the input and output speeds of the transmission, the neutral position of the gear lever, and the position of a special shift intent switch on the side of the gear knob. The engine controller processes the information and sends a message to the fuel control system to automatically increase or decrease the engine speed to synchronize with the road speed during shifting. In essence, it turns a nonsynchro box into a synchronized one. The driver has the option of turning the system off and operating the transmission as a fully manual box.

### Shifting Pattern

ESS is fitted to either the Rockwell 9-speed or Rockwell 10-speed manual transmissions. It allows the driver to move through the standard shifting pattern. Both transmissions are nonsynchro boxes with range-change shift patterns. (See Figure 7-15)

### Shifting Procedure

- Starting out, the driver turns the ESS switch on the side of the gear knob to the on position.

- The clutch pedal is depressed, first gear is selected, and the clutch is released. After that, the clutch only needs to be used again when coming to a complete stop.
- To shift up, the driver puts the *shift intent* switch on the side of the gear knob in the up position.
- At the appropriate engine speed (around 1,500 rpm) the driver applies light force on the shift lever toward neutral while in gear. The transmission should allow a shift to neutral.
- The engine automatically synchronizes with the road speed and allows the driver to move to the next gear without touching the throttle or the clutch.
- Downshifting is similar, except you put the shift intent switch in the down position before making the shift. The engine automatically increases its speed to match the road speed for a smooth shift.
- While in the ESS mode, the range control function is automated, so the driver does not have to flip from low to high or high to low.
- Any time the driver uses the clutch while the truck is moving or turns the ESS switch off, the transmission reverts back to fully manual operation, and the driver must use the clutch and throttle to shift gears.

## Shifting Fully Automatic Transmissions

Fully automatic transmissions do not require the use of a clutch. Instead, they use a torque converter to transfer power. These converters provide a fluid coupling instead of a hard frictional coupling provided by a clutch. Some newer transmissions also have lock-up functions that lock the converter mechanically when the transmission in in top gear. This provides a more solid coupling and helps improve fuel mileage.

Many automatic transmissions have a lever to change gears. But some newer models with electronic controls use buttons instead. To select a gear position, the operator pushes a button instead of moving a lever.

## Range Selector Positions

### Neutral (N)
Neutral is used for starting, standing, and parking the vehicle. The parking brake should be set when the vehicle is standing or parked. Never coast in neutral because transmission damage and loss of control of the rig can result.

### Reverse (R)
Reverse is used to back the rig. There is one gear in the reverse range. The vehicle must be stopped (no movement) before shifting into reverse. A reverse warning signal sounds when the gear is placed in reverse.

### 2-5 or Drive
This position is used for all normal driving conditions. It starts in 2nd and shifts up to 3rd, 4th, and 5th as you accelerate. Downshifting is automatic as your speed slows.

### 2-3/2-4 Lower Range
Some road, cargo, or traffic conditions make it desirable to restrict automatic shifting to the lower range. Low ranges provide greater engine braking. When the need for this range is over, shift back to high range (Drive or 2-5).

### 2/Low Gear

This gear is used for pulling through mud and snow or driving up a steep grade. It provides the most engine braking power. The lower ranges (2-3/2-4) will not upshift above the highest gear selected unless the engine governor speed for that gear is exceeded.

### 1/Creeper Gear

For off-highway use. Provides the greatest traction. You should never make a full power shift from creeper gear to a higher range.

## Upshifting and Downshifting with an Automatic Transmission

Upshifting using the accelerator

## CONTROLS AND SHIFT PROCEDURES FULLY AUTOMATIC TRANSMISSION

**Neutral**
Use When Starting, Standing, Parking
**Reverse**
Vehicle Must Be Completely Stopped Before Using
**2-5 or Drive**
All Normal Driving Conditions
**2-3 / 2-4**
Lower Range for Load Types, Driving Conditions
**2**
When Pulling Through Mud, Snow, Up Steep Hills
**1**
Creeper Gear for Off-Highway Use

© 1997 Career Publishing Inc.

**Figure 7-16**

- The pressure of the foot on the accelerator pedal influences automatic shifting.
- When the accelerator is fully depressed, the transmission automatically shifts up to the recommended speed of the engine.
- When partly depressed, upshifts occur sooner at a lesser engine speed.
- Either method provides the accurate shift spacing and control needed for maximum performance.

Downshifting
- Occurs automatically
- The transmission prevents downshifting when the engine speed is too high.

### SUMMARY OF GOOD SHIFTING HABITS

1. Know the shift pattern of the vehicle.
2. Start the rig in the lowest gear.
3. Use the clutch brake properly.
4. Upshift smoothly.
5. Downshift at the precise point and time required.
6. Use double clutching.
7. Avoid snapping or riding the clutch.
8. Use the tachometer and speedometer to time shifts.
9. Avoid lugging or revving the engine.
10. Do not force the transmission into gear.
11. Avoid overloading the rig.

## KEY WORDS

**Automatic transmission** — One that, when set for a certain speed range, will not exceed that speed and the engine automatically shifts through the gears until it reaches that speed.

**Manual transmission** — One that must be shifted by the driver through the different gears. A clutch must be used.

**Nonsynchronized transmission** — One that does not have thin plates between the gears to assist in shifting. The driver must double-clutch.

**Semi-automatic transmission** — One that is essentially a manual transmission, but uses electronic controls to automate some of the gear changes.

**Synchronized transmission** — One that has thin plates between the gears called synchronizers. Allows shifting without double-clutching.

# LEARNING ACTIVITIES

## True-False Questions

If the statement is true, circle the T. If the statement is false, circle the F.

(T)  F    1.   The clutch connects and disconnects the engine and transmission.

T   (F)   2.   Pushing down on the clutch pedal engages the engine.

(T)  F    3.   A standing vehicle requires more power to get it moving than to keep it moving once it is underway.

(T)  F    4.   Nonsynchronized transmissions require double clutching.

(T)  F    5.   Double clutching enables the driver to control engine rpms and the gear so the gears can be engaged smoothly.

TRUE (T) (F)   6.   Double clutching, though an obvious action, is not the main shifting event.

(T)  F    7.   Bringing the teeth of the driving gear and those of the driven gears to the same speed (synchronizing) requires special shifting skills.

T   (F)   8.   Nonsynchronized gears can be synchronized easily without double clutching.

(T)  F    9.   In double clutching, the driver disengages the clutch after shifting into neutral and accelerates to increase the tooth speed of the driving gear. *(p. 7.8)*

(T)  F   10.   When a vehicle with a nonsynchronized transmission is rolling in neutral, the driver must hunt, find, or hit a gear.

(T)  F   11.   The ability to find the synchronizing rpm under all possible shifting conditions is the major skill necessary in handling a nonsynchronized transmission.

(T)  F   12.   Controls differ for the many different transmissions, but all work on the principle of providing power and speed as needed for driving conditions.

# Chapter Eight
# BACKING

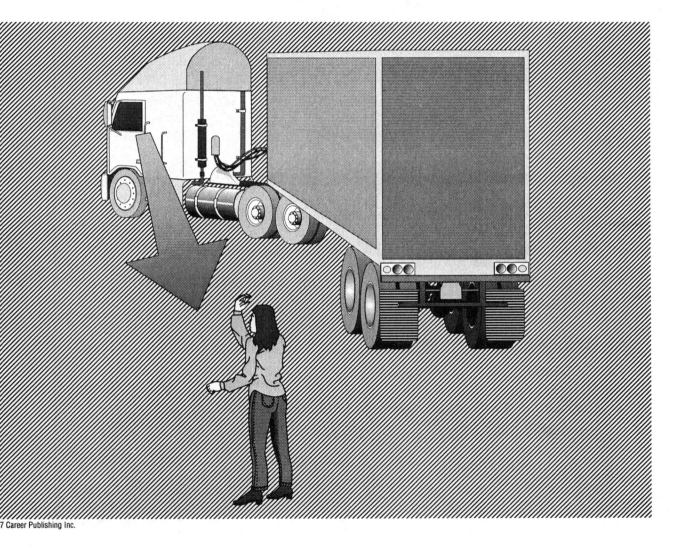

**Backing Principles and Rules • Steering Principles • Backing Safely • Inspect Intended Path • Use a Helper • Use Four-Way Flashers and Horn • Start in Proper Position • Back Slowly • Start Over if Necessary • Straight-line Backing • Alley Dock Backing • Parallel Parking**

**FROM NOW ON,**

**ONLY THE BEST WILL DRIVE**

# OBJECTIVES

When you have mastered this chapter, you will be able to:

- Describe the procedures for backing and parking

- Explain the correct method to prepare for backing maneuvers

- Explain the principles of reverse steering when driving an articulated vehicle

- Avoid the hazards of backing

- Understand the importance of using a helper

- Explain why drivers should avoid unnecessary backing and blind-side backing

- Show how to check the area before backing

# CHAPTER EIGHT

# BACKING

## INTRODUCTION

Backing a 48-foot (or longer) trailer into position, without any problems, is a satisfying accomplishment. It is a skill you must develop if you drive a rig. You will learn to back under careful supervision in the practice driving area.

## BACKING PRINCIPLES AND RULES

There are, however, principles and rules you should know before you get in the cab and try to back a vehicle on your own. This chapter contains some of the information you need to know. Studying it will help you master this very necessary skill.

### Steering Principles

Proper backing is important to safe and efficient operation of a tractor-trailer. Unless enough time and attention are devoted to mastering this skill, maneuvering the rig can be very difficult.

Most people feel comfortable backing a car. A car has two axles. In most cars, the front axle is used for steering, and the rear axle has fixed wheels that cannot steer. They simply follow the direction the car is headed.

The techniques involved in backing a tractor-trailer are much different. Backing is more complicated because the rig is made up of two units. The tractor steers both vehicles. The trailer, with its fixed wheels, depends on the tractor for direction. In other words, the tractor steers the trailer.

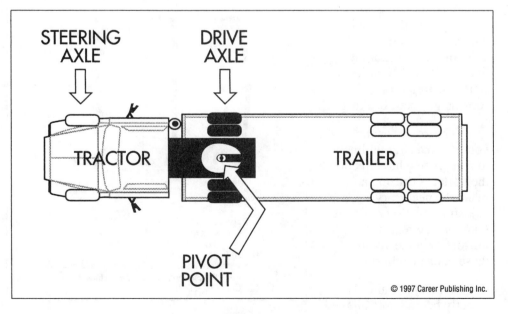

© 1997 Career Publishing Inc.

**Figure 8-1**

The rear tractor axle becomes the trailer's steering axle. In backing, when the tractor moves in one direction, the front of the trailer moves in the same direction. This forces the rear of the trailer in the opposite direction. When you turn the steering wheel to the right, the rear of the trailer goes to the left. When you turn the steering wheel to the left, the rear of the trailer goes to the right.

Backing in a straight line is the easiest backing maneuver to perform with a tractor-trailer, and also the basis of all other backing maneuvers. The point where the trailer is connected to the tractor becomes the pivot point for the vehicle.

A pivot point (or point of articulation) is extremely sensitive to movement. For example, if the tractor and trailer are exactly aligned and you hold the steering wheel as straight as possible when you begin to move back, the whole unit will rarely, if ever, move in a straight line. Usually, the trailer will start to drift left or right as soon as you start backing.

The key to backing your rig in a straight line is to recognize what direction the trailer is drifting and make the necessary adjustments. You must use *both* outside rearview mirrors to guide you in these delicate adjustments.

When the trailer is directly behind you, aligned and straight, the picture you

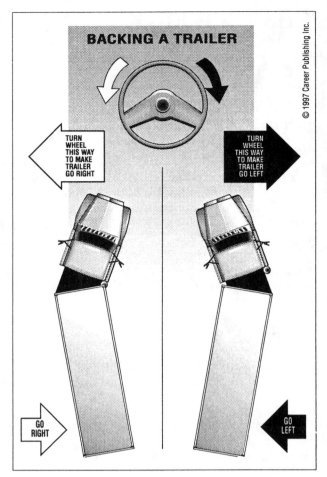

**Figure 8-2**

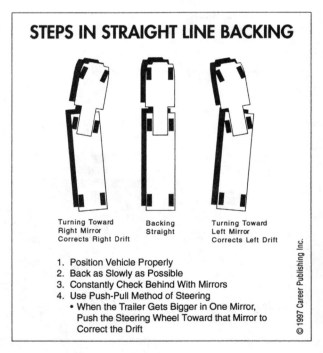

**Figure 8-3**

see in both mirrors will be the same. When the trailer starts to drift, the pictures will begin to change. If the trailer starts drifting to the right, you will start seeing more of the trailer in your right mirror and less of the trailer in your left mirror.

To correct the drift, turn the steering wheel toward the drift. In this case, turn the steering wheel to the right. It takes very little movement of the steering wheel to correct a drift if you adjust early. Do not oversteer.

When the trailer begins to respond to the correction, begin turning the wheel in the opposite direction to remove the initial corrrection. Depending on the length of the trailer, it takes 8 to 12 feet for the trailer to respond. Shorter trailers react faster than longer trailers.

Be patient. Think your moves through carefully. If you find the trailer has gone too far out of line, pull forward and position the rig for another try.

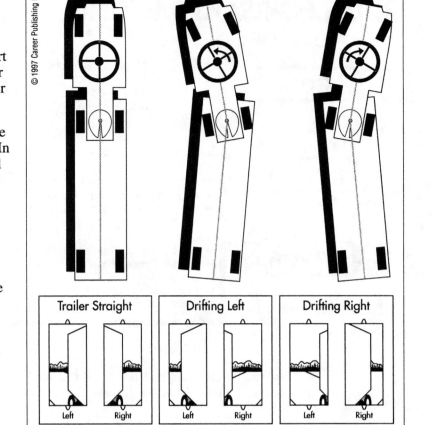

© 1997 Career Publishing Inc.

**Figure 8-4**

## General Rules for Backing Safely

Because you cannot see directly behind your vehicle, backing is always dangerous. Common sense dictates that you avoid backing whenever possible. For example, when you park the rig, try to park so you will be able to pull forward when you leave.

Even though you can reduce the need to back by planning ahead, almost everyone who drives a tractor-trailer will have to back it at times. When you do have to back, there are a few simple rules that will help you do it safely.
- Inspect your intended path.
- Use a helper.
- Back and turn toward the driver's side whenever possible.
- Use your four-way flashers and horn.

## Inspect Your Intended Path

Whether you will be backing in a straight line or backing and turning, inspect the line of travel before you begin. Get out and walk around the vehicle. Check the clearance of the path your vehicle will make. Make sure the road, parking, or docking areas will be able to support your vehicle. Look for low

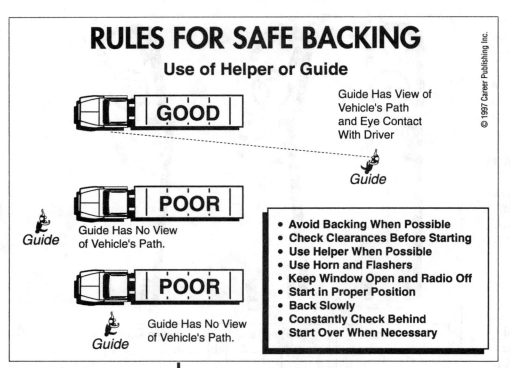

# RULES FOR SAFE BACKING

## Use of Helper or Guide

**GOOD**

Guide Has View of
Vehicle's Path
and Eye Contact
With Driver

*Guide*

**POOR**

*Guide*

Guide Has No View
of Vehicle's Path.

**POOR**

Guide Has No View
of Vehicle's Path.

*Guide*

© 1997 Career Publishing Inc.

- • **Avoid Backing When Possible**
- • **Check Clearances Before Starting**
- • **Use Helper When Possible**
- • **Use Horn and Flashers**
- • **Keep Window Open and Radio Off**
- • **Start in Proper Position**
- • **Back Slowly**
- • **Constantly Check Behind**
- • **Start Over When Necessary**

**Figure 8-5**

clearances e.g. wires, roof overhangs, etc. Check for debris in your path, other parked vehicles, or any potential hazards that may be moving into your path; e.g., fork trucks, people, and yard jockeys. Is your path sloped down to the dock? Is it into an enclosed area? You need to get a mental picture before you start backing.

## Use a Helper

Use a helper when you have to back. You cannot see behind the vehicle, and there are blind spots in the mirrors. A helper is always needed for blind-side backing. The helper should stand near the back and to the side of the vehicle so that the driver has a clear view of the helper's directions and the helper will not be run over by the truck.

Hearing a helper's spoken directions is sometimes difficult. Before you begin backing, work out a set of hand signals that you both understand. Agree on signals for directions such as "turn," "more turn," "less turn," "back," "clearance," "forward," and "stop." Remember, even though a helper is needed, the driver is responsible for any problems.

## Back and Turn Toward the Driver's Side

When you have to back and turn, try to back toward the driver's (left) side of the vehicle.

© 1997 Career Publishing Inc.

**Figure 8-6**

You will have a better view of what you are doing. You will also avoid the dangers of backing to your blind side.

If you back toward the driver's side, you can watch the rear of the vehicle by looking out the side window and by using your left mirror. In a tractor with a box trailer, you can see only the side of the trailer in the right mirror during blind-side backing. Do not become focused on one mirror. Always use both mirrors.

Avoid backing into the street if possible. Back into an alley so that you can drive out forward. If you must back into the street, driver-side backing lets you block off the whole street and protect other drivers who might otherwise try to pull around you before you get into position on your side of the street. DO NOT drive into an alley; backing into it is safer. Whenever possible get someone to watch your blindside; other vehicles and people may try to get around you.

When you know that you will have to back, plan ahead so you can use driver-side backing. This may mean going around the block to put your vehicle in the right position. The added safety and ease of operation is worth the extra time and effort.

## Use Your Four-Way Flashers and Horn

When you have inspected your intended backing path, without delay, get back into your cab, and turn on your four way flashers. If your truck is not equipped with a backup alarm, blow your air horn 2 to 3 times, and then start backing. Check both mirrors and the front of the tractor constantly.

## General Backing Rules

The four general rules for backing your vehicle are:
• Start in the proper position.
• Back slowly.
• Constantly check behind your vehicle.
• Start over when necessary.

### Start in the Proper Position

The most important maneuver in backing is starting with the proper setup. Without being set up properly, the best of drivers cannot dock the trailer. The instructor will illustrate this in the classroom and demonstrate it on the backing range.

You must position your rig before beginning to back. You reach the right position by moving forward. When you think the vehicle is in the right spot, stop and secure it. Get out, and check your position from all angles. Try to limit the distance of the pull-up. The farther you pull up, the farther you must back up.

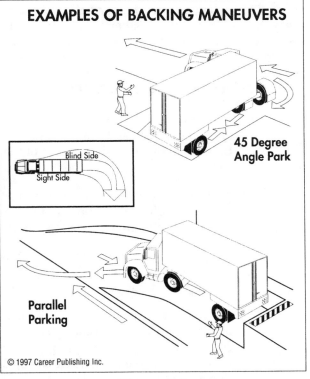

**Figure 8-7**

## Back Slowly

Use the lowest reverse gear and back slowly. Be patient. If possible, stay off the accelerator. Avoid riding the clutch.

## Constantly Check Behind the Vehicle

Backing a tractor-trailer is done with mirrors. You should know what the trailer looks like in the mirrors at all times. Use both mirrors. Do not become focused on one mirror and use minimal steering correction. It takes 8 to 12 feet for the tractor to react to the driver's direction. Be patient.

## Start Over When Necessary

If the trailer gets out of position, pull forward and start over. It is better to pull forward and try again instead of continuing to back from the wrong position.

# BASIC BACKING MANEUVERS

You will need to master four basic backing maneuvers.
1. Straight-line backing
2. 45-degree angle parking
3. Straight back parking
4. Parallel parking

## Straight-line Backing

The key to backing a tractor-trailer in a straight line is to recognize which way the trailer is drifting and make adjustments to correct it immediately. Be sure the tractor is directly in front of the trailer before starting to back. Back slowly in the lowest possible gear. Visualize a straight line as the trailer's path.

## 45-Degree Angle Parking

1. Pull forward, in a straight line, near the parking space. You should be about 3 to 5 feet out from the parked vehicles. When the front of the trailer is in line with the left side of the parking space, turn hard to the right.

2. You should now be going about 3 to 5 miles an hour. When the tractor is at the 12 o'clock position, straight away from the parking space, turn to the left until the steering wheel is in the 10 o'clock position.

3. Keep moving this foward position until the trailer is near a 45° angle. When the tractor is at a slight angle to the left of the trailer and the parking space can be seen from the driver's window, stop the tractor.

4. Set your brakes and get out of the cab. Your tractor tandem should be about 12 to 15 feet in front of the left side of the parking space. Be sure the steering tires are straight. Get back in the cab and start backing. Straighten out the rig as you enter the space and watch the direction of the rear tandem. Correct its movement as needed.

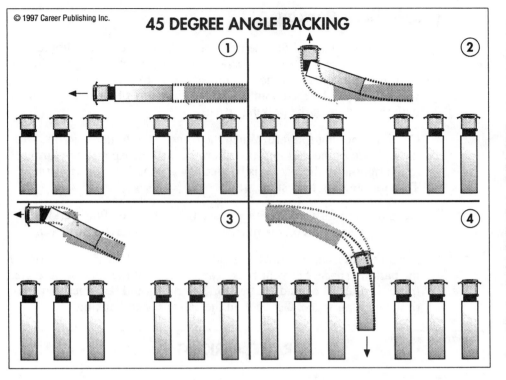

**45 DEGREE ANGLE BACKING**

Figure 8-8

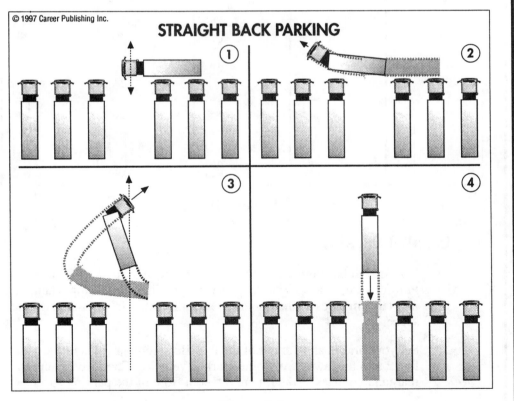

**STRAIGHT BACK PARKING**

Figure 8-9

## Straight Back Parking

1.  Pull forward in a straight line near the parking space. You should be about 3 to 5 feet out from the parked vehicles. Stop when your line of sight is in the middle of the parking space. Look out your right window for a reference point that is within a line of sight and even with the middle of the parking space.

2.  Continue moving forward. When the front of the trailer is in line with the left side of the parking space, turn hard to the right. Keep turning to the right until the tractor is headed toward the 2 o'clock position. Turn the steering tires straight.

3.  Keep moving forward. When you see the right side of the parking space in your right convex mirror, turn back to the reference point.

4.  Straighten the steering tires and pull forward until the rig is in front of the parking space. Set your brakes and get out of the cab. Be sure the trailer is directly behind the tractor. The rig should be directly in front of the parking space. Get back in the cab and start backing.

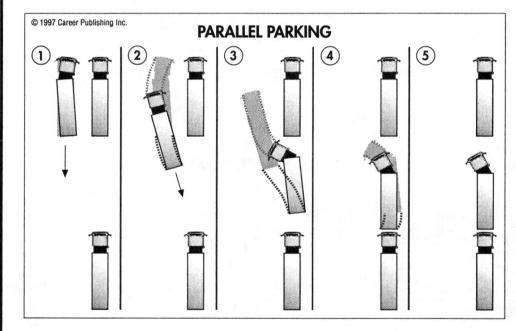

**Figure 8-10**

## Parallel Parking

1.  You should be about 2 to 3 feet out from the other parked vehicles. Pull forward, in a straight line, near the parking space. Stop when the rear tandem axles of the trailer are about 8 feet in front of the parking space.

2.  Set your brakes and get out of the cab. Be sure your rig is in a straight line 2 to 3 feet away from other parked vehicles. Check to be sure the rear tandem axles of the rig are 8 feet in front of the parking space.

3.  Get back in the cab and start backing with the steering wheel turned to the left. The angle between the left side of the tractor is about 12° to 15° away from the front of the trailer.

4.  Turn hard to the right and continue backing until the tractor and the trailer are in a straight line. The middle of the rig should be in the parking space. (See position #2 in Figure 8-10). Continue backing until the front of the trailer is even with the front of the parking space (See position #3).

5.  Turn hard to the right and continue backing until the trailer is parallel inside the parking space. The tractor should be at an 85° to 90° angle to the left. Leave the tractor in this position. This will make it easier for you to exit the space.

## SUMMARY

In this chapter you have learned the correct procedures for backing in a tractor-trailer safely and correctly. You also learned that tractor-trailer combinations have different backing characteristics from automobiles. How to use backing in helping you to master 45-degree angle backing and parallel parking were also explained.

## KEY WORDS

**45-degree angle parking:** An alley dock backing technique in which the rig is pulled forward at a 45-degree angle to the target, then backed in.

**Articulated vehicle:** A vehicle that contains a pivot point. In the case of a tractor-trailer, it is the point where the tractor and trailer are coupled.

**Blind-side backing:** Backing toward the right (blind) side of the rig.

**Driver-side backing:** Backing toward the left (driver) side of the rig. Also called sight-side backing.

**Maneuver:** To make a series of planned changes of direction a vehicle is moving for a specific purpose.

**Straight back parking:** An alley dock backing technique in which the rig is pulled forward so that the rear is facing the target, then backed in.

# LEARNING ACTIVITIES

## Review Questions

1.  Why is backing a tractor-trailer different from backing a car?

2.  When you want the trailer to move to the right, which way should you turn the steering wheel? Why?

3.  You are attempting to back in a straight line and the trailer begins to drift to the left. Which way should you turn the steering wheel to correct the drift?

4.      Explain what is meant by oversteering.

         _____

         _____

5.      List the four general rules for backing safely that you should observe before you start. Give a brief explanation of each.

         _____

         _____

         _____

         _____

         _____

         _____

6.      List and explain the four general backing rules.

         _____

         _____

         _____

         _____

         _____

         _____

7.      What is the key to backing a tractor-trailer in a straight line?

         _____

8.      What is the difference between sight-side backing and blind-side backing?

         _____

         _____

         _____

9.      Why is parallel parking a very difficult maneuver?

         _____

         _____

         _____

## True-False Questions ✓

If the statement is true, circle the T. If the statement is false, circle the F.

T  F    1.   To correct a trailer drift when attempting to back straight, turn the steering wheel toward the drift.

T  F    2.   When backing into an alley, you can see best if you back toward the driver side.

T  F    3.   Before backing, check behind the vehicle by getting out of the cab.

T  F    4.   When backing a tractor-trailer, the front tractor axle becomes the steering axle for the trailer.

T  F    5.   Turning the steering wheel to the left when backing will force the rear of the trailer to the right.

T  F    6.   Turning the steering wheel to the right when backing will force the rear of the trailer to the left.

T  F    7.   It is better to pull into an alley cab first, so that you can back into the street when you leave.

# Chapter Nine
# COUPLING AND UNCOUPLING

Overview of Coupling • Step-by-Step Coupling Procedure • Overview of Uncoupling
Step-by-Step Uncoupling Procedure • Coupling Procedure Checklist • Uncoupling
Procedure Checklist

**FROM NOW ON,**

**ONLY THE BEST WILL DRIVE**

## OBJECTIVES

When you have mastered this chapter, you will be able to:

- Explain the correct way to couple a tractor with a trailer

- Show the proper way to uncouple a rig

- Describe the controls used when coupling or uncoupling

- Explain the hazards of coupling and uncoupling improperly

# CHAPTER NINE

# COUPLING AND UNCOUPLING

## INTRODUCTION

A tractor and trailer are two separate and independent units. They become a tractor-trailer, or rig, only when they are brought together and joined, or coupled. The driver is responsible for bringing them together and coupling them.

The purpose of this chapter is to help you learn how to couple and uncouple a rig correctly. This information will be presented in a step-by-step sequence.

Coupling is a basic skill in operating a tractor-trailer. Federal Motor Carrier Safety Regulations require you to be qualified in this operation. The best way to learn coupling is in a step-by-step sequence. This approach protects you and others from injury and your vehicle from damage.

Trying to couple or uncouple a rig without knowing what you are doing can be dangerous. You can be hurt. The tractor or trailer can roll into you or others. It can also damage property. The tractor, trailer or the contents can be damaged.

The 15 basic steps that make up a proper coupling sequence follow.

## STEP-BY-STEP COUPLING PROCEDURES

### Step 1. Inspect the Fifth Wheel

When inspecting the fifth wheel you should check:
- For damaged or missing parts
- The mounting of the fifth wheel on the tractor to be certain it is secure and not damaged
- For proper lubrication

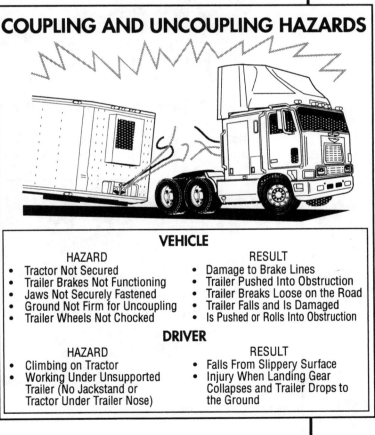

**COUPLING AND UNCOUPLING HAZARDS**

**VEHICLE**

| HAZARD | RESULT |
|--------|--------|
| • Tractor Not Secured | • Damage to Brake Lines |
| • Trailer Brakes Not Functioning | • Trailer Pushed Into Obstruction |
| • Jaws Not Securely Fastened | • Trailer Breaks Loose on the Road |
| • Ground Not Firm for Uncoupling | • Trailer Falls and Is Damaged |
| • Trailer Wheels Not Chocked | • Is Pushed or Rolls Into Obstruction |

**DRIVER**

| HAZARD | RESULT |
|--------|--------|
| • Climbing on Tractor | • Falls From Slippery Surface |
| • Working Under Unsupported Trailer (No Jackstand or Tractor Under Trailer Nose) | • Injury When Landing Gear Collapses and Trailer Drops to the Ground |

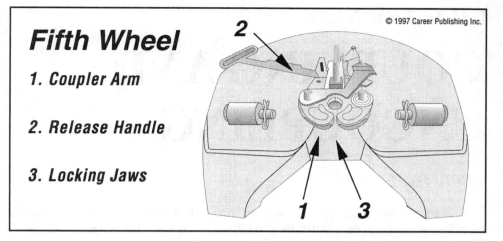

**Figure 9-2**

- To be sure the fifth wheel is in position for coupling
- Tilted down toward rear of tractor
- Jaws open
- The safety release handle is in the automatic lock position
- Make sure the slider locks are in place
- Make sure the fifth wheel position will allow coupling without allowing the rear end of the tractor to strike the landing gear

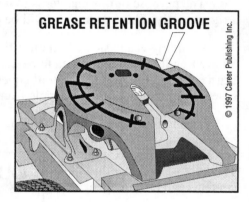

**Figure 9-3**

## Step 2. Inspect and Chock the Trailer Wheels

Be sure the area is clear. Then chock the trailer wheels. Check the cargo to be sure it will not move when the trailer is coupled to the tractor.

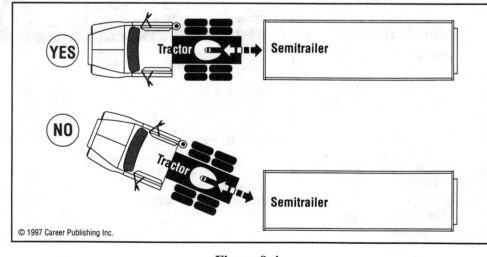

**Figure 9-4**

## Step 3. Position the Tractor

The tractor should be placed squarely in front of the trailer. Do not back the tractor at an angle. The wrong approach by the tractor can push the trailer backwards or sideways. This can break the landing gear and cause the trailer to fall.

To be sure the tractor and trailer line up properly, use the outside edge of your drive axle tires and the edge of the trailer as guide points. The tractor, outside edge of the drive axle tires, and edge of the trailer should form a straight line.

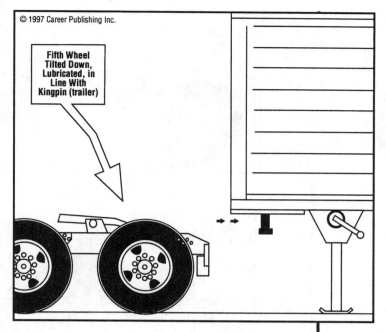

© 1997 Career Publishing Inc.

Fifth Wheel Tilted Down, Lubricated, in Line With Kingpin (trailer)

**Figure 9-5**

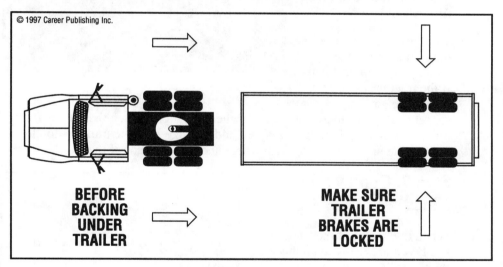

© 1997 Career Publishing Inc.

BEFORE BACKING UNDER TRAILER

MAKE SURE TRAILER BRAKES ARE LOCKED

**Figure 9-6**

## Step 4. Back Slowly Until the Fifth Wheel Just Touches the Trailer

Back slowly toward the nose of the trailer and stop just before the fifth wheel reaches the trailer. You should be close enough to hook up the air lines and to compare the fifth wheel height with the trailer height.

## Step 5. Secure the Tractor

Shift into neutral. Put on the tractor parking brake. Exit the cab.

**Figure 9-7**

## Step 6. Check the Trailer Height

Inspect the height of the trailer nose compared to the fifth wheel. The nose should be slightly higher than the fifth wheel. To couple properly, the nose of the trailer should touch the middle of the fifth wheel.

To adjust the height of the trailer, crank the landing gear up or down. If the tractor has an adjustable air

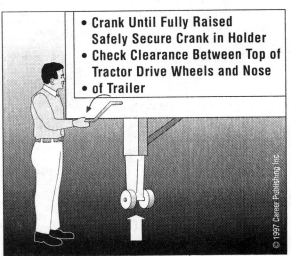

**Figure 9-8**

suspension, you can adjust the fifth wheel height to match the trailer. If the trailer is too low, the tractor may hit and damage it. If the trailer is too high, it may ride up and over the fifth wheel and into the rear of the cab.

## Step 7. Connect the Air Lines

When the height of the trailer is right, you are ready to connect the tractor's air lines to the trailer. There are two air lines running from the tractor to the trailer. They are called the SERVICE and EMERGENCY air lines. Normally, one will be stamped SERVICE and the other EMERGENCY. Glad hands connect the air lines.

Sometimes the air lines are coded differently. They may be:

* Color-coded: Red for emergency and blue or black for service.

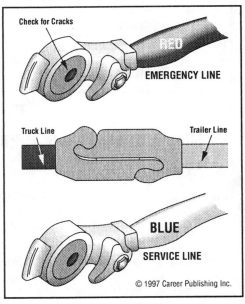

**Figure 9-9**

- Shape-coded: Round gladhands for the emergency air line, and square gladhands for the service air line.

For the brakes to work properly, the air lines must be connected right. You need to match the plug to the connector. Do not force it if it does not fit. Sometimes, the tractor's connectors and the trailer's connectors do not match. Use a converter if this happens. Firmly seat the plug in the receptacle. Put on the safety catch, or latch, to keep them from accidentally separating.

## Step 8. Supply Air to the Trailer

After the air lines have been connected and secured, get back in the cab. With the truck engine off, push in the red "Trailer Air Supply" valve to supply the trailer brakes with air. Listen for escaping air. If you hear a leak or if the air

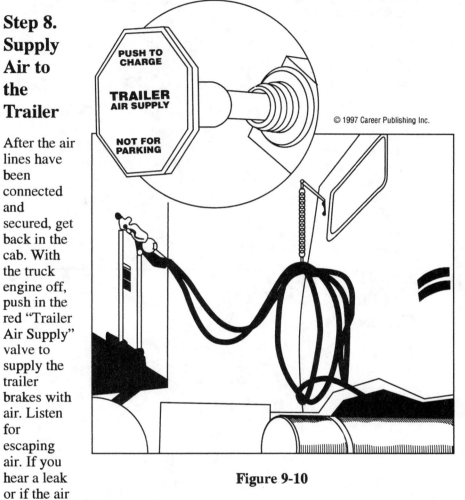

**Figure 9-10**

pressure gauge registers too much loss of air, correct the problem. You will notice air leaking if you have connected the air lines incorrectly.

## Step 9. Release the Tractor Parking Brake and Put on the Trailer Brake

You are now ready to back the tractor under the trailer.
- Start the truck engine.
- Release the tractor parking brake (yellow valve).
- Pull out the trailer air supply valve (red) to apply the trailer brakes.

## Step 10. Back Under the Trailer

Use the lowest reverse gear and back the tractor slowly under the trailer. Stop when you feel or hear the kingpin lock into the fifth wheel.

Do not hit the kingpin too hard. This could:
- Bend the kingpin
- Buckle the upper plate
- Jump the pin (kingpin over the fifth wheel causes the trailer to hit the tractor)
- Push the trailer away
- Damage cargo in the trailer

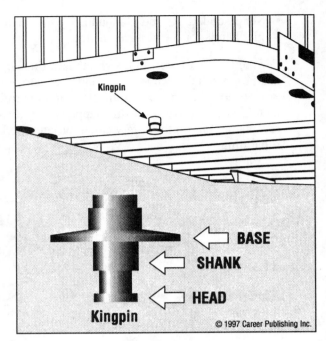

**Figure 9-11**

## Step 11. Test the Connection

Test the hookup by pulling the tractor gently forward in low gear while the trailer hand brake is on. As soon as resistance to forward motion is felt, disengage the clutch. Accelerate just enough to keep the engine from stalling. Then test the connection again.

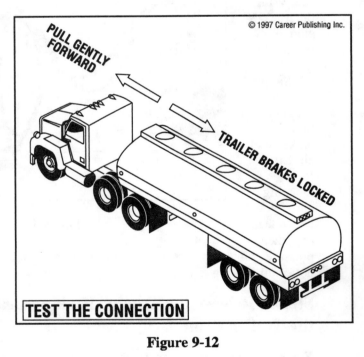

**Figure 9-12**

## Step 12. Secure the Vehicle

When you are sure of a solid hookup, put on the parking brake. Get out of the cab. Turn off the engine.

## Step 13. Inspect the Coupling

You will now need to go under the trailer and use a flashlight to get a good look at the coupling. Check to see if the:
*   Fifth wheel jaws have engaged the shank of the kingpin and not the head. If the jaws are closed around the head, the trailer will bounce the kingpin out of the jaws.
*   Jaws are closed and locked. The safety catch is over the locking lever.
*   Upper fifth wheel plate is in full contact with the lower trailer plate. If there is a space between the two, stop and fix the problem before doing anything else. The space may be due to uneven ground surface. Move the rig to flat ground and check again.

**CHECK THE COUPLING**
© 1997 Career Publishing Inc.

**No gap between fifth wheel and trailer upper plate**

**Figure 9-13**

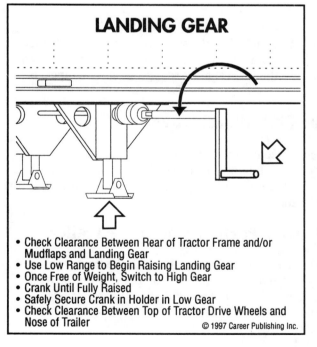

**LANDING GEAR**

*   Check Clearance Between Rear of Tractor Frame and/or Mudflaps and Landing Gear
*   Use Low Range to Begin Raising Landing Gear
*   Once Free of Weight, Switch to High Gear
*   Crank Until Fully Raised
*   Safely Secure Crank in Holder in Low Gear
*   Check Clearance Between Top of Tractor Drive Wheels and Nose of Trailer
© 1997 Career Publishing Inc.

**Figure 9-14**

## Step 14. Connect the Electrical Cord. Then Check the Air Lines

Plug the electrical cord into the trailer. Then fasten the safety catch. Be sure neither the electrical cord nor the air lines are damaged. These lines must not hit any moving parts of the rig.

## Step 15. Raise the Landing Gear

You are now ready to raise the landing gear. Most crank handles have a low speed and a high speed. Use the low speed to start raising the landing gear. Switch to high speed when the trailer weight is off the landing gear. Keep on cranking until the landing gear is fully raised.

Never drive your rig with the landing gear partly raised. It can catch on railroad tracks, dips in the road, etc. Make sure the crank handle is safely secured to prevent damage to other vehicles or injury to pedestrians.

## STEP-BY-STEP UNCOUPLING PROCEDURES

### Step 1. Position the Vehicle

To prepare for uncoupling, place the tractor directly in line with the trailer. This is to keep from damaging the landing gear when pulling the tractor from under the trailer.

Make sure the surface where you plan to uncouple the trailer will support the rig. Use a level surface.

### Step 2. Secure the Vehicle

Place the tractor protection valve in the emergency position. This cuts off the air supply between the tractor and trailer. Make sure you have backed tightly against the pin. If you have not, it will bind and not release properly. Put on the tractor parking brake. Exit the cab.

### Step 3. Lower the Landing Gear

Lower the landing gear until both supports touch the ground. If one touches the ground but not the other, find a more level location to drop the trailer. Crank until you see the trailer begin to rise off the fifth wheel.

### Step 4. Disconnect and Store the Air Lines and Electrical Cable

Disconnect the air lines and electrical cable. Place the air line gladhands on dummy couplers behind the cab. Hang the electrical cable down to avoid moisture on the plug. Secure the lines against snagging, cuts, scrapes, or other damage.

### Step 5. Release the Fifth Wheel Latch

To release the fifth wheel, raise the release handle lock pin and pull to the open position. On a single axle tractor, this is usually not hard. On tandem axle tractors, however, the release handle is sometimes hard to reach. If it is hard to reach, use a pull handle or hook.

### Step 6. Pull the Tractor Partly Clear of the Trailer

Get back in the cab and release the parking brake. Pull the tractor forward until the fifth wheel begins to clear the trailer apron plate. Stop the tractor while its frame is still under the trailer. This will keep the trailer from falling if the landing gear collapses or sinks.

### Step 7. Secure the Tractor

Put on the tractor parking brakes. Exit the cab.

## Step 8. Inspect the Trailer Supports

Be sure the landing gear is supporting the tractor and is not damaged.

## Step 9. Pull the Tractor Clear of the Trailer

Release the parking brake. Check the area ahead of the tractor and pull the tractor slowly away from the trailer. Uncoupling is now safely completed.

## SUMMARY

In this chapter you learned how to couple a trailer to a tractor and how to uncouple the rig. The controls that must be used when coupling or uncoupling were explained. How to test the connection was also shown.

## KEY WORDS

**Coupling** — Joining a tractor to a trailer.

**Fifth wheel** — The tractor support plate and locking jaws for the trailer kingpin.

**Gladhand** — A device that connects the air lines.

**Landing gear** — A support for the trailer to rest on when uncoupled.

**Uncoupling** — Separating a tractor from a trailer.

# LEARNING ACTIVITIES

## Review Questions

1. When preparing to couple, how should the tractor be placed in relation to the trailer?

   _____

   _____

2. Why is the height of the trailer nose an important part of the coupling process? What happens if it is too high? Too low?

   _____

   _____

   _____

3. What is the proper position for the fifth wheel before coupling?

   _____

   _____

4. Why is it dangerous to back under the trailer at an angle when coupling?

   _____

   _____

5. Name the two types of air lines found on a tractor-trailer air brake system.

_____

6. List three ways the air lines may be coded. Why is it important to be able to tell them apart?

_____

_____

_____

7. You have crawled under the trailer with a flashlight to inspect the coupling. List three things you should look for.

_____

_____

_____

8. As you lower the landing gear before uncoupling, you notice that one support touches the ground before the other. What does this tell you? What action, if any, should you take?

_____

9. Why should you place the tractor protection valve in the emergency position before uncoupling?

_____

10. What is a gladhand?

_____

## Review Quiz—PART A

List the following steps in the correct order for coupling a tractor to a trailer. Each step is used only once, so you can cross them off as you list them.

A. Secure the tractor.

B. Test the connection.

C. Connect the air lines.

D. Inspect the area, chock the wheels, and then place the tractor in front of the trailer.

E. Release the tractor parking brake and put on the trailer brake.

F. Raise the landing gear.

G. Inspect the fifth wheel.

H. Inspect the coupling.

I. Check the trailer height.

J. Back slowly until the fifth wheel just touches the trailer pickup apron.

K. Put on parking brake. Exit cab.

L. Back slowly until the fifth wheel locks

1. _____

2. _____

3. _____

4. _____

5. _____

6. _____

7. _____

8. _____

9. _____

10. _____

11. _____

12. _____

## Review Quiz—PART B

List the following steps in the correct order for uncoupling a tractor from a trailer. Each step is used only once, so you can cross them off as you list them.

A.  Lower the landing gear.                                       1.  _____

B.  Place the tractor in line with the trailer.                   2.  _____

C.  Inspect the trailer supports.                                 3.  _____

D.  Pull the tractor partly clear of the trailer.                 4.  _____

E.  Release the fifth wheel latch.                                5.  _____

F.  Secure the tractor.                                           6.  _____

G.  Disconnect and store the air lines and electrical cable.      7.  _____

H.  Secure the vehicle.                                           8.  _____

I.  Pull the tractor clear of the trailer.                        9.  _____

## True-False Questions ✓

If the statement is true, circle the T. If the statement is false, circle the F.

(T) F  1.  When coupling a rig, the nose of the trailer should be slightly higher than the midpoint of the tractor's fifth wheel.

(T) F  2.  When coupling, the tractor should be placed squarely in front of the trailer.

(T) F  3.  When coupling, you should bring the upper fifth wheel plate into contact with the lower trailer plate.

T (F)  4.  Moving the tractor protection valve to the normal position before coupling cuts off air pressure to the trailer.

T (F)  5.  In the final coupling inspection, make sure you have a solid hookup. You must inspect it from the side of the trailer.

(T) F  6.  To prepare for uncoupling, the tractor should be placed directly in line with the trailer.

(T) F  7.  Moving the tractor protection valve to the emergency position before uncoupling cuts off air pressure to the trailer.

(T) F  8.  To safely support the trailer, lower the landing gear with the crank until both supports touch the ground.

T (F)  9.  For proper coupling to take place, the jaws of the fifth wheel must engage the head of the kingpin.

(T) F  10.  For the brakes to work properly, the air lines must be connected properly.

# PROCEDURAL STEPS AND CHECKLISTS

The following lists are included to give you a handy reference, You may cut out the guide and take with you when you practice coupling and uncoupling a rig.

## Coupling Procedures Checklist

1. Inspect the Fifth Wheel
   - Check for damage, missing parts, and proper lubrication.
   - Check mounting.
     - Is it tilted down toward the rear of the tractor?
     - Jaws open?
     - Is the safety release handle in the automatic lock position?
2. Inspect the Area, and Chock the Wheels
   - Be sure the area is clear.
   - Chock the trailer wheels to keep the rig from rolling.
   - Check the cargo. Be sure it will not move when the trailer is coupled to the tractor.
3. Position the Tractor
   - Place the tractor squarely in front of the trailer, not at an angle.
   - Use the outside edge of the drive axle tires and the edge of the trailer as reference points.
   - Check the alignment by looking down the side of the trailer. The tractor, outside edge of the drive axles, and the edge of the trailer should form a straight line.
   - Make a final check with both mirrors to be sure the tractor and trailer are aligned.
4. Back Slowly
   - Stop when the lower plate of the fifth wheel just touches the trailer.
   - Back slowly. Do not jar the trailer.
5. Secure the Tractor
   - Apply the tractor parking brake.
   - Climb out of the cab.
6. Check the Trailer Height
   - Inspect the height of the trailer nose in relation to the fifth wheel.
   - The nose of the trailer should be slightly higher than the midpoint of the fifth wheel.
   - For proper coupling, the nose of the trailer should touch the middle of the fifth wheel.
7. Connect the Air Lines
   - Connect the service air line from the tractor to the service gladhand on the left side of the trailer.
   - Connect the emergency air line from the tractor to the emergency gladhand on the right side of the trailer.
8. Supply Air to the Trailer
   - With the truck engine off, push in the red Trailer Supply Valve
   - Check the system for signs of excessive air loss.
9. Release the Tractor Parking Brake, and Apply the Trailer Brake
   - Release the parking brake, allowing the tractor to move.
   - Put on the trailer brake to hold the trailer in place.
10. Back Under Trailer
    - Use the lowest reverse gear to back the tractor slowly under the trailer.
    - Stop when you feel or hear the kingpin lock into the fifth wheel.
11. Test the Connection
    - In low gear, pull the tractor forward gently while keeping the trailer hand brake applied.
    - As soon as resistance is felt, quickly disengage the clutch. Then test it again.
12. Secure the Vehicle
    - Put on the parking brake.
    - Climb out of the cab.

13. Inspect the Coupling
    • Using a flashlight, go under the trailer.
    • Check to see if the fifth wheel jaws have closed around the shank of the kingpin.
    • See if the upper fifth wheel plate is in full contact with the lower trailer plate.
    • Make sure the jaws are closed and locked, and the safety catch is over the locking lever.
14. Connect the electrical cord, and check the air lines
    • Plug the electrical cord into the trailer.
    • Then fasten the safety catch.
    • Be sure neither the electrical cord nor the air lines are damaged.
    • Be sure these lines will not hit any moving parts of the rig.
15. Raise the Landing Gear
    • Use the crank handle at low speed, and start raising the landing gear.
    • As soon as trailer weight is off the landing gear, switch to high speed and continue cranking until the landing gear is fully raised.

## Uncoupling Procedures Checklist

1. Position the Vehicle
    • Position the tractor directly in line with the trailer.
    • Make sure the surface where you will uncouple the trailer is level and capable of supporting the rig
2. Secure the Vehicle
    • Place the tractor protection valve in the emergency position.
    • Apply the tractor parking brake.
    • Climb out of the cab.
3. Lower the Landing Gear
    • Lower the landing gear until both supports touch the ground.
    • Continue cranking until you see the trailer begin to rise off the fifth wheel.
4. Disconnect and Store Air Lines and Electrical Cable
    • Secure the air lines against snagging, cuts, scrapes, or other damage.
    • Hang the electrical cable down to avoid moisture on the plug.
5. Release the Fifth Wheel Latch
    • Raise the release handle lock pin and pull the release handle to the open position.
    • If you cannot reach the release handle, use a pull handle or hook.
6. Pull the Tractor Partly Clear of the Trailer
    • Return to the cab.
    • Pull the tractor forward and stop while its frame is still under the trailer.
7. Secure the Tractor
    • Apply the tractor parking brake.
    • Leave the cab.
8. Inspect the Trailer Supports
    • Check the landing gear for damage.
    • Make sure it is supporting the trailer. Check the surface.
9. Pull the Tractor Clear of the Trailer
    • Get in the cab. Release the parking brake.
    • Drive the tractor slowly away from the trailer.

# Chapter Ten
# VISUAL SEARCH

**Importance of Seeing • Systematic Seeing • Looking Ahead • Scanning and Searching • Intersections • Mirrors • Field of View • Using Mirrors When Making Changes and Turning Corners**

FROM NOW ON,

ONLY THE BEST WILL DRIVE

# OBJECTIVES

When you have mastered the chapter, you will be able to:

• Show the importance of knowing what you are seeing when you drive

• Look ahead and scan the environment

• Explain the different types of mirrors, their adjustments, and how to use them

• Describe the truck driver's responsibilities to other drivers

# CHAPTER TEN

# VISUAL SEARCH

## INTRODUCTION

To drive a rig with success, the driver needs to know what is going on around the vehicle. Imagine you are looking down on your rig from a few hundred feet above. See the space in front of the rig? To the sides? To the rear? This is the *environment*, or area, you must see, hear, feel, and sense when driving. It changes all the time as you move. This chapter will help you learn what you need to know to search the environment and drive defensively.

## THE IMPORTANCE OF SEEING

The driver's view from a tractor cab is much different from what he or she would see from a car. You can see farther ahead because you are sitting above traffic. You see *over* the traffic. This is a plus for the driver. On the other hand, you cannot see as well to the sides and rear. It is hard to see the right side of the tractor-trailer and along the drive wheels on both sides. It is also hard to see small vehicles.

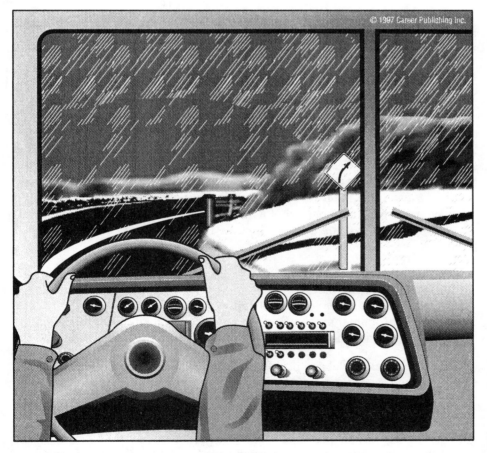

**Figure 10-1**

The driver must be able to get a clear, complete, and accurate picture of the traffic scene. To find out what is happening around you in traffic, you must use your senses of sight, sound, and smell. Pay attention to movement, balance, and the *feel* of things.

Sight is the most important sense in driving. It is your best source of information about the traffic scene. Seeing what is there, however, is not enough. You must also understand what you see and apply what you *sense* to the traffic situation. To know what you see quickly and correctly, you must use a visual search pattern, or routine. This is called **systematic seeing**. It helps you know:
- What to look at
- What to look for
- Where to look

Look ahead of where you intend to travel. Search the traffic scene ahead of the rig and to the sides. Use your mirrors to see to the rear.

## LOOKING AHEAD

Looking ahead of your rig helps you to drive better. Steer toward an imaginary target or reference point in the center of your lane of travel. Having a target will help keep your vehicle centered in the lane.

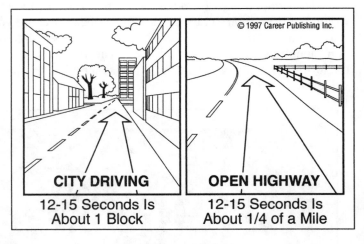

© 1997 Career Publishing Inc.

**CITY DRIVING** — 12-15 Seconds Is About 1 Block

**OPEN HIGHWAY** — 12-15 Seconds Is About 1/4 of a Mile

**Figure 10-2**

A good rule of thumb for deciding how far ahead you should look is to have the target at least the distance you will travel in 10 or 12 seconds. This is called eye lead time. In city driving, 12 seconds is equal to about one block. On the open highway, it is about 1/4 of a mile. If you cannot look ahead one block in the city or 1/4 of a mile on the open highway, slow down and be extra alert.

Looking far enough ahead will give you time to:
- Identify problems
- Prepare for trouble
- Decide how to avoid the problem
- Check for anything that may keep you from making the proper change
- Take the right action

Looking well ahead and having enough visual lead time increases safety, saves fuel, and saves time.

**Safety**: You can see hazards early enough to give you time to react properly. There will be fewer close calls and accidents.

**Fuel**: When you can see far enough ahead, you can avoid quick speed adjustments and stops that waste fuel. You can adjust smoothly.

**Time**: Spotting situations early will help keep you from being trapped behind turning vehicles, getting stuck in the wrong lane, or missing your exit.

## Scanning and Searching the Traffic Scene

As important as it is to have a 12-second visual lead time, do not stare off into the distance all the time. You must know what is going on *all* around you. Keep your eyes moving. After you have chosen a reference point, scan and search around your rig. Look far ahead, just ahead of the rig, and on both sides. Look away from your reference point. Quickly scan and search. Then return to your reference point.

When scanning, look for anything that can affect your travel path.

- People
- Traffic signs
- Signals
- Slick spots
- Intersections
- Merging lanes
- Road shoulders
- School zones
- Construction sites
- Stopped vehicles

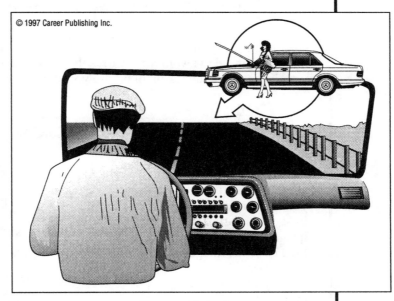

© 1997 Career Publishing Inc.

**Figure 10-3**

Always look for bail-out areas. Bail-out areas are places you can use to avoid a crash. Your scanning pattern and what you look for will vary depending on traffic and your driving situation.

## Looking at Intersections

After stopping at an intersection, it is important for you to know how to look before you move into and across the traffic lanes. These general guidelines should be helpful.

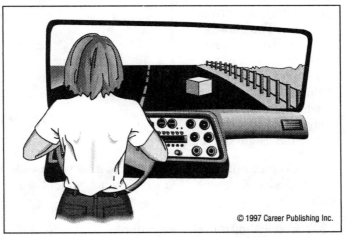

© 1997 Career Publishing Inc.

**Figure 10-4**

- Move your rig forward very slowly. Give other drivers a chance to see you. The slow, controlled speed will also let you stop again before pulling into the path of cross traffic.

- Look in the right order.
  Left
  Right
  Then left again as you begin to move forward

The reason you look in this order is that the first lane you cross carries traffic from the left. Until that lane is clear to enter, you cannot move forward. If your search shows the right lane is also clear, you can safely begin to move forward. At this point, the second look to the left assures you there are no changes in that direction. You can now go through the intersection.

- Finally, be aware of the blind spots created by the mirrors and the corner posts of your cab.

**Mirrors**: From your seat in the cab, you can see behind you only in your left and right side-view mirrors. Check these mirrors when you scan and search. It is very important to check them before you slow down, stop, or change direction.

## Field of View

You will have the biggest field of view in the left mirror. The closer the mirror is to you, the larger the image. The larger the image, the bigger the field of view. Images will appear similar to those in the side view mirror of a car.

## MIRRORS

There are two types of side mirrors, plane (flat) and convex (curved). The **plane mirror** gives the best view of the rear of the trailer and the roadway behind. It does not give a wide view. It can leave blind spot areas along the length of the rig.

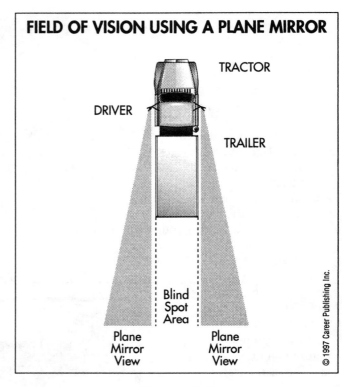

**Figure 10-5**

**Convex mirrors** have a curve to give you a wide angle view. They are best used for side close-ups. You have a much wider field of view than with a plain mirror.

Convex mirrors eliminate most, but not all, of the blind area created by the plane mirror. The images you see, however, will be smaller and appear farther away than they really are.

With plane mirrors, the blind areas are too large. Using only the convex mirror creates too much distortion. So the best way is to have both plain and

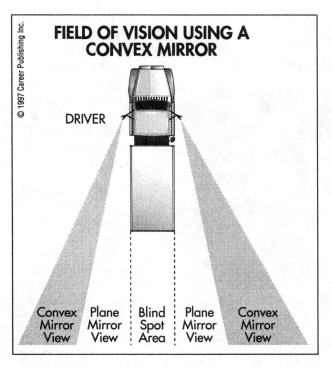

## FIELD OF VISION USING A CONVEX MIRROR

© 1997 Career Publishing Inc.

DRIVER

Convex Mirror View | Plane Mirror View | Blind Spot Area | Plane Mirror View | Convex Mirror View

**Figure 10-6**

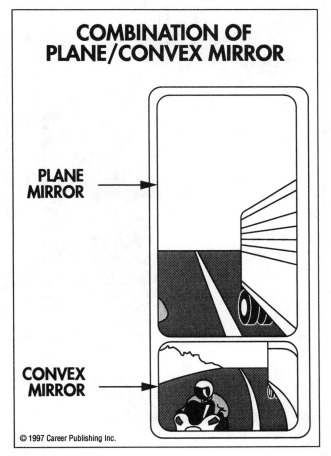

## COMBINATION OF PLANE/CONVEX MIRROR

PLANE MIRROR

CONVEX MIRROR

**Figure 10-7**

convex mirrors. Many rigs have this combination. It gives drivers the best side and rear vision.

Remember, though, blind spots are still there. Adjust your mirrors. Check both mirrors often. It is the only way to know if something is in a blind area.

A **fender mirror** is mounted on the fender of a regular long nose tractor. Its use requires less eye movement, so you can watch the road ahead better.

Wide angle (convex) fender mirrors let you see more when you are making right turns. This is really helpful in a tight turn. The view of the road is similar to what you see with a convex side mirror, but there is less distortion.

## Adjusting Mirrors

Every driver needs to learn to adjust both the left and right mirrors to get the best view of the sides and rear of the rig. All mirrors should be adjusted to show some part of the vehicle (trailer body, tires, etc.). This will give you a reference point for judging the position of the other images. Adjust mirrors when the rig is straight for the best image.

Some rigs have motorized mirrors that allow you to adjust them from inside the cab. They can also be used to get a wider view when needed, and then returned to the normal position.

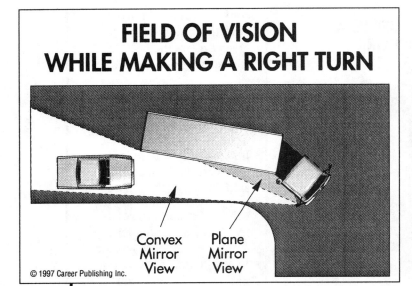

# FIELD OF VISION WHILE MAKING A RIGHT TURN

Convex Mirror View     Plane Mirror View

© 1997 Career Publishing Inc.

**Figure 10-8**

**Left Side Mirrors**: (Plane) The inside, vertical edge of the mirror (about 3/4 to 1 inch) should show the trailer body. The remaining part will show what is beside and behind the trailer. The range of view to the side will be about 15 feet.

(Convex) The inside, vertical edge of the mirror should show part of the trailer. The top, horizontal edge should show a view overlapping that of the plane mirror by about five feet and going back to the end of the trailer.

**Right Side Mirrors**: (Plane) The inside, vertical edge of the mirror (about 3/4 inch to 1 inch) should reflect the trailer body. The rest will show what is on the side (for about 15 feet) and behind the trailer.

(Convex) The inside, vertical edge of the mirror should reflect part of the trailer. The top, horizontal edge should show a view overlapping that of the plane mirror by five feet and extend to the end of trailer.

**Fender Mirrors**: The convex fender mirrors on both the right and left sides should be adjusted so you can see the trailer tires, curbs, and other objects when turning.

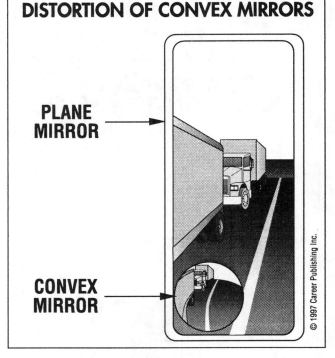

# DISTORTION OF CONVEX MIRRORS

PLANE MIRROR

CONVEX MIRROR

© 1997 Career Publishing Inc.

**Figure 10-9**

## Seeing to the Rear

Checking your rig's mirrors is a part of scanning and searching. Check:
- How secure your load is
    Is it loose or falling?
- Your tires for fire

In addition, your mirror checks can tell you:
- If there are any hazards around your rig
- What is beside or behind the rig that may be affected by a sudden move
- If your trailer has struck anything

## Using Mirrors When Making Changes

Before making any sudden changes in speed or direction, check the traffic behind you.

**Changing Lanes**: Always use both the plane and convex mirrors when you change your path of travel. Be aware there are blind spots behind and to the sides of your rig. You may need to make many checks to be sure of the traffic situation. Remember, it takes longer to check to the rear when you are driving a rig than it does when you are driving a car. Properly checking the left mirrors takes almost 1 second. Checking those to the right side takes nearly 1-1/2 seconds.

Be sure it is safe to look away from the front of the rig before making the mirror checks. At 55 mph, you travel 80 feet in 1 second. Keep enough space between yourself and the vehicle in front of you. Do not take chances. If there is not enough space or time, delay the lane change.

**Turning Corners**: When coming to a corner where you want to turn, check your side-view mirrors before slowing down. Then check them again as you are turning. After completing the turn, check the mirrors to be sure:

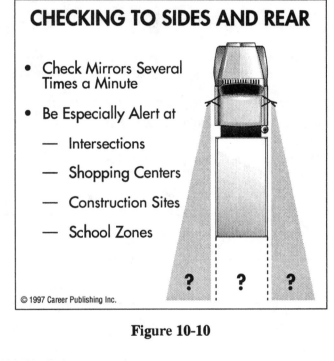

## CHECKING TO SIDES AND REAR

- Check Mirrors Several Times a Minute

- Be Especially Alert at
  - — Intersections
  - — Shopping Centers
  - — Construction Sites
  - — School Zones

© 1997 Career Publishing Inc.

**Figure 10-10**

- Your rig is not entangled with or dragging anything
- Your rig has not damaged anything

## SUMMARY

In this chapter you have learned how to systematically search the environment around your tractor-trailer. You have learned the value of looking ahead and planning for hazards. You were taught the correct methods of crossing an intersection and making lane changes. The differences in the reflected image in a plane mirror and a convex mirror were explained. You also learned how to adjust the mirrors for maximum visibility. Finally, you learned what things you should look for when you check your mirrors.

## KEY WORDS

**Convex Mirror:** A curved mirror that gives the driver a wide-angle view to the rear of the rig.

**Environment:** The area around the rig that you must see, hear, feel, and sense when driving.

**Plane Mirror:** A flat mirror for seeing to the rear of the rig.

**Systematic Seeing:** A driver's visual search pattern that helps him or her know what to look at, what to look for, and where to look.

# LEARNING ACTIVITIES

## Review Questions

1.   What is systematic seeing?

   _____

2.   Explain the term, eye lead time. Why is it important?

   _____

   _____

3.   List three ways a driver can benefit by looking ahead properly and maintaining enough visual lead time.

   _____

   _____

   _____

   _____

4.   Why is it important to scan and search the area around your rig?

   _____

   _____

5.   Explain what is meant by the left, right, left concept? Why does it make sense? Why is it important?

   _____

   _____

   _____

6.     What are the two basic types of side mirrors?

_____

_____

7.     Which type of side mirror provides the best view of the rear of the trailer and roadway behind?

_____

8.     Which type of mirror is best for side close-ups?

_____

9.     Images will appear smaller and more distant than they really are in which type of mirror?

_____

10.    What is a fender mirror? How is it used? Is it commonly used on all tractors?

_____

_____

11.    Explain the importance of mirror checks in lane changing.

_____

_____

12.    How long should it take to check the right side mirror? The left side mirror? Why is the time it takes
       important?

_____

_____

13.    Explain how to adjust the side mirrors.

_____

_____

_____

_____

## Traffic Situations

Explain what traffic problem can occur in each of the traffic situations shown in the drawings. Write your solution to the problem. Be sure to include how to avoid such a problem if there is a way.

1. _____
   _____
   _____
   _____
   _____
   _____
   _____

2. _____
   _____
   _____
   _____
   _____
   _____
   _____
   _____
   _____

3. _____
   _____
   _____
   _____
   _____
   _____
   _____
   _____

4. _____
   _____
   _____
   _____
   _____
   _____
   _____

5. _____

_____

_____

_____

_____

_____

_____

_____

6. _____

© 1997 Career Publishing Inc.

_____

_____

_____

_____

_____

_____

_____

_____

_____

_____

## True/False Questions ✓

Circle the T if the statement is true. Circle the F if the statement is false.

T **(F)** 1. The image in a convex mirror will appear closer than it really is.

**(T)** F 2. The image in a convex mirror will appear smaller than it really is.

**(T)** F 3. In city driving, it is best to look ahead at least one full block.

**(T)** F 4. You should establish an eye lead time by looking ahead 10 to 12 seconds.

T **(F)** 5. At highway speeds, you should try to look ahead about 1/8 of a mile.

T **(F)** 6. With the mirrors properly adjusted, a driver can see the same image in both the left and right mirrors.

**(T)** F 7. A plane (flat) side mirror gives the best view of the rear of the trailer and roadway behind.

**(T)** F 8. A convex mirror is best used for side close-ups of the trailer.

**(T)** F 9. Fender mirrors require less eye movement than side mirrors.

**(T)** F 10. Properly checking the right side mirror takes more time than checking the left mirror.

# Chapter Eleven
# COMMUNICATION

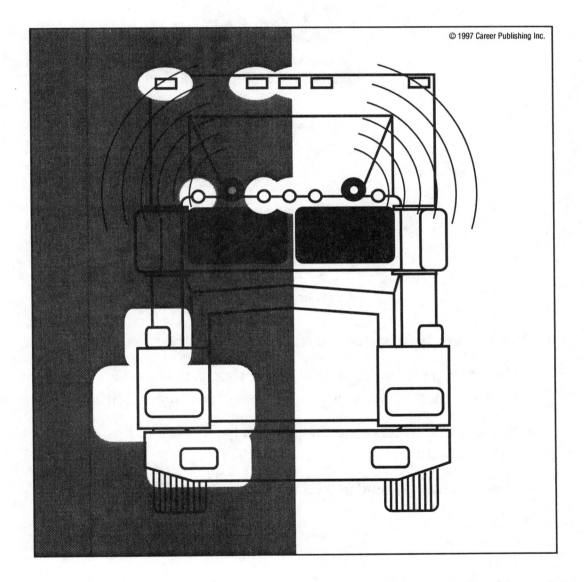

© 1997 Career Publishing Inc.

**Tell Your Intent • Signaling for Turns • Signaling for Lane Changes
Slowing Down • Directing Traffic • Overtaking Other Vehicles
When It Is Hard to See • Stopping Beside Highways**

FROM NOW ON,

ONLY THE BEST WILL DRIVE

# OBJECTIVES

When you have mastered the chapter, you will be able to:

• Understand the importance of using signals to tell other highway users when you plan to change position in traffic

• Explain why good communication helps to avoid collisions and traffic violations

• Describe how to send and receive communications

# CHAPTER ELEVEN

# COMMUNICATION

## INTRODUCTION

If travel is to be safe and smooth, highway users need to *talk to each other*. Drivers of rigs must do their share. Tell others what you intend to do as you move your rig through traffic. At the same time, be alert for messages from other highway users.
- Drivers
- Pedestrians
- Bicyclists

How we manage this information while driving is called communication.

Good communication calls for knowledge, foresight, and understanding of our own needs as well as those of others. In its simplest form, communication is trying to help one another get the job done. In addition to using turn signals, there are other ways to help highway users know of your presence and intentions. This chapter outlines those ways.

It may be difficult to believe that people cannot see a big rig, but there are times when this happens. When you communicate your presence (let others know where you are), you may help prevent an accident.

## TELL YOUR INTENT

You know where you are and what you are going to do. Others usually do not know what you are going to do unless you tell them. Remember the concern you felt when a bicyclist was in your lane on the highway? That concern is a good example of why it is important to tell your intentions to others.

To signal what you intend to do before you do it is important for all highway users, but there are some

**SIGNAL EARLY.** Signal for some time before you turn. It is the best way to keep others from trying to pass you when it is not safe.

**SIGNAL CONTINUOUSLY.** Do not cancel the signal until you have completed the turn.

**CANCEL YOUR SIGNAL AFTER YOU HAVE TURNED.** Turn off your signal if you do not have self-cancelling signals.

**Figure 11-1**

special rules for signaling when you drive a rig. The size of your rig, blind spots, and the space you need for turning mean you must do everything you can to help others know what you intend to do.

# SIGNALING

## Signaling for Turns

There are three special rules for signaling for turns.
1. Signal early
2. Signal continuously
3. Cancel your signal

**Signal Early:** The size of your rig makes it hard for you to see someone who is about to pass you or who may already be doing so. The best way to keep others from trying to pass you when you are turning is to give plenty of advance warning. Put on your turn signal early. The general rule-of-thumb is to turn on the signal one-half block before an intersection or about 500 feet on the open highway.

The FMCSR says you must signal at least 100 feet in advance. State requirements vary from 100 to 500 feet. Keep in mind that the legal requirements are minimums. 100 feet may not be far enough in advance for many conditions.

**Signal Continuously:** You may find that after turning on your signal, you must stop and wait for a safe break in traffic. Keep the signal on. It tells everyone what you are going to do. Remember when making a turn in a big rig, keep both hands on the wheel.

© 1997 Career Publishing Inc.

**CHANGING LANES:**
• Check traffic to the front and rear, especially in your blind spot.
• Signal the lane change.
• Do not tailgate while waiting to change lanes.
• Make a smooth lane change, maintain your speed, and allow the correct distance between all vehicles.
• Cancel your signal.

**Figure 11-2**

**Cancel Your Signal:** When you have completed the turn, cancel the signal. Do not cancel the signal until you *have* completed the turn. One good way to remember to cancel the signal is to connect it in your mind with the upshift. After completing a turn, speed up, cancel the signal, and upshift. Soon this routine will become a habit.

## Signaling for Lane Changes

Lane changes need the same early signals as turns. They also need one more signal — the motion of your vehicle. Once you have started your lane change, pause for a few seconds as you enter the new lane. This will catch the attention of those who did not notice your earlier signal. It will give them a chance to react.

## Slowing Down

Highway users expect vehicles ahead of them to keep moving. Any time you slow suddenly, give the driver behind you some warning. A few light taps on the brake pedal — enough to flash the brake lights without exhausting your air supply — should do the trick. Give a warning in any of the following situations.

**Trouble Ahead:** The size of your rig may make it impossible for drivers of vehicles that are following your rig to see around you.

**Tight Turns:** Few car drivers realize how hard it is to make a tight turn in a big rig. Often they are not prepared when a truck ahead of them slows to nearly a stop before starting a turn. Give them a warning.

**Stopping on the Road:** Unfortunately, truck drivers are sometimes forced to stop in a traffic lane when others may not be expecting it. It may be a case of having to unload cargo when there is no space at the curb. Sometimes it is at a railroad crossing. Maybe the driver is getting ready to back into a driveway. In any case, the drivers that are following can be caught off guard. Give them a warning.

**Driving Slowly:** Sometimes drivers overtaking a slow vehicle do not know how quickly they are closing in on it. Often they are too close before they can react. If you are being slowed by hills or heavy cargo, tell other drivers by turning on your emergency flashers.

Laws regarding the use of flashers differ from state to state. Know the laws in your own state. Check on the laws of other states before driving through them.

## Do Not Direct Traffic

Some truck drivers try to help other drivers by signaling when it is safe to pass. While they mean well, their judgment is poor. If there is another vehicle the truck driver did not see, the *help* can cause an accident. The truck driver is then held liable. It is very costly for the truck driver or his or her employer. Signaling others to pass is illegal and dangerous. Signal only to tell others what *you* plan to do. Leave directing traffic to the police.

## Overtaking Other Vehicles

**Avoid Guiding Others**

DO NOT SIGNAL OTHERS TO PASS OR CROSS

© 1997 Career Publishing Inc.

**Figure 11-3**

Whenever you are overtaking another vehicle, a pedestrian, or a bicyclist, it is best to assume they do not see you. If they do not see you, there is also a chance they will suddenly move into your path. Tell them you are there with a light tap on the horn. *Note, we said light tap.* At night, flashing your lights with the dimmer switch also works.

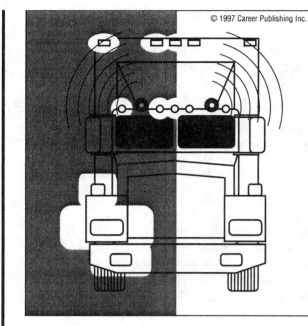

**Figure 11-4**

A light tap on your eletric horn is enough to tell others you are there. Avoid a loud blast on the air horn that may startle them and cause them to swerve into your path. Loud blasts of the horn are for emergencies only.

Signal any time you overtake and pass pedestrians or cyclists. Obviously, you cannot signal every time you overtake another vehicle. It is a good idea to do it, though, whenever you approach a driver who is signaling a lane change or starting to pull into your path.

## When it is Hard to See

It is hard to see:
- At dawn or dusk
- In rain or snow
- On cloudy days

A truck can be just as hard to see as any other vehicle. If you are having trouble spotting oncoming vehicles, you must assume other drivers are having a tough time seeing you. Turn on your lights. Use your headlights, not just ID or clearance lights. Use your low beams. High beams can be as annoying in the day as at night.

## At the Side of the Road

Any time you pull off the road and stop, be sure to turn on your emergency flashers. This is really important at night when a driver who has not seen you decides to pull off the road in the same spot. Do not trust your taillights to provide a warning. Many drivers have crashed into the rear of a parked truck simply because they were not warned properly.

**Figure 11-5**

If you are forced to stop on or near the road, you will need more than emergency flashers. Approaching drivers need advance warning to get around you. Put out reflective triangles. For better safety at night, also use flares or fusees. Do not use flares or fusees if you are carrying hazardous cargo or there is spilled fuel.

Place reflective triangles at the following locations if you must stop on an undivided highway.

**Figure 11-6**

- On the traffic side, 10 feet (4 paces) to the rear of the rig. This marks the location of the vehicle.
- About 100 feet (40 paces) behind the rig on the shoulder or in the lane in which the rig is stopped to give overtaking drivers plenty of warning.
- About 100 feet in front of the rig on the shoulder to give oncoming drivers plenty of warning.

If you must stop on a one-way or divided highway, place the triangles at the following locations.

- About 10 feet behind the rig. This will show approaching traffic the rig's location.
- About 100 feet behind the rig.
- About 200 feet (80 paces) behind the rig. This will give oncoming drivers plenty of warning there is a stopped rig.

Always also place reflective triangles beyond a hill, curve, or anything that keeps drivers of overtaking vehicles from seeing your rig when they are 500 feet away.

If you have to double-park on a city street, triangles and flares are not practical. You must, however, turn on your emergency flashers so approaching drivers will know your rig is stopped.

## SUMMARY

In this chapter, you learned the importance of communicating with other road users. You also learned that communication is a key to highway safety. The correct ways to signal a turn or lane change, slowing down, and overtaking another road user were explained. You also now know how to place warning devices correctly if you must stop your truck by the side of the road. Finally, you learned that truck drivers have a responsibility to communicate with the driving public as a whole.

## KEY WORDS

**Communication:** Telling other drivers what you are going to do.

**Reflective triangle:** A warning device carried on big rigs that is placed to warn other drivers when the rig is stopped. It is usually bright orange with red borders.

# LEARNING ACTIVITIES

## Review Questions

1.  What does communicating your intent mean? Why is it important?

    _____

    _____

2.  What are the three special rules for signaling turns? Explain each.

    _____

    _____

    _____

    _____

    _____

    _____

    _____

3.  Explain why the laws for signaling may not be safe enough in many cases.

    _____

    _____

    _____

4.  In addition to using your turn signals to communicate your intent to change lanes, what additional signal should you use? Why?

    _____

    _____

5.  Any time you slow down suddenly, you should give some warning to the driver behind you. Tell of three situations in which this would apply.

    _____

    _____

    _____

6.  If you are being slowed by hills or oversize cargo, what should you do?

    _____

    _____

7.  Why is signaling others to pass you illegal and dangerous?

    _____

    _____

8.  What does communicating your presence mean? Why is it important?

_____

_____

_____

9.  What are three situations in which communicating your presence is necessary. Explain each.

_____

_____

_____

_____

_____

_____

# DIAGRAMS

Place reflective triangles in the correct places if a rig is stopped on an undivided highway. Be sure to tell how far away from the rig the triangle is.

Place reflective triangles in the correct places if a rig is stopped and there is something to block the view of oncoming drivers. Be sure to tell how far away from the rig the triangle is.

Place reflective triangles in the correct places if a rig is stopped on a divided highway. Be sure to tell how far away from the rig the triangle is.

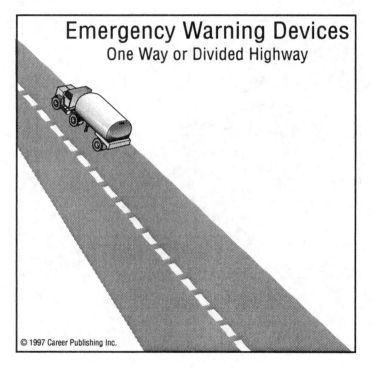

## True-False Questions

If the question is true, circle the T. If the question is false, circle the F.

T  F  1.  The major reason for using turn signals is to obey the law.

T  F  2.  Turning on your turn signal is enough communication for most situations.

T  F  3.  Reducing speed unexpectedly can create problems for drivers following your rig.

T  F  4.  Emergency flashers are helpful in filling some communication needs but are of limited use in other situations.

T  F  5.  Helping others pass you by waving them on is both courteous and proper because it can help prevent long streams of slow moving traffic behind you.

T  F  6.  Even though your vehicle is large in comparison to many others on the road, you should use special methods to let other highway users know of your presence.

T  F  7.  When stopping beside a well-traveled highway during daylight hours, your emergency flashers are enough warning for other drivers.

T  F  8.  For better safety at night, you should use flares or fusees in addition to the emergency flashers.

T  F  9.  Hills and curves present special communication problems when parking beside a roadway.

# Chapter Twelve
# SPACE MANAGEMENT

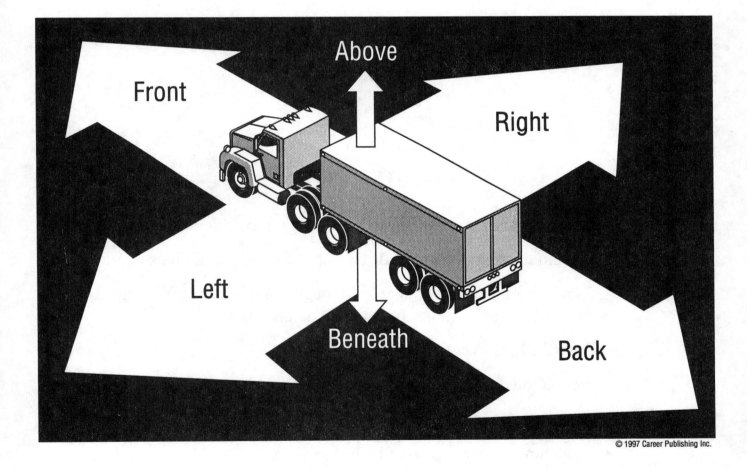

© 1997 Career Publishing Inc.

**Importance of Space Management • Space Ahead • How Much Space • Space Behind
Space to the Sides • Space Overhead • Space Below • Space for Turns
Space to Cross or Enter Traffic**

**FROM NOW ON,**

**ONLY THE BEST WILL DRIVE**

## OBJECTIVES

When you have mastered the chapter, you will be able to:

- Explain the right following distance for different conditions

- Show the importance of keeping enough room between your rig and other vehicles to be able to drive defensively

- Describe how to control your space

- Present the dangers of overhead obstructions

- Explain the correct way to make turns

- Show how to manage space in intersections

# CHAPTER TWELVE

# SPACE

# MANAGEMENT

## INTRODUCTION

What makes a good driver? An accident and ticket-free record? An undamaged vehicle? Being able to handle all driving conditions? The answer is probably yes, but there are other things a good driver does.

One of the most important things a good driver does is to keep a *cushion* of air around his or her vehicle at all times. We call this **space management**. This chapter is about managing space to make your driving smooth, comfortable, and uneventful.

## THE IMPORTANCE OF SPACE MANAGEMENT

You need space all around your vehicle — in front, to the sides, and to the rear. When things go wrong on the road, space gives you time to adjust. Many times, other vehicles will stop unexpectedly or turn in front of you. You may need space to change lanes, stop, or slow down. If, for instance, you must change lanes or swerve right or left, you will need to check your side-view mirrors. That takes time, and time requires space.

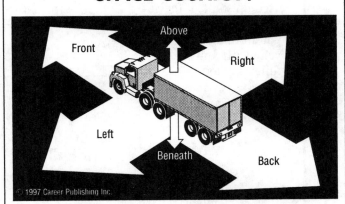

**SPACE CUSHION**

Figure 12-1

You need to be concerned with space in all directions — ahead, behind, to the sides, and even above and below. You also need to be aware of the space needed for turning, crossing roads, or entering traffic.

In order to have the space you need when something goes wrong, you need to manage space well at all times. While this is true for all road users, it is especially important for those who drive big rigs. They take up more space to begin with, and they need a great deal more space for stopping and turning.

## SPACE AHEAD

Of all the space around your rig, the space ahead is the most important. This is the amount of space you need to be able to stop.

We know from accident records that the vehicle most likely to be hit by a tractor-trailer is the one in front of it. The most common cause is that the rig follows too closely.

If the vehicle ahead of you is lighter than yours, it can stop faster and in less space than yours. That vehicle may begin to slow down without your noticing it at once. By the time you realize what is happening and decide to put on your brakes, you have used up some of the space that separates you from the other vehicle. If you are following too closely, you may not be able to avoid hitting it.

## How Much Space?

How much space do you need in front of you? A good rule is that you need 1 second for each 10 feet of your rig's length. If you are driving a 40-foot rig, leave at least 4 seconds between your front bumper and the vehicle ahead. In a 60-foot rig, leave 6 seconds.

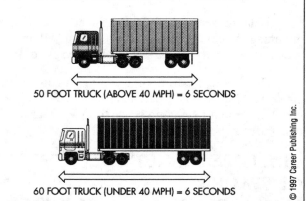

# HEAVY VEHICLE FORMULA
## For timed interval following distance

• 1 Second Required for Each 10 Feet of Vehicle Length at Speeds Under 40 MPH

• Above 40 MPH Use Same Formula. Then Add 1 Second for the Additional Speed

40 FOOT TRUCK (UNDER 40 MPH) = 4 SECONDS

50 FOOT TRUCK (ABOVE 40 MPH) = 6 SECONDS

60 FOOT TRUCK (UNDER 40 MPH) = 6 SECONDS

© 1997 Career Publishing Inc.

**Figure 12-2**

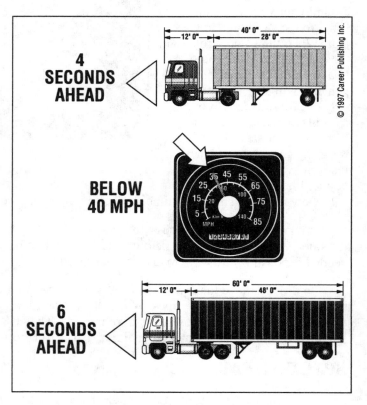

**Figure 12-3**

To measure your following distance, note when the rear end of the vehicle ahead passes a marking on the road. Then count off the seconds, 1,001, 1,002, 1,003, and so on, until the front of your rig reaches the same spot. Compare your count with the rule of 1 second for every 10 feet of your rig's length.

If you are driving a 40-foot rig and count less than 4 seconds, you are following too closely. You must drop back a bit. Then count again. Until you have at least 4 seconds of space, you are in danger, and so are all other road users near you.

For speeds above 40 mph, add 1 second to the basic amount of space needed.

---

Example: 50-foot rig traveling at 48 mph
- Basic amount of space needed — 5 seconds (50/10 = 5)
- Above 40 mph — Add 1 second

Total following distance needed — 6 seconds (5 + 1 = 6)

---

For bad weather, poor visibility, or bad road conditions, you should add at least one more second.

---

Example: 60-foot rig with poor visibility traveling at 55 mph
- Basic amount of space needed — 6 seconds (60/10 = 6)
- Above 40 mph — Add 1 second
- Poor visibility — Add 1 more second

Total following distance needed — 8 seconds (6 + 1 + 1 = 8)

---

The times listed above are the **absolute minimums** to insure:
- Seeing time
- Thinking time
- Reacting time
- Braking time

# SPACE BEHIND

As you know, you cannot completely control the space behind your rig. There are, however, a number of things you can do to control the space to the rear.
- Stay to the right
- Be careful when changing lanes
- Expect tailgating
- Respond safely to tailgaters

**Stay to the right**: Sometimes going uphill or when a load is very heavy, a rig cannot keep up with traffic. At these times, it is best to use the special truck lanes or stay as far to the right as possible. However, remember driving on the shoulder is illegal in some states.

When going uphill, do not try to pass a slower vehicle unless it can be done quickly. Being caught behind two trucks that are side by side is very annoying to other drivers.

**Changing lanes:** The length of a tractor-trailer makes it hard to judge whether a lane change can be made safely. Here are a few hints:

- When in doubt, leave plenty of space. Wait a little longer before pulling in front of the vehicle you have passed. On a multi-lane road, there is no need to rush your return to the right-hand lane.

**Figure 12-4**

- Do not always trust the signals of other drivers. They may have the best intentions, but you really have no idea what they will do.

**Anticipate tailgating:** In large vehicles, it is often hard to know when you are being tailgated. A good rule is to expect to be tailgated in these situations.

- When you are traveling slowly: Drivers trapped behind slow-moving vehicles tend to edge up close even though some states have minimum following distances.
- Bad weather: Many drivers follow large vehicles closely in bad weather, especially when visibility is poor.

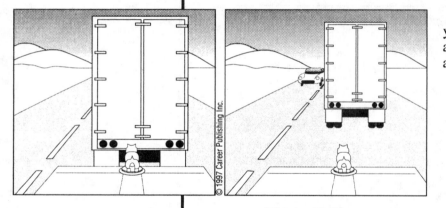

**Figure 12-5**

**Respond safely to tailgaters:** If you find yourself being tailgated, some actions can help reduce the chance of an accident.

- Reduce your speed slowly. This will encourage the tailgater to pass you.
- Avoid quick changes. If you have to slow down or turn, signal your intentions early and make the change very slowly.
- Increase your following distance. Arrange for more space in front of your rig. This will help you avoid having to make sudden changes in speed or direction. It also makes it easier for a tailgater to get around you.
- Do not speed up. Tailgaters often tend to stay close no matter how fast you go. It is better to be tailgated at a low speed than a high speed.
- Avoid tricks. Do not turn on your headlights or flash your brake lights to shake up the tailgater. You could make the situation worse by angering or confusing him or her.

## SPACE TO THE SIDES

The wider the vehicle, the less space it has to the sides. To protect yourself on both sides, you need to manage space with care. To do this, keep your rig centered in your lane. Avoid driving alongside others. Overtake and pass others carefully.

## Staying Centered in the Lane

There is usually little more than a foot between the sides of your trailer and the edges of the lane in which you are driving. Keeping the rig centered is important for safety.

Keep as much space to the sides as possible. Concentrate on keeping your vehicle centered whenever you are meeting, passing, or being passed by another vehicle.

Do not move to the right simply because of an approaching vehicle. This may put you too close to the other side of your lane. Of course, you must try to avoid an oncoming vehicle if it moves over into your lane.

Check your mirrors often to be sure the trailer has not drifted out of line. If it has, get in front of it and pull it back into the center of the lane.

## Traveling Beside Others

Two dangerous situations can develop any time you travel alongside other vehicles:
1. Another driver may change lanes suddenly and turn directly into you.
2. You may need to change lanes and find there is no opening. You are trapped.

The best way to avoid either situation is not to *travel with the pack*. Find an open spot where you have the road pretty much to yourself. Of course, there are times when traffic is so heavy you cannot find an open spot. Then you have no choice except to be alert and careful. If you have to travel near other vehicles, stay out of their blind spots. Drop back or pull forward so the other drivers can see you.

## SPACE OVERHEAD

Hitting overhead objects is a major cause of damage — both to rigs and done by them. Make sure you have enough space above your rig at all times.

Most overhead collisions are with low-hanging wires, marquees, signs, and air-conditioning units. Check the heights of any overhead structures before driving under them. If there is any doubt about

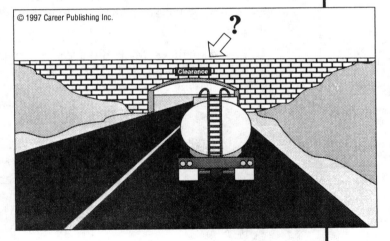

**Figure 12-6**

being able to pass below an object, slow down and drive very carefully. If any question remains, stop, get out, and check the clearance.

Do not rely entirely on posted heights at bridges and overpasses. Repaved roads or packed snow may have reduced the clearance since the signs were posted.

The weight of the vehicle affects its height. The fact that you were able to drive under a bridge when you were fully loaded does not mean that you can do it on the return trip when your rig is empty or lightly loaded.

Sometimes your rig may tilt toward the side of the road because of a high crown or different levels of paving. You may not clear signs, trees, or other objects along the side of the road. When this is a problem, drive a little closer to the center of the road.

Backing can be very troublesome. Before you back into an area, get out and check any overhanging structures. It is easy not to see them while you are backing.

## SPACE BELOW

Many drivers overlook the importance of the space beneath their rigs. That space can be *squeezed* when a vehicle is heavily loaded and the springs are compressed. The space below is especially important when you are driving low-bed hauling equipment. Some of the situations where there may not be enough clearance beneath the rig are listed below.

**Railroad tracks:** Railroad tracks can extend inches above the surface of the road. This is often a problem on dirt roads and in unpaved yards where the surface around the tracks can wear away. Do not take the chance of getting hung up halfway across. Get out and measure the clearance.

**Soft surfaces:** One way to lose clearance is to sink down until the truck frame is resting on the surface. Make sure it will hold the weight of your truck before driving onto the surface.

**Shopping center parking lots**: Many parking lots are not made for large, heavy trucks. Look for signs indicating weight limits. If you have to make a shopping center delivery, check ahead to be sure the surface can handle your loaded rig.

**Unpaved surfaces**: Many dirt surfaces will support your truck in good weather but not in bad weather. After a rainstorm, dirt can turn quickly to mud. Check before driving onto unpaved surfaces, especially if they are covered with grass or gravel. They may not be as firm as they look.

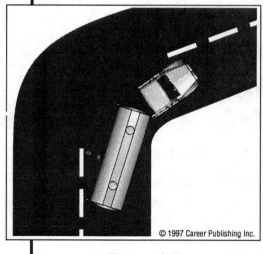

© 1997 Career Publishing Inc.

**Figure 12-7**

**Excavated areas**: Excavated areas can be dangerous for big rigs. They may be covered over with planks that will not hold a truck. Sometimes they are filled in with loose dirt. Use care when you have to drive near road work or construction.

## SPACE FOR TURNS

Having enough room on the sides of your rig when you turn is important. Because of their wide turning radius and off-tracking, trucks frequently sideswipe other vehicles or run over things during turns.

## Right Turns

Because most right turns are tighter than the turning radius of your truck, you have to swing a little wide for a successful turn. Timing is a key factor. Stay to the right as long as possible if you have to swing out to the left for the turn. Otherwise, the driver of a vehicle following you may not realize you plan to turn and will try to move by you on the right. These steps can be useful:

- Approach the intersection in the right lane.
- Switch on your right turn signal.
- Swing left just as you approach the intersection.
- Turn sharply to the right.

Timing the left swing is critical. Wait until the last possible moment. You can keep people from passing on the right by staying to the right and using your trailer to block traffic. If you do this, by the time the trailer begins to move left, the tractor will be well into the turn and will keep anyone from passing.

If the turn is particularly sharp or difficult, swing out into the street you are about to enter. Watch your off-tracking to avoid running over the curb or a grassy area. Grassy areas often hide things, such as sprinkler heads. Return to the right lane as soon as possible. Remember, it is better to make three left turns to get onto the street you want than to endanger others.

## Left Turns

When you make a left turn, be sure you reach the center of the intersection before turning left. If you turn too soon, the side of the trailer, as it off-tracks, may hit an object or a vehicle waiting to enter the intersection.

**Left Turns from Two Lanes:** The choice of lanes is very important in a left turn. If there are two turning lanes, use the right lane. If you start in the left lane, you will have to swing out in order to make the turn. A driver on your right may not expect you to turn and may drive into the side of your rig. Keep traffic in the next lane on the sight side where you see it best. A vehicle to your right is very hard to see.

## SPACE TO CROSS OR ENTER TRAFFIC

New drivers often do not allow for the size and weight of their rigs when they cross or enter into traffic. Remember these things.

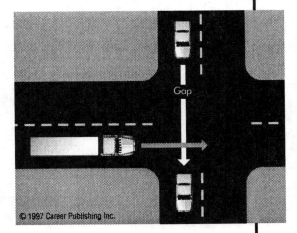

**Figure 12-8**

- Because your rig accelerates slowly, it requires more space than a smaller, more responsive vehicle. You need a much larger gap than a car does to cross or enter traffic.
- Acceleration varies with the weight of the vehicle. Allow more room if you have a heavy load.
- Before you start across a street, think about the length of the rig. Make sure there is enough space for you to clear the intersection completely.

## SUMMARY

In this chapter, you learned there is space all around your tractor-trailer. There is space in front of it, behind it, to both the right and left sides, and above and below the vehicle. You also learned the types of hazards you may encounter if you do not manage these spaces correctly. You were taught how to determine time and turn it into distance, thus being able to decide if you are a safe distance from another road user. The types of road surfaces that may present a danger were described. Finally, you learned how to make both right and left turns correctly and enter or cross traffic safely.

## KEY WORD

**Space management:** Keeping a *cushion* of air around the rig at all times.

# LEARNING ACTIVITIES

## Review Questions

1. Of all the space around your vehicle, which is the most important? Why?

   _____

   _____

2. When driving a big rig, what is the general rule for how much space to have in front of the vehicle?

   _____

   _____

   _____

3. If you are driving a 60-foot rig at 55 mph on a clear day, how much following distance should you maintain?

   _____

   _____

4. What can you do to help keep enough space behind your vehicle?

   _____

   _____

   _____

5. Does the weight of your load affect the trailer's height? Explain.

   _____

   _____

   _____

6. When making a right turn, what should you do to make sure you have enough space?

   _____

   _____

7.   Describe how to make a left turn in a tractor-trailer?

_____

_____

_____

8.   When you are turning left and there is more than one turning lane, which lane should you use? Why?

_____

_____

9.   You need a much larger gap to cross or enter traffic with a tractor-trailer than with an automobile. Why?

_____

_____

## True-False Questions

Circle the T if the statement is true. Circle the F if the statement is false.

T  F   1.   Space management is keeping a cushion of air around your rig.

T  F   2.   Because bridges and overpasses have carefully posted heights, drivers of big rigs do not have to worry about hitting them.

T  F   3.   When we speak of space when driving, we are also talking about time.

T  F   4.   The most common cause of rear-ending another vehicle is following too closely.

T  F   5.   The space in front of your rig is the only area you need to be concerned with in managing the space around your rig.

T  F   6.   When making a right turn, one of the most dangerous things faced by the driver is striking a vehicle that tries to pass on the right during the turn.

T  F   7.   Left turns are safe because the driver has a good view of the space all around the rig.

T  F   8.   The only space that is constant and unchanging is the space under the rig.

## Special Activity

Explain the reason for your answer to true-false statement number 3.

_____

_____

_____

_____

_____

_____

_____

_____

# Chapter Thirteen
# SPEED MANAGEMENT

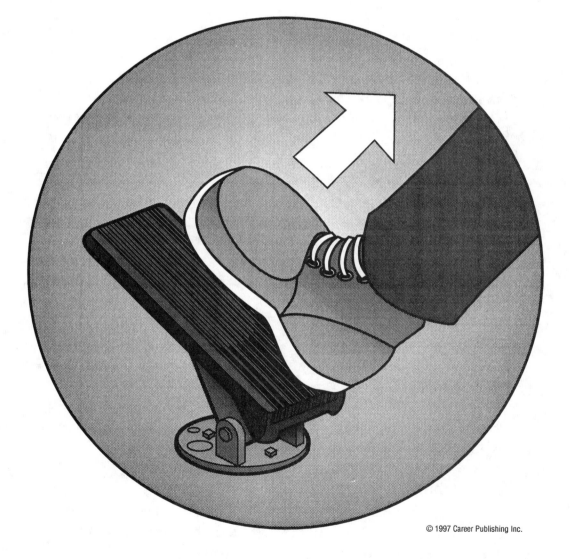

**Speed and Stopping Distance • Road Surfaces • Hydroplaning • Taking Curves • Hills • Speed and Your Field of Vision • Night Driving • Bad Weather • Speed and Traffic**

FROM NOW ON,

ONLY THE BEST WILL DRIVE

# OBJECTIVES

When you have mastered the chapter, you will be able to:

- Explain the relationship of speed to:
  Stopping distance
  Hydroplaning
  Accidents
  Ability to control the rig
  Fuel economy

- Discuss the effect of speed on:
  The rig's weight
  The rig's center of gravity
  Loss of stability

- Show how the driver's available sight distance and the road
  surface conditions affect choosing a safe speed

# CHAPTER THIRTEEN

# SPEED MANAGEMENT

## INTRODUCTION

The word speed usually suggests quickness. **Speed** is really the rate of motion of your rig. You can be driving at a high speed or low speed. What may be thought of as speedy or swift in some cases may be quite moderate in others.

In this chapter, we will discuss how speed must be adjusted to each traffic condition. Distances are given but they are only approximate and not exact. They will help you understand the principles of speed management.

As the driver of a big rig, you must use your best judgment while in traffic. There is no place in this profession for cowboys or show offs.

## SPEED AND STOPPING DISTANCE

**Speeding** is defined as exceeding, or driving faster than, the legal or posted speed limit. You also speed when you drive too fast for the conditions. The second part of the definition — *driving too fast for the conditions* — is harder to define, but just as important.

Managing speed is a big part of driving safely. The faster you go, the less time you have to react to what is happening around you. Conditions can change in a split second.

The faster you go, the longer it will take you to stop. It takes over eight times more distance to stop at 50 mph than it does at 15 mph. The following chart will give you an idea of the distance it takes to stop a tractor-trailer on dry pavement. Remember, the distances are not exact.

| Miles Per Hour | How Far the Rig Will Travel in One Second | Driver Reaction Distance | Vehicle Braking Distance | Total Stopping Distance |
|---|---|---|---|---|
| 15 mph | 22 ft. | 17 ft. | 29 ft. | 46 ft. |
| 30 mph | 44 ft. | 33 ft. | 115 ft. | 148 ft. |
| 45 mph | 66 ft. | 50 ft. | 260 ft. | 310 ft. |
| 50 mph | 73 ft. | 55 ft. | 320 ft. | 375 ft. |
| 55 mph | 81 ft. | 61 ft. | 390 ft. | 451 ft. |

The three distances are defined as:

**Driver Reaction Distance**: The distance your rig travels during the time you identify a hazard to the time you apply the brakes.

© 1997 Career Publishing Inc.

Empty trucks need greater stopping distances because an empty vehicle has less traction. The brakes, tires, springs, and shock absorbers on heavy vehicles are designed to work best when the vehicle is fully loaded.

**Figure 13-1**

**Vehicle Braking Distance**: The distance your rig travels from the time you apply pressure to the brake pedal until the rig stops.

**Total Stopping Distance**: The driver reaction distance plus the vehicle braking distance.

The weight of the rig as well as how well the brakes are working will affect the braking distance.

There is no speed that will always be a safe speed. Speed must be adjusted to the conditions. These conditions can and do change often during a trip — even a short one.

# ROAD SURFACES

To steer your rig or stop it, you need **traction**. Traction is the contact between your tires and the road surface. Sometimes, it is defined as the *grip* of the tires on the road. Some road surfaces keep the tires from having good traction. Then you must slow down. The sections that follow discuss some of these surfaces.

© 1997 Career Publishing Inc.

THE POINTS OF FRICTION (TRACTION) BETWEEN THE TIRES AND ROAD ARE SMALL

**Figure 13-2**

**Slippery Surfaces**: It takes longer to stop when the road surface is slippery. It is also harder to turn your rig. This is because the tires lose their grip on the road. If you are to control your rig, slow down when the road is slippery. This is called **managing your speed**.

If your rig has antilock brakes, do not expect to stop any quicker. All antilock brakes do is allow you to stay in control while braking.

How much you slow down depends on the conditions. If the surface is wet, you need to reduce your speed by about one-fourth. If you are driving 55 mph, slow down to about 40 mph. On packed snow, reduce speed by about one-half. That means at 55 mph, you slow to about 28 mph.

If the surface is icy, you will need to cut back speed by about two-thirds. At 55 mph, you slow to about 18 mph. The following chart tells, generally, the speed that will let you drive safely in different kinds of bad weather.

| Normal Driving Speed | Driving in Rain | Driving in Snow | Driving on Ice |
|---|---|---|---|
| 55 mph | 40 mph | 28 mph | 18 mph |
| 50 mph | 35 mph | 25 mph | 17 mph |
| 45 mph | 33 mph | 23 mph | 15 mph |
| 40 mph | 30 mph | 20 mph | 13 mph |

## Identifying Slippery Surfaces

Sometimes it is hard to know if a road is slippery. Certain clues can help you identify bad spots. When you see any of the following, slow down!

**Shaded area:** When the sun begins to melt the ice and snow, the shaded areas of the road stay icy long after the open areas are clear. Examples are around bridges and trees.

**Bridges:** Because air can circulate over, under, and around bridges, they tend to freeze more quickly than other parts of the road. Be very careful when the temperature is right around $32^0$. When the ice begins to melt, bridges will be wet and even more slippery.

**Figure 13-3**

**Black ice:** A thin layer of ice clear enough to let you see the road underneath is called *black ice*. It makes the road look wet. Any time it is below freezing and the road looks wet, watch out for black ice. Another way of detecting black ice is to watch tire spray. If it disappears when the weather is cold enough, you may be on black ice.

On rainy days when the temperature is near or below freezing, look for ice beginning to form on your vehicle. An easy way to check for ice is to open the window and feel the front of the mirror. If you feel ice, the road surface is probably getting icy. Ice build-up on the antennas of other vehicles is another sign.

**Just after rain begins:** When rain begins to fall after a period of dry weather, it mixes with dirt, grit, oil, and other road particles. Then the surface becomes very slippery. For the first 15 minutes of rain, the road will be very slippery. On hot days, this is a special problem on asphalt roads because the oil tends to rise to the surface. This is called bleeding tar. As the rain continues, the mixture is washed away. When there are leaves on the road, they are very slippery — even after the rain has stopped — from the oil and water trapped between them and the surface of the road.

## Hydroplaning

When water and slush collect, your wheels may lose contact with the road. This loss of traction is called **hydroplaning**. It is much like water skiing. A thin film of water separates the tires from the road and your rig simply slides along the water. Under these conditions, you lose much of your ability to steer, brake, or control the rig.

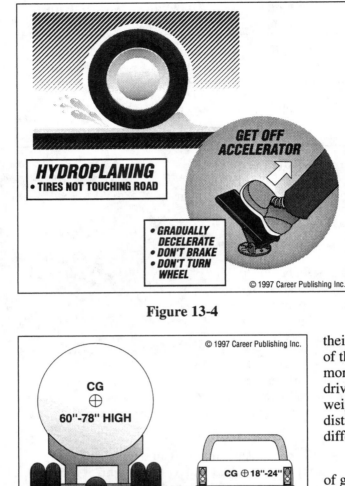

**Figure 13-4**

Your rig can hydroplane on even a very thin layer of water. Usually it occurs at higher speeds, but it can happen at speeds below 30 mph. This will depend on how much water is on the road and the condition of your tires.

# TAKING CURVES

## The Center of Gravity

All drivers must adjust their speed to the condition of the road. This is even more important when you are driving a big rig. How the weight of the load is distributed also makes a difference.

How high your center of gravity is will help decide your speed when you take curves. One layer of crates of equal weight will keep the

**Figure 13-5**

center of gravity lower than the same number of crates stacked on top of each other in an 8-foot stack. The higher the load is stacked, the higher the center of gravity. The higher the center of gravity, the more likely the rig will be to tip over during turns. How the load is secured is also important. A shifting load can cause serious problems of control for the driver.

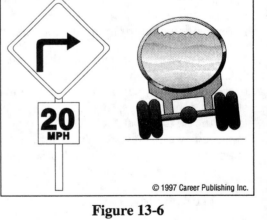

**Figure 13-6**

## Adjusting Your Speed

Trying to take a curve too fast can cause you to lose control. This happens in one of two ways.

1. The wheels lose traction and continue straight ahead. This is a skid.
2. The wheels may keep their traction, but the rig will not turn. This can cause a rollover.

Braking in a curve is dangerous because the wheels can lock. Slow to a safe speed before entering a curve. Ease off the accelerator or downshift. If you downshift, slow down enough before you shift to be in the bottom of a usable engine rpm when you shift. This will allow you to speed up when you need to. You can then speed up slightly in the curve. This will help keep your rig stable. When you are through the curve, bring your rig back up to speed.

## HILLS

### Adjusting Your Speed

**Gravity** affects speed on upgrades and downgrades. On upgrades, your rig is working against gravity. To maintain speed, you must increase pressure on the accelerator.

Going downhill, your vehicle is working with gravity to increase your speed. You must be careful to slow your rig to a safe speed to keep it under control. This will be discussed in detail in a later chapter.

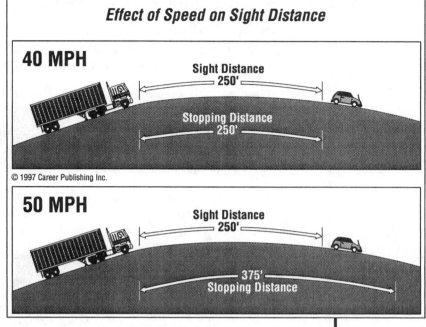

**Figure 13-7**

## HOW FAR CAN YOU SEE?

How far you can see and your field of vision require speed adjustments. You must adjust your speed to how well you can see ahead of your rig. Driving at 45 mph, you will need 310 feet to stop your rig. If, because of fog or rain, you can see ahead only 100 feet, you are in a dangerous situation. Imagine a stalled vehicle on the road just beyond the limit of your vision! A general guideline is that you should always be able to stop within the distance you can see ahead.

### Night Driving

You can apply the same general guideline to night driving. Low beams let you see about 250 feet ahead. If you drive faster than 40 mph at night with low beams, you will not be able to stop in time to keep from hitting something that

**Figure 13-8**

suddenly appears on the road in front of you.

## Bad Weather

Heavy rain, snow, fog, and smog can reduce your visibility a great deal. Really bad conditions can limit what you see ahead to a very few feet. You must slow down as much as you need to drive safely. Remember, when it is hard for you to see other vehicles, other drivers are having trouble seeing you.

## Speed and the Field of Vision

Your **field of vision** includes everything you can see (front and both sides) while looking straight ahead. The faster you go, the less you can see to the sides. As your speed increases, your field of vision decreases.

In order to see something clearly, you must stop your eyes from moving and fix them on the object you want to see. Try this experiment.
- Look in a mirror.
- Try to see your eyeballs move.

That's right! You can see them only when they stop moving.

Remember this when you are looking for cross traffic or at the scene around you. Moving eyes do not see clearly. You cannot react to what you do not see. You cannot see it if you are not looking at it. Fix your eyes where you want to see.

## SPEED AND TRAFFIC

The safest speed in traffic is usually the same speed other vehicles are going. Accidents happen more often when vehicles are traveling at different rates. As a general rule, it is best to blend with other traffic. Adjust your speed to match that of others. Some drivers try to save time by speeding. This really does not pay because:
- Speeding is risky and often leads to accidents.
- When there is other traffic, you usually cannot save more than a couple of minutes in an hour of driving.

It simply is not worth the extra risk to speed.

If you drive faster than the other traffic:
- You will have to pass many other vehicles. Each time you change lanes to pass, there is the risk of an accident.
- You become more tired from driving.
- You will be more likely to attract the attention of the police or highway patrol.
- You will waste fuel and increase the wear on your brakes.
  Going with the flow is safer, easier, and cheaper.

## SUMMARY

Now that you have completed this chapter, you have learned the importance of speed management. You now understand and can explain the relationship of speed to stopping distance, hydroplaning, fuel economy, and accidents. You have also learned how speed affects your ability to control the rig. Because you have completed this chapter, you can now discuss the effect of speed on the rig's weight and center of gravity and loss of stability. You can also show how the driver's available sight distance and the road surface conditions affect choosing a safe speed.

# KEY WORDS

**Black ice:** A thin layer of ice clear enough to let you see the road underneath.

**Driver reaction distance**: The distance your rig travels during the time it takes to identify a hazard.

**Field of vision**: Everything you can see (front and both sides) while looking straight ahead.

**Gravity**: The force that pulls things toward the center of the earth.

**Hydroplaning**: A road condition in which a thin film of water separates the tires from the road and the rig simply slides along on top of the water.

**Managing your speed**: Adjusting your speed for the road, weather, and traffic conditions.

**Speed**: The rate of motion of your rig.

**Speeding**: Driving faster than the legal or posted speed limit or driving too fast for the conditions.

**Total stopping distance**: The driver reaction distance plus the vehicle braking distance.

**Traction**: The contact between the tires and the road surface.

**Vehicle braking distance**: The distance your rig travels from the time you apply pressure to the brake pedal until the rig stops.

# LEARNING ACTIVITIES

## Review Questions

1. What is speeding?

   _____

   _____


2. What are the two parts of stopping distance? Explain each.

   _____

   _____

   _____

   _____


3. Name two things besides speed that affect braking distance.

   _____

   _____


4. What is black ice?

   _____


5. What happens when your rig hydroplanes?

   _____

   _____

6.   What are two things that can happen if you enter a curve too fast?

_____

_____

7.   What is the best rule to follow about seeing and speed? Explain the rule and give an example.

_____

_____

_____

8.   What is a driver's field of vision?

_____

_____

9.   How does speed affect your field of vision?

_____

_____

10.   What is the safest speed when driving in traffic?

_____

_____

## Case Study

This is an outline of a trip in which two drivers followed the same route for 1,000 miles.

| **Driver A** | **Driver B** |
|---|---|
| Drove as fast as possible | Adhered to the speed limit |
| Driving time: 20 hours and 12 minutes | Driving time: 20 hours and 43 minutes |
| Braked 1,339 times | Braked 645 times |
| Overtook 2,004 vehicles | Overtook 645 vehicles |
| Four emergency stops | No emergency stops |

Do these figures suggest anything about:

Time and speed?

_____

_____

Fuel economy and speed?

_____

_____

Safety and speed?

_____

_____

What could have happened by having to pass so many other vehicles?

_____

What possible damage to the rig could have happened?

_____

_____

Why did the carrier possibly have to pay an extra cost for this trip?

_____

_____

For what traffic violations could the driver have been cited?

_____

_____

_____

_____

## True-False Questions ✓

Circle the T if the statement is true. Circle the F if the statement is false.

**T** F 1. The total stopping distance is the driver reaction distance plus the vehicle braking distance.

**T** F 2. Traction is the contact between the tires and the road.

T **F** 3. Hydroplaning is not like water skiing.

T **F** 4. Your control of the rig depends on the tires keeping a good grip on the road.

T **F** 5. Keeping the brakes applied in a curve is wise because it can cancel out the effects of a top heavy load.

**T** F 6. Very little time can be saved by speeding on long trips.

T **F** 7. Your field of vision increases as you speed up.

T **F** 8. The safest speed in traffic is the same speed as most other vehicles are traveling.

**T** F 9. A person who drives according to the existing conditions and within the posted speed limits is managing speed properly.

**T** F 10. Your field of vision includes everything in front and on both sides that you can see.

# Chapter Fourteen
# NIGHT DRIVING

© 1997 Career Publishing Inc.

**Night Driving Factors • Lack of Experience • Your Vehicle • Night Driving Procedures • Night Driving Adjustments**

FROM NOW ON,

ONLY THE BEST WILL DRIVE

# OBJECTIVES

When you have mastered this chapter, you will be able to:

- Show how the amount of light affects your ability to see

- Describe the need for and use of high-beam headlights

- Present the three factors that most affect night driving
    1. The driver
    2. The road
    3. The rig

- Detail how to get your rig ready for night driving

- Explain how headlight glare can cut the vision of other drivers

- Describe the general factors affecting night vision

- Show how sunglasses help night vision

## CHAPTER FOURTEEN

# NIGHT DRIVING

## INTRODUCTION

Night driving presents problems that require special attention by the driver. Changes occur in:
- Inspection routines
- Scan and search
- Communication
- Speed control
- Space management

This chapter will tell you how to meet the special demands of night driving.

## NIGHT DRIVING FACTORS

You cannot see as well at night because there is less light. In order to see possible hazards, you must be closer to them. Not being aware of this simple fact causes more than one-half of all traffic accidents to occur at night. Four factors contribute to the night driving problem.
1. Driver
2. Road
3. Vehicle
4. Weather

### The Driver

As a beginning tractor-trailer driver, you should be aware of factors that can affect your driving at night. They include:
- Vision
- Glare
- Fatigue
- Lack of experience

### Vision

Eyes need time to adjust to the change between daylight and darkness. Even after they adjust, you cannot see as well at night as you can during the day. Things are harder to make out. You cannot see as well to the sides. In other words, you have limited vision at night.

### Glare

Glare from oncoming headlights and other lights can cause temporary blindness. Recovering from glare takes time. Unfortunately, while your eyes recover, you and your rig are moving along the road.

## Fatigue

Fatigue is always a concern when you drive, but more so at night. You do not see as clearly when you are tired. You become less alert, are slower to see hazards, and you do not react as quickly.

## Lack of Experience

Lack of experience driving a rig and the problems of reduced vision, glare, and fatigue help to account for the fact that

Figure 14-1

new drivers have higher nighttime accident rates than more experienced drivers. You must learn how to adjust your:
- Speed
- Space management
- Driving techniques

to night conditions as soon as possible.

## The Road

Five road conditions can affect night driving. They are:
1. Low-level light at night
2. Changes in levels of light
3. How well you know the road
4. Other road users
5. Drivers who are under the influence of alcohol or drugs

**Low-level Light at Night:** Lighting on two-lane roads depends on headlights. Headlights are useful for a short and narrow path directly ahead of your vehicle. They do not bend around corners. Much of the light from streetlights is fair to poor.

**Changes in levels of light:** You must adjust your eyes to different types and degrees of light all of the time. Flashing lights distract as much as they illuminate. Traffic signals are hard to see against a background of other lights in towns and cities.

Going through a business district in the rain can be very difficult because of the extra glare. You may also need extra stopping distance.

**How Well You Know the Road:** You need to be extra alert on roads you have never driven during the day. Do not take even familiar roads for granted. Your view of the road will not be the same at night. Situations on the same road will also change.

**Other Road Users:** Some other road users are not easily seen at night. They include pedestrians, joggers, bicyclists, and animals. All are hazards, and you must watch for them.

**Drivers Who Are Under the Influence:** It is always possible to meet a driver on the road who is under the influence of drugs or alcohol. Your chance of meeting one increases after sundown. Keep this in mind when driving past roadside taverns and similar places.

## Your Vehicle

As a driver, you must be sure your rig is safe for night driving. Check the:

- Headlights
- Auxiliary lights
- Turn signals
- Windshield
- Side windows
- Rearview mirrors

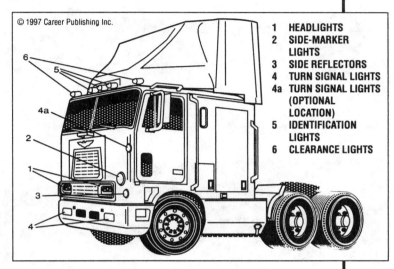

© 1997 Career Publishing Inc.

| 1 | HEADLIGHTS |
| 2 | SIDE-MARKER LIGHTS |
| 3 | SIDE REFLECTORS |
| 4 | TURN SIGNAL LIGHTS |
| 4a | TURN SIGNAL LIGHTS (OPTIONAL LOCATION) |
| 5 | IDENTIFICATION LIGHTS |
| 6 | CLEARANCE LIGHTS |

**Figure 14-2**

**Headlights:** Your tractor's headlights are the best source of light for you to see. They are also the main sign to other road users of your rig's location. Be sure your headlights are clean and properly adjusted.

The distance you can see ahead is much less at night than during the day. Low beam headlights light a path about 250 feet ahead of your rig (less than the length of a football field). High beams light 350 to 500 feet.

Your sight distance is limited to the range of your headlights. You must drive at a speed that will allow you to stop within your sight distance. If your speed is greater than this, you are *overdriving* your headlights. Driving within your headlight or sight distance is your best bet for avoiding accidents with objects or other road users.

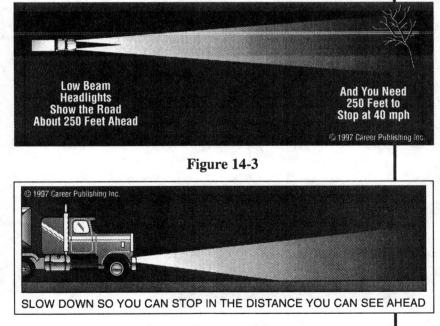

Low Beam Headlights Show the Road About 250 Feet Ahead

And You Need 250 Feet to Stop at 40 mph

© 1997 Career Publishing Inc.

**Figure 14-3**

© 1997 Career Publishing Inc.

SLOW DOWN SO YOU CAN STOP IN THE DISTANCE YOU CAN SEE AHEAD

**Figure 14-4**

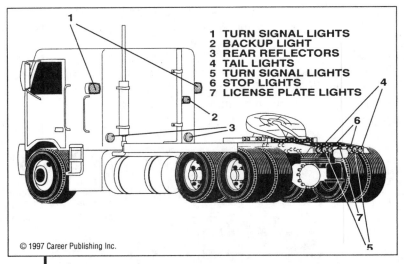

1 TURN SIGNAL LIGHTS
2 BACKUP LIGHT
3 REAR REFLECTORS
4 TAIL LIGHTS
5 TURN SIGNAL LIGHTS
6 STOP LIGHTS
7 LICENSE PLATE LIGHTS

© 1997 Career Publishing Inc.

**Figure 14-5**

**Figure 14-6**

**Auxiliary Lights:** When all lights are working, big rigs can be easily seen by other highway users. The following lights must be clean and working.

- Reflectors
- Marker lights
- Clearance lights
- Taillights
- ID lights
- Brake lights

**Turn Signals:** How well you can communicate with other road users depends on your turn signals. Turn signal lights that are not working or are dirty do not let you tell your intent. This increases the risk of an accident.

**Windshield:** A clean windshield is a must for safe driving. Even a clean windshield shuts out 5% of the available light. Dirty windshields block light. They also cut your ability to see and relate to traffic. Clean the inside and outside of the windshield so you can see as well as possible.

**Mirrors:** Mirrors help you see what is going on around you. Unless you can see the other vehicles, you cannot relate to the other road users. Be sure to keep your mirrors clean and properly adjusted at all times.

**Figure 14-7**

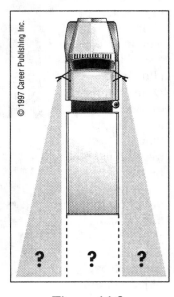

**Figure 14-8**

# NIGHT DRIVING PROCEDURES

Before you attempt to drive at night, you must prepare yourself and your rig. If you wear glasses, be sure they are clean. Dirty or scratched glasses increase the effects of glare. Do not wear sunglasses at night. Wear sunglasses during the day, when you must also drive that night, to help your night vision. Your eyes will need less time to adjust to the darkness.

Plan your route. Know where the rest stops are. Think ahead to known hazards along your route. Where are the:
- Unlighted areas?
- Exit ramps?
- Construction areas?

Keep your eyes open for new changes.

Check all lights on the rig. Clean them or replace them as needed. Make a pre-trip inspection.

## Do Not Blind Other Drivers

Headlight glare from oncoming and following vehicles can be a problem. The Federal Motor Carrier Safety (FMCS) regulation says a driver must dim the headlights 500 feet before meeting an oncoming vehicle. This regulation meets all state laws as well. It is also common sense to be considerate. If your lights make it hard for an oncoming driver to see, you and your rig are in danger.

Dim your headlights before they bother other drivers. Although not required by FMCS regs, you should also dim your headlights 200 feet before overtaking another vehicle. In addition to helping others, this action meets most state laws.

## Avoid Blinding Yourself

Keep the inside of the cab as dark as you can. Adjust the instrument panel lights to a low level. Yet be sure they are bright enough to read them easily. Keep the dome light off! The brighter the inside of the cab, the harder it is to see outside.

Use high-beam headlights when it is safe and legal to do so. Many drivers always drive with low beams. This seriously cuts down their vision. Most nighttime accidents happen because a driver cannot see. Always try to give yourself the best night vision.

Take advantage of headlights from the vehicles ahead to spot hazards. Let road signs and reflectors act as visual guides.

USE HIGH BEAMS WHEN SAFE AND LEGAL TO DO SO

© 1997 Career Publishing Inc.

**Figure 14-9**

## NIGHT DRIVING ADJUSTMENTS

Some basic driving techniques must be modified for nighttime driving.

**Communicating**: Make sure your signals to reduce speed, stop, or turn are clear and in time. It is wise to signal earlier than you do during the daytime.

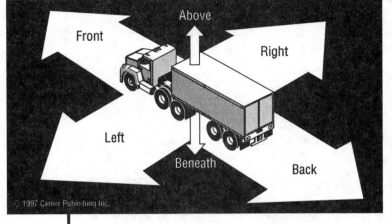

**Figure 14-10**

Check to be sure your taillights, back-up lights, and turn signal lights are working.

Signal your presence since eye contact is not possible at night. Light use of the horn can be helpful. Do not hurt the vision of others by using your headlights to signal.

**Space**: Since you cannot see as well or as far at night, you need more time to react to events around your rig. Get the needed time by increasing the space around your rig. Increase your following distance at night by at least one second more than the normal daytime following distance (review Chapter 12, Space Management).

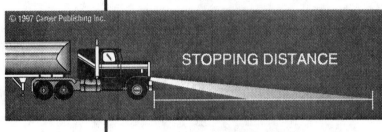

**Figure 14-11**

**Speed**: Adjust your rig's speed to keep the stopping distance within the sight distance. Do not overdrive your headlights. The lower speed is needed to keep from hitting objects after they come into view. If you do not adjust your speed to nighttime conditions, you will have too little time and space to react to hazards.

## SUMMARY

In this chapter, you have learned there are many differences between driving during daylight hours and driving at night. You learned that the inspection routines must be altered, communication with other drivers must be done by signaling because you cannot have eye contact at night. You also learned that you must slow down so that you will be able to stop within the distance you can see ahead. The reasons for allowing more space around the tractor-trailer were explained. Finally, you learned that the changes while driving at night are made for safety. As a responsible professional truck driver, you want to create the safest conditions on the road that you can for yourself and for other drivers.

## KEY WORDS

**Fatigue**: Being weary and tired.

**Glare**: Shine with a harsh light.

**Overdriving**: Driving at a speed that will not let you stop within your sight distance.

**Vision**: The ability to see, or sight.

# LEARNING ACTIVITIES

## Review Questions

1. What are the four driver factors that affect night driving?

   _____

   _____

   _____

   _____

2. What are the five road factors that affect the way you drive at night?

   _____

   _____

   _____

   _____

   _____

3. How far ahead will your low beam headlights project light?

   _____

4. Explain the phrase *overdriving your headlights.*

   _____

   _____

5. FMCS Regulations say you must dim your headlights before meeting oncoming vehicles. When must you dim them? Why is this important to other drivers? To you?

   _____

   _____

   _____

   _____

6. How does wearing sunglasses during the day, when you must also drive that night, affect night vision?

   _____

   _____

7. In overtaking another vehicle, when should you dim your headlights? Why?

   _____

   _____

   _____

8.    What should you do to keep from being blinded by the headlights of oncoming vehicles?

     _____

     _____

9.    Name two things you can do to improve your visibility when driving at night.

     _____

     _____

10.   Why are signaling your presence and what you intend to do more important at night?

     _____

     _____

11.   How should following distance be adjusted at night?

     _____

     _____

12.   Why should you drive at a lower speed at night?

     _____

     _____

## True-False Questions ✓

Circle the T if the statement is true. Circle the F if the statement is false.

T **(F)**   1.   At night, low-beam headlights let you see about 350 feet ahead of your rig.

**(T)** F   2.   High-beam headlights let you see about 350 to 500 feet ahead of your rig.

**(T)** F   3.   The FMCSR say you must dim your headlights 500 feet before meeting an oncoming vehicle.

**(T)** F   4.   You should dim your headlights 200 feet before overtaking another vehicle.

**(T)** F   5.   If your speed keeps you from stopping within the distance you can see ahead, you are overdriving your headlights.

## Discussion Topic

Break into small groups of three to five people. Create a driving situation of about 100 miles that includes city, highway, and rural driving. List the conditions a driver may encounter, such as pedestrians, an accident, narrow streets, etc. Describe how he or she may have to adjust for night driving. Do not leave out any small details when telling how the driver will have to react. Include the proper speed for each incident.

After you have created the situation and sent the driver through it, come back together as a class. Each group can then share with the others their situation and the driver's reaction to it. Ask each other questions. Share other possible solutions to the problems that were created.

# Chapter Fifteen
# EXTREME DRIVING CONDITIONS

**Extreme Weather • Vehicle Checks • Weather Reports and Road Conditions • Tire Chains
Starting Your Engine in Cold Weather • Engines That Won't Start • Bad Weather Operating
Hazards • Skidding • Slippery Surfaces • Wet Brakes • Freeing a Stuck Rig • Towing
Breaking Down in a Remote Area • Hot Weather Driving • Desert Driving • Mountain
Driving • Auxiliary Brakes and Speed Retarders • Escape Ramps**

FROM NOW ON,

ONLY THE BEST WILL DRIVE

# OBJECTIVES

When you have mastered this chapter, you will be able to:

- Discuss conditions that reduce traction, such as rain, snow, ice, and mud

- Show the effects of rain, snow, and ice on your ability to control your rig

- Describe the causes of skidding and jackknifing and how to avoid them

- Show the effects of ice, snow, water, mud, and debris on the rig's brakes

- Understand hot weather driving procedures

- Discuss the best ways of driving in the mountains

## CHAPTER FIFTEEN

# EXTREME DRIVING CONDITIONS

## INTRODUCTION

The words *extreme driving conditions* are easy to say, but what do they really mean? Extreme means the worst; it refers to the most difficult driving conditions: when it is cold, wet, dry, hot, windy, snowing, or foggy. Driving in the mountains is also considered an extreme driving condition.

No one can learn how to drive in all these conditions by reading a book or sitting in a classroom. On the other hand, you can learn many useful facts by studying this chapter. Since you may be driving a rig in all of these conditions, you will want to read it very carefully.

## EXTREME WEATHER

Knowing the rig's parts, systems, and how they work is critical when you drive in extreme weather conditions. Less traction and poor visibility are two major safety hazards. Less traction increases the stopping distance and decreases the driver's ability to control the rig. Reduced visibility means you will not see hazards as soon; you will have less time to respond.

### Vehicle Checks

You must be sure both you and your rig are ready before you drive in winter weather. Make a regular pre-trip inspection. This pre-trip inspection should include the following items.

---

### SPECIAL EXTREME WEATHER CHECKLIST FOR PRE-TRIP INSPECTION

- Antifreeze
- Heater/Defroster
- Wipers/Washers
- Tires
- Chains
- Brakes
- Lights
- Windows, Mirrors, and Reflectors
- Hand and Toe Holds
- Radiator Shutters
- Exposed Wiring and Hoses
- Fuel Tank
- Muffler and Exhaust System
- Fifth Wheel
- Personal Gear and Supplies
- Weather Reports — Road Conditions

© 1997 Career Publishing Inc.

**Figure 15-1**

**Coolant Level and Antifreeze Concentration:** Make sure the cooling system is full. A low coolant level affects the operation of the heater and defroster. If the coolant level is very low, the engine will not perform as well as it should. The antifreeze concentration should be checked with a tester (see vehicle or company specs).

**Figure 15-2**

**Heating Equipment:** A badly heated cab can reduce your ability to do your job. Be sure to check the heater hose for wear. The controls and fans should work. The operator's manual will tell you how to operate them. Check the window defrosters. Include the heaters for the mirrors, battery box, and fuel tanks in your check.

**Wipers/Washers:** Check the washer reservoir for cracks, collapsed areas, and loose clamps. Make sure it is full and the fluid is not frozen. In the winter, add antifreeze to the reservoir. Do the washers work?

Test the condition of the rubber blades on the wipers. They should operate at the manufacturer's recommended arm pressure. The wrong pressure will let the blades slide over the snow instead of sweeping it off.

**Tires**: Check the mountings. Look for any flaws on the sidewalls or tread. Check the air pressure with a gauge. Are all tires inflated properly? Check the tread depth also. You should have at least 4/32-inch tread in every major groove on the front wheels, and at least 2/32-inch on the other

**Figure 15-3**

wheels. The tires must have enough traction to push the rig over wet pavement or through snow.

**Chains**: Nobody likes to have to use tire chains, but you must be prepared. Carry the correct number of properly fitting chains and extra cross-links. Watch for broken hooks, worn or broken cross-links, and bent or broken side chains. (Tire chains will be covered in greater detail later in the lesson.)

**Brakes**: Check the brake balance. The brakes should all apply pressure equally and at the same time. If a wheel stops turning before the others, it may cause a skid or handling problems. Check the adjustment and take up the slack if needed.

If your rig has a front brake limiting valve, turn it on. Do this with the hand switch located in the cab. The valve limits air pressure to the brake chambers. This helps keep the wheels from locking up.

Check the brake linings for ice. Ice can cut the braking power and cause the shoes to freeze to the brake drums.

Finally, drain the moisture from both the tractor and trailer air tanks. Water in the air lines can cause the brakes to freeze. If your rig has other moisture controls such as spitter valves or alcohol evaporators, check to be sure that they are operating properly.

**Lights and Reflectors:** Be sure they are not dirty, muddy, salty, icy, or snowy. Check often during a trip. How well you can see, and others can see you, depends on how clean the lenses are.

**Hand and Toe Holds:** You can enter and leave the cab much more safely if you keep the hand and toe holds free of ice and snow. If you need to, use a brush to clean them before getting out of the cab.

**Radiator Shutters and Winterfront:** Remove the ice from the radiator shutters. Ice can keep the shutters from opening and cause the engine to overheat. Keep a close check on the engine temperature when driving. If the engine overheats, you may need to adjust the shutters and winterfront to maintain proper operating temperature. Close them if the engine is too cold. Open them if it gets too hot.

Winterfronts that have to be checked are not recommended for engines with air-to-air after coolers. Some winterfronts must have air flow through to the automatic fan activator sensor.

**Exposed Wiring and Air Lines:** Be sure all wiring and lines are properly supported. Remove any ice or snow before and during a trip. Snow and ice buildup can cause the lines to sag and snag on the tire chains.

**Fuel Tank:** Make sure the fuel tank is full before you start on a trip. If bad weather is expected, top off the tank frequently. If you do not, you can run out of fuel and be stranded without power.

Beware of low quality fuel. It can freeze (jell) in the fuel lines and filters. It is wise to fill the tank at the end of a trip to reduce the build-up of moisture. Also, it is best to drain water from the bottom of fuel tanks.

**Engine and Exhaust Systems:** The exhaust connections must be tight to keep carbon monoxide or other dangerous gases from leaking into the rig.

**Coupling Devices:** Make sure the fifth wheel is coated with a winter-grade lubricant to prevent binding. This will also help steering on slippery roads. Double-check the locking mechanism.

**Interaxle Differential Lock (if your rig has one):** Check the operator's manual for the proper operation. If it is air operated, check for water in the air lines when you are stopped.

**Emergency Equipment:** Driving in the winter without proper clothing and equipment can be deadly. You need drinking water, extra food, medicine (as needed), hats, boots, gloves, extra pants, and proper outerwear. You should also have a windshield scraper, snow brush, flashlight, fuses, and a small folding shovel (available through army surplus stores).

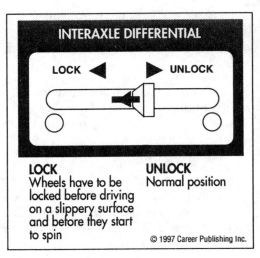

**LOCK**
Wheels have to be locked before driving on a slippery surface and before they start to spin

**UNLOCK**
Normal position

© 1997 Career Publishing Inc.

**Figure 15-4**

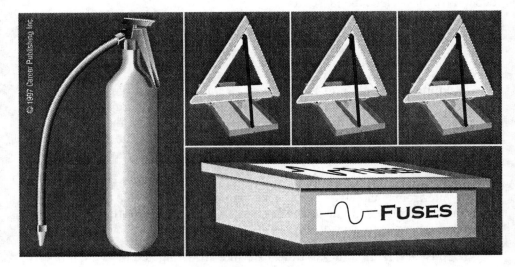

**Figure 15-5**

## Weather Reports and Road Conditions

Drivers should keep informed of the latest weather and road conditions. The National Weather Radio Service broadcasts on 162.40-162.55 MHz. They constantly update weather forecasts from many locations around the country. Be alert. Conditions often change quickly. Plan your route accordingly.

## TIRE CHAINS

Tire chains are a must for driving in many areas. Chains increase traction by as much as 500%. They can be the difference between driving and not driving. Chains improve the pulling power of the drive wheels when going uphill. When going downhill, they improve the trailer wheel braking. They also help prevent stalls, skids, and jackknifes.

Mount your chains at the first sign of slippery conditions. To continue driving without them is to take the chance of skidding, damaging your rig, or getting stuck.

## Using Chains

Chains are most effective in heavy, wet snow. If you drive on a heavy ice accumulation or in freezing rain on top of snow, you will probably need reinforced chains (see *How Chains are Made*). Conventional chains provide little traction. In light snow, chains do not help traction much, but they do provide some stability for the rig. Most chains are not effective on glare ice.

## Installing Your Chains

Do not be afraid to install your chains. Once you have learned how, it is pretty easy. A few guidelines will help.
* Properly installed chains should be snug, not rigid.
* Chains are designed to *creep*, or move. This prevents tire damage.
* Tighten your chains after driving 5 miles. This will keep them from slapping against the trailer or catching on the suspension.

Be careful when you put on your chains. When you are outside the rig, other drivers may not see you or they see you and may put on their brakes but slide into you. Remember slow moving vehicles, even with chains, are very quiet in the snow. New snowfall absorbs sounds. There is danger, also, from your own rig. Hot tires melt snow. The surface can get quite slippery and cause your rig to slide sideways when it is parked.

When getting ready to put on chains, you should:
* Pull well off the road.
* Park on a level surface.
* Be careful; footing can be slippery.
* Work facing traffic.
* Plan where to go if there is an out-of control vehicle or one whose path suggests the driver may not see you.
* Make sure your own rig does not slide into you.
* Be sure you put on the chains right-side out.

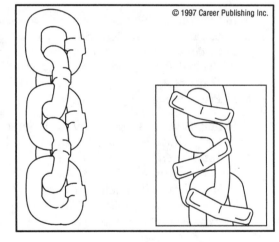

© 1997 Career Publishing Inc.

**Figure 15-6**

## How Chains are Made

Cross chains go across the tread of the tire and provide traction. Side chains go around the tires in the same direction as the sidewalls. They hold the cross chains. The cross chains are made with two types of links. One type is an ordinary, or conventional, link. The other type is a reinforced link. This link has V-lugs or cleats welded to cross links to improve the chain's grip.

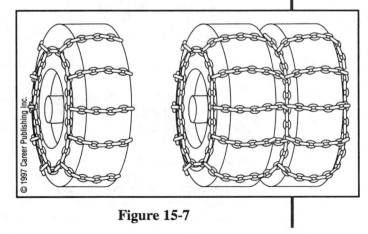

© 1997 Career Publishing Inc.

**Figure 15-7**

Chains may be single and made to go over a single tire. The chain is used on the outside tire of dual wheels. Double chains are made to go over a complete set of duals.

## When to Use Your Chains

Many mountain states have rules for using chains in certain kinds of weather. Drivers should know the rules of the states in which they operate.

Many states have laws that say where the chains must be installed on the rig. In some western states, the locations may vary from one part of the state to another. Again, it is the driver's duty to know the regulations.

You may enter a *chain control area.* This is simply a highway area on which it is illegal to drive without chains. Check points usually are set up ahead of chain control areas. Trucks are stopped and checked to see that the proper number of chains are on board. If not, the inspectors will not let the rig into the chain control area. It is the driver's duty to be prepared.

*Chains advised* means it is your choice. Be careful in these areas because there can be large fines if you spin out or cause an accident and do not have chains on.

## STARTING YOUR ENGINE IN COLD WEATHER

In the winter, all engines are harder to start. The lower the temperature, the harder they are to get started. Big rigs are no exception. There are, however, a number of devices that can be very helpful.
- Special starting substances like ether or an ether-based fluid
- Glow plugs
- Pre-heaters

**Ether**: Ether has a very low flash point. It ignites easily even at sub-zero temperatures. Since it is such a high energy fuel, using ether has some drawbacks.
- If not used properly or used too often, ether can damage the engine by cracking cylinder heads, breaking pistons, or snapping connecting rods.
- It is highly flammable. If you should spill any on your clothes, change as soon as possible. Stay away from open flames, matches, cigarettes, or hot exhaust pipes and heaters. They could easily catch your clothing on fire.

Ether is packaged in a number of forms.
- Aerosol spray cans
- Pressurized cylinders
- Driver-controlled injection systems
- Capsules

It can be applied both manually (by hand) and automatically.

Capsules, aerosol sprays, and pressurized cylinders are used manually. One advantage of using a capsule is that only one person is needed to start the engine. The capsule is placed in a special holder attached to the air cleaner. Each capsule provides one start. Do not place it in the air cleaner. It could be sucked into the engine and damage it.

Aerosol sprays or pressurized cylinders need two people to start the engine. One person sprays ether into a rag hung in front of the air cleaner. The other starts the engine. It takes *very little* ether to start the engine. Be careful! Too much spray may cause a flashback or engine damage.

Automatic injection systems need only the driver to start the engine. Ether is put into the engine in one of two ways.

1. The driver turns on a switch in the cab and ether is injected into the engine.
2. Ether is injected into the engine automatically when the engine is started.

Because the amount of ether is regulated, there is no danger of injecting so much ether it can damage the engine. Do not use this system with either a glow plug or pre-heater.

**Glow Plugs**: Glow plugs are simply electric heating elements that warm the air coming into the engine from the air intake. They can be mounted in the intake manifold or in each combustion chamber. On diesel engines, they are sometimes located in a pre-combustion chamber.

Before operating a glow plug, consult the operator's manual and/or the instrument panel for instructions. The plug may need a pump that is hand primed to spray the fuel into the combustion chamber.

Glow plugs raise the temperature in the combustion chamber. It is the hot compressed air that ignites the fuel. This usually takes about 60 seconds. *Never use ether and glow plugs at the same time.*

**Pre-Heaters**: Pre-heaters keep the engine warm while parked for the night. There are two types.

1. In-block
2. Immersion

Most of the pre-heaters used on truck tractors are the **in-block** type. They fit into the freeze plug holes in the lower water jacket. The other end of the pre-heaters heat the coolant to approximately 160°, which is near normal operating temperature. The coolant circulates through the engine and keeps it warm.

The **immersion** type of pre-heater is used on off-highway construction vehicles and mining equipment.

When you use a pre-heater, you do not need a warm-up period. You can use normal starting procedures. In extremely cold areas, heaters are often used with battery box heaters, oil sump heaters, and fuel heaters. Do not use a pre-heater without instruction. Consult your company's maintenance people.

## An Engine That Will Not Start

If your engine will not start when you use starting aids, check to be sure the engine is getting fuel.

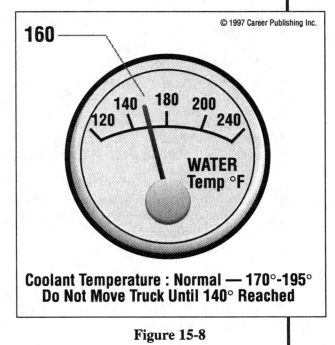

Coolant Temperature : Normal — 170°-195°
Do Not Move Truck Until 140° Reached

**Figure 15-8**

To check for fuel, look at the exhaust stack while you crank the engine. If there is no vapor or smoke, the engine is not getting fuel. Do not keep on cranking the engine. This will not start the engine, it will only run down the battery. Check the fuel tank and lines to be sure they are not blocked by ice. Also check the fuel tank vent.

Never crank the engine more than 15 seconds at a time. If the engine is getting fuel and still will not start, check the electrical system. If the rig has an electrical starter, remember the battery does not operate at full capacity in cold weather. The battery must be in the best possible condition. Check for:
- Corrosion on the terminals
- Loose connections
- Cracks in the cables
- Moisture in the cables

If the rig has an air starter, the engine will not start unless there is an air supply. If there is no air, the air supply can be restored from another tractor or an air compressor. Check the operator's manual for the best way to do this.

## BAD WEATHER OPERATING HAZARDS

There are two major hazards when driving in bad weather:
1. Less visibility
2. Less traction

### Less Visibility

Ice and snow can build up on windows and mirrors. Of course, you do not see as well. When this happens, you must stop often to clean the windows and mirrors. Do not drive with your side or rearview mirrors blocked. All lights and reflectors should be free of ice, snow, and mud. Stop and clean them when you need to.

**PRIMARY HAZARDS**

Reduced Visibility
Reduced Traction
- Road Surface
  — Different Surfaces — Different Degrees of Traction
  — Be Aware of Changing Conditions
- Speed
  — Speed Magnifies Mistakes
  — Determine the Speed at Which the Wheels Roll Without Spinning
  — Adjust Speed to Changing Road Surfaces and Conditions

© 1997 Career Publishing Inc.

**Figure 15-9**

Even when your windows, lights, and reflectors are clean, how far you can see is sometimes limited by rain, snow, or fog. Slow down and drive very carefully (see the chapter on Speed Management).

Sometimes visibility is almost zero. This happens at night in heavy snow, a downpour of rain, or dense fog. Driving is not safe in these conditions. Stop. Wait until you can see better before continuing.

### Less Traction

Remember, traction is the *grip* of the tires on the road. Different surfaces have different amounts of traction. Concrete provides greater traction than asphalt. This holds true whether the roads are wet or dry. If there is ice or packed snow, about 80% of the traction is lost.

If a road is slippery, the drive wheels spin easily. This results in less control of the rig. Watch for changing conditions. Put on your brakes every so often to check the traction.

Proper tire inflation, tread, and weight on the drive wheels gives you better traction and lets you control the rig better.

Speed is another factor in traction. As the rig's speed increases, traction decreases. When traction is poor for any reason, slow down until you have the rig well under control.

If the road is wet, reduce your speed by one-fourth. This means if you are driving 55 mph, slow down to about 40 mph. On packed snow, reduce your speed by 50%. At 55 mph, slow to about 27 mph. On icy surfaces, cut down to about one-third of your normal speed. At 55 mph, slow to about 18 mph.

THE POINTS OF FRICTION (TRACTION) BETWEEN TIRES AND ROAD ARE SMALL

**Figure 15-10**

**Figure 15-11**

Remember, these are general guidelines. Exact speeds will vary with the conditions. The following are also factors in deciding what is a safe speed.
- Weight of the rig
- Type of rig
- Condition of the tires
- Type of road surface
- Temperature
- Type of snow or ice

Black ice is so clear you can see the road surface under the ice. This makes it very hard to spot. It usually occurs:
- On bridges
- Beneath overpasses
- In dips in the road (where water collects)
- In shaded areas
- On the lower sides of banked curves

Black ice is also very hard to spot at night. If a driver is not aware of the black ice, it can be very dangerous. When you are driving in near-freezing rain, feel for ice along the front of a mirror. If ice is there, there also may be ice on the road. When in doubt, check your traction by putting on the brakes gently to see if the vehicle skids. Before you perform this check, be sure no one is behind you.

### Skidding

A skid happens when a rig's tires lose traction on the road. There are four basic causes of skids:
1. Driving too fast
2. Over-acceleration
3. Over-braking
4. Over-steering

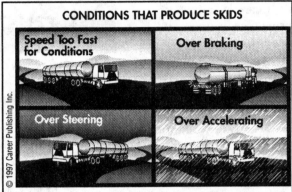

**Figure 15-12**

**Driving too fast** for the road conditions causes most of the serious skids. Drivers who adjust their driving to the conditions do not over-accelerate and do not have to over-brake or over-steer from too much speed.

**Over-acceleration** puts too much power to the drive wheels. This causes the tires to spin and may cause a skid.

**Over-braking** is braking too hard for the surface conditions. Using the service brakes too much is one cause. Suddenly releasing the accelerator can cause a braking effect that throws the rig into a skid. Skids can also be caused by using the engine brake incorrectly.

Drivers over-brake when they:
• Drive too fast for the conditions.
• Do not look far enough ahead.
• Do not leave enough following distance.

# SKIDDING AND JACKKNIFING

## Causes:

Over-acceleration
Over-braking
Over-steering
Speed too fast for conditions

**Figure 15-13**

**Over-steering** occurs when a driver tries to go around a turn too fast and turns the steering wheel too quickly. The drive wheels want to continue to move straight ahead. Then there is too little grip between the tires and road. The result is a skidding trailer and a tractor-trailer jackknife.

### Jackknifing

When the drive wheels lock up, they cause the tractor or trailer to skid. This skid can result in a jackknife. Be careful not to make things worse by putting on the brakes in a skid.

## OPERATING IN BAD WEATHER

Drivers need to realize that trips on icy roads will take longer. This section will make a number of points about driving on slippery surfaces, the problem of wet brakes, and present a brief summary of operating in bad weather.

### Driving on Slippery Surfaces

- Start gently. At the beginning of the trip, get a feel for the road. Don't hurry.
- Adjust turning and braking to the conditions. Make turns as gradually as possible. Do not brake any harder than you need to. Do not use the engine brake if possible.
- Check your mirrors. Check the trailer when you brake to be sure it is not drifting to one side. You can prevent a jackknife by acting when there is still time to recover. At night, if your trailer's lights begin to show in the mirror, it may mean a jackknifing trailer.
- Adjust your speed to the conditions. Do not overtake and pass other vehicles unless you have to. Slow down. Select a safe speed.

Caution. When your drive wheels have poor traction, the retarders may cause them to skid. Turn off your retarders when the road is wet, icy, or snow covered. © 1997 Career Publishing Inc.

**Figure 15-14**

- Watch far enough ahead to flow with the traffic. This will help you avoid the need to change speeds.
- Take curves and turns at slower speeds. Brake before curves. Be in the right gear before you enter a curve. Speed up slightly in the curve.
- As it gets warmer, ice melts and becomes more slippery. Slow down even more.
- Avoid driving beside other vehicles. Keep out of the pack. Leave yourself room for emergencies.
- Keep a longer following distance.
- When traffic looks congested ahead, fall back. Stop if needed and wait for things to clear up.
- Plan ahead for stops to avoid panic stopping.
- If your truck does not have antilock brakes, pumping them will allow you to stop more safely. If it does have antilock brakes, do **not** pump the brakes. Apply them hard and hold. This will provide the safest stop.

## Wet Brakes

When you drive in heavy rain or deep standing water, the brakes will get wet. Then the linings may slip on the drum or disc. This can cause uneven braking. The final result can be losing your brakes, wheel lockup, veering from one side of the lane to the other, or a jackknife.

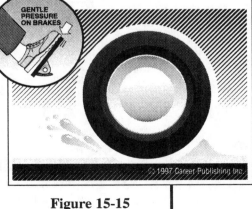

**Figure 15-15**

It is best to avoid standing water. If you must drive through water:
- Slow down.
- Shift to a lower gear.
- Place your foot lightly on the brake.
- Increase engine speed (rpm).
- Accelerate through the water.

After you are out of the water:
- Stay in the low gear.
- Keep your foot on the brake.
- Increase the rpm to prevent stalling.
- Keep a light pressure on the brakes for a short distance to dry them out.
- Release the brakes.

Check behind to make sure no one is following too closely. Then make a test stop to be certain the brakes are working properly.

## Summary: Operating in Bad Weather

Both the driver and rig have limits. As a tractor-trailer driver, one of your duties is to know these limits and adjust your driving to the changing conditions. The best way to prevent accidents in bad weather is to adjust your speed, braking, steering, and space cushion. When it is too dangerous to drive, stop and wait until the conditions are safe to drive in again.

## A Vehicle That is Stuck

The best advice about a stuck vehicle is, "Don't get stuck!" You can often keep from getting stuck by smarter driving.

Stay away from things that can cause a rig to get stuck.
- Soft berm (dirt on the roadside)
- Deep snow
- Mud
- Icy, slippery surfaces

When in doubt, avoid any suspicious surface. Be very alert when you leave the main road to make a delivery or when you pull off the road for rest, repair, or a vehicle check.

## Freeing Your Stuck Rig

- Do not spin the drive wheels or rock back and forth. These actions will simply dig the vehicle in further. On ice, spinning the wheels will cause heat. This will warm the ice under the tires and reduce traction by about 50%.

- Use traction aids. Dig out from under the front of the rig's wheels. Scatter sand or gravel in the path of the wheels. Lay loose chains in front of the wheels.

- Lock the interaxle differential (if your rig has one).

- Use a higher gear. For example, use the second or third gear. This will help keep the wheels from spinning because it reduces the force and applies it more smoothly.

- Start with the steering wheels straight ahead. If you have to start with the wheels turned, accelerate gently. Turn the steering wheel back and forth gently (less than an inch). This prepares a path for the wheels.

- As you begin to move, accelerate smoothly and gently. Ease off the accelerator if you start to slip.

## Towing

If your efforts to drive free fail, call a tow truck. Remember you are responsible for the equipment and cargo. You, not the tow truck driver, should supervise the operation. If the tow truck driver starts to do something you think is wrong or unsafe, stop him or her. Then correct the problem.

Agree on the procedure before beginning the hook-up or towing operation.
- In what direction will the tow truck pull?
- In what direction will you steer?
- When is the tow truck to stop?

The driver of the rig should signal the tow truck to stop. Agree on a signal such as the horn.

It is best for you to hook the chain or cable yourself.
- Pass it through the hole in the front bumper. Do not to hook it to the bumper.
- Attach the chain or cable to the tow hooks on the frame. If there are not any hooks, fasten it to a solid portion of the frame. Be careful not to hook it around the steering tierod or spring shackles.
- From the rear, secure the cable or chain to the tow hooks or frame.
- Leave enough slack in the cable or chain to keep the rig, once it is freed, from lurching into the tow truck.
- The tow truck should accelerate gently.
- When you have been pulled clear, signal the tow truck driver to stop.
- Put on the tractor-trailer brakes. When the rig's brakes are applied, they will prevent the tractor-trailer from rear-ending the tow truck. Bring both the rig and the tow truck to a stop.

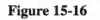

**FREEING A STUCK VEHICLE**

**AVOID IF POSSIBLE**
- Soft Berm
- Deep Snow
- Muddy Road
- Slippery Driving Surface

**WHEN STUCK**
- Do Not Spin Wheels
- Use Traction Aids
- Lock Interaxle Differential
- Place in Higher Gear
- Accelerate Gradually

**WHEN USING TOW TRUCK**
Remember:
- You Are Responsible for Your Vehicle and Cargo
- You Should Maintain Control
- You Should Hook the Cable or Chain to Vehicle

© 1997 Career Publishing Inc.

**Figure 15-16**

© 1997 Career Publishing Inc.

**Figure 15-17**

## If Your Rig Breaks Down In A Remote Area

If your rig should break down or you are stranded because of the weather, stay in the cab. Being out in the wind and cold can be dangerous. Put on extra clothing to stay warm. Do not try to walk for help. You may not make it. Stay with your rig so you can move it after it is freed.

If you must leave your rig, leave a note on the steering wheel telling:
• When you left
• Where you went
• When you think you will be back
If your engine will run, do not let exhaust fumes stay in the cab. Keep a window slightly open.

Smart drivers prepare for emergencies by carrying a supply of drinking water, candy bars, fruit, and extra clothing when bad weather may be expected.

# HOT WEATHER

In hot weather, you must be certain your rig is prepared for the worst. There are several areas that you must watch very carefully.

## Vehicle Inspection

This is an important non-driving duty. You are the one who will be out there with the rig. If the heat gets severe, you must deal with it. Be sure your rig and all the equipment can stand the heat. Check the following very carefully.

**Tires:** Check the mounting and inflation. Inspect them every two hours or 100 miles. An increase of 10-15 psi is common. Check the heat of the tire with the back of your hand, not the palm. If the pressure increase is more than 15 psi or if a tire becomes too hot to touch, stop driving. The tire could blow out or catch fire. Let it

**Figure 15-18**

cool off. Never bleed air from tires when they are hot. Let them cool and then recheck the pressure.

**Engine Lubrication:** Oil helps cool the engine. Keep the oil at the proper level. Do not overfill. Check it before you start and often while driving. Check the oil temperature gauge regularly. See the manufacturer's specs.

**Engine Cooling System:** Engines are big and powerful, but they are delicate. They need heat to run, but too much heat can damage or ruin them quickly. The engine cooling system is vital to proper engine operation and should be kept full and clean. Watch your water temperature gauge. Some types of engines tend to run warmer than others. Read your operator's manual to find the correct temperature for your engine.

Always carry coolant. If you must add coolant, let the engine cool. Then run the engine at high enough rpms to circulate the fluid. Very carefully remove the coolant reservoir cap with a heavy cloth. Keep your face and body clear because the coolant may spray. Add the new coolant slowly.

**Engine Belts:** Check the belt tension. Then check the belts for cracking, fraying, or wear. Slipping belts can cause the fan or water pump to stop operating. Then you will have an overheated engine.

**Hoses:** Check for cracks, fraying, and kinks. Be sure they do not collapse when the engine accelerates. The coolant must circulate freely to keep the engine operating at the right temperature.

© 1997 Career Publishing Inc.

**Figure 15-19**

# DRIVING IN THE DESERT

**Washes**: Secondary roads often are built through dry riverbeds. In heavy rains, the roads can flood very quickly. When it looks like rain, get to a main road as soon as possible.

**Bleeding Tar**: Tar in roads often rises to the surface when it is very hot. Spots where tar is bleeding become very slippery. Watch for them. Avoid them if you can.

**High Speeds:** High speeds create more heat for the tires and engine. Avoid continuous high speed driving under hot, desert conditions. The heat cannot be disposed of by the engine cooling system. Tires simply have no way of giving off the heat.

**Vehicle Breakdown**: If your rig breaks down in a remote area, do not leave it. Your body will not be able to stand the heat and sunlight. Body fluids are used up rapidly in the desert. You will become dehydrated. You also can suffer sunstroke. Stay in the cab, or sit under the trailer. Wait for help to come.

# MOUNTAIN DRIVING

Mountain driving is different from other driving. You and your rig must deal with gravity. Gravity is the force that pulls objects toward the center of the earth. It changes normal driving patterns. It does not matter whether you are going uphill or down a grade. The pull of gravity is so severe you must adjust your driving. Failing to adjust can make your trip harder. It can even damage your rig.

**Figure 15-20**

When you climb a grade, gravity adds to the weight of the load. This pulls the rig down. It will take more horsepower to move the rig. You cannot pass other vehicles as easily.

When you go downhill, gravity pulls the rig toward the earth. This increases your momentum. If the grade is steep, gravity can pull the vehicle off the road on curves, bumps, or where there is loose gravel on the road.

### Inspections

If your rig has air brakes, check the system carefully before driving in the mountains.

Check:
*   The compressor to be sure it can maintain full reservoir pressure.
*   The pressure drop when the brakes are fully applied to be sure it is within the limits.
*   The slack adjusters for correct adjustment.
*   To see if you can hear any air leaks. Check when the brakes are on and then again when they are off.
*   To be sure the glad hands and air lines are secured.
*   The brake drums for overheating. Do not touch a drum. It can burn your hand. Hold the back of your hand close to the drum. Some heat is normal, but not a high temperature.
*   To be sure the trailer supply valve is working.

### Upgrades

- **Shifting**: If the rpm falls, downshift to the next lower gear. Gravity will cut your speed during the downshift. Complete the shift quickly before the rpm reaches the bottom of the range. Downshift until you reach a gear that will maintain the rpm.
- **Position**: Drive on upgrades with patience. Move your rig to the far right or truck lane. Stay in this lane. Do not try to pass if you cannot do so quickly. Remember, a slow uphill truck creates a negative reaction to our industry. Other drivers can lose patience and drive recklessly.
- **Watch your gauges**: Pulling a heavy load up a long grade can cause overheating. Check the coolant and water temperature gauges often. Shift a few hundred rpms earlier than the lowest rpm for that gear. This will help compensate.

### Downgrades

Watch for signs showing the angle and length of the grade. These will help you decide on the correct speed for going downhill. Never go faster than the posted Maximum Safe Speed. Talk with other drivers who have made the same downhill runs before. They can often offer helpful hints.

Because gravity plays a big part in mountain driving, you must allow for the pull of gravity on your rig when going downhill. Make sure your brakes are properly adjusted. Check your brakes before starting downhill. Check the traffic pattern in your mirrors — especially to the left and rear.

Downshift before you start down the hill. Never downshift while going downhill. If you try to downshift, you will not be able to get into a lower gear. You might not even be able to shift at all. If that happens, you will lose all braking effect from the engine.

If you try to force an automatic transmission into a lower gear at high speed, you can damage the transmission. If you damage the transmission, you may lose all engine braking.

If you drive an older truck, a general rule is to use the same gear going downhill that you used going uphill. If you drive a newer truck, choose a lower gear because the truck is more streamlined and may have a more powerful engine.

When you are in the right gear, your engine will not race. Be sure your speed is not too fast for the:
- Total weight of the vehicle and cargo
- Length of the grade
- Steepness of the grade
- Road conditions
- Weather

Use your engine as the primary way to control your speed. The braking effect of the engine is the greatest when it is near the governed RPMs and the transmission is in a lower gear. Save your brakes for when you really need them. **Never Shift into neutral and coast.** It is **illegal** and **unsafe** to do so.

© 1997 Career Publishing Inc.

**Figure 15-21**

If you use your brakes too much, they may get hot and fade. Then you will have to apply them harder to get a braking effect. If you keep on using them, they may fail completely, and then you will have no brakes.

In an effort to determine the best way to brake when going down hills, the **University of Michigan Transportation Research Institute (UMTRI)** in cooperation with the **National Highway Traffic Safety Administration (NHTSA)** has performed experiments and has released these findings (March, 1992).

**CHECKLIST FOR MOUNTAIN DRIVING**
UPGRADES
• Downshift Until You Find Gear That Will Maintain RPM's
• Position Vehicle in Right Lane
• Do Not Pass
DOWNGRADES
• Never Downshift While Descending
• Use a Low Gear
• Go Slow
• Use Close to Rated Engine Speed to Maximize Drag
• Use Snubbing Method When Braking

© 1997 Career Publishing Inc.

**Figure 15-22**

*The right way to go down long grades is to use a low gear and go slow. Use close to rated engine speed to maximize drag. If you go slowly enough, the brakes will be able to get rid of enough heat so they will work as they should. The driver's most important consideration is to pick a control speed that is not too fast for the weight of the vehicle, the length of the grade, and the steepness of the grade.*

*Drivers who are unfamiliar with routes in mountainous regions need to select a low speed to be safe. . . However, if the driver is not familiar with which grades are long ones, the driver needs to proceed with caution – perhaps at a low speed of no more than 20 mph. . .*

*To control speed going down a mountain, some people favor using a light, steady pressure to drag the brakes while others favor a series of snubs, each sufficient to slow the vehicle by approximately 6 mph in about 3 seconds. The snubbing strategy uses pressure over 20 psi for heavy trucks while the light drag may involve pressures under 10 psi. Tests have shown that either method will result in approximately the same average brake temperature at the bottom of the mountain as long as the same average speed is maintained. However, the snubbing method, due to the higher pressure involved, will aid in making each brake do its fair share of the work. Hence, the snubbing method will result in more uniform temperatures from brake to brake and thereby aid in preventing brakes from overheating.*

*Furthermore, light, steady pressure at highway speeds on short grades of roughly one mile in length can lead to problems with 'hot spotting' and drum cracking and fragmenting if the brake linings are new.*

*In summary, the most important considerations are to go slow enough and use the right gear. Remember that compared to a strategy based upon light pressure dragging, the snubbing strategy will aid in making each brake do its fair share of the work and reduce the tendency for hot-spotting and drum-cracking of new or recently relined brakes.*

The **American Association of Motor Vehicle Administrators (AAMVA)** in their **Model CDL Drivers Manual** makes this recommendation:

*Once the vehicle is in the proper low gear, the following is a proper braking technique:*
  1. *Apply the brakes just hard enough to feel a definite slowdown.*
  2. *When your speed has been reduced to approximately 5 mph below your safe speed, release the brakes. The brake application should last for about three (3) seconds.*
  3. *When your speed has increased to your safe speed, repeat steps 1 and 2.*

*For example, if your safe speed is 40 mph, do not put on the brakes until you reach 40 mph. Then brake hard enough to reduce your speed to 35 mph. Release the brakes. Repeat this as often as you need to until you reach the end of the downgrade.*

## AUXILIARY BRAKES AND SPEED RETARDERS

Auxiliary brakes and speed retarders reduce the rig's speed without using the service brakes. This saves wear and tear on the brakes. The retarders help control the rig on long grades. They can often keep the rpms within a safe range. If they do not, the service brakes will also have to be used to keep the rig under control.

### Types

There are four basic types of auxiliary brakes and speed retarders.
  1. Engine brakes
  2. Exhaust brakes
  3. Hydraulic retarders
  4. Electric retarders

  1. **Engine brakes** (for example, the *Jake Brake*) eliminate the power stroke. They convert the engine to an air compressor for braking purposes. Fuel injection is stopped. The exhaust valves open. Compressed air is expelled and slows the piston movement.

  2. **Exhaust brakes** (for example, the *Blue Ox*) back exhaust gases into the engine to create the pressure (40-50 psi) that slows the piston movement. You often control engine and exhaust brakes with an on/off switch in the cab. Other types operate by an automatic switch that is turned on by releasing the accelerator pedal or depressing the clutch pedal. Some may have controls for the amount of retardation.

  3. **Hydraulic retarders** (examples, the *Cat Brakesaver* and *Allison's Brake Preserver*) are mounted between the engine and transmission. They use engine oil pumped against the stator, a fan-like device, or the cavity between the stator and the rotor to slow the rig.

Hydraulic retarders can be adjusted manually in the cab to different levels of operation. The higher they are turned up, the more effective they are. They also have a treadle valve and may have a clutch switch.

4.  **Electric retarders** (examples, the *Jake ER Brake* and *Telma Retarder*) are mounted in the drive line. They slow the drive shaft rotation with an electromagnet that can be turned on or off. There is no in-between setting. The Jacobs Jake ER Brake retarder has a 4-position steering column switch and no throttle or clutch switch.

### Operation and Control

Because these devices can be noisy, be sure you know where they are permitted. You will also need to know:
*   With which gears they may be used.
*   What is the proper rpm for their use.
*   In what kind of weather you may use them.

Speed retarders are useful any time the service brakes are used continually. This may be in the mountains or on long, downhill grades.

## ESCAPE RAMPS

Escape ramps are designed to stop a vehicle safely without injuring people or damaging the cargo. They are built to stop a 50 thousand pound GVW tractor-trailer traveling at 55 mph about 450 feet into the ramp. Stopping feels like a hard lock wheel stop on dry pavement.

Ramps either sink the rig in loose gravel or sand, or send it up an incline. The grade may be up to 43 percent. Either way, damage to the rig and cargo is limited to minor scratches, nicks, lost battery covers, etc.

**Figure 15-23**

### How Ramps Work

At Rabbit Ear Pass, a 9,650 foot summit on U.S. Route 40 in Colorado, a 40,000 lb. rig carrying steel beams was on a 7% downgrade when it had a drive-train failure. The brakes did not work. It was a runaway vehicle. The driver entered the escape ramp at 100-110 mph. The rig came to a stop 1,300 feet into the ramp. Both the driver and a passenger walked away unhurt. Damage to the rig was a dent in the cab and a missing battery cover. The total cost of the accident was $10 for two ramp markers and the price of a tow truck to free the rig.

There are four basic types of escape ramps:
1.  **Gravity**: These ramps have a loose material surface such as pea gravel. The grade will be from 5%-43%.
2.  **Sand piles**: These are mounds or ridges built high enough to drag the undercarriage of the rig. They are from 85 feet to 200 feet long.
3.  **Arrester beds**: These flat beds are masses of loose material, usually pea gravel. They are from 300 feet to 700 feet long.
4.  **Combination ramp and arrester bed**: These types rely on the loose surface material to stop the rig. They have a grade of 1.5%-6.7% and are from 500 feet to 2,200 feet long.

If you think you are in trouble:
*   You can use an escape ramp.
*   Try to enter the ramp squarely and not at an angle.
*   You will most likely save your own life and maybe the lives of others.
*   You will save your rig and its cargo.
*   You may have to pay to have your rig towed back onto the highway.
*   Know where escape ramps are located.
*   If you are in any trouble, remember, things are not going to get better.
*   When in doubt, use a ramp.
*   You may not have another chance.
*   Escape ramps save lives and cargo. Use them when you lose your brakes.

## SUMMARY

In this chapter, you learned that driving in adverse conditions differs greatly from driving in good weather or on good roads. You were taught the inspection procedures that differ from a normal inspection. You learned how to become aware of possible bad weather conditions and what you should do when you encounter them. You learned several methods of starting the truck's engine in cold weather and what to do if it will not start.

How to avoid skids was presented as well as how to dry out the truck's brakes should they become wet. You also learned what is your responsibility should your rig become stuck and need to be towed. The hazards of driving in hot weather or the desert were explained. Finally, you learned that driving in the mountains takes special care. Auxiliary braking systems, the best way to drive downgrades, and the use of escape ramps were explained.

## KEY WORDS

**Auxiliary brakes or speed retarders**: Devices that reduce the rig's speed without using the service brakes.

**Chain control area**: A highway area on which it is illegal to drive without chains.

**Escape ramps**: Areas used to stop runaway rigs by either sinking the rig in loose gravel or sand or sending it up an incline.

**Extreme driving conditions**: The worst possible driving conditions.

**Jackknife**: A type of accident in which the tractor and trailer turn to make a V-shape.

# LEARNING ACTIVITIES

## True-False Questions   ✓

If the question is true, circle the T. If the question is false, circle the F.

(T) F   1.   Ice, snow, mud, salt, or dirt on your lights and reflectors can cut down how much you can see and how well others can see you.

T (F)   2.   Reinforced chains are effective on glare ice.

T (F)   3.   If you install tire chains the right way, you do not need to be concerned about them for the rest of the trip.

(T) F   4.   Ether, while it can be helpful for starting in the winter, can be dangerous to both the driver and the engine.

T (F)   5.   The only major hazard of driving in extreme weather conditions is less traction.

(T) F   6.   In snow, the tires can lose as much as 80% of the normal traction.

(T) F   7.   As the rig's speed increases, traction decreases.

(T) F   8.   Skids can be caused by driving too fast and over-steering.

(T) F   9.   Letting up on the accelerator can cause a skid.

T (F)  10.   Once your brake pads or linings get wet, there is nothing you can do to dry them out.

(T) F  11.   The best advice about a stuck vehicle is to avoid getting stuck.

T (F)  12.   If you are stuck, a good way to get the rig loose is to rock it gently back and forth.

T (F)  13.   If you need a tow truck, remember, the tow truck operator is a professional and should take charge of the operation.

(T) F  14.   If your rig breaks down in bad weather, it is best to stay with it.

T (F)  15.   If tire inflation pressure increases more than 15 psi, immediately let some of the air out before you drive again.

(T) F  16.   Do not shift gears on downgrades.

(T) F  17.   A major part of downhill braking should be done by the engine.

T (F)  18.   Since escape ramps are for true emergencies, you should not use them unless you have tried all other ways of bringing your truck under control.

T (F)  19.   Speed retarders use the service brakes to reduce speed.

## Discussion Questions

Divide the class into four groups. Have each group discuss one question. Then have them share their solutions to the problem with the class. After they have presented their solutions, give the question to the class for other possible solutions. Some of the class members may have actually had these experiences. Encourage them to share them with the class.

1.  You are driving in the barren desert on a side road. You notice storm clouds on the horizon. Describe what can happen. Be sure to include why it can happen. What should you do? What would you do if there was no main highway close by?

2.  Although only light snow was predicted when you began your trip, it has now turned into a blizzard. It is very important that your cargo reaches its destination as soon as possible. What should you do? Where should you go?

3.  You have been broken down for three hours in the desert. What should you have been doing during those three hours? What are the dangers of the desert? What can you do to avoid them? Where should you go? What types of emergency supplies should you have? How can you get help?

4.  You are going downhill on the Grapevine, a steep grade on I-5 between Los Angeles and Bakersfield. Describe how you should take the grade. What are the things you should be sure to do? What are the things you should never do? If you think your brakes are fading, what should you do? Describe the solution in detail.

# Chapter Sixteen
# HAZARD AWARENESS

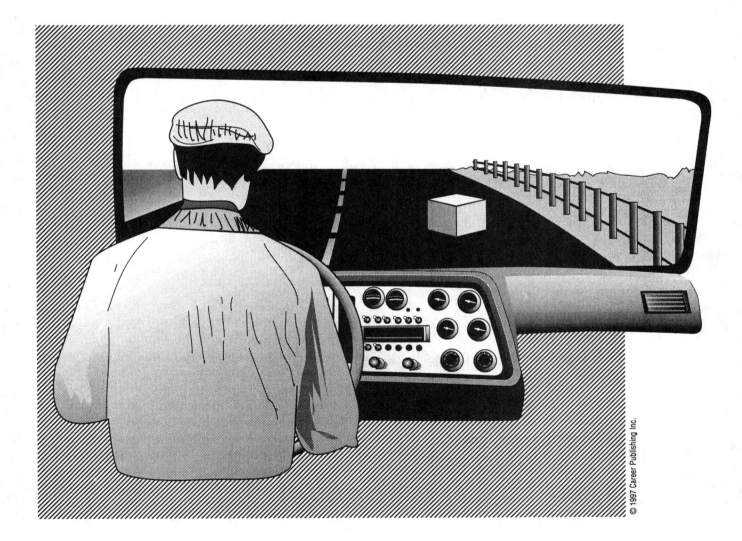

**Importance of Recognizing Hazards • What is a Hazard? • Learning to Recognize Hazards • Clues • Road Conditions • Road User Appearances • Road User Activities**

**FROM NOW ON,**

**ONLY THE BEST WILL DRIVE**

# OBJECTIVES

When you have mastered this chapter, you will be able to:

- Help drivers recognize possible hazards

- Explain how to tell when the road or the surroundings may be a danger

- Describe why a driver must always be alert to the changing scene

- Explain dangerous road conditions:
  Slippery surface        Uneven surface        Curves
  Soft surface        Sloping road

- Describe threats from the scene:
  Debris        Obstructions to visibility        Cross winds

- Present clues that tell a driver when other road users may be a possible safety hazard

- Explain why hazards must be recognized early

# CHAPTER SIXTEEN

# HAZARD AWARENESS

## INTRODUCTION

In addition to your vehicle, one other major element affects your driving. That is the scene (your surroundings, or environment). It includes the roadway, weather, buildings, trees, hills, people, and animals.

You must know each of these parts of your environment if you are to drive safely. This chapter is about the scene and how you must see and interpret it so your driving will fit in. Some of what you see will be friendly. Some will be neutral, and some will be dangerous. When you understand what you are seeing, you can adjust your driving.

**Figure 16-1**

**Figure 16-2**

## IMPORTANCE OF RECOGNIZING HAZARDS

To drive safely, you must train yourself to be aware of clues from your environment. They are always there and are always changing. Your job is to see and interpret them, so you can handle whatever may develop.

### What is a Hazard?

A **hazard** is any road condition or road user (driver, cyclist, pedestrian, or animal) that presents a possible danger to you or your rig. Possible is the key word. The hazard may become a danger, or it may not. Either way, you must know that it can be a danger.

The brake lights of a nearby vehicle as it approaches an exit ramp are an example of a possible danger. You really do not know what the other driver intends to do. The brake lights may mean the driver does not know what to do. The vehicle can quickly move to another lane. If this happens, the vehicle is no longer a hazard. It is a danger.

This simple example zeros in on the whole idea of recognizing hazards. A driver who did not understand the vehicle was a hazard would not respond until it started to change lanes. The driver might then brake suddenly or change lanes. This could cause an accident.

## Learning to Recognize Hazards

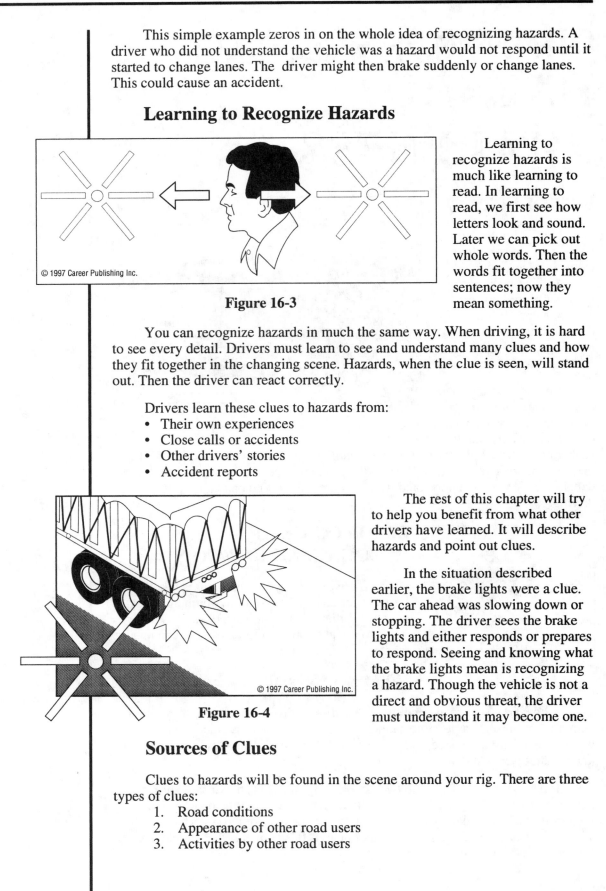

Figure 16-3

Learning to recognize hazards is much like learning to read. In learning to read, we first see how letters look and sound. Later we can pick out whole words. Then the words fit together into sentences; now they mean something.

You can recognize hazards in much the same way. When driving, it is hard to see every detail. Drivers must learn to see and understand many clues and how they fit together in the changing scene. Hazards, when the clue is seen, will stand out. Then the driver can react correctly.

Drivers learn these clues to hazards from:
- Their own experiences
- Close calls or accidents
- Other drivers' stories
- Accident reports

Figure 16-4

The rest of this chapter will try to help you benefit from what other drivers have learned. It will describe hazards and point out clues.

In the situation described earlier, the brake lights were a clue. The car ahead was slowing down or stopping. The driver sees the brake lights and either responds or prepares to respond. Seeing and knowing what the brake lights mean is recognizing a hazard. Though the vehicle is not a direct and obvious threat, the driver must understand it may become one.

## Sources of Clues

Clues to hazards will be found in the scene around your rig. There are three types of clues:
1. Road conditions
2. Appearance of other road users
3. Activities by other road users

# ROAD CONDITIONS

Road conditions are a major factor in tractor-trailer accidents because:
1. Big rigs travel more miles and travel more in bad weather than do most cars. This exposes them to more danger.
2. Big rigs are less stable because of a higher center of gravity. This makes them tip over more easily.
3. Tractor-trailers have longer stopping distances than cars.

Road characteristics that can be hazardous to rigs include:
- Surface conditions
- Shape
- Contour

Road surfaces may be hazardous if they are:
- Slippery
- Soft
- Sloping
- Uneven
- Littered with debris

## Slippery Surface

Sometimes it is hard to tell if roads are slippery. The following sections describe some of the weather in which there may be slippery roads.

**Wet Weather:** In wet weather, many surfaces are more slippery than they look.
- Patches of oil dripped from vehicles are very slippery just after it starts to rain.
- Painted or paint-striped areas, railroad tracks, and construction plates can also be slippery.

**Cold Weather**: In cold weather, look out for:
- Black ice
- Shaded areas
- Bridges

Figure 16-5

Figure 16-6

Black ice is a thin, clear coating of ice that looks wet. Shaded areas can freeze in wet weather when the rest of the roadway is dry. Bridges, both the traveled surface and the roadway below, freeze more quickly than the rest of the road. Be extra careful when cold weather, wet surfaces, bridges, and shade are combined.

**Hot Weather**: In hot weather, oil may come to the surface of an asphalt road and make it slippery. Be very careful when it starts to rain. The water mixes with this surface oil and reduces traction. The surface stays very slippery until the oil is washed away.

Figure 16-7

## Soft Surfaces

Some surfaces will not bear the weight of a fully loaded rig.

Examples are:
• Asphalt
• Construction areas
• Shoulders

On very hot days, the asphalt on some roadways may become soft and let the truck sink into it. In construction zones, surfaces that cover filled-in sewer trenches and septic tanks are seldom strong enough to hold a truck. Graded shoulders may be very soft after heavy rains or the snow thaws. There is danger the rig may sink in or turn over.

## Sloping Surfaces

The slope of the road can greatly affect a rig's handling. The force that *pushes* a vehicle off the road in a curve is called **centrifugal force**. Proper banking of the curve helps overcome this force and keeps the vehicle from *sliding* off the road. Proper banking allows you to take curves at a higher speed.

Figure 16-8

A curve that is not properly banked is a hazard. Your wheels are more likely to slide on the curve, so you must take the curve at a lower speed. Learn to know when a curve is not properly banked. Roads that are flat or slope the wrong way on the curves are not built right. Roads that are high in the middle and low on each side (high-crowned roads) are worse than flat roads. On curves, a *wrong-way slope* can cause severe front-end dip, front wheel lockup, or loss of control.

Another clue is pavement that drops off or slopes near the edge of the road. This *dip* can cause the top of the trailer to hit objects such as signs or tree limbs that are near the road.

## Debris

No matter what size your vehicle is, debris on the road is a hazard. A small box may contain heavy material that can cause control problems or damage your rig if it is hit by the debris. If a box does not move with the wind, think of it as a hazard. A pile of rags and paper or cloth sacks can also be a hazard. They may contain cement or another hard substance. If you hit them, you can damage tires, wheel rims, air lines, electrical lines, or fuel cross-over lines.

## Uneven Surfaces

Bumps in the road can hang up a low trailer and damage the undercarriage or tear off the dolly wheels. Try not to drive through puddles. They may be potholes filled with water. Potholes can cause you to lose control of your rig and cause damage.

## Contour of the Road

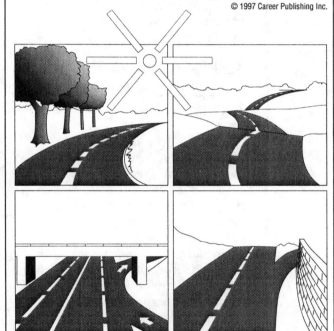

The shape, or contour, of a road can create hazards. The most common problems result from curvature, restrictions to visibility, and crosswind areas.

**Curvature:** Curvature is the amount of curving the earth does in your line of sight. Trees, power lines, or buildings can be clues to a curving road before you reach them. Are they in a straight line? Do they go up and down toward the horizon?

Expressway ramps can be dangerous for all drivers, but they are worse for tractor-trailer drivers. Curving, downhill ramps are especially bad because the weight and high center of gravity of the rig work with the centrifugal force pulling your rig to the outside of the curve to make holding onto the road harder. See the chapter on *Speed Management*.

**Figure 16-9**

**Restrictions to Visibility:** Many road characteristics restrict the driver's vision. Be prepared for these situations.
- At sunrise or sunset, you can be faced with extreme glare at the crest of a hill. It may help to lower your visor and put on sunglasses before you need them.
- At nighttime as you approach a hilltop, lights from the other side warn you of oncoming traffic. Be ready for headlight glare and protect yourself by looking to the right edge of the road.

- When approaching a tunnel in daylight, remember your eyes adjust slowly to changes in light. Take off your sunglasses before entering the tunnel. Put them back on after you leave the tunnel. Do the same when you enter a warehouse or dark alley on a sunny day.

**Crosswind Areas**: On windy days, you can be hit with a violent crosswind when moving from a protected area into an open area. A sudden crosswind can cause you to lose control of your rig. Look for the absence of trees, hills, or other protection when you come out into the open.

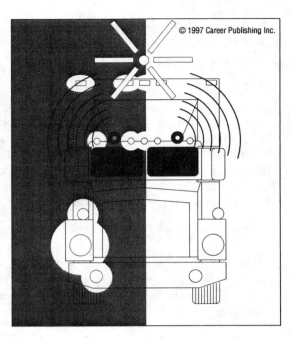

**Figure 16-10**

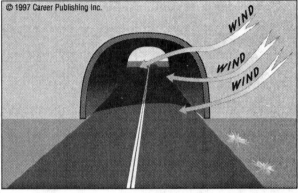

**Figure 16-11**

# APPEARANCE OF OTHER ROAD USERS

Drive defensively! While no driver can watch every move of every other road user, he or she can drive so that if the other driver makes a dumb or dangerous move, an accident can be avoided. Other drivers really are not bad drivers. They are often only careless. It makes sense to watch for the clues that tell you other road users may be ready to do something unexpected. Big rig drivers must be ready to deal with any sudden change of speed or direction.

Among the clues you should watch for in other drivers are:
- Obstructed vision
- Distraction
- Confusion
- Slow travel
- Impatience
- Impairment

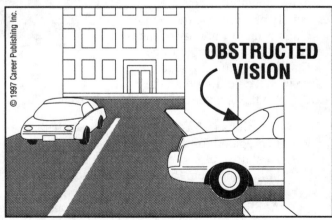

**Figure 16-12**

## Obstructed Vision

People who cannot see the road well are a serious hazard. This section will discuss clues that will help you identify drivers who may have obstructed vision. You should also be aware there may be hazards on the shoulder that are out of your line of sight when you are passing another vehicle.

**Vehicles with Limited Visibility:** Vans, loaded station wagons, and cars with obstructed rear windows are examples of some vehicles whose drivers may have limited ability to see the road around them. Drivers of rental trucks are often not familiar with their limited vision. Be alert for these drivers.

Sometimes vehicles are partly hidden by a blind intersection. You can see the other vehicle, but you know the other driver cannot see you. Look out!

A good example of this is when you are entering an intersection with the intention of turning left. If oncoming traffic in the nearest lane is stopped to let you turn, you may not be able to see vehicles passing to the right of the stopped vehicles. They, of course, are a danger if you turn in front of them. While the height of your cab can be helpful, it does not prevent other roadway users from being hidden.

The vision of drivers of delivery trucks is sometimes blocked by packages or vehicle doors. Drivers of step vans, postal vehicles, and local delivery trucks may leave their vehicles in a hurry. This often occurs when they are double parked. Watch out for these drivers.

**Parked Vehicles:** People in parked vehicles should always be considered a hazard. You never know when a driver may climb out in front of you. Watch for movement inside the vehicle and shaking or rocking of the vehicle. Parked vehicles may also move out into your lane of traffic.

When police units or emergency units are along the side of the road, move as far left as possible as soon as you can. Slow down if you can because anything can happen. Someone may even run out or be pushed into the traffic lanes.

Watch for:
- Brake and backup lights
- Exhaust gases
- A driver behind the wheel
- Turn signals
- Movement of the front wheel

**DISTRACTED DRIVERS**
© 1997 Career Publishing Inc.

**Figure 16-13**

## Distraction

If a driver is looking at, thinking about, or reacting to anything else, he or she may not see your rig. This is a distracted driver. A driver can attend to only those parts of the scene that he or she sees, hears, or senses. Therefore, you must help others to see and pay attention to you and your rig. On the next page are some common clues to distraction.

**Lack of Eye Contact:** Road users who are looking elsewhere may not be aware of your rig and pull right into your path. Always try to make eye contact with others. Even positive eye contact is no guarantee. Pedestrians or cyclists may assume you will yield or give them room. Remember, some states have pedestrian-right-of-way laws.

**Talkers:** Drivers or pedestrians who are talking may not be aware of you and your rig. They are paying attention to the person to whom they are talking.

**Workers:** Highway, construction, road repair, and utility workers often are not concerned about traffic. They may think someone else is directing the traffic. Delivery people may be distracted by their work, especially when they are loading and unloading. The presence of road repair equipment or delivery trucks is a clue for you to be alert.

**Figure 16-14**

**Vendors:** A vendor's vehicle is a clue to a hazard. People seem to forget there is traffic when they deal with a neighborhood street vendor. They walk or run across streets and roads without paying attention to the other vehicles. Ice cream trucks and small children are also a very dangerous combination.

**Objects Appearing From the Side:** A ball or other object appearing in the street usually means there is a child following. Be prepared to stop.

**Disabled Vehicle:** A vehicle being worked on beside a road or street is always a hazard. Drivers changing a tire or tinkering with an engine are usually not thinking about traffic. Passengers often leave the vehicle to walk around or supervise. They, like the person working on the vehicle, tend to ignore traffic. Therefore, you must protect them from their carelessness.

**School bus:** Slowing or stopped school buses almost always mean children on the move. They may come out from in front of or behind the bus. From either side of the road, expect the unexpected.

**Toll Booths:** Always check ahead as well in your rearview mirors for pedestrians at toll booths. These may be drivers who have gotten out of their cars or toll booth employees. Often they do not realize the danger of walking near tractor-trailers and may be run over by the trailer's wheels.

## Confusion

Confused drivers often drive more slowly than the other traffic. They tend to stop or change direction without warning. Clues that a driver may do something unexpected include:

**Figure 16-15**

- Cars topped with luggage
- Cars hauling a camping trailer
- Cars full of luggage or recreational gear
- Cars with out-of-state license plates
- Unexplainable actions such as the car stopping in mid-block, changing lanes for no apparent reason, or backup lights suddenly going on
- Hesitation, very slow driving, frequent braking, or stopping in the middle of an intersection
- Destination seeking: looking at street signs, maps, and house numbers

## Slow Travel

Motorists who do not travel at the normal speed are a hazard. Sometimes it is hard to judge how fast you are closing in on or overtaking a vehicle. Following too closely can create a problem. Identifying a slow driver early can prevent an accident. Some helpful clues to slow moving vehicles include:

- Underpowered vehicles such as some sub-compacts, recreational vehicles (RVs), or any vehicle towing a house trailer or other heavy load
- Farm or construction machinery such as tractors and bulldozers
- Mopeds
- Vehicles with the slow moving vehicle symbol (orange triangle with red sides). At night the triangle may look like an orange blob.
- Vehicles signaling a turn: turns into alleys or driveways may be very tight. Vehicles entering shopping centers may make sudden stops for pedestrians. Vehicles turning left may pause for oncoming traffic.

## Impatience

Some impatient drivers view all trucks as slow moving. They do not want to be caught behind a tractor-trailer and may recklessly try to get in front of it. Watch for drivers who overtake and pass you and then cut back over too quickly. They may even slow down after making the pass.

At intersections, be alert for drivers who pull out before they should, so they can avoid waiting until you and your rig pass through.

A commercial vehicle driver whose income depends on speed sometimes becomes impatient. They see you and your rig as getting in the way of their job. A taxi driver, messenger or any worker who is behind schedule and in a hurry can be a hazard.

## Impairment

While you may meet an impaired driver at any time, you are more likely to meet one late at night. Two common forms of impairment are:
1.   Being under the influence of drugs or alcohol
2.   Fatigue

Some clues to a driver's being under the influence of alcohol or drugs are:
*   Weaving across the lane(s)
*   Running off the right side of the road
*   Going over a curb while turning
*   Stopping for a green light or sitting too long at a stop sign with no cross traffic in the vicinity
*   Driving with the window open in cold weather
*   Erratic speed: too fast, too slow, or changing from fast to slow often
*   The driver talking to him- or herself
*   Throwing material (lighted) out the window
*   Acting unusually happy (false sense of well being)

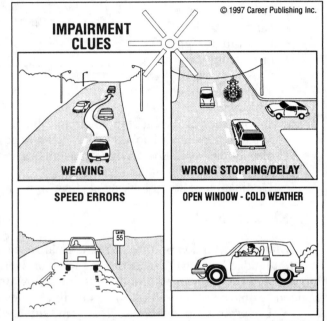

Figure 16-16

Such clues may not mean that a driver is impaired, but your job is to be alert for such clues and drive your rig defensively. If the clues are strong enough, you may want to contact the authorities. Remember, however, you are reporting only unusual or strange behavior! Do not suggest that the other driver may be impaired. The strange driving could be a result of some other condition.

Drowsiness, like being under the influence, has a number of clues. Among them are:
*   Weaving across lanes
*   Running off the right side of the road
*   Slowing down and speeding up

Remember, these clues may also mean something other than sleepiness.

## ACTIVITIES BY OTHER ROAD USERS

Any road user can be a hazard. Clues to hazards are often seen in the activities of road users. Some examples are:
*   Movement by the driver
*   Movement of the vehicle
*   Pedestrian and cyclist activities
*   Conflicts

## Movement by the Driver

Before doing something hazardous, a driver often makes some sudden movement of his or her body. Watch other drivers' heads, body, and vehicles.

**Head Movement:** Looking to the side may mean the driver plans to change direction. Drivers usually look in the direction they are going to turn. A turn of the head, therefore, may warn of a possible turn of the vehicle. You may notice a driver look at the rearview mirror. This may also indicate a lane change.

**Body Movement:** Drivers often straighten up just before turning to brace themselves for the turn and to get better control of the steering wheel.

**Vehicle Movement:** Drivers often edge across a lane in the direction of an intended turn. This sideways, or lateral, movement may be a clue for a lane change or turn.

As you know, big rig drivers, because of the length of their rigs, often make a *button hook* on tight right turns. That is, they swing out to the left to gain turning space before starting the right turn. Other drivers may do it too, especially older drivers. The key is to look out for button hooks. Do not try to pass a vehicle on the right that has swung out to the left just before an intersection.

## Buses and Taxis

Passengers leaving buses may cross the roadway in front of or behind the bus. In many cases, they cannot see your rig, so it is up to you to see and protect them. A taxi that is reducing speed is a clue to possible danger. Drivers looking for passengers or following a passenger's directions often act in ways that create hazards. Slow movement, U-turns, quick stops, and changes in direction are common. Pass cabs carefully because passengers may leave a taxi from either side as soon as it stops. A pedestrian may run out to catch a slow-moving taxi.

**Figure 16-17**

## Pedestrians and Cyclists

Pedestrians and cyclists can be a hazard for many reasons.
- They may travel with their backs to traffic.
- In rainy weather, they often think about the rain.
- Sometimes, they are careless.
- They do not always look around as well as they should.
- Their clothing or something they are carrying can limit their vision. Examples are a hat pulled too low over their eyes or an umbrella.
- They may not realize where they are and move directly into your path.

Watch for people on the sidewalk, shoulder of the road, or road itself.

Always remember children are easily distracted. They tend to act quickly without thinking or looking around. When kids are playing, they do not think about the traffic.

### Emergency Areas

Accident scenes and hospital emergency areas are dangerous for all drivers because of the lookie-lou's. People look away from the road and traffic to see what is happening. This is also true in slow-moving traffic. People become stressed out and try to see the reason for the delay.

### Conflicts

A conflict occurs when a vehicle is on a collision course with an object or another road user. Problems of other road users become your problems when you have to make a sudden change in direction or stop. Such actions can damage your rig or cargo if you are not careful. Being able to see and understand conflicts early is to your benefit. You can then plan what you will do and perhaps avoid the conflict.

### Obstructions

Examples of common obstructions are:
- The end of a lane
- A barricade
- Slow-moving or stalled traffic
- A disabled vehicle
- An accident

Obstructions may be in your lane or another lane. If the obstruction is in your lane, you must see the hazard in time and avoid conflict with it. If the obstruction is in a lane going the same direction as yours or in an opposing lane, you must watch for other road users who may move into your path.

### Merging

Certain merge situations may force another vehicle into your path. Examples include a car that is:
- Entering a freeway
- Pulling out from a driveway or side street
- Moving out of a parallel parking space

### Intersections

When streets or roads come together, conflicts can develop. Other road users may

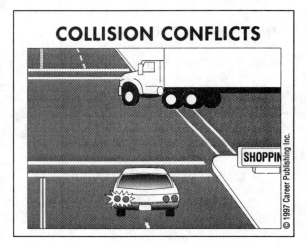

**Figure 16-18**

not stop or yield the right of way. They may be in your blind spot or hidden by shrubbery or buildings. Road users in conflict with you and your rig may come from the right, left, or opposite direction. At times, you may even find yourself in conflict with more than one other road user.

© 1997 Career Publishing Inc.

**Figure 16-19**

# SUMMARY

Blending with other roadway users depends on how well you see and understand the scene and the activities of other road users. The scene, or your environment, includes the:

- Roadway
- Curvature of the road
- Surface condition of the road
- Immediate area around the road

You must watch for and interpret the intentions and actions of other road users. Watch for the clues to guide you and help pinpoint possible hazards.

You should understand that driving is a social act. It involves you, everyone, and every object in your area. Your success as a driver will depend on how well you see and identify the potential hazards and react by adjusting your driving.

# KEY WORDS

**Button hook**: When a driver swings out to the left to gain turning space before starting a right turn.

**Centrifugal force**: The force that *pushes* a vehicle off the road in a curve.

**Clue**: Anything that alerts you to a possible hazard.

**Conflict**: When a vehicle is on a collision course with an object or another road user.

**Hazard**: Any road condition or road user (driver, cyclist, pedestrian, or animal) that presents a possible danger to you or your rig.

**Scene**: The surroundings, or environment, in which the driver operates. It includes the road conditions, weather, scenery, people, animals, and other road users.

**Under the influence**: Refers to any driver operating under the influence of alcohol or drugs.

# LEARNING ACTIVITIES

## Commentary Driving and Hazard Perception

Commentary driving is talking, or making comments, about what you see as you drive. During the on-street part of your instruction, you may be asked to try this exercise. It will help you identify hazards and let your instructor know what you are seeing and how you react to it.

In commentary driving, you do not discuss what you see at length. Your job is to see and identify any possible hazard. Use brief statements such as:

"Boy on right...could come in front of me."

Such statements tell the instructor that you are aware of a possible hazard.

This simple example makes commentary driving sound quite easy. Depending on the situation, it may not be. Seeing and talking about *a boy beside the road* is easy when it is the only thing you have to do. When you add the many other driving tasks, commenting can become very demanding.

Some people find it helpful to identify hazards out loud. Other people, including some instructors, do not like this method. Even though it may seem hard at first, you will find it will help you become a driver who is more aware of his or her surroundings.

## Guidelines for Commentary Driving

1. Identify in your mind any hazard (object, road condition, or road user) that is a possible threat to you. Identify and describe only those hazards to which you must be prepared to respond.
2. Describe the hazard in a few words. Tell what and where it is.
   **Examples:**   "Child in the street on the left."
   "Yellow car on the right."
   "Pavement in the shade of that bridge."
3. Describe in a few words what makes the hazard.
   **Examples:**   "...is looking the other way."
   "...is going to move backward."
   "...might be very slippery."
You do not have to describe how you are going to respond to the hazards.
4. In conflict (possible crash) situations, comment only on the object or vehicle in conflict with your vehicle. Do not bother to comment on the reason the conflict occurred.
   **Examples:**   "...car in my lane."
   "...bicyclist with back toward me in my lane."
   "...wind blowing debris across the road."
   "...cattle in unfenced field."
5. When the object, road condition, or person is not a hazard, say nothing.

## Diagrams

*What is the hazard in each drawing? Draw a circle around it. Comment and tell why it is a hazard on the lines below each drawing.*

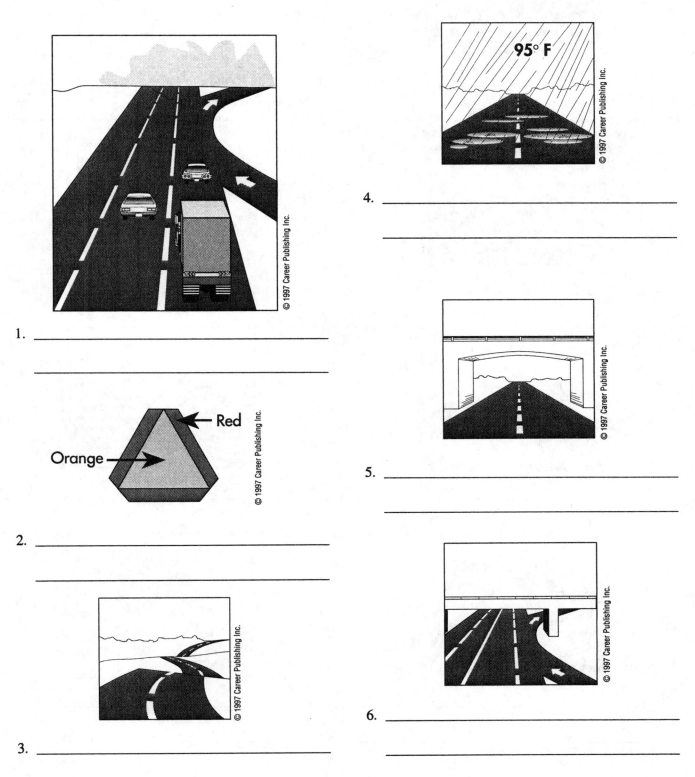

1. _____

_____

2. _____

_____

3. _____

_____

4. _____

_____

5. _____

_____

6. _____

_____

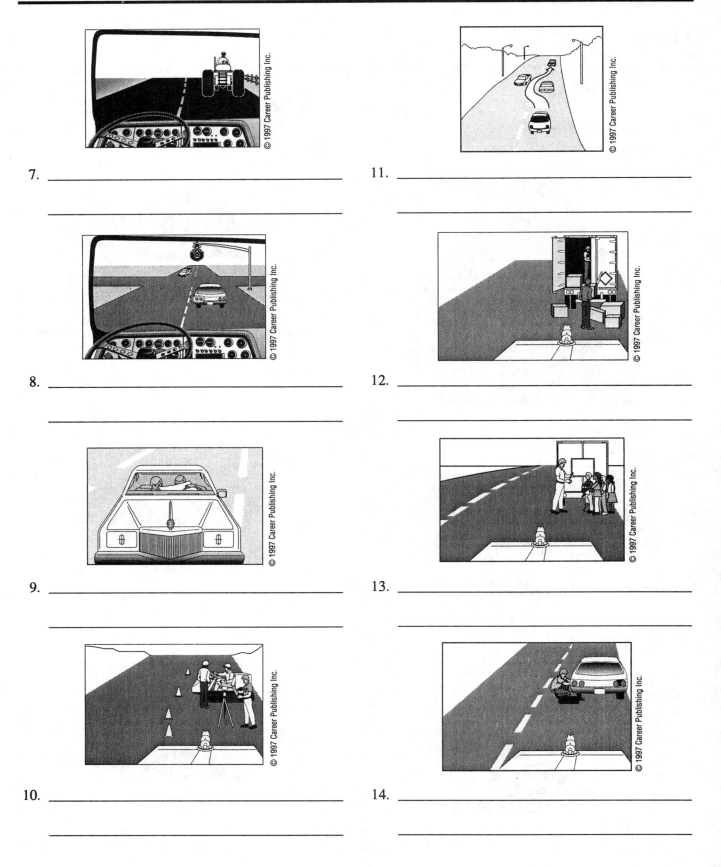

7. _____

_____

8. _____

_____

9. _____

_____

10. _____

_____

11. _____

_____

12. _____

_____

13. _____

_____

14. _____

_____

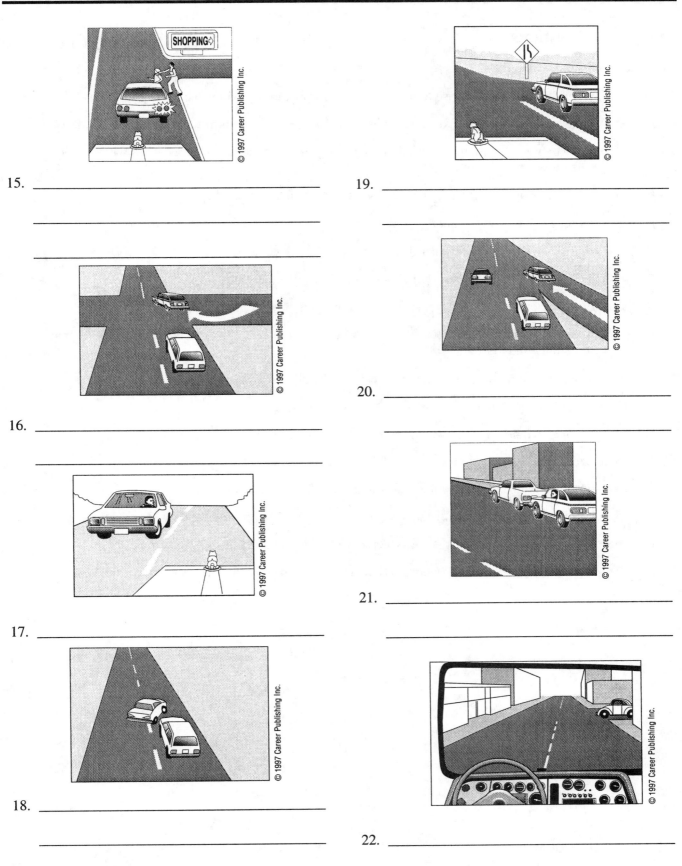

15. _____

_____

_____

16. _____

_____

17. _____

18. _____

_____

_____

19. _____

_____

20. _____

_____

21. _____

_____

22. _____

_____

_____

## True/False Questions

If the question is true, circle the T. If the question is false, circle the F.

T  F    1.   When it is hot, oil may rise to the surface of an asphalt road and make it slippery.

T  F    2.   If the road is properly banked on a curve, vehicles can make the turn at a faster rate of speed.

T  F    3.   Since expressway ramps are properly banked, you do not need to be concerned with your speed when entering a ramp.

T  F    4.   Since your rig is so large and heavy, wind is not likely to affect it.

T  F    5.   As long as you can see another vehicle, you may assume its driver sees you, too.

T  F    6.   You should be very careful when driving near step vans, postal vehicles, and local delivery trucks.

T  F    7.   People in parked vehicles should always be considered hazards.

T  F    8.   Eye contact with other drivers is an important part of avoiding hazards.

T  F    9.   A vehicle carrying luggage on the roof or pulling a trailer is a clue to a hazard. Its driver may do something unexpected.

T  F  10.   Vehicles that travel slower than the speed of the other traffic are possible hazards.

T  F  11.   Some impatient drivers view all trucks as slow moving.

T  F  12.   An open window in cold weather may be a clue that the driver is under the influence.

T  F  13.   Drowsiness, like being under the influence, has a number of clues.

T  F  14.   Fortunately, the clues of intoxication and drowsiness are different.

T  F  15.   Head and body movement can give clues as to what a driver intends to do.

T  F  16.   Since most pedestrians and cyclists travel on the sidewalk, they are not likely to be hazards.

T  F  17.   Traffic merging, such as meeting at intersections, can be hazardous.

# Chapter Seventeen
# EMERGENCY MANEUVERS

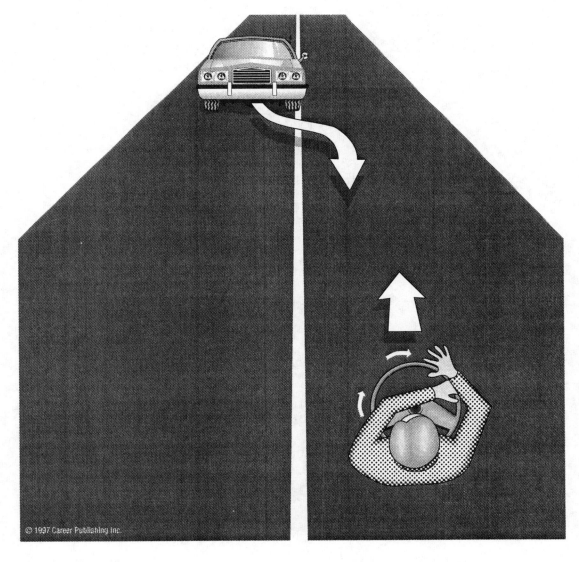

**Avoiding Emergencies • Emergency Maneuvers • Evasive Steering**
**Off-Road Recovery • Emergency Stopping • Brake Failure • Blowouts**

**FROM NOW ON,**

**ONLY THE BEST WILL DRIVE**

# OBJECTIVES

When you have mastered this chapter, you will be able to:

• Think ahead to avoid possible emergencies when driving

• Show how driving through an emergency may be better than trying to stop

• Explain the reasons why leaving the road is safer than a head-on collision

• Describe the correct ways to make quick stops and quick turns off the road

• Describe the safe way to return to the highway

• Explain the methods of handling brake failure and blowouts

# CHAPTER SEVENTEEN

# EMERGENCY MANEUVERS

## INTRODUCTION

Ideally, road users should avoid one another. Drivers of cars, vans, trucks, buses, motorcycles and bicycles should keep space between themselves and other users to avoid problems. In real life, it does not always work that way.

We all make mistakes that can create emergencies. This chapter will help you prepare for, recognize, and react to those emergencies. It will help you learn how to:
- Handle difficult situations.
- Maintain control of your rig.
- Avoid other road users through quick turns and changes in speed.

## AVOIDING EMERGENCIES

The best way to handle an emergency is to avoid it. This sounds simple, but most emergencies happen when drivers make mistakes. These mistakes often create unsafe situations. If we do not **drive defensively,** accidents can occur.

Professional drivers reduce their chances of an accident by using the knowledge and skill described in this book. They recognize possible emergencies and react to them in a way that avoids the problem.

There are a number of safe driving practices that will reduce your chances of an emergency. They include:

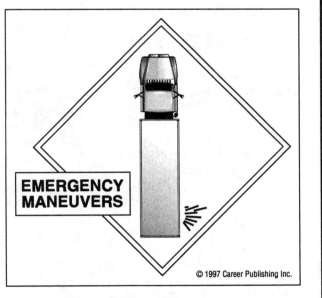

Figure 17-1

- Vehicle inspection
- Visual search
- Recognizing hazards
- Communication
- Speed management
- Space management
- Familiarity with night operations
- Skill in driving during extreme operating conditions
- Maintaining good health
- Observing safety practices

An Indiana University study has shown that 1/3 of all vehicle accidents could have been avoided with the proper driving techniques. Though an escape route, or *out*, was usually available, the study found that most drivers hit the brakes and let their vehicles skid out of control. Panic braking is a result of habit. Drivers tend to put on the brakes in emergencies and tight situations.

## TYPES OF EMERGENCY MANEUVERS

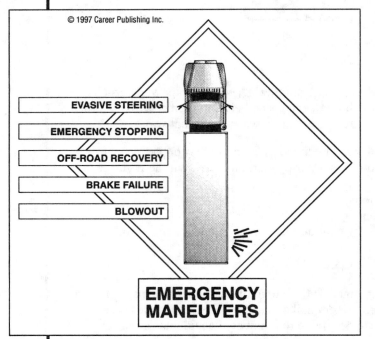

© 1997 Career Publishing Inc.

EVASIVE STEERING

EMERGENCY STOPPING

OFF-ROAD RECOVERY

BRAKE FAILURE

BLOWOUT

**EMERGENCY MANEUVERS**

**Figure 17-2**

Five emergency maneuvers will be reviewed in this section. They include:

1. **Evasive Steering:** Steering out of an emergency situation.
2. **Off-road Recovery:** Using the roadside as an escape path and safely returning to the highway.
3. **Emergency Stopping:** Stopping quickly while keeping the vehicle under control.
4. **Handling Brake Failure:** Stopping the truck when the brakes fail.
5. **Blowout:** Maintaining control when a front tire blows.

## EVASIVE STEERING

Evasive steering is a safe and important way to get out of an emergency situation.
- It reduces the chances of an accident.
- It reduces the severity of the accident.
- It allows the use of possible escape routes.

**Reducing the chance of an accident:** You can usually turn a truck quicker than you can stop. Often you can turn far enough to avoid the emergency.

**Reducing the severity of an accident:** If evasive steering is used, any accident that occurs

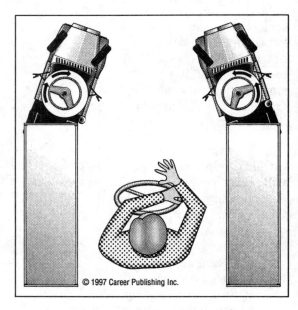

© 1997 Career Publishing Inc.

**Figure 17-3**

will probably be less severe than a head-on collision. With the size, weight, and height of a truck, a head-on or rear-end collision is more likely to be fatal.

**Using possible escape routes:** Another lane or the road shoulder are possible escape routes. If a lane is available, a quick lane change is often the best escape route. If there is not a lane available, the shoulder of the road is sometimes a suitable escape route.

If there is a choice between a collision and trying evasive action, trying to evade the collision is usually safer. A sharp turn of the steering wheel can cause a roll-over, so other evasive actions are probably safer.

If you are hauling a stable load and your rig has a low center of gravity, you have the best chance of avoiding an accident when using evasive action. Firm traction on the road or shoulder offers added safety.

## General Procedures for Evasive Steering

- When you use evasive steering, turn as little as possible to avoid the emergency. Turn quickly. Be sure to use correct braking while you are turning. Countersteer when you have passed the emergency. **Countersteering** means turning back toward your intended path of travel.

- To turn as quickly as possible, hand-over-hand steering is best. Placing the hands in the 9:00 - 3:00 position lets the wheel turn 180° without releasing either hand. If you always make sure you drive with your hands in this position, you will be ready if a quick turn is needed.

- Brake before turning. If you can, avoid braking in a turn. Braking in a turn can cause the tractor and trailer wheels to lock up. By braking before the turn, a sharper turn can be made. Also there is less chance of a roll-over or jacknife.

- After making an evasive turn, be ready to countersteer at once. Do it smoothly to keep your rig from going out of the escape path and off the road. Timing is very important. Begin to countersteer as soon as the front of the trailer clears the obstacle.

**Seatbelts:** Most people do not know all the benefits of wearing a seatbelt. When you turn the steering wheel of a rig quickly, you can slide out from under the wheel and lose control if you are not wearing a seatbelt.

Many **secondary collisions** occur when a driver swerves to avoid an emergency and slides out of the correct seating position. The driver is not able to countersteer and loses control of the rig. Always wear your seatbelt.

## Evasive Driving in Specific Situations

Different evasive techniques are used for different situations. Some of the most common situations are those that deal with:
- An oncoming vehicle
- A stopped vehicle
- A merging vehicle

## Oncoming Vehicle

This is one of the most frightening emergencies. Another vehicle comes right toward you from the opposite direction. Driver error is nearly always the cause of this problem. The driver may be:

- Impaired
- Not paying attention
- Asleep
- Under the influence
- Ill
- Simply reckless

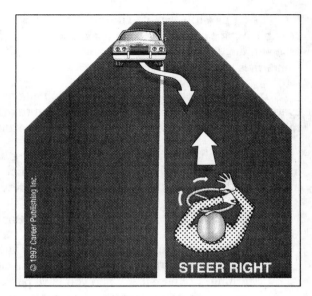

**Figure 17-4**

In any event, you must try to prevent a collision. The best move is usually to try to move to your right. A blast of your horn may startle the other driver into corrective action. Remember, leaving the road on the right is nearly always better than a head-on collision.

Steering to the left is usually a bad move. The other driver may try to correct position by pulling back into their lane. Then you will still be on a collision course — but on the left side of the road.

## Stopped Vehicle

This situation usually happens in one of two ways.
1. You may be following the car ahead of you too closely and they suddenly stop.
2. You may come over the top of a hill to find a stopped vehicle in your lane.

You can take three possible evasive actions when this happens.

**Figure 17-5**

1. If the lane to your left is clear, you can turn into that lane and avoid the obstacle. This move is usually better than a swerve to the right; it prevents side-swiping a vehicle on your right. The height of the cab lets you see if the oncoming lane is clear. This is one emergency situation in which it can be safe to turn left into an oncoming lane.
2. If you are along a clear shoulder with a good surface, you can swerve to the right. Side-swiping another vehicle on a shoulder is rare.
3. If you are in one of the middle lanes of a multi-lane road, move into whichever lane is clear. Otherwise, evade to the right. If there is a vehicle in the right lane, it is better to force it over than to force another vehicle into an oncoming lane.

### Merging Vehicle

This situation can develop in a number of ways.
*   Another vehicle may try to change lanes and move into your lane.
*   Another vehicle may try to merge onto the highway without yielding to you.
*   A vehicle may pull out from a side street, driveway, or parking space.
*   Another road user, such as a pedestrian or cyclist, may enter the highway.

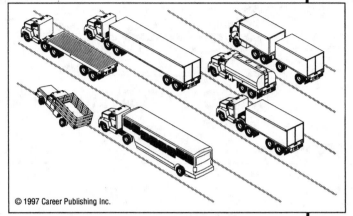

© 1997 Career Publishing Inc.

**Figure 17-6**

Blasting your horn can startle the other person and cause them to make a sudden stop. If this happens, you may have to do less evasive steering to avoid the problem. Studies show that drivers often do not use their horn because other drivers do not like it. Annoying other drivers with your horn is better than a collision.

## Stopping Instead of Evasive Steering

If there is **enough space**, a *quick* stop is always safer than an evasive turn. Then there is no risk of collision with a vehicle you did not see. Also, such a stop is not likely to cause a jacknife or roll-over.

When evasive steering is not possible, braking is your only option. Even if you cannot bring your rig to a full stop, the impact of the collision will not be as hard, and both vehicles will have less damage. There will also be less chance of an injury or death.

If your truck has antilock brakes, it will be possible to brake and make an evasive turn at the same time without losing control.

## OFF-ROAD RECOVERY

When the area beside the road provides the best escape path, it may be either the right shoulder of the road or the shoulder of the median strip.

Most drivers fear leaving the road. This is because staying on the road is a strong habit. Drivers often fear the shoulder will not support their rig. Drivers also sometimes hear of a crash when the roadside is used for evasive action. The truth is most roadside crashes result from drivers being distracted or falling asleep. Keep in mind that many evasive actions are successful and do not result in an accident. These are not reported.

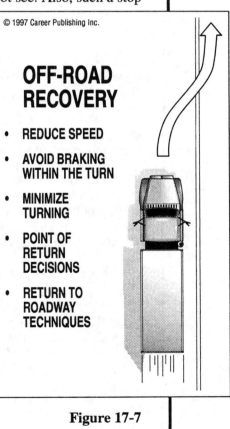

© 1997 Career Publishing Inc.

**OFF-ROAD RECOVERY**

*   **REDUCE SPEED**
*   **AVOID BRAKING WITHIN THE TURN**
*   **MINIMIZE TURNING**
*   **POINT OF RETURN DECISIONS**
*   **RETURN TO ROADWAY TECHNIQUES**

**Figure 17-7**

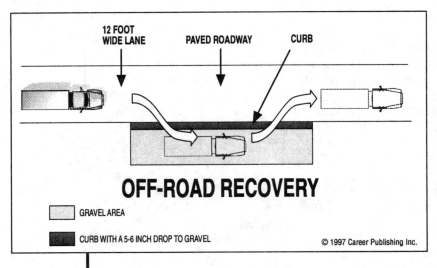

**Figure 17-8**

Sometimes drivers wait too long to leave the road. Successful off-road recovery often means the driver must leave the road at once. Most accidents that result from using the roadside are caused by the driver's poor technique. Generally, off-road recovery is safe when the roadside is wide enough and firm enough to handle the rig, and the driver uses good judgement.

## Procedure

If you see the need to leave the road to avoid a collision, remember to:
• Brake before turning.
• Avoid braking in the turn.
• Turn as little as possible, unless your rig has antilock brakes.

You also need to think about:
• Whether the roadside is clear
• When and how to countersteer
• How to handle the wheel-drop that often happens as the wheels leave the road

**Brake before turning:** When you plan to leave the road, slow down as much as you can. Use controlled braking or stab braking to keep control of your rig.

**Avoid braking in the turn unless your rig has antilock brakes:** If you brake in a turn and the brakes lock, you may go into a skid. Control of steering is very important when you enter the roadside.

**Turn as little as possible:** If possible, keep one set of wheels on the pavement. You will keep better control of the steering. Traction is better on the pavement because gravel and dirt reduce your traction. Reduced traction causes skids. Turn as little as possible on the roadside. Maintain as straight a course as possible. Remember, each turn creates a chance for a skid.

## Returning to the Highway

After leaving the road, drivers often try to return too quickly. You should grasp the wheel firmly and think about steering straight ahead. Stay on the roadside and allow the engine compression to stop the rig. Put on the brakes only when you have slowed enough to stop safely. Signal and check your mirrors before you return to the road.

If there is a telephone pole, sign, parked vehicle, or other obstacle in your path, stay off the road until your view is clear. Then turn back sharply onto the road.

Attempting a gradual return may cause you to lose control of your rig and go into a skid. The skid may make your rig cross into an oncoming lane, jacknife, or roll over. Turning sharply lets you countersteer and decide the point where you will return to the road.

### Countersteering

When you return to the road, **countersteer** (turn quickly away from the road). Countersteer as soon as the right front wheel rides up onto the surface of the road. Both turning back on the road and countersteering should be done as a single steering move.

### When the Wheels Drop Off the Road

Wheels sometimes drop off the pavement when a rig is too close to the edge. Drivers often try to return at once. Do not do this. With one side of the rig on the pavement, controlling your rig is easy. Trying a quick return has caused many drivers to roll over or skid into oncoming traffic. **Come to a complete stop before you attempt to return to the road.**

Follow the same procedure as you do for an off-road recovery. If the path ahead is clear, let the vehicle slow to a complete stop. Then return to the road when it is safe.

## EMERGENCY STOPPING

By using your brakes properly, you can maintain control of the rig and shorten the distance required for stopping. There are two ways of braking, depending on your rig's braking system. If it does not have antilock brakes and you brake too much or too hard, you can lock the wheels and cause a skid. A skid can produce a jacknife in which the trailer may hit the tractor. Either the tractor or trailer may then collide with other roadway users, trees, or buildings. If your rig has antilock brakes, hit them hard and hold down the pedal. The system's electronic controls will ensure the wheels do not lock.

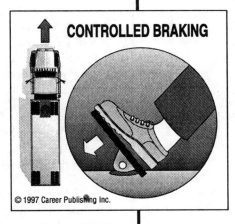

If a vehicle pulls in front of you and you are going to overtake it quickly at your present speed, you can:
- Steer to the left or right (evasive steering) without braking in vehicles without antilock brakes.
- Brake quickly.

If oncoming traffic and vehicles on the right prevent evasive steering, you have no choice but to brake quickly. For rigs with antilock brakes, either of two emergency braking techniques can be used.
1. Controlled braking
2. Stab braking

They both prevent a skid or jacknife.

**Figure 17-9**

### Controlled Braking

In controlled braking, put on the brakes with a steady pressure just short of wheel lockup. The point of lock-up differs among vehicles and it is hard to find the exact point. Practice in your rig to find the lock-up point. If you do not know where the lock-up point is, stab braking is best.

### Stab Braking

When you use stab braking, apply the brakes fully. Then release the pedal partly when the wheels lock. Put on the brakes again when the wheels start to roll. Repeat the stab braking sequence until you can safely stop or turn.

Remember, putting on the brakes again before the wheels begin to roll can cause a skid. Stab braking lets you have maximum braking when the brakes are applied. It then avoids a skid when the brakes are released.

**Figure 17-10**

## BRAKE FAILURE

Well maintained brake systems rarely fail completely. Several devices are designed to prevent brake failure from causing an accident. However, brake failure can occur in a runaway vehicle. If you keep cool, you can usually bring your rig under control.

Brakes can fail because of:
• Loss of air pressure
• Air blockage
• Brake fade
• Mechanical failure

### Loss of Air Pressure

If a leak occurs in the air system, a warning buzzer will sound when the air

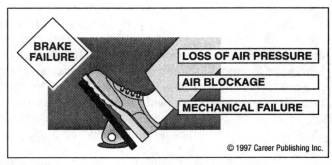

**Figure 17-11**

pressure gets too low. When this happens, you should stop at once. If you do not stop, you may lose more air from the system. Then your brakes will fail, and you cannot stop.

A built-in safety system automatically puts on the brakes when the air loss reaches a critical level. This happens while there is still enough air in the system to stop the rig. However, if the loss is too fast, the air supply may be used up before the rig is stopped.

The independent trailer brake valve will not put on the trailer brakes because they depend on the air system. If the rig has spring loaded parking brakes, the brakes will come on automatically when the air pressure fails. They will generally stop the truck unless it is on a steep downgrade.

### Air Blockage

Air blockage happens when air is kept from reaching the brakes. A common cause is water freezing in the air system.

## Brake Fade

Brake fade occurs when the brakes overheat and lose their ability to stop the truck on a downgrade.

## Mechanical Failure

Some part in the braking system may not work. Usually, this will not affect all of the brakes at the same time; the rig can then be stopped.

**Figure 17-12**

## Procedures to Follow if the Brakes Fail

If your brakes fail, you must do two things.
1.  Reduce speed as much as possible.
2.  Find an escape path and follow it.

## Reduce Speed

If your rig is on a level surface, try to downshift. This will let the engine act as a brake to slow the rig. It also raises the rpm and increases the air pressure. Keep on downshifting until your rig is moving slowly enough you can stop it with the spring loaded parking brake. Do not downshift on a downgrade (see the chapter on Extreme Driving Conditions).

## Find an Escape Path

Begin looking for an escape path at once. Do not wait to see if the rig can be stopped. If you do so, you may go past the only available escape path. Some safe escape paths include:
*   A side road (particularly if it runs uphill)
*   An open field (even though you may damage the undercarriage)
*   A runaway vehicle escape ramp

## Other Things to Do

**Create Drag:** You may have to take other actions to slow down. Rubbing tires along the curb can help. In open country, you may be able to drive into heavy brush or small bushes. Remember, the main idea is to prevent serious damage to the rig or injury to yourself and others by avoiding a collision with other vehicles.

**Inspect the Brakes:** After escaping the emergency, pull over to the side of the road. Stop and inspect your rig to find out what caused the brake failure. Do not return to the road until the brakes are working properly. This may require road service. Some drivers try to *nurse* the rig along to a repair station. This is a bad move. You may have another failure and be unable to avoid serious damage or injury.

## BLOWOUTS

A blowout occurs when a tire suddenly loses air. This can happen because the tire may:

- Be worn to the point that it is too thin to hold air
- Have a crack in the tire casing
- Be damaged from debris, potholes, curbs, nails, etc.

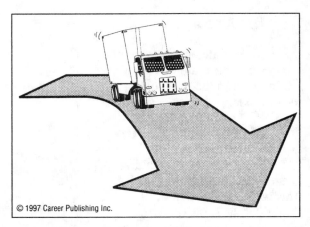

© 1997 Career Publishing Inc.

**Figure 17-13**

You can prevent blowouts resulting from wear by careful pre-trip inspections and proper braking.

### What Happens When a Tire Blows Out

A front tire blowout will cause steering problems so the rig will veer to the side. Blowout to a rear tractor tire may produce a vibration in the cab. This can cause the rear of the tractor to pull in the direction of the air loss. Trailer tire blowouts can generally be identified by handling difficulties or sound. If it is an outside tire, you may be able to see it in your mirrors.

### Front Tire Blowout

If a front tire blows, you usually hear a loud bang. Remember, a tire can also deflate without a sound. Grasp the wheel tightly so it will not be jerked from your hands. You may have steering problems. You want to keep the rig from veering off to the side. Speed up to stop the side force and regain control. Then bring the vehicle to a gradual, controlled stop.

Having to grasp the wheel tightly in an emergency is one reason to hold the wheel at the 9:00 and 3:00 positions at all times. When holding the wheel at the 9:00 and 3:00 positions, the thumbs should be facing up. The force of a blowout can break a thumb wrapped around the wheel or under a wheel spoke.

By speeding up at once when you have a blowout, you help keep the rig moving in a straight line. Slow down gradually when you have the rig under control. Braking after a front tire blowout is dangerous because it shifts weight to the front of the vehicle and makes steering more difficult.

After the engine has slowed down the rig, it is safe to gently put on the brakes. You can then slowly pull off the road and brake gently to a stop.

**Front Tire Blowout: AVOID BRAKING**

© 1997 Career Publishing Inc.

**Figure 17-14**

## Rear Tire Blowout

A blowout of a tire on the rear of the tractor is not as dangerous as one on a front wheel. You usually will not feel any pull on the steering wheel, but the truck may pull to the side of the flat. The trailer can, however, lean toward the side of the blown tire.

Do not brake at once. Let the rig slow down gradually. Then brake slowly and pull off the road before gently braking to a stop.

The tire should be changed as soon as possible. Check for damage the blown tire may have done. Check:
- The air lines and other parts
- The tire rim
- For fire
- For damage to other vehicles

NOTE: Remember, it is illegal to drive on damaged tire rims. If a rim is damaged, have it fixed before driving further.

## SUMMARY

In this chapter, you learned how to avoid some emergencies. You were shown how to steer evasively, how to recover when your rig goes off the road, and how best to stop in an emergency. You were also taught the reasons for brake failure and what to do when it occurs. Tire blowouts were described and so were the safest ways to deal with them.

## KEY WORDS

**Countersteering**: Turning sharply in one direction and then quickly turning back in the other direction.

**Defensive driving**: Driving to avoid or get out of problems that may be created by other drivers.

**Secondary collision**: A collision that results from either being involved in an accident or taking evasive action to avoid an emergency.

# LEARNING ACTIVITIES

## Problem Solving — Emergencies

The emergency situations described here are examples of some of the problems that can develop during routine driving. The instructor will describe the conditions and then ask the class to discuss how to solve the emergency. He or she may also show you a visual. The class will review the correct procedures and suggest how the problem might have been avoided through safe driving practices. These include communication, speed and space management, and a careful search of the scene.

The correct procedures for avoiding the accident are found at the end of the chapter.

## A.  Oncoming Car Passing

You are traveling 55 mph when an oncoming car tries to pass two vehicles. The lead car is a compact and was not seen at first by the driver who is now committed to overtaking and passing both vehicles. A high curb runs along the right side of the road. Trees on the right are an additional hazard.

Name two things you should do.

1.  _____

2.  _____

3.  Do not _____

4.  Why? _____

## B.  Pedestrian in Street

You are traveling at 35 mph on a four-lane divided highway. A pedestrian runs into the road 75 feet in front of your rig. There is a low curb to your right. There is not enough time to brake.

1.  What can you expect the pedestrian to do? _____

2.  What is your best escape route? _____

3.  Do not _____

4.  Why? _____

## C.  Car Turning Left

While traveling at 40 mph, you see a car parked on the right moving out to cut across the road and make a left turn. There is not enough time to brake and trying to will put you into a skid. There are no other vehicles parked on the right.

1.  One good action is _____

2.  Do not _____

3.  Why? _____

## D.  Bicyclist

You are moving at 30 mph and a bicyclist 75 feet ahead swerves in front of your rig. There are no oncoming vehicles.

Name three things you can do.

1.  _____

2.  _____

3.  _____

## E.   Car Pulling Out

You are moving along a two-lane street with cars parked parallel to the curb. On the right side, a car pulls out about one car-length ahead of you. There are no oncoming vehicles.

Name two things you should do.

1. _____

2. _____

3. What may happen if you put on your brakes? _____

    _____

## F.   Head-on Collision

While traveling 55 mph on a two-lane road, an oncoming vehicle moves out of its lane and into your path. There are no obstructions on the right shoulder.

Name two things you can do to encourage the other vehicle to return to its lane.

1. _____

2. _____

3. What else should you do? _____

## G.   Fallen Motorcyclist

You are moving at 45 mph and are being passed by an oncoming car. At the same time, a car is passing you on the right. There is a grassy shoulder on the right. A motorcycle rider falls down ahead of you.

Name two things you should do.

1. _____

2. _____

3. Why will you not honk the horn? _____

## H.   Ice Cream Truck

You are moving at 25 mph when an ice cream truck stops about 100 feet ahead because a child has run in front of it. A parked car and an oncoming car prevent evasive steering.

1. What should you do?_____

## I.   Hillcrest

While traveling on a two-lane highway at 50 mph, you go over the crest of a hill and see an on-coming car 150 feet ahead in your lane.

Name two things you can do to avoid a collision.

1. _____

2. _____

## True-False Questions

If the statement is true, circle the T. If the statement is false, circle the F.

T  F     1.   When there is a hazard, it is usually easier to stop a rig than to steer around the hazard.

T  F     2.   When you must swerve off the right side of the road to avoid a collision, it is best if only the wheels on the right side of the rig leave the road.

T  F     3.   When you leave the road, you should return as soon as you have passed the hazard.

T  F     4.   You should avoid a head-on collision even if you must leave the road to do it.

T  F     5.   A driver usually has to train him- or herself to think of how to avoid an emergency rather than slamming on the brakes when the hazard appears.

T  F     6.   A rig can be stopped more quickly than it can be turned.

T  F     7.   The safest way to handle an emergency is to keep it from happening in the first place.

T  F     8.   Most emergencies occur because of mechanical failure.

T  F     9.   Speed management helps the driver handle possible emergencies.

T  F    10.   With knowledge and experience, you can usually stop your rig safely even though the brakes have failed.

## Answers to Problem Solving — Emergencies

### A.   Oncoming Car Passing

1.   *Reduce speed as much as possible.*
2.   *Squeeze as far to the right of the road as possible.*
     Oncoming cars (those being overtaken and passed) will also squeeze to their right. This should result in an alley for the passing car.
3.   Do not *try to climb the curb.*
4.   Why? *Your rig can bounce back into the center of the road.*

### B.   Pedestrian in Street

1.   *Continue, stop, or turn around and try to return to the side of the road.*
2.   *The roadside to the right.* The curb can be easily mounted and there is plenty of open space beyond the curb.
3.   Do not *use your horn.*
4.   Why? *It can cause the pedestrian to turn back.*

### C.   Car Turning Left

1.   *To angle to the right just far enough to pass behind the car.*
2.   Do not *use the horn.*
3.   Why? *It can frighten the other driver and cause him or her to stop and block your escape route.*

## D. Bicyclist

1. *Slow down.*
2. *Keep as far behind the bicyclist as possible.*
3. *Sound your horn.*
   Sounding your horn should cause the cyclist to swerve back to the right. This will create space for you to move by on the left.

## E. Car Pulling Out

1. *Swerve to the left.*
2. *Sound your horn.*
3. *Braking may cause a skid.*
   Sounding your horn may cause the driver pulling out to stop and reduce the amount of swerve you will need to make.

## F. Head-on Collision

1. *Blast your horn.*
2. *Flash your headlights.*
3. *Swerve to the right.*
   When you swerve to the right, try to keep your left tires on the pavement. Concentrate on steering. After the oncoming vehicle has passed, let your rig come to a complete stop. When it is safe, pull back onto the highway.

## G. Fallen Motorcyclist

1. *Brake hard.*
2. *Ease off the brakes and start swerving to the right.*
   Swerving to the right will force the car on your right to swerve to the right also. Side-swiping the passing car is better than hitting either the motorcyclist or the oncoming car.
3. *It will not communicate a definite message and may only confuse the other driver.*

## H. Ice Cream Truck

1. *Brake to a stop.*
   You have enough room between you and the ice cream truck to stop. Use either controlled braking or stab braking.

## I. Hillcrest

1. *Brake hard to slow down as much as you can.*
2. *Swerve to the right if the car does not return to its lane.*
   There is not enough room to brake to a stop but you should brake hard to reduce speed. If necessary, drive off the right side of the roadway. You have done everything possible to avoid a head-on collision in this situation.

# Chapter Eighteen
# SKID CONTROL AND RECOVERY

© 1997 Career Publishing Inc.

**Vehicle Control Factors • Traction • Wheel Load • Force of Motion • Preventing Skids • Causes of Skids • Types of Skids • Tractor - Trailer Skids • Jackknife • Front Wheel Skid • All Wheel Skid • Skid Recovery**

FROM NOW ON,

ONLY THE BEST WILL DRIVE

## OBJECTIVES

When you have mastered this chapter, you will be able to:

- Show how skid control can prevent accidents

- Explain vehicle control factors, including traction, wheel load, and force of motion

- Describe the causes of skidding

- Illustrate a tractor jackknife, front wheel skid, and an all wheel skid

- Explain recovery techniques

- Show why most skids can be prevented and can occur at any speed

- Describe the ways to recover from a skid if it is detected early and corrected properly

# CHAPTER EIGHTEEN

# SKID CONTROL

## INTRODUCTION

Everyone knows that vehicles can skid. When a vehicle skids, it is out of control. What many people do not know is that the driver can prevent most skids. It is much easier to prevent a skid than to correct one.

Almost all skids happen because the driver makes a mistake. The most common mistake is trying to quickly change speed or direction. The driver may speed up or slow down too quickly. He or she may try to make too tight a turn for the conditions.

Most skids happen when the road is slippery. It may be:
• Raining
• Snowing
• Icy

Loose material on the pavement like gravel or wet leaves can also make the road slippery. Because the major cause of skids is a sudden change in speed or direction, drivers must always be aware of the road surface and adjust their speed to it.

In this chapter, you will learn:
• About skids
• How skids happen
• How they can be prevented
• How to correct them

You will discuss skid prevention and recovery in the classroon. Hands on experience should be practiced only in the skid pan or on a special driver training range.

NOTE: Most of the instruction in this chapter assumes that neither the tractor nor the trailer has antilock brakes. If you drive a newer truck, it will probably have antilock brakes. Many of the same principles of motion apply, but you will need to brake differently to achieve the shortest stopping distance.

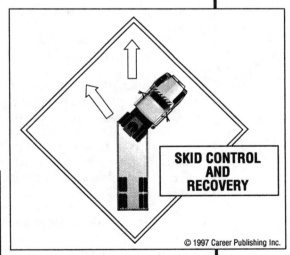

© 1997 Career Publishing Inc.

**Figure 18-1**

## VEHICLE CONTROL FACTORS

Factors that affect control of the vehicle include:
• Traction
• Wheel load
• Force of motion
When the vehicle control factors are not in balance, a skid will occur.

## Traction

Traction is the *grip* between the tires and the road surface. It is the only contact the rig has with the road. Traction determines how much control the driver has over the rig. If the tires have good traction, the driver can speed up, steer, and stop properly. If there is poor traction, the driver cannot control the rig and may go into a skid.

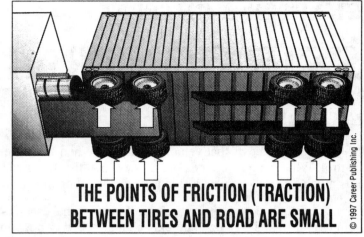

THE POINTS OF FRICTION (TRACTION) BETWEEN TIRES AND ROAD ARE SMALL

© 1997 Career Publishing Inc.

**Figure 18-2**

- When you speed up, traction between the tires and the pavement causes the vehicle to move.
- When you steer, the traction of the tires on the road surface resists the sideways (lateral) movement. This traction helps control the direction in which the rig will go.
- When you brake, the friction of the brake system slows the turning of the wheels. The traction of the tires against the pavement slows down the rig.

There are two types of traction the wheels can have with the surface of the road.

1. Rolling traction
2. Sliding traction

**Rolling Traction:** Rolling traction is the friction of one surface rolling over another. The friction of a rolling tire moving over the road in the same direction the rig is moving is an example.

**Sliding Traction:** Sliding traction is the friction of one surface sliding across another. This occurs when other forces acting upon surfaces are greater than the traction between them. This can happen whether the wheels are locked or turning.

The tires may slide in any direction when they lock from too much braking. Too much outward force may cause tires to slide sideways even though the wheels are turning.

## Wheel Load

Wheel load is the downward force of weight on a wheel. The greater the load on the wheel, the better the traction. Wheel load is determined by the weight of the vehicle and the weight and distribution of the load.

## Force of Motion

The force of the motion of the rig is determined by the weight and speed of the rig. The heavier the rig and load and the faster it is going, the greater the force that moves the rig.

To keep the rig under control, you must avoid skids as you drive. Remember, the major cause of skidding is a sudden change in either speed or direction.

**Speed**: A sudden change in speed can result from either too much braking or speeding up too fast. If the forces of motion are more than the traction of the tire against the pavement when you brake, the rig will skid instead of stopping.

Most people know that braking too hard will cause a skid. Not as many know that speeding up too fast increases the wheel speed to a point where the tires cannot provide traction. When this happens, a skid occurs. In some cases, such skids will simply be a spinning of the drive wheels. In more severe cases, the tractor may skid sideways or even jackknife.

**Direction**: Changing the direction of your steering too quickly can cause the rolling tires to lose their friction with the road surface. When this happens, the rig continues in the direction it is moving instead of changing to follow the direction of the steering wheel.

## PREVENTING SKIDS

It is better to keep skids from happening than to try to get out of them. Safe driving practices discussed in earlier chapters can help prevent skids.

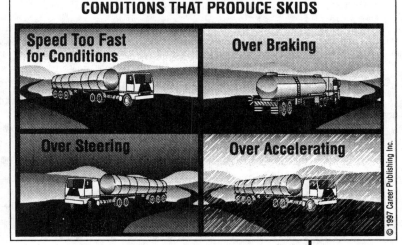

**Figure 18-3**

- Adjust your speed to curves. This will reduce your chances of a cornering skid.
- Drive within your sight distance. This reduces the need for sudden stops and the chances of a braking skid.
- Maintain enough following distance so you will not have to stop quickly.
- Do not drive too fast on slippery surfaces.
- Adjust your speed to the surface condition and curvature of the road.
- Do not over-brake.
- Do not suddenly downshift.
- Use the brake limiting valve correctly.
- Inspect the air system and brake adjustment before and during each trip. All wheels should start stopping at the same time. If they do not, a skid can result when you brake.
- Inspect the tires, front wheel alignment, and suspension system.
- Load the cargo properly.

## CAUSES OF SKIDS

To review, there are two basic causes of skids. They are sudden changes in:
1. Speed
2. Direction

## Change in Speed

Skids involving speed may be from braking or acceleration. Braking skids result in:

- Wheel lock-up
- Tire slides

These increase the rig's stopping distance and can cause the driver to lose control.

**Wheel lock-up** happens when you:

- Put on the service brakes, exhaust brakes, or speed retarder too hard.
- Downshift too much.
- Slow down suddenly.

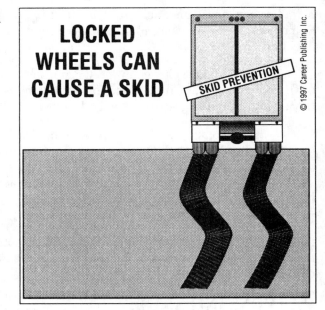

**LOCKED WHEELS CAN CAUSE A SKID**

SKID PREVENTION

© 1997 Career Publishing Inc.

Figure 18-4

You lose control when the locked wheels slide and the rig skids out of control. The skid may be straight ahead, sideways, or a jackknife. The unit will be out of control until the driver corrects the problem or a collision occurs.

**Tire slides** occur when the forces from weight and acceleration of the rig are greater than the tires' ability to maintain traction. Wheel lock-ups and tire slides increase the rig's stopping distance. Remember, sliding tires do not slow a vehicle as well as rolling tires will.

Spinning of the tires occurs when the force from acceleration on the drive wheels is more than the tires' ability to provide traction. The wheels spin, but the vehicle does not move. The spinning continues until the driver stops accelerating. The rear of the tractor may also move in a sideways spin. This is called a **power skid**.

Slowing down too fast can also cause a skid. If a rig has moved onto ice and the driver suddenly recognizes the problem, he or she may quickly react by removing their foot from the accelerator. This action may reduce the wheel speed too fast and cause a skid. If possible, slow down before reaching an icy spot.

## Change of Direction

When a vehicle makes a turn, centrifugal force makes it want to keep going in the same direction. As a result, the vehicle tends to slide outward in a turn.

If the rate of speed or the sharpness of the turn is too great, force exceeds traction. This causes the tires to skid sideways. A new driver may put on the brakes suddenly. The wheels will then lock up. This will make the skid worse. The driver will then have even less control of the rig.

# TRACTOR-TRAILER SKIDS

Tractor-trailer skids are grouped by what happens to the rig. There are four major types of skids.

1. Trailer jackknife
2. Tractor jackknife
3. Front wheel skid
4. All wheel skid

## Trailer Jackknife

A trailer jackknife is caused by too much braking or cornering. In either case, the trailer tires skid because they are locked. The force of locking them has overcome the traction with the surface of the road.

**Over-Braking**: A driver can over-brake by putting on the foot brake too hard or not using the trailer brake correctly. The trailer brake should not be used for stopping.

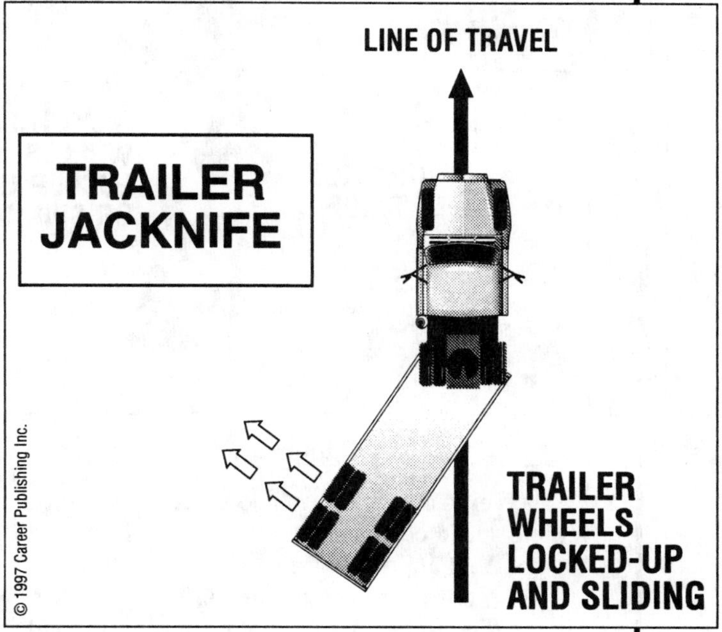

**TRAILER JACKKNIFE**

LINE OF TRAVEL

TRAILER WHEELS LOCKED-UP AND SLIDING

© 1997 Career Publishing Inc.

**Figure 18-5**

Sometimes, the driver uses the brakes too much because there is a mechanical problem such as:

- A faulty air system that sends too much pressure to the trailer wheels
- Not adjusting the brakes on the trailer properly
- Worn trailer brake linings that cause brake seizure
- A light trailer load

**Excessive Cornering:** If a rig enters a curve too fast for the surface conditions, the tires may lose traction. The rig may jackknife or go out of control. Adjust your speed before you enter the curve.

A trailer jackknife can be prevented by adjusting speed to the surface conditions and curvature of the road. Inspect the air system and brake adjustments before and during each trip.

## Tractor Jackknife

A tractor jackknife (drive wheel skid) happens when the tractor drive wheels lose traction because of:

- Wheel lock-up
- Over-acceleration
- Trailer override

When any of these three conditions happen, the drive wheels have less traction than the front wheels. They then try to overtake the front wheels. As a result, the rear of the tractor tends to swing out. As it swings out, the tractor pulls the trailer outward. The trailer then pushes the tractor outward and a jackknife results.

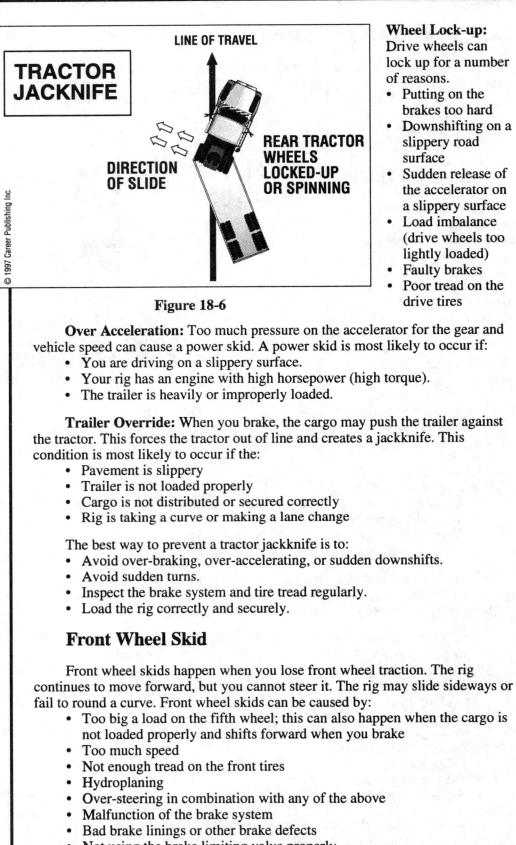

**Figure 18-6**

**Wheel Lock-up:**
Drive wheels can lock up for a number of reasons.
• Putting on the brakes too hard
• Downshifting on a slippery road surface
• Sudden release of the accelerator on a slippery surface
• Load imbalance (drive wheels too lightly loaded)
• Faulty brakes
• Poor tread on the drive tires

**Over Acceleration:** Too much pressure on the accelerator for the gear and vehicle speed can cause a power skid. A power skid is most likely to occur if:
• You are driving on a slippery surface.
• Your rig has an engine with high horsepower (high torque).
• The trailer is heavily or improperly loaded.

**Trailer Override:** When you brake, the cargo may push the trailer against the tractor. This forces the tractor out of line and creates a jackknife. This condition is most likely to occur if the:
• Pavement is slippery
• Trailer is not loaded properly
• Cargo is not distributed or secured correctly
• Rig is taking a curve or making a lane change

The best way to prevent a tractor jackknife is to:
• Avoid over-braking, over-accelerating, or sudden downshifts.
• Avoid sudden turns.
• Inspect the brake system and tire tread regularly.
• Load the rig correctly and securely.

## Front Wheel Skid

Front wheel skids happen when you lose front wheel traction. The rig continues to move forward, but you cannot steer it. The rig may slide sideways or fail to round a curve. Front wheel skids can be caused by:
• Too big a load on the fifth wheel; this can also happen when the cargo is not loaded properly and shifts forward when you brake
• Too much speed
• Not enough tread on the front tires
• Hydroplaning
• Over-steering in combination with any of the above
• Malfunction of the brake system
• Bad brake linings or other brake defects
• Not using the brake limiting valve properly

Front wheel skids can be prevented:
- Slow down when driving on wet pavement.
- Load your cargo correctly.
- Inspect your tires, front wheel alignment, and suspension system. Correct any problems you find.
- Use the brake limiting valve properly.
- Use good braking techniques.

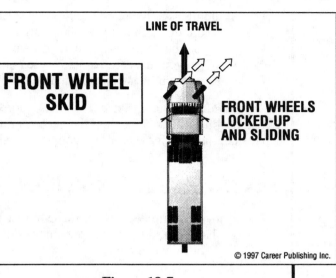

**Figure 18-7**

## All Wheel Skid

When all the wheels lock and do not roll, you lose traction. You stop rolling and start to slide. The rig usually continues in a straight line, but without traction, the driver loses control.

The major causes of this kind of skid are:
- Excessive speed
- Over-braking on a slippery surface

**Figure 18-8**

In cases of over-braking, one set of wheels generally locks up before the others. In some situations, even light brake pressure can cause lock-up.

The best prevention for all wheel skids is to control your speed and not brake too much on slippery surfaces. If you must brake, use stab braking to keep control of the rig.

### Summary of Skid Prevention

How to prevent skids was discussed previously in this chapter. You learned that managing your speed and space, especially when driving in extreme conditions, is very important in helping you control your rig.

Most skids result from sudden changes in speed or direction. Over-braking and over-steering as well as fast acceleration or deceleration cause these sudden changes. Avoid them.

Skidding usually occurs on slippery surfaces.
- Avoid quick braking or quick turns on slippery pavements.
- If you must turn or brake, do no more than you have to.
- When you must stop quickly, use controlled braking or stab braking.
- Keep the brakes adjusted and balanced.

Reducing your speed and allowing more space is vital to safety when the road is slippery. It can prevent the need for quick turning or braking. If the pavement is wet, snowy, or icy, you need to slow down and leave more following distance.

## ANTI-JACKKNIFE DEVICES

Anti-jackknife devices are made to restrict trailer swing and prevent damage. However, they do not prevent skidding. There are two basic types.
1. Fifth wheel devices
2. Cable devices

The **fifth wheel devices** are automatic and restrict the rotation of the kingpin. This prevents a collision between the trailer and the cab. They are mounted on the tractor and can be used with any kind of trailer.

The **cable devices** are mounted on the trailer and connected to the tractor. They are activated by hard braking and keep the trailer and tractor in line. Their disadvantage is that using them conflicts with skid recovery. The hard braking prevents the use of controlled braking. Cable devices may actually make a skid worse.

## ANTILOCK BRAKES

Antilock brakes are becoming more and more common on tractors and trailers. The Federal Government has mandated them on all new tractors built after March 1, 1997 and on all new trailers built after March 1, 1998.

Antilock systems use electronic controls to read wheel speed and prevent the brakes from locking up the wheels under hard braking. This increases driver control during braking but does not necessarily shorten stopping distances. Also, if the tractor has antilock brakes and the trailer does not or vice-versa, you need to apply the normal skid control procedures in this chapter to prevent jackknifing. Antilock is most effective when you hit the brake pedal and hold it down.

## SKID RECOVERY

Almost all tractor skids are corrected by the same general responses:
- Disengage the clutch
- Get off the brakes
- Countersteer
- Stab the brakes for control

Most skids happen when you try to change speed too quickly for the conditions. Remove your foot from the brake pedal to reduce skidding. Then you can more easily gain control of the direction the rig is going. Do not put on the independent trailer brake. If the trailer has started to jackknife, putting on the trailer brake can make it worse.

If over-braking resulted from downshifting:

- Depress the clutch quickly.
- Use the foot brake for stab braking.

If over-acceleration has been the cause of the skid, you should:

- Ease off the accelerator.
- Depress the clutch pedal to remove engine power from the drive wheels.

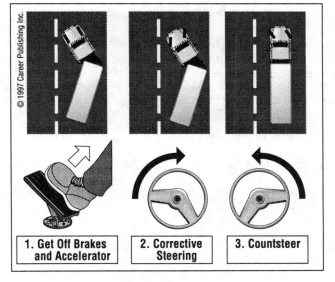

| 1. Get Off Brakes and Accelerator | 2. Corrective Steering | 3. Countsteer |

**Figure 18-9**

## Corrective Steering

In a tractor jackknife, corrective steering is needed to put the tractor back on course. Steer toward the direction the rear of the rig is moving. Steer in the line of travel as shown in Figure 18-6 on page 18.8, and Figures 18-7 and 18-8 on page 18.9.

**Over-steering:** On a slippery surface when you lose control of your steering and traction, you must over-steer. Turn beyond the intended path of travel. You must do this because you do not have full traction. Unless you over-steer, you will not regain control of the rig.

**Countersteering:** When you try to correct a skid, little traction makes the rig slow to respond. As the vehicle resumes the correct course, the driver must counter-steer early. Do this to avoid a new skid. Continue countersteering until the rig is on a straight path. Each counter steering movement should get smaller until the rig is going straight again.

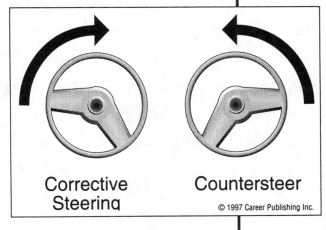

Corrective Steering          Countersteer

**Figure 18-10**

If a new skid happens because you countersteered too late, the rig may turn beyond the intended path and spin out. Although it may not spin out the first time you countersteer too late, each correction may make it get worse until a spin-out occurs.

## Braking to a Stop

Once the vehicle is on a straight path, you can brake to a stop. It is best to use stab braking.

## SUMMARY

In this chapter, you learned the types of skids and what can be done to prevent them. You also learned that there are ways to recover from each type of skid and prevent damage to your rig and injury to yourself or others. The conditions that cause skids were also discussed.

## KEY WORDS

**Centrifugal force:** The force that pushes objects away from the center of rotation.

**Drive wheel skid**: (Tractor jackknife) A skid that occurs when the tractor drive wheels lose traction.

**Force of motion**: Movement determined by the weight and speed of an object as it moves along.

**Power skid**: A skid that happens when the drive wheels spin and the rear of the tractor moves sideways.

**Rolling Traction:** The friction occurring when one surface rolls over another.

**Sliding Traction:** The friction occurring when one surface slides across another.

**Wheel load**: The downward force of weight on a wheel.

# LEARNING ACTIVITIES

## True-False Questions

If the question is true, circle the T. If the question is false, circle the F.

T   F   1.   The major cause of skids is a sudden change in speed or direction.

T   F   2.   Traction is the grip, or grab, between the tires and the pavement.

T   F   3.   The amount of traction determines how much control the driver has over the rig.

T   F   4.   The force of motion is controlled by the weight and speed of the rig.

T   F   5.   If the force of motion is greater than the traction of the tire on the pavement, the vehicle skids.

T   F   6.   When the wheels lock, the driver loses control of the rig.

T   F   7.   Locking the wheels decreases stopping distance.

T   F   8.   Drive wheel skids occur when the amount of force applied to the drive wheels is more than the traction between the tires and the pavement.

T   F   9.   Accelerating too fast can cause a skid.

T   F   10.   When a vehicle turns, centrifugal force tends to pull it toward the center.

T   F   11.   It is easier to recover from a skid than to prevent it.

T   F   12.   A trailer jackknife is caused by over-braking or excessive cornering.

T   F   13.   Over-braking can result from a mechanical brake problem.

T   F   14.   If you enter a curve too fast, traction may be overcome by centrifugal force.

T   F   15.   If you realize you are going too fast while in the curve, it is best to slam on your brakes to bring the rig under control.

T  F  16.  A tractor jackknife results when the tractor's drive wheels have more traction than the front wheels.

T  F  17.  A tractor jackknife can result from wheel lock-up, over-acceleration, or trailer override.

T  F  18.  If a tractor jackknifes, it is best to avoid over-braking, over-accelerating, or suddenly downshifting.

T  F  19.  During a front wheel skid, the rig continues to move forward, but you cannot steer.

T  F  20.  Driving slower on wet pavement is vital if you want to prevent front wheel skids.

T  F  21.  When wheels lock-up, the movement of the rig is changed from rolling to sliding.

T  F  22.  The major cause for all wheel skids is over-steering.

T  F  23.  The best way to prevent all wheel skids is to avoid too much braking on slippery surfaces.

T  F  24.  Most skids happen when you over-control the rig (sudden changes in speed or direction).

T  F  25.  Skidding generally occurs on slippery surfaces because traction is easily lost.

T  F  26.  Fortunately, anti-jackknife devices prevent skidding.

T  F  27.  In a tractor jackknife, use corrective steering to put the tractor back on course.

## Name the Skid

Write the name of the skid and tell what happens in this kind of skid on the lines to the side of each drawing. Then tell how to prevent the skid.

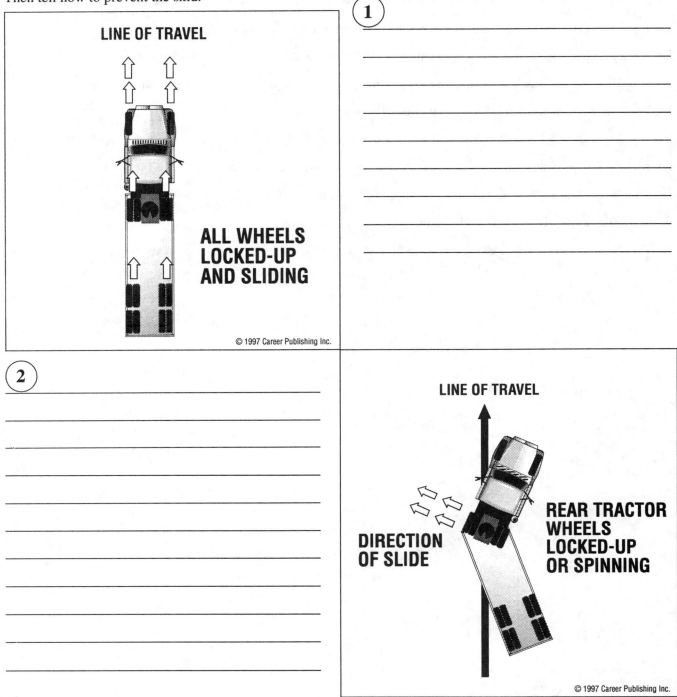

**LINE OF TRAVEL**

**ALL WHEELS LOCKED-UP AND SLIDING**

© 1997 Career Publishing Inc.

**①** _____
_____
_____
_____
_____
_____
_____
_____
_____

**②** _____
_____
_____
_____
_____
_____
_____
_____
_____

**LINE OF TRAVEL**

**DIRECTION OF SLIDE**

**REAR TRACTOR WHEELS LOCKED-UP OR SPINNING**

© 1997 Career Publishing Inc.

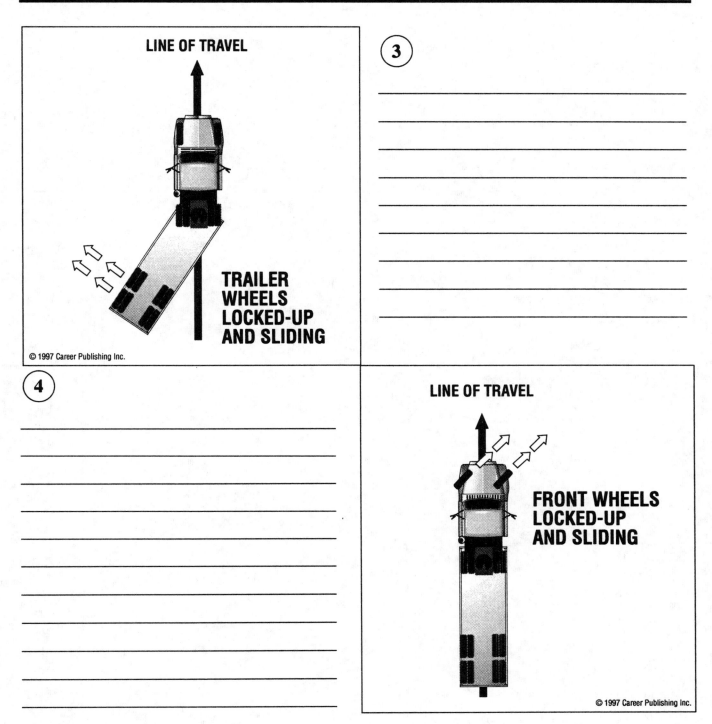

**LINE OF TRAVEL**

**TRAILER WHEELS LOCKED-UP AND SLIDING**

© 1997 Career Publishing Inc.

③

④

**LINE OF TRAVEL**

**FRONT WHEELS LOCKED-UP AND SLIDING**

© 1997 Career Publishing Inc.

# Chapter Nineteen
# ACCIDENT PROCEDURES

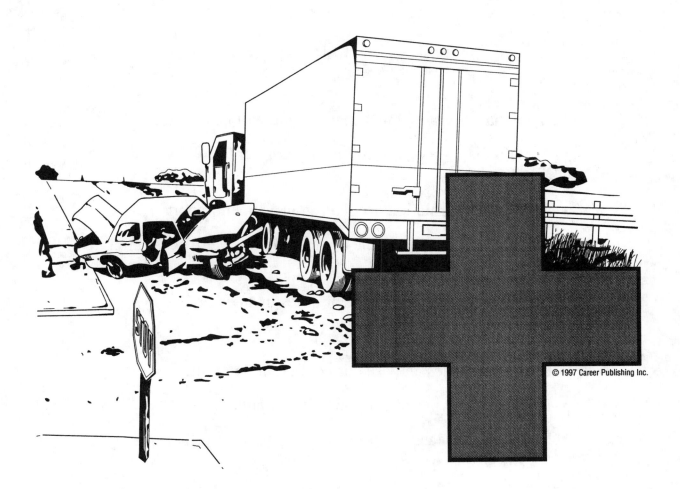

© 1997 Career Publishing Inc.

**Scene of the Accident • Accident Reporting**
**Accidents Involving Hazardous Materials • Warning Devices**
**Driver's Responsibilities • Giving First Aid • Fires and Fire Fighting**

**FROM NOW ON,**

**ONLY THE BEST WILL DRIVE**

# OBJECTIVES

When you have mastered this chapter, you will be able to:

- Explain the correct procedures for a driver to follow at an accident scene

- Detail the information needed for an accident report

- Explain which subjects the driver should never discuss after an accident

- Describe the driver's responsibilities in an emergency

- Explain how to protect the scene

- Evaluate injuries and use correct first aid measures

- Describe the types of fires and how to put them out

- Explain the special skills needed if there is a spill of hazardous materials

- Detail the special reports needed when hazardous materials are involved

# CHAPTER NINETEEN

# ACCIDENT PROCEDURES

## INTRODUCTION

Unfortunately, accidents do happen. When they happen, the driver must know what to do and what not to do. This chapter will explain the driver's responsibilities at the scene of an accident. You will learn:

© 1997 Career Publishing Inc.

**Figure 19-1**

- What you should do about your rig.
- How to report the accident.
- How to help other people.
- How to prevent a fire or control it if one does start.
- What equipment to use.
- How to use your common sense.
- How to act safely.
- What you need to do to stay within the law.

## ACCIDENTS

If an accident occurs, a driver must know what to do at the scene and how to report the accident. He or she should also know what being in an accident means to a driver's record.

### Steps to Take at the Scene of an Accident

Drivers must know there are important actions to take at the scene of an accident. They should also be aware that leaving the scene is against the law.

FMCSR 392.40 requires drivers involved in an accident to:
- Stop immediately.
- Protect the scene to prevent further accidents.
- If diesel fuel is spilled, remember it makes the road very slippery.
- Provide reasonable assistance to injured persons.
- Protect injured persons. Do not move them unless they are in danger. Let trained emergency personnel move them. This will reduce the chance of further injury.

- Get the following information from the other persons involved in the accident.
  - Name and address of drivers
  - Name and address of the motor carrier if any other commercial vehicles were involved
  - Vehicle registration or license plate number
  - Driver's license number and the state issuing it
  - The name and address of their insurance company and the policy number
- Give this information to the other persons involved in the accident.
  - Your name and address
  - The name and address of your carrier
  - Your vehicle registration or license plate number
  - Your driver's license number and the state that issued it
  - The name and address of the company insuring your rig and the policy number
- Report the accident to your motor carrier as soon as possible.

You can expect to be tested for drugs or alcohol in your system after an accident. It is the driver's responsibility to be tested for drugs and alcohol if:

- Someone dies as a result of the accident.
- Anyone is injured and must receive treatment.
- The vehicle is damaged so much it must be towed away.
- The driver of the CMV receives a citation for a moving violation.

Carriers must make sure their drivers know the rules for drug testing.

Follow these steps if there is an accident.

© 1997 Career Publishing Inc.

**Figure 19-2**

- Identify the other drivers and vehicle owners.
- Help anyone who is injured.
- Remember, anything the driver says or does can affect his or her liability for the accident.
- The driver's actions can also affect future relations of the trucking industry with the public.

If a CMV hits an unattended vehicle, FMCSR 392.41 requires the driver to stop and make a reasonable effort to locate the driver of the other vehicle. If he or she cannot be located, the driver must leave a note on the other vehicle where it will be easily seen. The note should contain the driver's name and address as well as the name and address of the carrier. Be sure to attach the note in such a way it will not blow away or fall off. Put it where the driver can see it easily. If it appears there was no note, you could be charged with hit and run.

Some drivers carry Polaroid-type cameras with them so they can take photographs if they are in an accident.

## What to Do When You Have an Accident

The law, common sense, and most company policies require drivers to do the following if they are in an accident.
- Stop.
- Shut off the engine and all electrical components if you have a flammable load.
- Turn on the 4-way flashers.
- Protect the scene to prevent further accidents.
- Aid the injured.
- Notify the police. Send someone else to report there has been an accident. The driver should remain at the scene whenever possible.
- Call for an ambulance if one is needed.
- Notify the company.
- Collect the facts.
  - Names of others involved in the accident, their addresses, their driver's license numbers and states issuing them, and the vehicle registration number and expiration date for each vehicle involved.
  - Names of witnesses and their addresses.
  - Draw a sketch of the scene.
- Conduct themselves properly.
- Stay calm and be courteous.
- Say nothing about who is at fault. Do not offer to pay for damage. Do not accept payment from anyone else involved.
- Give the required identification to anyone requesting it.
- Remain at the scene until their company instructs them to leave.
- Make sure any cargo that is spilled is cleaned up.
- Check the rig over carefully before they drive it again to be sure it is in condition to be driven.
- Expect drug or alcohol testing.
- File a complete accident report when they arrive at their destination.

## Accidents While Transporting Hazardous Materials

A driver who has a cargo of hazardous materials should be aware that any accident can be very dangerous. Check the shipping papers in advance so that you know what class of hazardous material and the approximate amount you are hauling. The driver must make sure shipping papers for hazardous materials are within reach during the trip and can be read easily.

**Figure 19-3**

If the driver of hazardous materials has an accident, he or she should:
- See if there are any leaks or cargo has spilled, and assume it is hazardous material. Do not allow anyone to walk or drive through spills.
- Keep on-lookers away.
- Stay upwind of any spills. Do not allow anyone to eat, drink, or smoke in the area.
- Advise emergency responders there are hazardous materials and allow them to check the shipping papers. Always check to be sure they are legible when you accept the shipment.

- Set out warning devices to protect the scene.
- Notify local authorities. If he or she cannot leave the scene, the driver should ask a passing driver to notify them. Be sure they understand the truck is transporting hazardous materials. Tell them the classes and quantities on board.
- Contact the motor carrier. Make sure the carrier also understands hazardous materials are involved and whether there has been a spill. If the accident is near water, inform the carrier.
- Follow the Company's policy for what the driver is supposed to do at the accident scene.

## ACCIDENT REPORTING

When a vehicle transporting hazardous materials is involved in an accident, additional reports must be made. Usually, the carrier handles these reports, based on the information given by the driver. The driver should not handle any of this reporting except when:

- The driver is an owner/operator.
- The driver cannot contact the motor carrier for whom he or she is driving.
- The shipper's instructions require reporting by the driver.
- Authorities at the scene request the driver to make the report.

### Emergency Procedures

Because the laws are constantly changing, always check with your employer before you begin a trip hauling hazardous material to learn what you must do if there is an accident or spill. Some of the agencies you may need to notify are listed in the following paragraphs.

The **U.S. Coast Guard National Response Center** helps coordinate emergency forces in response to chemical hazards. Their number is 1-800-424-8802. The **Chemical Transportation Emergency Center** (CHEMTREC) can tell emergency personnel what they need to know to make the proper notifications. Their

© 1997 Career Publishing Inc.

| NATIONAL RESPONSE CENTER (800) 424-8802 | CHEMTREC (800) 424-9300 |
|---|---|

**CHEMICAL EMERGENCY**

You need to know and understand what these agencies do and what they cannot do.

**Figure 19-4**

24-hour number is 1-800-424-9300 (emergency calls only). You can call 1-800-226-8200 for information.

The **National Response Center** must be notified if there is an accident that results in:
- A fatality
- An injury requiring hospitalization
- Property damage of $50,000 or more
- Fire, breakage, spillage, or contamination from radioactive materials or etiologic (disease-causing) agents
- A situation presenting a continuous danger to life
- Discharge of a hazardous substance
- Public evacuation that lasts one hour or more
- A major transportation artery is closed or shut down for more than one hour

If you need to call CHEMTREC, be sure to include:
- Your name and a call-back number
- The name of the motor carrier and the unit number
- The name of the consignee
- The name of the shipper or manufacturer
- A description of the accident scene

If the load is a disease-causing agent, then you should call the **Center for Disease Control (CDC)** at 1-404-633-5313 or 1-202-267-2675.

For more specific information about reporting accidents involving hazardous materials, refer to CFR Section 171.15.

Federal laws also require filing a written **Hazardous Materials Incident Report** (Form 5800.1, Rev 6-89) for any unintended release of hazardous materials (with limited exceptions). The

© 1997 Career Publishing Inc.

**Figure 19-5**

report must be filed within 30 days. The driver must report any such release and give the necessary information to the supervisor for preparing this report. For more specific information, refer to 49CFR Section 171.16.

## How to Protect the Scene

The driver, or someone acting for him or her, warns oncoming traffic to prevent further accidents. To do this, a driver must know:
- The types of warning devices that should be used to protect the scene
- How to set up the warning devices quickly
- How to place the warning devices correctly

## Types of Warning Devices

**Emergency Triangles:** FMCSR 393.95 requires reflective triangles to be carried on all current commercial vehicles. The triangles are better warning devices because they:

- Have a unique appearance
- Can be used in the day or at night
- Are self-illuminating at night and have an orange border that is easy to see during the day
- Can be used more than once

**Fusees:** Because of the danger of fire, fusees or other flame-producing warning devices cannot be used under certain conditions. Also, because of the fire hazard, fusees should not be used when flammable liquids or gases may be present.

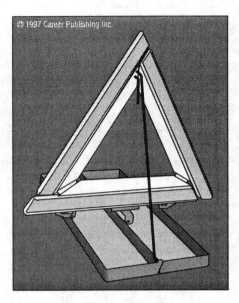

**Figure 19-6**

Fusees or other warning devices or signals produced by a flame must not be used with:

- Any vehicle hauling Class A or Class B explosives (Explosives 1.1 through 1.3)
- Tanks used for flammable liquid or compressed gas (whether loaded or empty)
- Vehicles powered by compressed gas

To give the red signal, fusees burn at a very high temperature. To light a fusee, read and follow the instructions printed on the fusee. After they are lighted, molten material can drip and cause severe burns. When lighting or using a fusee, turn your back to the wind, point the lighted end away from yourself, and hold it at an angle that will keep the

Fusees Are Ignited by Striking the Cap Along the Striker Button on the Side. Place Your Back to the Wind, and Hold Fusee Well Away From Body or Clothing.

**Figure 19-7**

molten material from dripping. Although larger sizes are available, fusees generally have a 15-minute burning time.

You must keep fusees dry, or they cannot be lighted. They should be stored in a rack or container that is easy to reach from outside the cab.

To light a fusee:
- With your back to the wind, remove the cap and expose the friction surface. This also exposes the igniter button at the top of the fusee.
- Grasp the bottom one-third of the fusee with one hand. Point it away from yourself at a 45-degree angle.
- To light the fusee, use your other hand to rub the friction surface of the cap firmly across the igniter button. Keep clear of the flame.
- Set the lighted fusee on or near the pavement. Use the spiked end, wire, or cardboard prop provided to keep the lighted end off the pavement.
- Never attach a lighted fusee to a vehicle.

When you use a fusee to signal by hand:
- Hold the lighted end away and keep clear of any dripping molten material.
- Avoid breathing the fumes.
- Do not look into the glare.

To put out a lighted fusee, press the burning end into dirt or rub it against a paved surface. Do not use water. Do not leave hot residue in the grass or anything else that will burn.

## Placing Warning Devices

The reason for using warning devices is to warn approaching vehicles of a problem and guide them around the scene. Properly placed warnings can be easily seen and do not confuse other motorists.

© 1997 Career Publishing Inc.

**Figure 19-8**

When setting up triangles, it is best to walk well off the road and hold the triangle out in front of you so that approaching traffic can see it. This will make you more visible and help protect you from being hit by oncoming traffic.

When you stop your rig:
- Turn on the 4-way flashers as a warning to traffic.
- While the flashers are on, put out the emergency warning devices. This should be done within 10 minutes after you stop.
- After the warning devices are in place, turn off the 4-way flashers to save the battery.
- When you are ready to start again, turn on the warning flashers.
- Pick up the emergency warning devices and put them in the cab.

Always place flares or warning reflectors at least 100 feet from the accident or disabled vehicle. On a two lane highway, place:

- One device on the traffic side within 10 feet (4 paces) of the rear of the truck
- One device about 100 feet (40 paces) from the truck in the center of the traffic lane or shoulder where the truck is stopped
- One device 100 feet from the truck in the other direction

On one-way or divided highways, place:

- One device no more than 10 feet from the rear of the truck
- One device 100 feet (40 paces) and one 200 feet (80 paces) from the truck toward the approaching traffic. Place them in the center of the lane or on the shoulder where the truck is stopped.

In business or residential districts, use emergency devices when there is not enough light to give oncoming drivers a view of your truck from 500 feet away.

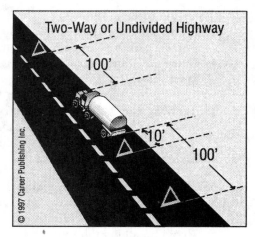

**Figure 19-9**

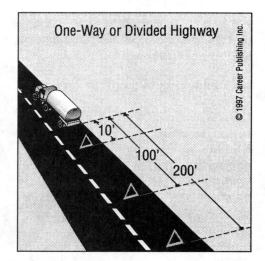

**Figure 19-10**

## Handling the Accident Scene

If an accident occurs, it is your duty to assist the injured, call the police and ambulance (if necessary), conduct yourself properly, collect the facts, use accident packets, diagram the accident, identify witnesses, provide proper identification, and remain at the scene until all requirements are met.

### Assist the Injured

After stopping and protecting the scene, your first priority is to help anyone who is injured. But beware! Know your limitations!

- Do not try to do anything you are not trained to do.

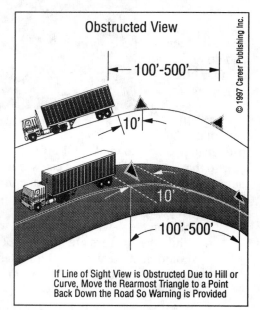

If Line of Sight View is Obstructed Due to Hill or Curve, Move the Rearmost Triangle to a Point Back Down the Road So Warning is Provided

**Figure 19-11**

- Do not move the injured unless they are in danger.
- Avoid doing anything that could bring additional liability.
- Insist that anyone who claims to be injured get medical help because a doctor's record is the best protection against future claims. If a person refuses treatment, be sure to report this fact.

### Call Police and Ambulance

If it appears to be needed, call for an ambulance. Give the exact location of the accident. If you are not familiar with the area, ask others at the scene if they can help you determine the location. Use the CB emergency channel or send someone to call for help if a phone is not available.

### Conduct Yourself Properly

An accident can be a very emotional experience. Much depends on keeping your cool. Remain polite and calm even if others try to blame you. Do not debate right or wrong or admit in any way you are at fault. Remember, legal liability for what happened will be determined later (sometimes much later). What you do or say can affect the decision. Do not give or accept money. Do not sign any type of release form. The only paper you must sign is a traffic citation from a police officer.

### Collect the Facts

The facts listed earlier will be very important when the others involved in the accident, your employers, and the authorities work to set responsibility for the accident.

Basic facts to collect include the:
- Date, place (specific street location), time of day, weather, and driving conditions
- Name, address, and license number of other drivers
- Name and address of the owner of the other vehicle and the vehicle registration number
- Description and license plate number(s) of other vehicle(s)
- Description of the damage to the other vehicle(s) or property
- Name and address of all injured persons, description of injuries, and the name of the hospital where they were taken
- Name and badge, or ID number, and department of the police officer(s) investigating the accident

## ACCIDENT REPORTING KIT

### In case of Accident:
**Attended Vehicle**

- Stop your vehicle and investigate. Do not move vehicle until police arrive.

- Use 4-way flashers and set up warning devices.

- Assist the injured - DO NOT move injured - call for medical assistance.

- Notify police and supervisor.

- If no phone is available, ask a bystander to contact your supervisor with an ACCIDENT NOTIFICATION CARD.

- Do not make any statements or sign anything.

- If the other driver says you are not at fault, be sure to have him or her sign the EXONERATION CARD.

- Supply name, address, company name and address, vehicle registration number, operator's license number, and insurance information to police and other party.

- Have witnesses complete WITNESS CARDS to obtain names and addresses.

- Complete the accident report at the accident scene.

- If the vehicle cannot operate under its own power, secure from theft and further damage.

- Give the completed packet to your supervisor.

### Unattended Vehicle

- If you strike an unattended vehicle and cannot locate the owner, leave your name and company address with the vehicle. Attach the note securely.

© 1997 Career Publishing Inc.

**Figure 19-12**

Most companies give drivers accident packets to help them handle their responsibilities at the scene of an accident. Check for this packet during your pre-trip inspection. Packets usually contain:

- Basic instructions for handling the scene of an accident
- Preliminary accident report or memo
- Witness cards

# Accident Memorandum

| Date of Accident | _____ , 19 | Day of Week _____ | Hour _____ | a.m. p.m. |

| ☐ CITY ☐ SUBURBAN ☐ RURAL | PLACE WHERE ACCIDENT OCCURRED County _____ | | City, town or township _____ |

If accident was outside city limits indicate distance from nearest town. Use two distances and two directions if necessary.  _____ miles _____ north-south  _____ miles _____ east-west  of  ☐ Limits of ☐ center of  _____ City or Town

ROAD ON WHICH ACCIDENT OCCURRED _____ Give name of street or highway number (U.S. or State)

☐ AT ITS INTERSECTION WITH _____
  OR   _____ feet _____ north-south
☐ NOT AT INTERSECTION   _____ feet _____ east-west
  (Check and Complete One)

of   Name of intersecting street or highway number
Show nearest Intersecting Street or Highway, House number, Curve, Bridge, Rail Crossing, Alley, Driveway, Culvert, Milepost, Underpass, Numbered Telephone Pole, or Other Identifying Landmark. Show Erect Distance, Using Two Directions and Two Distances If Necessary.

OTHER DRIVER'S NAME

ADDRESS

CITY                          STATE                DRIVER'S LICENSE No.

OTHER VEHICLE OWNER'S NAME

ADDRESS

CITY                          STATE                VEHICLE LICENSE No.

TYPE VEHICLE          MAKE          YEAR          No.

DAMAGE TO OTHER VEHICLE AND/OR PROPERTY

| INJURED PERSONS | AGE | SEX | INJURIES |
|---|---|---|---|
| Name | | | |
| Address | | | |
| Name | | | |
| Address | | | |
| POLICE Name | | | Badge No. |

| BE SURE WITNESS CARDS ARE COLLECTED | PLACE THEM IN THIS FOLDER |

INDICATE ON THIS DIAGRAM WHAT HAPPENED

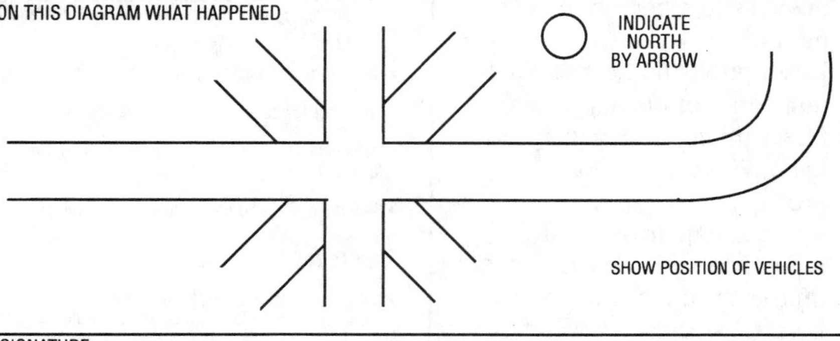

INDICATE NORTH BY ARROW

SHOW POSITION OF VEHICLES

DRIVER'S SIGNATURE

**Figure 19-13**

### Draw a Diagram

If possible, photograph the scene before any of the vehicles are towed or moved. Draw a diagram of the scene showing the positions of the vehicles before, during, and after the accident. Include:

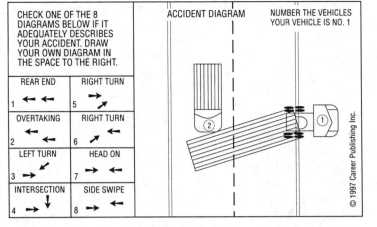

**Figure 19-14**

- A description of the damage to other vehicles and property
- An estimated amount of property damage (if possible)

### Witnesses and Witness Cards

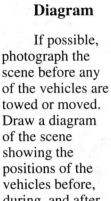

**Figure 19-15**

Try to get witnesses who can verify the vehicles' positions, speed, use of turn signals, skid marks, etc. Sometimes drivers of cars that were near you can verify your speed. If your company supplies an accident packet, use the witness cards from it to get the names and addresses. If no one volunteers as a witness, write down the license plate numbers of possible witnesses. Note the addresses of nearby buildings from which someone may have seen the accident.

### Give Required Information

A driver must provide the following information.
- Name and address
- Company name and address
- Vehicle owner name and address if he or she is driving a leased vehicle
- CDL number
- Vehicle registration number(s)

Some states require you to give the name and address of your insurance carrier.

**Remain at the Scene Until Your Carrier Instructs You to Leave**

Do not leave the scene until your carrier instructs you to leave. Be sure you have given all of the required information to the authorities and to others involved in the accident. If there is a cargo spill, remove the unbroken packages as safely as possible.

Clean up the contents of broken packages as soon as you can. If you are hauling hazardous material, you will need specialized clean up. Do not handle the product unless you have been trained to do so and have the necessary special equipment.

Give your rig a pre-trip type of inspection to see if it is safe to drive. If it is not safe, call a mechanic to make repairs or a tow truck to remove the rig from the scene.

Figure 19-16

**Call the Company for Instructions**

When you call your company for instructions:
- Tell them whether or not you are injured.
- Report any damage to the truck and cargo.
- Ask for help if it is needed. For example, you may need another rig or a crew to transfer the cargo.
- Be sure to tell them what your cargo is, so they can make any special arrangements if needed.
- Get instructions from your supervisor as to whether you should continue the trip or return to the terminal.

**Legal Requirements**

By law, every accident must be reported regardless of how bad it is. Leaving the scene of an accident is a major traffic violation. A conviction for leaving the scene of an accident while driving a CMV will result in losing your CDL for one year in addition to any other penalties imposed by state law.

The failure of a driver to report an accident to the motor carrier will almost always result in the driver's losing his or her job. The driver will also be subject to prosecution.

### Importance of the Driver's Information

You must be very careful when you get information at the scene of the accident. This information will affect everything that occurs as a result of the accident. Your information is needed by the company to prepare the required reports for the:

- Carrier's insurance company
- State agencies
- U.S. Department of Transportation (if required)

The driver's information is also important to the company so they may determine their legal obligations. They also need to update the driver's record. They will also need the information to reach an equitable settlement if there are claims.

### SAMPLE SUPERVISOR'S INVESTIGATION REPORT

| | |
|---|---|
| COMPANY<br>Safe Company Trucking | TERMINAL OR DIVISION<br>Tenth Street Terminal |
| DRIVER<br>M. Peachy | TYPE OF VEHICLE IDENTIFYING NO.<br>Single Truck |
| LOCATION OF ACCIDENT *(Street, town, state)*<br>Tenth Street Terminal Yard | DATE AND TIME OF ACCIDENT<br>February 6, 199X 8AM |

NO. OF PERSONS INJURED AND EXTENT OF PROPERTY DAMAGE *(Company and other)*
No injuries.

Left rear fender (apx. $50.00 damage)

No damage to truck, bumper contacted car.

DESCRIPTION OF ACCIDENT *(State in detail what occurred just before, and at the time of the accident)*
Truck rolled away from loading dock, no chocks were placed at rear

wheels. Truck was not in gear, parking brake was not securely set.

(Truck brakes were out of adjustment.) Truck rolled apx. 10 feet and

struck rear fender of parked car in yard. Car was parked illegally

in yard.

UNSAFE CONDITION *(Describe unsafe conditions such as faulty brake, light, etc. contributing to accident)*

No chock blocks on truck.

Brakes out of adjustment.

UNSAFE ACT *(Describe the unsafe action of driver as turning from wrong lane, speeding, failing to signal, etc.)*

Brakes not secured when parked. Truck not in gear.

Car parked in truck area.

REMEDY *( As a supervisor, what action have you taken or do you propose taking to prevent a repeat accident)*

Check truck dock for chocks. Require chocks at loading dock and stops.

Driver issued warning. Keep private vehicles out of loading area.

| SUPERVISOR<br>R. Ray | REVIEWED AND APPROVED BY | DATE REPORT PREPARED<br>February 8, 199X |
|---|---|---|

*(Use reverse side for sketch and additional detail)*

**Figure 19-17**

What the driver tells them may also be used to see if there are measures that can be taken to prevent similar accidents in the future. This information may also be used to assess the company's overall accident experience and trends in accidents.

## Summary of Accident Reporting Requirements

Unless he or she is an owner/operator, the driver does not prepare the reports for the insurance company or state or federal agencies. However, the driver should understand the state and federal reporting requirements.

**Federal Requirements:** A motor carrier operating in interstate or foreign commerce must report accidents to local authorities if they result in:
- A fatality
- An injury requiring treatment away from the scene
- Disabling damage to one or more vehicles requiring the vehicle to be towed from the scene

Local authorities are responsible for notifying the U.S. DOT. An accident does not have to be reported to the DOT if it involves only getting on or off of a vehicle or loading or unloading cargo unless the accident releases hazardous material. Then it must be reported.

**State Requirements:** Every accident that results in a fatality or personal injury must be reported to state authorities. Each state has its own limit for reporting property damage accidents. The amounts range from $50 to $2,000. The driver involved in a property damage accident should be sure to check with the police about reporting requirements.

## Accidents and the Professional Driver

Nothing is more important to the professional truck driver than having a driving record that is free of accidents and violations, either in a CMV or a personal vehicle. The FMCSR require interstate motor carriers to review the record of each driver every year. They must evaluate each driver's accident record and number of traffic violations.

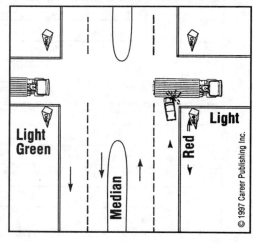

**Preventable or Not?**

© 1997 Career Publishing Inc.

**Figure 19-18**

Every accident costs the carrier money even though the truck driver may not be to blame. If the driver is at fault in any way, the cost is much greater to the company.

Usually the trucking industry decides whether an accident could have been prevented. This is more than just a question of whether the truck driver was issued a citation. They decide if the driver failed to take any action that could have prevented the accident.

Under trucking industry standards, an accident is considered preventable:
1. If the truck driver did anything that contributed to it
2. If the driver did not try to avoid it

## GIVING FIRST AID

**First aid** is immediate and temporary care given to a victim until professional help arrives. This section will help you understand the need to learn basic first aid and how to treat blocked airways, serious bleeding, and shock.

This overview will only be an introduction to first aid. You should have more training such as the Red Cross course, *Essential First Aid and CPR,* so you can be of real help in an emergency. After such a course, you will also be able to help your family, friends, and co-workers.

As a driver, your job at the scene of an accident is to stop and help. If help is already there, you do not need to stop. If you stop when you are not needed, you will only add to the congestion.

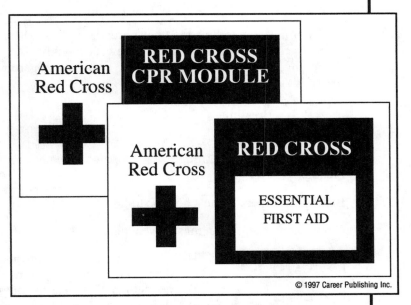

© 1997 Career Publishing Inc.

**Figure 19-19**

### Limitations

A person's ability to help is limited by skill and how much he or she knows about first aid. Know your company's policy and the state's laws for limits they place on you. Learn about each state's *Good Samaritan* laws, which protect a person giving first aid. Learn also about each state's requirements for persons who are trained in first aid and CPR.

### Basic Principles of First Aid

It is very important to stay calm and not move anyone who is injured unless there is danger to the person from fire, heavy traffic, or other serious threat. You should:
- Get help.
- Keep on-lookers back.
- Make the person(s) comfortable.
- Give immediate attention to the most serious injuries:
    - Breathing
    - Bleeding
    - Shock
- Keep the injured person warm.
- Never give water or other liquids to an unconscious or partly conscious person.
- Talk calmly to the victim. Get the person's permission to help.
- Do not discuss the extent of injuries.

## Types of Severe Injuries

Call for help if there is anyone nearby, so you will not be alone as you try to help the injured people. You also want emergency response personnel there as soon as possible. Another person can call them while you help those who are hurt.

You must take care of the worst injuries first. Some injuries can cause a person to die very quickly if they are not treated at once. First of all:
- Check to see if the person is breathing.
- Check the vital body functions.

For a person to live, they must breathe and their heart must beat. Severe bleeding can also cause a person to die very quickly. To find out if the respiratory (breathing) system and the circulatory (heart) system are working, check the person's ABCs.
- **A** Airway
- **B** Breathing
- **C** Circulation

Airway: The passage through which a person breathes must be clear so they can breathe.

Breathing: A person must breathe to live.

Circulation: The person must have a pulse and not be bleeding severely.

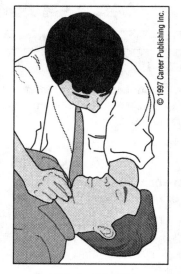

**Figure 19-20**

To find out if a person is **conscious**, gently ask them, "Are you OK?" If they do not answer or do not act like they hear the question, check to see if they are breathing. If they are not breathing, you must start rescue breathing at once.

Find out if the person has a pulse by pressing the neck as shown in the illustration. Place your fingers (not your thumb) in the groove between the voice box and the muscles of the neck. The carotid artery is there. If the heart is beating, you should be able to feel the pulse.

If there is no pulse, begin chest compressions with rescue breathing. This is known as **CPR** (cardiopulmonary resuscitation). Take a class offered by the Red Cross to learn the different methods that should be used for adults and children. Because of the danger of contracting a disease, use a device called an airway when administering rescue breathing or CPR.

If the person is **unconscious**, check their condition in this way.
- Check for neck and back injury. If you suspect a spinal injury, do not move the person while you check the ABCs. If there does not seem to be a spinal injury, gently roll them on their back. Support their head as you roll them.
- Open the airway by tilting their head back and lifting up the chin if there does not seem to be a spinal injury. If you think there is a spinal injury, use only the chin lift. Do not tilt the head.

• Look, listen, and feel for breathing. See if the chest is rising and falling. Can you hear breathing? Can you feel air against your cheek?

If you do not think the person is breathing, begin rescue breathing at once by giving two full breaths. See Figure 19-21. If the chest does not rise and fall, tilt the person's head farther back and give two more breaths. If the chest does not rise and fall, the airway is obstructed. You will have to clear it before they will be able to breathe.

**Figure 19-21**

## How to Give CPR

For an adult or child over the age of 8:
1. After you have placed the head as described previously, straighten the person's legs.
2. Kneel next to the person about halfway between the person's head and chest.
3. To open the airway:
   • Put one hand on the person's forehead.
   • Put two fingers of your other hand under the bony part of their chin.
   • Push on the forehead, and lift the chin to tilt the head back.

Pinch the nose shut and seal your lips around their mouth. Give 2 breaths that last 1 to 1 1/2 seconds. Let the chest fall before you give another breath.

If the chest does not rise, tilt the person's head and try again.

If the person begins to breathe and has a pulse, watch them closely until help arrives. If they have a pulse, but are not breathing:
   • Give 1 breath every 5 seconds.
   • Check the pulse after every 12th breath (1 minute).

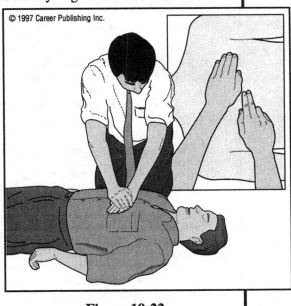

If the person is not breathing and does not have a pulse:
1. Place middle finger on the notch where the ribs and the breastbone (sternum) meet. Put the heel of your other hand next to and above your index finger as shown in Figure 19-22.

**Figure 19-22**

2. Remove your fingers and put the heel of this hand over the heel of the other hand. Hold your fingers up. Do not let them press into the chest.
3. Give 15 chest compressions. To do this, press hard on the sternum. Use the weight of your body to do this. Depress the sternum 1-1/2 to 2 inches. Release your weight, but do not remove your hands. Do not rock back and forth. Push straight down. Give the 15 chest compressions at a rate of 80-100 a minute. Count aloud one and two and three and . . .
4. Open the airway with the head tilt/chin lift. Give 2 breaths.
5. Repeat the 15 chest compressions and 2 breaths 4 times.
6. Check the pulse.

If the person is breathing and has a pulse:
• Stop giving CPR.

If the person has a pulse but is not breathing:
• Continue rescue breathing. If the pulse stops, resume CPR.

If the person has no pulse and is not breathing:
• Continue CPR until the person revives or help arrives.

## Severe Bleeding

Damage to blood vessels causes bleeding which can be minor or can kill a person. Bruises are blood under the skin. You can see external bleeding and know where the wound is.

You may not know there is bleeding inside a person (internal bleeding). Often when a person is in an accident, there are internal injuries. Then the person bleeds inside and may even die.

Blood from an artery is bright red and spurts with each heartbeat. A person can die very quickly unless this bleeding is stopped.

Blood from a vein flows steadily and is darker in color. It does not spurt but bleeding can be severe.

Because of the danger of AIDS and other diseases, wear sterile gloves when you are helping people if it is possible. If you do not have gloves, you can put several layers of dressing or a layer of plastic wrap between you and the wound. Wash your hands before and after helping someone.

The best way to help someone is to care for them in this way.
• Calm the person down if they are frightened. The sight of blood scares many people.
• Find out where the blood is coming from.
• Remove any loose debris near the wound.
• Use a sterile dressing or clean cloth. Apply direct pressure to stop the bleeding. See Figure 19-23.
  **Do not** apply pressure:
  • On an eye injury
  • If you know there is something in the wound
  • If the wound is to the head and you think there may be a skull fracture
• Raise the bleeding part above the head if the bone is **not** broken or if raising it does not cause pain.

## To apply direct pressure:

1. Place dressing over the wound.
2. Press firmly on the dressing with one hand and elevate the wound higher than the person's heart.
3. If blood soaks the dressing, place another dressing on top of the first one.
4. If bleeding continues, press harder. Use both hands if you need to.
5. Keep applying pressure for 15 minutes.

© 1997 Career Publishing Inc.

**Figure 19-23**

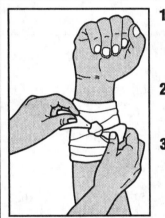

1. Wrap a roller bandage or long strip of cloth around the wound. Secure in place. Use overlapping turns around a limb. Do not wrap the bandage over and over the same spot.
2. Split the ends of the bandage into 2 strips. Tie the ends tight. Tie the knot directly over the wound.
3. Be sure it is not too tight. You should be able to feel the pulse beyond the wound unless it is too tight. If the skin turns blue, it is too tight.

© 1997 Career Publishing Inc.

**Figure 19-24**

- If bleeding does not stop after 15 minutes of direct pressure or the wound is too large to cover, use pressure point bleeding control. See Figure 19-24.
- If the bleeding is severe, you may have to prevent shock. Lay the person flat with feet raised 8-12 inches. Cover the person. **Do not** raise the feet if you suspect any hand, neck, back, or leg injury, or the person seems to be uncomfortable.

**Do Not**
- Feel around in a wound or pull out anything that is in it. This will cause more bleeding and may harm the person.
- Try to clean the wound.
- Use a tourniquet.
- Remove a dressing if it becomes soaked in blood. Just add another dressing on top of the first one.
- Check a wound to see if it has stopped bleeding. This could cause it to start bleeding again.
- Give the person anything to drink if you think there are internal injuries.

If the bleeding has stopped, you may put on a pressure bandage. To apply a pressure bandage:

**Pressure Points:** If direct pressure does not control the bleeding, put pressure on the artery (pressure point) closest to the wound.

The locations of arteries follow:
- Temporal artery: Just in front of the ear.
- Facial artery: In the small crevice about one inch from the angle of the jaw.
- Carotid artery: Deep and back on each side of the Adam's apple.
- Subclavian artery: Deep in the hollow near the collarbone.
- Brachial artery: On the inner side of the upper arm about three inches below the armpit.
- Femoral artery: In the groin between the crotch and hip (for leg injuries).

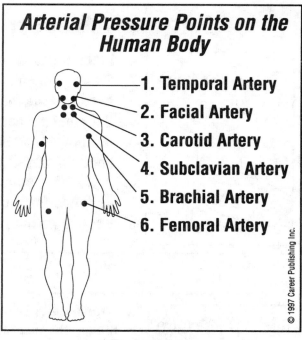

**Arterial Pressure Points on the Human Body**

1. Temporal Artery
2. Facial Artery
3. Carotid Artery
4. Subclavian Artery
5. Brachial Artery
6. Femoral Artery

© 1997 Career Publishing Inc.

**Figure 19-25**

## Shock

Shock happens when something reduces the flow of blood throughout the body. It can kill a person. Keep the person warm and quiet. You can tell someone is in shock when there is:
- Weakness; dizziness
- Decreasing alertness
- Cold, clammy skin
- Extreme paleness
- Bluish lips and fingernails
- Chest pain
- Rapid, shallow breathing
- Numbness; paralysis
- Nausea; vomiting
- Intense thirst
- Unconsciousness

Shock often results from burns, drug overdose, electrical injury, heart attack, heatstroke, low blood sugar, hypothermia, overwhelming infection (septic shock), poisoning, severe allergic reaction, severe bleeding, severe vomiting and/or diarrhea, and spinal injury.

Any person who has been in an accident may very easily go into shock. Shock can also be caused by shallow breathing, loss of blood, or unsplinted fractures. If shock is not treated quickly, it can cause death even if the injury that caused the shock is not severe.

To treat a person is in shock and who does not appear to have a spinal injury:

- Check the person's ABCs.
- Lay the injured person down.
- Raise the feet and legs 12". This will help the flow of blood to the heart and head. Do not raise the legs if it makes the person uncomfortable or if they have trouble breathing.
- Keep the person warm but not hot.
- Keep the person calm and quiet.
- If they vomit, turn their head to the side.

If you suspect a spinal injury, do not move them unless you have to. Do not raise their legs.

## First Aid Summary

It is best to get training from the Red Cross or other agency before you need to give first aid. If you do have to give first aid, you should:

- Know your limits.
- Know the state and federal laws for treating victims.
- Follow company policy.
- Know when not to apply first aid.

# FIRES AND FIRE FIGHTING

It is always better to prevent a fire instead of having to put one out. Ways to prevent fires and methods for putting them out will be explained in this section.

While there is a fire in only a small percentage of truck accidents, such accidents usually cause

© 1997 Career Publishing Inc.

**Figure 19-26**

deaths, severe injuries, and property damage. For this reason, drivers should know what types of fires they may encounter, and how to safely deal with them.

Knowing how to use a fire extinguisher effectively can let a driver save someone's vehicle or control a fire long enough to rescue a trapped accident victim.

To burn, a fire needs:

1. Fuel
2. A source of heat
3. Oxygen
4. Chemical chain reaction

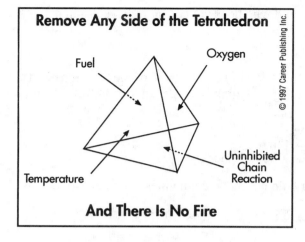

**Remove Any Side of the Tetrahedron**

Fuel

Oxygen

Temperature

Uninhibited Chain Reaction

**And There Is No Fire**

© 1997 Career Publishing Inc.

**Figure 19-27**

If you remove one of the elements, there will be no fire. You can put out a fire by cooling it to the point it will not burn. You can usually do this by putting water on it. You can also put out a fire by smothering it. This will cut off the supply of oxygen. You can do this with a gas or powder. The powder releases a gas when heated and smothers the flames. Certain agents, such as halon and some dry chemicals extinguish the fire by interrupting the chain reaction.

Different types of fires must be put out using different methods. For example, using a stream of water on a burning liquid, or on a water-reactive hazardous material will make the situation worse. On other types of fires, such as a burning tire, water is needed to cool the burning material even though smothering may temporarily control visible flames.

There are different types of fires. They are divided into four classes: A, B, C, and D.

**Class A fire:** A fire in ordinary combustibles such as wood, paper, and cloth.

**Class B fire:** A fire in flammable or combustible liquids and gases such as gasoline, diesel fuel, alcohol, paint, acetylene, hydrogen.

**Class C fire:** A fire in live electrical equipment. You must put it out with something that does not conduct electricity. After the electricity is cut off, extinguishers suitable for Class A or Class B fires may be used.

**Class D fire:** A fire in combustible metals such as magnesium and sodium. These fires can only be put out with special chemicals or powders.

*Classes of Fires*

Ordinary **A** Combustibles

Flammable **B** Liquids

Electrical **C** Equipment

Combustible **D** Metals

A. Wood, Paper, Ordinary Combustibles **Extinguish by Cooling and Quenching** Use: Water or Dry Chemicals

B. Gasoline, Oil, Grease, Other Greasy Liquids **Extinguish by Smothering, Cooling, or Heat-Shielding** Use: Carbon Dioxide or Dry Chemicals

C. Electrical Equipment Fires **Extinguish with Nonconducting Agents: Carbon Dioxide or Dry Chemicals** DO NOT USE WATER

D. Fire in Combustible Metals **Extinguish by Using Specialized Extinguishing Powders**

| Fire Extinguisher Type | For | Class of Fire |
|---|---|---|
| Regular Dry Chemical | | B,C |
| Multi-Purpose Dry Chemical | | A,B,C, or B,C |
| Purple-K Dry Chemical | | D |
| KCL Dry Chemical | | B,C |
| Dry Powder Special Compound | | D |
| Carbon Dioxide (Gas) | | B,C |
| Halogenated Agent (Gas) | | B,C |
| Water | | A |
| Water With Anti-Freeze | | A |
| Water, Loaded Stream Style | | A,B |
| Foam | | B, Some Use on A |

© 1997 Career Publishing Inc.

**Figure 19-28**

## Fire Extinguishers

Most fire extinguishers are marked by a letter and symbol to indicate the classes of fires for which they can be used. Every truck or truck-tractor with a gross vehicle weight rating (GVWR) of 10,001 pounds or more must have a fire extinguisher. The extinguisher must be checked as part of the pre-trip inspection.

**Figure 19-29**

If the vehicle is used for transporting hazardous material that requires placards, the extinguisher must have an Underwriter's Laboratory (UL) rating of 10B:C or more. If the vehicle is not used for hazardous materials, an extinguisher with a UL rating of 5B:C may be used. The rating is usually shown near the UL certification on the extinguisher. If the rating also shows a 1A or 2A, it indicates the extinguisher can be used for fires of ordinary combustibles.

The extinguisher must be securely mounted so the driver can get it easily. If the extinguisher is not in the driver's compartment, (e.g. the luggage compartment of a sleeper cab) the outside of the vehicle should be marked showing its location. This is required by law in some states.

Every extinguisher has an instruction plate. The driver should read it to know how to operate the extinguisher in the event of a fire. Extinguishers for trucks are most effective for putting out small fires in their early stages. Because they do not hold a large quantity, the driver must plan how to use it to the best advantage. The stream range and discharge time are listed on the extinguisher. These vary, but generally they are as follows:

- Stream range — 5-12 feet
- Discharge time — not less than 8 seconds

To put out a fire, aim the extinguisher at the base of the flames and spray back and forth in a sweeping motion. Be sure not to leave pockets of fire that may flash again later.

The driver must not risk his or her personal safety trying to put out a fire. If the driver decides to fight the fire, he or she must be careful not to get surrounded and cut off by it. The driver should fight the fire with the wind at his or her back, if possible.

**Figure 19-30**

## Additional Information About Truck Fires

If your tractor-trailer should catch on fire, drive it to the nearest safe place and stop. Stay as far away from buildings as possible. Get help as soon as you can. If the tractor can be unhooked from the trailer safely, do so. You may stop the spread of fire by doing this.

**Tire Fires:** Tire fires usually occur because the air pressure in the tire is too low. Tires that are low or flat flex too much. This lets heat build up inside the tire. When it gets hot enough, the surface will burst into flame. You can control the flames with a fire extinguisher, but large quantities of water must be poured on the tire to cool it down. Then the fire can be finally put out. Tires can easily catch on fire again because heat builds up between the plies.

© 1997 Career Publishing Inc.

**Figure 19-31**

These fires can be prevented by checking to be sure the tires are properly inflated. Tires can be checked best by using a truck tire gauge. It is the only way to be sure the air pressure is balanced for dual tires. Because of the dangerous cargo, drivers transporting hazardous materials are required to check the tires every 2 hours or after each 100 miles of travel.

**Cargo Fires:** In a closed van, you may not know there is a cargo fire until smoke seeps out around the doors. To keep the fire smoldering instead of burning, keep the doors closed. This will limit the oxygen that can reach the fire.

Stop in a safe location and get help. Let the fire department open the cargo doors when they arrive. This will lessen the flare-up of fire. If you can safely do so, remove the undamaged cargo before fire fighters put water on the fire.

**Fuel Fires:** In a serious accident, there is a great risk of fire if the gas tank ruptures or a fuel line breaks. The leaking fuel may be ignited by sparks from the accident or another source. The truck's fire

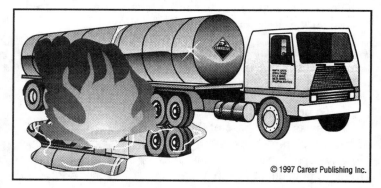

© 1997 Career Publishing Inc.

**Figure 19-32**

extinguisher may not control a fire from a large fuel spill. Although diesel fuel does not burn as easily as gasoline, it will burn if it gets hot enough.

If you find any fuel leaks during a pre-trip inspection, correct them before you start your trip. Be sure the caps are securely on fuel tanks. When you refuel, do not smoke or allow others to do so. Metal-to-metal contact must be maintained between the nozzle and the fill-pipe.

Federal laws say you cannot fill any fuel tank to more than 95% of its capacity. This will prevent spills when the fuel expands as it warms. If the cargo is hazardous material, a person must control the flow of fuel when the truck is being refueled.

**Electrical Fires:** Electrical fires can happen when the insulation on wiring is worn or frayed. If the bare wires touch each other or other metal parts of the truck, a fire can result. In an accident, damaged wiring can short circuit and cause a fire. If you can safely disconnect the battery when there is an electrical fire, this will remove the source of heat.

## SUMMARY

In this chapter, you learned how a driver should act if there is an accident: 1) what information to be sure to obtain; 2) what information you must give to others involved in the accident; 3) subjects you must not discuss; and 4) how to give first aid. The requirements for hazardous material spills were outlined. The types of fires and ways of fighting them were also explained. You also learned there are different types of fire extinguishers and they are used on different types of fires.

## KEY WORDS

**Accident packet:** Given by most companies to drivers to help them handle their responsibilities at the scene of an accident. Packets usually contain basic instructions for handling the scene of an accident, a preliminary accident report or memo, and witness cards.

**Center for Disease Control (CDC):** Agency to be notified if a cargo spill is a disease causing agent.

**Chemical Transportation Emergency Center (CHEMTREC):** Tells emergency personnel what they need to know to take care of a chemical problem. It also helps make the proper notifications and supplies the emergency personnel with expert technical assistance.

**First Aid:** Immediate and temporary care given to a victim until professional help arrives.

**Hazardous Materials Incident Report:** A written report that must be filed within 15 days if there is an unintended release of hazardous materials.

**National Response Center:** Helps coordinate the emergency forces in response to major chemical hazards.

**U.S. Coast Guard National Response Center:** Helps coordinate emergency forces in response to chemical hazards.

# LEARNING ACTIVITIES

## What to do in an Emergency

1.   Below are several different types of fires. On the lines below each drawing, identify the fire, tell how you would fight it, and what you would use to put out the fire.

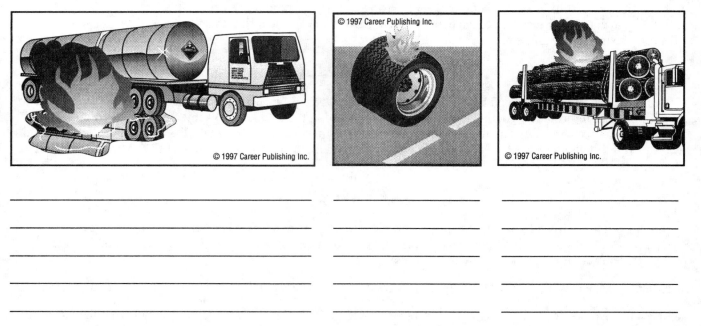

_____   _____   _____

_____   _____   _____

_____   _____   _____

_____   _____   _____

_____   _____   _____

2.   In the pictures shown below, draw reflective markers at the locations where they should be placed if the rig is stopped. Mark the distance they are from the truck.

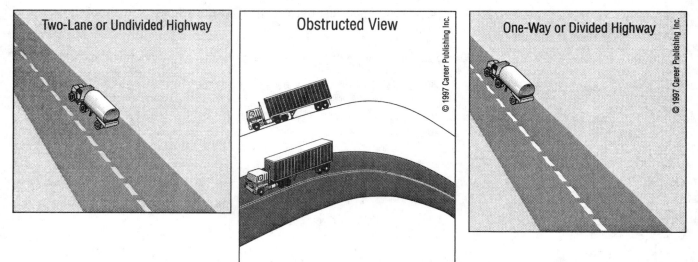

3.  You have been in an accident. You were driving in your correct lane. As you came over the crest of a hill, you side-swiped an on-coming car that had strayed into your lane. Draw a diagram of the accident using the instructions given in this chapter.

4.  What four elements are necessary for a fire to continue burning?

    A. _____  B. _____  C. _____  D. _____

5.  What information should you collect from the other people involved in an accident?

    _____

    _____

    _____

    _____

    _____

6.  What information should you give to those involved?

    _____

    _____

    _____

7.  List the subjects you should not discuss if you are involved in an accident.

    _____

    _____

8.  What are the three major types of injuries for which you may have to give first aid.

    A. _____  B. _____  C. _____

9.  One of the injured seems badly hurt. His face is turning blue, and he is bleeding badly from his upper leg. List in the order of importance how you would give him first aid.

    _____

    _____

    _____

## Discussion Questions

Discuss the following statements in class. Determine whether they are true or false. If they are false, give the correct answer. If they are true, explain why.

Most truck fires occur from failure in the exhaust system.

A bent or loose exhaust pipe may get too close to the gas tank or tires and cause a fire or explosion.

If an engine catches fire, you should raise the hood and smother the flames with an extinguisher.

## True-False Questions

T  F  1.  When there is an accident, it is the driver's responsibility to warn oncoming traffic to prevent further accidents.

T  F  2.  Fusees can be used for hand signals to warn of an accident scene.

T  F  3.  After stopping and protecting the scene, your first priority is to assist the injured.

T  F  4.  You should not try to do anything you are not adequately trained to do.

T  F  5.  When someone is injured and you want to help, it is important you know your limitations.

T  F  6.  If a person is injured, your first effort should be to move him or her to a warm, calm place.

T  F  7.  Because accident scenes are usually hectic and disorganized, it is best if you wait to prepare a diagram of what happened until later when you can approach it calmly and without interruption.

T  F  8.  One use for accident reports is to aid in driver improvement and prevention of future accidents.

T  F  9.  An accident is judged preventable if there was at least one thing the driver could have done to prevent the accident and failed to do.

T  F  10.  If no one has stopped to help, you should drive by an accident where there are injuries without stopping to offer assistance.

T  F  11.  Your ability to assist is limited by how much you know about first aid and your skill in using it.

T  F  12.  You should not move an injured person even if there is danger from fire, heavy traffic, or some other serious threat.

T  F  13.  Injuries that require immediate attention are severe bleeding, stopped or troubled breathing, and shock.

T  F  14.  Shock, if not treated properly, can cause death even if the injury that caused the shock is not severe.

T  F  15.  A fire can start and continue to burn only if heat, fuel, and oxygen are present or there is a chain reaction.

T  F  16.  If your rig catches fire and you are near a service station, you should pull in and get help at once.

T  F  17.  If a tire catches fire, you should keep using large amounts of water even after the flames are out.

# Chapter Twenty
# SLIDING FIFTH WHEELS AND TANDEM AXLES

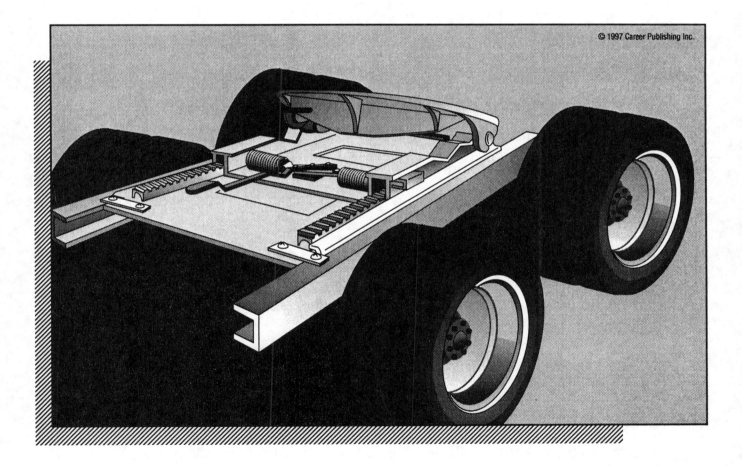

© 1997 Career Publishing Inc.

**Overview • Shifting Weight • Maneuverability • Off-tracking
The Fifth Wheel • Sliding The Fifth Wheel • Trailer Tandem Axles
Sliding The Trailer Tandem Axles**

# OBJECTIVES

When you have mastered this chapter, you will be able to:

• Describe the reasons for sliding the fifth wheel or trailer tandem axles

• Explain the concept of shifting weight between the tractor and trailer

• Explain the effects of sliding the fifth wheel or trailer tandem axles on:
    Overall length
    Maneuverability
    Off-tracking

• Describe the procedure for locking and unlocking a sliding fifth wheel

• Explain the correct way to slide the fifth wheel of a tractor with a trailer attached

• Describe the procedure for locking and unlocking a sliding tandem axle

• Explain the correct way to slide the tandem axles of a trailer with a tractor attached

• Explain the hazards of sliding the fifth wheel or trailer tandem axles improperly

# CHAPTER TWENTY

# SLIDING FIFTH WHEELS AND TANDEM AXLES

## INTRODUCTION

Many tractor-trailers have a sliding fifth wheel on the tractor and sliding tandem axles on the trailer. Tractor-trailers can have either one or both of them.

The sliding fifth wheel can:
- Adjust the overall length of the tractor-trailer.
- Adjust the turning radius of the vehicle.
- Adjust and balance the weight on each of the axles.

The sliding tandem axles on the trailer can:
- Adjust the tracking angle of the trailer.
- Adjust the turning radius of the vehicle.
- Adjust and balance the weight on each of the axles on the trailer.

As you can see, wheels and axles have similar effects on both the tractor and trailer. Their positions are very important to the driver if he or she wishes to safely and legally haul a load. Remember, the driver is responsible for:
- The legal gross vehicle weight of the vehicle
- The amount of weight per axle
- The overall length of the vehicle
- The rig's maneuverability and ability to turn safely, should state or local restrictions apply

The purpose of this chapter is to help you learn how to slide the fifth wheel and the trailer tandem axles. You will also learn some of the basic reasons for making these adjustments to a rig.

## SHIFTING WEIGHT

When a trailer is coupled to a tractor, some of the weight of the trailer is transferred to the tractor through the connection with the fifth wheel. If the freight is evenly distributed in the trailer, standard trailer axle and fifth wheel settings will properly distribute the weight on each axle.

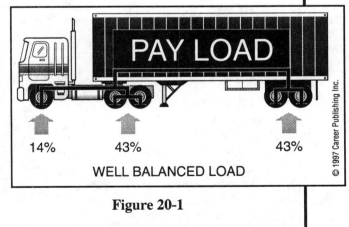

© 1997 Career Publishing Inc.

**Figure 20-1**

14%          43%                    43%

WELL BALANCED LOAD

Some trailers have sliding tandem axles to transfer weight to the tractor if the load in the trailer is not evenly distributed. The amount of weight transferred to the tractor can be adjusted by sliding the tandem axles on the trailer toward the *rear*. This will increase the amount of weight on the drive and steering axles of the tractor.

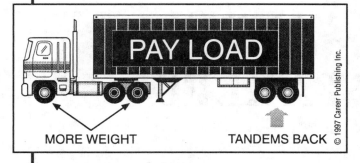

**Figure 20-2**

By sliding the trailer tandems *forward*, you can shift weight off the tractor. This causes the weight behind the trailer's tandem axles to actually tip the weight off the tractor. Shifting the weight decreases the amount of weight on the drive and steering axles of the tractor.

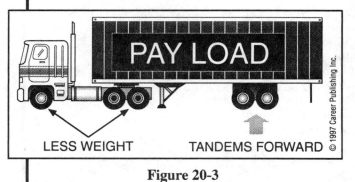

**Figure 20-3**

Some tractors have a sliding fifth wheel. This can adjust the length of the tractor-trailer and balance, or shift, some of the weight from the trailer to between the steer axle and drive axles of the tractor.

By sliding the fifth wheel on the tractor *forward*, you can transfer weight to the steer axle and also shorten the overall length of the vehicle. If too much weight is shifted to the steer axle, the tractor will be hard to steer. It will also be harder to maneuver. If you shift too much weight, the rig may also be overweight according to regulations on the steer axle. At night, your headlights will not be aimed properly, and you will not see as well.

**Figure 20-4**

If you slide the fifth wheel on the tractor toward the *rear*, you can reduce the amount of weight on the steer axle, but you will increase the total length of the tractor. If too much weight is shifted off of the steer axle, the

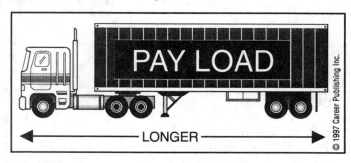

**Figure 20-5**

steering will *feel* light, and you will
not have as much control over the
steering. Shifting too much weight
off the steer axle can also make the
rig overweight on the drive axles.
At night, your headlights will be
aimed at the sky instead of on the
road ahead.

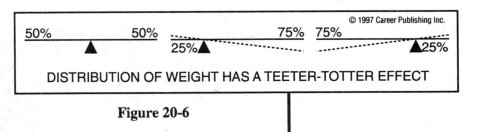

DISTRIBUTION OF WEIGHT HAS A TEETER-TOTTER EFFECT

**Figure 20-6**

As you can see, the positions of the fifth wheel and the trailer tandem axles
have a lot to do with the weight per axle and handling of the rig.

## THE BRIDGE FORMULA

To achieve the maximum legal weight on each axle, you will need to pay
attention to the Bridge Formula. This is a national formula for axle spacings
designed to protect the country's road and bridges. All trucks operating on
interstate highways and on some state highways must comply with this formula.
Under the formula rules, tractors must have a minimum outer spread of 14 feet to
scale the maximum 46,000 pounds (12,000 pounds on the steer axle, 34,000
pounds on the tandems). The outer spread is the distance between the center of
the front axle and the center of the rearmost axle. This distance is not affected by
sliding the fifth wheel forward or back. But two other distances are affected.
These are the **inner bridge** (between the center of the rearmost tractor axle and
the center of the leading trailer axle) and the **outer bridge** (between the center of
the forward tractor tandem and the rearmost trailer axle). Sliding the fifth wheel
or a trailer slider will change these distances and may affect your legal load
carrying capacity. For example, a five-axle tractor trailer must have an outer
bridge of at least 51 feet to haul the maximum allowable 80,000 pounds.

## MANEUVERABILITY AND OFF-TRACKING

The **maneuverability** and
**off-tracking** of the tractor-
trailer are affected by the
position of the trailer tandems
and the position of the fifth
wheel. When you slide the fifth
wheel to the *rear* of the tractor,
the overall length of the vehicle
*increases*. The distance between
the steer axle and the kingpin
also increases along with the
distance to the trailer tandem
axles.

When you turn, the greater
the distance between the steer
axle and the pivot point
(kingpin) of the trailer, the
further the trailer will off-track.

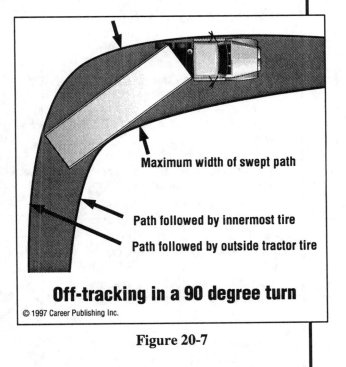

**Maximum width of swept path**

**Path followed by innermost tire**

**Path followed by outside tractor tire**

## Off-tracking in a 90 degree turn

**Figure 20-7**

The swept path of the trailer will *increase*. You will need more space to make a
turn.

The position of the tandem axles of the trailer also affects off- tracking and the space needed to turn. When you slide the tandem axles all the way to the *rear*, the distance between the kingpin and the rear axle wheels *increases*. The overall length of the vehicle does not change, but the amount of space needed to turn *increases*.

When the tandem axles are all the way back, trailer off-tracking *increases* and so does the swept path of the vehicle. The sharper the turn, the *more the rear wheels will off-track*.

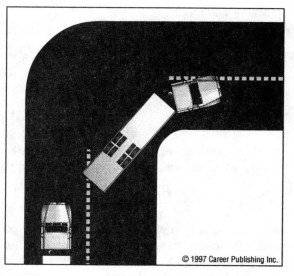

**Figure 20-8**

When you slide the tandem axles *forward* and the distance between the kingpin and the rear axles *decreases*, the rig is *easier to maneuver*. There is also *less trailer off-tracking*. This is very helpful when you are making deliveries. You must also be very careful when the tandem axles are all the way forward because there is a *trailer overhang*.

As you can see, the benefits of sliding the tandem axles forward when you drive in downtown traffic can be offset by the possible dangers of trailer overhang.

## THE FIFTH WHEEL

There are two types of fifth wheels.
1.   Fixed (stationary)
2.   Sliding

A **fixed**, or **stationary, fifth wheel** is usually mounted directly on the frame rails of the tractor by a bracket assembly. The bracket assembly allows the fifth wheel to *rock* up and down. The stationary fifth wheel is placed to get the best weight distribution between the tractor's steer axle and the drive axle(s) of a properly loaded trailer. Weight adjustments are made by sliding the tandem axles of the trailer.

**Sliding fifth wheels** are attached to sliding bracket assemblies. The sliding bracket assemblies can be attached to a base that has a sliding rail assembly built

**Figure 20-9**

**Figure 20-10**

into it. The base is then attached to the frame rails of the tractor. Sometimes the sliding rails are attached directly to the frame rails of the tractor. Then the fifth wheel and sliding bracket assembly are attached directly to them.

The fifth wheel has a locking device that holds the sliding assembly in place. There are two types of locking assemblies.
1.  Manual release
2.  Air operated release

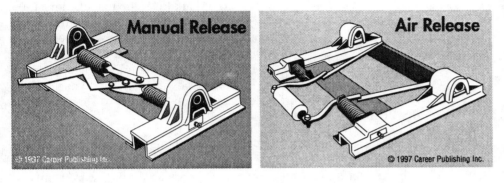

| **Figure 20-11** | **Figure 20-12** |

The **manual release** allows you to release, or unlock, the sliding mechanism by pushing or pulling a release handle. This release handle may be on the driver's side of the fifth wheel or directly in front of the fifth wheel. When the handle is pulled to the unlock position, the locking pins are released from the locking holes, or notches, on the mounting base or sliding rail assembly.

The **air operated release** lets you release the locking device on the sliding fifth wheel by moving the fifth wheel release lever in the cab to the unlocked position. When the lever is in the unlocked position, air is forced against a piston on the fifth wheel locking device. The piston forces the locking pins to release from the locking holes, or notches, on the mounting base or sliding rail assembly.

## SLIDING THE FIFTH WHEEL

Sliding the fifth wheel is not very hard. It should be done on a level surface, off the road, and away from hazards. The trailer must be properly connected to the locked fifth wheel, and the kingpin locked into place. The air and electrical lines should be connected to the trailer. If the trailer has a sliding tandem axle, it should be locked into place. Be sure to put on the tractor parking brake before getting out of the cab for any reason. This will keep the tractor from rolling away.

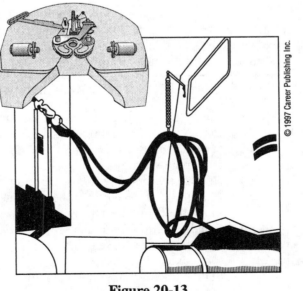

**Figure 20-13**

© 1997 Career Publishing Inc.

TO SLIDE FIFTH
WHEEL BACKWARD
PULL GENTLY FORWARD
IN LOW GEAR

TO SLIDE FIFTH
WHEEL FORWARD
EASE BACK IN REVERSE

**Figure 20-14**

Test the connection to the trailer by gently pulling forward with the trailer brake on. If you have just made the connection to the trailer, look at the connection to make sure the fifth wheel jaws are locked around the kingpin of the trailer. Then crank up the landing gear of the trailer.

The next step is to place the fifth wheel release lever, or handle, in the unlocked position. Put on your trailer brakes either by pulling down your trailer brake hand valve (if you have one) or by pulling out the red trailer air supply valve. Release the tractor parking brake valve. Your tractor brakes are now released and your trailer brakes engaged. You are ready to slide the fifth wheel.

If you are going to slide the fifth wheel forward, put the tractor into reverse. If you want to slide the fifth wheel backward toward the rear of the tractor, use low gear. With the tractor in gear, ease the tractor forward or backward gently. You may have some resistance from the sliding assembly when you do this.

If the fifth wheel has not been moved for quite some time, you may have what is called *binding*. Look at the fifth wheel locking pins first to be sure they have unlocked, and the fifth wheel is free to slide. Pressure on the pins may be holding them in place. If the pins appear to be stuck or binding, you can usually free them by gently rocking the tractor. Corrosion, dirt, or grime may have gotten into the mechanism causing it to lock up. You may have to clean some of the road grime off the mechanism so it can work correctly. You may want to lower the landing gear, also. It can help relieve binding and stress, allowing the fifth wheel to move easier.

Once you have moved the fifth wheel to where you want it, place the fifth wheel release lever, or handle, in the locked position. With the trailer brakes still set, gently tug or push against the trailer. This will let the fifth wheel locking pins or lugs seat themselves.

Set the tractor brakes. Look at the fifth wheel slider to make sure it is properly locked into place. Now that you are done, remember you have just changed your overall length. This will make a difference in your ride, weight distribution, and maneuverability.

---

**QUICK REVIEW — Sliding the Fifth Wheel**

1. Make sure the tractor is properly *coupled* to the trailer.
2. Place the fifth wheel release in the *unlocked* position.
3. *Set the trailer brakes* using the hand valve or by pulling the red trailer air supply valve.
4. *Release the tractor brake* or parking brake system.
5. *Ease the tractor gently* in the opposite direction in which you want to move the fifth wheel.
6. Place the fifth wheel release in the *locked* position.
7. With the trailer brakes still set, gently *tug or push* against the trailer to seat the locking pins.
8. Set the tractor brakes and *visually check* that the fifth wheel slider is properly locked into place.

Remember you have just *changed the rig's overall length.*

# TRAILER TANDEM AXLES

Not all trailer axles are tandem axles. A light duty trailer may have just one axle. In this case, the axle is usually stationary, or fixed. Trailers with a high-rated cargo carrying capacity usually have tandem axles. All trailer axles are attached to a suspension system and sub-frame.

© 1997 Career Publishing Inc.

ONE-AXLE TRAILER      TANDEM-AXLE TRAILER

**Figure 20-15**

Trailer tandem axles can be grouped into two types:
1. Fixed (stationary)
2. Sliding

A **fixed**, or stationary, trailer tandem axle assembly includes the suspension and sub-frame. The assembly is usually mounted directly on the frame rails of the trailer. The stationary tandem axle assembly is placed to get the best weight distribution between the tractor and the trailer. Weight adjustments between the tractor and the trailer are then made by moving, or shifting, the load inside the trailer.

The **sliding** trailer tandem axle assembly is also mounted directly on the frame rails of the trailer. The difference is that the sub-frame assembly allows the trailer axles and suspension to slide, or move along, the frame rails of the trailer. The part of the sub-assembly that slides is called the **tandem axle slide**. There is one slide on each side of the trailer.

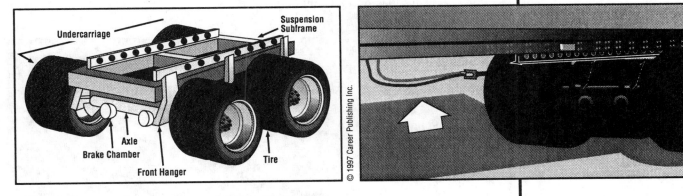

**Figure 20-16**

You will notice there are evenly placed holes along the length of the slide. The holes are designed to seat four locking lugs or pins. These locking pins or lugs are attached to a lever, or handle, called the lug control lever. You engage the lug control lever manually. There is no cab control switch as with an air operated assembly. At the ends of the sliding rails, there are stops that keep the assembly from coming apart when you slide the axles.

## SLIDING THE TRAILER TANDEM AXLES

Sliding the **trailer tandem axles** is very similar to sliding the fifth wheel. This also should be done off the road, on a level surface, and away from hazards.
- The trailer must be properly connected to the fifth wheel.
- The kingpin should be locked into place.
- The air and electrical lines should be connected to the trailer.
- The sliding fifth wheel and the trailer's sliding tandem axle assembly must also be locked.

If you must get out of the cab for any reason, be sure to put on the tractor parking brake. This will keep the tractor from rolling away. Now you are ready to test the connection to the trailer by gently pulling forward with the trailer brake in the *on* position. If you have just made the connection to the trailer, look at the connection to make sure the fifth wheel jaws *are locked* around the kingpin of the trailer. Then *raise* the landing gear of the trailer.

**Figure 20-17**

The next step is to locate the pin or lug control lever. It is usually on the driver's side of the trailer and just in front of the trailer wheels. The lever is usually inside the lever guide that serves as a support. Some units have a safety pin or lock on the lever guide that keeps the lever from bouncing up and down while traveling.

You will note the lever controls four locking pins, two on each side of the trailer. Lift and pull this lever toward you until the grooves on the lever line up with the slot on the lever guide. Then slip the lever into the sideways slot. The slot will hold the lever in the *unlocked* position. Make sure the lever is firmly seated in the slot.

Now that you have unlocked the slides, it is important to make sure all four locking lugs are completely out of the holes in the slides. Check the lugs on each side of the trailer. If any are not all of the way out of the holes, you will have to repeat the unlocking procedure.

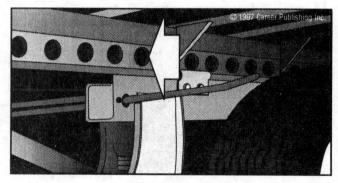

**Figure 20-18**

Get in the cab again. *Engage* the trailer brakes by either pulling down the trailer brake hand valve or by pulling out the red trailer air supply valve. *Release* the tractor parking brake valve. You now have your tractor brakes released and your trailer brakes engaged. You are ready to slide the tandem axles. If you have wheel chocks, use them. They will keep your locked wheels from dragging along the pavement and scuffing the tires.

To the right of the driver on the control panel are two push-pull type valves. The red knob on the bottom is called the Trailer Supply Valve. When this knob is pulled, only the trailer brakes are applied.

© 1997 Career Publishing Inc.

**Figure 20-19**

If you are going to slide the tandem axles *forward*, put the tractor into *reverse*. If you want to slide the tandem axles *backward* toward the rear of the trailer, use *low gear*. With the tractor in gear, ease the tractor forward or backward gently.

If the tandem axle assembly has not been moved for quite some time, the sliding assembly may resist (bind) when you do this. To let the assembly move freely, you will need to find out why it is binding.

Look at the locking pins first to be sure that they have *unlocked*, and the tandem axles are free to *slide*. There may be pressure on the pins holding them in place. If the pins appear to be stuck or binding, you can usually correct this problem by gently rocking the tractor against the trailer.

Corrosion, dirt, or grime may have worked their way into the slides themselves. This creates more friction and can cause them to lock up. You may have to *clean* some of the road grime off the slides so they will work properly.

Once you have moved the sliding tandem axle to the position where you want it:
- Put on the parking brakes.
- Climb out of the truck.
- Release the lug control lever, and place it into the locked position.
- Get back in the tractor.
- Release the tractor brakes.

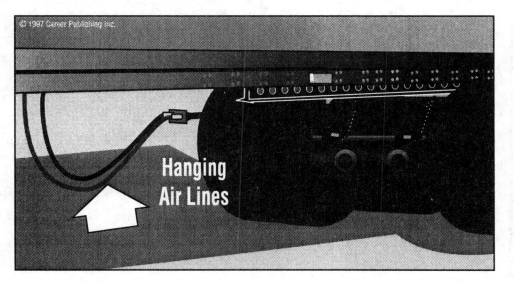

**Figure 20-20**

With the trailer brakes still *set*, gently tug or push against the trailer. This will let all four locking pins or lugs seat themselves. *Set* the tractor brakes, and *look* at all four lugs or pins to be sure they are firmly seated through the holes in the tandem axle slides. Make sure the lug control lever has remained locked and is secured. If you have moved the tandems forward, make sure the air supply lines under the trailer are not hanging down. If they are hanging down, something along or in the road can damage or cut the lines.

Now that you have moved the sliding tandem axle, remember you have just changed your axle dimensions. This will make a difference in your ride, weight distribution, and maneuverability.
- If you moved the tandems *forward*, you now have an *overhang* that you must pay attention to on curves and turns.
- If you slid it toward the *rear*, your *off-tracking* will increase. You will have to compensate for this when maneuvering and turning.

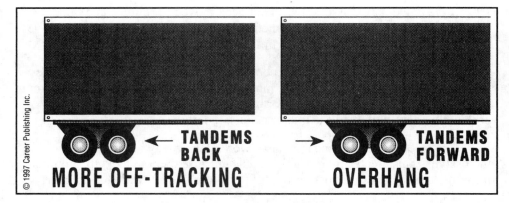

**Figure 20-21**

Decide how you want to set up your rig for loading before it is actually loaded. It is easier to make adjustments on any empty unit than on a loaded one. Even though it may be hard in the beginning, try to become skilled in doing this.

A good way to learn is to keep a notebook on each customer. In it, describe how you set up your rig for the load, as well as directions for getting to the stop, their phone number and the person to talk to, the days and hours they ship, whether they are seasonal, and is an appointment needed. Then you will be able to set your rig before it is loaded because you have a diary of the loads you have already hauled.

How you adjust your fifth wheel and axles depends on a combination of factors.
- Distribution of weight
- Overall length laws
- Legal axle weight limits
- Bridge weight laws
- Handling stability
- Maneuverability
- Preventing damage to the cargo

**QUICK REVIEW — Moving the Sliding Tandem Axle**

1. Make sure the cab is properly *coupled* to the trailer.
2. *Set* the tractor brakes.
3. *Lift and pull* the lug (locking pin) control lever until the grooves slip into the sideways slot on the lever guide. This will disengage the locking pins/lugs.
4. *Check* to make sure all four lugs are retracted properly.
5. *Set the trailer brakes* by pulling out the red trailer air supply valve or pulling down the trailer brake hand valve.
6. *Release the tractor brakes* by pushing in the yellow parking brake valve.
7. *Ease* the tractor forward to slide the tandem backward. Ease the tractor backward to slide the tandem forward.
8. *Reset* the tractor brakes by pulling out the yellow parking brake valve.
9. *Release* the lug/pin control lever. Place it into the *locked* position.
10. *Release* the tractor brakes.
11. With the trailer brakes still *set*, gently tug or push against the trailer to seat the locking lugs.
12. *Reset* your tractor brakes.
13. *Look* at all four lugs/pins to make sure they are firmly seated through the holes in the tandem axle slides. Make sure the lug control lever has remained locked and is secured.
14. *Inspect* the trailer air supply lines for clearance under trailer. Be sure they are not hanging down.

Remember that you have just made changes to your tandem axle setting. This will affect the handling of the tractor-trailer.

## SUMMARY

In this chapter, you have learned the reasons for sliding either the fifth wheel or the trailer tandem axles. You have also learned that doing this will change the distribution of weight as well as the overall length of the rig, maneuverability, and off-tracking of the trailer wheels. The correct ways to slide the fifth wheel and the tandem axle assembly were explained and illustrated. Finally, you found there can be hazards if these procedures are not done correctly.

## KEY WORDS

**Air operated release**: The device on a fifth wheel that allows you to release the locking mechanism on the sliding fifth wheel by moving the fifth wheel release lever in the cab to the unlocked position.

**Frame Rails**: Steel beams that run the length of the tractor and trailer.

**Inner bridge**: The distance between the center of the rearmost tractor axle and the center of the leading trailer axle.

**Lug lever:** The device that unlocks locking lugs on a sliding tandem axle.

**Manual release**: The device on a fifth wheel that allows you to release, or unlock, the sliding mechanism by pushing or pulling a release handle.

**Maneuverability**: The ability of the tractor-trailer to change direction while moving.

**Off-tracking**: When the rear wheels of a tractor-trailer follow a different path than the front wheels while making a turn.

**Outer bridge**: The distance between the center of the forward tractor tandem and the rearmost trailer axle.

**Release**: The device that unlocks locking pins on a sliding fifth wheel.

**Slides**: Sliding assemblies for the fifth wheel and the tandem axle.

**Sliding fifth wheels**: Fifth wheels that are attached to sliding bracket assemblies and can be moved.

**Stationary fifth wheel**: A fifth wheel that is placed to get the best weight distribution between the tractor's steer axle and the drive axle(s) of a properly loaded trailer, and is fixed in that position.

# LEARNING ACTIVITIES

## Review Questions

1. Who is responsible for the gross vehicle weight and the weight per axle of the tractor-trailer?

   _____

2. What is the purpose of the sliding fifth wheel?

   _____

   _____

3. Explain what happens to the weight per axle of the tractor when you move the fifth wheel forward toward the cab.

   _____

4. Explain what happens to the weight per axle of the trailer when you move the fifth wheel forward toward the cab.

   _____

5. Explain what happens to the weight per axle of the tractor when you move the fifth wheel rearward toward the trailer.

   _____

6. Explain what happens to the weight per axle of the trailer when you move the fifth wheel rearward toward the trailer.

   _____

7. What is the purpose of the sliding tandem axle?

   _____

   _____

8. Explain what happens to the weight per axle of the tractor when you move the sliding tandem axle forward toward the cab.

   _____

9.     Explain what happens to the weight per axle of the tractor when you move the sliding tandem axle rearward toward the trailer.

       _____

10.    Explain what happens to the weight per axle of the trailer when you move the sliding tandem axle rearward toward the trailer.

       _____

11.    Will off-tracking increase or decrease when you move the fifth wheel rearward toward the trailer?

       _____

12.    Will off-tracking increase or decrease when you move the sliding tandem axle forward toward the tractor?

       _____

13.    Name the two types of locking devices that lock and unlock the sliding assembly.

       _____

14.    What is the name of the locking device that locks and unlocks the trailer sliding axle?

       _____

15.    How many locking lugs or pins are part of the sliding tandem axle? Where are they located?

       _____

16.    What should you do if the sliding fifth wheel is binding?

       _____

17.    What should you do if the sliding tandem axle is binding?

       _____

       _____

18.    What four things will change when you move the fifth wheel?

       _____

19.    What four things will change when you move the sliding tandem axle?

       _____

## Review Quiz
## PART A: Sliding Fifth Wheel

List the following steps in the correct order for sliding the fifth wheel. Each step is used only once, so you can cross off the steps as you use them.

A.  Remember you have just changed the rig's overall length.
B.  Set the tractor brakes and visually check that the fifth wheel slider is properly locked into place.
C.  With the trailer brakes still set, gently tug or push against the trailer to seat the locking pins.
D.  Set the trailer brakes using the hand valve or pulling the red trailer air supply valve.
E.  Make sure the cab is properly coupled to the trailer.
F.  Ease the tractor gently in the opposite direction from which you want to move the fifth wheel.
G.  Place the fifth wheel release in the locked position.
H.  Release the tractor brake or parking brake system.
I.  Place the fifth wheel release in the unlock position.

### Sliding Fifth Wheel Procedure

1. _____     2. _____     3. _____     4. _____     5. _____

6. _____     7. _____     8. _____     9. _____

## Review Quiz
## PART B: Sliding Tandem Axle

List the following steps in the correct order for sliding the tandem axle. Each step is used only once, so you can cross off the steps as you use them.

A.  Ease the tractor gently in the opposite direction you want the sliding tandem axles to move.
B.  Release the tractor brakes. With the trailer brakes still set, gently tug or push against the trailer to seat the locking lugs.
C.  Inspect the trailer air supply lines for clearance under the trailer. Be sure they are not hanging down.
D.  Reset your tractor brakes and look at all four lugs/pins to make sure they are firmly seated through the holes in the tandem axle slides.
E.  Remember that you have just made changes to your tandem axle setting. This will affect the handling of the tractor-trailer.
F.  Make sure the tractor is properly coupled to the trailer.
G.  Lift and pull the lug (locking pin) control lever until the grooves slip into the sideways slot on the lever guide disengaging the locking lugs.
H.  Release the lug/pin control lever. Place it into the locked position.
I.  Release the tractor brakes by pushing in the yellow parking brake valve.
J.  Set the tractor brakes.
K.  Reset the tractor brakes by pulling out the yellow parking brake valve.
L.  Set the trailer brakes by pulling out the red trailer air supply valve or pulling down the trailer brake hand valve.
M.  Check to make sure all four lugs are retracted properly.

### Sliding Tandem Axle Procedure

1. _____     2. _____     3. _____     4. _____     5. _____

6. _____     7. _____     8. _____     9. _____     10. _____

11. _____     12. _____     13. _____

# Chapter Twenty-One
# SPECIAL RIGS

© 1997 Career Publishing Inc.

**Characteristics of Special Rigs • Multiple Articulation Vehicles • Twin Trailers
Western Doubles • Turnpike Doubles • Triple Trailers • B-Trains • Special Trailer
Types • Low Clearance Vehicles • High Center of Gravity Vehicles • Unstable Loads
Special Cargo Vehicles • Special Handling Vehicles**

# OBJECTIVES

When you have mastered this chapter, you will be able to:

- Identify common special rigs

- Describe the function, operating characteristics, size, special features, and hazards of special rigs

- Explain the special skills and training needed to operate some rigs

- Understand the hazards of operating a rig when not qualified

- List some of the types of cargos that are carried

# CHAPTER TWENTY-ONE

# SPECIAL RIGS

## INTRODUCTION

A special rig is any combination vehicle that differs from the standard tractor and 48-53 foot dry freight trailer van with five axles and 18 wheels. In this section, you will learn about the most common special rigs. We will describe these rigs. Their handling characteristics will be discussed in detail. The special skills and training needed by drivers will be noted.

No one should drive any commercial vehicle without additional training. It is very important for drivers of all special rigs to receive training by either a school or employer. The following is limited information that is only intended to familiarize you with the unusual nature and driving requirements associated with some special rigs.

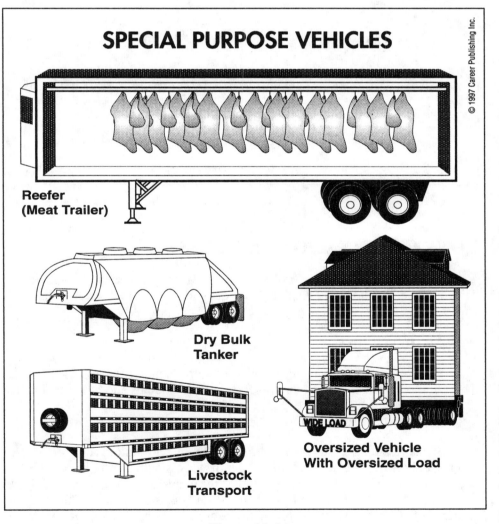

## SPECIAL PURPOSE VEHICLES

Reefer (Meat Trailer)

Dry Bulk Tanker

Livestock Transport

Oversized Vehicle With Oversized Load

WIDE LOAD

© 1997 Career Publishing Inc.

**Figure 21-1**

You will learn about a wide variety of tractors and trailers. Among the special rigs are those:
- With more than one point of articulation (multiple-articulation)
- That are overlength, overheight, overwidth, or overweight
- With a very low vehicle-to-ground clearance
- That have a high center of gravity when loaded
- With load stability problems
- That are used for special cargos
- That require special handling

NOTE: The word *articulate* means consisting of segments separated by joints. A multiple-articulation rig is one that has several parts connected by joints. A typical tractor-trailer has just one joint. It connects the tractor to the trailer.

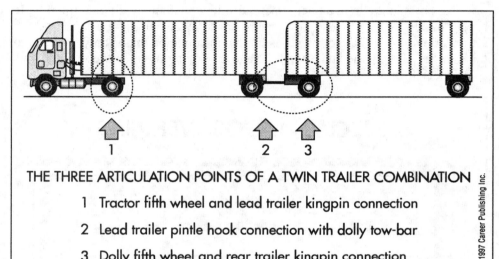

THE THREE ARTICULATION POINTS OF A TWIN TRAILER COMBINATION

1  Tractor fifth wheel and lead trailer kingpin connection

2  Lead trailer pintle hook connection with dolly tow-bar

3  Dolly fifth wheel and rear trailer kingpin connection

© 1997 Career Publishing Inc.

**Figure 21-2**

# LONG COMBINATION VEHICLES

Rigs with more than one trailer are known as long combination vehicles. They include doubles, turnpike doubles, Rocky Mountain doubles, B-trains, and triples.

## Twin Trailers

These rigs are also known as double-bottoms, doubles, or set of joints. There are two basic types of twin trailers: standard doubles and turnpike doubles.

### Standard Doubles

Standard doubles use two semitrailers. The second trailer is converted into a full trailer by using a converter dolly (a set of wheels with a fifth wheel). The second semi couples with the fifth wheel of the converter. Most converters have a drawbar with one eye that connects to the pintle hook on the back of the first trailer. These are known as A-dollies. Some converters have a set of two parallel eyes that hook into two pintle hooks on the back of the first trailer. These are known as B-dollies. A rig with an A-dolly is also known as an A-train and a rig with B-dollies can be called a C-train.

### Identifying Characteristics

Doubles have three points of articulation.
1. The first trailer kingpin and the fifth wheel
2. The pintle hook and eye
3. The converter dolly fifth wheel and the kingpin of the second trailer

### Other Major Characteristics

Trailer lengths vary from 26 to 28 feet with overall lengths from 65 to 75 feet. Trailers may be:
- Vans
- Flatbeds
- Tankers

Used throughout the country.

Cargo: Many types

### Handling

Driving doubles requires some special handling techniques.
- Always hook the heavy trailer as the lead trailer.
- The driver must avoid backing. The vehicle is not designed for this maneuver.
- Steering must be smooth. Jerking or whipping the steering wheel causes the second trailer to overreact.
- Do not put on the brakes in a curve. This will cause the second trailer to dip.
- Be aware of the rig's greater length when passing other vehicles, changing lanes, or crossing intersections and railroad tracks.

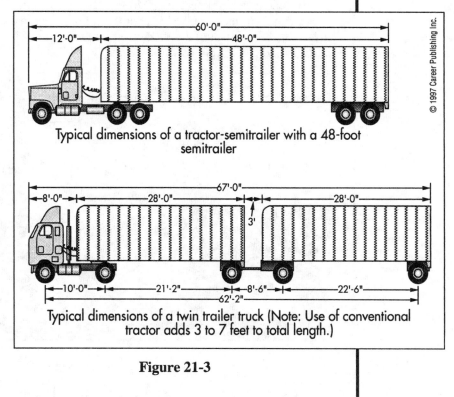

Typical dimensions of a tractor-semitrailer with a 48-foot semitrailer

Typical dimensions of a twin trailer truck (Note: Use of conventional tractor adds 3 to 7 feet to total length.)

**Figure 21-3**

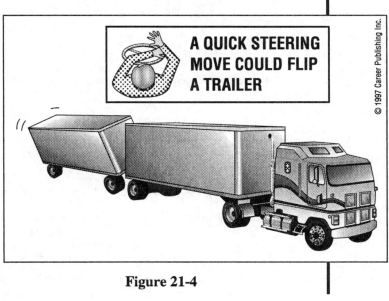

A QUICK STEERING MOVE COULD FLIP A TRAILER

**Figure 21-4**

- You cannot make tight turns with these closely coupled rigs.
- Be aware of bumps, potholes, etc. This can cause the tops of the trailers to hit one another.
- Be aware of where your wheels are tracking. It is harder to stay in your lane when taking curves.

### Special Requirements

A driver must have a Doubles/Triples Endorsement on his or her CDL. A driver needs special knowledge and skills to safely drive double rigs. These rigs may be used in many states. Check the regulations in each state in which you will drive for the maximum allowed length and weight. Also check for needed permits and use requirements.

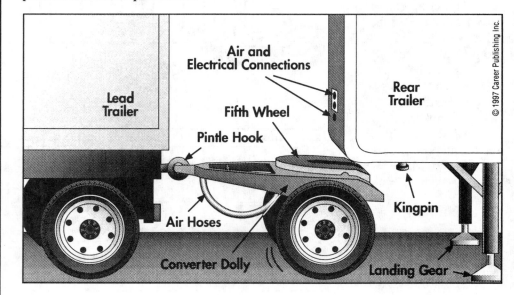

**Figure 21-5**

During pre-trip and enroute inspections, the driver must inspect the drawbar and pintle hook articulation, safety chains, light cords, air line hookup, and valve positions with care. More difficult coupling and uncoupling procedures must also be mastered.

## Turnpike Doubles

Commonly used on turnpikes in eastern states, these are typically nine-axle rigs.

### Identifying Characteristics

Trailer lengths: 40 to 48 feet
Overall length of the rig: Over 100 feet
Usually have high powered engines and multiple gear transmissions

### Other Major Characteristics and Handling

Same handling characteristics as standard doubles. Longer trailers require more room for manuevering.
Trailer lengths: 26 to 28 feet may also be used
Overall length of the rig: Some states allow lengths of over 100 feet.

The trailers may be:
* Vans
* Flatbeds
* Tankers

Used mostly in the western states
Cargo: Many types

### Special Requirements

A Doubles/Triples Endorsement is also required on the driver's CDL for these rigs. More knowledge and skills are needed for driving a turnpike double than for a standard double.

If a special permit is held, turnpike doubles can be used on certain toll roads. For more information, see each state's regulations.

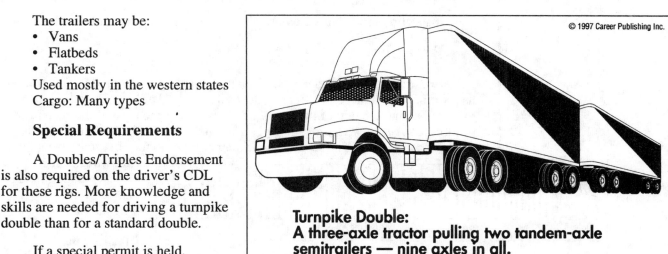

© 1997 Career Publishing Inc.

**Turnpike Double:
A three-axle tractor pulling two tandem-axle semitrailers — nine axles in all.**

**Figure 21-6**

Inspection procedures are basically the same as for standard doubles. Toll road authorities sometimes require special, more demanding routines.

## Rocky Mountain Doubles

These are larger than standard doubles, but smaller than turnpike doubles. The lead trailer is typically longer than the second trailer.

### Identifying Characteristics

Trailer lengths: 40 to 53 feet for the semitrailer; 26 to 29 feet for the full trailer.
Overall length: 80 to 100 feet

### Other Major Characterisitcs and Handling

Same handling characteristics as standard doubles, but long lead trailer requires extra space for maneuvering.
The trailers may be:
* Vans
* Flatbeds
* Tankers

### Special Requirements

A Doubles/Triples Endorsement is required in addition to the standard CDL. More knowledge and skills are needed for driving Rocky Mountain doubles than are needed for driving standard doubles.

Special permits are needed to operate them. They are most commonly permitted on limited access roads in western states and western Canada.

Inspection procedures are basically the same as for standard doubles.

Inspection procedures are basically the same as for standard doubles.

## B-Trains

A B-train is a rig with two semitrailers pulled by a tractor. The first trailer has two or three axles on the rear of the trailer body. The second or third axle extends beyond the rear of the trailer body and under the nose of the second semitrailer. A fifth wheel is mounted above the second axle. This removes the need for a converter. The second semitrailer couples to the first semi using the fifth wheel. This arrangement eliminates one point of articulation.

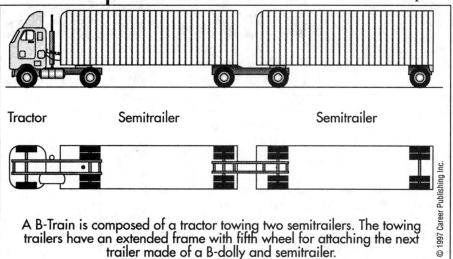

Tractor          Semitrailer                    Semitrailer

A B-Train is composed of a tractor towing two semitrailers. The towing trailers have an extended frame with fifth wheel for attaching the next trailer made of a B-dolly and semitrailer.

© 1997 Career Publishing Inc.

**Figure 21-7**

### Identifying Characteristics

Combinations with one tractor and one semitrailer have one point of articulation. Doubles have three. B-trains have two.

When a semitrailer has tandem axles, they are usually located all the way under the trailer. In B-train rigs, the second axle extends beyond the rear of the first semi.

### Other Major Characteristics

The trailers and overall length vary depending on the state or province in which they are driven. For example, there may be two 40-foot trailers or one 40-foot and one 27-foot trailer. The trailers may be vans, tankers, flat beds, dumps, etc. B-trains have been used in Canada for some time, but now are also being seen in the U. S. They carry many types of cargos.

### Handling

In addition to the safe driving practices for regular combinations, there are a number of special handling points:
- Backing is difficult and should be avoided. B-trains are easier to back than doubles.
- Steer smoothly. Jerking or whipping the steering wheel causes the second trailer to overreact.
- The driver must be aware of the greater length when overtaking and passing other vehicles, lane changing, and crossing intersections.
- Must be aware of tracking to be able to stay in the lane through curves.

### Special Requirements

Driving a B-train rig requires special training, skill, and knowledge. A Doubles/Triples Endorsement on the driver's CDL is needed. With special

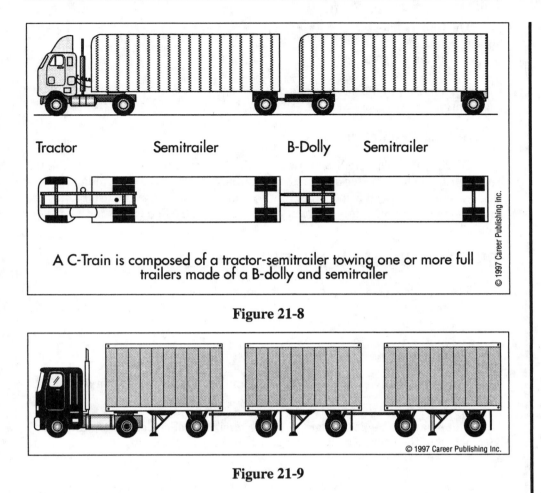

A C-Train is composed of a tractor-semitrailer towing one or more full trailers made of a B-dolly and semitrailer

© 1997 Career Publishing Inc.

**Figure 21-8**

© 1997 Career Publishing Inc.

**Figure 21-9**

## Triple Trailers

Other names for triple trailers are triples, triple headers, triple bottoms, or set of joints.

### Description

Triple trailers are combination rigs that have three semitrailers pulled by a tractor. The second and third semis are converted to full trailers by converters. They are connected by drawbars and pintle hooks.

### Identifying Characteristics

Similar to doubles, there are a number of connection points. Triples have five. They are:
• Three kingpin and fifth wheel connections
• Two eye and pintle hook connections
Length of each trailer: 26 to 28 feet

### Other Major Characteristics

These are also the same as for doubles.
Trailer lengths: 26 to 28 feet
Overall length of the rig: Some states allow lengths up to 100 feet.

The trailers may be:
- Flatbeds
- Tankers
- Boxes, etc.

Used mostly in the western states
Cargo: Many types

### Special Requirements

Drivers of triples need to know more things than those who drive doubles. They must also have better driving skills. Triples are operated only in the far western states and need a special permit for certain highways. The driver must have a Doubles/Triples Endorsement on his or her CDL. See each state's regulations.

## SPECIAL TRAILER TYPES

These trailer types are for oversized loads. They include:
- Lowboys
- Drop frames
- Flat beds
- Open top vans

They have many wheels and axles depending on the vehicle, cargo weight, and state laws.

Many have outriggers to support the oversized loads. Converter dollies may be attached in the usual way or to the cargo itself. They help distribute the weight over more axles and support longer loads.

These rigs haul many types of large, overweight loads.
- Power plants
- Nuclear reactors
- Industrial dryers
- Heavy construction equipment

## Special Requirements

Special training, added skills and knowledge are needed by the driver. The driver must have a Doubles/Triples Endorsement on his or her CDL. With special permits, these rigs may be operated on certain highways. For more information, see each state's laws.

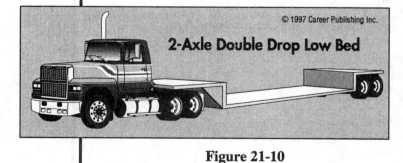

**Figure 21-10**

## Examples

Two axle, double drop, low bed with outriggers: This rig has a double-top frame and two rear axles. Outriggers are attached to each side of the trailer. When they are extended, they support wider loads.

**Five-axle, removable gooseneck, low bed detachable, two axle dolly:** This low bed frame has three rear trailer axles. A two-axle dolly is attached to the rear of the trailer. The detachable gooseneck lets the trailer rest on the ground when loading heavy equipment like bulldozers, front loaders, backhoes, etc.

**Custom trailer and dolly for hauling large diameter and long items:** This rig has a drop frame and two rear axles.

**Two-axle float:** This rig has a flat bed frame with two rear axles and no landing gear. It is used mostly in oil fields for hauling drilling equipment, pipes, etc.

**Four-axle, removable gooseneck, low bed with outriggers:** This rig has a low bed frame, four rear trailer axles and a detachable gooseneck. This allows the trailer to rest on the ground for loading heavy equipment like bulldozers and cranes. For wide loads, outriggers may be used.

**Multi-wheel low bed trailer with jeep dolly:** This rig has a low bed frame and two rear trailer axles.

A **two-axle dolly** is attached to the trailer using the actual cargo. One end of the cargo rests on the dolly. The other end rests on the trailer.

A **two-axle jeep dolly** can be attached to the fifth wheel. The fifth wheel is between the tractor and trailer.

© 1997 Career Publishing Inc.
**5-Axle Removable Gooseneck Low Bed With Detachable 2-Axle Dolly**

**Figure 21-11**

**Custom Trailer and Dolly for Hauling Large-Diameter and Long Commodities**
© 1997 Career Publishing Inc.

**Figure 21-12**

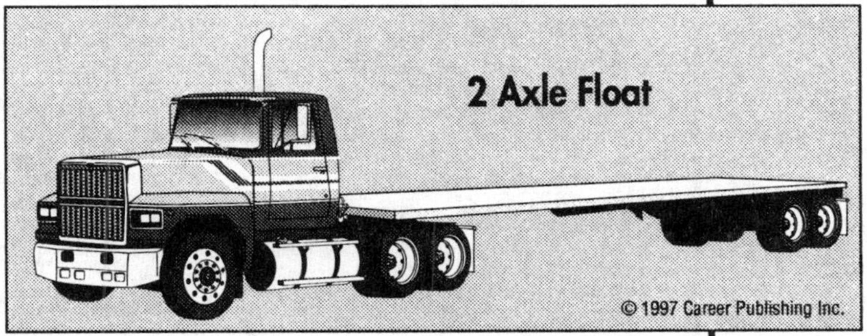

**2 Axle Float**
© 1997 Career Publishing Inc.

**Figure 21-13**

**4-Axle Removable Gooseneck Low Bed With Outriggers**
© 1997 Career Publishing Inc.

**Figure 21-14**

**Multi-Wheel Low Bed Trailer With Jeep Dolly**
© 1997 Career Publishing Inc.

**Figure 21-15**

## LOW CLEARANCE VEHICLES

There are two types of low clearance vehicles: drop deck and double drop deck. The double drop frame drops close to the ground. The single drop frame drops about half the distance. Both drop far enough behind the kingpin plate to keep the tractor hookup from hitting the trailer drop. Be sure the fifth wheel is not too far forward. The tractor frame must not hit the trailer drop, and the rear wheel must not hit the trailer on hard turns. Drop frames haul heavy, oversized cargos or larger, space demanding loads such as van-type trailers on low beds.

### Special Requirements

They are similar to other special rigs. Special training, added skills, and knowledge are needed by the driver. With special permits, these rigs may be operated on certain highways. For more information, see each state's laws.

© 1997 Career Publishing Inc.

**Double Drop Low Bed**

**Double Drop Furniture Van**

**Figure 21-16**

### Double Drop Frame

Low beds are also known as flat beds or low boys. They haul heavy equipment such as bulldozers, cranes and earth movers. They also haul oversized items such as equipment for power plants, boilers, and generating stations. They may have as many as four axles and 24 wheels. These trailers can have bottom clearance problems at railroad crossings, curbs, and large potholes.

Warehouse or furniture vans are the most commonly used vans in the household goods moving industry. The drop-in frame provides a greater load capacity. For instance, a drop of 27 inches gives an additional 3,000 cubic feet of cargo space. Generally, these vehicles are easier to load by hand because of the drop. The wheel housing can be a problem if a forklift is used.

Electronics vans were designed to handle delicate electronic equipment. They have air ride or soft ride suspension to protect fragile loads. Now they are also used to haul high bulk, low weight items such as clothing, potato chips, and plastics.

These vans have a smaller drop (21 inches) than a warehouse van. They have smaller wheels (15 inch), which let them have a flat floor with no wheel wells. The drawback to these vans is less space for the cargo. More heat buildup in the brake drums and tires also occurs.

Livestock transports are designed to carry live animals: cattle, sheep, hogs, etc. See the section on Unstable Loads.

## Single Drop Frame

The low bed is also known as the flat bed. These can haul higher loads without going over the height limits set by law. Bottom clearance problems are not as bad as those of double drop frames. These trailers can have many axles and wheels depending on type and weight of load. See the Oversized Vehicle section.

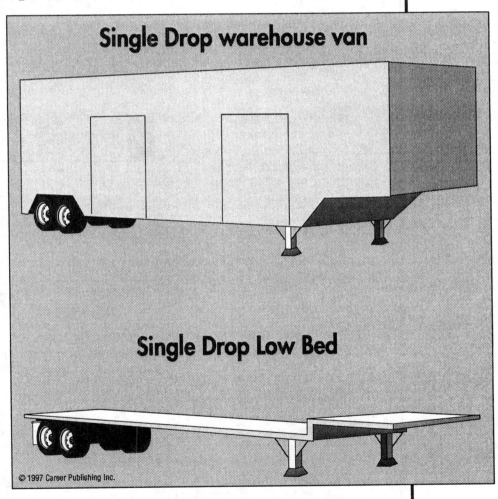

Figure 21-17

Warehouse, furniture, or electronics vans can have either a single drop frame or double drop frame design.

# HIGH CENTER OF GRAVITY VEHICLES

As the name suggests, the bulk of the weight of the cargo in these rigs is high in the load. The center of gravity, therefore, is farther from the road. This makes the trailer more likely to roll over when taking curves.

## Dry Bulk Tankers

The shape of the semitrailer varies but is usually cylindrical. It may be high at each end and slope to a center bottom discharge gate. Trailer lengths vary. The high center of gravity requires careful speed control, particularly on curves.

They are used to haul dry bulk cargo.
- Flour
- Sugar
- Powdered milk
- Ground limestone
- Cement
- Fly ash
- Plastic pellets

These rigs are usually loaded through openings in the top. They are unloaded by a blower from the tractor or through the bottom of the tanker.

**Figure 21-18**

## Liquid Cargo Tankers

Milk tankers are rarely used for other cargos. They do not have baffles or bulkheads. Their smooth linings must be kept very clean. These rigs can be difficult to handle because they must be driven with partial loads. As deliveries are made and the cargo is reduced, the handling characteristics change.

The smooth interior of the tanks and partial loads make driving very challenging. Drivers should accelerate slowly. Avoid braking in turns. Turn only at safe speeds. The greater the speed, the greater the force of the load.

## Special Requirements

There are special requirements for drivers of liquid tankers.  They:
- Must be familiar with the vehicle
- Must have experience with unstable loads
- Must know each state's requirements for road use and permits including those for transporting hazardous materials
- Must have a Tank Vehicles Endorsement on their CDLs
- Must have a Hazardous Materials Endorsement on their CDLs if they are hauling hazardous materials

Pre-trip and enroute inspections should include the standard semitrailer inspection. Check the tank for leaks. Also, check all hoses, valves and fittings. Finally, a check of the emergency valve release is very important.

### Livestock Transport Trailer

These are semitrailers with either a flat floor or double drop frame design. They are used to carry live animals such as cattle, sheep, hogs, etc. Slots or holes in the sides allow the livestock to breathe. Many have side doors rather than rear ones. Some may have both.

### Characteristics

The length may vary between 27 feet and 45 feet. They carry a fixed tandem axle in the rear. These rigs can be changed to have two or three decks for smaller animals such as sheep or pigs. Some can be converted into dry freight vans for the backhaul (return trip).

Livestock trailers can have special handling problems. Live cargo shifts about and that changes the balance and stability. Drivers should drive at the speed that lets them keep the vehicle under control at all times. When braking, tap the brakes lightly to set the animals. Then slowly put on the brakes. Do not attempt to drive one of these rigs without proper training.

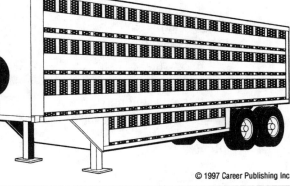

**Figure 21-19**

### Special Requirements

The driver needs more knowledge and skill than for a regular rig. The driver is responsible for the cargo's health and safety. Road use and permits vary. See each state's requirements for transporting livestock.

Oversized vehicles sometimes carry loads with the cargo resting much higher on the trailer than normal. This raises the center of gravity. Any livestock transport that has two or three decks has a high center of gravity when loaded. The animals on the top level cause the high center of gravity.

## UNSTABLE LOADS

The most common unstable loads are of two general types: liquid in tankers and livestock or carcasses.

### Liquid Tanker

Liquid tankers are used to transport liquid cargo such as gasoline, asphalt, milk, orange juice, or liquefied gases. The tanker itself may be hot, cold, or pressurized. The type of tanker used will depend upon the cargo.

The semitrailers of these rigs are usually oval (most common), circular, or square shaped. The load/unload mechanism may or may not be connected to the tractor.

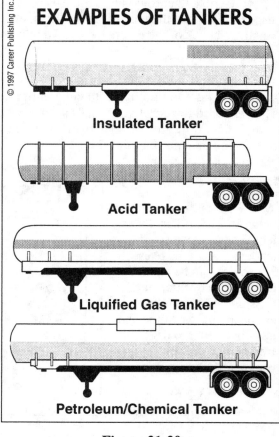

**Figure 21-20**

The number and lengths of compartments vary. There may be one compartment or many. Some contain baffles (walls with holes to reduce surge) or bulkheads to prevent the liquid from surging front-to-back. Handling these vehicles can be very difficult. Surging loads create an unstable vehicle.

Petroleum or chemical tankers may have one to five compartments and may or may not have baffles. Their capacity can be as high as 9,500 gallons.

Acid tank rigs have a small diameter tank with outside stiffener rings and a variety of linings or baffles. They are sometimes insulated and can carry up to 6,000 gallons of liquid.

Liquefied gas tankers are designed for high pressure. They carry butane, propane, oxygen, hydrogen, and other gases in a liquid state.

Insulated tankers carry heated material. Steel tankers can carry materials as hot as 500°F (260°C).  Aluminum ones can carry loads up to 400°F (204°C).

## Refrigerated Trailer (Reefer)

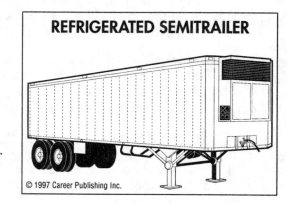

**Figure 21-21**

There are two types of reefers: nose mount and belly mount. Nose mount trailers have the refrigeration unit at the upper front of the trailer. In belly mount trailers, the unit is under the trailer.

Both are box-type semitrailers. Some have racks or rails suspended from the roof. Beef, pork, and lamb are hung from these racks or rails. Others have separate compartments. Some cargo can be kept frozen while other cargo is only cooled. These units have slotted floors and canvas ducts in the ceiling to let air or gas circulate.

## Characteristics

The refrigeration units have their own engines. They may be powered by gasoline, diesel fuel, or liquefied petroleum gas. They also have their own fuel tanks. The floors, sides, and roofs are thickly insulated.

Refrigerated trailers, or reefers, that have rails attached to the trailer roof from which to hang meat have a special problem. The high hanging meat raises the center of gravity.

## Handling

Loosely packed, swinging meat loads create very dangerous stability problems. Swinging meat is more of a handling problem than sloshing liquid. Safe loading procedures are vital.

## Special Requirements

These are similar to those of most other special rigs. Special training, added skills, and knowledge are needed by the driver. A Doubles/Triples Endorsement on the driver's CDL may also be needed. With special permits, these rigs may be operated on certain highways. For more information, see each state's laws.

Inspections should include a careful check of the trailer for holes in walls. Also check ceiling and floor ducts, doors and door gaskets, the fuel level of the reefer, and the reefer's engine coolant, oil, and refrigerant level. The driver should also monitor the operation of reefer unit.

## SPECIAL CARGO VEHICLES

Any rig designed to haul one certain type of cargo is special. For example, a tanker designed to transport edible cargo should not carry any loads that cannot be eaten. Reefers cannot backhaul garbage or trash.

### Pole Trailer

A pole trailer carries long, narrow cargo. A pole trailer can be telescoped, or made longer or shorter to fit the load. Cargo may be poles, timbers, logs, steel girders, or concrete beams.

The load carrying bed is made of two U-shaped cradles (bunks) connected by a steel pole (reach). The

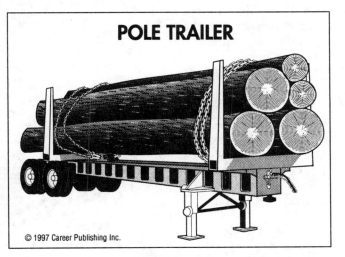

**Figure 21-22**

reach is the part that can be lengthened or shortened. Some rigs do not have a reach. If this is the case, the load becomes the body. Sometimes a straight truck is used as the tractor and the front bunk of the trailer is mounted on the flat bed of the truck body.

## Auto Transport Trailer

This rig hauls cars and pickup trucks. It can carry six full size cars or up to ten subcompacts. Sometimes another car is mounted on a rack above the tractor. A rear ramp that can be raised or lowered lets the cars be driven on and off the transport.

**Figure 21-23**

# SPECIAL HANDLING VEHICLES

These rigs have special handling problems because of visibility, location of the steering axle, etc.

### Low Cab Forward

The cab is in front of the engine on this small diesel used for city pick-up and delivery work. A heavy duty diesel may be used as a combination city and short distance haul rig.

### Snub Nose Tractor

The engine extends back into the cab in this otherwise conventional tractor. It is often used for close clearance city work.

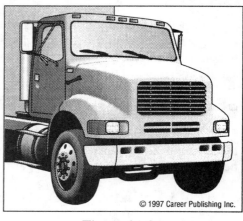

**Figure 21-24**

### Yard Tractors

Sometimes known as a cab-beside-engine, this heavy duty diesel is most frequently used as a yard horse or goat. Its job is to shuttle, or transfer, trailers from one part of the yard to another.

### Dromedary Tractor

**Figure 21-25**

This is a tractor with a cargo body mounted just behind the cab and ahead of the fifth wheel. Its cargo space, or drom box, may be loaded from the rear or through side doors.

## SUMMARY

Many of the special rigs described in this section are dangerous in the hands of an untrained driver. All require special instruction and training. Most special rigs also require special permits and endorsements.

## KEY WORDS

**Articulate**: Consisting of segments separated by joints.

**Baffle**: A wall that has holes in it through which the liquid can flow in a tanker.

**Bulkhead**: A solid wall that divides a large tank into smaller tanks.

**High center of gravity**: The bulk of the weight of the load is high off the ground.

**Liquid surge**: The wave action of the cargo in a tanker.

**Overlength load**: Cargo that is longer than the legal limit permits.

**Overweight load**: Cargo that weighs more than the legal limit permits.

**Overwidth load**: Cargo that is wider than the legal limit permits.

**Smoothbore tank**: A tank that has no bulkheads or baffles.

# LEARNING ACTIVITIES

### Identify These Vehicles

Write the correct name for each of the vehicles on the line below each drawing.

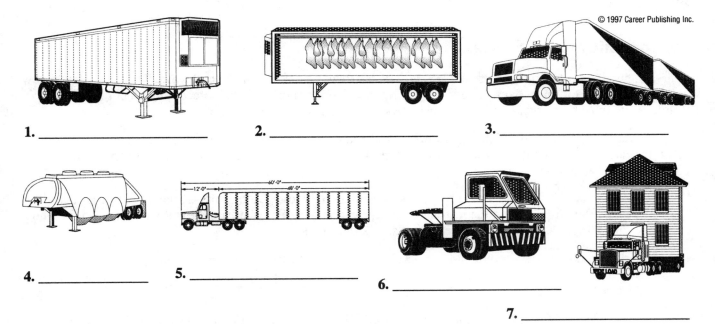

© 1997 Career Publishing Inc.

1. _____

2. _____

3. _____

4. _____

5. _____

6. _____

7. _____

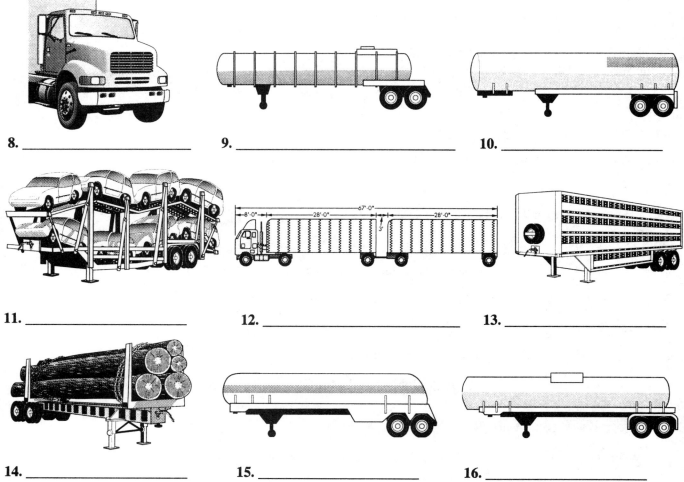

8. _____   9. _____   10. _____

11. _____  12. _____  13. _____

14. _____  15. _____  16. _____

## Identification of Special Rigs

The best way to learn about special rigs is to watch them on the streets and highways. There are, as you now know, special rigs for many hauling needs. Carrying raw milk from the farm to a processing plant requires different equipment than would be used to haul new, boxed TV sets to retail outlets.

Having read about many of the rigs, you can know and understand them better by seeing and identifying them. Discuss them with other learners or instructors. The purpose of this exercise is to identify special rigs during the on-road lessons.

**Directions**: As you see other tractor-trailers, look them over to see if they are special or different in any way. Point them out to the instructor. Describe what you see, what you think it was designed for, and any special handling features it requires. Ask questions.

This exercise, of course, should not interfere with the major purpose of an on-road lesson.

## Field Trip

If time and a suitable site to visit are available, you may want to join other students in observing rigs at a manufacturing site or local transportation firm.

Contact the company you wish to visit, explain the purpose of your visit, number of visitors, and arrange for a time and length of stay. Ask for a company representative to accompany you. After the visit, one person from your group should write a letter of thanks to the host company.

# True-False Questions

If the question is true, circle the T. If the question is false, circle the F.

T  F  1. A special rig differs from the standard tractor that has a 48-53 foot dry weight trailer van and five axles and 18 wheels.

T  F  2. A point of articulation is a joint or connecting link between two different parts of a rig.

T  F  3. Special rigs do special hauling jobs.

T  F  4. Refrigeration vans are sometimes called reefers.

T  F  5. Rigs with a low center of gravity are easier to handle than those with a high center of gravity.

T  F  6. Load stability problems occur when liquid is being transported.

T  F  7. The center of gravity is higher in reefers hauling more than one level of hanging meat.

T  F  8. Livestock is an unstable load because the animals can move around during a trip.

T  F  9. When hauling dual trailers, the heavier trailer should be in front.

T  F  10. Turnpike doubles and standard doubles are different names for the same rig.

T  F  11. Tracking is more difficult with a set of doubles because you have more equipment following you around a curve.

T  F  12. The difference between a reefer and semitrailer is that the reefer has a lower bed or cargo space.

T  F  13. Drivers must avoid backing double or triple bottom rigs.

T  F  14. Beware of bumps, potholes, etc. because the tops of the trailers can hit one another.

T  F  15. Generally speaking, if you can handle one tractor-trailer combination, you have the skills necessary to handle any of the special rigs without additional instruction or training.

T  F  16. Smooth steering is very important with a set of doubles because any jerking or whipping causes the second trailer to overreact.

T  F  17. Rigs that haul bulldozers, cranes, and earth movers can have bottom clearance problems at railroad crossings, curbs, and large potholes.

T  F  18. A surging load is dangerous because the shifting cargo weight can cause handling problems.

T  F  19. When hauling cattle, hanging meat, or liquid cargo, vehicle speed is critical because of the possibility of shifting or surging cargo.

T  F  20. Most special rigs require special permits and/or endorsements on the driver's CDL.

# Chapter Twenty-Two
# PREVENTIVE MAINTENANCE AND SERVICING

**Preventive Maintenance • Routine Servicing • Unscheduled Maintenance and Repair FMCSR Requirements • Vehicle Condition Report Checking the Fuel Level Inspecting the Fuel Tanks • Checking the Oil Level • Checking the Coolant Level Changing Filters • Checking the Battery • Checking the Power Steering Fluid Level Replacing Light Bulbs • Fuses and Circuit Breakers • Checking Tire Air Pressure Changing Tires • Adjusting the Brakes**

FROM NOW ON,

ONLY THE BEST WILL DRIVE

## OBJECTIVES

When you have mastered this chapter, you will be able to:

- Explain the different types of maintenance

- Describe how to do various simple maintenance procedures

- Know your responsibilities in maintenance

- Show dangers of certain types of maintenance

- Understand the inspection, repair, and maintenance requirements of the Federal Motor Carrier Safety Regulations

## CHAPTER TWENTY-TWO

# PREVENTIVE MAINTENANCE AND SERVICING

## INTRODUCTION

A tractor-trailer that is well cared for will do its job much better than one that is neglected. To keep it in good shape, a driver must know how to inspect the vehicle and its parts.

While some routine servicing tasks can be done by the driver, most service and repair work should be done by trained personnel. When someone who is trained for the job does the servicing, it costs less and takes less time. If someone who is not trained attempts to work on the rig, the work may not be done right. This can result in:

- Accidents
- Injuries
- Death

**Preventive Maintenance and Servicing**

© 1997 Career Publishing Inc.

**Figure 22-1**

A driver must know and understand what should be and what should not be part of his or her job.

This chapter has three goals.
1. To teach you the basic checks and servicing needed for the engine and vehicle.
2. To show you how perform some preventive maintenance and simple emergency repairs.
3. To show you that drivers are not expected to be mechanics. They should not try to do any maintenance or repair work unless they have been taught how to do it and have had experience repairing it under the guidance of a trained person.

**MAINTENANCE PROCEDURES**

© 1997 Career Publishing Inc.

**Figure 22-2**

## PREVENTIVE MAINTENANCE

**Preventive maintenance** is the servicing done at regular intervals on a truck. By servicing the truck regularly, many costly emergency repairs are avoided. Small problems can be fixed before they develop into big ones.

In many fleets, even the most routine maintenance is performed by the fleet's maintenance department, the dealer, an independent garage, or a truck leasing company. Drivers are not permitted to do any maintenance.

Other carriers, however, require drivers to perform certain maintenance tasks as part of their job. Independent owner/operators generally do more preventive maintenance than do drivers in larger companies. Owner/operators also have some work done by a garage or dealer.

## TYPES OF MAINTENANCE

Maintenance includes:
- Routine servicing
- Scheduled preventive maintenance
- Unscheduled maintenance and repair

### Routine Servicing

**Routine servicing** tasks can be done by drivers. Drivers often:
- Add fuel
- Add oil
- Add coolant
- Drain moisture from fuel and air systems

### Scheduled Preventive Maintenance

**Scheduled preventive maintenance** is servicing that is based upon time or mileage since the last scheduled maintenance. Most fleets have a regular preventive maintenance schedule. This maintenance is often set up under four levels and is not performed by drivers.

# SCHEDULED PREVENTIVE MAINTENANCE

- **Based on Time or Mileage or a Combination of Time/Miles**

- **Usually Set Up on Four Levels**
  - **Level A — Perhaps Grease and Oil Change Only**
  - **Level B — Same as A but More Involved**
  - **Level C — All of A, plus B and an Engine Tune-Up**
  - **Level D — All of A, B, and C plus a Major Overhaul of Engine**

© 1997 Career Publishing Inc.

**Figure 22-3**

**Level A**
Grease job
Oil change
Filter change
Checking all fluid levels

**Level B**
Includes all of Level A
Inspection and maintenance of key
    components such as
    lubricating water pump shaft

**Level C**
Includes all of Level A and Level B
Engine tune up
Detailed inspection of all major
    components
Road test

**Level D**
Includes all of Levels A, B, and C
Complete overhaul of the engine
Rebuilding parts
Fuel pump
Alternator

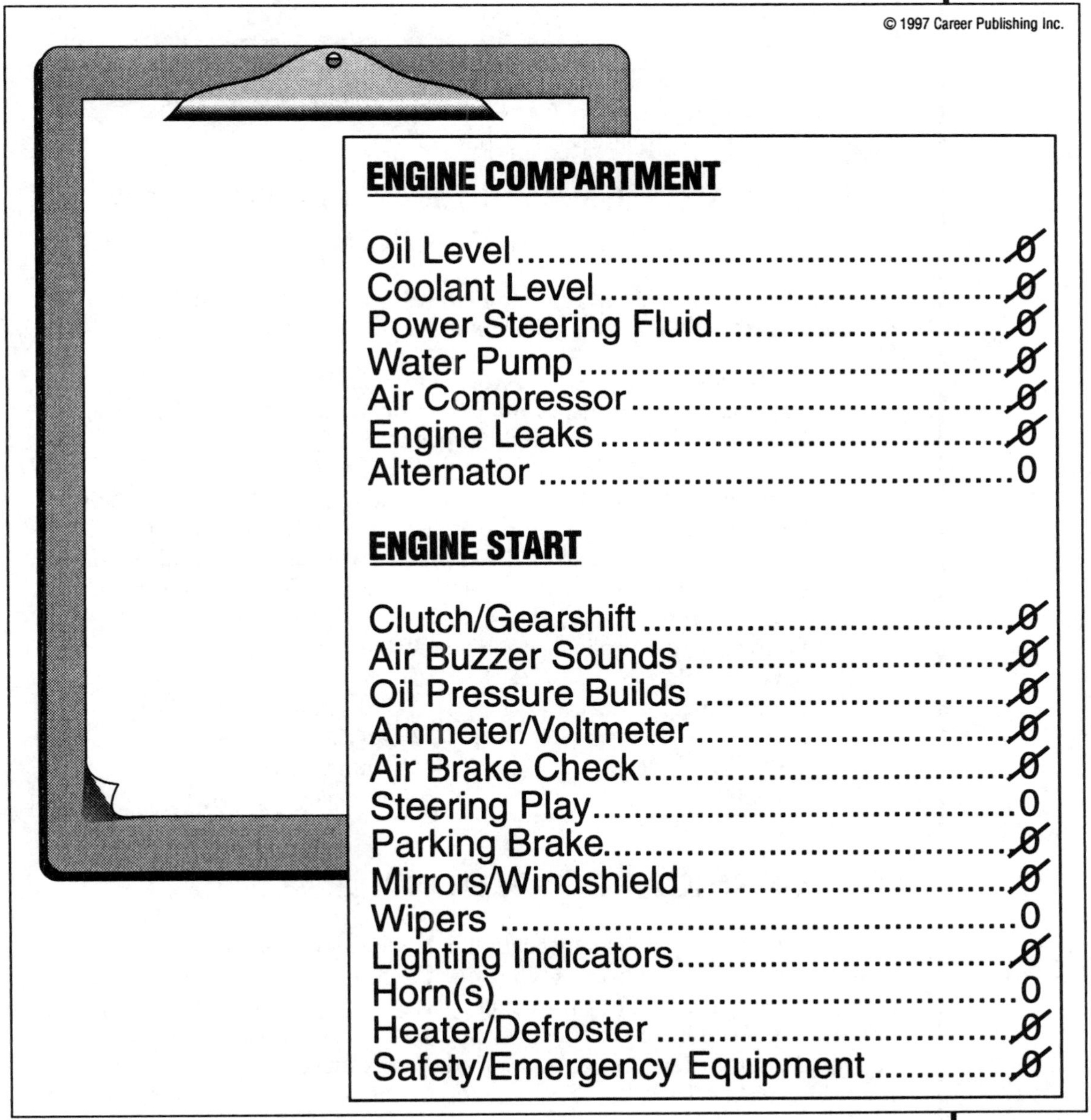

© 1997 Career Publishing Inc.

**ENGINE COMPARTMENT**

Oil Level...............................................∅
Coolant Level.......................................∅
Power Steering Fluid..........................∅
Water Pump.........................................∅
Air Compressor...................................∅
Engine Leaks.......................................∅
Alternator ............................................0

**ENGINE START**

Clutch/Gearshift.................................∅
Air Buzzer Sounds.............................∅
Oil Pressure Builds ...........................∅
Ammeter/Voltmeter ...........................∅
Air Brake Check..................................∅
Steering Play......................................0
Parking Brake.....................................∅
Mirrors/Windshield ...........................∅
Wipers ................................................0
Lighting Indicators............................∅
Horn(s)................................................0
Heater/Defroster ...............................∅
Safety/Emergency Equipment ..........∅

**Figure 22-4**

## Unscheduled Maintenance and Repair

**Unscheduled maintenance and repair** occurs when unexpected breakdowns or emergencies require immediate maintenance.

- Breakdowns on the road
- Repair of accident damage
- Problems listed in a driver's pre-trip or post-trip inspection report

**Figure 22-5**

# FEDERAL MOTOR VEHICLE INSPECTION AND MAINTENANCE REQUIREMENTS

All drivers must learn what the **Federal Motor Carrier Safety Regulations (FMCSR)** say and follow them.

Part 392 and Part 396 of the FMCSR require drivers to:
- Perform a pre-trip inspection before operating a vehicle.
- Review the last daily vehicle inspection report.
- Sign the report to indicate they have reviewed it. The driver also confirms that a mechanic has completed any needed work on the rig.
- Perform enroute inspections (see section 392.9) after the vehicle has been driven for 3 hours or 150 miles — whichever occurs first. If the driver is hauling hazardous materials, see part 397 for more requirements.
- Perform a post-trip inspection on the:

| | |
|---|---|
| Service brakes | Horn |
| Parking brakes | Wind shield wipers |
| Steering mechanism | Rear-view mirrors |
| Lights and reflectors | Coupling devices |
| Wheels and rims | Emergency equipment |
| Tires | |

# DAILY VEHICLE CONDITION REPORT

Results of the post-trip inspection must be entered on an official daily **Vehicle Condition Report (VCR)** form. The report must be completed even if no defects were found. The driver must make an accurate report of everything he or she finds. Then he or she must sign and date it. The report must then be delivered to the supervisor. Every day all drivers must complete this report for each vehicle they drive. Laws and the report help the mechanics keep equipment in top condition.

# VEHICLE CONDITION REPORT

## DRIVER'S INSPECTION REPORT

MAINTENANCE

(SEE INSTRUCTIONS ON REVERSE SIDE)

CHECK DEFECTS ONLY. Explain under REMARKS

COMPLETION OF THIS REPORT REQUIRED BY FEDERAL LAW, 49CFR 396.11 & 396.13.

Mileage (No Tenths)

Truck or
Tractor No. _____  |__|__|__|__|__|  Trailer No. _____

Dolly No. _____  Trailer No. _____  Location: _____

### POWER UNIT

| GENERAL CONDITION | IN CAB | EXTERIOR |
|---|---|---|
| ☐ 02 Cab/Doors/Windows | ☐ 03 Gauges/Warning Indicators | ☐ 34 Lights |
| ☐ 02 Body/Doors | ☐ 02 Windshield Wipers/Washers | ☐ 34 Reflectors |
| ☐ ____ Oil Leak ____ | ☐ 54 Horn(s) | ☐ 16 Suspension |
| ☐ ____ Grease Leak ____ | ☐ 01 Heater/Defroster | ☐ 17 Tires |
| ☐ 42 Coolant Leak | ☐ 02 Mirrors | ☐ 18 Wheels/Rims/Lugs |
| ☐ 44 Fuel Leak | ☐ 15 Steering | ☐ 32 Battery |
| ☐ ____ Other ____ | ☐ 23 Clutch | ☐ 43 Exhaust |
| ____ | ☐ 13 Service Brake | ☐ 13 Brakes |
| (IDENTIFY) | ☐ 13 Parking Brake | ☐ 13 Air Lines |
| | ☐ 13 Emergency Brake | ☐ 34 Light Line |
| ENGINE COMPARTMENT | ☐ 53 Triangles | ☐ 49 Fifth-Wheel |
| ☐ 45 Oil Level | ☐ 53 Fire Extinguisher | ☐ 49 Other Coupling |
| ☐ ____ Belts ____ | ☐ 53 Other Safety Equipment | ☐ 71 Tie-Downs |
| ☐ ____ Other ____ | ☐ 34 Spare Fuses | ☐ 14 Rear-End Protection |
| ____ | ☐ 02 Seat Belts | ☐ ____ Other ____ |
| (IDENTIFY) | ☐ ____ Other ____ | ____ |
| | ____ | (IDENTIFY) |
| | (IDENTIFY) | ☐ NO DEFECTS |

### TOWED UNIT(S)

| | | | |
|---|---|---|---|
| ☐ 71 Body/Doors | ☐ 16 Suspension | ☐ 77 Landing Gear | ☐ 79 Rear-End Protection |
| ☐ 71 Tie-Downs | ☐ 17 Tires | ☐ 59 Kingpin Upper Plate | ☐ ____ Other ____ |
| ☐ 34 Lights | ☐ 18 Wheels/Rims/Lugs | ☐ 59 Fifth-Wheel (Dolly) | ____ |
| ☐ 34 Reflectors | ☐ 13 Brakes | ☐ 59 Other Coupling Devices | (IDENTIFY) |

☐ NO DEFECTS

REMARKS: _____

_____

_____

_____

| REPORTING DRIVER: | Date _____ | MAINTENANCE ACTION: | Date _____ |
|---|---|---|---|
| Name _____ | Emp. No. _____ | Repairs Made ☐   No Repairs Needed ☐ | |
| | | R.O.#s _____ | |
| REVIEWING DRIVER: | Date _____ | Certified By: _____ | |
| Name _____ | Emp. No. _____ | Location: _____ | |

SHOP REMARKS: _____

_____

**Figure 22-6**

## Importance of Preventive Maintenance

Failure to perform preventive maintenance can increase the cost of operation. For example, breakdowns on the road may include these extra costs:
- Cargo transfer charges
- Late delivery charges
- Expensive road services (towing; out of town repair)
- Driver expenses (salary while not driving; living expenses)

Preventing part failure costs less than repairing or replacing a damaged part. Unscheduled maintenance disrupts the schedule of preventive maintenance for other parts and vehicles.

## Operating Costs

Vehicles that are poorly maintained cost more to operate. For example, fuel costs are higher. A poorly tuned engine gets fewer miles per gallon and has longer trip times.

A breakdown on the road can result in an accident. Of course, this adds to expenses and decreases trip efficiency. The extra costs can include:
- Repairing the damage
- Lost work time
- Medical expenses
- Increase in company insurance rates

**Figure 22-7**

© 1997 Career Publishing Inc.

# BASIC SERVICING AND ROUTINE MAINTENANCE

Drivers should understand and be able to perform some basic servicing and routine maintenance. They should be able to:
- Inspect and change the engine fluids, certain filters, lights, and fuses.
- Change a tire (change a wheel) in an emergency.
- Drain the moisture from air reservoirs and the fuel system.

Why should drivers learn this if they are going to work for a carrier that has a policy of not allowing drivers to do any servicing or adjustments to their trucks? A few good reasons are:
- If a mechanic is working on your rig and is doing something wrong, you should be able to recognize the error.
- If your rig breaks down at 2:00 a.m., it is -10° F., and you are 15 miles from the nearest telephone, you will be glad to have some basic mechanical knowledge.
- As a professional driver, you should know as much about your rig and its parts as possible. In this way, you can detect systems or parts that are in danger of failing.
- You may not always work for a carrier that does not permit the driver to do maintenance. You may go to work for one who expects the driver to do basic servicing.

# CHECKING AND CHANGING ENGINE FLUIDS, FILTERS, LIGHTS, AND FUSES

This section will explain the correct maintenance procedures for the:

- Fuel tank, fuel level, and filter
- Oil level and filter
- Coolant level and filter
- Battery fluid level
- Power steering fluid level
- Air filter element
- Lights and bulbs
- Fuses and circuit breakers

## Checking the Fuel Tank and Fuel Level

### Fuel Tanks

- Open the drain cocks on the bottom of the tanks, and drain out any water.
- Tighten all fuel tank mountings and brackets. Be careful not to tighten them so much you crush the tank. These systems are designed with some flexibility.
- Check the seal in the fuel tank cap and check the breather hole.

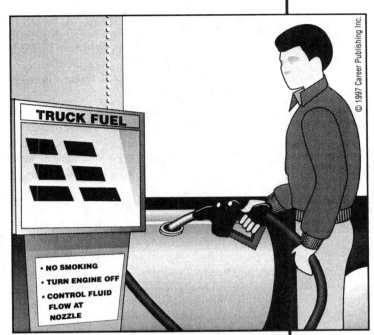

**Figure 22-8**

### Fuel Level

- Park the rig on level ground.
- Open the fuel tank cap.
- Check the fuel level by looking at it.
- Make sure the level matches the gauge reading in the cab.

## Changing the Fuel Filter Element

- Turn the fuel filter element counter-clockwise until it comes off of the base. If you use a filter wrench, be sure to use it at the bottom of the filter, so you will not crush the filter shell.
- Discard the filter element according to EPA standards.
- Clean the surface of the seal on the filter base. Be sure to always remove the old seal and use a new one.
- Wipe up any fuel that spilled when you took off the filter.
- Fill the new filter with clean fuel.
- Coat the seal of the new filter with clean diesel fuel or engine oil.
- Screw the filter onto the base until the seal touches the base.
- Tighten the filter 1/2-turn.
- Start the engine. Check for leaks.

## Replacing the Filter

The following method of replacing the filter is general in nature. There are many types of fuel filter systems. To find the correct way to replace your filter, read the instructions on the filter.
- Turn off the fuel supply from the fuel tanks.
- Place a container under the filter.
- Open the drain cock in the filter housing base.
- Drain the filter.
- Remove the filter body with the element. If you use a filter wrench, be sure to use it at the bottom of the filter, so you will not crush the filter shell.
- Discard the filter element according to EPA rules.
- Clean the housing. Make sure the old filter came out.
- Close the drain cock.
- Install a new filter in the housing.
- Fill the housing with clean fuel.
- Install the filter housing containing the new filter element with a gasket. Always use a new seal. An old seal can leak.
- Lubricate with fuel or engine oil and tighten.
- Open the fuel line shut-off valve.
- Start the engine.
- Check for leaks.

## Draining the Fuel Filter

To drain a fuel filter:
- Locate the filter and water separator.
- Remove the drain plug at the bottom of the filter.
- Allow the water to drain.
- Replace the drain plug.

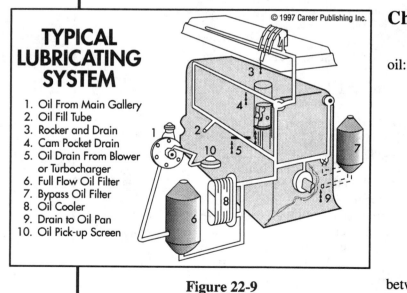

**TYPICAL LUBRICATING SYSTEM**

© 1997 Career Publishing Inc.

1. Oil From Main Gallery
2. Oil Fill Tube
3. Rocker and Drain
4. Cam Pocket Drain
5. Oil Drain From Blower or Turbocharger
6. Full Flow Oil Filter
7. Bypass Oil Filter
8. Oil Cooler
9. Drain to Oil Pan
10. Oil Pick-up Screen

**Figure 22-9**

## Checking the Oil Level

To check the level of the oil:
- Park the vehicle on level ground.
- Shut off the engine.
- Wait a few minutes for the oil to drain down.
- Find the dipstick.
- Remove the dipstick.
- Wipe it clean and replace it.
- Pull it out again.
- Check the oil level.

The level should be between the full and add marks. Do not overfill or drive when the oil level is below the add mark. Be careful not to overfill when you need to add oil.

## Changing the Oil Filter

Changing oil filters on a truck is messy. It is far harder than changing a car's filter. Like fuel systems, what is right for changing the filter on one system may be wrong for another type of system. Change filters only after you have been trained and checked out by your supervisor or a mechanic.
- Remove the drain plug from the bottom of the filter housing.
- Drain the oil.
- Remove the filter housing that contains the filter element. Consult the manufacturer's guide for how to remove the filter element. Most filters today are one piece and disposable.
- Discard the filter according to EPA standards.
- Fill the new filter element with clean oil and install it.
- Secure the housing.
- Replace the drain plug.
- Start the engine.
- Check for leaks.
- Turn off the engine.
- Wait 10 minutes.
- Check the oil level.
- Add enough oil to bring it to the proper level on the dip stick.

## Checking the Coolant Level

© 1997 Career Publishing Inc.

**Figure 22-10**

To check the coolant level:
- Shut off the engine.
- Wait until engine is cool.
- Put on thick cloth gloves to protect your hands.
- Remove the radiator cap very carefully. Turn the cap slowly to the first stop. Step back while pressure is released from the cooling system.
- When all of the pressure has been released, press down on the cap and remove it.
- Look at the level of the coolant.
- Add coolant if needed. Check the operator's manual for specific instructions for your truck.

Many trucks now have sight glasses or see-through containers for checking the level of the coolant. If your rig has one, you will not need to go through the previous routine to check the level of the coolant. If the coolant level is too low, you simply add coolant to the reservoir.

## Changing the Coolant Filter

To change the coolant filter, follow these steps.
- Shut off the engine.
- Wait until the engine is cool.
- Put on thick cloth gloves. Do not handle a hot filter with your bare hands.
- Turn the filter element counter-clockwise to remove it.
- Replace it with a new filter element and a new cover gasket.
- Start the engine.
- Check for leaks.

## Checking the Battery Fluid Level

© 1997 Career Publishing Inc.

**Figure 22-11**

You must be very careful when you are checking the level of the battery fluid. Follow these safety rules.
- Protect your eyes with goggles or glasses.
- Protect your hands. Batteries contain acid that can severely burn you if it touches your skin.
- Do not smoke. Batteries give off explosive gases.

Some batteries are maintenance free and do not need to have the level of the fluid checked. Others are not and must have the level of the fluid in the battery checked. To check the level of the fluid in the battery:
- Open the battery caps.
- Check the fluid level.
- If the battery needs fluid, use distilled water.
- Fill to the bottom of the split ring in the cell filler well.

## Checking the Power Steering Fluid Level

With the engine running at normal operating temperature, turn the steering wheel back and forth several times to stabilize the fluid level. To check the fluid level:
- Turn off the engine.
- Remove the dipstick.
- The fluid should be between the bottom of the dipstick and the full mark.
- If fluid is needed, add enough to raise the level to the full mark. Do not overfill.

## Changing the Air Filter Element

Dust, dirt, grease, or other grime can get into an engine when you change the air filter. Be careful to keep things as clean as you can.

On air cleaners with a restriction indicator, change the element or clean it when the indicator shows red. On trucks that have an air filter restriction gauge, consult the manufacturer for information on when to change the element.

To change the air filter element:
* Remove the end covering from the housing.
* Make sure your hands are clean.
* Remove the filter element.
* Inspect the end cover and gasket surfaces for dents or possible air leaks.
* Check the outlet tube to be sure it is clean and undamaged.
* Check the filter element for wear.
* Replace it if it is damaged.
* If the filter is not damaged, clean with compressed air. Always blow the air in the opposite direction of the normal cleaner flow. Some filters should not be blown out. If your unit does not have an indicator or air filter restriction gauge, find out how often to replace it.
* Wipe away any dirt in the filter housing.
* Install the filter element.
* Replace the end cover and secure it.

**Figure 22-12**

Always handle the filter element carefully to keep dirt from shaking loose onto the clean side of the filter system.

## Changing a Bulb in a Headlight or Clearance Light

To change a headlight bulb or a bulb in a clearance light:
* Park the rig and turn off the engine.
* Remove the trim ring from the burned out light.
* Unfasten the mounting screws.
* Disconnect and remove the light from the socket.
* Clean any dirt or bugs off of the socket area.
* Plug in the new headlight bulb.
* Test the light to see if it works properly.
* Fasten the mounting screw.
* Make sure the new light is clean.
Some lights have lenses that snap off to let the bulbs be replaced.

NOTE: Do not touch the headlight adjusting screws when you are changing the bulb.

## Changing Fuses and Resetting Circuit Breakers

**Fuses**: Always use a fuse that is the right size and has the same amp rating as the fuse it replaces. To change a fuse:
* Check the fuse and clip holder to be sure they are clean and do not have any burrs.
* If the holder is dirty, touch up the contact points with a coarse cloth.
* Gently but firmly snap the new fuse into the clip holder.
* Make sure there is a good connection between the fuse ends and the clip holder.

**Circuit breakers**: To reset a circuit breaker:
* Remove the circuit breaker cover panel.
* Flip the circuit breaker switch back. This will reset it.
* Replace the panel.
* Some circuit breakers reset themselves.

# CHECKING THE AIR PRESSURE AND CHANGING TIRES

This section explains the correct way to check tire inflation pressure and change a flat or damaged tire and wheel assembly. Actually changing a tire (wheel) — removing it from the rim and installing a new one on the rim — is not taught in this book. Only a trained mechanic with the proper tools and safety equipment should replace wheels. Drivers, however, must know how to remove a flat tire and replace it with a spare tire in a roadside emergency.

## Checking the Air Pressure

Check the air pressure when the tires are cool. Readings made when the tires are heated (immediately after a trip) do not give the correct pressure.

When the tires are cool, the correct way to check the pressure is to:
- Remove the valve stem cap.
- Place the air gauge over the valve stem opening.
- Read the inflation pressure from the gauge.
- Compare the tire's pressure with the correct pressure listed on the sidewall of the tire or in the operator's manual.
- Replace the valve stem cap.

## Changing a Wheel With the Tire Mounted

Drivers can learn the right way to change a tire from watching someone else do it. Changing a tire can be dangerous. If possible, it should be done by a trained professional. Remember, a driver should change tires only in an emergency.

Drivers should, however, know what type of tire and wheel style their rig has. They should also know the manufacturer's specs for them. Drivers must understand great care is needed when handling an inflated tire/wheel assembly. Tires explode with great force.

© 1997 Career Publishing Inc.

**Figure 22-13**

To change a tire:
- Park the rig on level ground.
- Put on the parking brake.
- Place the transmission in the lowest forward gear.
- Chock the front tractor wheels.
- Inspect the tires.
  - Check for over-inflation.
  - Compare the side and lock rings.
  - On duals, check the seating of the inner tire.

NOTE: If the tire seems over-inflated or the seating does not look normal, do not attempt to change the tire. Get the help of an expert.

- Refer to the owner's manual for the correct way to place the jack.
- Put a hardwood plank or block under the base of the jack, no matter what type of surface you have parked the rig on.

To remove the wheel/tire assembly:
- Jack up the truck enough to remove the weight from the studs. Be sure to stand clear of the truck when you use a jack. The truck could slip and hurt you.
- Loosen the wheel nuts.
- Observe direction of rotation.
- Examine the thread. On some wheels, the direction is indicated on the end of the stud (**R** means right, or clockwise; **L** means left, or counter-clockwise).
- Stand to one side of the tire because parts of the wheel assembly can fly off and hurt you when the stud bolts are loosened.
- Turn the wheel nuts by hand until they are flush with the end of the stud.
- Loosen the clamp on cast-type wheels. Tap with a hammer. Do not remove the stud nuts until the clamp is free so it will not fly off the studs.
- Remove the air lines from any wheels that have a tire pressure sensor. Cap the line and actuator.
- Jack up the truck to let the tire clear the surface. Stand clear of the rig while raising the jack. The truck can slip off and severely hurt you.
- Remove the wheel assembly by removing the wheel nuts and pulling the wheel from the hub.

**Figure 22-14**

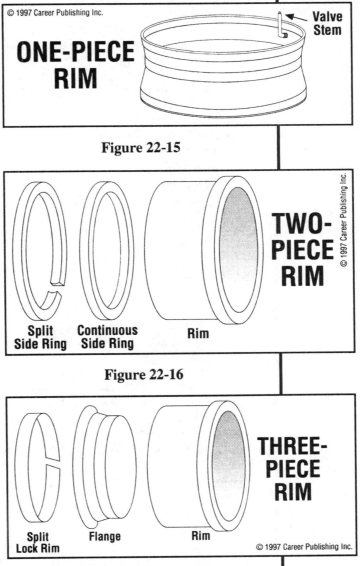

**Figure 22-15**

**Figure 22-16**

**Figure 22-17**

You can remove the inside wheel of a dual wheel assembly by following the same steps.

## Replacing Wheels

You should replace the inside wheel of duals first. To do this:
1. Mount the wheel by placing it on the hub.
2. Push the wheel all the way back.
3. Place the spacer ring on the hub. Push it back against the wheel.
4. Mount the outer wheel on the hub. Push it all the way back.
5. Install the spoke rim clamp on cast-type wheels.
6. Install and tighten the wheel nuts.

Use steps 1,2,5, and 6 for single wheel units.

To mount Budd type wheels (shown in Figure 22-13 and Figure 22-14), follow these steps. Replace the inside wheel of the duals first.
- Mount the wheel's concave side in by placing it on the studs.
- Install and tighten the flair wheel nuts.
- Mount the outside wheel's concave side out.
- Install and tighten the nuts.

Check the owner's manual for the right way to tighten the wheel nuts. If you do not have an owner's manual, tighten them by following these steps.

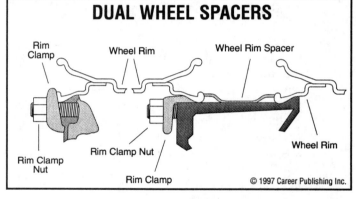

**DUAL WHEEL SPACERS**

Rim Clamp

Wheel Rim

Wheel Rim Spacer

Rim Clamp Nut

Rim Clamp Nut

Rim Clamp

Wheel Rim

© 1997 Career Publishing Inc.

**Figure 22-18**

- If the wheel is free to rotate, move the wheel until the nut to be tightened is on top.
- Tighten with a lug wrench.
- Use a torque wrench for the final tightening. Do not over-tighten or under-tighten.

NOTE: Never interchange ball seat wheel nuts with flange nuts. If you do, the wheel will not receive adequate clamping force, and it may fly off while you are driving down the road.

If a tire has a pressure sensor:
- Remove the caps and connect the air line to the actuator.

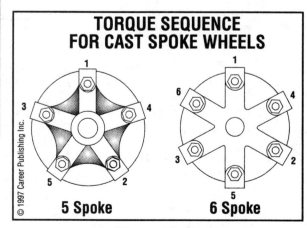

**TORQUE SEQUENCE FOR CAST SPOKE WHEELS**

© 1997 Career Publishing Inc.

**5 Spoke**

**6 Spoke**

**Figure 22-19**

- Lower the truck until the tire supports the weight of the vehicle.
- Remove the jack.

Be sure to put away all equipment you have used.

The rotation of the wheel usually loosens the wheel nuts. They will fall off unless they are tightened. To recheck the torque:
- Stop after you have driven a few miles.
- Check the wheel nuts.
- If the nuts need to be tightened, use a torque wrench to tighten them.
- Stop again in 100 miles.
- Tighten the nuts if needed.

> NOTE: Never use oil or grease on the wheel nuts.

# DRAINING THE AIR RESERVOIRS

If your air tanks have drain valves, drain them in this way:
- Park the truck on level ground.
- Chock the wheels.
- Open the drain cocks by twisting the valve on the bottom of the tank.
- Allow all of the air pressure to escape. The air pressure gauge will read 0 psi. This will let the moisture drain out.
- Close the valve.

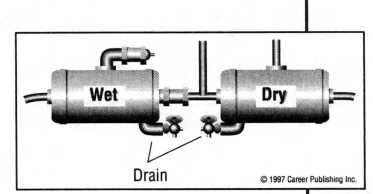

**Figure 22-20**

# ADJUSTING THE TRACTOR-TRAILER BRAKES

Some carriers want their drivers to make certain minor adjustments to the brakes. Others do not. Because instruction in this area is lengthy and manufacturer-specific, this book will not attempt to teach you how to adjust your brakes.

You should know that many trucks and trailers now have automatic slack adjusters. However, these still need to be checked regularly for proper adjustment.

Learn what your employer expects from you as a driver in adjusting the brakes. Learn what type of braking system your rig has. Remember, a person who is well-trained for one type of braking system may not understand what is required for another system. Be sure the person who works on your brakes is qualified for the type of braking system on your rig. Brakes that have not been adjusted correctly can cause an accident.

## SUMMARY

In this chapter, you have learned what types of maintenance are needed for the various systems on your rig. You have learned that preventive maintenance keeps unscheduled or emergency maintenance to a minimum. The types of reports that you, as a driver, will be expected to fill out and turn into your carrier were described. You also were taught how to do the basic, routine servicing expected of a driver. You now know how to change a tire if an emergency arises.

## KEY WORDS

**Preventive maintenance**: Servicing that is done at regular intervals on a truck.

**Routine servicing**: Tasks that can be done by drivers, such as add fuel, oil, and coolant, or drain the moisture from the fuel and air systems.

**Scheduled preventive maintenance**: Servicing that is based upon time or mileage since the last scheduled maintenance.

**Unscheduled maintenance and repair**: Occurs when unexpected breakdowns or emergencies require immediate maintenance.

**Vehicle Condition Report (VCR)**: A daily report filed with the supervisor by each driver that states the true condition of each truck they drove that day.

# LEARNING ACTIVITIES

## Written Reports

Your instructor will give you a practice VCR. Below the letters VCR, write what the letters stand for. Then fill out the report based on the information given to you by your instructor.

## Danger Points

On the lines after each servicing procedure, tell why it can be dangerous.

1. Changing a tire

   _____

   _____

2. Changing an oil filter

   _____

   _____

3. Checking the battery

   _____

   _____

4. Changing the air filter element

   _____

   _____

5.  Adjusting the brakes

_____

_____

## Lab Exercise

For this exercise, you will need a truck or models of truck systems provided by your school. Divide into groups of three. Each group is given a part to be serviced or examined.

The first person is to have a paper with the correct steps to complete the servicing operation written on it. The second person is to actually perform the routine, explaining each step as it is done. The third person is to carefully watch the second person and correct any mistakes that are made. If the third person does not catch an error, the first person should read the correct step from the paper. The second person corrects his or her error and continues with the servicing.

When the servicing is complete, the three people change roles and repeat the routine. This continues until all three people can perform the servicing correctly. Then the group goes on to another system. This continues until all groups can correctly service each system.

## True-False Questions

If the statement is true, circle the T. If the statement is false, circle the F.

T   F   1.   Future tractor-trailer drivers must know how to perform inspections and authorized maintenance and repairs.

T   F   2.   Once a student has learned the repairs presented in this lesson, he or she must always handle such repairs on a tractor-trailer.

T   F   3.   It is the driver's responsibility to insure the vehicle is safe to drive and will operate economically.

T   F   4.   Some carriers require drivers to perform certain routine maintenance tasks as part of their jobs.

T   F   5.   In some fleets, drivers cannot do any of the routine maintenance tasks.

T   F   6.   The Federal Motor Carrier Safety Regulations (FMCSR) require drivers to perform a pre-trip inspection and to review the last daily report (VCR) on the rig.

T   F   7.   Most drivers can safely remove a tire from the rim after they have been taught how.

T   F   8.   Most drivers have the skill to adjust tractor-trailer brakes because it is not hard to do.

T   F   9.   Brakes that are not properly adjusted can result in accidents.

T   F   10.  Air tanks should be drained only by a trained mechanic.

# Chapter Twenty-Three
# RECOGNIZING AND REPORTING MALFUNCTIONS

© 1997 Career Publishing Inc.

**Detecting Problems • Troubleshooting • Reporting Problems • Driver Responsibility
Maintenance Department Responsibility • Written Reports • Oral Reports
Emergency Starting Procedures • Troubleshooting Guide**

**FROM NOW ON,**

**ONLY THE BEST WILL DRIVE**

# OBJECTIVES

When the you have mastered this chapter, you will be able to:

- Explain how to know when vehicle systems and parts are not working correctly

- Show how the driver can use the senses of sight, sound, feel, and smell to detect problems

- Define both the driver's and the mechanic's responsibilities in vehicle maintenance

- Demonstrate how to troubleshoot problems

- Show the importance of a driver's being able to completely and accurately describe to maintenance personnel how the vehicle is functioning

- Explain to other drivers why they should not try to do any maintenance unless they are qualified

- Describe how to safely start a vehicle with a dead battery or without air pressure if it has an air starter

## CHAPTER TWENTY-THREE

# RECOGNIZING AND REPORTING MALFUNCTIONS

## INTRODUCTION

Most tractor-trailer drivers are not expected to be mechanics. Most companies have a policy stating clearly what repairs and adjustments may and may not be done by drivers. This chapter will help you understand what is expected of a driver. You will learn about common mechanical problems.
- How to find them
- What to do if they occur

The chapter will show you ways to find out exactly what is causing the problem. After you find the cause, you will be shown what to do. In some cases, the correct action will be to adjust a part. In other cases, you will be told to move on to the nearest truck stop, or call the company maintenance department for instructions.

You will learn how to use common sense and apply what you know. You will also learn to:
- Do only what you are capable of doing.
- Be concerned about safety.
- Follow company policies.
- Be concerned about yourself, others, your rig, and the cargo.

---

## Driver Responsibilities

- Know Company Maintenance Policy
- Identify Sources of Problems
- Diagnose and Fix Simple Problems When Policy Permits
- Report Symptoms Correctly

© 1997 Career Publishing Inc.

---

**Figure 23-1**

## DIAGNOSING AND REPORTING MALFUNCTIONS

Many newer trucks have electronics controls that will detect problems and sound buzzers or light up warning lights. From these warnings drivers can often diagnose a problem. While you are not expected to become a mechanic, you should be able to find the source of a problem. You will be shown how to gather information and report it to a mechanic. If this is done correctly, the mechanic can usually pinpoint the problem in the shop and come to the site with the proper tools and parts.

### Driver Awareness

Drivers can be aware of the rig's condition at all times by using their senses.

**Figure 23-2**

- Seeing
- Hearing
- Feeling
- Smelling

Look at the:
- Instrument gauges
- Exhaust smoke

Look for:
- Fluid leaks
- Damaged tires
- Missing wheel lugs

Listen for:
- Unusual engine noises
- Air leaks
- Any unusual noise

You can feel:
- Vibrations
- Thumps
- Swaying that is not natural for your truck

Be aware when you smell:
- Diesel fuel
- Smoke
- Burning rubber

Report any of the symptoms to your service department. In some cases, you may be able to make an adjustment and cure the problem.

By using these senses, you can notice a defect before it develops into:
- A breakdown
- A costly repair
- An accident

Also, if you understand the electronic diagnostics on a truck, you can help the mechanic pinpoint the problem to be repaired.

## Early Detection of Malfunctions

By using your senses and noticing symptoms early, you can cut repair costs. Problems are found and fixed before major damage occurs. This means repairs will be minor and the vehicle will spend less time in the shop. This all means the truck is being operated more efficiently. If you own the truck, you will be happy. If you work for someone else, your carrier will be pleased with you.

## Early Detection of Malfunctions

Early Detection of Malfunctions Results in:
- Lower Maintenance Expense
- Minimum Downtime
- Fewer Accidents
- Longer Vehicle Life
- Lower Operating Cost

© 1997 Career Publishing Inc.

**Figure 23-3**

When problems are noticed early and corrected, there is not as much of a chance for equipment to fail or accidents. The truck will probably also last longer. You may even avoid being stranded on the road.

## Driver Responsibility

Your company will have a **maintenance policy**. You should know what they expect of you. You will not have to be an expert, but you should be able to:
- Identify the sources of malfunctions.
- Diagnose and fix simple problems.

How much you may do and what you do will depend on:
- Company maintenance policy
- Your knowledge and mechanical experience
- Whether the carrier has an approved repair service
- Your access to tools

Do not try to fix any problem unless you really know how to.

## Mechanic's Responsibility

The mechanic should:
- Learn about system failures from driver reports.
- Diagnose the causes of the problems.
- Correct the malfunctions.
- Insure that a problem or failure has been fixed before releasing the truck.

## Driver and Mechanic Joint Responsibility

Drivers and mechanics must work together if the company is to benefit. A driver can be very helpful to the mechanic by knowing the rig and reporting all problems — large or small — at once. The mechanic can make sure all problems are fixed as soon as possible. When drivers and mechanics work closely together, they can prevent serious damage to the equipment.

© 1997 Career Publishing Inc.

**Figure 23-4**

## Troubleshooting

As a driver, you need to know:
- About your vehicle's systems
- Where the systems are located
- The parts of each system
- Where the parts are located
- How each system works

Understanding how a system works is the first step in knowing when it is not working properly or is in danger of failing. A vehicle will, in most cases, alert you to trouble by warning signals such as:
- A sharp drop in fuel mileage
- Erratic gauge readings
- A temperature gauge reading that is too high or too low
- A thump, bump, whine, grind, rattle, etc.

If you know how your vehicle's systems work, you can know the danger signals, trace a problem to its source, report your findings to a qualified mechanic, or make the repair yourself if you are permitted.

Figure 23-5

## Detection of Problems

When you notice a symptom, stop the truck as soon as possible (or as soon as the seriousness of the problem dictates). Then think the problem through before starting to **troubleshoot**. Start with the most likely cause of the problem. Keep these points in mind.
- You are not a mechanic or a mechanical expert.
- You should not try to do the mechanic's job.
- If you cannot trace the problem and identify the exact source of the trouble — actually see the part that is broken or not working — do not try to guess.
- Carefully describe the problem when you report it. Report what was checked, what you found, observed, smelled, etc.

## Reporting Requirements

**Driver's Job:** If you find something wrong, and you are capable of and permitted to repair it, you should. If you cannot repair it, report the symptoms and findings to the maintenance department.

**Written Report:** The **FMCSR** requires drivers to submit a **Vehicle Condition Report (VCR)** for each trip or 24-hour period within a trip. Include any problems in this report. Drivers must also review previous VCRs to verify that all problems have been corrected.

**Oral Report:** It often helps to discuss the problem with the mechanic. This gives the mechanic a chance to ask questions about the written report and helps him understand the problem.

**Limitations:** Remember, it is important to report *only* the facts about the symptoms and what your troubleshooting turned up. Guessing helps no one. The mechanic's job is to use the details you have given to solve the problem.

## Vehicle Condition Report

Each company has its own condition report forms. The data the driver gives should be accurate so the maintenance department can locate defects quickly and easily. If there are no problems, your report should say so. If problems did occur, the driver should:

- Check the appropriate place on the form to show what system or part was involved.
- Describe the symptoms and troubleshooting in as much detail as possible.
- Not overlook a discussion with the mechanic, if company policy permits.

Useful items for the remarks or comments section include:

- Symptoms
  A description of the way the problem appears to the driver.
  How did it start?
  Did it start suddenly or gradually?
  If it came on gradually — over what period of time?
  Several minutes, hours, days?
  When did it appear?

**Daily Vehicle Condition Report Form Correctly Filled Out**

DRIVER'S INSPECTION REPORT
(SEE INSTRUCTIONS ON REVERSE SIDE)
CHECK DEFECTS ONLY. Explain under REMARKS
COMPLETION OF THIS REPORT REQUIRED BY FEDERAL LAW, 49CFR 396.11 & 396.13.
Mileage (No Tenths)

Truck or Tractor No. 1250 | 1 0 1 5 9 9 | Trailer No. 26000

Dolly No. ______ Trailer No. ______ Loacation: ______

POWER UNIT

GENERAL CONDITION
- ☐ 02 Cab/Doors/Windows
- ☐ 02 Body/Doors
- ☐ ___ Oil Leak
- ☐ ___ Grease Leak
- ☐ 42 Coolant Leak
- ☐ 44 Fuel Leak
- ☐ ___ Other ______ (IDENTIFY)

ENGINE COMPARTMENT
- ☐ 45 Oil Level
- ☐ ___ Belts
- ☐ ___ Other ______ (IDENTIFY)

IN CAB
- ☐ 03 Gauges/Warning Indicators
- ☐ 02 Windshield Wipers/Washers
- ☐ 54 Horn(s)
- ☐ 01 Heater/Defroster
- ☐ 02 Mirrors
- ☐ 15 Steering
- ☐ 23 Clutch
- ☐ 13 Service Brakes
- ☐ 13 Parking Brakes
- ☐ 13 Emergency Brakes
- ☐ 53 Triangles
- ☐ 53 Fire Extinguishers
- ☐ 53 Other Safety Equipment
- ☐ 34 Spare Fuses
- ☐ 02 Seat Belts
- ☐ ___ Other ______ (IDENTIFY)

EXTERIOR
- ☐ 34 LIGHTS
- ☐ 34 Reflectors
- ☐ 16 Suspension
- ☐ 17 Tires
- ☐ 18 Wheels/Rims/Lugs
- ☐ 32 Battery
- ☐ 43 Exhaust
- ☐ 13 Brakes
- ☐ 13 Air Lines
- ☐ 34 Light Line
- ☐ 49 Fifth Wheel
- ☐ 49 Other Coupling
- ☐ 71 Tie-Downs
- ☐ 14 Real-End Protection
- ☐ ___ Other ______ (IDENTIFY)

☐ NO DEFECTS

TOWED UNIT(S)
- ☐ 71 Body/Doors
- ☐ 71 Tie-Downs
- ☐ 34 Lights
- ☐ 34 Reflectors
- ☐ 16 Suspension
- ☐ 17 Tires
- ☐ 18 Wheels/Rims/Lugs
- ☐ 13 Brakes
- ☐ 77 Landing Gear
- ☐ 59 Kingpin Upper Plate
- ☐ 59 Fifth-Wheel (Dolly)
- ☐ 59 Other Coupling Devices
- ☐ 79 Rear End Protection
- ☐ ___ Other ______ (IDENTIFY)

REMARKS: *Braking response time gradually increased over the course of the day. Vehicle pulled to the right when brakes were applied. This happened each time brakes were applied. Condition gradually kept getting worse. Road conditions were excellent throughout the day. Vehicle was carrying a 65,000 pound payload.*

REPORTING DRIVER: Date *12/10/98*
Name *John Doe* Emp. No. *26*
REVIEWING DRIVER: Date ______
Name ______ Emp No. ______

MAINTENANCE ACTION: Date ______
Repairs Made ☐ No Repairs Needed ☐
R.O.#'s ______
Certified By: ______
Location: ______

SHOP REMARKS: ______



Figure 23-6

• Conditions
    What were the conditions when the symptoms occurred?
    How long had you been driving?
    Was it hot or cold?
    What type of cargo and vehicle weight were you carrying?
    How far did your troubleshooting go?
    What did you find?
    Did you repair or try to repair anything?

## Example:

A driver notices the braking response time is getting slower and the vehicle pulls to the right when the brakes are applied.
    It came on gradually during the morning of the trip.
    The weather was moderate.
    The cargo was a max load of vegetables.
    Troubleshooting consisted of:
    Checking the tires, suspension, and brakes.

Results:
    Tire inflation OK.
    No broken or bent springs, shock absorbers, etc.
    Must be the brakes or front-end alignment.
    Called dispatcher for aid.
    Told to bring truck in at once for servicing.

## Troubleshooting Guide

You can find a **Troubleshooting Guide** in Appendix A. It is organized by sense; that is, IF YOU SEE, IF YOU HEAR, IF YOU FEEL, or IF YOU SMELL... It lists the systems that may be affected, what to look for, and what to do. Learn to relate the signals picked up by your senses with the kinds of problems they may indicate.

The following are examples of two signals or symptoms. One is something you can hear (a dull thud). The other is something you can see (gauge reading).

**A dull thud:** Suppose you hear a dull thud in time with the turning of the wheels. What is causing the problem?

**Possible systems involved**
Tires
Wheels/rims/lugs

**Possible cause**
Flat tire
Loose wheel or tire lugs
Rock between duals

**Proper action**
• Stop as soon as you can find a safe place.
• Decide what is the logical starting point for troubleshooting. Start with the simplest reason first. In this case, do you have a flat tire?

**If this is not the reason**
• You may need to tighten the lugs or remove a rock from between tires.

**Note**: Do not, for any reason, try to remove the tire from the rim.

**Gauge reading:** Your ammeter shows a continuous maximum charge. Your signals are crossed.

© 1997 Career Publishing Inc.

**Figure 23-7**

| Possible systems involved | Possible cause |
|---|---|
| Electrical | Short circuit in wiring |

**Proper action**
Disconnect the battery terminal until the short is repaired by a mechanic.

# PROBLEM SOLVING EXERCISES

There are twelve (12) problems presented in this section. After the instructor has set the scene, discuss and troubleshoot the following problems. Follow these three steps when solving the problem.
1. *Identify* the systems that may be involved.
2. *Trace* the problem toward its source.
3. *Decide* the best course of action.

Following the problems, the solutions are presented. The systems that may be causing the problem are identified. The possible source of the problem is noted. The best course of action is discussed. Compare these solutions with the class discussion. Was anything important overlooked?

## Problem 1
Each time you stop, the tractor is bumped or pushed in the rear by the trailer.

## Problem 2
Your mirrors are adjusted properly but you can see more of one side of the trailer than the other side (this is called trailer dog-tracking).

## Problem 3
Your coolant temperature suddenly rises, and the oil pressure is falling fast.

## Problem 4
The trailer sways too much when you take turns.

## Problem 5
The low air warning buzzer keeps sounding for a split second at a time.

## Problem 6
The circuit breaker for the trailer running lights keeps tripping.

## Problem 7
When you make sharp turns on slippery road surfaces, the steering wheel is turned but the tractor continues moving straight ahead. In other words, the tractor does not turn fully in response to the turning of the steering wheel.

## Problem 8
While coupling your tractor to the trailer, the tractor protection valve opens. There is a severe loss of air pressure.

## Problem 9
You hear a loud snap or click when you start the truck from a dead stop.

## Problem 10
You notice exhaust odor in the cab.

**Problem 11**

As you drive, you notice the ammeter registers discharge or there is a low reading on the voltmeter.

**Problem 12**

Excessive smoke is coming from the exhaust pipe.

## Solutions

**Problem 1:** Each time you stop, the tractor is bumped or pushed in the rear by the trailer.

**Possible systems involved**
- Trailer air brakes
- Coupling

**Probable cause**
- Slow timing of the trailer brakes. The driver cannot adjust the brake timing between the tractor and trailer.
- A brake valve with the wrong crack pressure is installed
- Air line connections between tractor and trailer
  - Loose glad hand connections
  - Worn or missing O-ring
- Air lines from glad hands to brake chambers
  - Holes or cracks in the line
  - Kinked hose
- Brake chambers
  - Air leaks
  - Slack adjuster
- Fifth wheel locking mechanism loose
- Fifth wheel slack adjuster needs adjusting
  - More than 1/2" horizontal movement between the upper and lower halves will cause the unit to be put out of service.

**Proper action**
- Stop at the first safe place where you can pull the truck off the road.
- Check for the causes.
- If you can, move to the next truck stop or available telephone where you can call the maintenance department. Be sure all the details are correct.

© 1997 Career Publishing Inc.

**Figure 23-8**

**Problem 2:** Your mirrors are adjusted properly but you can see more of one side of the trailer than the other side (this is called trailer dog-tracking).

**Possible system involved**
- Axles

**Probable cause**
- Tractor not aligned right.
- Sliding tandems
  - Lock pins that hold the tandems in place are not in the holes. One may be in place, but the other is not.
  - Lost pins
  - Pins are jarred loose
- Axles are not aligned properly

**Proper action**
- Slow down at once.
- Find a safe place to pull off the road.
- Locate the problem areas.
- If you have sliding tandems:
  - Make sure the lock pins are in place in the holes opposite each other.
  - Replace the pins if they are gone.
  - Tighten the pins if they are loose.
- If you have fixed tandems:
  - Get to the first available phone so you can call your maintenance department.

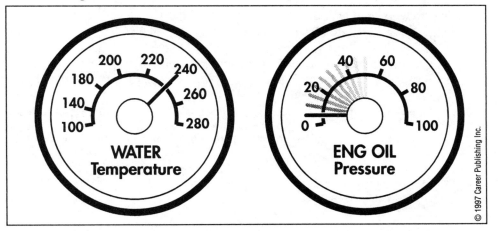

**Figure 23-9**

**Problem 3:** Your coolant temperature suddenly rises and the oil pressure is falling fast.

**Possible system involved**
- Lubrication

**Probable cause**
- Low oil level due to:
  - Lost oil drain plug
  - Oil filter not properly secured or tightened
  - Broken oil line
  - Blown gasket

**Proper action:**
- Pull off the road at once.
- Stop and turn off the engine.
- Check the engine oil level. CAUTION - the engine is very hot.
- Check all of the probable causes.
- Check for oil leaks in the engine compartment and under the truck.
- Call your maintenance department for assistance. Be accurate.
- Do not restart your engine!

**Problem 4:** The trailer sways too much when you take turns.

**Possible systems involved**
- Suspension
- Tires

**Probable cause**
- Cargo has shifted
- Broken or loose shock absorbers
- Broken or shifted spring or spring hanger
- Underinflated or flat tires

© 1997 Career Publishing Inc.

**Figure 23-10**

**Proper action**
- Slow down at once.
- Drive to first safe place and pull off the road.
- Check out the possible causes.
- If the cargo has shifted, move it back and secure it.
- If the problem is a shock absorber, go to the first truck stop and call your maintenance department.
- If the problem is a flat tire, call for help; Change it if you are permitted.

**Problem 5:** The low air warning buzzer keeps sounding for a split second at a time.

**Possible system involved**
- Air brakes

**Probable cause**
- Severe air leak
- Loose compressor belt
- Ruptured air line
- Disconnected air line
- Petcock open on air reservoirs
- Malfunctioning compressor
- Loose glad hand connections
- Worn or missing O-ring on glad hand
- Blown brake chamber diaphragm

LOW AIR PRESSURE WARNING

© 1997 Career Publishing Inc.

**Figure 23-11**

**Proper action**
- Stop at once.
- Park your rig.
- Locate the problem.
- Call for assistance.
- Correct the problem before resuming your trip.

**Problem 6:** The circuit breaker for the trailer running lights keeps tripping.

**Possible system involved**
- Electrical

**Probable cause**
- Exposed or hanging wire: the insulation may have worn off exposing the bare wire
- Broken ground wire

**Proper action**
- Stop your truck at the first safe spot off the road.
- Turn engine off. Check out the problem.
- Repair the wire if you are permitted. You can splice a broken ground wire and tape it.
- Tape any bare exposed wire.
- Reset the circuit breaker.
- Drive to the first available truck stop and have the electrical system checked by a qualified mechanic. Taping is only a temporary repair!

**Problem 7:** When you make sharp turns on slippery road surfaces, the steering wheel is turned but the tractor continues moving straight ahead. In other words, the tractor does not turn fully in response to the turning of the steering wheel.

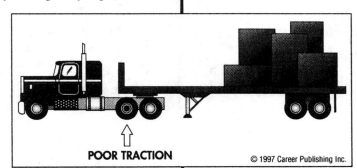

**Figure 23-12**

**Possible system involved**
- Steering

**Probable cause**
- Steering axle too lightly loaded

**Proper Action**
- Slow down at once and look for a safe place to pull off the road.
- Move the load to get more weight on the fifth wheel.
- If your truck has a sliding fifth wheel, move the fifth wheel forward.
- If the truck does not have a sliding fifth wheel but has sliding tandems on the trailer, move the tandems to the rear. This will put more weight on the fifth wheel by transfering weight to the steering axle.

NOTE: This is usually a problem on tandem axle tractors with a short wheel base. The tandems are a very short distance behind the steering wheel and they tend to take control of the vehicle and keep it from moving straight ahead.

**Problem 8:** While coupling your tractor to the trailer, the tractor protection valve opens. There is a severe loss of air pressure.

© 1997 Career Publishing Inc.

**Figure 23-13**

**Possible system involved**
• Air brakes

**Probable cause**
• Glad hands are not seated properly or they have a bad O-ring.
• Air lines are crossed. The service line is connected to the emergency line, and the emergency line is connected to the service line.
• Trailer air tank petcock is open.
• Broken air lines

**Proper action**
• This problem must be found and corrected before you drive from the yard.

**Problem 9:** You hear a loud snap or click when you start the truck from a dead stop.

**Possible system involved**
• Drive train

**Probable cause**
• Loose universal joint
• Excessive wear on universal joint or differential

**Proper action**
• Be very careful when you put the truck into motion.
• Proceed to the nearest truck stop.
• Have the drive train checked by a qualified mechanic.

**Problem 10:** You notice exhaust odor in the cab.

**Possible system involved:**
• Exhaust

**Probable cause**
• Loose connection in the exhaust system
• Cracked or broken exhaust pipe
• Leaking muffler
• Rusted out exhaust system
• Cracked exhaust manifold

**Proper action**
• Open all of the cab windows.
• Stop at the next truck stop.
• Have the exhaust system checked and repaired by a qualified mechanic as soon as possible.

**Problem 11:** As you drive, you notice the ammeter registers discharge, or there is a low reading on the voltmeter.

### Possible system involved
• Electrical

### Probable cause
• Loose or broken alternator belt
• Loose wiring connection
• Burned out generator or alternator
• A generator or alternator that is not adjusted right
• Defective voltage regulator

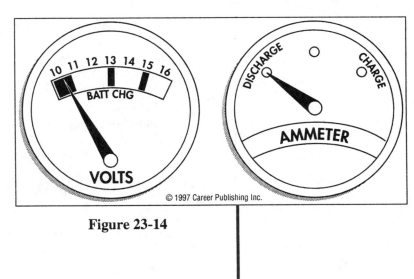

**Figure 23-14**

### Proper action
• Do not shut off the engine.
• Pull off the road at the first safe spot.
• Look for any obvious cause.
   • Missing belt (keep hands away from any moving belts and pulleys)
   • Loose connections
   • Bare insulation or a worn wire
   • Short circuit in the wiring
• Go to the first available truck stop or area where expert mechanical assistance is available.

**Problem 12:** Excessive smoke is coming from the exhaust pipe.

### Possible systems involved
• Exhaust
• Fuel

### Probable cause
• Dirty air cleaner
• Poor grade fuel
• Return fuel line is blocked, bent, or squeezed together
• Fuel pump malfunction
• Engine over fueled

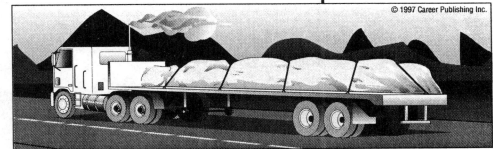

**Figure 23-15**

NOTE: These are some of the most common causes. There are a number of other possibilities.

### Proper action
• Continue your run only if there is not too much smoke, and is not very black.
• Carefully watch the smoke.
• Pull into the next truck stop or place where you can call your maintenance department.

## Troubleshooting Summary

A good troubleshooter:
- Knows his or her vehicle and its systems
- Uses common sense
- Is always aware when driving
- Knows the company maintenance policy
- Does not attempt to make repairs for which he or she is not trained
- Keeps good records

## EMERGENCY STARTING PROCEDURES

In this section, you will learn the correct and safe way to start a truck that has a dead battery. If a truck has an air starting system and has lost air pressure, it will also have to be manually started. The correct way to do so is explained in this section as well.

© 1997 Career Publishing Inc.

**Figure 23-16**

## Jump-Starting Dead Batteries

There are three things to always remember when jump-starting a truck that has a dead battery. They are:
1. Observe safety rules.
2. Prepare the truck.
3. Properly hook up the jumper cables.

### Observe Safety Rules
- Shield your eyes or wear safety goggles.
- Do not smoke.
- Make sure the batteries of both vehicles are negatively grounded and carry the same voltage (use a 12 volt battery to charge a 12 volt battery).
- Keep battery acid away from your skin and clothing.
- Never jump start a battery if the battery fluid is frozen.

### Prepare the Truck
- Align the vehicles so the jumper cables will reach without strain. Do not let the vehicles touch each other.
- Set the parking brake and chock the wheels.
- Shift into neutral.
- Add distilled water to the dead battery if it is needed.

### Hook Up the Cables Properly
- Clamp one cable to the positive (+) pole of the dead battery.
- Clamp the other end of the cable to the positive (+) pole of the booster battery.
- Connect the second cable to the negative (-) pole of the booster battery.
- Attach the other end of the cable to the stalled truck's frame, engine block, or other metal part as a ground.
- Start the booster truck.
- Start the disabled truck.
- Remove the cables in reverse order.

## Starting Trucks That Have Air Starters

To start a truck that has an air starter, there are fewer safety precautions you have to take. You should remember, though, that it is never a good idea to smoke when checking over or working on a vehicle.

### Prepare Vehicle
- Align the truck with the charged air supply.

### Hook Up the Air Line Properly
When you are using a compressor, follow these steps.
- Hook up an air line from the compressor to the glad hand of the disabled truck's air reservoir.
- Fill the reservoir.
- Start the disabled tractor's engine.

When you are using another tractor, supply the air in this way.
- Hook up an air line from one reservoir to the other.
- Start the booster tractor's engine.
- Fill the empty air reservoir of the disabled truck.
- Start the disabled tractor's engine.

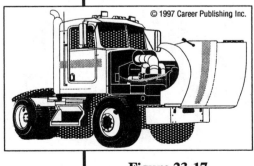

© 1997 Career Publishing Inc.

**Figure 23-17**

# SUMMARY

In this chapter, you have learned what a driver's responsibilities are in maintaining and servicing his or her truck. You know there are some repairs a driver should let a trained mechanic perform. You were taught how to troubleshoot and report on malfunctions. As a driver, you may have a truck that will not start, so you were shown safe and correct emergency starting procedures.

# KEY WORDS

**Maintenance policy:** Guidelines companies set up that tell drivers and mechanics what their responsibilities are in servicing and maintaining their vehicles.

**Malfunction:** When a part or system does not work properly.

**Troubleshoot:** Search out the source of a problem and to attempt to solve it.

**Vehicle Condition Report (VCR):** A written report each driver must file on the vehicles driven that day.

# LEARNING ACTIVITIES

## Troubleshooting Guide

The troubleshooting guide in Appendix A includes 33 symptoms that will help you search out, identify, and take proper action with mechanical problems. Use it to sharpen your skills in troubleshooting and know your responsibility as a driver.

## TRUE-FALSE QUESTIONS

If the question is true, circle the T. If the question is false, circle the F.

T  F  1.  Few companies have a policy on what drivers may and may not do in the way of minor repairs and adjustments.

T  F  2.  If you find a mechanical problem, you should do only what you are qualified to do. Keep in mind company policy, safety, your rig, your load, and the well being of yourself and others.

T  F  3.  Drivers and mechanics must work together to insure the safe and economic operation of a rig.

T  F  4.  Though drivers are not mechanics, they should notice unusual noises and the need for abnormal handling of the vehicle.

T  F  5.  If you use your senses of sight, sound, feel, and smell to notice a defect before it develops into a breakdown, you may prevent costly repairs and accidents.

T  F  6.  One problem with detecting malfunctions early is that your truck may have to go into the shop. This will cause too much *down time*.

T  F  7.  Finding problems early and repairing them leads to better operation and lower operating costs, which are good for everyone.

T  F  8.  If you are careless or do not pay attention, serious damage can disable your truck before the mechanic is aware a problem exists.

T  F  9.  If you find something wrong with your rig, you should fix it.

T  F  10.  You should report only the facts about the symptoms and what your troubleshooting has turned up.

T  F  11.  You should not try to repair brake problems. Leave them to a qualified mechanic.

T  F  12.  A good troubleshooter drives with a high degree of awareness.

T  F  13.  Good troubleshooters do not need to worry about company repair policies.

T  F  14.  One of the most important marks of a good troubleshooter is that he or she uses common sense.

T  F  15.  When you jump-start a dead battery, hook up one cable to the positive pole of the dead battery and the positive pole of the booster battery. Hook up the other cable to the negative pole of the dead battery and the negative pole of the booster battery.

# Chapter Twenty-Four
# HANDLING CARGO

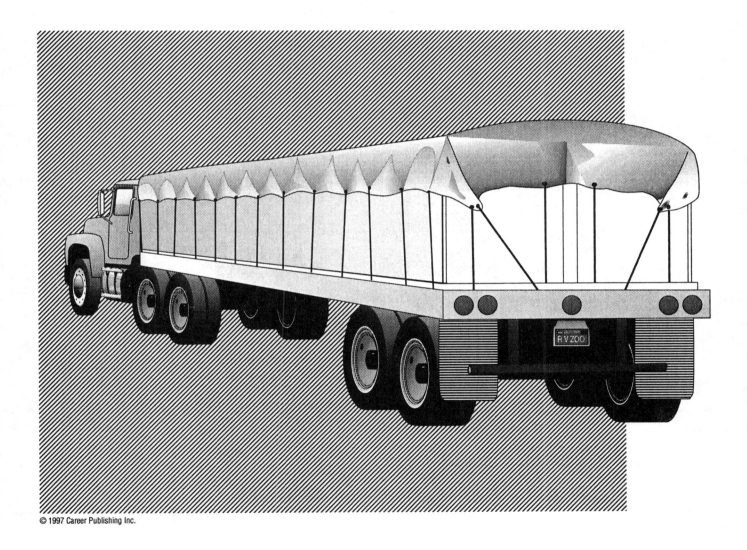

**Handling Cargo Correctly • Driver Responsibilities • Carrier Responsibilities Federal Regulations • State and Local Regulations  Securing Cargo • Covering Cargo • Loading Tools • Distribution of Weight • Hauling Hazardous Materials**

**FROM NOW ON,**

**ONLY THE BEST WILL DRIVE**

# OBJECTIVES

When you have mastered this chapter, you will be able to:

- Explain the importance of handling cargo correctly

- Specify the driver's responsibilities

- Outline the carrier's responsibilities

- Describe methods of containing and securing cargo

- Identify the federal and state regulations that control how cargo is shipped

- Explain distribution of weight

- Describe the special handling for certain materials

# CHAPTER TWENTY-FOUR

# HANDLING CARGO

## INTRODUCTION

Professional truck drivers know they have more responsibilities than just being able to drive a truck. Properly loaded cargo is less likely to be damaged and can help make the truck operate more efficiently. Freight that is not correctly loaded is unsafe and a danger to you and other road users. Because of the danger a truck that is overloaded or has improperly secured cargo presents, the FMCSR has set specific vehicle weight limits and methods for securing cargo. This chapter will teach you how to load a truck correctly so the weight is distributed evenly.

Most states have adopted the federal regulations as state laws through the Motor Carrier Safety Assistance Program (MCSAP). Enforcement of the law is, therefore, the duty of both federal and state officials.

© 1997 Career Publishing Inc.

**Figure 24-1**

## IMPORTANCE OF HANDLING CARGO PROPERLY

To **handle cargo** is the reason a carrier will hire you as a tractor-trailer driver. Carrying goods safely and as cheaply as possible to every community is the backbone of the trucking industry. Americans have learned they can rely on trucks to carry goods from manufacturers to consumers in the shortest possible time. They also know the goods will have the best chance of arriving safely and in good condition.

Today's tractor-trailers are designed to safely carry maximum payloads because they are built with strong light-weight materials. Drivers need to know how to protect their vehicles and the roads and bridges over which they drive from costly damage. This chapter will help you learn how to do this.

You will learn the basics for loading *general freight*. Cargo such as liquids in bulk, livestock, and unstable loads need special handling when they are loaded. How to handle these cargos was described in an earlier chapter.

Hazardous materials also require special handling and loading. Your safety, the public's safety, and the good name of the trucking industry depends on your knowing and complying with good industry practice and hazmat rules. Many states have adopted the **Federal Regulations for Hazardous Materials Transport** law and check trucks on the highway randomly.

## THE DRIVER'S RESPONSIBILITIES

Figure 24-2

Many drivers do not load or supervise the loading of the trailer they pull. These drivers still must check the cargo to see that it is properly secured and the weight is evenly distributed.

Checking a flat-bed or open trailer or the quantities in each compartment of a cargo tank is fairly easy. An enclosed van trailer that is loaded and has locking security seals needs a more creative method. The check should include:
- A visual check of the springs and tires for signs of overloading
- Checking for any noticeable sagging or bowing of the trailer
- Driver awareness of whether there is enough engine power to move the rig
- General handling characteristics
- Checking for leaks that could mean the cargo is damaged
- Figuring the weight of the load by adding all the weights shown on the shipping papers
- Comparing the segregation charts against the shipping papers

If the trailer is an open type or a van without seals or restricted access, the driver is responsible for checking the load for:
- Weight distribution: are heavy items loaded close together?
- Heavy freight loaded high in the trailer or in a position where it could fall on other cargo
- Fragile or hazardous material
- Loose freight that is not properly secured by holding devices or **dunnage** (a filler material loaded in empty spaces to keep cargo from moving or falling)
- Materials that are not compatible
- Regulated or restricted material

The driver is also responsible for checking all parts that are required by law to contain or protect the cargo. These may include:
- Tailgates
- Tailboards
- Doors
- Headerboards
- Tarps

Certain hazardous materials may need special equipment or protection from the weather as specified in 49 CFR Part 166. Some states also require additional equipment to guard against falling cargo. Drivers of trucks hauling loose cargo in dump trailers, log and lumber trailers, or pole trailers should know all federal, state, and local requirements that apply.

# REGULATIONS

In order to load a tractor-trailer correctly or to inspect one that has already been loaded, you must know the regulations. All drivers are responsible for knowing and complying with federal, state, and local laws. All Commercial Driver License (CDL) applicants must take **The General Knowledge Test** to see how much they know about the laws. Knowing the law helps promote safer operation of heavy trucks and tractor-trailers.

**Figure 24-3**

## Federal Regulations

The **FMCSR, Section 392.9** protects a driver from driving a truck that is not correctly loaded or does not have the load secured properly. You cannot drive, and your company cannot make you drive, any truck unless:
- The cargo is properly distributed and secured as specified in Section 393.100 to 396.106 of the FMCSR.
- Equipment such as tailgates, tailboards, doors, tarps, spare tires are secured.
- The cargo is loaded so it does not interfere with the driver's vision or control of the truck.
- The driver has easy access to emergency equipment.
- The driver and passengers can readily get out of the cab.

Except for trailers that have had the doors sealed or are loaded in such a way that you cannot see the load, the driver must:
- Check the vehicle before driving it to be sure:
  - The cargo is properly distributed and secured.
  - The vehicle components are secure.
  - The cargo does not interfere with operating safety.
- Check the cargo and adjust the securing devices within the first 25 miles of the trip.
- Check and adjust the cargo and securing devices when any of these conditions occur.
  - Change of duty status
  - Completion of 3 hours or 150 miles of driving (whichever happens first)

## State Regulations

As well as adopting federal regulations for safe handling of cargo, many states have their own laws. States regulate the gross weight of vehicles that travel intrastate. A rig that never leaves a state must follow its regulations. The Federal regulations set a gross vehicle weight for interstate hauling. The laws limit both the gross vehicle weight and the weight for each axle. Many states also require a cover on loose loads such as sand, gravel, and crushed stone. This is to keep the cargo from falling and damaging cars or leaving debris on the highway. Know the laws of all the states in which you will drive.

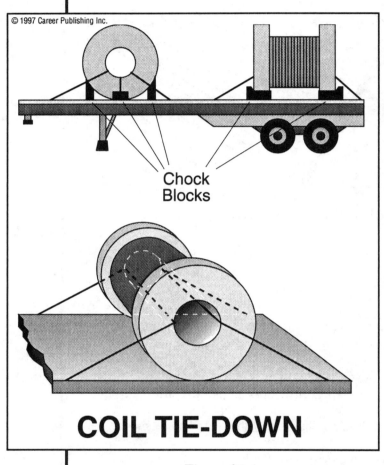

© 1997 Career Publishing Inc.

Chock
Blocks

# COIL TIE-DOWN

**Figure 24-4**

## SECURING CARGO

Federal regulations for protecting cargo from shifting or falling require specific methods of tie-down, blocking and bracing, and vehicle construction.

To keep cargo from falling off, the law requires a trailer to have:
• Both sides and ends.
  or
• Enough tie-downs to hold the cargo in place.

Certain types of cargo such as metal pipes, coils, bars, rods, sheets, slabs, and ingots must have special tie-downs.

Intermodal cargo containers, such as those that are taken from a ship and placed on a trailer, must be firmly locked to the chassis so they cannot move or accidentally come unfastened.

Federal laws also specify the types of devices that may be used to tie down freight and specify the minimum strength for the devices. Devices that may be used are:
• Hooks and chains
• Binders
• Nylon and metal straps
• Ropes
• Cables

You will study the advantages and disadvantages of using these devices later in this chapter.

INTEGRAL TYPE CONTAINER AND CHASSIS

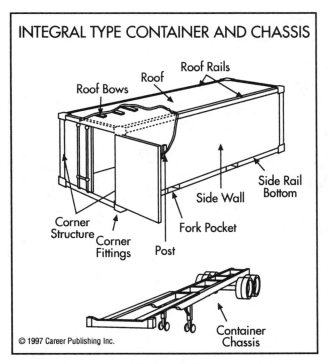

© 1997 Career Publishing Inc.

**Figure 24-5**

## Front End Structures on Trailers

Federal laws require trailers to have a header-board between the cargo and the driver. Van trailers satisfy this requirement if the front wall of the trailer is strong enough to protect the driver if the load shifts and crushes the cab.

Flatbeds, log trailers, and similar types of trailers must have a headerboard or enough height and width to keep the cargo from shifting forward. The laws specify the strength requirements.

Some tractors may have protective devices instead of a headerboard. Car carriers with vehicle tie-downs do not have to have headerboards.

## Blocking and Bracing

Federal regulations set the standards for keeping loose cargo from moving. Devices used to secure cargo include:
- Blocking: Pieces of wood nailed to the floor
- Dunnage: Filler material, such as sheets of plywood, padding, inflatable bags, etc., used to fill voids in the load
- Bracing: Pieces cut to fit and nailed or otherwise secured
- Cargo retainer bars
- Built-in lockable bulkheads
- Use of freight to prevent movement of other freight
- Tie-downs
- Cargo netting
- Shrink-wrapped pallets

Later, this chapter will cover the special requirements for hauling hazardous material.

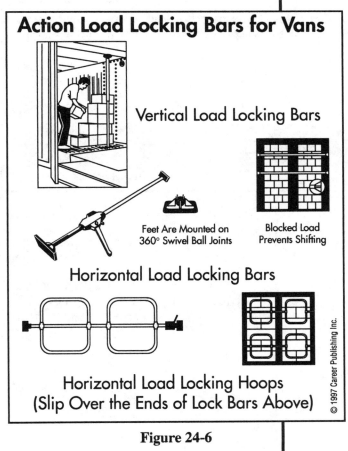

© 1997 Career Publishing Inc.

**Figure 24-6**

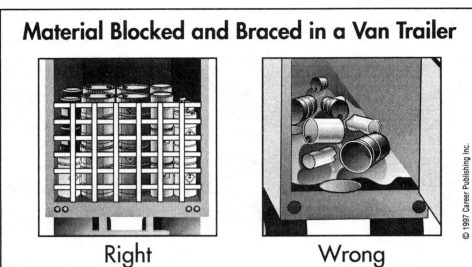

**Figure 24-7**

### Tie-Down Devices

Several types of tie-down devices may be used to secure cargo. The load may need any one of these devices or a combination of several. It is important to choose the right type. It must be strong enough to hold the load in place. You also must be able to adjust it during transport.

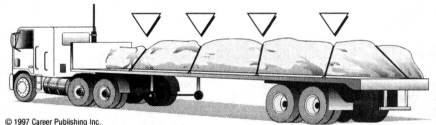

Cargo should have at least one tie-down for each 10 feet of cargo. Make sure you have enough tie-downs to meet this need. No matter how small the cargo is, there should be at least two tie-downs holding it.

© 1997 Career Publishing Inc.

**Figure 24-8**

You must know how to keep the cargo from moving around or falling off. You should also know the working load limits for chains, cables, ropes, straps, and binders. Never exceed the manufacturer's ratings. Federal laws require chains used as tie-downs to meet the specs set by the National Association of Chain Manufacturers. Hooks, binders, and connectors must be at least as strong as the chain required. Steel straps must also meet federal specs.

Lever or ratchet type binders used with strong chains are the strongest and most easily adjusted means of securing cargo.

Ratchets and winches used with strong nylon strapping provide an adequate, easily adjusted cargo tie-down for loads such as lumber, gypsum board, plywood, or other cargo that can be damaged by chain tie-downs.

# Approximate Safeworking Loads for Some Types of Wire Rope

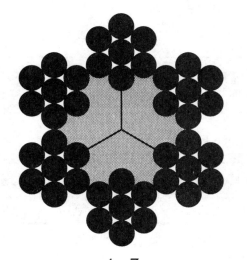

6 x 7
Wire Rope With 3 Strand Fibre Core

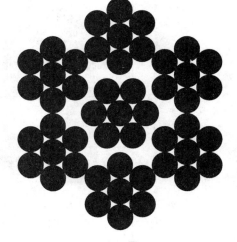

6 x 7
Wire Rope With 7 Strand Rope Core

| Diameter in Inches | Improved Plow Steel | Plow Steel | Mild Plow Steel |
|---|---|---|---|
| 1/4 | 5,280 Lbs | 4,600 Lbs | 4,000 Lbs |
| 3/8 | 11,720 | 10,200 | 8,860 |
| 1/2 | 20,600 | 17,920 | 15,580 |
| 3/4 | 45,400 | 39,600 | 34,400 |

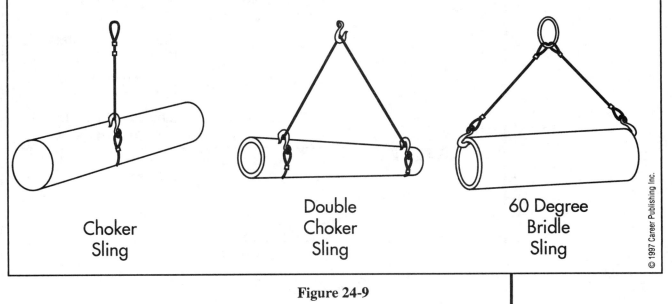

Choker Sling

Double Choker Sling

60 Degree Bridle Sling

© 1997 Career Publishing Inc.

**Figure 24-9**

**Approximate Safe Working Loads for Various Fibre and Synthetic Ropes**

| Size in Inches Diameter | Manila First Grade | Filament Nylon | Filament Dacron | Poly-ethylene | Poly-propylene |
|---|---|---|---|---|---|
| 1/4 | 60 Lbs | 360 Lbs | 240 Lbs | 210 Lbs | 250 Lbs |
| 3/8 | 135 | 800 | 520 | 420 | 540 |
| 1/2 | 265 | 1,460 | 900 | 720 | 900 |
| 5/8 | 440 | 2,180 | 1,380 | 1,080 | 1,320 |
| 3/4 | 540 | 3,120 | 1,900 | 1,400 | 1,600 |
| 7/8 | 770 | 4,280 | 2,520 | 1,900 | 2,150 |

NOTE: Protect ropes from moisture, dragging in sand or grit and from exposure to sunlight and chemicals. When not in use should be coiled and put in dark storage with good air circulation. If a wet rope becomes frozen, do not disturb it until completely thawed out otherwise frozen fibers will break when subjected to bending.

**Figure 24-10**

## EVALUATION OF TIE-DOWN DEVICES

| TYPE | ADVANTAGES | DISADVANTAGES |
|---|---|---|
| Nylon Rope | Easily installed and adjusted | Stretches and becomes loose |
| Wire Rope | Very strong | Difficult to handle |
| Web (nylon) Straps | Strong, lightweight, easily adjusted | May become frayed or cut by sharp edges |
| | May be used with ratchet or winch assemblies | Sunlight rots nylon fibre |
| | Inexpensive and easy to store | May not be used to secure steel machinery or certain metal products |
| Steel Straps | Good for securing boxes on pallets or wooden crates on vehicle | No means of adjustment during transport |
| | | Vibration can cause failure |
| | | Straps over 1" wide need 2 pairs of crimps |
| | | May cut into cargo and become loose |
| Hooks & Chains | Strong and durable | May damage cargo if too tight |
| | Readily available | Not of equal strength for rated load |
| | Hooks may be replaced and easily checked | |
| | Easily adjusted during transport | |

## COVERING CARGO

There are two basic reasons for covering cargo.
1.  To protect the cargo.
2.  To prevent spills of loose cargo.

Carriers use covers to protect the cargo because they:
*   Keep metal from rusting.
*   Prevent damage to fiberboard containers.
*   Keep loads such as bagged cement from being destroyed.
*   Keep cargo that can absorb water from welting.
*   Cut down on claims for damaged freight.

Carriers want to keep cargo from spilling because:
*   They want to protect both the company and driver from liability for any injury or damage caused by spilled material.
*   There are laws against littering.
*   Many states have laws that require cargo covers.

Figure 24-11

### Types of Coverings

The most common coverings are called tarpaulins, or tarps. There are many durable, lightweight materials that can be used for covering loads. The most common tarp materials are:
*   Cotton canvas
*   Rubberized or plastic coated canvas
*   Nylon or other synthetic fabrics
*   Polyethylene
*   Vinyl
*   Plastic coated paper with fiber plies

For long hauls and continued use a tarp should be of good quality. Short trips or a one-time use may permit use of a less expensive tarp that is not as durable.

You must store and maintain tarps that are used a lot to prolong their life. If tarps are not cared for, they may mildew and rot. If the tarp is a good one, it is expensive to replace.

Federal laws require tarps to be properly tied down. They cannot obscure the driver's vision or the lights on the vehicle. Always tie a tarp snugly in place. Ballooning or flapping in the wind can damage a loose tarp. Check tarp tie-downs often.

# Trucker's Draw Hitch

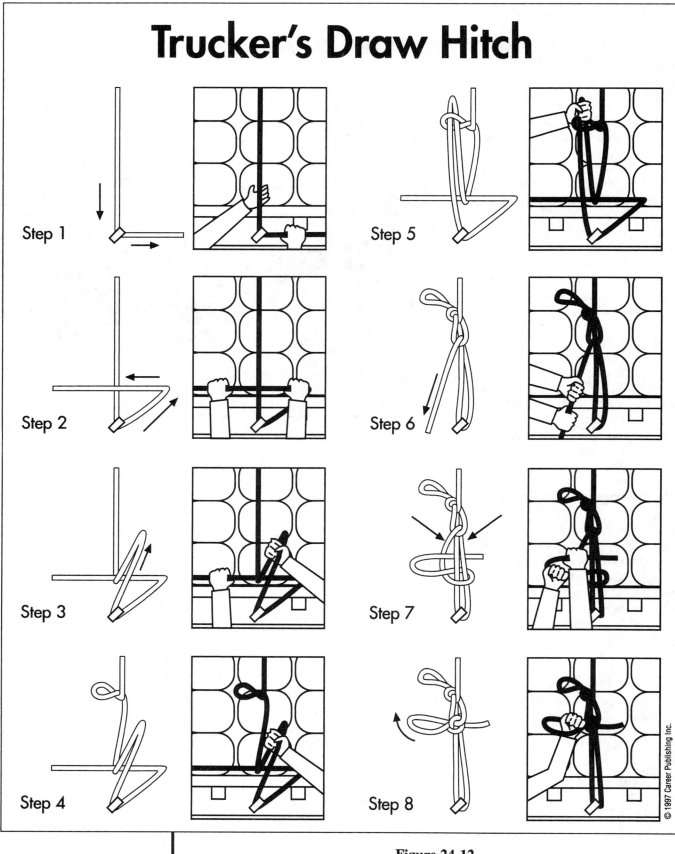

Step 1
Step 2
Step 3
Step 4
Step 5
Step 6
Step 7
Step 8

**Figure 24-12**

# ACCEPTING AND LOADING FREIGHT

When you accept freight for your trailer, you become responsible for safely delivering the load in good condition. Always inspect cargo for:
- The condition of the packages
- Any leaking contents
- Broken palettes or torn shrinkwrap
- The proper container for the material
- Proper quantities as listed on the shipping documents
- Compatibility with the other freight
- Identification marks and addresses
- Weight: will the rig be overweight?
- Identification of any hazardous materials
- Any packages marked glass or fragile

Bring any damage or inaccurate counts to the shipper's attention at once! Usually there is a company policy on accepting such shipments. Contact your supervisor when in doubt about accepting any shipment.

## Loading Cargo

Always chock the trailer wheels, put the tractor in gear, and put on the parking brake while loading or unloading. If the loading dock has a dock lock, you may not need to use wheel chocks. Never attempt to load freight on your trailer without the proper tools. Some common tools for loading cargo are described in the sections that follow.

© 1997 Career Publishing Inc.

**Figure 24-13**

### Forklifts

Forklifts are used for loading pallets or heavy objects. Listed next are some basic rules for using forklifts.
- Do not operate a forklift unless you are qualified to do so.
- Make sure the forklift is rated for the load.
- Check the overhead clearance.
- Operate the forklift carefully.
- Use dockboards when they are available to bridge between the loading dock and your trailer.
- Do not damage the freight with the forks.
- Do not raise it higher than you have to.
- Avoid tilting it. You might drop the freight.
- Do not damage the trailer.

© 1997 Career Publishing Inc.

**Must Tilt Back Slightly to Cradle Load**

**Figure 24-14**

### Pallet Jacks

Pallet Jacks are used for loading palletized cargo. They are similar to a forklift only smaller. Use the same safety rules you would use if you were operating a forklift.

### Cranes and Hoists

Cranes and hoists are often used to load cargo. There are some things you have to watch so you will not get hurt or the cargo will not be damaged.
- Check the load rating of winches, cables, chains, etc.
- Never exceed the rated load.
- Do not stand under raised cargo.
- Provide protection in case the chain or cable breaks and whips around.
- Never drop freight roughly on your trailer.

### Hand Trucks

Hand trucks are often used to carry small loads from the trailer to a storage area. There are certain safety rules you must follow when using them.
- Never stack the boxes so high they obstruct your vision.
- Do not stack the boxes so high they can topple over.
- Use ramps or dockboards between the trailer and the dock.
- Never load an object that is too big for the hand truck.

**Drum Trucks:** Never roll drums to load them. Use a drum truck, and secure the locking strap. Do not try to move a drum alone that is too heavy for you to handle.

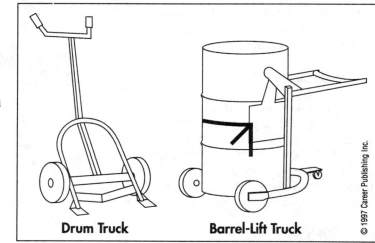

**Carton Truck**   **Utility Truck**

**Figure 24-15**

**Drum Truck**   **Barrel-Lift Truck**

**Figure 24-16**

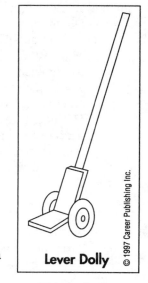

**Lever Dolly**

**Figure 24-17**

**Levers:** Use levers or Johnson bars to lift the edges of crates, etc. Use care so you will not damage the freight.

**Hand Tools or Hooks:** Do not damage the outside packaging. Learn to identify fragile cargo. Use tools only for the purpose for which they were designed.

NOTE: For more information on proper lifting techniques, see Chapter 26 on Personal Health and Safety.

# HAZARDOUS MATERIALS

**Hazardous material** is any material that may pose a risk to health, safety, or property while being transported. It is sometimes called hazmat. Materials and substances that have been designated as hazardous are listed in Title 49 of the Code of Federal Regulations (49CFR). They should be handled and transported only by trained and qualified persons.

**Figure 24-18**

This section will teach you the basic requirements for transporting hazardous materials. If you are employed by a carrier to haul hazardous materials, they must provide additional training. In addition, you will have to obtain the **Hazardous Materials Endorsement** for your CDL. If the hazardous material is carried in a tanker, you will also need the **Tank Vehicles Endorsement** on your CDL.

If you work for a carrier that does not haul hazardous materials, you must be able to identify such shipments so you will not accidentally load them.

Hazardous material is classified by hazard class. There are 9 hazard classes. Some of the classes are further broken down into divisions. Each hazard class has requirements for labeling containers. The hazard classes are listed below.

## Hazard Classes

### Class 1 Explosives

| | |
|---|---|
| Division 1.1 | Explosives (with a mass explosion hazard) |
| Division 1.2 | Explosives (with a projection hazard) |
| Division 1.3 | Explosives (with predominantly a fire hazard) |
| Division 1.4 | Explosives (with no significant blast hazard) |
| Division 1.5 | Very insensitive explosives; blasting agents |
| Division 1.6 | Extremely insensitive detonating substances |

### Class 2 Gases

| | |
|---|---|
| Division 2.1 | Flammable gas |
| Division 2.2 | Nonflammable compressed gas |
| Division 2.3 | Poison gas |
| Division 2.4 | Corrosive gases (Canadian) |

**Class 3 Flammable and combustible liquid**

**Class 4 Flammable solids; spontaneously combustible materials; dangerous when wet**

Division 4.1     Flammable solid
Division 4.2     Spontaneously combustible material
Division 4.3     Dangerous when wet material

**Class 5 Oxidizers and organic peroxide**

Division 5.1     Oxidizer
Division 5.2     Organic peroxide

**Class 6 Poisonous material and infectious substances**

Division 6.1     Poisonous materials
Division 6.2     Infectious substance (Etiologic agent)

**Class 7 Radioactive material**

**Class 8 Corrosive material**

**Class 9 Miscellaneous hazardous material**

Some hazardous materials, when they are packaged in small quantities, may be shipped as *Consumer Commodities* and are not required to display hazard class labels. Examples of *Consumer Commodities* are some paints, hair spray, drain cleaners, cleaning products, and all aerosols. Be alert for packages marked *Consumer Commodity ORM-D.* Use care in handling and loading.

Some classes of hazardous material cannot be shipped together in the same vehicle. There are charts you can use as a guide when you load different classes of hazardous materials so you will not make a mistake.

For example, packages with a flammable solid label cannot legally be transported in the same vehicle with explosives. Packages with poison labels cannot be shipped in the same vehicle with food intended for humans or animals, unless they are packed in special containers.

## Shipping Papers

Hazardous materials require special shipping papers. Items must be identified by the proper shipping name, hazard class, identification number, and packing group.

Hazardous material shipping papers must be in clear view and within the driver's reach when driving. When the driver is not behind the wheel, the papers must be on the driver's seat or in the driver's door pouch.

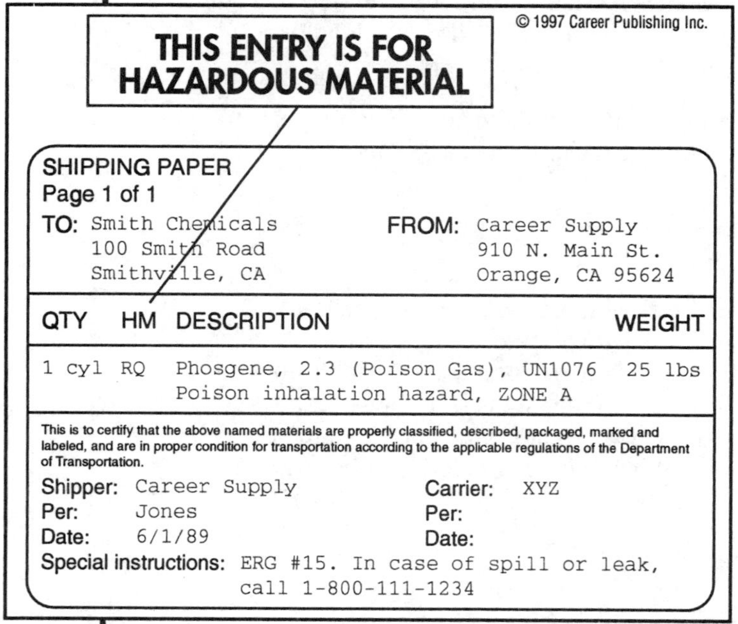

---

**THIS ENTRY IS FOR HAZARDOUS MATERIAL**

© 1997 Career Publishing Inc.

SHIPPING PAPER
Page 1 of 1

TO: Smith Chemicals     FROM: Career Supply
     100 Smith Road         910 N. Main St.
     Smithville, CA         Orange, CA 95624

| QTY | HM | DESCRIPTION | WEIGHT |
|-----|----|-----|-----|
| 1 cyl | RQ | Phosgene, 2.3 (Poison Gas), UN1076 Poison inhalation hazard, ZONE A | 25 lbs |

This is to certify that the above named materials are properly classified, described, packaged, marked and labeled, and are in proper condition for transportation according to the applicable regulations of the Department of Transportation.

Shipper: Career Supply     Carrier:  XYZ
Per:    Jones          Per:
Date:   6/1/89         Date:
Special instructions: ERG #15. In case of spill or leak, call 1-800-111-1234

**Figure 24-19**

These papers may be inspected by officials at any time.

**REFUSE TO HAUL THE LOAD!**

Figure 24-20

Carefully check shipping documents to see if any hazardous materials are in the shipment before you load freight. **Refuse to carry placarded loads of hazardous material if you do not have a Hazardous Materials Endorsement on your CDL.**

## Loading and Unloading

Federal laws require special handling for certain hazardous materials.

**NO SMOKING** while loading or unloading explosives, flammable materials, or oxidizers. Keep anyone away who is smoking or carrying lighted smoking materials.

Tanks, barrels, drums, cylinders, or packages containing flammable liquid, compressed gas, corrosive materials, poisonous materials, or radioactive material must be secured so they cannot move while being transported. Valves and fittings must be protected from damage.

Hazardous materials cannot be loaded into a trailer unless the parking brake is set. The truck must not move, so the wheels must be chocked. Do not use any tools to load or unload hazardous materials that may damage the containers.

Certain hazardous materials may not be transported in trailers with cargo heaters. If your trailer has a heater, check the regs before loading any hazmat.

The truck's engine must be shut off before you can load explosives or flammables. Explosives may not be transported in certain types of vehicles, such as doubles containing certain other hazardous materials. Check the inside of the trailer to be sure there are no nails or projections that can damage the containers of explosives.

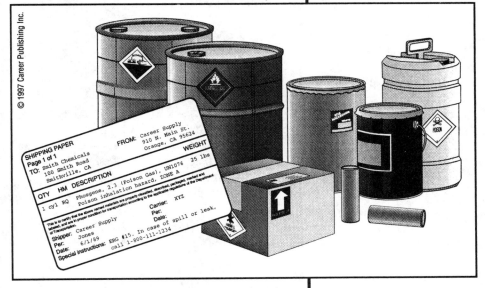

Figure 24-21

Tightly close or cover packages and make sure they do not leak before hauling explosives, corrosives, oxidizing materials, or flammable solids. Batteries and corrosive acids must be specially stacked. Securely lock, box and rack cylinders of compressed gas. Protect the valves from damage.

Trailers that have carried certain poisons or radioactive material must be thoroughly cleaned before they can be loaded with other freight.

### Accidents or Spills

Whenever you have a spill of any hazardous material, federal regulations require you to make certain reports. Notify your supervisor at once if you have an accident involving a spill of hazardous materials. Follow the instructions your company gives you. Keep on-lookers away. In some cases, you may even have to notify Chemtrec or the National Response Center.

**CHEMICAL EMERGENCY**

**Figure 24-22**

### Refueling

When you refuel your truck, be sure the engine is shut off. Federal law says that it must be. Do not smoke. The person who fills the tank is to be in control of the nozzle or pump.

### Tires

When hauling hazmat in a trailer that has dual wheels, you must stop the truck in a safe place and check all tires:
- At least once every two hours or
- After 100 miles of travel

**Figure 24-23**

If you find an overheated tire, remove it and place it a safe distance from the truck. Inflate any tires that need it. Change any tire that is flat.

## Placards

Federal laws specify when placards must be displayed on vehicles transporting hazardous materials. They are 10-3/4" square and turned upright on a point in a diamond shape. The placards must be securely attached to all four sides of your vehicle and the hazard class or UN number readable from all four directions.

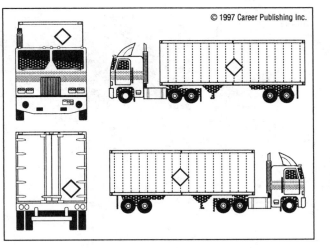

© 1997 Career Publishing Inc.

**Figure 24-24**

Shippers must furnish placards when they are needed, but you are responsible for putting them on your trailer. Check the shipping papers and package labels to determine if placards are required for the load.

## Driving

Certain highways are off limits if you are hauling hazardous materials. Often tunnels and bridges prohibit any vehicle loaded with these materials from using them. Before you start a trip, make sure you will be permitted to travel on your intended route. It is your responsibility to obtain any needed permits. Avoid heavily populated areas, bridges, tunnels, and narrow streets and roads.

# VEHICLE WEIGHT

Today's tractor-trailers are designed to safely, efficiently, and economically carry heavy payloads. The horsepower, gear ratios, and brake systems of these vehicles have improved greatly in recent years.

Increased use of the public highway system in America has made it hard for state and federal engineers and maintenance crews to keep up

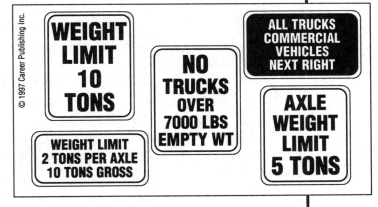

**Figure 24-25**

with the wear and tear on road surfaces and bridges. Very heavy wheel and axle loads can cause severe damage to deteriorating bridges and road surfaces.

Cargo loads that exceed the manufacturer's weight limits for vehicles and tires can damage parts or even make new equipment unsafe.
- Tires may overheat and blow out.
- Springs, bearings, or the suspension may break.
- Frames and couplers may break.
- The rig may not accelerate safely to operating speeds.
- Brake systems may fail.
- Steering control may be affected.

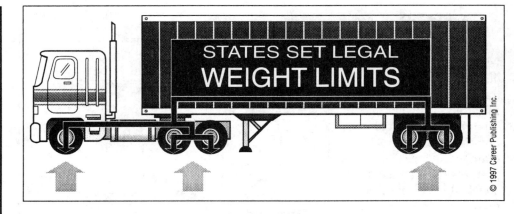

**Figure 24-26**

Limits on the weight and size of vehicles are up to each state. Federal guidelines and federal grant programs for highways have tried to make these state requirements uniform. Some states have lower limits than others. Check the regulations for each state you will drive through. Violations for the truck's being overweight are often expensive and can reflect on your driving record.

Officials can detain an overweight vehicle. They may make the driver off-load or redistribute the weight in addition to fining him or her. A rig that is detained for an overload results in great expense for the trucking company. It also means a late delivery to the customer.

Weights are usually checked in the following ways.

**Individual wheel weight**: Wheel weight is usually checked by state or local officials with a portable scale that measures the load on each wheel. Wheel weights are then checked against the permitted load for the tire.

**Axle weight**: Axle weight can also be checked with a portable scale. The weight of each wheel on an axle is recorded. The weights are then added to find the axle weight. At weigh stations, drive each set of axles on the scale to measure the axle weight.

**Combined axle weight**: Tandem or triple axles can have a different weight per axle than a single axle. To find the total combined weight, add the weights of all the axles. You can also find the total weight by driving the whole rig onto the scale platform.

**Gross Vehicle Weight (GVW)**: The total weight of a straight truck and load.

**Gross Combination Vehicle Weight Rating (GCWR)**: The total weight of a tractor, trailer, and load. Local or state officials may check the GCWR by weighing each wheel or axle individually and adding the total, or by having you drive the entire rig onto the platform scale to be weighed as a unit.

There are more restrictions placed on short, heavy rigs for wheel, axle, and gross weights. The reason is because the total load is distributed over a shorter surface. This increases the stress placed on bridges and other highway structures. If you pull a heavy cargo in an intermodal container on a short trailer or chassis, you may exceed the weight limit for a bridge.

Manufacturers' warranties and liabilities may be affected if you exceed the rated weight for each part. Limits include the following:
- Tires: Maximum load at specified inflation
- Suspension System: Maximum for spring assembly
- Axle weight: Rated weight for single or combination
- Fifth Wheel: Maximum pull weight
- GCWR: Recommended gross weight

## DISTRIBUTION OF WEIGHT

If the weight is not distributed properly, the rig will be harder to handle. **Distribution of weight on a tractor** depends on the location of fifth wheel.

- With a single rear axle, it should be slightly in front of the axle.
- With a tandem rear axle and a stationary fifth wheel, it should be slightly in front of the tandem center line.
- With a tandem rear axle and a sliding fifth wheel, the last notch of the slider adjustment should be just ahead of the tandem center line.

With a movable fifth wheel:
- Move it forward, and the load shifts more to the steering axle(s).
- Move it back, and the load shifts to the tractor drive axle(s).

You can make the rig handle differently by the way you distribute the weight. When the load is moved forward, the rig will handle better and give you better cornering. If too much weight is shifted forward, you can lose traction on the rear axles and have hard steering. When you move a load forward, be careful not to exceed the legal weight limits for the front axle.

Weight shifted too far back causes light steering with poor control. It can also overload the drive axles.

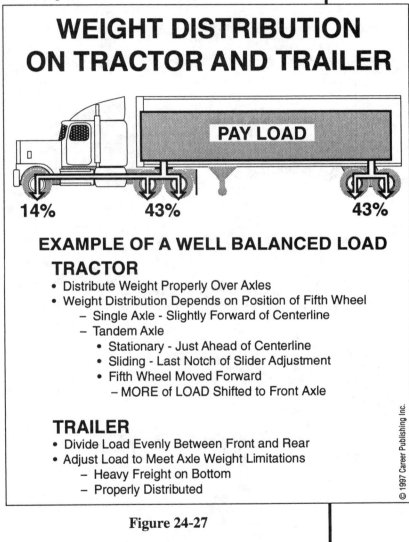

**WEIGHT DISTRIBUTION ON TRACTOR AND TRAILER**

PAY LOAD

14%     43%     43%

**EXAMPLE OF A WELL BALANCED LOAD**

**TRACTOR**
- Distribute Weight Properly Over Axles
- Weight Distribution Depends on Position of Fifth Wheel
    - Single Axle - Slightly Forward of Centerline
    - Tandem Axle
        - Stationary - Just Ahead of Centerline
        - Sliding - Last Notch of Slider Adjustment
        - Fifth Wheel Moved Forward
            - MORE of LOAD Shifted to Front Axle

**TRAILER**
- Divide Load Evenly Between Front and Rear
- Adjust Load to Meet Axle Weight Limitations
    - Heavy Freight on Bottom
    - Properly Distributed

© 1997 Career Publishing Inc.

**Figure 24-27**

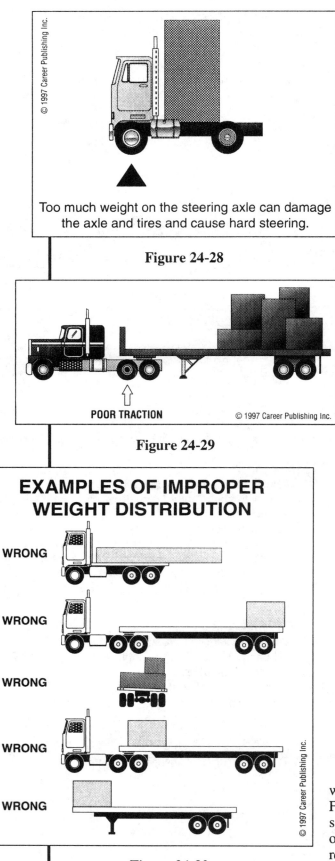

© 1997 Career Publishing Inc.

Too much weight on the steering axle can damage the axle and tires and cause hard steering.

**Figure 24-28**

POOR TRACTION                    © 1997 Career Publishing Inc.

**Figure 24-29**

## EXAMPLES OF IMPROPER WEIGHT DISTRIBUTION

WRONG

WRONG

WRONG

WRONG

WRONG

© 1997 Career Publishing Inc.

**Figure 24-30**

**Distribution of weight in a trailer** is just as important. Use care when you load the cargo. Distribute the weight as evenly as possible between the trailer's rear axle(s) and the tractor's drive axle(s). If you are pulling double trailers, center the weight on the converter dolly.

When you load the trailer:
- Find out the total weight of the cargo.
- Load 1/2 in the front and 1/2 in the rear (if possible).
- Spread the load evenly over the floor from side to side to prevent shifting.
- Keep heavy freight as low as possible. This will help to keep the vehicle's center of gravity low.
- Spread out any heavy cargo to prevent concentrated stress on the trailer floor.
- Do not load heavy objects where they can fall on other freight.
- Move the heavy freight as needed to keep the weight evenly distributed after part of the cargo has been unloaded.
- The weight can be adjusted in trailers with sliding rear axles by moving the axle.
- Slide the axle forward to shift more weight to the trailer axle and off of the tractor drive axle.
- Slide to the rear position to shift the most weight to the tractor drive axle.

With sliding axles or fifth wheels, be aware of the Bridge Formula laws that dictate axle spacings. On interstate highways and on some state routes, you are required to have certain axle spacings to haul maximum allowable weights.

## High Center of Gravity

Some vehicles have a high center of gravity. This means the weight is carried high off the road. Such rigs are top heavy. These vehicles carry:

- Hanging loads such as meat.
- Tiered loads such as livestock.
- Liquids in bulk such as milk or gasoline.

They require special loading and driving techniques. The trailers have a high center of gravity that is always moving as they travel. They are more apt to roll over.

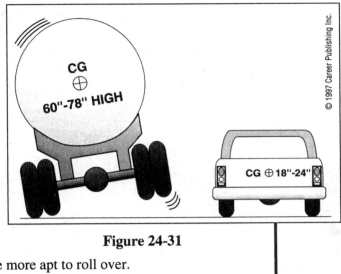

**Figure 24-31**

## SUMMARY

In this chapter, you learned why it is important to handle cargo properly. You have also learned what the driver's responsibilities are regarding the cargo. You discovered there are laws that determine the way cargo is shipped and how it must be secured. You now know certain types of cargo are hazardous materials and have their own rules for the way they must be shipped and the routes the driver can use. Weight limits and distribution of weight were also discussed.

## KEY WORDS

**Dunnage**: A filler material loaded in empty spaces to keep cargo from moving or falling.

**Federal Regulations for Hazardous Materials Transport**: Federal laws that regulate the manner in which hazardous materials must be shipped.

**FMCSR, Section 392.9**: The part of the federal law that protects the driver by prohibiting driving a truck that is not loaded or secured properly.

**General Knowledge Test:** The written test all CDL applicants must take to see how much they know about the laws regulating the trucking industry.

**Hazardous material**: Material that may pose a risk to health, safety, and property while being transported.

**Hazardous Materials Endorsement:** An endorsement on a CDL that all drivers who transport hazardous material must obtain.

**Tank Vehicles Endorsement**: An endorsement on a CDL that all drivers who transport liquids in bulk must obtain.

# LEARNING ACTIVITIES

In the following drawings, the cargo is **not** loaded correctly. On the lines beside each drawing, tell why it is not loaded properly and what may happen.

**1**

_____

_____

_____

_____

_____

**2**

_____

_____

_____

_____

_____

**3**

_____

_____

_____

_____

**4**

_____

_____

_____

_____

_____

## True-False Questions

T  F  1.  The backbone of the trucking industry is the safe, efficient transport of products.

T  F  2.  All over-the-road or long-haul drivers must personally load the cargo they haul or supervise the loading of trailers they pull.

T  F  3.  All drivers are responsible for knowing and complying with federal, state, and local laws.

T  F  4.  Federal regulations for protecting cargo from shifting or falling specify the methods for tie-down and blocking and bracing, and how the vehicle is to be constructed.

T  F  5.  Federal regulations require trailers to have headerboards between the cargo and driver.

T  F  6.  Federal laws set the standards for preventing movement of loose cargo.

T  F  7.  Only chains may be used to secure cargo on a flat bed trailer.

T  F  8.  There is only one reason for covering cargo, and that is to prevent dangerous spills.

T  F  9.  Tying a tarp securely in the first place saves time because you will not have to check it again.

T  F  10.  When a driver accepts freight for loading on a trailer, he or she becomes responsible for its safe delivery in good condition.

T  F  11.  Any damage to freight, shortage or overage on count, or other discrepancies should be brought to the shipper's attention at once.

T  F  12.  If a drum is too heavy to lift onto a drum truck, the only thing left to do is to roll it into place.

T  F  13.  Hazardous materials should be handled and transported only by trained and qualified persons.

T  F  14.  If you are employed by a carrier of hazardous materials, additional training and guidebooks must be provided.

T  F  15.  Each hazard class has requirements for labeling and marking containers.

T  F  16.  Hazardous material shipping papers must be within a driver's reach at all times and may be inspected by officials at any time.

T  F  17.  Federal regulations require the engine to be shut off while refueling. The person filling the fuel tank must be in control of the nozzle or pump.

T  F  18.  When hauling hazardous materials in a trailer that has dual wheels, the driver must stop the vehicle in a safe location and check all tires at least once every two hours or after 100 miles.

T  F  19.  Shippers are required to place placards when they are needed.

T  F  20.  When hazardous materials are loaded, the driver should check the regulations to determine placard requirements.

T  F  21.  Overweight violations are often expensive and can affect a driver's professional record.

T  F  22.  Distribution of weight on the tractor will have an effect on handling.

# Chapter Twenty-Five
# CARGO DOCUMENTATION

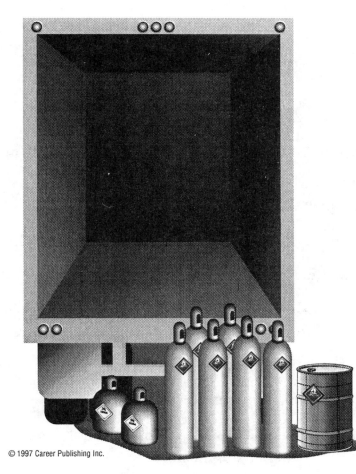

**Shipping Term Definitions • Transportation Charges • Surcharges • Transportation Rates • Bills of Lading • Cargo Manifest • Driver's Responsibilities • Shipper's Responsibilities • Freight Bills • Trailers Previously Loaded • Interline Carriers Security Seals • Hazardous Material Shipments Labels • Placards • ID Numbers Shipping Papers**

**FROM NOW ON,**

**ONLY THE BEST WILL DRIVE**

## OBJECTIVES

When you have mastered this chapter, you will be able to:

• Describe how to check the shipping documents to verify the cargo and quantity to be shipped

• Explain how to check documents for compliance with the law

• Understand the legal terms of shipping contracts

• Explain how drivers how can protect themselves and their companies from loss claims

• Specify how shipping document copies are to be distributed

• Explain what possession of the papers means

• Specify the documentation and communication requirements for hazardous material shipments

# CHAPTER TWENTY-FIVE

# CARGO DOCUMENTATION

## INTRODUCTION

The documentation that accompanies shipments serves many purposes. Its most important use is to provide an accurate record of the cargo. In some cases, it also serves as a contract for transportation services. You must be able to understand the terms and content of the shipping documents and your legal responsibilities in order to get a job as a tractor-trailer driver.

If you do not understand how to properly prepare and handle the papers, you may:

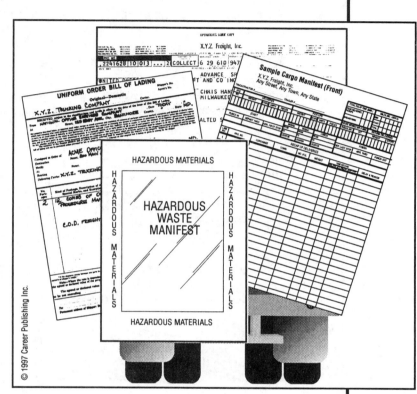

Figure 25-1

• Be liable for civil or criminal penalties if there is cargo loss or shortages
• Damage your reputation as a professional tractor-trailer driver
• Be fired from your job
• Endanger public health and safety by not properly communicating the dangers of hazardous materials cargo

## DEFINITION OF TERMS

In order for you to better understand certain words used by the shipper, carrier, or the person to whom the delivery is made, you will need to know exactly what they mean. The following terms have special meanings when referring to the trucking industry.

**Shipper, or Consignor:** The person or company who offers the goods for shipment.
**Receiver, or Consignee:** The person or company to whom the goods are being shipped or consigned.

**Motor Carrier, or Carrier:** The person or company that is in the business of transporting goods. In this chapter, carrier may mean:
- Private carrier
- For-hire carrier
  - Common carrier
  - Contract carrier
  - Exempt commodity carrier

**Freight Broker:** A person or company that arranges for transporting freight.

**Freight Forwarder:** A person who gathers small shipments from various shippers and puts them together into larger shipments. These shipments then may go to a break-bulk facility where they are broken down for delivery to the consignees.

**Originating, or Pickup, Carrier:** The carrier that first accepts the shipment from the shipper.

**Connecting Carrier:** Any carrier that transports freight to an interchange location and then transfers the cargo to another company to continue the shipment.

**Delivery, or Terminal, Carrier:** The carrier that delivers the shipment to the consignee.

**Bill of Lading:** A written contract between the shipper and the carrier for transporting a shipment. The paper that identifies all freight in the shipment, the consignee, the delivery location, and the terms of the agreement.

**Straight Bill of Lading:** A contract that provides for delivery of a shipment to the consignee. The driver does not need to get a copy from the consignee when the goods are delivered.

**Order Notify Bill of Lading:** A bill of lading that permits the shipper to collect payment before the shipment reaches the destination. The driver must pick up the consignee's copy of the Bill of Lading before he or she delivers the shipment.

**Through Bill of Lading:** A Bill of Lading used for shipments transported by more than one carrier that has a fixed rate for the service of all of the carriers.

**Manifest:** A list describing the entire shipment on the vehicle.

**Packing Slip:** A detailed list of packed goods that is prepared by the shipper.

**Freight Bill:** A bill submitted by a common carrier for transport services. The Freight Bill contains much of the same information as a Bill of Lading. A copy usually serves as a receipt for services when signed by the consignee.

**Delivery Receipt:** A paper signed by the consignee or an agent of the consignee accepting the shipment from the driver. The driver keeps the receipt as proof of delivery.

© 1997 Career Publishing Inc.

**Figure 25-2**

**Warehouse Receipt:** A receipt kept by the driver to prove the shipment was unloaded at a warehouse.

**Agent:** A person or company that acts as the official representative of another, such as a consignee's agent.

**Hazardous Materials Shipping Paper:** A Bill of Lading that describes hazardous materials by the proper shipping name, hazard class, identification number, and the quantity being shipped. This form must be legible.

**Hazardous Waste Manifest:** A form (EPA-8700-22) that describes hazardous waste and identifies the shipper, carrier, and destination by name and by the identification numbers assigned by the Environmental Protection Agency. The shipper prepares, dates, and signs the Manifest. All carriers of the shipment must sign the paper. It must also be signed by the consignee. The driver keeps a copy.

# TRANSPORTATION CHARGES AND SERVICES

Transportation charges are the fees for transportation services. They may also include payment for the goods shipped (COD shipments). It is very important to understand the terminology about the charges and payment for services. You must understand all the terms of each agreement to protect yourself from liability and personal expense.

Usually the cost for the goods in the shipment is agreed upon by the shipper and the customer before the shipment is offered for transport. Sometimes the carrier will also have to collect the payment for the goods being shipped and return this payment to the shipper. The shipper and carrier usually agree on the transportation charges before the freight is loaded.

## Types of Payment

**Prepaid:** The transportation charges are paid at the shipping point.

**COD**: These are Collect On Delivery shipments. The driver must collect payment before the cargo can be unloaded. The payment may be for the transportation charges only or also include the cost of the goods. A driver must know the company's policy for the types of payment that can be accepted, such as certified check, money order or cash.

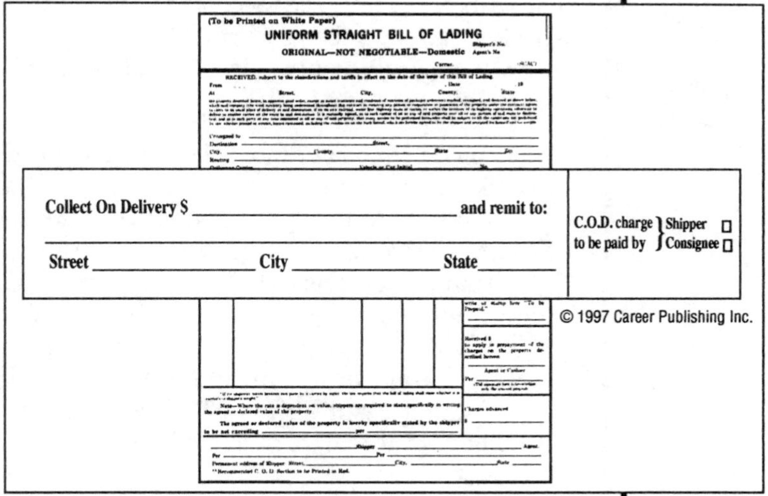
(To be Printed on White Paper)
UNIFORM STRAIGHT BILL OF LADING
ORIGINAL—NOT NEGOTIABLE—Domestic

Collect On Delivery $ ______ and remit to:
______
Street ______ City ______ State ______

C.O.D. charge to be paid by: Shipper ☐ Consignee ☐

© 1997 Career Publishing Inc.

**Figure 25-3**

**Order notify shipment:** Payment for the goods is made when the driver gets a copy of the Order Notify Bill of Lading from the consignee. He or she must get the bill from the consignee before delivering the shipment.

## Transportation Rates

Charges for transportation are figured by multiplying the rate by the weight of the cargo and distance the load will be shipped. Rates are based on the value of the cargo and services performed by the carrier.

The value of the cargo used for rate purposes is either the:

- Actual value of goods as shown on the Bill of Lading
  or
- Value shown on the Bill of Lading that is set by the shipper as the limit for carrier liability.

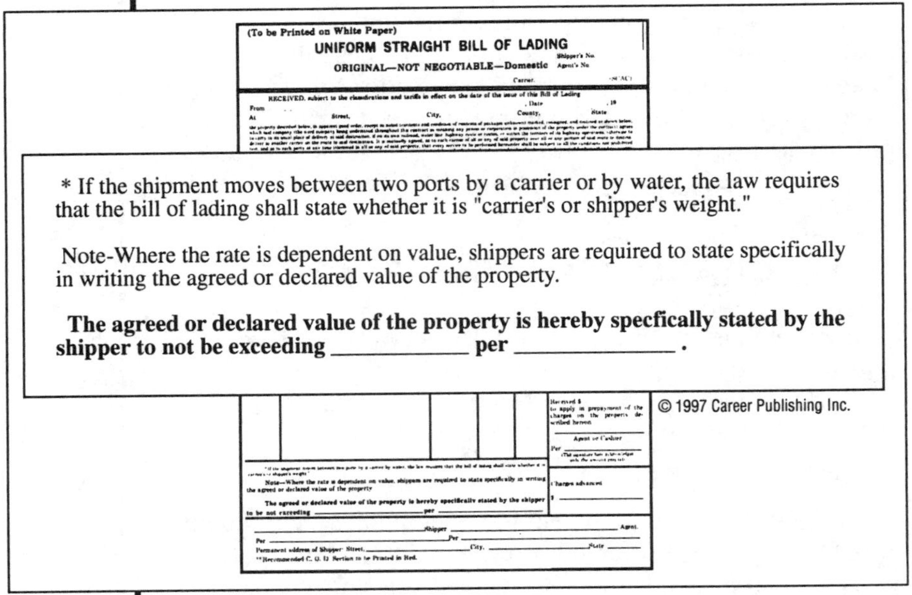
(To be Printed on White Paper)

UNIFORM STRAIGHT BILL OF LADING

ORIGINAL—NOT NEGOTIABLE—Domestic

* If the shipment moves between two ports by a carrier or by water, the law requires that the bill of lading shall state whether it is "carrier's or shipper's weight."

Note-Where the rate is dependent on value, shippers are required to state specifically in writing the agreed or declared value of the property.

**The agreed or declared value of the property is hereby specfically stated by the shipper to not be exceeding __________ per __________ .**



**Figure 25-4**

Services to be performed by the carrier are based on special handling requirements and tariffs. Tariffs are lists of services common carriers perform for the public and the rates charged for them.

## Services and Surcharges

Rates for services and surcharges or additional charges are negotiated between the shipper and the carrier before the carrier accepts the shipment. Surcharges may include those for special services to be performed by the driver when delivery is made. You must know the meaning of the terms that describe certain services. The services should be clearly stated on the Bill of Lading.

**Inside Delivery:** Indicates the freight is to be delivered inside instead of unloaded at the curb.

**Tailgate Delivery:** The freight is unloaded and delivered at the tailgate (the back of the truck).

**Helper Service:** A helper is to be provided for loading or unloading freight. The Bill of Lading specifies who will pay for the helper.

**Residential Delivery**: The Bill of Lading will specify the address and method of collecting payment if the shipment is to a residence.

**Dunnage and Return:** The weight of the dunnage will be listed on the Bill of Lading. If the shipper wishes it to be returned, this will be stated on the Bill of Lading.

**Storage and Delay Charges:** An additional amount to be paid to the carrier if a delivery is postponed by the consignee or shipper or a shipment must be stored before it can be delivered. These terms are stated in the Bill of Lading.

**Detention Time or Demurrage:** Detaining a vehicle beyond a given time. Payment is made to the carrier when delivery is delayed.

# BASIC SHIPPING DOCUMENTS

A **Bill of Lading** is a contract between a shipper and a carrier. It lists all the goods in the shipment and any special handling requirements or conditions for transportation. It is a legally binding document that is regulated by federal law.

There are several different types of Bills of Lading, which serve many purposes.
- Identifies the type and quantity of freight being shipped
- Shows the ownership of the goods
- States the value of the freight in case of loss or damage
- Establishes the rates and freight charges
- Serves as a legal contract
- Identifies the point of origin of the shipment and the destination to which it is being shipped
- States the method of payment for all charges
- Serves as a permanent record of the transaction

**Uniform Straight Bill of Lading**: The most common type of Bill of Lading is the Uniform Straight Bill of Lading. It is a contract that the parties cannot change. The goods must be delivered to the consignee or an authorized representative. There are usually three copies of the Bill, distributed as follows:
- Copy 1 (original): Sent to the consignee
- Copy 2 (shipping order): Carrier copy
- Copy 3 (memorandum): Shipper copy

*A Uniform Straight Bill of Lading* (see Figure 25.5) will have the:

1. Motor carrier's name
2. Shipper's name
3. Date the goods were accepted by the carrier
4. The number of items in the shipment and a description of each
5. Condition of all packages or goods in the shipment
6. Space for the driver to note damage, shortages, or packages not properly packed
7. Name of the consignee
8. Address to which the shipment is to be delivered
9. Routing, if more than one carrier will transport
10. Identification of connecting carriers, if there are any
11. Freight charges and the method of payment, such as COD or prepaid
12. Special handling or services
13. Signatures of the shipper and the driver as agents for the carrier, the Bill is NOT VALID without SIGNATURES

Contract information will be detailed on the back of Copy 2 in case the driver must check for specific duties on delivery.

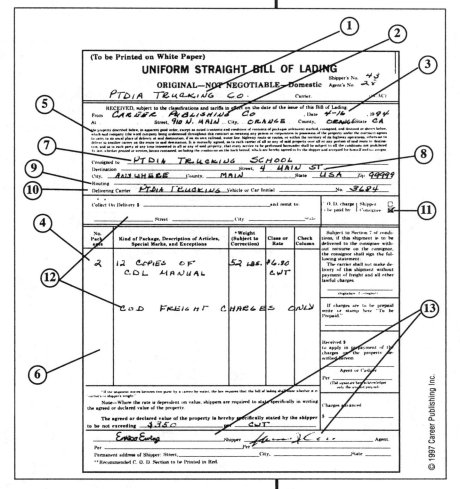

**Figure 25-5**

**Order Notify Bill of Lading:** An Order Notify Bill of Lading is a special type of Bill of Lading. Ownership of the shipment can be transferred by the valid sale of this document. There will be three copies.
- Copy 1 (original): Yellow
- Copy 2 (shipping): Blue
- Copy 3 (memo): White

The information that describes the freight in the shipment will be the same as for a Uniform Bill of Lading.

The driver must check the back of the yellow page (original) to be sure it is signed by the shipper and any bank or financial institution that has paid the shipper.

If there is any question about the validity or proper preparation of the Order Notify Bill of Lading, contact the financial department or billing agent for your company.

The driver must not deliver any part of the shipment unless he or she has the original copy (Copy 1) of the Bill. After delivery, the original copy of the Bill is given to the consignee. The holder of the Order Notify Bill of Lading is the legal owner of the freight.

**Household Goods Bill of Lading:** A Household Goods Bill of Lading is used by moving companies for their shipments. This type of bill serves as a legal contract between the shipper and the carrier. The Household Goods Bill of Lading lists the carrier and the customer. It is a combined Bill of Lading, Freight Bill, and record of the items in the shipment stating:
- Their appearance
- Their condition
- How they are packaged

Legal requirements for weighing a load with a Household Goods Bill of Lading differ from those for ordinary freight.

**Freight Bills:** Freight Bills are prepared by the carrier from the Bill of Lading. Drivers are mostly concerned with Copy 1, which serves as the delivery receipt copy. The driver must have the consignee sign the bill, showing that he or she accepts the shipment, before it can be unloaded.

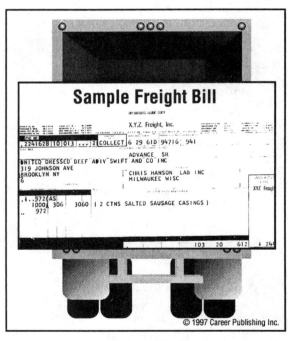

**Figure 25-6**

The Freight Bill will tell the driver if:
- The carrier charges are prepaid.
- There is a COD payment due upon delivery.

Freight Bills are usually preprinted with **pro numbers** (progressive numbers). The numbers are in front of the Freight Bill numbers. Often the driver will have to identify the bill by its pro number. Sometimes, drivers refer to Cargo Manifests as pro bills or pro sheets because the manifest lists all Freight Bills.

## Other Documents

**Invoice:** A bill from the shipper that lists the goods, prices, and total due. This may be mailed to the consignee, or the driver may have to give it to the consignee if it is a COD shipment.

**Packing Slip:** A list of the total parts packaged in a shipment. The responsibility of opening packages and checking the contents against the packing slip belongs to the consignee.

## DRIVER'S SIGNATURE AND RESPONSIBILITY

Your signature on a shipping document as the driver actually puts you and your company on the line! **Never sign** a shipping document unless you understand all terms and conditions completely. Be sure you compare all descriptions with the freight offered for loading.

Your signature on a Bill of Lading means:

- You and your company are legally responsible for fulfilling all the terms and conditions of the contract.
- You and your company agree to the methods and rates of payment for the services as stated.
- You and your company are responsible

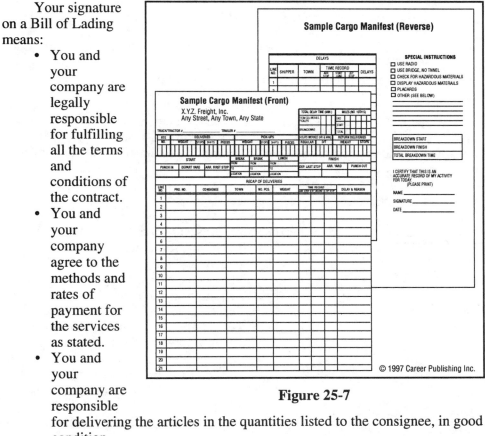

**Figure 25-7**

for delivering the articles in the quantities listed to the consignee, in good condition.
- You have inspected the shipment and found all items to be in good condition. The count is correct.
- You have noted any shortages, damages, or mistakes before signing the Bill.

by:

As a professional tractor-trailer driver, protect your reputation and your job

- Never taking the word of someone else for the freight count or the condition of the shipment
- Always observing the loading of cargo to ensure all pieces are loaded
- Checking the descriptions on the packages against the Bill of Lading
- Learning the way to quickly and correctly count palletized packages
- Checking the address on the freight against the delivery address of the consignee to avoid loading the wrong cargo
- Handling fragile goods properly when you load them; if they are loaded by others, watch out for rough handling and breakage
- Never loading or permitting someone else to load leaking packages or drums; the leakage could damage other freight
- Noting freight that is poorly packaged and could come out of the package during transport
- Knowing the policies of your company for refusing damaged or incomplete shipments; if you accept these for shipment, it could result in freight claims

## PREVIOUSLY LOADED TRAILERS

Before signing a *Bill of Lading* for a shipment that was not loaded in your presence:

- Inspect the load, if possible.
- Check the *Bill of Lading* for incompatible freight, overweight shipments, etc.
- Check the general appearance of the load for proper blocking and bracing.

If the trailer is sealed with a security seal or you cannot visually inspect it, make a note on the *Bill of Lading* "shipper's weight, load, and count." This releases you and your company from responsibility for any shortage or damage unless it is caused by an accident.

### Security Seals

For trailers that have been equipped with security seals by the shipper:

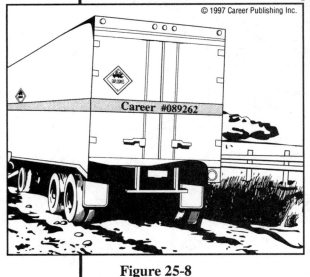

© 1997 Career Publishing Inc.

Career #089262

**Figure 25-8**

- Record the serial number of the seal on all copies of the Bill of Lading.
- Note on the Bill of Lading "shipper's weight, load, and count."
- Check the seal to be sure it is properly locked. The serial number must match the number noted on the Bill of Lading.
- Have the consignee sign for the shipment upon delivery before breaking the seal.
- If the seal is broken enroute for inspection by enforcement officials, obtain their signature, badge number, department, and get a replacement seal.
- If the seal is broken enroute by someone other than an enforcement official, notify your dispatcher or supervisor at once.

# DELIVERY OF FREIGHT

When you deliver freight, remember you are responsible for the shipment until it is accepted by the consignee.
- Make sure delivery is to the proper consignee.
- Obtain the correct signature on Freight Bills, Bills of Lading, receipts, or other documents before you unload the shipment.
- Collect COD payments before unloading the cargo.
- Obtain the properly signed Order Notify Bill of Lading before you unload the shipment.
- Check to be sure the entire consignment is delivered.
- Any differences, shortages, or changes in the method of payment should be reported to your dispatcher or supervisor before you release the shipment to the consignee.
- Know your company policy on freight delivery problems.

# INTERLINE FREIGHT

Pick up freight from an interline carrier in the same way you would from a shipper. Deliver freight to an interline carrier like they were a consignee.
- Always inspect the shipment for damage or shortages.
- Compare the Bill of Lading with the freight.
- Do not sign Freight Bills, Bills of Lading, or receipts until you note any shortages or damages and they are signed by the interline carrier.
- Make sure you thoroughly understand any special services and the method of payment.
- Get signatures and receipts before you release the shipment to the connecting carrier.
- If there is an equipment interchange with the connecting carrier, know the policy of your company. Always follow the established procedures.

Remember, you are responsible not only for the freight but also for making sure the trailer is within legal limits. Check the weight of the shipment on the papers, so you will not accept an overloaded trailer.

# HAZARDOUS MATERIAL AND HAZARDOUS WASTE

Hazardous materials shipments must be specially:
- Labeled
- Prepared
- Handled
- Documented
- Placarded

**Figure 25-9**

Communication of hazards in transportation is vital to public health and safety. If there is an accident or spill, police, fire, and emergency crews must be able to quickly recognize the presence of these materials.

As a professional driver, you must know how to recognize hazardous materials shipments and be aware of the dangers of each hazard class.

## Shipper's Responsibilities

The shipper is required by federal law to:
- Train all employees involved in Hazmat functions.
- Identify all hazardous materials by hazard class.
- Properly pack the material in the correct packaging.
- Prepare the shipping papers, which list in this order, the:
  1. Proper shipping name
  2. Hazard class
  3. Identification number
  4. Packing group
- State the total quantity or volume of the material.
- Properly label each package with the correct hazard class label if one is required.
- Mark each package with the proper shipping name and identification number for the contents.
- Provide placards for the carrier.
- Provide the emergency response telephone number.

## Driver's Responsibilities

Drivers are required by federal law to be trained before they can accept shipments of hazardous materials. They may also need the Hazardous Materials endorsement on their CDL. A properly trained tractor-trailer driver has the ability as well as the legal responsibility to:
- Check the Bill of Lading for hazardous material cargo.
- Make sure the shipping papers are complete and accurate.
- Check the shipping papers to be sure the shipper's certification form is signed.
- Check the packages for proper labeling and marking.
- Check compatibility and segregation requirements for the materials.
- Observe the special handling and loading requirements.
- Properly placard the vehicle as required:
- Comply with Federal Motor Carrier Regulations.

## Placards

Placards are diamond-shaped signs (10-3/4" on a side) that tell the hazard class of the shipment. They are similar in design to labels, except they are larger in size. They must be displayed on each side of the vehicle. Placards communicate the hazard. From a safe distance, they tell others about the hazards aboard a trailer. This is important to emergency responders if the rig is in an accident.

Figure 25-10

Due to changes in the Hazardous Materials Regulations, two types of placards are being used by the trucking industry today. Although new placards are being used elsewhere, trucks may continue to display the old placards until the year 2001.

Cargo tanks that have multiple compartments and are used for hauling hazardous material have special requirements for placards. When you haul these products, you must learn the special placarding regulations.

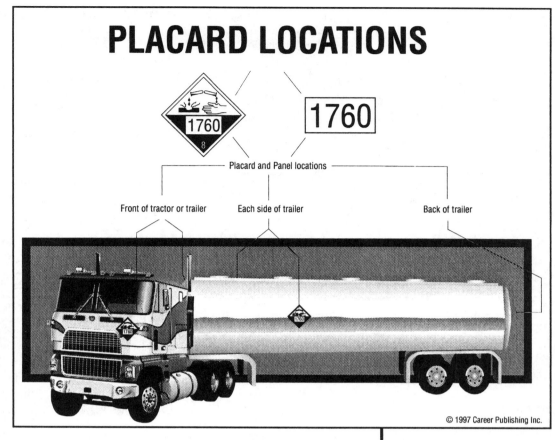

**PLACARD LOCATIONS**

1760

Placard and Panel locations

Front of tractor or trailer    Each side of trailer    Back of trailer

© 1997 Career Publishing Inc.

**Figure 25-11**

Placards must be visible on all four sides of the tractor-trailer. They must be easily seen. Place them so the words and numbers are level and read from left to right. They must be at least three inches away from any other markings.

Portable tanks and van trailers carrying bulk shipments that require placards and ID numbers must also have them on all four sides of the trailer.

The importance of placards to the driver's safety, that of emergency responders, and the public is obvious. The driver has the legal responsibility to display the proper placards on the tractor and trailer when required and to remove them when hazardous materials are no longer aboard. Placards must remain on empty tank trucks and tank trailers until they are cleaned.

## Labels

Labels and placards for each hazard class look very much alike. Labels resemble small placards and must be placed on packages near the proper shipping name and identification number. You should have a chart that tells the proper color and format for each hazard class when you load freight. Some shipments of hazardous materials can be shipped as a Consumer Commodity, Limited Quantity, or Small Quantity and do not need labels on the package.

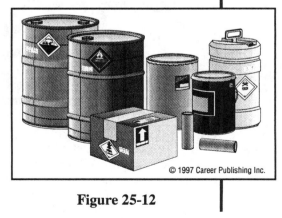

© 1997 Career Publishing Inc.

**Figure 25-12**

Federal laws require certain materials that meet the definition of more than one hazard class to display multiple labels. You must know the procedures for checking labels on packages.

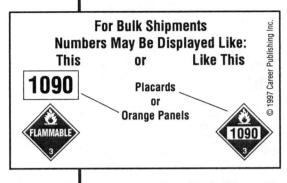

**Figure 25-13**

## Identification Numbers

All hazardous materials are identified by a four-digit identification (ID) number. The four-digit number is preceded by either the letters UN or NA.

UN means the United Nations uses the number for that material worldwide. NA means the number is used only in North America.

The ID number is used by emergency response crews and police to identify the material in the Emergency Response Guidebook so they can take the proper action at an accident.

ID numbers are required on all hazardous materials shipping papers. They must also be marked on all packages along with the proper shipping name.

ID numbers must be marked on two opposite sides of the following:
- Liquids: Bulk packaging with a capacity of over 118.9 gallons
- Solids: Bulk packaging weighing over 881.8 pounds
- Gases: Bulk packaging with over 1,000 lbs. water capacity

ID numbers must be marked on all four sides of the following:
- Liquids: Bulk packaging with a capacity of over 1,000 gallons
- Solids: Bulk packaging of over 133.7 cubic feet

For bulk shipments, the numbers can be on orange panels with black numerals or on the required placard(s).

## Hazardous Material Shipping Papers

Hazardous materials, when listed on shipping papers or Bills of Lading with other non-hazardous materials, must be clearly distinguished by one of the following methods:
- Listing the hazardous materials first on the paper
- Highlighting the entry
- Identifying the shipper with an X before the shipping name in the column titled HM; The letters RQ may be used instead of X if the shipment is a reportable quantity.
- Printing the entry in a contrasting color

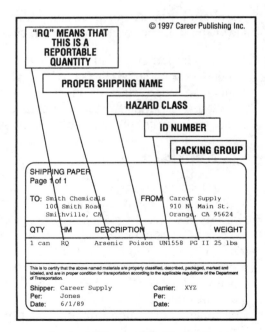

**Figure 25-14**

When hauling both hazardous and non-hazardous materials together, the documents identifying the hazardous materials must be marked in one of the following ways.
• On top of all other papers
• Flagged with an easily recognized tab
• Enclosed in an envelope clearly marked HAZARDOUS MATERIALS

The shipping papers must be easy to see and find.
• When driving: Within the driver's reach with his seatbelt fastened
• Empty cab: Either on the driver's seat or in the pouch on the driver's door

The papers must be available for inspection by an official at any time.

Shipments must have emergency response information included. This information can be printed on the shipping papers or contained in another document attached to the shipping papers. The information should include the data about the material being shipped and an emergency response phone number.

Always remember to check all labels, markings, placards, and shipping papers to be sure they are correct. Any errors should be brought to the shipper's attention and corrected before the materials are loaded.

Figure 25-15

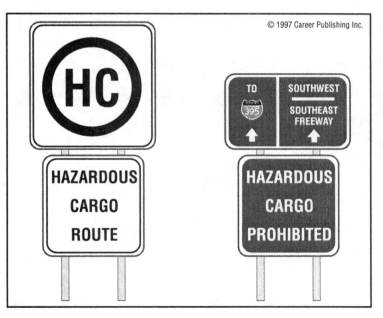

Figure 25-16

Because vehicles carrying hazardous materials cannot use certain highways, always check the shipping papers for special routing instructions. If the driver plans the route, be sure to avoid restricted roads, bridges, tunnels, or heavily populated areas.

## SUMMARY

In this chapter, you have learned the importance of cargo documentation: Bills of Lading, Freight Bills, Cargo Manifest, Invoices, Packing Slips, and Hazardous Material Shipping Papers. The responsibilities of both the shipper and driver were explained. How to accept a load for shipment and the correct way to deliver it were described. The special requirements for loads of hazardous material were also explained.

Figure 25-17

## KEY WORDS

**Bill of Lading:** A contract between a shipper and a carrier.

**COD shipments:** Shipments in which the driver Collects payment On Delivery for freight or cargo and freight.

**Documentation:** The papers that accompany shipments and provide an accurate record of the cargo. In some cases, it also serves as a contract for the transportation services.

**Freight Bills:** Bills prepared by the carrier from the Bill of Lading that must be signed by the consignee before the cargo can be unloaded and indicate whether the charges are prepaid or COD.

**Identification (ID) number:** Four-digit numbers used to identify all hazardous materials.

**Interline carrier:** One that accepts or delivers shipments for only part of the trip. Another carrier either begins or completes the trip.

**Hazmat Labels:** Labels resembling small placards that are placed on packages near the proper shipping name and identification number.

**Order notify shipment:** One in which payment for the goods is made when the driver gets a copy of the Order Notify Bill of Lading from the consignee.

**Prepaid shipments:** Ones in which the transportation charges are paid at the shipping point.

**Placards:** Diamond-shaped signs (10-3/4" on a side) that tell the hazard class of the shipment and are displayed on each side of the vehicle.

**Pro numbers:** Preprinted numbers on freight bills that are often used to identify the freight bill.

**Security seals:** Seals placed on cargo containers by shippers that do not let the driver fully inspect the load.

**Transportation charges:** Fees for transportation services.

# LEARNING ACTIVITIES

## Fill-Out-The-Form

Put a check mark in each blank that must be filled out by the shipper before a driver can accept the shipment for transport.

---

**(To be Printed on White Paper)**

# UNIFORM STRAIGHT BILL OF LADING
### ORIGINAL-NOT NEGOTIABLE-Domestic

Shipper's No. _____
Agents No. _____

_____ Carrier _____ (SCAC)

RECEIVED, subject to the classifications and tariffs in effect on the date of the issue of this Bill of Lading.
From _____, Date _____, 19 _____
At _____ Street, _____ City, _____ County, _____ State ____

the property described below, in apparent good order, except as noted (contents and condition of contents of packages unknown) marked, consigned, and destined as shown below, which said company (the word company being understood throughout this contract as meaning any person or corporation in possession of the property under the contract) agrees to carry to its usual place of delivery at said destination, if on its own railroad, water line, highway route or routes, or within the territory of its highway operations, otherwise to deliver to another carrier on the route to said destination. It is mutually agreed, as to each carrier of all or any of said property over all or any portion of said route to destination and as to each party at any time interested in all or any of said property, that every service to be performed hereunder shall be subject to all the conditions not prohibited by law, whether printed or written, herein contained, including the conditions on the back hereof, which are hereby agreed to by the shipper and accepted for himself and his assigns.

Consigned to _____
Destination _____ Street _____
City, _____ County, _____ State _____ Zip _____
Routing _____
Delivering Carrier _____ Vehicle or Car Initial _____ No. _____

Collect On Delivery _____ and remit to:

_____ Street _____ City _____ State

C.O.D. charge } Shipper ☐
to be paid by } Consignee ☐

| No. Packages | Kind of Packages, Description of Articles, Special Marks, and Exceptions | * Weight (Subject to Correction) | Class or Rate | Check Column | |
|---|---|---|---|---|---|
| | | | | | Subject to Section 7 of conditions, if this shipment is to be delivered to the consignee without recourse on the consignor, the consignor shall sign the following statement: The carrier shall not make delivery of this shipment without payment of freight and all other lawful charges. |
| | | | | | |
| | | | | | _____ (Signature of consignor) |
| | | | | | If charges are to be prepaid write or stamp here "To be Prepaid.". |
| | | | | | _____ |
| | | | | | Received $ _____ to apply in prepayment of the charges on the property described hereon. |
| | | | | | _____ Agent or Cashier |
| | | | | | (The signature here acknowledges only the amount prepaid) |

\* If the shipment moves between two ports by a carrier or by water, the law requires that the bill of lading shall state wheter it is "carrier's or shipper's weight."

Note-Where the rate is dependent on value, shippers are required to state specifically in writing the agreed or declared value of the property.

The agreed or declared value of the property is hereby specifically stated by the shipper to not be exceeding _____ per _____

Charges advanced:

$ _____

_____ Shipper _____ Agent
Per _____ Per _____
Permanent address of Shipper: Street, _____ City, _____ State _____

**Distributing Copies**

You have a Uniform Straight Bill of Lading. There are three copies of the Bill. Fill in the name of the person who gets the copy on the line beside the copy.

Copy 1 (original): _____

Copy 2 (shipping order): _____

Copy 3 (memorandum): _____

You have an Order Notify Bill of Lading. There are three copies. Fill in the color of the copy on the line beside the copy.

Copy 1 (original): _____

Copy 2 (shipping): _____

Copy 3 (memo): _____

**Delivery of Freight**

When you deliver freight, remember you are responsible for the shipment until it is accepted by the consignee. Put the following steps in the correct order by placing a number on the line beside the step. Put a 1 for the first step, 2 for the second step, etc.

_____ Check to be sure the entire consignment is delivered.

_____ Any differences, shortages, or changes in method of payment should be reported to your dispatcher or supervisor before you release the shipment to the consignee.

_____ Make sure delivery is to the proper consignee.

_____ Collect COD payments before unloading the cargo.

_____ Obtain the correct signature on Freight Bills, Bills of Lading, receipts, or other documents before you unload the shipment.

_____ Obtain a properly signed Order Notify Bill of Lading before you unload the shipment.

## True-False Questions

Circle the T if the statement is true. If the statement is false circle the F.

T  F  1.  A driver must completely understand the terms of all agreements in order to protect himself or herself against liability and personal expense.

T  F  2.  Surcharges on rates may include special services to be performed by the driver when the shipment is delivered.

T  F  3.  A Bill of Lading is a legally binding document that is regulated by federal law.

T  F  4.  Freight bills are prepared by the driver from the Bill of Lading.

T  F  5.  The driver must determine from the freight bill if the carrier charges are prepaid or if the payment is due on delivery (COD).

T  F  6.  The driver's signature on the Bill of Lading means the driver and his or her company are legally responsible for fulfilling all terms and conditions of the contract.

T  F  7.  It is safe to take the word of a highly regarded shipper for the count and condition of the freight.

T  F  8.  Before signing a Bill of Lading for a shipment not loaded in your presence, you should inspect the load if possible.

T  F  9.  If the trailer is sealed with a security seal or cannot be visually inspected and quantities verified, a driver should note on the Bill of Lading, "shipper's weight, load, and count."

T  F  10.  When a trailer has a security seal placed by the shipper, the driver should check the seal to be sure it is locked and the serial number matches the number on the Bill of Lading.

T  F  11.  Hazardous materials shipments require special preparation, handling, documentation, and communication of hazard.

T  F  12.  It is the driver's responsibility to properly label each package with the proper hazard class label.

T  F  13.  Placards are signs shaped like triangles that are similar in design to labels except for their large size.

T  F  14.  Only some of the more dangerous hazardous materials are identified by an assigned, four-digit identification number.

T  F  15.  Cargo tanks that have multiple compartments, or those used for hauling petroleum products, have special placarding requirements.

T  F  16.  Shipping papers must be made available for inspection by officials at any time.

# Chapter Twenty-Six
# PERSONAL HEALTH AND SAFETY

© 1997 Career Publishing Inc.

**Physical Requirements for Drivers • Fatigue and Driving**
**Alcohol and Driving • Drugs and Driving • Safety Practices**
**Safety Equipment • Accidents • On- and Off-Duty Stress**

# OBJECTIVES

When you have mastered this chapter, you will be able to:

• Show why a truck driver's job demands good physical condition

• Describe the causes of and cures for fatigue

• Explain the FMCSR with regard to alcohol or drug use

• Describe the effects of fatigue and alcohol on the body

• Show the benefits of a good diet, exercise, and plenty of rest

• Identify danger zones for drivers and show how to use safety measures

• Describe how to lift objects safely

• Explain the value of the right protective gear (hard hat, respirators, etc.) in the prevention of injury

• List the causes of stress

• Show causes of accidents

# CHAPTER TWENTY-SIX

# PERSONAL HEALTH AND SAFETY

## INTRODUCTION

Your personal health affects your driving. Drivers need to stay in shape by getting enough rest, eating the right foods, and exercising. Drivers also need to know the effects of fatigue, alcohol and drugs. What the law has to say about a driver's using alcohol and drugs and driving when tired is important for all drivers to know. This chapter will explain these points.

© 1997 Career Publishing Inc.

**Figure 26-1**

## PHYSICAL CONDITION

In order to be a commercial driver, a person must pass a physical examination and get a certificate from a doctor. This exam includes a vision test.

Good vision is one of the most important physical requirements for driving. Being able to see well includes good side vision, color recognition, and night vision. The federal law says only that a driver must be able to see clearly. Night vision and glare recovery are also very important, although not covered by federal laws. A driver must also hear well and have stamina.

A tractor-trailer driver must stay in shape to be able to drive safely and avoid the medical problems that could cause him or her to fail a physical exam. Plenty of rest and exercise are needed. Not using drugs or drinking will help you be alert and in good health.

*Physical Requirements for Interstate Truckers*

- Vision
  - 20/40 Vision
  - Peripheral Vision-at Least 70 Degrees in Each Eye
  - Distinguish Red and Green
  - Eye Check Every 24 Months

- Hearing
  - Hear Forced Whisper at 5 Feet

- Stamina
  - To Meet Job Requirements, e.g. Loading, Unloading

- Disqualifications
  - Loss of Limb(s) or Disease That Limits Limbs
  - Chronic Illness That Seriously Affects Driving
  - Examples:
    - Diabetes
    - Heart Disease
    - Alcoholism

- Required Physical Examination
  - Every 2 Years
  - At Carrier's Discretion
  - After Serious Injury or Illness

- Certification by Physician
  - Must Be Carried at All Times
  - As Important as Driver's License

**Figure 26-2**

## Eating Habits

Some truck drivers have poor eating habits. Not eating well can affect:
• Alertness
• Reaction time
• Perception
• Overall driving ability
• Health in later years

Bad habits include eating:
• The wrong foods
• Too much
• Too fast

A poor diet can cause:
• Fatigue
• Headaches
• Lack of energy
• Indigestion

Over time, a poor diet can lead to:
• Being overweight
• Nervous disorders
• High blood pressure
• High cholesterol level

© 1997 Career Publishing Inc.

**Figure 26-3**

All of these can lead to problems with your circulation and heart. A good diet, on the other hand, helps a driver stay alert and have enough energy to do a good job.

## Exercise

It is important to get enough exercise. Regular exercise:
• Tones the muscles
• Reduces fat
• Helps keep your reflexes and reactions sharp
• Helps you relax
• Helps prevent heart and circulatory problems

Eating the wrong food, lack of exercise, and smoking are major causes of heart disease.

Be sure to get enough exercise both when you are off duty and when you are on the job.

## Rest

Truck drivers need to be alert and well-rested. It is best for all drivers to avoid too much activity, parties, alcohol, and stressful situations during their off-duty time just before driving.

The FMCSR calls for eight hours of rest before driving. Some people, of course, need more than eight hours. Time off-duty is not rest time if the driver has been partying, working hard around the house, etc. Be sure you use your rest time resting.

# FATIGUE

As a driver, you are responsible for your condition when you report for work. You must do your best to stay rested. Fatigue can be a dangerous problem for truckers. It is the underlying cause of many accidents. Fatigue is often a real problem for long-haul drivers who have irregular schedules.

© 1997 Career Publishing Inc.

**Figure 26-4**

Fatigue can be caused by:
- Lack of sleep
- Long, tedious tasks, such as long periods of driving
- Illness — even a cold
- Being out of shape or overweight
- A sleep disorder, such as sleep apnea.

Fatigue usually occurs in the early morning hours, especially around 4:00 am and 6:00 am. A fatigued driver loses some basic skills, such as:
- Judgment
- Ability to react
- Perception

**Judgment:** A fatigued driver will not recognize hazards and will tend to misjudge clearances, gaps, and speed. He or she may not know how fast they are driving or be able to judge the speed of others.

**Ability to React:** A fatigued driver may not be able to respond quickly to situations. He or she may not even realize they are reacting in slow motion.

**Perception:** A fatigued driver may distort the overall picture of the traffic situation. Depth perception is less accurate. He or she may misjudge speed and distance. Normal reaction time is 3/4 of a second. If you are driving at 50 mph, you will travel 55 feet during that time. A driver who is fatigued may take 1 second to react. He or she will then travel 74 feet. Those 19 feet may make the difference in whether or not an accident can be avoided.

Fatigue can cause drivers to fall into micro-sleeps. These are short unintended naps that may last only a second or so. Imagine what can happen if you are driving 30 mph and you sleep for only 1/2 second. You will drive blind for 22 feet.

Fatigue also causes drivers to imagine they see hazards that really are not there: another vehicle, an animal, a tree or building, or even people. The driver then swerves to avoid the object, and often loses control of the vehicle. This is a cause of many accidents.

**Stress:** Stress increases the chance of fatigue. Causes of stress include:
- Tension on the job or at home
- Improper diet and lack of exercise
- Use of alcohol, cigarettes, or drugs
- Loneliness and boredom
- Worry
- Varied sleep patterns

## How to Deal with Fatigue

The best way to deal with fatigue is to prevent it. If it does occur, you must recognize it and deal with it at once. You can cut the chances of fatigue if you get plenty of rest, eat the right foods, and get plenty of exercise. When you are on the road, try to remain active. If you become tired, stop and get some rest. Do not risk falling asleep at the wheel. A quick nap (10 to 15 minutes) is the best remedy. If you sleep longer, you may feel more tired.

The major signs of fatigue are obvious. Your eyes get heavy and dull. Tired eyes mean a tired body and that fatigue is setting in. You may become cross and cranky. You may even feel unable or unwilling to do anything.

## Fatigue and Myths

When you deal with fatigue, knowing what not to do is as important as knowing what to do. There are a number of things that have been guaranteed to ward off fatigue. Do not believe them. The most common myths are:
- Open a window.
- Turn up the radio.
- Stop for something to eat.
- Talk to someone.
- Take a pill.
- Have a drink.
- Have a cup of coffee.

**Figure 26-5**

Fresh air may actually lull a driver to sleep unless it is cold air. The sound of the radio may also lull you to sleep, even if it is loud. Eating a heavy meal actually increases the chances of falling asleep. Statistics show that many accidents occur roughly 30 minutes after a meal. After you eat, your body's circulatory system works hard to digest the food. This causes less blood to go to your brain, so it wants to rest.

Pills do not remove fatigue. Non-prescription pills are illegal for drivers, and prescription medications should not be taken while on duty unless your doctor OKs it. Pills that keep you awake can be dangerous as they wear off.

It is against the law for a commercial driver to drink alcohol while on duty. Even if it were not illegal to drink and drive, alcohol is a downer and will put a driver to sleep. Though coffee may stimulate for a short period, it lets the driver down as it wears off. This increases the chances of falling asleep.

## The Cure for Fatigue

So what should you do if you feel fatigue coming on? In a word, SLEEP. Sleep is the best solution. There is no substitute.

Pull off the road. Be sure you stop in a safe, legal place. Secure the vehicle properly. Get comfortable. Napping over the steering wheel is usually not helpful. Try to lie down and rest. Take a short nap. 20-30 minutes is usually enough. Sometimes, though, a second nap is needed.

© 1997 Career Publishing Inc.

**TAKE SHORT BREAKS**

**Figure 26-6**

If short naps do not rest you enough, stop driving. Pull into a rest stop or motel. Get the rest you need! Depending on your schedule, you may have to call your supervisor. If you are afraid you will be fired if you fail to keep up with your schedule, remember, it is better to lose your job than your life. It is even better to lose your job than to risk major losses because you fell asleep at the wheel.

Other Aids: Air conditioning can help prevent fatigue. Keep the cab cool. Warm air can make you sleepy. Walk and stretch for a few minutes every so often.

## ILLNESS

A person should not be on the road if they are ill or have an injury that interferes with their driving ability. Conditions that should keep a driver off the road include:
- A heavy cold or allergy: these can cause drowsiness.
- A painful, badly sprained ankle: this will prevent full movement of the foot.

FMCSR 392.3 states it is illegal to drive when impaired. Fatigue and illness are included as conditions that limit alertness and the ability to drive.

## ALCOHOL

We all know that drinking and driving is a serious problem. Each year, thousands of people are killed in accidents where a driver had been drinking.

There are a number of false beliefs about the use of alcohol. A person who believes these myths may be more likely to misuse alcohol. A few of the myths follow.

| Myth | Truth |
|---|---|
| Alcohol increases mental and physical ability. | Nonsense. It decreases both. A person under the influence of alcohol usually thinks he or she is doing better than they really are. |
| Some people can drink without being affected. | Not true. Any person who drinks is affected by alcohol. Some persons may be slower to show the effects because of greater body weight or experience. |
| If you eat a lot before drinking, you will not get drunk. | Not true. Food will slow down the absorption of alcohol, but it will not prevent it. |
| Coffee and fresh air will help a drinker sober up. | Not true. Only time will help a drinker sober up. Other methods just do not work. |
| Stick with beer, it is not as strong as wine or whiskey. | False. There is the same amount of alcohol in a:<br>• 12 ounce glass of 5% beer.<br>• 5 ounce glass of 12% wine.<br>• 1-1/2 ounce shot of 80 proof liquor. |

**Figure 26-7**

As a truck driver you should know:
• How alcohol works in the human body
• How alcohol affects your driving ability
• Laws regarding the use of alcohol (FMCSR 392.5)
• Legal, financial, and safety risks of drinking and driving

**Figure 26-8**

## How Alcohol Works

When a person drinks alcohol, it is rapidly absorbed into the blood stream and carried directly to the brain where it affects judgment, inhibitions, vision, coordination, and bodily functions. Unlike food, the alcohol does not have to be digested before it is absorbed. The drinker can control the absorption rate by drinking slowly and spacing drinks. Having some food in the stomach will slow the absorption rate.

The drinker cannot control the rate of elimination. Most of the alcohol (about 90%) is removed by the liver at the rate of about one drink per hour.

Alcohol builds in the blood stream, because it is absorbed faster than the drinker can get rid of it. The amount of alcohol in the bloodstream is measured as a percentage and is called the Blood Alcohol Content (BAC).

The Blood Alcohol Content (BAC) is determined by the:
- Amount of alcohol drunk
- Time it took to drink it
- Weight of the drinker

**Figure 26-9**

The faster you drink, the more alcohol your bloodstream absorbs. The more alcohol there is in your bloodstream, the higher your BAC. If there is food in your stomach, it will affect the BAC because it slows the absorption rate.

**Alcohol and the Brain:** As the BAC builds up, the brain's functions are affected more and more. The first parts to be affected are the higher learning centers. These areas control judgment (common sense) and inhibition (control of your actions).

Muscle control, vision, and coordination are affected next. The drinker may feel he or she is performing very well when they are really out of control.

Finally, bodily functions are affected. The drinker may even pass out.

As a person sobers up, the effects of alcohol disappear in the reverse order. Judgment is restored last.

**Other factors that affect a drinker:** A person's mood, experience in drinking, tolerance of alcohol, and whether they are tired can affect the amount of influence alcohol will have on their body. If a person is angry or depressed, the alcohol may affect them more than usual.

### Effects of Alcohol as BAC Increases

| BAC | EFFECTS |
|---|---|
| .01-.04 | Judgment and Inhibitions Are Slightly Affected. Drinker Is More Relaxed, Sociable, Talkative. Some Risk if Drinker Drives. |
| .05-.09 | Judgment, Vision, and Coordination Are Affected. Behavior Changes. Drinker Has False Sense of Security. Serious Risk if Drinker Drives. |
| .10 and Over (Legal level of intoxication in most states.) | Judgment, Vision, and Coordination Are Seriously Affected. Drinker Is Not Able to Drive Safely Because of Dangerously Lessened Abilities. |

**Figure 26-10**

People who usually do not drink generally have a very low tolerance of alcohol. They tend to show the effects quickly. Experienced or heavy drinkers may have a high tolerance. They may not appear to be affected, but they really are. If a person is tired, the effects of alcohol are quickly obvious.

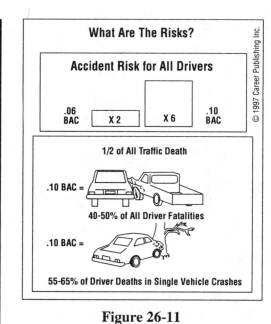

**Figure 26-11**

## Alcohol and Driving

Alcohol has bad effects on judgment, vision, coordination, and reaction time. All are critical when driving, so there is an increased danger if you drink. Driving at the wrong speed, loss of lane control, and dangerous passing often happen.

## Sobering Up

The body requires about one hour to get rid of each drink. If you have more than one drink per hour, alcohol builds up in your system. Time is needed to clear the alcohol out of your system. There is no shortcut.

## Alcohol and the Law

The alcohol regulations in FMCSR 392.5 state that:
- No person shall drink an intoxicating beverage or be under the influence of alcohol within four hours of going on duty.
- Driving while under the influence of alcohol is illegal.
- It is unlawful to drink any alcohol while on duty.
- A first violation can result in a one-year disqualification. A second violation can result in a lifetime disqualification.

Risks and penalties can be severe. Any time a vehicle is on the road, there is risk involved. If the driver is under the influence of alcohol, there is increased risk of accident and injury. Damage to the rig is more likely. Financial risks include fines and penalties, higher insurance rates, loss of license, jail sentence, and loss of job.

## DRUGS

Both legal and illegal drugs are common in our society. Many people take drugs under the direction of their doctors. Some individuals purchase over-the-counter substances that can affect behavior. Tractor-trailer drivers must not take any substance that can bring on drowsiness or affect driving.

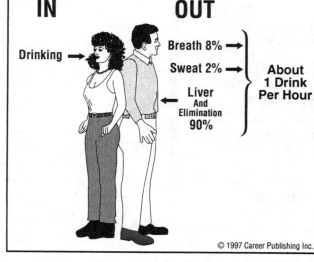

**Figure 26-12**

Every truck driver should realize that drugs, even legal ones prescribed by a doctor, can have bad effects on driving. One of the most common effects is drowsiness. Many cold and allergy over-the-counter remedies also have this side effect. Always check with your doctor before driving when using prescription drugs.

© 1997 Career Publishing Inc.

**Use of alcohol or drugs can lead to traffic accidents resulting in death or injury and property damage. It can also lead to arrest, fines, and jail sentences. Alcohol can mean the end of a person's driving career.**

Figure 26-13

Some pills that are legally used to treat overweight people and severe cases of depression are misused by drivers to stay awake. They are nicknamed bennies, pep pills, or co-pilots. They can increase alertness for a short period but can also cause headaches, dizziness and agitation. Even worse, they may hide fatigue and keep a person from knowing how tired they are. In other words, if you take drugs, you may think you are alert and driving well when you really are not.

Also, it is hard coming down from the pills. Fatigue is sometimes very severe, even overwhelming. A driver may have hallucinations, or visions, of something that is not there. Swerving into oncoming vehicles because of a vision is not uncommon.

## Illegal Drugs

Some prescription drugs are sold illegally at or near truck stops. Marijuana, cocaine, heroine, LSD, and other illegal drugs are also widely available. Any person who is capable of driving a big rig knows the danger of becoming involved with these drugs. Generally, people who buy drugs illegally have no idea what they are getting. Many times, they are contaminated, so the buyer cannot possibly know the side effects.

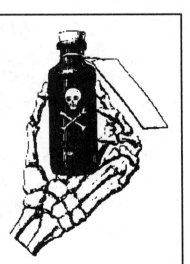

Figure 26-14

The best advice is to steer clear of drugs. Do not take chances. The risks are too great and the penalties too severe. Even if no accident occurs, the chance of losing your job, having a criminal record, being fined, or going to jail should be enough to cause any sensible trucker not to take illegal drugs.

**Figure 26-15**

## Legal Drugs

There are two kinds of legal drugs.
1. Prescription drugs
2. Over-the-counter drugs

Many people think anything prescribed by a doctor or sold over-the-counter at a pharmacy is safe to use. Some products, however, can be dangerous. This is especially true if they are used with other products.

**Prescription Drugs:** When a doctor prescribes a drug, always ask if there are any side effects. Ask if it is safe to drive when using the drug. Take only the amount prescribed and be aware that not all people react in the same way to drugs.

**Over-the-Counter Drugs:** Some products, like antihistamines used for colds and allergies, can make the user drowsy. Read all warning labels carefully. Some will say to avoid driving when using the product. If you are uncertain, check with a pharmacist or doctor.

## Drugs and Alcohol

Combining drugs and alcohol can be very dangerous. The best policy is not to mix any drug with alcohol.

Tranquilizers and alcohol can, when used together, have multiple effects on the user. The combined effect of one pill plus one drink can be rapid and unpredictable. Blackout, rapid intoxication, and even death are possible. Again, read all labels carefully. If taking the drug and alcohol are listed as a bad mix, do not mix them.

## The FMCSR and Drugs

FMCSR 392.4 prohibits driving while under the influence of any dangerous drug. These drugs include:
• Narcotics
• Morphine
• Heroin
• Codeine
• Amphetamines

The law does not prohibit possession and use of prescription drugs if a doctor has advised that it will not affect driving.

## Drug Testing

As of January 1, 1996, all truck drivers must be in a drug testing program.

### Summary — Drugs and Alcohol

• A professional driver is a safe driver.
• Anything that affects driving ability must not be used when driving.
• A driver who uses alcohol or drugs may be sued if an accident occurs.
• The driver's company can also be sued.
• A driver that uses drugs or alcohol can lose his or her job, reputation, and chance of future employment.

# HAZARDS TO SAFETY

The purpose of this lesson is to review common safety hazards found in the trucking world. The need for safety equipment and safe practices while performing non-driving parts of the job will also be covered. This section will deal with safe dress, proper equipment, danger zones, falling hazards, lifting, roadside emergencies, and avoiding crime.

Many accidents and injuries happen while the trucker is working around the vehicle or with cargo. These non-driving accidents can be costly in a number of ways. They can even put the driver out of work because of an injury.

## Safety Dress and Proper Equipment

Dressing properly for the job requires that the body be covered. Shorts and T-shirts are not enough. Heavy denims offer the best protection. In cold weather, wear warm clothes.

**Protect Your Hands:** Many hand injuries occur to truckers each year because there are so many hazards. Some of these hazards include:
- Sharp steel bands used to tie boxes and crates
- Nails, broken glass, and pointed wire
- Irritating or corrosive chemicals

Avoid wearing jewelry or rings because they can get snagged and cause serious injuries. Always wear gloves when handling cargo. Selecting the right gloves is important:
- Gloves should have a good gripping surface.
- Hazardous materials or wastes usually require special gloves. Ordinary gloves may trap corrosives. Rubber or latex gloves do not.

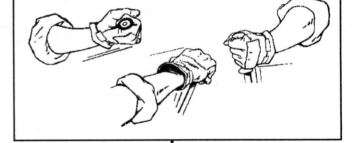

**Figure 26-16**

**Protect Your Eyes:** If you wear glasses, make sure they are shatterproof. Wear sunglasses to protect your eyes from glare. Be sure they are high quality and will filter out infrared rays. Protective goggles or a face shield are needed with some cargo. For example, goggles will protect your eyes when dealing with dust, flour, or cinders.

**Protect Your Feet:** Safety shoes protect your feet from falling objects. Steel-tipped shoes or work boots are best and required by some trucking companies. Do not wear sandals or tennis shoes.

## Special Equipment

Some circumstances require special equipment. Special cargo like hazardous material or waste may mean you will need special equipment for protection. Find out what is needed and then use it properly. The special equipment needed may include:
- Hard hats to protect your head from chains and falling cargo at construction and delivery sites.
- Respirators to prevent being overcome by fumes when handling chemical loads, and liquified chemicals. Some chemical loads require a self-contained breather (air supply). Find out what is needed. Take nothing for granted.

- Splash aprons to prevent liquids from splashing on your skin and causing burns.
- Goggles or a face shield to prevent severe eye damage from flying particles. Chemical face shields that have a splash guard may be needed for some acids or dangerous chemicals. Do not wear contact lenses. Fumes can get trapped under them and cause blindness.

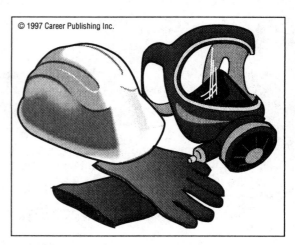

**Figure 26-17**

- Dust masks to prevent respiratory problems when handling dry chemicals or similar loads. Some companies require drivers to be clean shaven with no facial hair so dust masks and face shields will fit tightly.
- Shin guards that have heavy metal plates to protect the front of the leg and tips of the shoes from rolling steel bars.
- Special coveralls to protect the body from corrosives and other hazardous materials.
- Gas masks to protect from poisonous gases and other hazardous materials.

## Danger Zones

There are many hazards when you work around a tractor-trailer or with cargo. A driver can be seriously injured if he or she falls, trips, or gets bumped. A driver must use care when jumping down from the cab or trailer. Most accidents in the vehicle and cargo danger zones can be avoided if the driver is aware of the possible dangers and is not careless. Using common sense is the best way to prevent these accidents.

Use great care when you are in the following five areas.
1. Cab
2. Coupling and uncoupling area
3. Rear end of the trailer
4. Cargo area
5. Around the vehicle

You also must be very careful when you are cleaning the windshield.

## The Cab

The height of the cab presents the greatest danger to the driver. Some cabs do not have handholds or steps. If there are handholds or steps, they may be slippery from fuel, oil, water, ice, or snow.

When getting in or out of the cab, look at the surfaces. Always enter and exit the cab facing the inside of the cab area. Smooth surfaces will be more slippery than ribbed surfaces. Be particularly careful of ice, grease, or oil on the surface or on your shoes. Check for grease or oil on your gloves. Then get a good hand grip.

Always keep a 3-point contact with the vehicle when climbing into or out of the rig. A 3-point contact means at least two hands and one foot or two feet and one hand in contact with the vehicle at all times. Do not jump down from the cab. Debris or a pothole could be in the landing area. Watch for stones. They too can cause you to sprain or turn your ankle.

Other injuries that can happen in and around the cab include:

- Injury from a falling hood while you are looking at, or working on, the engine. Be sure the hood (or raised cab in cab-over-engine) is properly secured and the safety locks or pins are in place.
- Thumb injuries from the steering wheel can occur if the wheel is not gripped properly. The hands should be on the outer edge in the 3:00 and 9:00 positions. If the truck hits a pothole or obstacle, the steering wheel can spin out of control. If the thumbs are between the spokes, they may be broken. The driver can then lose control of the vehicle.

**Getting In and Out of Cab Safely**

**Climb in Safely**
- **Look Before Climbing**
- **Watch for Slippery Surfaces, Gloves, Boots**
- **Use 3-Point Contact**

**Get Out Safely**
- **Do Not Jump Out of Cab**

© 1997 Career Publishing Inc.

**Figure 26-18**

© 1997 Career Publishing Inc.

**Danger Areas**

**Figure 26-19**

## Coupling and Uncoupling Area

The coupling/uncoupling area may be dangerous because of grease and oil. If you have to stand on the vehicle to connect the air lines or electric cables, be careful of slippery surfaces such as the fuel tank or battery box. These are especially dangerous when they are wet or covered with ice, oil, or grease. If possible, use surfaces that have been treated with a rough material or have ribbed plates. Pulling the release latch handle during coupling or uncoupling is dangerous because you may be thrown off balance and injure your back.

## Rear of the Trailer

Open and close the swinging cargo door with great care. If you do not, you may be injured or damage the freight. When you open the door, remember the cargo may have moved and be resting against it. If it is, the door will pop open from the force of the cargo as soon as the latch is released. If that happens, you could be knocked down and have cargo fall on top of you. Be careful when it is windy. The doors can break your fingers and hands, or knock you down.

Many drivers have been hurt closing the door because they stood on the trailer deck, grabbed the strap, and jumped to the ground. If the strap breaks or the driver loses hold of it, he or she may fall to the ground. If you add a length to the strap, you can pull it down while standinging on the ground.

The power lift or elevating tailgate used for heavy cargo is another source of danger. Use common sense and care when you load or unload, and you will prevent serious problems. Keep your hands, feet, and cargo from the shearing, or pinching, areas. When loading with a liftgate, be sure the cargo is secure and will not fall off.

Other dangers at the rear of the trailer include:
- Slippery surface: you may slip and fall even if the surface is not slippery if your shoes have a slick sole or slippery substance on them.
- No handhold
- Nails or splinters in the trailer floor: these can hurt the driver when he or she gets off.

Always use the proper handholds and steps when they are available. Also, wear gloves when getting off so you will not hurt your hands. Never jump down from a trailer.

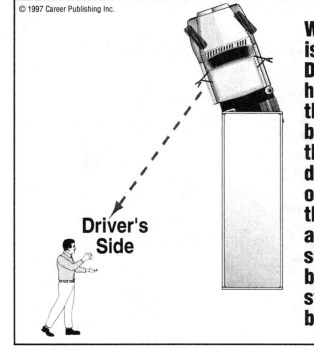

© 1997 Career Publishing Inc.

Driver's Side

**Walking backward is very dangerous. Drivers have been hurt or killed when they were pinned between the rear of the trailer and the dock while guiding others. Stand off to the side when you are guiding someone who is backing up. Never stand directly behind the trailer.**

**Figure 26-20**

## Cargo Area

Various types of trailers and cargoes have different kinds of hazards. For instance, working with a tanker sometimes requires climbing to the top to hook or unhook dome covers. Flatbeds have no sides, so you can fall off while tying down the cargo. Open top vans mean you may have to climb up the side to tie down the tarp cover.

Working inside a van is dangerous for many reasons.
• You may have to climb in, over, and around cargo to find a piece that is to be unloaded.
• You can be bruised or cut from nails or broken glass.
• You can bump into the sharp edges of cargo.
• Cargo can fall on you when you are climbing around.

## Around the Vehicle

Damaged rigs can cause injury. Tears in the trailer skin and unrepaired accident damage to the fenders, bumpers, or hood can cut if you rub against or bump into them.

When working at night, a flashlight is a must. You cannot possibly couple a rig or do a pre-trip inspection without light.

Working under the rig is always dangerous. Make sure the vehicle cannot roll. Use wheel chocks when necessary. Be sure, too, that the keys are in your pocket. Then, no one can hop in the rig and move it while you are underneath.

## Cleaning Windshields

If possible, use an extension handle on the squeegee. Then you can stand on the ground instead of having to climb onto the tractor when you clean the windshield. If you must climb up to clean it, be careful of slippery surfaces. Keep both feet and one hand securely on the vehicle while cleaning the windshield.

## Lifting

Many injuries occur when objects are not lifted properly or safely. All cargo handlers need to know how to safely and correctly lift to avoid back injury, hernia, or injuries to their hands or feet.

**Figure 26-21**

The first rule in lifting is:
• Do not try to lift something if it is too heavy or not in a position to be moved. Get someone else to help you or use mechanical assistance.

Also, before lifting anything, remember to protect your hands and feet.

---

### Eight Steps to Safe Lifting

1. Feet should be parted - one alongside and one behind the object.
2. Turn your forward foot in the direction of movement.
3. Keep your back straight.
4. Tuck in your chin.
5. Grip the object with your whole hand.
6. Tuck in your elbows and arms.
7. Put your body weight directly over your feet.
8. Avoid twisting – a common cause of back injuries.

---

To protect your hands, remember:
- A good grip is a must for safe lifting.
- To use gloves that will help with the grip and protect your hands.
- To guard against pinching your hands in the cargo when lifting.

Most foot injuries result from dropped cargo. To protect your feet, be sure to:

- Wear safety shoes.
- Keep your feet clear of the object being lifted in case it drops.
- Get a good grip and lift properly. This will reduce the chance of dropping the cargo.

## Lifting with Others

When two or more persons lift cargo, they must work together. They should all use the basic safe lifting techniques and safety precautions. Make sure each person has a good grip and can handle their share of the load. An unbalanced load is more likely to be dropped. If one person cannot hold up his or her share of the load, stop lifting and ease the item down. If you continue to lift, the load may drop and injure someone. And remember, be alert. Watch your fellow workers.

To safely lift cargo as a group, follow these guidelines.
- Get a comfortable hold on the object.
- Do not try to carry it too high.
- Carry freight the shortest distance possible.
- Talk to your partners. Let them know when you are going to put your end down. Never drop your end without warning!.
- Choose the route before you start. Never climb over freight, cars, etc.
- If two people are carrying an object, one may have to back up. Do not force this person to move too fast. Let them set the pace.
- Guide the person who is backing because they cannot see where they are going. Then follow their path.
- Beware of horse play. It can cause tragedy.
- Keep your back as straight as possible.
- Lift the load with your legs.

## ROADSIDE EMERGENCIES

When you must stop for an emergency, be careful. How, where, and under what conditions you stop can make the difference between safety and serious problems.

There is great danger of being rear-ended if you park on the shoulder of the road. Pull off the road as far as possible.

- Look for a truck stop or rest area.
- Be especially alert when there is no breakdown lane or adequate area to stop. Rural roads and city streets do not have breakdown lanes.

© 1997 Career Publishing Inc.

**Figure 26-22**

Check before stopping. Be particularly careful in the dark when you cannot see the surface. Be sure the surface can support the rig. During or after a heavy rain or snow, a road shoulder may be too soft to support it. A rig pulled onto a soft shoulder may get stuck or even roll over.

## Stopping on Slippery Hills

Many drivers have been injured while checking a vehicle that is stuck on an icy or slippery hill or was spinning its wheels. Even after properly securing the vehicle (transmission in gear, emergency brake set, wheels chocked), there is danger. A rig can slide downhill and roll over the driver. For example, on a very slippery surface, both the wheels and the chocks may slide.

## Get Out of the Cab Safely

Many drivers who have stopped properly in an emergency get hurt while leaving the cab. Do not jump out of the cab. Do not get out on the driver's side into the path of oncoming traffic. Remember, if you are not in a breakdown lane, there is great danger. Anything you do, such as jumping out, can increase the danger. Turn on the emergency flashers. After you get out of the cab, put out flares or triangles to warn other drivers of a problem.

## Minor Repairs and Maintenance

Follow the guidelines for getting out of the cab safely when you install chains, change a tire, or make other roadside repairs. You should also:
- Make sure you are complying with company policies.
- Face oncoming traffic.
- Be especially alert in wet or icy weather.

**Cold Metal:** When you stop to check your rig in freezing weather, your hands can freeze to cold metal. You may even rip your skin when you try to move them. Wear gloves to prevent this problem.

**Hot Tires:** You can be badly burned when checking hot tires. First, feel the heat without touching the tire, and then slowly move your hand closer to the tire to touch it. Touching the sidewalls or tread with the palm of your hand can burn you before you can pull away your hand. Use the back of your hand. Your reflexes will pull away your hand more quickly in that position if the tire is too hot.

**Live Wires:** Bad storms sometimes knock down live electrical wires. They are very dangerous. If they land on your rig, do not try to get out of the cab. Do not move around in the cab or touch anything you are not already in contact with. Sit and wait for someone else to help. If you have a CB, radio for help.

**Figure 26-23**

## Avoiding Crime

In addition to driving hazards, truck drivers must be aware of and know how to avoid other problems. Among the other hazards you face are hijacking and robbery. You can best avoid them by knowing and following company policy. Be aware of crime areas and know which types of cargo are more likely to be targets.

Protect your truck by parking and securing it safely in a well lighted area or rest stop. Never leave the truck unattended while the motor is running. Always close and lock all the doors when you leave. Drivers who leave their vehicles unsecured can be regarded as accomplices to crime and prosecuted.

Padlock all the doors of the trailer or van to protect the cargo. Drop a trailer only in a secure area. Use a kingpin lock to secure it. Do not discuss your cargo or flash the shipping papers when you are carrying high value cargo.

Do not set yourself up for crime. Do not carry a lot of cash. Stay away from dangerous areas. If something looks suspicious, use the CB radio to call for help.

Do not pick up hitchhikers. It is illegal (FMCSR) and asking for trouble. Finally, do not carry a gun. It is illegal without a permit, and a permit is valid only in the state in which it was issued.

## CAUSES OF ACCIDENTS

Most over-the-road accidents are preventable. There are three main causes of traffic accidents. They are:
1. Vehicle defects
2. Road or weather conditions
3. Driver error

Of the three, driver error is the main cause.

### Vehicle Defects

Mechanical defects, poor maintenance, vehicle abuse, and poor inspections are common causes of accidents. Parts that are failing or in danger of failing often do so while the driver is on the road. Parts can also fail because they have been abused. Bad parts that are overlooked when the driver is inspecting the rig can let him or her down out on a run. Overloaded or improperly loaded vehicles can and do also lead to accidents.

## Road or Weather Conditions

Slippery roads, poor visibility, lack of light (especially at dusk or dawn) and headlight glare can lead to accidents. Accidents can also be caused by poorly designed or maintained roads and signals. Examples are potholes, stop signs hidden by branches, and exit ramps that are too sharp for heavy duty vehicles.

## Driver Error

The major cause of accidents is driver error. Stress, both on-duty and off-duty, can lead to driver error. Staying in good condition is the responsibility of every professional driver.

The driver is the only person who can prevent an accident. By being aware of what is going on around the rig, thinking ahead, and using good judgment,

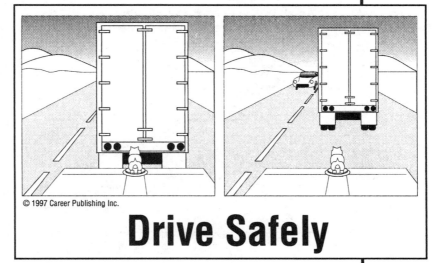

© 1997 Career Publishing Inc.

**Drive Safely**

**Figure 26-24**

the driver can adjust to problems before they happen. Statistics show that 80-90% of accidents involve one or more errors by the driver.

A driver's errors are usually caused by one or more underlying causes.
- Not being aware of what is happening
- Thinking of other things instead of the job at hand
- Driving while impaired (fatigued, ill, under medication, or under the influence of alcohol or drugs)
- Trying to make up lost time
- Emotional immaturity (showing off, being aggressive)
- Lack of technical knowledge of the vehicle
- Lack of driver training
- Failing to recognize personal limitations

Driving a tractor-trailer is a full-time job that takes 100% of the driver's attention at all times. Nobody can drive a problem and a rig at the same time. It is up to the driver to park either the problem or the rig.

## ON-DUTY AND OFF-DUTY JOB STRESS

Both the stresses of living and the job are often underlying causes for drivers' errors. Whatever the source, stress leads to fatigue, lack of attention, nervousness, poor physical and mental habits, and emotional breakdowns. This, in turn, leads to errors by drivers, which may cause accidents.

**Job Related Stress:** Normal job demands stress the driver physically, mentally, and emotionally. Any added stress increases the chance for driver error.

Among job conditions that can lead to physical, mental, and emotional fatigue are:
- Schedules that are always changing
- Frequent short notices to report for a run
- Economic pressures
- Delays at the terminal and enroute
- Poor lay-over conditions
- Physical demands of the job
- Over-the-road vibration
- Administrative duties

**Figure 26-25**

**Changing Schedules and Short Notices:** New drivers may have to fill in on short notice for sick or vacationing drivers or for unexpected runs. This can result in lack of sleep and not being able to look after personal affairs. This creates worry.

**Economic Pressures:** Demands to meet the schedule or lose their job lead to anxiety. Warning letters make matters worse. Trying to get in an extra trip during the week means driving longer hours, driving faster, and having less time off. Any existing physical or mental condition will get worse.

**Delays:** Delays occur at the terminal waiting to be loaded or dispatched. Delays enroute lead to hasty loading and unloading, driving too fast, and tailgating. The final result is added physical, mental, and emotional stress.

**Poor Lay-Over Conditions:** Noisy, uncomfortable hotels or truck stops often keep a driver from resting, relaxing, and eating properly. Loneliness encourages poor health habits. Poor health habits include:
- Not getting enough sleep
- Poor meals
- Too much drinking
- Watching TV instead of resting
- Playing pinball and video games instead of sleeping

## PHYSICAL DEMANDS OF THE JOB

Being a truck driver is a very demanding job. The driver needs to be in good physical condition. Some of the demands, which can be very tiring, are:
- The need to always pay attention to what is going on around him or her (looking and listening)
- Sitting up and steering an oversize wheel for long periods: a driver can become quite tired and uncomfortable as a result.
- Having to pay attention to the details of shifting, backing, and parking
- Non-driving tasks such as inspecting the rig, handling cargo, and coupling and uncoupling the rig
- Loading and unloading cargo

## Over-the-Road Vibration

Road vibration can drain a driver's physical strength and bring on physical problems. Noise levels can dull the driver's mind, making him or her feel very tired. Although today's trucks are more comfortable than ever before, they can still be noisier and rougher riding than cars, particularly on long-distance runs.

## Administrative Duties

Federal, state, local, company, and union rules change often. Such changes create paperwork such as filling out logs, trip reports, shipping papers, mileage reports, keeping track of tolls, etc.

## Off-Duty Causes

Poor health habits such as not eating the right foods, little or no exercise, and not enough rest can all add to a driver's stress level. Even well-trained, experienced, and physically fit drivers are affected by personal problems. Worrying about what is happening also adds to stress and can make a driver perform badly.

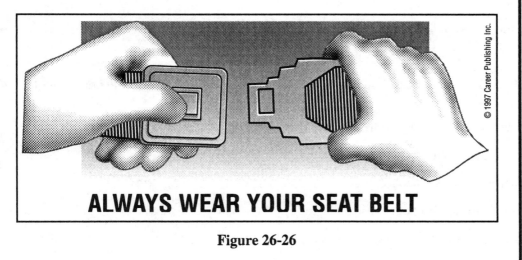

**Figure 26-26**

## SUMMARY

Anything that interferes with a driver's physical, mental, or emotional state can lead to poor performance. You have learned that drivers must stay away from drugs and use alcohol wisely. A driver must also stay physically fit and eat the right foods. Trying to avoid the causes of stress also helps a driver do a better job.

## KEY WORDS

**Blood Alcohol Content (BAC):** The amount of alcohol in the bloodstream. Determines the level of intoxication.

**Fatigue:** Being very tired from overwork, stress, or lack of sleep.

# LEARNING ACTIVITIES

## True-False Questions

If the question is true, circle the T. If the question is false, circle the F.

T   F   1.   Good vision is one of the most important physical requirements for drivers.

T   F   2.   Although poor diet can cause a number of long-range physical problems, it has little or no short-term effect.

T   F   3.   Exercise, both on and off the job, is helpful for tractor-trailer drivers.

T   F   4.   Fatigue is the underlying cause of many accidents in the trucking industry.

T   F   5.   A fatigued driver loses some ability to judge and react well.

T   F   6.   Even though fatigue makes you physically weary, it does not cause drowsiness.

T   F   7.   Stress increases the chances of fatigue.

T   F   8.   The best way to deal with fatigue is to prevent it.

T   F   9.   In dealing with fatigue, knowing what not to do is as important as knowing what to do.

T   F   10.   Bringing fresh air into the cab is a sure way to keep from falling asleep.

T   F   11.   After you eat, the body's circulatory system works hard to digest food and makes the brain want to sleep or rest.

T   F   12.   Short 20-30 minute naps can relieve a driver's need for sleep.

T   F   13.   Some people can drink alcohol and not be affected.

T   F   14.   If you eat a lot before drinking alcohol, you will not get drunk.

T   F   15.   Neither coffee nor fresh air will help a drinker sober up.

T   F   16.   A few beers affect a person in the same way as a few shots of whiskey.

T   F   17.   Like food, alcohol must be digested before it can be absorbed into the blood stream.

T   F   18.   Alcohol builds in the blood stream when it is absorbed faster than the drinker can get rid of it.

T   F   19.   The BAC is determined by the amount of alcohol consumed, the time it took to drink it, and the weight of the drinker.

T   F   20.   The first parts of the brain affected by alcohol are those that control judgment and inhibitions.

T   F   21.   After a few drinks, a person is usually more relaxed and can control his or her muscles better.

T   F   22.   A person's mood can make a difference in how much effect alcohol will have.

T   F   23.   The body requires about one hour to eliminate the alcohol in one drink.

T   F   24.   Time is the key to clearing the system of alcohol.

T   F   25.   FMCSR regulations say that no person shall drink any intoxicating beverage or be under the influence of alcohol within four hours of going on duty.

T  F  26.  Bennies and pep pills should be used by drivers to help them stay awake.

T  F  27.  If an item is sold over-the-counter, it is sure to be safe because pharmacies and drug stores are so carefully regulated.

T  F  28.  When a doctor prescribes a drug, you should ask if there are any side effects.

T  F  29.  Pep pills and bennies can increase alertness for only a short period of time and then may bring on fatigue.

T  F  30.  Drugs and alcohol should not be mixed.

T  F  31.  When used together, tranquilizers and alcohol can multiply their normal effect on the user.

T  F  32.  Many accidents and injuries happen while the trucker is working around the rig or with cargo.

T  F  33.  The height of the cab can be a danger to the driver.

T  F  34.  When getting in or getting out of the cab, a driver is safe as long as both feet are firmly planted on a secure surface.

T  F  35.  The coupling/uncoupling area can be dangerous because of grease and oil.

T  F  36.  When pulling down the back door of the trailer, many drivers have been injured because they grab for the strap and jump to the ground.

T  F  37.  Different types of trailers and cargoes present different kinds of hazards.

T  F  38.  One reason it is dangerous to work inside a van is because cargo can fall on a person who is climbing around.

T  F  39.  When one person feels the load is too heavy, he or she should drop it quickly to avoid serious back injury.

T  F  40.  When there is an emergency, how, where, and under what conditions you stop can make the difference between safety and serious problems.

T  F  41.  When checking tires for overheating, you should use the palm of the hand because it is more sensitive to heat levels.

T  F  42.  If live wires fall on your rig, you should get out of and away from the rig.

T  F  43.  You can best avoid hijacking and robbery by knowing and following company policy.

T  F  44.  Drivers who leave their rigs unsecured can be regarded as accomplices to crime and prosecuted.

T  F  45.  Driver error is the main cause of accidents.

T  F  46.  Job related stress can increase chances for driver error.

T  F  47.  Poor health habits can increase stress levels and create problems for the driver.

# Chapter Twenty-Seven
# TRIP PLANNING

**Types of Runs • Local Operations • Peddle Runs • Shuttle Operations • Long-Distance Transport • Route Selection • Special Situations • Map Reading Calculating Travel Time • Fuel Consumption • Keeping Records • Vehicle Licensing Permits • Size and Weight Limits • Enforcement • Over-The-Road**

**FROM NOW ON,**

**ONLY THE BEST WILL DRIVE**

# OBJECTIVES

When you have mastered this chapter, you will be able to:

- Use a motor carrier road atlas

- Explain how to locate the starting point and destination of a trip on a map

- Plan trip routes

- Explain how to choose alternate routes

- Show how to estimate mileage and travel time

- Explain how to obtain the necessary permits

- Describe the types of vehicles and cargos most likely to have routing restrictions or special requirements

- Explain where to get information about special requirements

- Describe how to plan for personal needs and expense money for trips

- Describe the different types of enforcement procedures

## CHAPTER TWENTY-SEVEN

# TRIP PLANNING

## INTRODUCTION

As well as driving a rig safely, the driver must be able to plan trips. He or she must be able to read and understand maps, know the general size and weight laws, and registration and fuel tax requirements. The driver must also be aware there are special regulations to be followed when planning a trip.

The driver must understand how important it is to keep accurate records. The carrier may need the records to show they have complied with the regulations for hours of service, cargo, fuel tax payments, and registration fees.

A driver should be able to estimate:
• Mileage from point of origin to destination
• Trip time
• Fuel requirements
• Personal financial needs

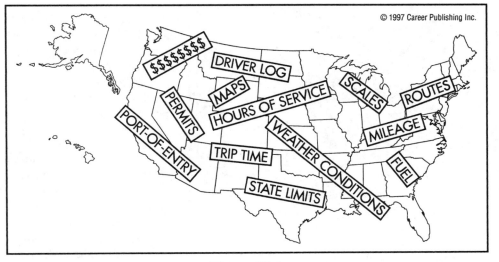

© 1997 Career Publishing Inc.

**Figure 27-1**

The driver may or may not be involved with these aspects of trip planning. Companies differ in what they require of the driver. It depends on the type of operation, the size and type of carrier, length of haul, territory covered, and so on.

This chapter will help you understand what to do when you are planning a trip. Knowing how to plan well for a trip will help you be a more responsible driver.

## TYPES OF TRUCK RUNS

This section is intended to give you an idea of the types of runs made in the trucking industry, and what they are like. Some carriers operate only a single type of run. Other carriers operate many types. The driver may or may not have a choice of the type of run assigned.

Many times, the driver will be given specific instructions about which routes are to be used. These instructions must be followed. In other cases, company management specifies the use of a particular route because other routes have been checked, and this one is the best. Going off an assigned route without a very good reason is a serious violation of company rules and may cause the driver to be disciplined.

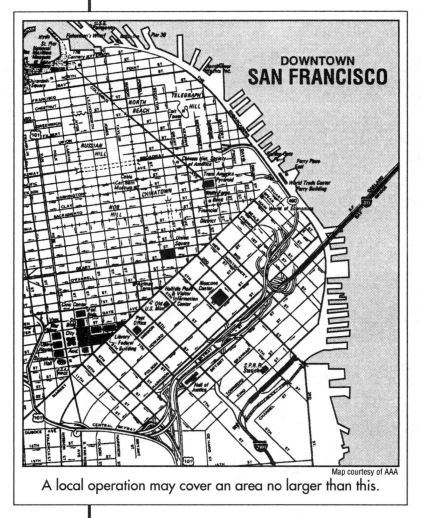

A local operation may cover an area no larger than this.

**Figure 27-2**

## Local Operations

**Local Pickup & Delivery:** In typical local pickup and delivery operations, the driver operates in and around cities. He or she will usually be delivering freight to its final destination (the consignee), and picking up freight from shippers. A local operation may represent the final step in delivering freight to its destination, after it has been brought into the area by a line-haul operation. It may also pick up freight that will be transported to a distant destination by another carrier. In other local operations, freight is moved between nearby points of origin and destinations.

The local driver must know the street system well, so pickups and deliveries can be made in the safest, quickest way. The driver must also know the local traffic patterns in order to avoid areas of congestion and delay whenever possible.

**Peddle Run:** This is a type of local pickup and delivery operation. Usually freight is hauled from the terminal to separate destinations in the nearby area. Peddle run drivers also pick up freight along the route and bring it back to the terminal. Because of frequent changes in the points to be served, drivers in this type of service may be asked to select their routes. Drivers should know how to select the safest and quickest route for each trip.

**Shuttle Operations:** In shuttle operations, some drivers move either empty or loaded trailers between nearby points such as terminals to customer, drop yards to customer, rail heads to customer, and vice-versa. The number of trailers a driver moves during a single driving period will depend on the distances involved.

## Long-Distance Transport

Long-distance trucking involves the transport of cargo from a point of origin to one or more distant destinations. Several types of operations fall within the general classification of a long-distance operation. In some cases, a long-distance driver may

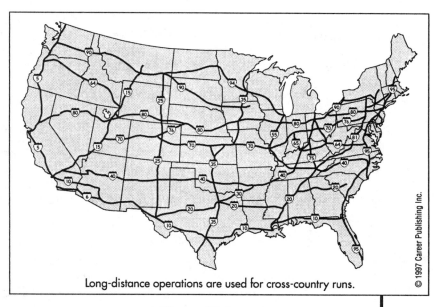

Long-distance operations are used for cross-country runs.

**Figure 27-3**

return to the home terminal at the end of about 10 hours of driving. In other cases, a driver may be on the road two days or more at a time. Brief descriptions of several types of long-distance operations follow.

**Regular Run**: The driver operates between the same points on each trip and may or may not have a regular starting and finishing time for each period of driving. Today, very few drivers have regular runs.

**Open Dispatch**: The driver goes from the point of origin to a distant point. Depending on the driving time and the need to comply with hours of service limits, the driver may take another unit to an additional destination. After driving for 10 hours, the driver must rest. When the driver can legally drive again, he or she may be given a run heading toward the home terminal or may be dispatched to another point. The cycle may be repeated for several days before the driver returns home.

**Regular Route**: A regular route refers to line-haul transport between given origins and destinations using assigned highways. Most less-than truckload fleets are regular route operations.

**Irregular Route**: An irregular route describes long-distance transport between a combination of origin and destination points using any suitable route. It is also referred to over-the-road trucking. Most truckload fleets are irregular route carriers. It is in this type of operation that the driver is most likely to be involved in selecting a route, but even in irregular route operations, management may have set the routes to be used by drivers. This is most likely to happen between the origins and destinations that are served most often. A driver must comply with the set routes.

**Relay Runs**: A relay run refers to a trip in which a driver drives for 10 hours and then goes off-duty as prescribed by the hours of service laws. Another driver takes the unit on to the next point. This cycle may be repeated several times as the truck is driven from origin to final destination by several different drivers.

**Meet and Turn**: Meet and turn is a type of relay run in which two drivers start toward each other from different points and meet at a chosen mid-point. At the meeting place, the drivers exchange complete units or only trailers. Then each driver goes back to his or her starting point.

**Turn-around**: In a turn-around run, a driver travels for about 5 hours to a destination and then returns to his or her home terminal. At the turn-around point, the driver may switch units or trailers for the return trip.

**Roll and Rest**: A single driver takes the truck from origin to destination in a roll and rest operation. At the end of each period of 10 hours of driving, the driver stops in a suitable location for the required off-duty time. The driver must plan the trip so there are suitable rest facilities at the intervals required by the hours of service regs.

**Sleeper Operations**: The driver of a rig that has a sleeper berth can accumulate the required off-duty time in two periods as long as neither period is less than 2 hours. To meet the requirements, the driver must use the sleeper berth. This is a special provision of the hours of service regulations. Sleeper operations may use a single driver or a two-driver team.

A single driver with a sleeper cab saves lodging costs on the road. If the driver arrives early at an origin or destination, having a sleeper berth can let him or her get the required rest while waiting to load or unload.

Sleeper teams are also used when speedy service requires the unit to be on the road as much as possible, or a second driver is needed for other reasons. In team operations, drivers usually exchange duties every 4-5 hours so one driver can rest while the other drives.

**Figure 27-4**

## ROUTE SELECTION

There are many types of highways. Selecting the right type often depends on how well you can read a map. Each type of highway is coded on a map. If you understand this code, you will be able to know what is an Interstate highway, what is a state highway, or what is only a country road. The types of highways are described in the following section. They are listed in the order of preference of use.

- Interstate routes
- Toll roads
- U.S. Numbered routes
- State Primary routes
- Other streets and highways

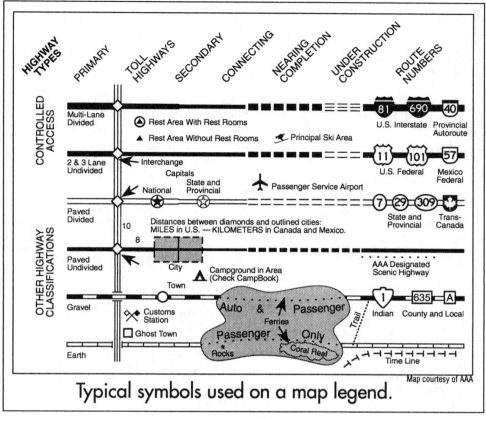

Typical symbols used on a map legend.

**Figure 27-5**

**Interstate Routes**: These routes are usually preferred because they separate opposing traffic, have limited access, and bypass many small communities. Although they are the safest type of highway, drivers must be aware that these highways can be snarled up by bad weather or traffic congestion, especially in urban areas. In selecting the Interstates, drivers should note other available routes in case of a major traffic problem on the Interstate.

**Toll Roads**: Except for having to pay a toll, these roads are similar to the Interstates. In many states, toll roads are part of the Interstate system. Whether to use a toll road must be based on many factors in addition to cost. Drivers should take into consideration:

- Differences in time and distance over alternative routes
- Terrain
- Road conditions
- The need to go through built-up areas
- The amount of stop-and-go driving
- Wear and tear on the equipment
- Fuel usage

**U.S. Numbered Routes**: These are the major through-routes. Those that parallel the Interstates may be good alternatives in case of delays on the Interstate.

**State Primary Routes**: Within each state, these are the major routes. In some instances, a state primary route may be as good as or even better than a nearby U.S. Numbered Highway.

**Other Streets and Highways**: Drivers will have to use other types of roads to reach a loading or unloading point. In general, choose county roads or other routes designated by number or letter. These are the through routes set by the local authorities and are generally better able than other local streets to safely handle truck traffic.

A driver must use extreme care when driving on local streets that often were not designed for truck traffic. Drivers should avoid using side streets because they may have hazards such as low clearances, unsafe railroad crossings, poor road surfaces, and sharp turns and local restrictions.

## Special Situations

It is not possible to foresee every problem a driver may encounter. Drivers must learn to approach new situations carefully and use common sense. Some of the special situations you may find are:
- Local truck routes
- Posted bridges
- Restricted routes

**Local truck routes**: Many cities and towns have designated routes for trucks. They are not always marked well. If you do not stay on the route, you may get a ticket.

**Posted bridges**: Many bridges have special weight restrictions. Do not cross a bridge if your rig's weight is more than the weight that is posted. Some fines are as much as $10,000.

Figure 27-6

**Restricted routes**: One reason for prohibiting trucks on some roads is a past history of accidents. Always heed posted prohibitions, even if it means driving on to a point where you can obtain information. If you do drive on the road, you may get a ticket, be faced with a hazardous condition, or be unable to avoid an accident.

There are many ways to get the information or help you need. Here are some suggestions:
- Use a CB. Talk to other truck drivers or local residents about the conditions.
- If you are near a destination, stop and call the shipper or consignee for directions.
- Stop and make inquiries about the local conditions at truck stops, service stations, firehouses, police stations, or other locations where there may be people who know the area.
- Look in a road atlas. Many have information on restricted routes, low clearances, etc.

# MAP READING

Being able to read maps is important to the professional truck driver. Sooner or later, the driver will have to locate unfamiliar pickup and delivery points. Maps are a good investment because they offer the driver a chance to save time and miles. There are several types of maps.
- Local or area map
- State map
- U. S. map
- Atlas

You may obtain maps from several sources.
- Bookstores
- Drug stores
- Discount stores
- Auto Clubs
- Filling stations
- Truck stops

Truck stops are the best place to get special atlases just for truckers. These have lots of extra information on restricted routes, weigh stations, etc.

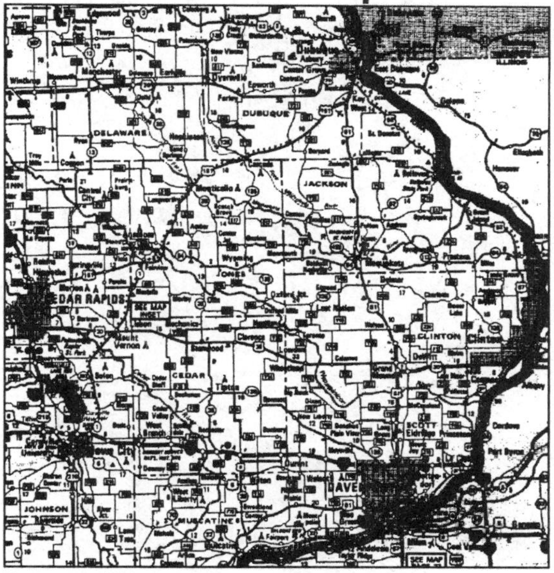

Map courtesy of AAA

## A portion of a state map.

**Figure 27-7**

**Local or area map:** A local or area map is very useful for the local driver because it will show local streets (see Figure 27-2 on page 27.4). You can get them in bookstores and in many drug stores and filling stations. Some show a single city, while other types may show one or two counties or a region. Because of the rapid growth in many urban areas, the driver should plan to obtain an updated map at least every year.

**State map:** Often a free state map is available at information centers along the Interstates. They are also for sale at other locations. When considering the purchase of a map, a driver should remember maps covering several states or an entire region may not show the minor roads the driver will need to reach some points.

**Atlas**: A driver who expects to cover a large territory should consider purchasing a trucking atlas. The atlas contains maps of all the states, the Canadian Provinces and Mexico (in some cases), and maps of major cities.

Atlases have been developed to meet the needs of the professional truck driver. In addition to state, city and area maps, these special atlases may include information about:

- The location of permanent scales
- Low underpasses
- Size and weight limits
- Fuel taxes
- Designated Routes for the operation of twin-trailers and 53/102 semitrailers
- State laws for access to the Designated Highway System

The following pointers will help you when reading a map.

- In most cases, **North** is at the top of the map. Often it is also indicated by an arrow symbol with the letter N or a symbol showing all four points of the compass. In some cases, a map of a small area may be printed with North to one side. North will always be shown by some symbol.

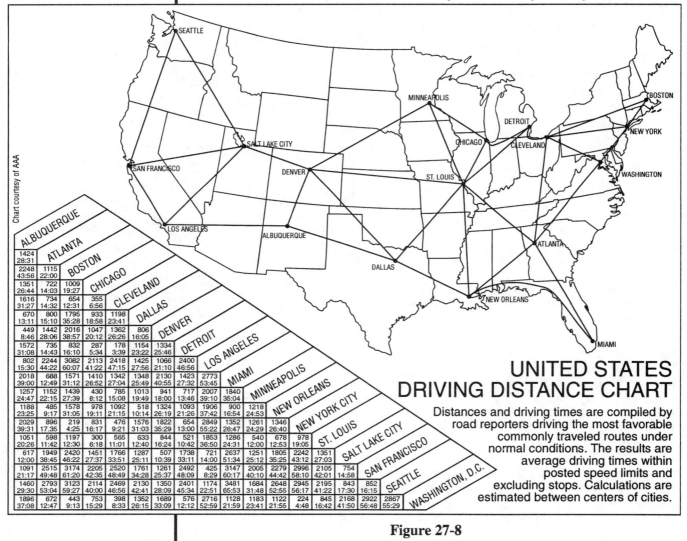

Chart courtesy of AAA

## UNITED STATES DRIVING DISTANCE CHART

Distances and driving times are compiled by road reporters driving the most favorable commonly traveled routes under normal conditions. The results are average driving times within posted speed limits and excluding stops. Calculations are estimated between centers of cities.

**Figure 27-8**

- Read the **key, or legend**, that explains the symbols and colors used to show the Interstates, federal, state, and local routes, rest areas, interchanges, distances, and other important features (see Figure 27-5 on page 27.7).
- Learn to figure the distance between points by adding the mileage figures shown along the route. Black numbers often refer to short distances between two black dots. Red numbers refer to longer distances between two red dots. Using the scale of the map is not accurate because measuring with a ruler will give only the air miles. Air miles are shorter than driving distance.

Many maps have mileage charts showing approximate distances between principal cities and towns. Many atlases have a special map showing distance and estimated driving times between principal cities. The driving times shown are usually for cars and light trucks. You should allow more time for driving a tractor-trailer.

- Learn to use the grid coordinates to locate points on the map. Numbers are printed across the top and bottom of maps, and letters are printed down each side. Most maps also have an index. On a state map, the index will list names of cities, towns, and villages. On the map of a city or region, the index will list street names. In each case, the location will show a letter and a number, for example C-6 or C6. To find the location, look down from 6 and across from C. The point will be near where the imaginary lines from the number and letter cross on the map.

## CALCULATING TRAVEL TIME AND FUEL USAGE

Knowing how to figure the distance, your average speed, and trip time will be helpful. The driver who wants to keep track of the average speed and fuel usage may want to buy a calculator. The following formulas are used often by truck drivers.

**Distance** = Speed multiplied by Time
50 mph x 9 hours = 450 miles

**Average Speed** = Distance divided by Time
450 miles / 9 hours = 50 mph

**Trip Time** = Distance divided by Average Speed
450 miles / 50 mph = 9 hours

### Travel Time

Drivers must comply with the DOT's regs for speed limits and hours of service. When a driver's record of duty status (driver's log) is checked, enforcement personnel will divide the miles driven by the number of hours of driving time to determine the average speed. This will tell them if the driver has been speeding.

Officials use these standards to decide if a driver has been speeding. Where the predominant speed limit is 55 mph:
- A trip of 450 to 500 miles in 10 hours is open to question. This means the driver had an average speed of 45-50 miles per hour.
- A trip of 500 to 550 miles in 10 hours, or any trip showing an average speed of 50 miles per hour or more may be considered not in compliance with the hours of service and the speed limit.

Where the predominant speed limit is 65 mph:
- A trip of 500 to 550 miles in 10 hours is open to question (average speed 50-55 miles per hour).
- A trip of more than 600 miles in 10 hours (average speed of 60 miles per hour or more) will raise a red flag for an officer.

Both drivers and motor carriers may be required to document runs to show they can be made without violating the hours of service rules or the speed limits.

The distance that can be covered in 10 hours of driving will depend on the speed limits and other factors such as heavy traffic, travel through urban areas, long upgrades, adverse weather, or anything that can reduce the safe operating speed. Generally, the average speed for a trip will be 5-15 mph below the cruising speed.

## Fuel Consumption

To figure the fuel consumption:
1. Fill the fuel tank and record the mileage shown on the odometer.
2. After driving, refill the tank and record the odometer mileage.
3. Record the amount of fuel put in the tank.
4. Subtract the odometer mileage at the first fill-up from the odometer mileage at the second fill-up. This will tell you the distance covered.
5. To determine the miles per gallon, divide the distance covered by the gallons of fuel used.

Example:

| | |
|---|---|
| Odometer reading - 1st fill-up | 65456 |
| Odometer reading - 2nd fill-up | 65956 |
| Gallons of fuel added | 90 |

**Distance covered** = odometer reading at 2nd fill-up (65956)
– odometer reading at 1st fill-up (65456)
= 500 miles

**Miles per gallon** = $\dfrac{500 \text{ miles (distance covered)}}{90 \text{ gallons (fuel added)}}$ = 5.5 mpg

If a driver knows the capacity of the truck's fuel tank(s) and the average fuel mileage, he or she can figure the cruising range by multiplying the tank capacity by the miles per gallon.

Example:

Cruising range = Tank capacity x mpg

Tank capacity = 100 gallons
Miles per gallon = 5.5

**Cruising range** = 100 (gallons) x 5.5 (mpg) = 550 miles

The driver must be aware that under actual operating conditions, many factors can easily increase fuel usage. Some of the more important factors include:
- Prolonged idling
- Driving too fast
- Extended operation in low gears
- Stop-and-go driving
- Mountainous terrain
- Headwinds
- Low tire pressure
- Defects in the engine or fuel system

# KEEPING RECORDS

A driver must always have on hand all the papers he or she needs when they are on duty. Each carrier has its own way of keeping records. It meets the information needs of that carrier and helps them remain within the law. You must learn the method your carrier uses.

If the driver does not carry the papers and keep the records the carrier requires, both the driver and the carrier can be penalized. Not carrying the right papers or keeping records may also cause delays in being paid.

The driver must have the following papers:
- Driver's license
- Medical certificate
- Driver's log
- Driver's inspection report

Law enforcement officers have the right to examine these documents.

**Driver's license**: Your CDL must be the type required for the equipment you are driving. You must also have the proper endorsements. Federal law prohibits a truck driver from having more than one license.

**Medical certificate**: This must be current and valid. The driver must be in compliance of any special requirements; i.e. glasses, hearing aids.

**Driver's Log** (Record of duty status): The record must be correctly completed and kept up to date to the driver's last change of duty status. The driver who has to keep a log must have the log for the current day and the 7 preceding days with him or her while on duty.

**Driver's inspection report**: The driver must keep a copy of the inspection report prepared by the previous driver and have a blank driver's inspection report available to prepare at the end of the trip or tour of duty.

The driver may also have other documents, including:
- Shipping papers
- Trip reports

**Shipping Papers**: There are many different forms that are used for this purpose. (See the chapter on *Cargo Documentation*.)

**Trip Reports**: Carriers usually develop the type of report that meets their needs. As a result, there are many types, and they provide different information. The following data is usually found on these reports.
- Name of driver
- Terminal
- Vehicle identification
- Departure time from terminal
- Routing instructions
- Address of each stop to deliver or pick up freight
- Times of arrival and departure for each stop
- Quantity of freight handled
- Time of return to terminal
- Space for remarks

Some trip reports have a space for entering the odometer reading when the driver crosses a state line or when going from origin to destination. Drivers must be very careful and accurate when noting these details. A driver must be sure to comply with the carrier's rules when preparing a trip report.

## On-Board Recorder

More and more carriers are now using on-board recording equipment. Some carriers use this equipment to show compliance with hours of service limits. If the carrier for which you work uses such devices, they will teach you how to use them properly.

Some trucks have recorders installed so the carrier can control how the truck is operated. Basic information recorded by these devices includes:
- Time the engine is running
- Whether the truck is stopped or moving
- Speed
- Miles driven

## Personal Needs

The driver must be able to meet his or her personal needs during trips. The driver should find out what expenses he or she must meet while on the trip that will be reimbursed by the motor carrier, how the payment is to be made; what paperwork must be kept to prove the expense; and if there are forms to be filled out. These expenses and who is usually responsible are listed below.

| | |
|---|---|
| Meals | Usually driver expense |
| Lodging | Usually carrier expense |
| Fuel | Carrier expense |
| Enroute repairs | Carrier expense |
| Tolls | Carrier expense if authorized |
| Permits | Carrier expense |
| Special fees | Carrier expense |

Carriers handle their expense accounts in different ways. Some companies have accounts with fuel stops, motels, repair shops, toll facilities, and for permits. Others use Comchecks. Some carriers give you cash advances for these expenses. Always find out how your company handles expenses before you start on a trip. Keep copies of all receipts for your records. Retain logbooks to document your daily expenses for tax purposes.

© 1997 Career Publishing Inc.

Some of the personal concerns of truck drivers on the road..

**Figure 27-9**

Drivers should know the kind of weather they may find during the trip. They should know where there may be extreme weather conditions and carry the right kinds of clothes with them for any situation. Clothes for working outside the truck during bad weather should also be included. Many drivers also carry blankets, a sleeping bag, and an emergency supply of food in case they are stranded out in the middle of nowhere.

# VEHICLE LICENSING AND PERMITS

Every vehicle must have a registration (license) plate (tag) in order to operate. Fees are paid each year, and registration plates are issued. The majority of trucks or truck or tractor combinations that weigh more than 26,000 pounds will be registered under the **International Registration Plan (IRP)**.

The IRP is a registration agreement among the states and Canadian provinces that is based on the percentage of miles driven in each state or province. License fees are paid to each state or province in which the vehicle operates. A cab card is issued to the vehicle. This card states the IRP areas in which the vehicle can operate.

Usually, the carrier obtains the registration plate. The driver is responsible for keeping mileage records. The percentage of fees paid to each state depends upon the number of miles driven in that state compared to the number of miles driven in all states and provinces.

**Figure 27-10**

If a truck that has IRP plates plans to operate in a state that is not shown on the IRP cab card, a trip permit must be obtained. The carrier is responsible for telling the driver how to obtain these permits. Permits are usually issued for a given period of time, ranging most often from 24-72 hours. Federal laws require all states to be members of IRP by Sepetember 30, 1996.

## Fuel Use Tax

In order to operate legally in a state, a truck must be registered for **fuel use tax** purposes. When it is registered, a fuel tax decal will be issued. This decal is then placed on the door of the tractor. The decal is evidence the vehicle is registered for fuel use tax purposes. The price of the decal varies considerably from state to state. The fuel use tax itself is paid by the carrier quarterly. The fuel tax registration law is usually enforced by the state revenue or taxation department.

The carrier pays the fuel tax in each state based on the number of miles driven in that state. If the carrier buys more fuel in a state than is needed to cover its fuel tax obligation, the carrier gets a tax credit. On the other hand, if not enough fuel is bought in a state, the carrier must pay more tax.

A driver must be sure he or she gets receipts for all fuel purchases and submits them to the carrier along with required record of miles operated. The information submitted by the driver forms the basis of the carrier's fuel tax report to each state.

## Weight Distance Taxes

Some states have **weight distance taxes**. They are also called mileage taxes, ton-mile taxes or axle taxes. These taxes are paid by the carrier and are based on the annual ton mileage. The carrier must also file a quarterly report. States often require trucks to be registered for the weight distance tax. The carrier usually obtains a decal or number for the tractor. These taxes are enforced by the state's highway department or transportation department.

# FEDERAL LENGTH AND WEIGHT LIMITS

The driver is responsible for staying within federal and state weight and length laws. All states must allow truck combinations of certain weights and lengths to operate on roadways that are part of the **National System of Interstate Highways**. This system is also known as the **Designated System** or **National Network**. Most of these highways are identified by the letter I and the number of the highway such as **I 80** or **I 5**. Many additional multi-lane, divided highways, such as the U.S. routes and turnpikes, are also part of this system.

In addition, states must allow federally authorized STAA truck combinations to have access to terminals and facilities for food, fuel, repairs, and rest. States are allowed to determine the distance off the designated system these vehicles may travel for such purposes. The distances currently range from a limit of 1500 feet off the New York State Thruway, for example, to unlimited access on state and local roads in Ohio.

Many state highways have requirements similar to the following federal weight and size limits, but it is always wise to check the applicable maps and charts for actual dimension limits.

### Vehicle Weight

A maximum of 20,000 lbs. may be carried on any one axle (except steer axles which are only allowed 12,000 lbs.) and 34,000 lbs. on a tandem axle. 80,000 lbs. overall gross weight is allowed on a typical five-axle tractor-semitrailer. The way the axles are spaced and the number of axles may lower the single and tandem axle limits. Rigs must also stay within weight-to-length limits based on the weight of groups of two or more adjacent (following) axles.

---

*Mileage Control Sheet*
*(Speedometer Mileage Readings)*

Destination _____

Date _____ Unit Nos. _____

Driver _____

New Jersey

     Beginning _____
     State Line OUT _____
     State Line IN _____
     Ending _____

New York

     State Line IN _____
     State Line OUT _____

Connecticut

     State Line IN _____
     State Line OUT _____

Pennsylvania

     State Line IN _____
     State Line OUT _____

© 1997 Career Publishing Inc.

**Figure 27-11**

The **Federal Bridge Formula** is used to calculate permissable gross loads. Ideally, a typical 80,000 lb. five-axle highway rig should get 12,000 lbs. on the front axle and 34,000 lbs. on each of the tandems. The tractor must have an **outer spread** (distance between the middle of the front axle and the middle of the rear-most axle) of at least 14 feet. The formula also requires minimum distances between the tractor and trailer axles (**inner** and **outer bridge**).

The following are limits that some states have imposed for the length of semitrailers. Note the difference in requirements.

### Vehicle Length

There is no limit on the overall length of a tractor-semitrailer on the Interstates and designated highways. But some states do limit lengths. These are typically measured from the center of the trailer tandems. Pay special attention if the trailer is over 48 feet long. Some states may require a permit.

States cannot limit the length of trailers to less than 28' for doubles (semi-trailer and trailer). States must also continue to allow 28 1/2' double trailers if they were in operation before 1983.

No state can prohibit doubles on the Interstate and Designated Highway System. Longer doubles (more than 28' per trailer) and triple trailer combinations usually operate under special permits.

| Vehicle Lengths — Maximum Limits | | |
|---|---|---|
| | Interstates | State Highways |
| Alaska | 48' | 45' |
| Arizona | 51' | 51' |
| Delaware | 53' | Not Specified |
| Georgia | 48' | 48' |
| Idaho | 48' | 48' |
| Kansas | 53' | 53' |
| Michigan | 50' | 50' |
| New Jersey | 48' | 48' |
| Ohio | 53' | 53' |
| Oklahoma | 52' | 52' |
| Texas | 57' | 57' |
| Wyoming | 60' | 60' |

© 1997 Career Publishing Inc.

**Figure 27-12**

## STATE LIMITS

Unless they are controlled by federal interstate law, weight and size limits vary from state to state. If a driver is not sure of a state's limits, he or she should find out about the limits before entering the state. Dispatchers usually have this information. So do most trucker atlases. The State Police, Highway Patrol, Department of Transportation, and state trucking associations can also usually provide accurate information.

When deciding whether a tractor-trailer is within limits, there are three key factors to be considered.
1. Vehicle Weight
2. Number of Axles
3. Vehicle Length, Height, and Width

**Vehicle weight:** Many state agencies provide color coded maps (red, green, purple) that identify load maximums that can be carried on various roads. These maximums are generally based on the condition of the road and the weight that can be supported by the bridges. You can weigh your rig at fleet or shipper terminals or you can use public scales at truck stops. Some public scales will certify the weight and even pay overweight fines if they are wrong.

TRUCKS WEIGH ON CERTIFIED SCALES TO BE SURE THEY ARE WITHIN LEGAL LIMITS.

**Figure 27-13**

**Number of axles:** States have bridge laws that limit the maximum weight that may be carried. The laws are determined by the number of axles and the distance between them. While most states have adopted **Federal Bridge Formula** to determine axle weight limits and gross weight limits, some states have other means of figuring these limits.

**Vehicle length:** Vehicle length is regulated by both state and local governments. They also set the maximum load, length, and overhang (the distance beyond support of the load bed) that is permitted. The legal length may be set either in terms of overall length (from bumper to bumper) or trailer length.

**Vehicle height and load:** While some states permit vehicle heights of 14', most restrict heights to 13'6". This limit includes the load. Overpasses on most Interstates have clearances of 16'6", but some are only 13'6". Always check to make sure.

## Special Permit Hauling

Loads that are larger than either the state or local laws allow need special permits. You can get these permits from state agencies and police departments. Typical loads that need these permits include machinery, buildings, and bridge construction girders.

Some permits limit hours of operation (before sundown, after sunup, rush hours, etc.) and the routes to be used. Permits may:

- Be limited to specific vehicles
- Require the use of special signs (oversize load, etc.)
- Require the use of escort vehicles both in front of and behind the load
- Require using special lights such as rotating amber lights
- Specify the route to be followed

**Hauling this load requires a special permit**

© 1997 Career Publishing Inc.

**Figure 27-14**

Drivers may have to submit their planned route before they can get a permit. If a detour or delay occurs, the driver may have to call the state or local agency that issued the permit to request a change in time or route.

## HAZARDOUS MATERIAL

If you haul hazardous material, trip planning will be affected. You must first know the cargo is hazardous. Second, you must follow federal regs for trip planning. Finally, you will need to know in advance which highways and facilities you may use and which ones restrict or prohibit hazardous materials. You may not use certain bridges or tunnels.

**Federal Regulations:** You must obey Part 397 of the Federal Motor Carrier Safety Regulations (FMCSR). These regulations deal with driving and parking vehicles that contain hazardous materials. You must understand and follow sections 397.3, 397.5, and 397.7.

**FMCSR 397.3** requires all vehicles carrying hazardous materials to comply with state and local restrictions on routes and parking.

The safe haven regulation is **FMCSR 397.5**. It requires all vehicles carrying Class A or Class B explosives (Explosives 1.1 through 1.3) to be attended at all times. They may be parked in a safe haven. A **safe haven** is an area approved in writing by local, state, or federal officials in which unattended vehicles carrying Class A or Class B explosives may be parked.

## Restrictions on Hazardous Material Transportation: State: Hawaii

| Facility Name and Location | Are Cargos With the Following Allowed to Pass Through the Tunnel or Highway Facility? | | | | | | | | | |
|---|---|---|---|---|---|---|---|---|---|---|
| | Explosives A (Explosives 1.1-1.3) | Explosives B | Compressive Gas | Combustible | Poison | Flammable | Flammable Gas | Oxidizers | Radioactive | Dangerous |
| **Oahu** | | | | | | | | | | |
| Pali Tunnel — SR-61 Between Honolulu and Kailua | No | No | Yes | Yes | Yes | Yes | Yes | Yes | Yes | Yes |
| Wilson Tunnel — SR-63 Between Honolulu and Kaneohe | No | No | Yes | Yes | Yes | Yes | Yes | Yes | Yes | Yes |

**Remarks:**

Red Hill Tunnel on Proposed H-3 Route Will Have Similar Restrictions.
No Bridge or Highway restrictions on Kauai, Maui, or Hawaii.

© 1997 Career Publishing Inc.

**Figure 27-15**

**FMCSR 397.9** controls the routes. Trips must be planned in the best interest of public safety and not for the operator's convenience.

Vehicles carrying hazardous materials must, when possible, operate over routes that do not go through or near heavily populated areas and should avoid tunnels, narrow streets, alleys, or places where crowds are assembled.

Loads of Class A or Class B explosives require a written trip plan. The carrier must submit the plan in advance. The driver must then follow the plan. In some cases, the driver prepares the plan for the carrier.

There are also specific regulations dealing with routing decisions in the Hazardous Materials Regulations. **HMR 177.810** requires drivers of vehicles containing hazardous materials to obey state and local laws for the use of tunnels.

Planning for trips and hauling radioactive material is controlled by **HMR 177.825**. There are detailed instructions for routing loads of radioactive materials. A written route plan must be submitted in advance for highway route-controlled quantities of radioactive materials.

# ROADSIDE ENFORCEMENT

As well as the normal enforcement of traffic laws, there are three other types of controlling activities routinely carried on by states. Drivers need to be aware of:
- Scales
- Ports-of-entry
- Roadside safety inspections

**Figure 27-16**

In many cases, these functions are carried out at a single location.

## Scales

States usually enforce size and weight laws through a combination of permanent scales and the use of roving crews who have portable scales, or loadmeters. Permanent scales are often on the main highways at the state line. In some states, there are also scales at other key points. Not stopping at the scales is a serious offense and may result in a fine. Observe all signs, lights, and verbal commands when entering, weighing, and exiting the scales.

## Ports-of-Entry

These are locations where the driver must stop and prove the carrier has authority to operate in the state. In some cases, the driver may have to buy permits or pay fees. Weighing may also be done at the port-of-entry. Do not pull onto the scales. Park near the scales and walk up and get your permit. Some states will fine you if you pull onto the scales without a permit. In some states, the driver's log will be checked for hours of service violations and be time-stamped by the person on duty.

**Figure 27-17**

## Roadside Safety Inspections

These inspections are done at scales, ports-of-entry, special safety inspection facilities, or in a suitable safe area. The driver must show his or her license, medical certificate, driver's logs, and the shipping papers for the load. Inspectors have the authority to inspect the cargo, even if it is sealed. If a sealed load is inspected, a new seal will be put on by the inspector. The driver should record in the log the identification number of the seal that is removed and the number of the new seal that is put on.

The driver may be put out of service at once for certain violations. These include:
- Hours of service violations
- A vehicle so unsafe it is likely to be involved in an accident or breakdown
- Leaking hazardous material

At the end of a roadside inspection, the driver will be given a copy of the form filled out by the inspector. This form must be turned in to the carrier. If the driver will reach a company facility within 24 hours, the form may be turned in at that time. If not, the driver must mail the form to the carrier.

## SUMMARY

In this chapter, you learned about the different kinds of trucking operations and how to plan for a trip. The different types of roads were explained. The permits that may be required were described. How to read maps, figure travel time and fuel consumption, plan for personal needs on a trip, and keep records were also explained. Legal weight and length limits and enforcement agencies for them were presented. You also learned that when you haul hazardous material, you will have special regulations to follow.

## KEY WORDS

**Federal Bridge Formula:** A formula used to figure permissable gross loads. It also requires minimum distances between the tractor and trailer axles.

**Fuel Tax:** A tax based on the number of miles driven in that state that is paid by the carrier to each state.

**Inner bridge:** The distance between any two following axles. Determines weight limits.

**International Registration Plan (IRP):** An agreement among the states and Canadian provinces for paying registration fees that are based on the percentage of miles operated in each state or province.

**Interstate Operating Authority**: Issued by the DOT and permits trucks to cross state lines.

**Over-The-Road:** Cargo is hauled on regular routes. Drivers may be away for a week or more.

**Long-Distance Transport:** Cargo is transported from a point of origin to one or more distant destinations.

**National System of Interstate Highways**: Also known as the **Designated System** or **National Network**. Consists of the Interstates and many additional multi-lane, divided highways, such as the U.S. routes.

**Outer bridge**: The distance from the center of the steering axle to the center of the last axle in the combination. Determines weight limits.

**Safe haven**: An area approved in writing by local, state, or federal officials in which unattended vehicles carrying Class A or Class B explosives may be parked.

**Weight Distance Tax:** Also called a mileage tax, ton-mile tax or axle tax. A tax paid by the carrier that is based on the annual ton mileage.

# LEARNING ACTIVITIES

## Trip Planning

Break into small groups. Using what you learned in this chapter, plan the following trips.

### Trip #1

You are a delivery driver. You have goods to be delivered to ten different locations in the same city. What must you plan for before beginning your deliveries. What actions must you take to be sure the consignee receives the right items on time?

### Trip #2

You will be making an Open Dispatch Run. Your point of origin is New Orleans, LA. Your destination is Houston, TX. At Houston, you are assigned a run to Dallas, TX. In Dallas, you pick up a load for Oklahoma City, OK. In Oklahoma City, your load is headed for Wichita, KS. In Wichita, you are given a load for Kansas City, MO. In Kansas City, the load is going to Tulsa, OK. In Tulsa, you are dispatched to St. Louis, MO. From St. Louis, you are sent to Batesville, MS. At Batesville, you pick up a load for New Orleans. The run is during the month of March.

1. For how many days should you plan? _____
2. What paperwork should you be able to produce at any given time?
3. What special permits might you need?
4. How much money should you bring along? What other alternatives do you have to carrying cash?
5. What type of weather may you encounter? At what points?
6. Where can you find information about weather conditions?
7. What type of clothing should you bring along?
8. What type of supplies should you bring?
9. Will you need any special maps?
10. Fill out a Driver's Log for the trip.
11. What information will you need to supply to your carrier about your trip?

### Trip #3

You are carrying a load of radioactive material from White Sands, NM to Huntsville, AL. The cargo is sealed. At an inspection point, the cargo's seal is broken so the load can be inspected. Plan your trip. List all permits needed. List all prohibited routes. What special care must you take? Fill out a Driver's Log for the trip. Will you need special maps?

### Trip #4

You and another driver are assigned a run from Anacortes, WA to Houma, LA. You will be hauling drilling equipment. Your load is classed as overweight. Your cab has a sleeper berth. The run is being made in November. Plan your trip. List all permits needed. List all clothing, supplies, etc. you should take. Will you need special maps? Fill out a Driver's Log for the trip. What information should your carrier give you before you begin the trip? What information should you supply to your carrier when you return?

## Map Reading

For the following trips, find the best route. Tell what type of roads you will have to use. Note if there are any roads or bridges you cannot use. Will you need any special permits to make the run? What type of maps did you use to plan your route? How far did you travel? Your instructor may use different routes because there are more maps available for that run.

### Trip #1

You pick up a load in Carbondale, PA. Your final destination is Youngstown, OH with stops in Liberty, PA and Ridgway, PA.

### Trip #2

Your point of origin is Detroit, MI. Your destination is Traverse City, MI with stops in Midland, MI; Big Rapids, MI; and Grayling, MI.

### Trip #3

Your point of origin is Leadville, CO. Your final destination is Roswell, NM. You have stops in Aspen, CO; Gunnison, CO; Durango, CO; Shiprock, NM; Grants, NM; and Alamagordo, NM.

### Trip #4

Your point of origin is Mountain Home, ID. Your final destination is Spirit River, Alberta, Canada. You have stops in Grangeville, ID; Missoula, MT; Coeur d'Alene, ID; Bonners Ferry, ID; Lethbridge, Alberta; Calgary, Alberta; Edmonton, Alberta; and Slave Lake, Alberta.

## True-False Questions

Circle the T if the statement is true. Circle the F is statement is false.

T   F   1.   In addition to being able to drive safely, a driver must be able to plan trips and read maps.

T   F   2.   Commercial truck drivers do not have to know the size and weight laws, how to register a CMV, how to get permits, or fuel tax requirements.

T   F   3.   Drivers should be able to find the approximate mileage from origin to destination.

T   F   4.   Drivers should know how to estimate trip time, fuel requirements, and personal financial needs.

T   F   5.   Drivers do not need to know which roads are prohibited. This is the job of the dispatcher.

T   F   6.   In all cases, the best routes for drivers to take are those using the U.S. numbered routes. These routes are always given priority in maintenance and repair.

T   F   7.   Only trucking company management is responsible for informing drivers of special weight restrictions on bridges.

T   F   8.   In areas where the speed limit is 55 mph, drivers should be able to travel 575 miles in 10 hours without breaking the speed limit and hours of service regulations.

T   F   9.   Drivers or motor carriers may have to document runs to show they can be made without violations of the hours of service laws or speed limits.

T   F   10.   If a driver knows how much fuel the truck's tank can hold and the average fuel mileage, he or she can figure out the cruising range of the truck by multiplying the tank's capacity by the miles-per-gallon.

T   F   11.   Low tire pressure and prolonged idling can help improve fuel mileage.

T   F   12.   Drivers must carry a valid CDL and medical certificate while driving.

T   F   13.   Federal law allows drivers to have CDLs from many states.

T   F   14.   Log books and driver inspection reports must be completed only when the driver is hauling hazardous materials.

T   F   15.   At roadside inspections, inspectors do not have the authority to inspect the cargo.

T   F   16.   If a vehicle is put *out of service* at a roadside inspection, the driver may continue to operate the vehicle for another 100 miles before any correction or repair is made.

T   F   17.   Drivers should not be concerned with the weight of the vehicle or federal size and weight limits. These concerns are the responsibility of the company.

T   F   18.   If you haul hazardous materials, there are no special route restrictions or regulations that you need to know.

T   F   19.   If you are transporting Class A or Class B explosives (Explosives 1.1 through 1.3), you must have a written trip plan. In some cases, the driver may prepare the plan for the company.

# Chapter Twenty-Eight
# PUBLIC RELATIONS AND EMPLOYER-EMPLOYEE RELATIONS

**Image of the Trucking Industry • Contact With the Public • Customer Relations • Employer Relations • Company Policy • Driver Qualifications Getting a Job • Interviews**

**FROM NOW ON,**

**ONLY THE BEST WILL DRIVE**

# OBJECTIVES

When the student has mastered this chapter, he or she will be able to:

- Communicate to other truck driver trainees the importance of presenting a good image to the public because they represent the trucking industry

- Explain the results of presenting a bad public image

- Describe what is included in a good image

- Explain the importance of good relations with customers

- Outline the proper procedures for applying for a job as a truck driver

- Describe a job interview and how the job applicant should act

- Explain the reasons for a driver being disqualified

CHAPTER TWENTY-EIGHT

# PUBLIC RELATIONS AND EMPLOYER-EMPLOYEE RELATIONS

## INTRODUCTION

Much of what people think of the trucking industry is a result of what they see drivers do on the roads. A few thoughtful or courteous acts by tractor-trailer drivers can create good will. On the other hand, one careless or rude driver can cause enough resentment to create laws that penalize the entire industry.

Tractor-trailer drivers are the front-counter people of trucking. Drivers are the ones the public notices. If the public does not like what they see, the trucking industry will hear about it in ways that hurt business, earnings, and jobs.

The purpose of this chapter is to help tractor-trailer drivers-in-training learn that how they look and act is the closest view most people get of the trucking industry. Employer-employee relations are also discussed including the driver's qualifications, and recommendations are made for job interviews.

© 1997 Career Publishing Inc.

**Figure 28-1**

## PUBLIC RELATIONS

How good the relations are between the trucking industry and the general public is often determined by how well truck drivers obey the laws and regulations meant to protect road users. Obeying the laws, being courteous, and using everyday common sense create good public relations. This chapter discusses some common public relations problems along with the steps drivers can take to improve the image of the industry.

## The Image of the Trucking Industry

The trucking industry operates under many state and federal laws and regulations. Most of the laws are made to protect the public. Some can be difficult for the industry, such as:

- High road use taxes
- Laws restricting vehicles from using certain roads
- Lower speed limits for heavy vehicles
- Old hours-of-service rules that make it hard to get the rest you need when you need it

How the public feels about the trucking industry influences all laws that could affect the industry.

The public image, whether it is accurate or not, results in letter writing campaigns in which the public and media come out for or against the trucking industry. The complaints create:

- Legislation that is unfavorable to the industry (higher use taxes, road restrictions, etc.).
- Less profit for the trucking industry. This often means a loss of jobs.

THE DRIVER AND HIS VEHICLE ARE THE IMAGE OF THE TRUCKING INDUSTRY TO THE PUBLIC.

## AVOID A BAD IMAGE!

| BAD IMAGE | RESULTS |
|---|---|
| ROAD HOG | PUBLIC COMPLAINS |
| SPEEDER | LETTERS TO LAWMAKERS |
| TAILGATER | LAWS RESTRICT ROAD USE |
| BAD LANGUAGE | LOWER SPEEDS |
| ROWDY BEHAVIOR | HIGHER USE TAXES |
| | TOUGHER TO MAKE A LIVING |

## MAINTAIN A GOOD IMAGE!

| GOOD IMAGE | RESULTS |
|---|---|
| SAFE, COURTEOUS | BENEFITS TO: |
| DRIVER | THE TRUCKING INDUSTRY |
| HELPFUL | YOUR COMPANY |
| PROFESSIONAL | YOUR FAMILY |
| BEHAVIOR | YOURSELF |

## BE A KNIGHT OF THE ROAD

© 1997 Career Publishing Inc.

**Figure 28-2**

One driver's bad performance can have a dramatic effect on the whole industry. The industry needs to be seen as a worthwhile profession. Courteous drivers, who know and practice safe driving at all times, can be the *knights of the road.*

## Contact with the Public

There are many chances for public contact. This contact can be in cooperation or conflict. Drivers must take great care to see that their conduct and actions create a good image. All of us, whatever our positions, have to deal with difficult situations and stress in our daily lives. The way truck drivers react to those situations is seen by others as an image of the industry and affects how they feel.

We all are responsible for maintaining a good image when driving. We can do this by obeying the laws, making a good appearance, and sharing the road.

**Obeying the law:** Laws are meant to protect everybody. They should be obeyed at all times. When drivers obey the law, they project the image of a true professional. Obeying the law also cuts down on incidents that make life harder for your fellow drivers, the industry, and yourself.

**Making a good appearance:** A clean, neat driver looks like a professional and gains respect for the industry. We need to be sure we stay in top physical, mental, and emotional shape.

We must be sure our rigs are in top shape, as well. A good pre-trip inspection may prevent an accident or breakdown. A clean, well maintained vehicle makes the industry look good. Flapping tarps, spilling cargo, and dragging chains or rope say we belong to a shoddy industry.

**Sharing the Road:** Most conflicts with the public occur while sharing the road. Some actions that cause public resentment are:

Figure 28-3

- **Space related:** Following too closely or driving in packs that prevent others from passing.
- **Speed related:** Speeding and cutting in and out of traffic.
- **Going uphill:** Attempting to pass another truck without enough speed. As a result, two trucks block the flow of traffic. You could block an unmarked emergency or police vehicle. The same type of situation can occur when trucks do not keep to the right and pull over to allow other vehicles to pass. Be careful, and do not pull onto a soft shoulder. The rig could sink, turn over, or throw gravel at following vehicles.
- **Passing:** The truck driver cuts off other drivers or does not signal.
- **At intersections:** Do not try to bluff your way through intersections. Trucks are very large and can frighten some people so that they may react in a way that causes an accident. Other drivers do not always leave enough room for a tractor-trailer to turn. Some truck drivers become angry. They should realize that most drivers do not understand how much room is needed to turn a big rig. Keep cool and do not get mad. Do not jump the light on left turns, this can lead to the end of your career as a trucker. When a light turns from red to green, do not go until it is safe to do so. Be sure there are no emergency vehicles approaching.
- **Use of headlights:** Not dimming lights when meeting or following other vehicles is very irritating and dangerous. Truck high beams are more annoying than those of automobiles. Shining high beams into vehicles ahead of you can confuse the driver and possibly cause an accident. This causes bad press for the trucking industry. Remember the posted speed is the maximum you should drive.

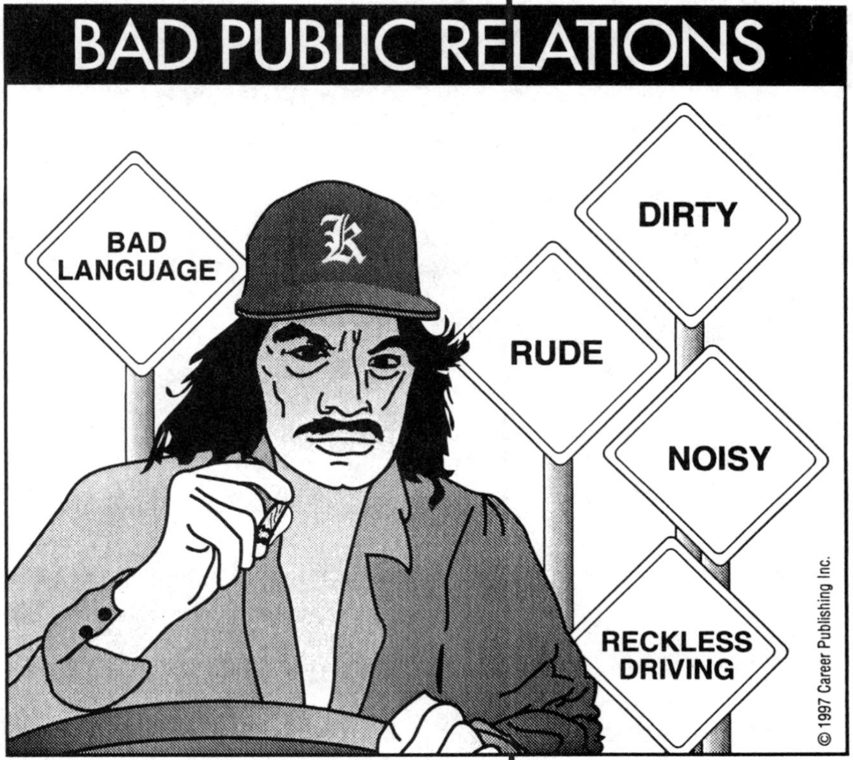

- **Noise:** Using your air horn when it is not needed. Mufflers that are damaged or not the right type create a lot of noise.
- **Parking incorrectly:** When you block traffic unnecessarily, people can think it is deliberate. This reflects badly on the industry.

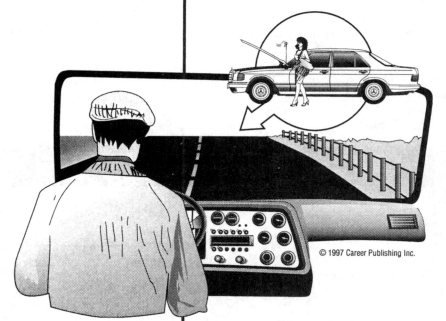

Improper actions by other drivers are often unsafe and frequently annoy truckers. Truckers must avoid trying to get even. Yelling, foul language, and obscene gestures accomplish nothing and can cause you to lose your job and hurt the image of the entire industry. Motorists sometimes report incidents to the company. The best policy is to act like a professional. Remember, many of the trucks on the road today have a phone number painted on them that people may call to report both good and bad driving.

© 1997 Career Publishing Inc.

Make a habit of being clean and neatly dressed whenever you are on duty. Be courteous, polite, and helpful. Avoid arguments and be a good representative for the industry.

**Figure 28-4**

Even when you are off duty, you can often be identified by appearance or uniform. Loud, rowdy behavior in restaurants or other public places causes people to think of truck drivers as rude and badly behaved.

If company policy permits, you should help other road users whenever possible. Giving directions, assisting stranded motorists by directing help to them, and treating others properly will all pay off in good PR for the industry.

## Results of Bad Public Relations

The bad actions of a few drivers reflect on the whole industry. None of us should encourage bad behavior by laughing, clapping, or showing approval. As a rule, most drivers do not like other drivers who are out of line. Bad drivers soon get poor records and may even lose their jobs. Remember, since actions and how things look do most of the speaking for the industry, one bad act can undo hundreds of good ones.

Because of one driver, a company may get a bad name and lose business. Sometimes, the driver or company may even be sued. Tough laws may be passed to prevent the situation from being repeated. These laws hurt financially and make our job more difficult.

## CUSTOMER RELATIONS

Drivers are the ones who are seen. They *are* the company as far as the public is concerned. As a driver, how you act can lose or gain business for your company. The little extra effort it takes to do a good job is well worth it in the long run. Both you and the company will benefit. Remember, how you and your equipment look is important, and first impressions count.

All the factors that affect your image as seen by the public mean more when the *public* is a customer. The image you project is the customer's closest view of the company.

Company rules and procedures were set up to improve and keep business. Follow the company policy for:
- Cargo and freight documentation and handling
- Dealing with customers
- Dealing with freight problems

Drivers who do not follow company policy give the company a bad reputation and can lose their jobs. If you have a problem, call your company. It is their job to help you.

**TIPS FOR GOOD CUSTOMER RELATIONS**
- FOLLOW COMPANY PROCEDURES
- DO NOT ARGUE OR LOSE YOUR TEMPER
- BE COURTEOUS
- BE POLITE, HONEST, AND HELPFUL
- ALWAYS THANK THE CUSTOMER

IF YOU GIVE THAT EXTRA CARE —
**YOU MAY GET MORE BUSINESS!**

REMEMBER... THE DRIVER HAS MORE CONTACT WITH CUSTOMERS THAN ANY OTHER PERSON IN THE COMPANY

© 1997 Career Publishing Inc.

**Figure 28-5**

A positive attitude is very important. Some signs of a positive attitude are:
- Promptness when picking up or delivering cargo
- Courtesy
- Politeness, helpfulness, and honesty at all times
- An easy manner; do not argue or allow yourself to be provoked.

# EMPLOYER RELATIONS

This section will help you know what qualifications employers are looking for in a driver. Also, it will help you understand how to act during an interview for a job.

## BASIC JOB REQUIREMENTS

A good attitude is a must for success in finding and holding any job. The general qualifications expected of an interstate tractor-trailer driver are listed below. The driver must:

- Meet the requirements of federal law, including the medical qualifications and having the correct CDL
- Meet the employer's needs and qualifications as stated in the company policy
- Know about the trucking industry and have the attitudes and interests suited to its environment

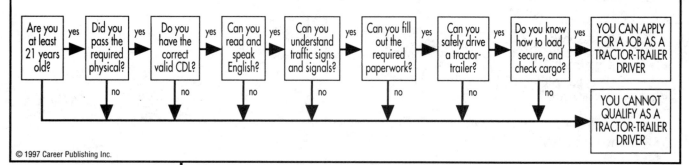

Figure 28-6

## Requirements of Federal Law

People who apply for tractor-trailer driving jobs must meet the U.S. Department of Transportation (DOT) qualifications as stated below. They must:

- Be at least 21 years old
- Be physically qualified (FMCSR 341.91)
- Have a valid CDL
- Be able to read and speak English
- Understand traffic signs and signals
- Be able to fill out the required paperwork
- Be able to safely drive a tractor-trailer
- Know and use the correct methods for securing cargo
- Be able to determine if cargo is properly loaded and secured

Tractor-trailer drivers must also pass certain tests and be able to fill out the applications that are required. They must:

- Fill out a job application that meets DOT requirement FMCSR 391.21 (carrier will supply the application).
- Take a written test and a road test given by the company. The DOT requires the company to keep the results on file.
- Have passed all the tests needed for their CDL.
  - General Knowledge Test
  - Air Brakes Test
  - Combination Vehicles Test
  - Pre-trip Inspection Test
  - Basic Control Skills Test and Road Test

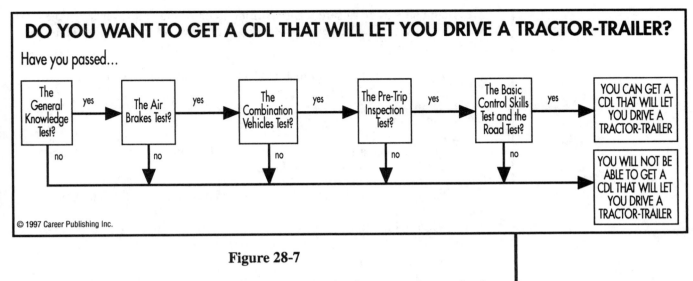

**Figure 28-7**

Drivers who operate double or triple trailer combinations or tankers or haul hazardous material must pass additional tests before they can drive these vehicles.

## Disqualifications

Under FMSCR 391.15, an applicant for a CDL that will let them drive a tractor-trailer must be disqualified for any of the following:
- Loss of license
- Operating a motor vehicle while under the influence of alcohol, amphetamines, or narcotics
- Transportation, possession, or unlawful use of a Schedule I drug
- Being in an accident that results in injury or death and leaving the scene
- Conviction of a felony involving the use of a commercial motor vehicle

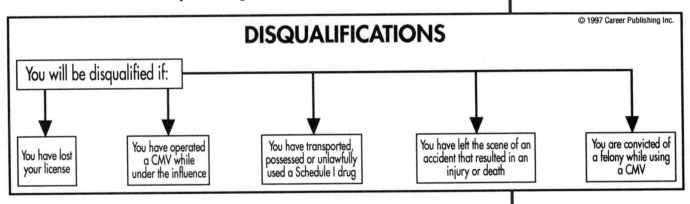

**Figure 28-8**

## General Qualifications

Truck driver applicants should know something about the various types of vehicles used in the industry. They should also be informed about their systems and components. They should be able to speak the language of the industry as well as know how to fill out the required paperwork. A knowledge of state and local traffic regulations and laws must be demonstrated. This includes the basic hazardous materials requirements.

Being able to drive safely and learning to drive the employer's vehicles safely are *must skills*. The driver must also know how to handle cargo using the correct handling methods.

To qualify, an applicant must have a positive attitude toward the:
- Trucking industry
- Employer
- Job

He or she must also be willing to follow company policies regarding hours of work, safety rules, and public relations.

Finally, the candidate must have a personality that suits the job. This includes:
- High job interest
- Maturity
- Safety awareness
- Enthusiasm
- A responsible nature

## Company Policy

Each company has its own policies. Company policy should be followed even if it differs from what you have learned in school or elsewhere. Find out what is expected during your job interview and then meet those expectations.

---

**Company Policies**

Most company policies have requirements that cover:
- Hours of work and benefits
- Basic work rules
  - Types of supervision
  - Requirements for advancement
  - Discipline including rules for dismissal
- Safety rules
  - Safety training
  - Safety meetings
  - Safe driving and cargo handling rules
- Vehicle inspection and maintenance requirements
  - Instructions
  - What is expected of the driver
  - Forms to be filled out
- Rules for trips
  - Driving rules for fuel economy
  - Where and when drivers can make fuel or rest stops
  - How drivers are to pay for fuel, food, etc.
  - Reimbursement policy for drivers
  - Use of credit cards
  - Cash advances
- Relations with the public and customers
  - Dress code
  - Conduct expected

## What Companies Cannot Require of a Driver

No driver can be required to work in violation of state, federal, or local regulations. Drivers must be provided with a safe place to work and a safe vehicle. No driver can be required to violate the hours of service regulations.

© 1997 Career Publishing Inc.

- If there is any violation of federal, state, or local laws
- If you are not qualified
- If you will violate the hours of service regulations
- If the rig is unsafe to drive

**REFUSE TO HAUL THE LOAD!**

**Figure 28-9**

## Drivers and Company Policy

The more a driver applicant knows about a company, the easier it is to get a job interview and do well during the interview. If possible, know the answers to the following questions in advance:
- Do you have the abilities the employer needs?
- If additional training is available, are you are willing to learn?
- Is this a place where you want to work?
- Are the hours, pay, and working conditions going to meet your needs?

Obviously, the greatest likelihood for success exists when the company and applicant agree on these needs. The job seeker should be aware that he or she will have to learn the company policies in depth and follow them.

Finally, a person's attitude is as important as their knowledge of company requirements. To review, the key attitudes you should have if you want to be successful on the job are:
- Working with a spirit of cooperation
- Loyalty
- Dependability
- Safety mindedness
- Honesty

## Opportunities for Advancement

There are many types of jobs in the trucking industry. Many new drivers today start out driving tractor-trailers over-the-road for large fleets. But some start driving locally in, perhaps, a smaller truck. They may even start as yard jockeys, freight handlers, and truck washers before moving up to local deliveries with straight trucks. Then they may move on to intrastate work.

You can gain valuable experience at the local level. Picking up freight in the morning, making local deliveries and pickups all day, following dispatch instructions, and dealing with the shipping papers is good training for tractor-trailer drivers. This is the time to do a good job, show enthusiasm, and learn all you can. While you wait for a chance to get the driving job you want, the experience you gain and a good record will help you qualify for the over-the-road jobs that require the most skill.

In trucking, most advancement is from within. One type of advancement within the trucking industry is being promoted to the longer hauls that carry more valuable cargo or hazardous materials. Other positions are dispatcher, terminal manager, or working in freight operations.

## APPLYING FOR THE JOB

Generally, an applicant for a job as a tractor-trailer driver must fill out an application, give references for the employer to check, have a job interview, and be tested.

The application form is the first impression you make on the potential employer. If your application is neat, accurate, and honest, you will usually make a good impression on the employer. However, whether you meet their requirements is not always easy to tell from the application.

For reference checks, you should have the names and addresses of previous employers. It is very important that you give an accurate account of your previous driving record.

Next to the road test, the interview is the most important part in finding a job, and you have a chance to sell yourself. There are three key rules for a good job interview:

1. Be prepared.
2. Know how to act during the interview.
3. End the interview well and thank the person for their time and consideration.

**Figure 28-10**

## Preparing for the Interview

To prepare for the interview:
- Learn all you can about the company.
- Be ready to ask intelligent questions such as:
  - What are the company policies?
  - What are the chances for training?
  - Is there opportunity for advancement?
- Know your own abilities and limitations.
- Know whether you can you drive the kind of vehicle used in this job and handle the cargo?
- Know whether you will need extra training.

Make sure you have all the necessary paperwork with you including the correct license, endorsements, certifications, and letters of reference.

Be ready for the interview; be on time or a bit early. Visit the location a day or so before the interview so you will not get lost or be delayed. Dress neatly but ready to drive if you are asked to take a road test.

## How to Act During the Interview

The interview is your chance to sell yourself. Be polite and courteous, and do not smoke unless you are invited to. When you are asked about your qualifications and experiences, present them clearly and honestly. Do not brag or stretch the truth. Be sure the interviewer knows what you have done in the past. Showing how your experiences and qualifications fit in with what the company needs is very important.

Most people are a little nervous before and during interviews. Do not let this bother you. Just try to relax and be yourself. Keep a positive attitude about the job. A good attitude is often what makes the difference in who gets the job.

Remember, the interviewer's job is to learn about you — to find out who you are and what you are like. Try to answer questions clearly, but do not volunteer unnecessary information. Try to keep talk fixed on the job and why you are the best candidate.

Ask questions. Find out about the company. Do not wait until you get the job to find out you do not like it. If the interviewer does not tell you about conditions that are important to an employee, he or she expects you to ask.

## End the Interview Well

Thank the interviewer for his or her time and interest. Show your interest in the company and the job and repeat how you can meet their needs. Ask how and when you will be informed of their decision.

You may not get the job. If you do not and you think the company is a place where you want to work, you may choose to accept a job as a helper or dock worker as a place to begin.

## Tests

Be prepared and well rested when you take the written and performance tests. To prepare for the written tests:
- Study the regulations about safe driving practices.
- Review the state driver handbook and FMCSR regulations.
- Review the safe driving information and procedures learned in school.

If you do not have a copy of a **Test Study Book** for the specific tests you must take, you may obtain them from Career Publishing Inc. by phoning (800) 854-4014. For tractor-trailer drivers, Test Study Books are available for the General Knowledge, Air Brakes, Combination Vehicles, Tank Vehicles, Hazardous Materials, Doubles/Triples, Pre-Trip Inspection, and Basic Control Skills and Road Tests. The types of questions and answers used on the tests are included.

The road test is a most important part of applying for a job. The test will probably include:
- A pre-trip inspection
- Coupling and uncoupling
- Backing
- Parking
- Driving in traffic

Be dressed and ready for the test. Ask about unfamiliar parts or accessories. If you feel you are not qualified to drive the rig, do not drive. **Do not take a risk with an unfamiliar vehicle**.

**Figure 28-11**

## Physical Examination

You must have a current, valid doctor's certificate stating you have passed a physical examination and meet the minimum qualifications. If you have not had one, you will need to have a physical exam. The company may also give its own physical.

# SUMMARY

In this chapter, you have learned how a truck driver acts has much to do with how the public views the whole trucking industry. You have also learned how to present a good image and how to avoid presenting a bad image. Ways to maintain good public relations were explained. The penalties for bad public relations were presented. You now know the minimum requirements for becoming a truck driver, and how to obtain your CDL. Ways to find a job and handle an interview were also explained.

# KEY WORDS

**Driver image:** The impression a truck driver makes on other people.

**Employer-employee relations:** How you, as a truck driver, get along with your employer, the carrier.

**Public relations:** How you, as a truck driver, get along with the public.

**Test Study Books:** Books sold by Career Publishing Inc. that will help you study for and pass your CDL tests.

# LEARNING ACTIVITIES

## Role Playing

You are to take part in an interview for a job as a tractor-trailer driver. The instructor will set the scene by telling you how you found out about this job, what you know about it, and any other items of importance that have occurred before the interview.

Divide into groups of five. One person will act as the interviewer. The second person will act as the job applicant. The other three people will listen to the interview and offer comments after it is over. It is helpful if the listeners make notes as the interview progresses so nothing is overlooked. Rotate these roles until everyone has had a chance to play each character.

Then come back together and share with the class in a discussion of what you have learned from the experience. Decide what was the most helpful part in preparing for an actual interview. Each class member should have a chance to discuss the interview.

## Good PR or Bad PR

### Part A

The public's image of the trucking industry is determined for the most part by how their drivers act in a situation. Several common examples are given below. Discuss what a truck driver's reaction might be. Then determine if it is going to create good Public Relations or bad Public Relations. If the class decides the reaction was bad PR, discuss what should have been done to turn it into good PR.

1.  You are driving on an Interstate Highway and most of the traffic in the right two lanes are trucks. Traffic is heavy but is flowing at the speed limit. In your rearview mirror, you see this little sports car weaving in and out of traffic. You see it is a hazard for the big rigs. Suddenly it disappears into your blind spot. You are trying to anticipate what its next move will be when it whips around you cutting you off as it zips into your lane. As the car passes you, the driver makes an obscene gesture. Your first thought is anger. After all, the sports car was a danger and you were going as fast as the law allows.

2.  You are in the second from the right lane on an Interstate Highway. Traffic is heavy, so it is very difficult to change lanes. You do notice that people in the lanes beside you are moving at a faster speed than you. One by one, the vehicles ahead of you change lanes. Then you see why. There is slow moving car ahead of you. As you become the first vehicle behind the car, you see the driver is an older person who is clutching the wheel and the car has out of state plates. You decide to show the slow driver what a hazard they are, so you ride the car's tail.

3.  You are driving on a secondary road when you see a car stopped off to the side of the road. There are two small children inside. There is a woman standing beside the car waving frantically. What are your choices? What does company policy say? Should you stop and help? What other possibilities are there?

4.  You are making local deliveries, and it has been a really trying day. The roads out there are a zoo. You are sure every loony was on them. You have two deliveries left, and you will be glad to be able to go home. You try to deliver the shipment, but the owner of the company says he never ordered the merchandise. You check the shipping papers. They seem to be in order. You tell the consignee this information. He then launches into a tirade against your stupid company and the even more stupid drivers who obviously cannot read, etc., etc. Your first impulse is to tell him what he can do with the shipment in no uncertain terms.

5.  You come upon an accident shortly after it has happened. You are running behind schedule and really do not want to stop and help. You glance at the scene and see someone should at least warn on-coming traffic there is a problem here. What actions might the driver take? What should he or she do that would create good PR? What things should be avoided so there is no bad PR?

## Part B

Have the class create additional situations and share normal reactions to them. Again, decide if the reaction is going to create good PR or bad PR. If it is bad PR, discuss how good PR could be produced instead.

Have the class bring in clippings from newspapers or magazine that tell of incidents involving trucks. Discuss the reasons for the incidents and possible public reaction to them.

## True-False Questions

If the statement is true, circle the T. If the statement is false, circle the F.

T   F   1.   How the public views the trucking industry influences laws that are passed related to the industry.

T   F   2.   Many people have a poor image of the trucking industry.

T   F   3.   Most conflicts between the public and the trucking industry occur in road sharing situations.

T   F   4.   All factors that affect the trucking industry's public image mean more when the public is a customer.

T   F   5.   Those who wish to drive a tractor-trailer must be at least 20 years of age.

T   F   6.   One important qualification for over-the-road driving is having a personality that suits the job.

T   F   7.   No driver may be required to work in violation of federal, state, or local regulations.

T   F   8.   Sometimes qualified drivers start out with a company as yard jockeys, freight handlers, or truck washers.

T   F   9.   The most important part of applying for a job is the list of references you give the employer.

T   F   10.  The interview is a good opportunity to brag about what you have done in the past.

T   F   11.  When being interviewed for a job, the candidate should answer questions but not ask the interviewer questions.

T   F   12.  The road test is a most important part of applying for a job.

T   F   13.  Even if you have a current valid doctor's certificate of a successful physical examination, you may be asked to take a physical exam given by a company appointed physician.

# Chapter Twenty-Nine
# THE COMMERCIAL DRIVER LICENSE

## YOUR COMMERCIAL DRIVER LICENSE

| I.D.NUMBER | HT. | WGT. | CLASS |
|---|---|---|---|
| | | | |

ENDORSMENT :
    Tanker N

SIGNATURE

NAME:
STREET:
CITY:                 ZIP

**The Law • Classes and Endorsements • CDL Knowledge Tests • CDL Skills Tests**
**Exceptions • Why So Many Different Tests? • Passing Scores • A Single License**
**A Classified License • A National License • CDL Test Study Book Series**
**CDL Videotapes • CDL Audiotapes**

# CDL WHAT COMMERCIAL DRIVER'S LICENSE WRITTEN KNOWLEDGE TESTS WILL YOU NEED TO PASS ?

*IT DEPENDS UPON THE TYPE OF COMMERCIAL MOTOR VEHICLE YOU DRIVE AND THE CARGO YOU HAUL. HERE ARE SOME EXAMPLES:*

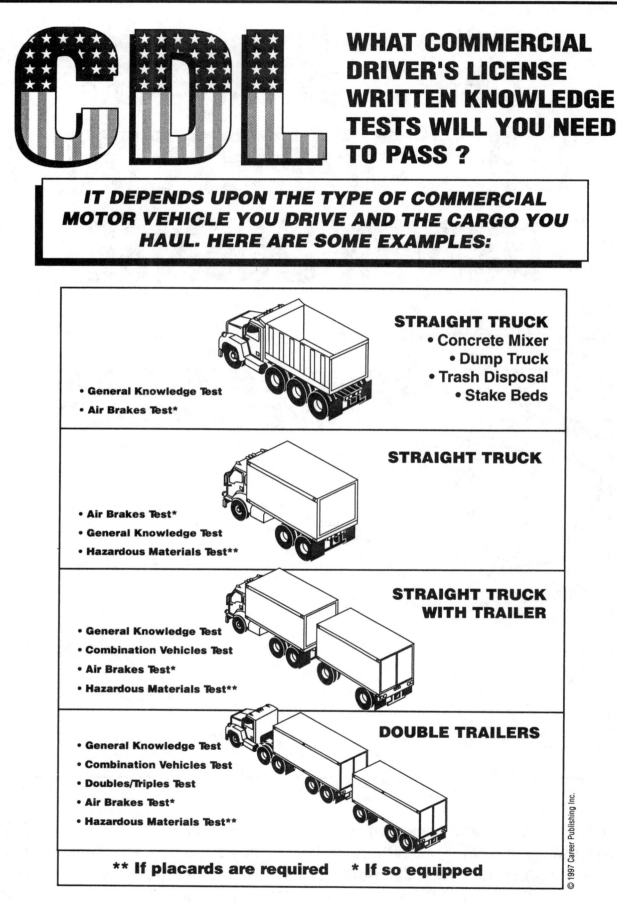

### STRAIGHT TRUCK
- Concrete Mixer
- Dump Truck
- Trash Disposal
- Stake Beds

- General Knowledge Test
- Air Brakes Test*

### STRAIGHT TRUCK

- Air Brakes Test*
- General Knowledge Test
- Hazardous Materials Test**

### STRAIGHT TRUCK WITH TRAILER

- General Knowledge Test
- Combination Vehicles Test
- Air Brakes Test*
- Hazardous Materials Test**

### DOUBLE TRAILERS

- General Knowledge Test
- Combination Vehicles Test
- Doubles/Triples Test
- Air Brakes Test*
- Hazardous Materials Test**

**\*\* If placards are required     \* If so equipped**

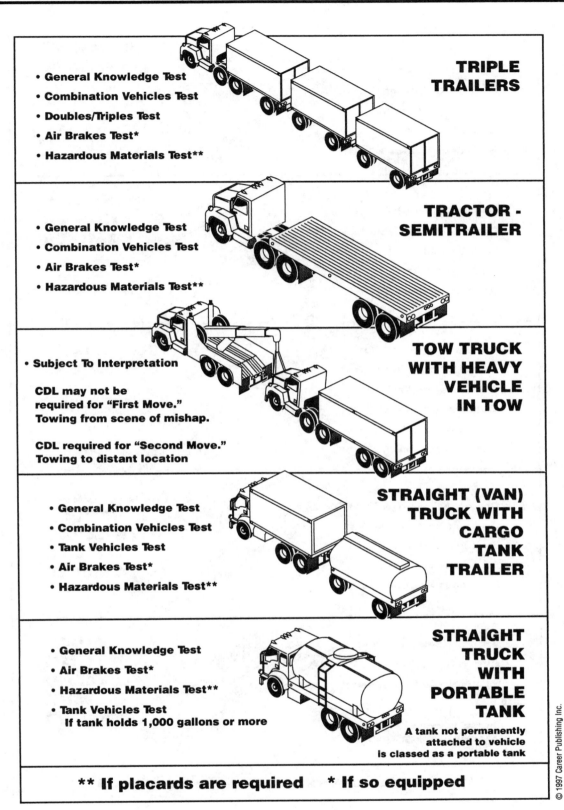

**TRIPLE TRAILERS**

- General Knowledge Test
- Combination Vehicles Test
- Doubles/Triples Test
- Air Brakes Test*
- Hazardous Materials Test**

**TRACTOR - SEMITRAILER**

- General Knowledge Test
- Combination Vehicles Test
- Air Brakes Test*
- Hazardous Materials Test**

**TOW TRUCK WITH HEAVY VEHICLE IN TOW**

- Subject To Interpretation

CDL may not be required for "First Move." Towing from scene of mishap.

CDL required for "Second Move." Towing to distant location

**STRAIGHT (VAN) TRUCK WITH CARGO TANK TRAILER**

- General Knowledge Test
- Combination Vehicles Test
- Tank Vehicles Test
- Air Brakes Test*
- Hazardous Materials Test**

**STRAIGHT TRUCK WITH PORTABLE TANK**

- General Knowledge Test
- Air Brakes Test*
- Hazardous Materials Test**
- Tank Vehicles Test
  If tank holds 1,000 gallons or more

A tank not permanently attached to vehicle is classed as a portable tank

## ** If placards are required      * If so equipped

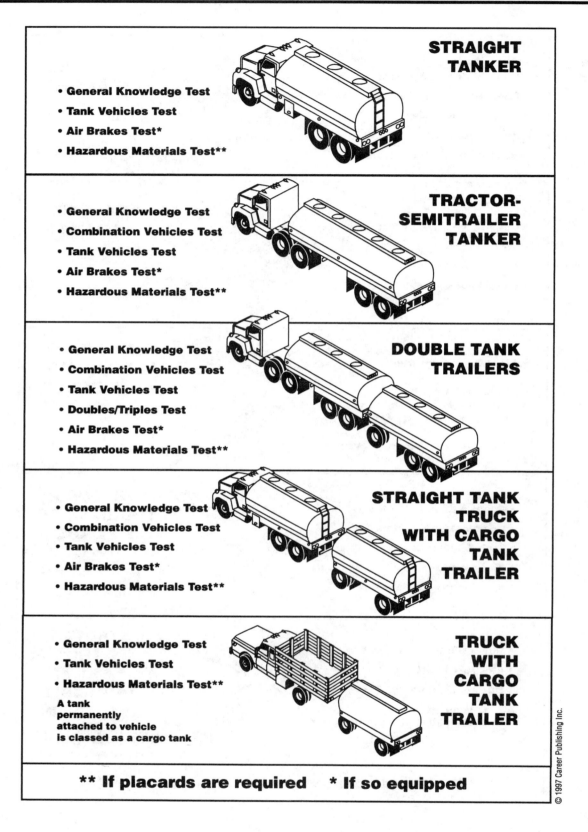

**STRAIGHT TANKER**

- General Knowledge Test
- Tank Vehicles Test
- Air Brakes Test*
- Hazardous Materials Test**

**TRACTOR-SEMITRAILER TANKER**

- General Knowledge Test
- Combination Vehicles Test
- Tank Vehicles Test
- Air Brakes Test*
- Hazardous Materials Test**

**DOUBLE TANK TRAILERS**

- General Knowledge Test
- Combination Vehicles Test
- Tank Vehicles Test
- Doubles/Triples Test
- Air Brakes Test*
- Hazardous Materials Test**

**STRAIGHT TANK TRUCK WITH CARGO TANK TRAILER**

- General Knowledge Test
- Combination Vehicles Test
- Tank Vehicles Test
- Air Brakes Test*
- Hazardous Materials Test**

**TRUCK WITH CARGO TANK TRAILER**

- General Knowledge Test
- Tank Vehicles Test
- Hazardous Materials Test**

A tank permanently attached to vehicle is classed as a cargo tank

**\*\* If placards are required    \* If so equipped**

## CHAPTER TWENTY-NINE

# THE COMMERCIAL DRIVER LICENSE

## INTRODUCTION

As a commercial vehicle driver, you should be aware that commercial driver licensing procedures have changed. In the past, states have been allowed to regulate and license operators of commercial vehicles under their own guidelines. But now, states must follow a new set of national minimum standards for licensing and testing commercial drivers. The national standards, set by the federal government, establish a new **Commercial Driver License (CDL)**. Since these are minimum standards, your state can make stricter rules for getting your CDL. You will need to read and study your state's commercial driver handbook to pass the required tests. You can also buy special Test Study Books, Videos, and audiotapes from Career Publishing.

You can help yourself by becoming familiar with the CDL facts on the following pages. They are based on the minimum federal standards, but they apply to all states.

## THE LAW

1.  On October 26, 1986 the **Commercial Motor Vehicle Safety Act** was signed into law. This law requires each state to meet the same minimum standards for commercial driver licensing.

2.  The federal standards require commercial motor vehicle drivers to get a Commercial Motor Vehicle Driver License (CDL).

3.  You must have a CDL to operate any of the following Commercial Motor Vehicles (CMVs):
    A.  A single vehicle with a gross vehicle weight rating (GVWR) of more than 26,000 pounds. The GVWR is the rating assigned by the manufacturer of the vehicle.
    B.  A trailer with a GVWR of more than 10,000 pounds if the gross combination weight rating is more than 26,000 pounds.
    C.  A vehicle designed to transport more than 15 persons (including the driver).
    D.  Any size vehicle that requires hazardous materials placards.

4.  Your state may have stricter definitions of CMVs. California, for example, defines a bus as any vehicle designed to transport 10 or more passengers, including the driver.

5.  The goals of the new standards set by the CMVSA of 1986 are to:
    • Improve driver quality
    • Remove problem drivers from the highways
    • Establish a system that will prevent operators of CMVs from having more than one license

6.  You cannot have more than one license, that is, licenses from more than one state. If you break this rule, a court may fine you up to $5,000 or put you in jail. Keep your home state license and return any others.

7.  If you are an experienced commercial driver and have a safe driving record, you may not need to take the skills test to get your CDL. Check with your driver licensing authorities.

8.  If you are employed as a commercial vehicle driver, you must tell your employer within 30 days of a conviction for any traffic violation (except parking). This must be done no matter what type of vehicle you were driving, even if you were driving your own car.

9.  You must notify your motor vehicle licensing agency within 30 days if you are convicted in any other state of any traffic violation (except parking). This is true no matter what type of vehicle you were driving.

10.  If you are employed as a commercial vehicle driver, you must notify your employer if your license is suspended, revoked, or canceled, or if you are disqualified from driving.

11.  If you are employed as a commercial vehicle driver, you must give your employer information on all driving jobs you have held for the past 10 years. You must also do this when you apply for a commercial driving job.

12.  No one can drive a CMV without a CDL. A court may fine you up to $5000 or put you in jail if you drive a CMV without a CDL.

13.  Your employer cannot let you drive a Commercial Motor Vehicle if you have more than one license or if your CDL is suspended or revoked. A court may fine the employer up to $5000 or put him or her in jail if they break this rule.

14.  All states will be connected to one computerized system to share information about CDL drivers. The states will check on drivers' accident records and be sure that drivers do not have more than one CDL.

15.  You will lose your CDL for at least one year for a first offense:
     • If you drive a CMV under the influence of alcohol or a controlled substance (for example, illegal drugs)
     • If you leave the scene of an accident involving your CMV
     • If you used a CMV to commit a felony; if the offense occurs while you are operating a CMV that is placarded for hazardous materials, you will lose you CDL for at least 3 years. You will lose your CDL for life for a second offense. You will also lose your CDL for life if you use a CMV to commit a felony involving controlled substances.

16.  You will lose your CDL:
     • For at least 60 days if you have committed two serious traffic violations within a 3-year period in a CMV
     • For at least 120 days for three serious traffic violations (involving any vehicle) within a 3-year period
       Serious traffic violations are excessive speeding, reckless driving, or traffic offenses committed in a CMV where there is a fatality.

17.  If you drive after drinking any amount of alcohol, you are driving under the influence of alcohol. You will lose your CDL for one year for your first offense. You will lose it for life for your second offense.

18.  These rules will improve highway safety for you and all highway users. Your State may have additional rules that you must obey.

## CLASSES OF LICENSES AND ENDORSEMENTS

19.  **Class A CDL**: Combination vehicles where the combined GVWR is 26,001 pounds or more and the GVWR of the vehicle(s) being towed is over 10,000 pounds.

20.  **Class B CDL**: Single vehicles with GVWR of 26,001 pounds or more. These vehicles may also tow trailers with a GVWR of 10,000 pounds or less.

21.  **Class C CDL**: Any vehicle with a GVWR less than 26,001 pounds if:
     • Designed to carry 16 or more persons including the driver; or
     • Transports hazardous materials requiring placards

22.  **ENDORSEMENT T**: Required when operating a double or triple trailer combination unit.

23.  **ENDORSEMENT P**: Required when operating a passenger vehicle designed to carry 16 or more persons including the driver.

24.  **ENDORSEMENT N**: Required when operating a tank vehicle designed to carry liquid in bulk or gases.

25.  **ENDORSEMENT H:** Required when operating a vehicle carrying hazardous material requiring placarding. If the driver is operating a tanker carrying harzardous material, **ENDORSEMENT X** is needed.

26.  **AIR BRAKES RESTRICTION:** Restricts operators to vehicles without air brakes.

## CDL KNOWLEDGE TESTS

27.  You will also need to take one or more knowledge tests, depending on what class of license and what endorsements you need. The CDL knowledge tests include the:
     **General Knowledge Test**, taken by all applicants.
     **Passenger Transport Test**, taken by all bus driver applicants.
     **Air Brakes Test**, which you must take if your vehicle has air brakes.
     **Combination Vehicles Test**, which is required if you want to drive combination vehicles.
     **Hazardous Materials Test**, required if you want to haul hazardous material or waste.
     **Tanker Test**, required if you want to haul liquids in bulk.
     **Doubles/Triples Test**, required if you want to pull double or triple trailers.

28.  All drivers must take the knowledge test(s). You may have to take from one to six written tests depending upon the endorsements requested. This requirement applies even if you presently hold a license.

## CDL SKILLS TESTS

**29.** If you pass the required knowledge tests, you can take the CDL skills and performance tests.

**30.** There are three types of CDL skills tests:
- The Pre-Trip Inspection Test
- The Basic Control Skills Test
- The Behind-the-Wheel Road Test

**31.** You must take these tests in the type of vehicle for which you wish to be licensed.

**32.** The purpose of the **Pre-Trip Inspection Test** is to check if you know whether or not your vehicle is safe to drive. During the Pre-Trip Inspection Test you will be asked to do a pre-trip inspection of your vehicle and/or explain to the examiner what you would inspect and why. You must demonstrate that you have a pre-determined or set routine for effectively conducting a pre-trip inspection.

**33.** Your vehicle must be in satisfactory condition at the time of the pre-trip test. All required equipment on your vehicle must be in place and in good working order. You must be able to demonstrate knowledge of your vehicle and its equipment.

**34.** For the Pre-Trip Test, the examiner will mark on a scoring form each item that you correctly inspect or explain. You and your vehicle must pass the pre-trip inspection, or you will not be allowed to take the Behind-the-Wheel Road Test.

**35.** The **Basic Control Skills Test** evaluates your basic skills in controlling the vehicle. This test consists of various exercises marked out by lines, traffic cones, or other boundaries. The exercises may include moving the vehicle forward, backing, parking, and turning maneuvers.

**36.** The examiner will explain to you how each exercise should be done. You will be scored on how well you control the vehicle, how well you stay within the exercise boundaries, and how many pullups you make. (A pullup is when you pull the vehicle forward in order to correct your position and continue the exercise.)

**37.** You must pass the Basic Control Skills Test if you intend to drive a Class A or Class B CMV. Your state may have you perform the Basic Control Skills Test exercises during the Road Test.

**38.** In some cases, when you apply for a Class A or Class B license, instead of taking a driving test, you may submit a Certificate of Driving. This certificate must be completed by your employer. The employer must be authorized by the state to issue such certificates. You can check with the state or your employer for more information on the Certificates of Driving Experience or Training.

**39.** **The Basic Control Skills Test** may include as many as seven test exercises.

A. **Measured Right Turn** — You must drive forward and make a right turn around a cone, marker, or curb. Your right rear wheels should come as close as possible to the cone, marker, or curb without touching it.

B. **Forward Stop** — You drive forward between lines (alley) and stop as close as possible to a stop line at the end of the alley. The alley will be about 100 feet long and 12 feet wide. After you stop, the examiner will measure the distance between the bumper and the stop line.

C. **Straight Line Backing** — This exercise tests your ability to back straight without touching or crossing boundary lines in an alley. The alley will be about 100 feet long and 12 feet wide. The examiner will check if you touch or cross the boundaries. Pullups will also be counted as errors.

D. **Alley Dock** — This exercise involves backing into an alley stall from the sight (left) side to simulate docking. The examiner will watch for pullups and hitting or crossing boundary lines or markers. When you stop at the end of the exercise, the distance between the rear of your vehicle and the stop line or dock marker will be checked.

E. **Parallel Park (Sight Side)** — For this exercise, you will park in a space that is on your left. The space you have to park in will be 10 feet longer than your vehicle. The examiner will look for pullups, hitting cones, and touching or crossing boundary lines. When you toot your horn at the end of the maneuver, the examiner will record the distance your vehicle is from the back, front, and curb lines.

F. **Parallel Park (Blind Side)** — In this exercise, the parking space is on the right side of your vehicle. The routine is the same as the sight side parallel parking exercise.

G. **Backward Serpentine** — This exercise requires backing around cones or markers, beginning and ending with markers on the left side. The serpentine layout is a row of three cones. You are to back around the three cones in a serpentine or snake manner without striking the cones or markers. One correction or pullup is usually allowed. In some tests, you may exit your vehicle to check your position.

40. Your state may require you to perform all seven of the skill exercises or only some of them. This will depend upon the space available at the examination site and the type of vehicle you are driving. A failure on any part of the skills test may cause you to fail the complete test, or points may be deducted for each error. Make sure you know how the test will be scored before you attempt the exercises.

41.  Once you have completed all other tests you are ready for the behind-the-wheel Road Test. The **Road Test** is also known as the "drive test." The Road Test is the test where you show your ability to drive in traffic. In this test, you demonstrate your safe driving skills. The test drive is taken over a route chosen by the examiner. As you drive, you must follow the instructions and directions given by the examiner. You will need to take the road test in the type of vehicle for which you intend to be licensed. Since safety is of highest priority, if you cause an accident or do not obey a traffic law during the test, you may automatically fail the test.

42.  The examiner will score you on how well you make turns, make lane changes, merge into traffic and control your speed at certain places along the test route. You will also be scored on how well you signal, search for hazards, shift gears, use mirrors, control speed, and position your vehicle in your lane.

43.  Like other CDL tests, your application fee generally entitles you to several attempts at passing the Road Test.

44.  During the Road Test, you will drive over a test route that has been planned and set up in advance. The ideal test route would include the **scoring locations** described in items 44A through 44N. The examiner will score certain driving performances at each location.

    A.  **Left and Right Turns**:  You will be asked to make turns at traffic lights, stop signs and uncontrolled intersections. The turns will range from easy to somewhat difficult for heavy vehicles. You can expect to make from four to eight left turns and four to eight right turns.

    B.  **City Business Streets**:  This section will be a one to two miles long, straight stretch in an urban business area. This test will contain uncontrolled intersections (no lights or stops) and controlled intersections. The traffic will be moderate. The section will require you to make lane changes somewhere along the route. This section will let you show how you cope with traffic in a typical business area.

    C.  **Intersections**:  These intersections may be located in the business area described. The test will include your driving through:
        •  Two uncontrolled intersections: these are through intersections — not controlled by traffic lights or stop signs.
        •  Two controlled intersections. These intersections are controlled by lights and signs. They are street corners where a stop may have to be made.

    D.  **Railway Crossings**:  The test will try to include one uncontrolled crossing and one controlled crossing. The crossings should have enough sight distance so that you can look for oncoming trains. You must look left and right as you approach the crossing. Your head movement is the only way the examiner can tell if you have noticed the crossing and are searching for hazards.

E.  **Left and Right Curves**: This section includes two curves, one to the left and one to the right. The curves will be fairly tight. Tight curves are used so that a noticeable off-tracking situation is produced. (Off-tracking occurs when the rear wheels do not follow the same path as the front wheels.)

F.  **Two-Lane Rural or Semi-Rural Road**: This section of the test will be about two miles long. If a rural road is not available in the test area, a street with few entrances and a higher speed limit will be used. This part of the test lets you show how you handle situations found on a two-lane rural road.

G.  **Freeway or Expressway**: This is where you show your ability to handle freeway or expressway driving. The sections should start with a ramp entrance and end with a ramp exit. The section should be long enough for a heavy vehicle to do two lane changes. A section of multi-lane highway may be used if there is no freeway or expressway available.

H.  **Downgrade**: The grade should be steep enough and long enough to require you to gear down and brake. If a long grade is not available, a steep, short hill will probably be used.

I.  **Upgrade**: The grade should be steep enough and long enough to require gear changing to maintain your speed. The same grade may be used for both the upgrade and downgrade sections of the test.

J.  **Downgrade for Stopping**: This is a grade where a bus or truck can be safely stopped and parked for a minute or so. The grade needs to be only steep enough to cause the vehicle to roll if you do not park properly. It only takes a gentle slope to cause a heavy vehicle to roll.

K.  **Upgrade for Stopping**: This section checks your ability to safely park on an upgrade. The same grade used for the downgrade stop may be used for this part of the test.

L.  **Underpass or Low Clearance and Bridge:** One underpass or low clearance and one bridge are used for this section. The underpass should have a posted clearance height. The bridge should have a posted weight limit. If an underpass or bridge is not available, the examiner will have you drive at places that have signs a heavy vehicle driver should heed. Examples of such signs are: "No Commercial Vehicles After 11:00 PM," or "Bridge With 10 Ton Weight Limit In 5 Miles."

M.  **Before Downgrade**: This is a flat section of road (1/4 mile long) where you are asked to go through the motions of driving down a steep grade. You will need to explain your actions. It may or may not be before a downgrade. If not, you are to pretend it is.

N.  **Other Railway Crossing**: When no actual railway crossing is available, a regular intersection may be used. You will be asked to pretend the intersection is a crossing. You must handle this as you would a real railway crossing. You will be scored as if you were driving at a real crossing.

45. As you can tell, these test route locations offer a wide variety of traffic situations. They also require you to perform certain driving tasks properly at each location. For instance, during each of four right turns, the examiner may grade your:

A. Speed
B. Position and lane usage:
   • Starts in wrong lane
   • Ends in wrong lane
   • Swings too wide
   • Swings too short
C. Mirror Checks
D. Signaling
E. Canceling signal
F. Gear Changes
G. Traffic checks

46. The Road Test course is planned so that certain tasks or maneuvers are scored only at selected locations during the test. You may make 10 right turns during the test drive. Yet only four of the turns may be used as scoring locations. The examiner will not deduct points for a maneuver that is performed improperly if this occurs at a location other than the pre-selected location for the maneuver to be performed. There is one big exception: an error that is grounds for immediate failure will be scored anywhere along the test drive course.

47. Each state will have its own special **Grounds For Immediate Failure (GFIF)** rules. Make sure you know your state's GFIF rules before you take the test. The GFIF rules deal with serious errors. As soon as an error of this type is made, the test is stopped. Here is a list of errors that may be grounds for immediate failure:

A. An accident during the test drive that involves any amount of property damage or personal injury.
B. Refusal to perform any maneuver that is part of the test.
C. Any dangerous action in which:
   • An accident is prevented by the actions of others.
   • The examiner must help the test driver avoid an accident.
   • The test driver drives over a curb or sidewalk and by doing so endangers others.
   • The test driver creates a serious traffic hazard, such as:
      a) Driving the wrong way on a one-way street;
      b) Driving on the wrong side of a two-way street;
      c) Stalling the vehicle in a busy intersection.
D. The test driver commits one of the following:
   • Passes another vehicle that is stopped at a crosswalk while yielding to a pedestrian.
   • Passes a school bus, with its red lights flashing, while the bus is loading or unloading students.
   • Makes or starts to make a turn from the wrong lane under traffic conditions that create a dangerous situation. An example of this would be a left turn from the right-turn lane or a right turn from the left-turn lane. This could be on a two-way street with several lanes, or it could be on a one-way street.
   • Running through a red light or stop sign. This applies if the test driver has to be stopped from running the light or sign.

E. The test driver is unable to properly operate vehicle equipment; or after a short distance on the test course, it becomes apparent that the test driver is dangerously inexperienced.

48. The national CDL system allows each state to make up its own tests and scoring systems. The national rules require the applicant to be able to perform certain skills, but the state may require more than the national rules. The applicant must successfully perform all of the skills in the road test to achieve a passing score. There are a number of road test scoring systems a state can use.

49. Before you take your road test, make sure you know:
- How you will be scored
- What performances will be graded
- What makes up a passing score
- The grounds for immediate failure
- The rules for repeating the test in case you fail

## EXCEPTIONS

50. There are exceptions to the national CDL rules. For instance, you may *not* have to take the Basic Control Skills Test and Road test because of your CMV driving experience or good safety record. Who you work for or the type of work you do may free you from some CDL requirements. Your state is given leeway in deciding this. Check your state's CDL rules. You may qualify for an exemption or be an exception to the CDL rule.

51. Exemptions and exceptions to CDL testing do not apply for the knowledge tests. The knowledge test requirements apply to all commercial drivers — experienced and new drivers alike.

## WHY SO MANY DIFFERENT TESTS?

52. It is easy to understand why there are three types of performance tests. Commercial drivers must be safe and skillful operators because of the valuable cargo they haul. But what about all the written exams?

Only one written exam would be needed if all commercial drivers drove the same type of vehicle and hauled the same type of cargo. The different vehicles and many cargoes they haul require different knowledge and skills. The CDL tests were made to handle these differences.

53. The General Knowledge Test samples what every driver should know. That is why it is given to all drivers applying for a CDL. The other tests are specialized because they deal with different types of vehicles and cargoes. For example, drivers of vehicles with air brakes need to know about operating air brakes safely.

It would be unfair to ask all drivers to pass a test about air brakes when some drivers have vehicles without air brakes. The same types of arguments can be made for the other specialized tests. Another way of looking at the different tests is that each test result supports a decision about you. Results of the General Knowledge Test support the decision of whether or not you should be licensed at all. Results of the Tank Vehicles Test support a decision whether you should be permitted to drive a tanker, and so forth.

## PASSING SCORES

54. Here are the general rules set by the U.S. Department of Transportation — the federal agency in charge — on passing the CDL tests:
    A. You must correctly answer at least 80 percent (80%) of the questions on each knowledge test in order to pass the test.
    B. To get a passing score on the performance tests, you must show that you can perform all the required skills for your vehicle.
    C. Two factors decide if you receive an air brake restriction on your CDL:
        1. The score you receive on the air brake test questions
        2. The type of vehicle you drive during the driving skills test

55. How the air brake restriction works:
    • If you score less than 80 percent (80%) on the air brake test questions, you will receive an air brake restriction on your CDL. That means you can only drive vehicles without air brakes.
    • If you take the driving skills test in a vehicle not equipped with air brakes, you will be restricted to driving vehicles without air brakes.

    This restriction is now used by nearly all states.
    • To avoid the restriction, take your driving skill test in a vehicle equipped with air brakes.
    • The air brake restriction will be shown on your CDL.

    For the driving skill test and restriction, air brakes mean any braking system that works fully or partly on the air brake principle.

    Your state may have a separate air brake knowledge test. If it does not have the separate test, air brake questions will be found in the General Knowledge Test.

## YOUR COMMERCIAL DRIVER LICENSE IS A:

56. **SINGLE LICENSE:** You hold only one license. There is no need for more than one license. In times past, you may have held an operator's license for your car and a chauffeur's license for your bus. When our national CDL system is fully in place, the chauffeur's license will no longer exist.

57. **CLASSIFIED LICENSE:** Your CDL authorizes you to operate a class of commercial motor vehicles. The CDL identifies the class of vehicle you are qualified to drive. To be issued a CDL you must be tested in a vehicle like the one you will operate.

58. **NATIONAL LICENSE:** Your CDL is a single, classified license. The assignment of the CDL is based on a uniform set of rules issued by the federal government. Your CDL is issued by a state. Each state may have their own test system, but each state must meet a common set of standards. Because the standards are the same throughout the nation, the CDL is a national license.

# Appendix A
# TROUBLE SHOOTING GUIDE

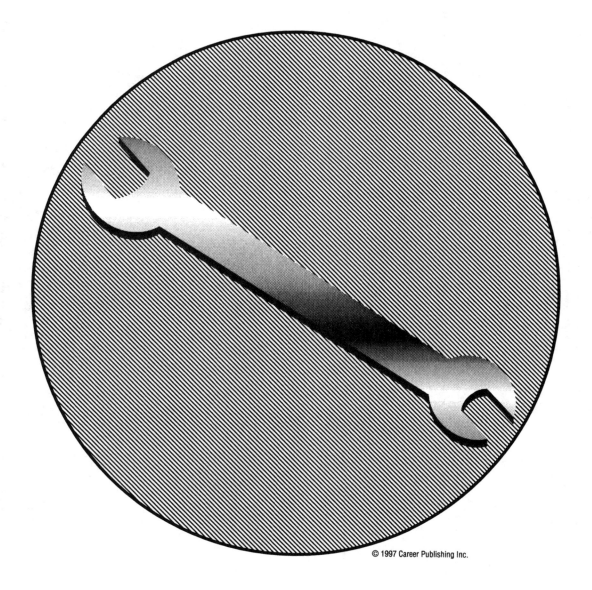

## ALWAYS FOLLOW YOUR COMPANY POLICY

Find out your company's rules for drivers doing any type of repairs to their equipment. Find out what they expect of you. Follow your company's policy. Do **not** do any type of repair work unless you have been authorized to do so.

**WARNING:** Before you jack up a cab-over-engine tractor cab, make sure you have been properly trained to do so. Always use the safety so the cab will not fall on you. Make sure nothing is loose and will fall from the cab or sleeper and break the windshield when the cab is jacked over. Lower the cab back into position very carefully.

| If You See... | System Affected | What to Look For | What to Do |
|---|---|---|---|
| 1. Ammeter shows continuous maximum charge | Electrical | Short circuit in wiring | Disconnect battery terminal until short has been repaired |
| | | Points in voltage regulator or cutout sticking | Have mechanic repair |
| 2. Ammeter shows discharge with motor running | Electrical | Loose connection or short in wiring | Tighten connection |
| | | Battery installed wrong | Have checked by a mechanic |
| | | Burned out or improperly adjusted generator or alternator | Have replaced or repaired by mechanic |
| | | Loose or broken alternator | Replace or tighten belt |
| 3. High engine temperature | Cooling | Low water level | Shut off engine. Allow to cool to normal. Add water. |
| | | Frozen radiator | Cover radiator, run motor slowly, add water as needed. |
| | | Broken fan belt | Replace fan belt |
| | | Slow water or oil circulation | Have checked and repaired by mechanic |
| | | Defective fan clutch or shutters | Have checked and repaired by mechanic |
| | | Blocked radiator | Have checked and repaired by mechanic |
| | | Defective thermostat or radiator hose suction side | Have checked and repaired by mechanic |

| If You See... | System Affected | What to Look For | What to Do |
|---|---|---|---|
| 4. Coolant, oil or fuel dripping | Cooling, Lubricating, or Fuel System | Check for source of leak | Have repaired by mechanic |
| 5. Gauge reading out of proper range | | Check the system that the gauge refers to | Have mechanic check gauge and appropriate system |
| 6. Excessive exhaust smoke | Exhaust or turbo system | Air cleaner dirty | Clean filter |
| | | Poor grade fuel | |
| | | Return fuel line blocked, bent or squeezed together | Let mechanic check and repair |
| | | Engine over-fueled | |
| | | Fuel pump malfunctioning | |
| | | Pollution controls malfunctioning | Have checked and repaired by mechanic |
| 7. Black exhaust smoke | Engine, fuel system | Overrich mixture due to | Clean or change filters. Let mechanic check |
| | | • restricted air supply | |
| | | • poor fuel spray distribution | |
| | | • improperly adjusted fuel control racks or | |
| | | • overloading or lugging the engine | Shift to lower gear to keep engine speed up |
| 8. White (sometimes grey) exhaust smoke | Engine, fuel system | Due to incomplete combustion in cold engine. Should clear up when engine warms. If it doesn't, look for misfiring due to | Have mechanic check |
| | | • Worn injector spray holes | |
| | | • Low cylinder compression | |
| | | • Faulty cooling system | |
| | | • Low fuel volatility | |

| | If You See… | System Affected | What to Look For | What to Do |
|---|---|---|---|---|
| 9. | Blue exhaust smoke | Engine, fuel system | Due to the burning of large quantities of lubricating oil as a result of<br>• Worn intake valve guides<br>• Poor oil control ring action<br>• Worn blower or turbo shaft seals<br>• Overfilled oil bath air cleaner | Have mechnic check |
| 10. | Low pressure | Lubricating system | Oil has become diluted by fuel or coolant leaks | Let mechanic check |
| | | | High oil temperature | Let mechanic check |
| | | | Worn oil pump | |
| | | | Wrong weight oil for type of weather conditions | Change oil |
| | | | Dirty filters | Clean or replace |
| | | | Worn bearings | Replace |
| | | | Oil and filter needs changing | Change oil and filter |
| | | | Oil leak | Let mechanic check |

| | If You Hear… | System Affected | What to Look For | What to Do |
|---|---|---|---|---|
| 11. | Metallic click in time with wheel revolutions | Suspension, wheels or tires | Wheel loose on axle | Tighten axle nut |
| | | | Loose wheel or tire lugs | Tighten lugs |
| | | | Piece of metal in tire | Remove metal or change tire |
| 12. | Dull thud in time with wheel revolutions | Wheels and tires | Flat tire | Change tire |
| | | | Loose wheel or tire lugs | Tighten lugs |
| | | | Rock between duals | Remove rock |
| 13. | Clanking noise in time with wheel | Tire on drive train system | Lock rim off tire | Change tire |
| | | | Loose drive shaft | Have tightened by mechanic |
| 14. | Dull thud or loud rap in time with engine | Engine | Burned out main or connecting rod bearing | Shut off motor. Contact garage for instructions |
| | | | Piston slap | |

| | If You Hear… | System Affected | What to Look For | What to Do |
|---|---|---|---|---|
| 15. | Air escaping | Tires, air system, braking system | Punctured or damaged tire | Change tire |
| | | | Open petcock on air | Close petcock |
| | | | Air lines or fittings leaking | Repair lines, tighten or change fittings |
| | | | Brake application or relay valve sticking | Apply air to brakes several times |
| | | | Ice on brake valves | Apply heat if you have been taught how to do this |
| 16. | Snap or click when starting from dead stop | Drive train system | Loose universal joint bolts | Tighten bolts |
| | | | Excessive wear in universal joint or differential | Report to mechanic |
| | | Fifth wheel | Worn or broken fifth wheel lock. Loose or broken mounting bolts | |
| 17. | Under floor noises | Drive train | Clutch trouble | Have mechanic check |
| | | | Bad throw-out bearing | |
| | | | Bent drive shaft | |
| | | | Broken teeth in transmission | |
| 18. | Whine — harsh with high pitch | Drive train on engine system | Worn accessory drive gears | Let mechanic check |
| | | | Loose belts | Tighten belts |
| 19. | Whine — short with high pitch | Engine | Ball bearing spinning in housing | Have mechanic check |
| | | | Generator or alternator malfunctioning | |
| | | | Water pump malfunctioning | Shut off engine immediately |
| 20. | Clicking sound in engine with loss of power, sluggishness and overheating | Engine | Broken valve spring | Have mechanic check |
| | | | Worn timing gear | |

A.5

| If You Feel... | System Affected | What to Look For | What to Do |
|---|---|---|---|
| 21. Sudden loss of power | Brake, drive train, engine or fuel system | Brakes dragging<br>Clutch slipping<br>Spark plug wire disconnected<br>Overheated engine<br><br>Vapor lock<br>Blocked fuel filter<br>Fuel pedal linkage failure | Have adjusted by mechanic<br>Have adjusted by mechanic<br>Replace wire<br>Determine cause of overheating and correct it<br>Let cool<br>Change filter or have it changed<br>Check linkage connectors |
| 22. Engine surges | Fuel or engine system | Air in fuel system<br>Worn gear on fuel pump<br>Throttle linkage loose<br>Low fuel supply<br>Buffer screw not properly set | Have mechanic check |
| 23. Brakes grab | Braking system | Grease on brake lining<br>Improperly adjusted brakes | Have grease removed by mechanic<br>Have readjusted by mechanic |
| 24. Brakes don't hold | Braking system | Brakes out of adjustment<br>Grease on linings<br>Water or ice on linings<br><br>Low air pressure<br>Air tanks full of oil or water<br>Master cylinder low on fluid<br>Worn brake linings<br>Hydraulic line broken<br>Broken air line or fitting leaking | Have readjusted by mechanic<br>Have removed by mechanic<br>Drive short distance with hand brake set<br>Check for air leaks<br>Bleed air tanks<br>Fill master cylinder<br>Have replaced by mechanic<br>Repair or install new line<br>Repair or install new air line or fitting |
| 25. Constant pull to right or left on steering | Tires, suspension, braking, or steering system | A soft tire<br>A broken spring<br><br>One front brake tight<br><br>Misadjusted tandem or front axle alignment | Repair or change it<br>Drive carefully until it can be replaced or repaired<br>Adjust or have adjusted by mechanic |

| If You Feel... | System Affected | What to Look For | What to Do |
|---|---|---|---|
| 26. Tractor does not want to come back straight after lane change or turn | Steering/Fifth wheel | Dry fifth wheel | Grease fifth wheel |
| 27. Vibration in engine | Engine system | One or more cylinders not firing caused by defective spark plugs, shortened spark plug wires, or wires off spark plug<br>Sticky valve<br>Broken valve<br>Blown cylinder head gasket<br>Vibration damper loose or worn<br>Unbalanced or damaged fan<br>Engine mounting loose or worn<br>Engine out of line in frame<br>Clutch out of balance<br>Drive line out of balance or line<br>Bad injectors<br>Air in fuel | Change plugs or make necessary adjustments<br><br>Have repairs made by mechanic |
| 28. Vibration in steering in time with rotation of wheels | Tire, wheel or rim | Wheels out of balance<br>Bubble on side of tire<br>Broken lock rim on tire<br>Bent wheels or rims<br>Uneven tire wear caused by other defects<br>Tire mounted on wheel incorrectly<br>Loose wheel lugs, broken studs | Have adjustments made by mechanic<br>Change tire<br>Change tire<br>Change tire<br>Have defects corrected by mechanic<br>Loosen tire lugs and tighten evenly<br>Tighten lugs, have broken studs replaced |

| | If You Feel… | System Affected | What to Look For | What to Do |
|---|---|---|---|---|
| 29. | Gradual loss of power | Fuel or engine system | Fuel filter dirty or clogged<br>Throttle linkage worn<br>Air filter clogged<br>Fuel pump gear worn<br>Dirty air filter<br>Cam lobes worn worn<br>Faulty valve<br>Jelling fuel<br>Blocked or freezing fuel filter | Clean or replace<br>Let mechanic check<br>Clean filter<br>Let mechanic check<br>Clean or replace<br>Clean or replace<br>Let mechanic check<br>Add anti-jell chemical to fuel<br>Change fuel filter |

| | If You Smell… | System Affected | What to Look For | What to Do |
|---|---|---|---|---|
| 30. | Burning rags | Drive train, engine, or brake system | Smoke or fire<br>Overheated engine<br><br>Clutch slipping (engine will race)<br>Hot or dragging brakes<br>Hand brake not released | Put out fire with fire extinguisher<br>Repair or replace part causing overheating<br>Have adjusted by mechanic<br>Have adjusted by mechanic<br>Release brake |
| 31. | Burning rubber | Brake system, tires, or electrical system | Tire on fire<br><br>Hot or dragging brakes<br>Short circuit in wiring<br>Belt slipping or frozen pulley bearing | Extinguish immediately and remove from vehicle<br>Have adjusted by mechanic<br>Disconnect battery terminal<br>Tighten or replace |
| 32. | Diesel fuel oil | Fuel system | Any leaks in system | Have repaired by mechanic |
| 33. | Burning oil (May also smell like burning rags) | Lubrication or engine system | Oil dripping on exhaust manifold or pipe<br>Overheated engine | Find source of oil leak and wipe off excess oil<br>Ascertain cause of overheating and repair or have repaired |
| 34. | Exhaust odor | | Cracked manifold<br>Loose connection in exhaust system<br>Leaking muffler<br>Improperly located tail pipe | Have repaired by mechanic<br>Keep cab well ventilated until repairs have been made |

# INDEX

## A

Accident memorandum, 19.12
Accident procedures, 19.3
    At the scene, 19.3, 19.10
    Causes, 26.20
    Diagram, 19.13
    Emergency procedures, 19.6
    First aid, 19.17
    Legal requirements, 19.14
    Reporting, 19.6
    Warning devices, 19.8
    When you are involved, 19.5
    With hazardous materials, 19.5
Accident reporting kit, 19.11
Accident witness card, 19.13
Agent, 25.5
Air brake system, 5.21-5.25
Air cleaner, 5.11
Air intake system, 5.10
Air lines, 9.7
Air pressure, checking 22.14
Air pressure gauge, 5.23
Air starters 23.17
Air suspension, 5.4
Air tank, draining, 5.22, 22.17
Airway, blocked, 19.18
Alcohol, 26.7-26.10, 26.12
Alignment, wheel, 5.32
Alley dock, 8.8
Alternator, 5.15
Ammeter, 5.15
Antifreeze, 15.4
Anti-jackknife devices, 18.10
Anti-lock (anti-skid) system, 5.25, 18.10
    brakes, 5.25, 18.10
Applying for job, 28.12
Auxiliary brakes, 15.21-22
Axles, 5.5
Axle weight, 20.5, 24.20, 27.17, 27.18

## B

B-train, 21.8
Backing, 6.7, 8.3-8.10
    Alley dock, 8.8
    Helper, 8.6
    Parallel park, 8.9
Bad weather, 13.5, 13.8
Bad weather driving, 15.3-15.16
Basic servicing, 22.8
Battery, 5.15
    Dead, 23.16-23.17
Battery fluid level, 22.12
Bearings, 5.12
Belted bias tires, 5.27
Bias ply tires, 5.27
Bill of lading, 25.4, 25.6
Bleeding, 19.20
Blocked airway, 19.18
Blocking and bracing, 24.7
Blowouts, 17.12
Brake controls, 2.6
Brake failure, 17.10
Brake inspection, 4.6, 15.5
Brakes, adjust, 22.17
Brakes, wet, 15.13-15.14
Braking, 15.10, 15.12, 15.20-15.21, 17.8, 18.6
    Controlled, 17.9
    Stab, 17.10
    Over, 18.7
Braking system, 5.20
Breathing, rescue, 19.18
Bridge Formula, 20.5, 27.18, 27.19
Bridges, 27.8
Broker, freight, 25.4
Budd wheel, 5.26
Bulb, changing 22.13
Bypass system, 5.13

## C

CDL (Commercial Driver License), 1.8, 24.5, 27.13, 29.2-29.14
    Disqualifications, 28.9
    Tests, 24.5, 24.15, 28.14, 29.2-29.4, 29.7-29.14
CMV (Commercial Motor Vehicles), 1.8-1.12
CMVSA/86 (Commercial Vehicle Safety Act of 1986), 1.8
Cab, 1.9, 26.14
Camber, 5.32
Cargo, 24.3-24.19, 26.13, 26.17
    Accepting, 24.13
    Covering, 24.11
    Loading, 24.13
    Securing, 24.6-24.12

Cargo documentation, 25.3-25.15
Cargo fires, 19.26
Carriers, 1.4-1.5, 25.4
Carrier's time record, 3.5-3.10
Caster, 5.32
Center of gravity, 13.6, 21.14, 24.23
Chains, 15.4, 15.6-15.8
Charging circuit, 5.15
Circuit breaker, resetting, 22.13
Clearance, 12.3-12.9, 21.12
Clothing, 26.13
Clutch, 5.17
Coil tie-down, 24.6
Cold weather driving, 15.3-15.16
Combination bypass/full flow system, 5.13
Combination vehicle, 1.8-1.12
Commercial Driver License (CDL), 1.8, 24.5, 27.13,
    29.5-29.14
Commercial Motor Vehicles (CMV), 1.8-1.12
Commercial Vehicle Safety Act of 1986 (CMVSA/86),
    1.8
Communication, 11.3-11.7, 14.8
Company policy, 28.10-28.11
Compressor, 5.22
Consignee (receiver), 25.3
Consignor (shipper), 25.3
Consumer Commodities, 24.16
Controlled braking, 17.9
Controls, 2.3-2.13
    Brake, 2.6
    Engine, 2.3
    Primary Vehicle, 2.4
    Secondary Vehicle, 2.8
    Transmission, 2.5
Converter dolly, 5.34
Converter dolly axle, 5.6
Coolant, 5.14, 15.4
Coolant filter, 22.12
Coolant level, 22.11
Cooling system, 5.13-5.14
Countersteering, 17.5, 17.9
Coupling, 9.3-9.10
    Area, 26.15
    Fifth wheel, 9.3-9.10
    Landing Gear, 9.5, 9.6, 9.9
    Procedures, 9.3-9.10
Coupling System Inspection, 4.9
Cranes, 24.14
Cranking circuit, 5.16

Crankshaft bearing, 5.12
Crime, 26.20
Curves, 16.6, 18.7
Customer relations, 28.6

**D**

DMV (Department of Motor Vehicles), 1.5
Dangerous areas, 26.14-26.18
    Accidents, 26.20
    Cab, 26.14
    Cargo, 26.17
    Coupling area, 26.15
    Crime, 26.20
    Emergencies, 26.18
    Lifting, 26.17-26.18
    Rear of trailer, 26.16
    Windshield, 26.17
Dayton wheel, 5.26
Dead axle, 5.5-5.6
Defensive driving, 17.3
Delivery, freight, 25.11
Delivery receipt, 25.4
Department of Motor Vehicles (DMV), 1.5
Desert driving, 15.17
Designated highway system, 27.17
Diesel engine, 5.8, 6.3-6.6
Diesel fuel, 5.10
Differential, 5.19
Disc brakes, 5.21
Disc wheel, 5.26
Distance, calculating, 27.11
Documentation, cargo, 25.3-25.15
Double clutching, 7.7-7.9
Downgrades, 15.19
    Braking, 15.19-15.23
Downshifting, 15.19
Drag link, 5.31
Drain cock, 5.22
Drive shaft, 5.19
Drive train, 5.16-5.19
Driver
    Alcohol, 26.7-26.10, 26.12
    Clothing, 26.13
    Drugs, 26.10-26.12
    Eating habits, 26.4
    Equipment, 26.13
    Exercise, 26.4

Illness, 26.7
Job demands, 26.22
Personal needs, 27.14
Physical requirements, 26.3
Rest, 26.4
Driver, professional truck, 1.13-1.17
Driver awareness, 23.4
Driver out of service, 3.10
Driver responsibility, 1.4, 10.3, 11.3, 12.3. 13.3, 14.3,
    15.15, 23.3-23.7, 24.4, 25.9, 25.12, 26.21
Driver restraints, 2.9
Driver's daily log, 3.6-3.10, 27.13
    Recap, 3.7, 3.8
Driver's health, 26.3, 26.7, 26.12
Driver's license, 1.8, 24.5, 27.13, 29.2-29
Drug testing, 19.4, 19.5
Drugs, 26.10-26.12
Drum brakes, 5.21
Dual tires, 5.30-5.31, 24.18
Dunnage, 24.7

## E

Eating habits, 26.4
Eaton Fuller, 7.12
    Nine Speed, 7.12
    Thirteen Speed, 7.15
    Super Ten, 7.13
Electrical fires, 19.27
Electrical system, 5.14-5.16
Emergencies, 17.3
Emergency equipment, 15.6
Emergency procedures, 17.3-17.13, 19.6, 26.18-26.19
Emergency relay valve, 5.24-5.25
Emergency stopping, 17.9
Employer-employee relations, 28.7-28.14
Engine, 5.7-5.8
    Belts, 15.17
    Cool down, 6.5
    Cooling system, 15.16
    Hoses, 15.17
    Lubrication, 15.16
    Non-starting, 15.9-15.10, 23.16-23.17
    Shutdown, 6.5
    Start up, 6.3-6.4, 15.8-15.10
    Warm up, 6.4-6.5
Engine block, 5.7-5.8
Engine brakes, 15.21
Engine controls, 2.3-2.4

Enroute inspection, 4.23
Escape ramps, 15.22-15.23
Evasive steering, 17.4
Exercise, 26.4
Exhaust system, 5.10-5.11
Exhaust system inspection, 4.8

## F

FHWA (Federal Highway Administration), 1.7
FMSCR (Federal Motor Carrier Safety Regulations),
    1.6-1.7, 24.5
Fan belt, 5.14
Fatigue, 14.4, 26.5-26.7
Federal Highway Administration (FHWA), 1.7
Federal Motor Carrier Safety Regulations (FMSCR),
    1.7, 24.5
Fifth wheel, 5.33-5.34, 9.10
    Sliding, 5.33-5.34, 20.3, 20.6-20.8
    Stationary, 5.33, 20.6
Filters, 5.9, 5.13
Fire, 19.23-19.27
    Cargo, 19.26
    Electrical 19.27
    Fuel, 19.26
    Tire, 5.30, 19.26
Fire extinguisher, 19.24-19.25
Firefighting, 19.23-19.27
First aid, 19.17
Flashers, 11.6-11.7
Fluid level, inspecting, 4.5
Force of motion, 18.4
Forklifts, 24.13
Frame, 5.3-5.4
Frameless construction, 5.3
Freight bill, 25.8
Freight broker, 25.4
Freight delivery, 25.11
Freight forwarder, 25.4
Fuel filter, 5.9, 22.9-22.10
Fuel fires, 19.26
Fuel level, 22.9
Fuel system, 5.8
Fuel tank, 5.9, 22.9
Fuel usage, 27.11, 27.12
Fuel use tax, 27.16
Full flow system, 5.13
Fuse, changing 22.13

# G

GCWR (Gross Combination Vehicle Weight Rating), 24.20
GVW (Gross Vehicle Weight), 24.20
Gasoline engine, 5.8
Gauges, 2.9-2.13
Generator, 5.15
Glad hands, 5.24
Glare, 14.3
Glow plugs, 15.9
Governor, 5.22
Gravity, 13.7
Gross Combination Vehicle Weight (GCWR), 24.20
Gross Vehicle Weight (GVW), 24.20

# H

Hand trucks, 24.14
Hazard awareness 16.3
Hazard classes, 24.15
Hazardous waste manifest, 25.5
Hazardous materials shipping paper, 24.16, 25.5, 25.14
Hazardous materials shipments, 24.15-24.19, 25.11-25.15, 27.20-27.21
    Accidents, 19.5-19.7, 24.18
Hazards, 15.10-15.16, 16.3-16.14
Headerboard, 24.7
Headlights, 14.5, 14.7
Health, driver, 26.3, 26.7, 26.12
Heaters, 15.4
High center of gravity, 13.6, 23.12, 24.23
Highways, 27.6-27.9
    Interstate, 27.7
    Posted bridges, 27.8
    Prohibited routes, 27.9
    State primary routes, 27.7
    Toll roads, 27.7
    Truck routes, 27.8
    U. S. numbered routes, 27.7
Hill driving, 13.7
Hoists, 24.14
Hot weather driving, 15.16-15.17, 16.6
Hours of service, 3.3-3.10
Hydroplaning, 13.5-13.6

# I

IRP (International Registration Plan), 27.16
Identification numbers, 25.14
Ignition circuit, 5.16
Illness, 26.7, 26.12
Independent trailer brake, 5.23
Inner bridge, 20.5, 27.18
Inserts, 5.12
Inspections, vehicle, 4.3-4.25, 15.18
    Air lines, 15.5
    Brakes, 4.6, 15.5
    Chains, 15.4-15.7
    Cooling system, 15.4, 15.16-15.17
    Coupling system, 4.9, 15.5
    Electrical system, 15.5
    Emergency equipment, 15.6
    Engine belts, 15.17
    Enroute, 4.23
    Exhaust system, 4.8, 15.6
    Fuel tank, 15.5
    Fluid level, 4.5
    Heating system, 15.4
    Hoses, 15.17
    Interaxle Differential Lock, 15.6
    Lights, 15.5
    Lubrication system, 15.16
    Pre-trip, 4.9, 15.3-15.6
    Post-trip, 4.23-4.24
    Radiator, 15.5
    Report, 4.24-4.25, 27.13
    Routine, 4.31
    Steering system, 4.8
    Suspension system, 4.8
    Tires, 15.4, 15.16
    Washers/Wipers, 15.4
    Wheels, 4.6
Instruments, 2.9
Integral container and chassis, 24.7
Internal combustion engine, 5.7
International Registration Plan (IRP), 27.16
Intersections, 10.5-10.6
Interstate Highways, 27.7
Interview, 28.13
Invoice, 25.9
Irregular Route, 27.5

## J

Jackknife, 15.12, 18.7-18.8, 18.10
Jifflox converter dolly, 5.34
Job application, 28.12
Job interview, 28.13
Job requirements, 28.8
    Disqualifications, 28.9
    Physical examination, 28.14
    Tests, 28.14

## K

Kingpin, 5.34

## L

Labels, 25.13
Landing Gear, 5.35, 9.9-9.10
Leaf spring suspension, 5.4
Length, vehicle, 27.18-27.19
Levers, 24.15
License, vehicle, 27.16
Lifting, 26.17-26.18
Lights, 14.5-14.6, 15.5
    Changing bulb, 22.13
Limits, vehicle, 27.17-27.19
Line-haul transport, 27.5-27.6
    Irregular route, 27.5
    Meet and turn, 27.6
    Open dispatch, 27.5
    Regular route, 27.5
    Regular run, 27.5
    Roll and rest, 27.6
    Sleeper operations, 27.6
    Turn around, 27.6
Live axle, 5.6,
Livestock trailer, 21.15
Load locking bars, 24.7
Local operations, 27.4
    Peddle run, 27.4
    Pick up and delivery, 27.4
    Shuttle operations, 27.4
Low pressure warning signal, 5.23
Lubrication system, 5.11-5.13
Lug tread, 5.28

## M

Malfunctions, 23.3
    Detecting, 23.4-23.6
    Diagnosing, 23.5
    Reporting, 23.6
Manifest, 25.4
Maps, 27.9-27.11
    Atlas, 27.10
    Legend, 27.11
    Local, 27.9
    State, 27.9
Mechanic's responsibility, 23.5
Medical certificate, 27.13
Meet and turn, 27.6
Meters, 2.9-2.12, 7.5-7.6
Mirrors, 10.6-10.10, 14.6
Mountain driving, 15.17-15.23
    Braking, 15.20-15.22
Multiple-articulation rig, 21.4
Multiple axle assembly, 5.6

## N

National Network, 27.17
National System of Interstate Highways, 27.17
Night driving, 13.7, 14.3-14.8
Nonsynchronized transmissions, 7.7-7.9

## O

Off-duty time, 3.4
Off-road recovery, 17.7-17.9
Off-tracking, 6.8-6.9, 20.5-20.6
Oil change, 5.12
Oil filter, 5.13, 22.11
Oil level, 22.10
Oil pan, 5.12
On-board recorder, 27.14
On-duty time, 3.4
One-way check valve, 5.22
Open Dispatch, 27.5
Operating costs, 22.8
Out of service, 3.10
Outer bridge, 20.5, 27.18

## P

Packing slip, 25.4, 25.9
Pallet jacks, 24.14
Parallel park, 8.9-8.10
Parking brake system, 5.20
Peddle run, 27.4
Penalties, 3.10
Permits, vehicle, 27.16, 27.19-27.20
Physical examinations, 28.14
Physical requirements, 26.3
Pick up and delivery, 27.4
Pinion gear, 5.19
Pitman arm, 5.31
Placards, 24.19, 25.12-25.13
Pre-heaters, 15.9
Pre-trip inspection, 4.9-4.22, 15.3, 15.16, 15.18
Preventive Maintenance, 22.3, 22.4
Primary vehicle controls, 2.4-2.5
Professional truck driver, 1.13-1.15
Progressive shifting, 7.10
Prohibited routes, 27.9
Ports-of-entry, 27.21
Post-trip inspection, 4.23-4.24
Public relations, 28.3-28.7
    Driver's role, 28.4-28.6
Pusher Tandem axle, 5.7
Pyrometer, 5.11

## Q

Quick-release valve, 5.24

## R

Radial tires, 5.27
Radiator cap, 5.14
Rear of trailer, 26.16
Receiver (consignee), 25.3
Recorder, on-board, 27.14
Records, 27.13
Reefer, 21.16-21.17
Regular route, 27.5
Regular run, 27.5
Regulating Agencies
    Department of Motor Vehicles (DMV), 1.5
    Federal Highway Administration (FHWA), 1.7
    U. S. Department of Transportation (USDOT), 1.5-1.6
Regulations
    Federal Motor Carrier Safety Regulations (FMSCR), 1.6-1.7, 24.5
    State, 1.6, 24.6
Relay valve, 5.24
Repairs, 22.6
Rescue breathing, 19.18
Rest, 26.4
Rib tread, 5.28
Ring gear, 5.19
Road condition, 13.4, 14.4, 15.10-15.12, 15.17, 16.5
    Reports, 15.6
    Slippery 13.5, 15.11, 15.13-15.14, 15.17, 16.5
Road users, 14.5, 16.8-16.14
Roadside enforcement, 27.21-27.22
Rockwell, 7.14, 7.18
    Engine Synchro Shift (ESS), 7.19
    Ten Speed, 7.14
Roll and rest, 27.6
Rope, 24.9-24.10
Routine maintenance, 22.4, 22.8
Route selection, 24.19, 27.6-27.11, 27.21

## S

Safe haven, 27.20
Safety, 1.15-1.17
    Clothing, 26.13-26.14
    Equipment, 26.13
    Inspections, 27.22
Scales, 27.21
Scanning, 10.5
Scheduled preventive maintenance, 22.4-22.8
Seatbelts, 2.9, 17.5
Secondary braking system, 5.20
Secondary vehicle controls, 2.8
Securing cargo, 24.6-24.12
Security seal, 25.10
Semitrailer, 1.11-1.12
Service brake system, 5.20
Servicing, 22.3, 22.7
Shifting, 7.3-7.21
    Controls, 7.3-7.4
    Double clutching, 7.7

Fully automatic transmission, 7.20
Nonsynchronized transmissions, 7.7
Patterns, 7.11-7.20
Semi-Automatic transmissions, 7.16
Shipper (consignor), 25.3
Shipper's responsibilities, 25.12
Shipping papers, 25.3-25.15, 27.13
Shipping papers, hazardous materials, 25.5, 25.14
Shock, 19.22
Shock absorbers, 5.5
Shuttle operations, 27.4
Sight distance, 13.7, 14.5
Signaling, 11.4
Single drive axle, 5.6
Skid, 15.12, 18.5-18.10
Cause, 18.5-18.6
Preventing, 18.5, 18.9
Skid control, 18.3, 18.10
Skid recovery, 18.10
Sleeper berth time, 3.8
Sleeper operations, 27.6
Sliding fifth wheel, 20.3, 20.6-20.8
Sliding tandem axles, 20.3, 20.9-20.13
Slowing, 11.5
Space management 12.3-12.9, 14.8
Special rigs, 21.3-21.18
Speed, 13.3, 15.11, 15.17, 16.11
Bad weather, 13.8
Calculating, 27.11
Field of vision, 13.8
Management, 13.3-13.8
Night driving, 13.7, 14.8
Skid cause, 18.5-18.6
Traffic, 13.8
Speed retarders, 15.21
Speeding, 13.3, 15.12, 18.8
Spicer AutoMate-2, 7.18
Spicer Pro-Shift Seven Speed, 7.11
Spoke wheel, 5.26
Spring brake system, 5.25
Stab braking, 17.10
State primary routes, 27.7
State Regulations, 1.6, 24.6, 27.18
Stationary fifth wheel, 20.6
Steering, 15.12
Corrective, 18.11
Evasive, 17.4

Over, 18.7, 15.12
Steering fluid level, 22.12
Steering system, 5.31-5.32
Steering system inspection, 4.8
Stopping, emergency, 17.9-17.10
Stopping distance, 13.3-13.4
Stress, 26.21-26.23
Stuck rig, 15.14-15.15
Remote area, 15.16
Towing, 15.15
Suspension system, 5.4
Suspension system inspection, 4.8

**T**

Tailgating, 12.6
Tag tandem, 5.7
Tandem axles, 5.6, 20.3, 20.9-20.13, 5.6
Tanker, 21.15-21.16
Taxes
Fuel use, 27.16
Weight distance, 27.17
Ten-Speed, 7.13
Eaton Fuller, 7.13
Rockwell, 7.14
Tests, 28.14
Thermostat, 5.14
Thirteen-Speed, Eaton Fuller, 7.15-7.16
Tie-down, 24.8-24.12
Tie rod, 5.31
Time, calculating, 27.11
Tire fires, 5.30, 19.26
Tire slide, 18.6
Tire tubes, 5.27-5.28
Tires, 5.27, 15.4, 15.10, 15.16
Dual, 5.30-5.31, 24.18
Inflation, 5.29-5.31
Toll roads, 27.7
Traction, 13.4-13.6, 15.10-15.12, 18.4
Tractor
Dromedary, 21.18
Low cab, 21.18
Snub nose, 21.18
Yard, 21.18
Tractor protection system, 5.24
Traffic, 12.7, 12.9, 13.8
Trailer hook-up, 6.6, 9.3-9.11

Trailer override, 18.8
Trailers, 1.10-1.12, 21.3-21.18
   Auto transport, 21.18
   B-trains 21.8
   Coupling, 9.3-9.10
   Doubles, 21.4-21.8
   Low bed, 21.10-21.13
   Pole, 21.17
   Refrigerated, 21.16
   Tank, 21.14
   Triple, 21.9-21.10
   Twin, 21.4
   Uncoupling, 9.10
Transmission, 5.18
Transmission controls, 2.5-2.8
Travel time, 3.5, 27.11-27.22
Tread, tire, 5.28, 5.31
Treadle valve, 5.23
Triangles, 11.7
Tri-drive axle, 5.7
Trip planning, 27.3
Trip report, 27.14
Triples, 21.9-21.10
Troubleshooting Guide, 23.8-23.16, Appendix A
Truck routes, 27.8
Truck tractors, 1.8-1.10
Trucking Industry, 1.3-1.10, 28.4
Trucks
   Combination vehicle, 1.8-1.12
   Hand, 24.14-24.15
   Truck tractors, 1.8-1.10
Tubes, tire, 5.27-5.28
Turn around transport, 27.6
Turn signals, 14.6
Turning, 6.8-6.13, 12.8-12.9
Turnpike doubles, 21.6-21.7
Twin screw axles, 5.7
Twin screw inter-axle differential, 5.20

## U

U.S. Department of Transportation (USDOT or DOT),
   1.4-1.5
U.S. numbered routes, 27.7
USDOT or DOT (U. S. Department of Transportation),
   1.4-1.5
Uncoupling, 9.10-9.11
Universal joint, 5.19

Unscheduled maintenance, 22.6
Upgrades, 15.19

## V

VCR (Vehicle condition report), 4.24-4.25, 22.6-22.7,
   23.7-23.8, 27.13
VLS (Variable load suspension) axle, 5.6
Variable load suspension axle (VLS), 5.6
Vehicle
   Break-down, 15.16, 15.17
   Inspection, 4.3-4.24, 15.3-15.6, 15.16-15.17
   Length, 27.17-27.20
   License, 27.16
   Permits, 27.16-27.20
   Stuck, 15.14-15.15
   Towing, 15.15
   Weight, 27.17-27.19
Vehicle condition report (VCR), 4.24-4.25, 22.6-22.7,
   23.7-23.8, 27.13
Vehicle systems, 5.3-5.35
Visibility, 15.10, 16.7-16.9
Visual search, 10.3-10.9
Voltage regulator, 5.15

## W

Warehouse receipt, 25.5
Warning devices, 11.7, 19.8-19.10
Weather reports, 15.6
Weight, axle, 20.5, 24.20, 27.17-27.18
Weight, distribution of, 20.3-20.5, 24.4, 24.21-24.23
Weight, vehicle, 24.19-24.23, 27.17-27.19
Weight distance taxes, 27.17
Wheel, changing 22.14-22.17
   Position, 5.28
   Replacing, 22.16-22.17
   Weight, 24.20
Wheel load, 18.4
Wheel lock-up, 18.6, 18.8
Wheels, 5.25-5.26
   Inspecting, 4.6
Windshield, 14.6, 26.17
   Washers, 15.4
   Wipers, 15.4
Wire rope, 24.9
Witness card, accident, 19.13
Wristpin, 5.12